COOK'S

ILLUSTRATED

~ 1994 ~

Published by

Boston Common Press Limited Partnership

17 Station Street

Brookline, MA 02445

ISBN: 0-9640179-1-1

ISSN: 1068-2821

To get home delivery of future issues of *Cook's Illustrated*, call 800-526-8442 inside the U.S.,
or 515-247-7571 if calling from outside the U.S.

In addition to the Annual Hardbound editions, *Cook's Illustrated* offers the following publications:

The *How to Cook* series of single topic cookbooks
Titles include *How to Make A Pie, How to Make An American Layer Cake, How to Stir-Fry, How to Make Ice Cream, How to Make Pizza, How to Make Holiday Desserts, How to Make Pasta Sauces, How to Make Salad, How to Grill, How to Make Simple Fruit Desserts, How to Make Cookie Jar Favorites, How to Cook Holiday Roasts & Birds, How to Make Stew, How to Cook Shrimp & Other Shellfish, How to Barbecue & Roast On The Grill, How to Cook Garden Vegetables, How to Make Pot Pies & Casseroles, How to Make Soup, How to Sauté, How to Cook Potatoes,* and *How to Make Quick Appetizers.* A boxed set of the first 11 titles in the series is available in an attractive, protective slip case. New releases are published every two months, so give us a call for our complete list of available titles.

The Best Recipe
This 560-page book is a collection of over 700 recipes and 200 illustrations from the past seven years of *Cook's.* We've included basics, such as how to make chicken stock, as well as recipes for quick weeknight meals and special entertaining. Let *The Best Recipe* become your indispensable kitchen companion.

Multi-Year Master Index
Quickly find every article and recipe *Cook's Illustrated* has published from the Charter Issue in 1992 through the most recent year-end issue. Recipe names, authors, article titles, subject matter, equipment testings, food tastings, cookbook reviews, wine tastings, and ingredients are all now instantly at your fingertips.

The Cook's Bible **and** *The Yellow Farmhouse Cookbook*
Written by Christopher Kimball and published by Little, Brown and Company.

To order any of the books listed above, call 800-611-0759 inside the U.S., or 515-246-6911 if calling from outside the U.S.

You can order subscriptions, gift subscriptions, and any of our books by visiting our online store at
www.cooksillustrated.com

BC=Back Cover

COOK'S ILLUSTRATED INDEX 1994

NUMBER SIX ◆ JANUARY/FEBRUARY 1994

$4.00 U.S./$4.95 CANADA

COOK'S
ILLUSTRATED

Tender, Moist
Pot Roast
Cook at a Subsimmer
for Succulent Meat

Homemade
Biscotti
Less Fat Means Crisper,
More Flavorful Cookies

How to Cook
Brown Rice
Boil, then Steam for
Tender, Separate Grains

Rating Juice
Extractors
$300 Winner,
$45 Best Buy

ROASTING ROOT
VEGETABLES
•
AUTHENTIC
HAND-FORMED PASTAS
•
BAKERY-STYLE
STICKY BUNS
•
MUSTARD FROM SCRATCH

JANUARY/FEBRUARY 1994

TABLE
OF CONTENTS

VOLUME TWO • NUMBER ONE

"Tropical Fruits"
See pages 16 and 17 for instructions on preparing many tropical fruits.

ILLUSTRATION BY
BRENT WATKINSON

Poached Pears on Salad Greens with Walnuts and Stilton,
inspired by a recipe from *Outdoor Entertaining* (Collins, 1992).

ILLUSTRATION BY
DAN BROWN

COOK'S
ILLUSTRATED

Publisher and Editor
CHRISTOPHER KIMBALL

Executive Editor
MARK BITTMAN

Senior Editor
JOHN WILLOUGHBY

Food Editor
PAM ANDERSON

Senior Writer
JACK BISHOP

Managing Editor
MAURA LYONS

Copy Editor
DAVID TRAVERS

Test Kitchen Assistant
VICTORIA ROLAND

Art Director
MEG BIRNBAUM

Food Stylist
MARIE PIRAINO

Circulation Director
ADRIENNE KIMBALL

Circulation Manager
MARY TAINTOR

Marketing Manager
NANCY HALTER-GILLIS

Circulation Assistant
JENNIFER L. KEENE

Production Director
JAMES MCCORMACK

Treasurer
JANET CARLSON

Office Manager
JENNY THORNBURY

Cook's Illustrated (ISSN 1068-2821) is published bimonthly by Natural Health Limited Partners, 17 Station Street, Box 569, Brookline, MA 02147. Copyright 1993 Natural Health Limited Partners. Application to mail at second-class postage rates is pending at Boston, MA and additional mailing offices. Editorial office: 17 Station Street, Box 569, Brookline, MA 02147; (617) 232-1000, FAX (617) 232-1572. Editorial contributions should be sent to: Editor, *Cook's Illustrated*, 17 Station Street, Box 569, Brookline, MA 02147. We cannot assume responsibility for manuscripts submitted to us. Submissions will be returned only if accompanied by a large self-addressed stamped envelope. Subscription rates: $24.95 for one year; $45 for two years; $65 for three years. (Canada: add $3 per year; all other foreign add $12 per year.) Postmaster: Send all new orders, subscription inquiries, and change of address notices to *Cook's Illustrated*, P.O. Box 59046, Boulder, CO 80322-9046, or telephone (800) 477-3059. Single copies: $4 in U.S., $4.95 in Canada and foreign. Back issues available for $5 each. PRINTED IN THE U.S.A.

EDITORIAL

LETTER TO MY YOUNGER DAUGHTER

Dear Caroline,

Caroline Kimball, age three

You were always a good eater. At age two, you ate your own bowl of cereal, then your older sister's, and then held out an empty bowl and demanded the hat trick. Like all kids, you preferred what was familiar and comforting. Small bits of bright color in a sea of ivory noodles were disturbing — an invading army that had to be picked out, one soldier at a time. You adored salads and fruit, but mistrusted chunky soups and their mysteries.

You loved to cook. You kneaded bread dough with gusto until it was as satiny smooth and plump as your belly. You stood on the trash can, wearing just your diaper, cutting out biscuits. You hid behind the kitchen counter and pilfered strips of pie dough. You loved to eat raw flour, licking it off the counter when my back was turned.

When you are older, you may have occasion to read this letter; you may in time have your own family. Your memories of sourdough, baked beans, corn muffins, apple pie, fresh-picked blueberries, and upside-down cake are part of your heritage. You were raised in New England and ate the same foods as our neighbors. Although you will doubtless eat sashimi and soba, skate and dim sum, it is Yankee food that dominates your past.

Compared to your grandfather's day, when the world was no larger than a neighborhood, you grew up at a time in which little was familiar. In the 1920s, our whole clan met at noon every Sunday at your great-great-great-grandmother's row house on Cathedral Street in Baltimore. Hair slicked back and shoes shined, your grandfather sat quietly in the thickly draped Victorian parlor with the grown-ups, bored and waiting for a dinner that was as predictable as the start of school — beaten biscuits, a roast, mashed potatoes, lima beans, followed by peach pie in season or a cake the rest of the year.

In the fifties, I spent summers in Vermont and remember midday dinners at a neighbor's farmhouse. Warm baking-powder biscuits (extras were stacked in a large tin), meat and mashed potatoes, a pitcher of fresh milk covered with a blue-and-white kitchen towel to keep out flies, a just-baked loaf of anadama bread, and molasses cookies with flour-dusted bottoms. Your grandmother had a full-time job, even back then; our own house had a

southern cook. Enormous pans of spoonbread, collard greens, black-eyed peas, giant popovers, and red snapper every Friday are as vivid to me now as the day they were served.

Today, a whole generation has grown up as a take-out culture. The food is convenient, and some of it is even good, but it has none of the ring of the familiar; it can never be personal enough to become part of our past. Your mother and I think about what we should pass on to your generation. Everyone talks values, as if they were computer skills. We would rather create memories: butter-dipping raw folds of Parker House Rolls on Thanksgiving morning; clipping sprigs of basil just before the first frost; stirring the batter for your sister's devil's food birthday cake. In food, there is so much to learn about life. As with good friends, the best foods are the simplest and most honest. Start out with memories of your dad's apple pie and then later on you can take the measure of a tarte aux pommes with crème anglaise. I'm betting that the deep-dish pie will stand the test of time because we made it together — your tiny hands on the axle-size rolling pin while you demanded, "Let me do it!"

I hope that the first splash of fall color will reawaken in you an urge to roll out your own round of pie dough, filling it with firm, juicy Northern Spys or Macouns and dad's special spice mixture. I hope that your best friends are as dependable and well-made as that pie. Before your mother and I got married, I invited her up for a weekend at the farm. She threw hay with the best of them and was no quitter — the last hay wagon wasn't empty until the barn swallows came out. That was the first day that I knew there would be a Caroline in my future.

As for the future, there will be many new memories to create. You and your family probably won't come to the farm as often as I'd like, but as soon as your kids can stand, they're going to get a good dose of rolling pie dough, kneading bread, and cutting cookies. Like the candyman, I'll lure them with a lick of the bowl and hook them with the magic of the kitchen. And after you've gone back home, your mom and I will sit together in front of the fire like coconspirators, with memories of small voices ringing out, "Let me do it!" And we will realize that, all this time, you were giving us the memories. Thank you.

Love, Dad

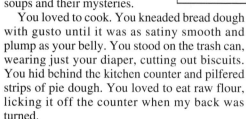

NOTES
FROM READERS

IS SCALDING MILK FOR BREAD ESSENTIAL?

In a recent issue you mentioned that scalding milk for custards is not necessary, but does help mix ingredients and shorten baking time. When making bread, it would save considerable time to omit the scalding process altogether. Many bread recipes call for scalded milk. What does scalding do to milk, and is it really necessary?

JILL CHESSMAN
Farmington, CT

If you are pleased with the results from recipes that call for scalded milk, don't make any changes. That said, scalding is nothing more than a method for increasing the temperature of milk or cream. Until early in this century, milk was often scalded — that is, brought to a temperature just below the boiling point — to kill bacteria which interfered with thickening, as in a custard or béchamel. Modern pasteurization makes this unnecessary.

However, many recipes still call for scalded milk in order to raise the temperature of the other ingredients. For instance, yeast thrives and causes maximum rise in a warm environment of about 80 degrees. While most cooks focus on the temperature of the kitchen, the temperature of the dough is equally important. If cold butter, eggs, and milk are used to make a yeast bread, the dough will be well below room temperature, thus slowing the rising process.

For this reason, many recipes call for warm (usually 105 to 115 degrees) or scalded liquids. Note that scalding is relatively imprecise. *The Joy of Cooking* defines scalding as the temperature at which tiny bubbles form around the edge of the pan, or about 180 degrees. Other sources define scalding as just below 212 degrees or when a thick skin develops on the milk surface. In either case, very hot milk will kill active yeast cells if not first combined with cooler ingredients.

CLEANING CUTTING BOARDS

In Notes from Readers in the September/October 1993 issue, you wisely advise readers to disinfect their cutting boards, whether wood or plastic, by soaking them periodically in a dilute solution of chlorine bleach. Unfortunately, no amount of rinsing with water

will remove every trace of chlorine odor, which can be transferred to foods.

There's a simple solution, however. A final rub with vinegar will kill all the chlorine odor because vinegar's acetic acid neutralizes the alkaline sodium hypochlorite of the bleach. This trick works well as a final rinse for bleached laundry, too.

ROBERT WOLKE
Professor Emeritus, University of Pittsburgh
Pittsburgh, PA

HOMEMADE LADYFINGER COOKIES

I used to make a great lemon meringue pie with store-bought ladyfingers as the crust. Recently, I have been unable to find large ladyfingers. All I can purchase are small cookies, which let the lemon filling seep through. Can you suggest a recipe? Also, where might I find a pan to make them in?

ELEANOR MARTELLI
Maspeth, NY

You are in luck. We have a great recipe for ladyfingers and you don't need to purchase a special pan. Just line a regular cookie sheet with parchment paper. You will need a pastry bag to pipe out the dough (*see* illustration, below).

LADYFINGERS
Makes about 30

Ladyfingers are simple to make if you use a good stiff batter that you pipe and bake immediately.

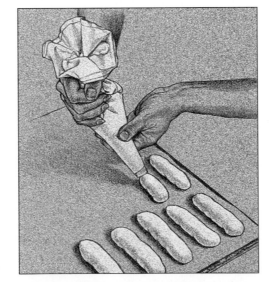

4   large eggs, separated
½   cup sugar
1   teaspoon vanilla extract
¾   cup flour
⅛   teaspoon salt
¼   cup confectioners' sugar

1. Beat yolks, sugar, and vanilla in a medium bowl until pale yellow. Sift flour and salt over yolk mixture; fold to combine.

2. Whip egg whites to stiff peaks, gradually adding 2 tablespoons confectioners' sugar after whites foam. Stir ¼ cup whites into yolk mixture; fold in remaining whites.

3. Heat oven to 350 degrees. Spoon batter into a pastry bag fitted with a ½-inch plain tube. Pipe 30, 3-by-1-inch strips of batter, about 1 inch apart, onto a cookie sheet lined with greased parchment. Sift remaining confectioners' sugar over strips of batter. Bake until golden, about 10 to 12 minutes. Cool on baking sheet for 5 minutes, then transfer them to a wire rack and cool completely. (Can be stored in an airtight container up to 2 days.)

CLOUDY OLIVE OIL

After reading your taste test of olive oils (Charter Issue), I was wondering why some oils seem to have so much sediment and cloudiness. Should I strain these oils?

ELSIE WHALEN
Roslindale, MA

Cloudiness in olive oil can result from naturally occurring sediment or from storage at cool temperatures. Some extra virgin olive oils are unfiltered and will appear cloudy at room temperature. This cloudiness is caused by sediment extracted from olives along with the oil during the pressing process. Arlene Wanderman of the International Olive Oil Council says this sediment — which is nothing more than very small pieces of olives — gives extra virgin oils added flavor and color. She notes that so-called "light" olive oils — mild oils with little flavor or color — are at the other end of the spectrum because they have been subjected to very fine filtration. Many unfiltered extra virgin oils are labeled as such and may have a stronger olive flavor than filtered oils. For this reason, do not filter cloudy extra virgin oils.

Cloudiness can also be caused by storage in the refrigerator or even in a cool basement.

ILLUSTRATIONS BY ALAN WITSCHONKE

This type of cloudiness is the result of congealing saturated fat. Just like butter or chicken fat, the saturated fat in olive oil will harden in the refrigerator. However, since the amount of saturated fat in olive oil is so much lower than that in butter, the oil turns cloudy as opposed to hardening fully and turning opaque. To clear chilled oils, simply pour the desired amount into a measuring cup and let stand at room temperature for 15 or 20 minutes.

CHINESE PANCAKES

I really enjoyed your Peking Duck article (September/October 1993) and was wondering if chef David SooHoo would share his recipe for the Chinese pancakes that accompany this dish, as shown in the color photograph.

MIRIAM NOVOGROTSKY
Gloucester, MA

SESAME CREPES
Makes about 18

The traditional recipe for this Chinese pancake is quite sturdy (it was often carried into the field by farmers for midday meals) and thus very chewy. For this dish, David SooHoo prefers a more delicate, European crepe that is not nearly as doughy or tough. He spikes the batter with sesame oil and sesame seeds to give the pancakes their Asian character.

- 1¼ cups flour
- ¼ teaspoon salt
- 2 eggs
- 1¼ cups milk
- 2 tablespoons sesame oil
- 2 tablespoons sesame seeds
-   Oil for coating pan

Whisk first 6 ingredients together in a medium bowl. Set a small nonstick skillet over medium-high heat; brush pan with oil. Pour 2 to 3 tablespoons batter into center of pan; swirl until bottom is coated. Cook until crepe edges start to brown, about 1 minute. Turn and brown other side, about 30 seconds longer. Remove crepe from pan and set aside. Repeat, oiling pan as necessary, until all the batter is used, stacking finished crepes on top of one another.

PITTING AVOCADOS

I read with some amusement the Quick Tip for pitting an avocado in the September/October 1993 issue. The method you describe is effective and one I have used myself. But I had to chuckle because the final step — the one I'm still looking for — was missing.

When the three steps you provided are completed, one is left with the following: a cleanly pitted avocado and a knife blade quite firmly embedded in an avocado pit. How do you suggest I remove the very sharp knife from the very slippery pit?

I take a wooden spoon and, aiming carefully,

just whack the pit from the blade and into a ready container. Do you have a more effective method of achieving the same end?

STEPHEN GLASS
Claremont, CA

We agree that removing the pit from a sharp knife requires caution. In fact, we use the same method you describe, since it is the only way that guarantees the safety of your hands and fingers.

EMULSIFYING SAUCES

My understanding is that emulsifying agents are used to combine oil and water in sauces. I know that the lecithin in egg yolks is an emulsifier and have heard that mustard and paprika also have emulsifying abilities. Because my wife is on a low-cholesterol diet (and by extension so am I), we generally avoid egg yolks. Is there some way to bind sauces without egg yolks? Also, are there emulsifiers without the flavor of mustard or paprika?

CHARLES RIGNALL
South Glastonbury, CT

An emulsion is a mixture of two liquids — such as oil and water — that would not ordinarily stay together. One liquid (often the fat) is broken into very small droplets that are suspended in the continuous liquid (often water). Many emulsions are created with mechanical force — shaking oil and vinegar together in a cruet; whisking oil into egg yolks, vinegar, and mustard to make mayonnaise. To maintain the emulsion — that is, to prevent the two liquids from separating — some sort of emulsifier is needed.

Lecithin, a phospholipid that is present in egg yolks, acts as an emulsifier by preventing oil droplets from coming together. As with all emulsifiers, one end of the lecithin molecule is attracted to water (hydrophilic) and the other is repelled by water (hydrophobic). The hydrophobic ends coat the oil droplets, thus preventing the oil droplets from coming together and falling out of the suspension. A simple vinaigrette breaks apart relatively quickly because there are no strong emulsifiers holding the oil and vinegar together. True emulsions, such as mayonnaise or milk (fatty acids and proteins keep the milk fat suspended in water), are much slower to separate.

In addition to phospholipids such as lecithin, some fatty acids, proteins, and plant materials (garlic and onions, for example) can act as emulsifiers. However, these materials (mustard and garlic are often used in a vinaigrette) usually lack the power of egg yolks.

For these reasons, individuals on low-cholesterol diets need to rethink sauce making. Sauces thickened by egg yolks, such as butter-rich béarnaise or hollandaise, are usually very high in fat and therefore not the best choices anyway. You may want to consider stock-based sauces thickened with starches, such as

flour, cornstarch, or arrowroot. Traditionally, these sauces are thickened by the addition of a roux — flour browned in fat. Instead, try whisking cornstarch, for example, with water or wine and using this paste, borrowed from Chinese stir-frying, to thicken reduced stock into a viscous sauce.

Perhaps even better is to consider vegetable- or fruit-based sauces — chutneys, relishes, and salsas. While not necessarily replacements for French sauces, these flavorful accompaniments are usually low in fat and cholesterol.

WHAT IS IT?

On the Julia Child birthday celebration broadcast some time ago on public television, I saw chefs Jimmy Burke and Dawn Sieber preparing a brandade wrapped in potato leaves. In the process, the potatoes were placed on an instrument that they called a "Japanese turning mandoline," and rotated with a crank. As the potato turned, a blade shaved off a continuous piece of potato that was several inches wide and paper thin. I have never seen anything like this and was wondering how this device works.

ANNE MORRISON
Northford, CT

Although the intricate cutting and slicing of vegetables key to Japanese cuisine is traditionally done by hand, in recent years the Japanese have turned to various devices to speed restaurant work. One of these high-tech tools is the Japanese turning mandoline used by Dawn Sieber on the Julia Child special. Hard vegetables such as carrots, turnips, and potatoes can be peeled and then put on a spindle attached to a crank — the turning mandoline actually resembles a manual pasta machine. As the vegetable turns it rubs against one of several blade attachments that shred and slice in various designs. Sieber, who is the chef at the Cheeca Lodge in Islamorada, Florida, cuts potatoes into long sheets — one potato can yield several feet — that can be used as food wrappers.

Most turning mandolines also come with attachments that cut vegetables into shapes that may resemble chrysanthemums or even a fisherman's net. Depending on the number of attachments, a good Japanese mandoline costs $300 to $400. Most home cooks can't justify the expense, but the next time you see an intricate vegetable presentation in a restaurant you will know the secret. Available from Mutual Trading Co., 431 Crocker Street, Los Angeles, CA 90013; 213-626-9458. ∎

Quick Tips

PEELING CHESTNUTS

The hard shell of a chestnut protects the tender meat. This technique removes in one piece both the shell and the thin membrane that covers the meat.

1. Score the shell of each chestnut around its equator. Do not cut into the meat.

2. Heat chestnuts in a 400-degree oven until the shells split, about 5 to 10 minutes. Remove the nuts from the oven. As soon as they can be handled, lift off shell and membrane (they should come off together) from each half.

KEEPING FISH FRESH

Air and warm temperatures are the enemies of fresh fish. As soon as you get fillets or steaks home from the market, follow this tip, which comes to us from Howard Raber, chef of the restaurant Two Twenty-Five in Dubuque, Iowa.

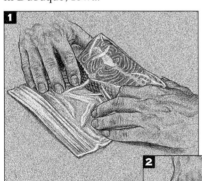

1. Place each piece of fish in a zipper-lock plastic bag. Press out as much air as possible from each bag, seal the bag, and roll the fish up in the remaining portion of the bag.

2. Place sealed bags in a large container and cover with ice. Set container in the coldest part of your refrigerator and refresh with new ice as needed. Depending on the quality of the fish, it should keep for a day or two.

CORING AND WASHING HEAD LETTUCE

This trick for cleaning head lettuce comes from three readers — Diane Boutotte of Sterling, Massachusetts; Lois Rutherford of Palatine, Illinois; and Milton Wilson of Vancouver, Washington.

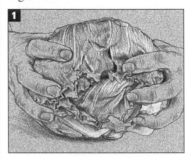

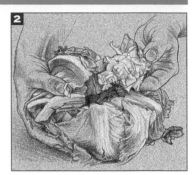

2. Pull out the core in one piece.

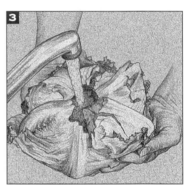

1. Remove bruised outer leaves from the head of lettuce. Rap the bottom of the lettuce sharply on the counter to loosen the core.

3. Fill the hole left by the extracted core with water to rinse soil from lettuce. Separate and dry leaves.

MELTING AND HOLDING CHOCOLATE

Melted chocolate begins to solidify as soon as it is removed from a double boiler or the microwave. When dipping cookies or fruit, frequent trips back to the stove or microwave to remelt the chocolate can become tiresome. Howard Raber, chef of the restaurant Two Twenty-Five in Dubuque, Iowa, uses a clever heating pad arrangement to avoid this problem.

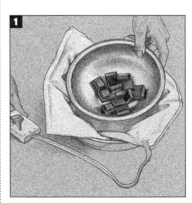

1. Line a metal bowl with a heating pad. Place a second metal bowl on top of the pad and put the chocolate to be melted into this bowl. Turn on the heating pad.

2. To melt chocolate quickly, cover the top bowl with plastic wrap, lifting the wrap occasionally to stir the chocolate until smooth. To keep the melted chocolate at an even temperature, remove the plastic wrap and set the heating pad to low.

ILLUSTRATIONS BY ALAN WITSCHONKE

TORTING A CAKE

Ken Mitchell of Redondo Beach, California, sent us this tip in which dental floss is used to cut a cake into two even layers. Once the cake is divided — professional bakers call this process "torting" — the layers can be filled with jam, buttercream, or whipped cream.

1. Place several toothpicks around the edge of the cake, halfway between the top and the bottom. Use a ruler to determine the midpoint, thus ensuring even layers.

2. Wrap a long piece of waxed dental floss around the circumference of the cake, making sure that the floss rests directly on top of the toothpicks. Cross ends of floss and pull. As floss tightens, it will cut through the cake.

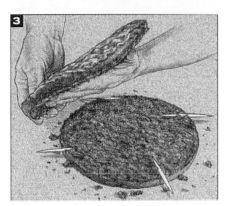

3. Once floss has cut through the cake, lift top layer and set aside. Remove toothpicks from bottom layer and proceed with filling and decorating the cake.

PREPARING BRUSSELS SPROUTS

Brussels sprouts are at their best when the heads are hard and the leaves tightly bunched. However, this quality may cause them to cook unevenly. To avoid this dilemma, follow this procedure.

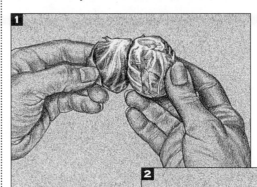

1. Remove any loose or wilted outer leaves from each sprout.

2. Cut off the stem of the sprout as close to the head as possible. Be careful not to cut into the leaves, or they will detach during cooking.

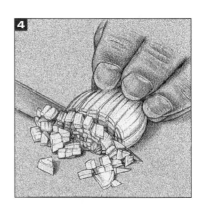

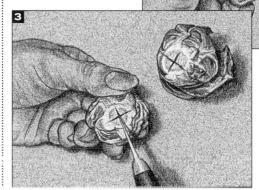

3. Using a paring knife, cut an X about three-eighths-inch deep into the stem end of each sprout. This will promote quicker and more even cooking.

DICING A SHALLOT

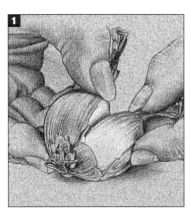

1. Separate shallot into individual bulbs.

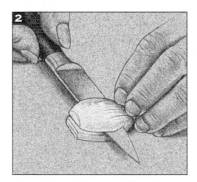

2. Peel skin from each bulb and lay flat side down on a work surface. Slice bulb crosswise almost to (but not through) the root end.

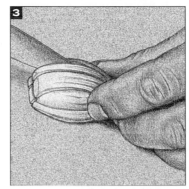

3. Make a number of parallel cuts through the top of the shallot down to the work surface.

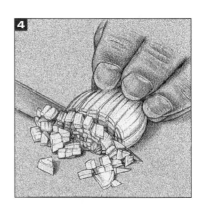

4. Finally, make thin slices perpendicular to the lengthwise cuts made in step 3.

Pot Roast Perfected

Start with the right cut and keep cooking temperatures low to get a tender, juicy pot roast that you can slice without shredding.

∽ BY STEPHEN SCHMIDT ∽

Pot roast is one of the first dishes most of us learn to cook, largely because we believe it is among the easiest. Just brown the meat with some vegetables, half cover it with water or stock, and simmer it, covered, until the meat begins to shred. The result — dry, stringy meat that has transferred its flavor to the now-delicious gravy — is pot roast as most of us have known it.

I wanted a pot roast, though, that wasn't dry, that didn't fall apart, and that retained some flavor. After conducting tests on some two dozen pot roasts, I'm pleased to report that there *is* a better pot roast, one in which the meat remains moist and flavorful. And the surprising news is that, although my method will sound strange at first, especially if you've been cooking pot roasts by the traditional method for years, it is not at all difficult.

Time vs. Temperature

Cooks have long been taught that tender cuts of beef — from the rib, loin, and sirloin, for example — are done when cooked to a certain internal temperature, as indicated on a meat thermometer. By contrast, tough pot-roasting cuts such as chuck have been considered done when cooked for a sufficient length of time — as long as it takes to make them tender. Half of this practice is correct: the best cuts for roast beef or grilled steak *are* juicy and tender at 125 degrees (rare) to 145 degrees (medium).

But conventional wisdom about pot-roasting cuts is only partially true. Although the doneness of pot roast cannot be gauged by a meat thermometer — many factors other than temperature affect the proper cooking of these cuts — temperature is not irrelevant. Pot roast becomes tough and dry if the internal temperature goes much beyond 160 degrees, which it assuredly will if you simmer the roast for hours, as most recipes recommend. In short, pot roast *can* be overcooked.

The best pot roasts are cut from well-exercised muscles of beef, muscles that contain a good deal of a connective-tissue protein called collagen, a major contributor to toughness. The trick to cooking tough cuts is to coax the collagen to solubilize, that is, to turn into gelatin, which is tender. Solubilization is a complex process which is dependent on a number of different factors, including time and temperature.

Optimal solubilization of collagen actually occurs when meat reaches an internal temperature near the boiling point of water. If gelatinizing the collagen were the only consideration, then the solution would be simply to throw the roast into a pot of boiling liquid and let it cook all day. Unfortunately, when meat is brought to such an extreme temperature, it loses almost all of its juice and develops a coarse, unpleasant texture.

Pot roasting, therefore, involves compromise. You must promote maximum collagen solubilization, knowing that complete solubilization is not possible without bringing on other unfortunate consequences. I eventually concluded that there are two things that will make the best of this less-than-ideal situation. First, start with a cut that will turn out palatably tender even if it is not brought to an extreme temperature. Second, bring the temperature of the meat to around 160 degrees over a very low flame and then, if necessary, hold it at that temperature for a relatively brief time. The slow heating helps the collagen shrink, and maintaining the temperature promotes solubilization. This low-temperature solubilization is not as complete as solubilization at the boiling point, but, then again, the meat will not suffer the ravages caused by high heat.

The Keys to Moist Meat

I began my tests with pot roast made by the traditional method, simmering several cuts for varying lengths of time. While the meat did indeed become tender, it also became fibrous, coarse, and dry. Thinking that the problem might be direct contact with liquid, I tried simmering small pieces of meat in self-sealing plastic bags; the results were identical.

Then, deducing that high temperature might be the culprit, I sealed four small chuck steaks and four small round steaks in eight separate plastic bags, then immersed them in a pot of water heated to exactly 160 degrees. After 30 minutes, I took out one chuck and one round steak and tasted them; the chuck was softer than the round but nei-

Use very little liquid with your roast and check often while cooking; the presence of even a few bubbles indicates that the liquid is too hot and the roast may dry out.

ther was yet quite tender. I raised the water temperature to 175 degrees and, one-half hour later, took out two more steaks. Neither the chuck nor the round was yet tender; on the other hand, neither had yet become stringy and dry in the way that my simmered roasts had. A half hour of additional cooking, this time at 190 degrees, rendered the chuck steak completely tender but left the round steak tough; neither steak had yet become fibrous. But when I raised the water temperature to 205 degrees and cooked the last two steaks just 15 minutes longer, I ruined both of them: the chuck had a coarse, shredded texture, and the round steak had become hard and dry.

Obviously, as the water approached simmering, the meat had become heated beyond the damage point. I did not yet know at precisely what temperature the damage had occurred, but I knew that it had to be well below the temperature of the water itself, for, no matter how small the piece, meat is never as hot as the liquid in which it is cooked. Still, I had already made a crucial discovery: Notwithstanding the advice given in most pot roast recipes (my own, of former times, included), the braising liquid of a pot roast should never be allowed to come near simmering.

But even when I conscientiously cooked below the simmer, my pot roasts still came out dry — they still seemed overcooked. I began to suspect that pot roasts respond to increased temperatures in much the same way that tender cuts of beef (and indeed all meats) do.

When meat is heated to an internal temperature of around 140 degrees — that is, the threshold between rare and medium — the fibers begin to toughen and shrink, expelling the juices. At temperatures of more than 160

PHOTOGRAPH BY ERIC ROTH

1. Using a piece of twine about four times the length of the roast, make a "lasso" by forming the fingers of one hand into a circle and running the twine around them.

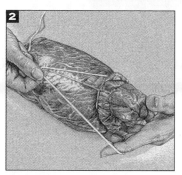

2. Widen the lasso enough to slip it around the roast.

3. Pull the loop tight several inches down the roast from the last such loop, and straighten the twine that now encircles the roast.

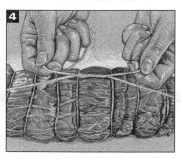

4. Continue until the entire roast has been firmly tied. Tie the ends of the twine firmly together on top of the roast.

degrees, there is a sharp tightening of the fibers, accompanied by an explosion of juice. Juice loss continues until around 180 degrees, at which point virtually all the moisture has been wrung out and the meat tastes dry. That is why, unless you dislike rare meat, tender cuts of beef should never be cooked beyond 140 degrees, when juice loss begins.

But pot roasts cannot be cooked to just 140 degrees because the pesky collagen would never break down. I tried heating the meat very slowly to 160 degrees, just shy of the end of the juice-expelling range. And, with the better pot-roasting cuts, such as the top blade, shoulder, and rump, this worked; at 160 degrees the meat was palatably tender, indicating a fair degree of collagen solubilization, yet still full of juice.

Now I reasoned that, in the case of a very tough cut, such as round, the trick might be to hold the meat at 160 degrees for an hour or more to further break down the collagen. When I tried this, the meat did become a little more tender, but it also hardened and dried out.

How could meat lose its juice before it had been heated to the end of the juice-expelling

temperature range? A chance occurrence shed some light on this riddle. I had been holding a fully cooked pot roast in the pot at a temperature well below 160 degrees and I noticed that in just 20 minutes it had begun to dry out, after an hour more it was almost juiceless. I was baffled; I knew from experience that a rare rib roast can be kept in a 120-degree oven for at least two hours without drying out.

I then consulted experts from the National Live Stock and Meat Board, who provided an explanation: Although 160 degrees is roughly 20 degrees short of the point where meat is cooked dry, tissues that have been subjected to such a relatively high temperature have become "denatured" to a greater extent than meat cooked only to rare. This means that, while rare-cooked meats still have a considerable capacity to retain moisture, well-done meat, because it has become unstable in this regard, quickly becomes dry even if it is not heated all the way to 180 degrees. Indeed, holding the thoroughly cooked meat at all, even at a low temperature, is ruinous.

Nor is juice the only component lost when

thoroughly cooked meat is kept over heat; the fat goes, too. The amount of fat left in the meat after cooking affects what meat professionals call perceived tenderness; it "lubricates" meat as it is chewed. A fair amount of fat makes meat seem tender; lesser amounts make meat difficult to chew and swallow. This is another reason why keeping well-cooked meat hot — or even warm — makes the meat seem dry, especially if the meat was very lean to begin with. All the fat melts out.

Finally, I began to understand why some chuck cuts make more succulent pot roasts than others and why none of the round cuts, with the exception of rump roast, are really suitable for pot roasting. First, the best of the chuck is not that tough to begin with, so, assuming that the temperature has been raised slowly, a sufficient proportion of the collagen will have solubilized by the time the meat reaches 160 degrees. By contrast, the tougher parts of the chuck and nearly all of the round need to be heated beyond 160 degrees and then held at a high internal temperature for a prolonged period if they are to be tender — at which point the fibers harden and the juices are expelled. That is, the meat is tough and dry.

In addition, the most desirable chuck cuts and the best part of the round — the rump — are naturally well marbled. So even when they are slightly overcooked or held after cooking, they will still seem juicy because they retain a fair amount of fat. The toughest cuts of the chuck, and all of the round except the rump, are lean; when they are overcooked they become unpalatably dry.

How to Cook Pot Roast

The way to cook perfect pot roast, although unusual, is quite simple. First, tie the roast to make it as compact and evenly shaped as possible (*see* illustrations 1 through 4, above); loose or protruding pieces of meat are likely to overcook. Dry the roast thoroughly with paper towels, then season it. Use a heavy pot with a tight-fitting lid to retain moisture and distribute heat evenly, and brown the roast to a deep mahogany color; if the roast is not thoroughly browned, the gravy will be pale and lacking in flavor. I prefer to brown in rendered pork or

WHICH GRADE OF BEEF IS BEST?

There are three common retail grades of beef — Prime, Choice, and Select, in descending order of quality. (Quality, in this case, is gauged by several factors, the most important of which is the degree of intramuscular marbling, or fat content.) Some supermarkets also carry ungraded beef, called "no roll" because there is no stamp — or roll — on the carcass. (You will rarely see a stamp even if the meat is graded, because it is usually trimmed off; ask the butcher what grade of meat the supermarket carries.) Most no-roll beef is comparable to

Select, but some is as well marbled as Choice or even Prime. The explanation: Although all beef must be inspected for wholesomeness, grading is entirely voluntary and is done only if the packer or processor pays for it. If there is a demand for beef of a certain grade, it becomes profitable to have the beef graded, but if there is no such demand, grading is unnecessary. Since no-roll beef can be of any quality, it makes sense to examine it carefully and to choose the piece that shows the most white flecks in the tissue. I actually had better luck with a visibly well-

marbled no-roll rump roast than with several Select and Choice cuts.

Choice cuts vary widely in their degree of marbling, and you can sometimes find a Select roast that is nearly as well marbled as a more expensive Choice roast of the same cut. Remember too that quality (as determined by grading) is not always crucial where pot-roasting cuts are concerned. Although I found that Choice shoulder roasts were more tender and juicier after cooking than Select shoulder roasts, that distinction was not evident with top blade roasts.

beef fat or in lard, all of which give better color and flavor than oil. Keep the flame moderately high, and keep an eye on the meat as it browns. If you blacken the pot, the dish will have a bitter flavor, and the exterior of the roast may become leathery.

After browning the vegetables, add just enough liquid to film the bottom of the pot — about two to five tablespoons. Submerging the meat in liquid leaches out the flavor components; the meat ends up tasting as though it has been soaked and boiled, which, in effect, it has. Remember, though, that when you use only a very little liquid, you must pay especially close attention to the heat under the pot. The less liquid you use, the more apt it is to come to a simmer, and when the liquid simmers the outer part of the roast is liable to toughen.

Using very low heat for the duration of the roasting is key to the entire process. Unless your burner can be turned way down, you must have a way to block the flame so that the liquid never comes anywhere near a simmer. You can use a store-bought flame-tamer — a solid piece of metal or an insulated metal heat diffuser — or you can improvise. Try stacking two burner grates, if you have a gas stove, or placing one or two beat-up pizza pans or cookie sheets over the burner.

You can also cook pot roast in your oven, but be sure to hold the heat to no more than 175 degrees. This is an almost unheard of oven temperature, and some ovens are incapable of holding it, regardless of what their thermostats might say (be sure to use a reliable oven thermometer). Check the roast frequently during cooking. If the steam rushes in your face when your remove the lid or — even worse — if the liquid has begun to simmer, turn the thermostat down.

Bubbling is a certain sign that the temperature is too high, for if there are bubbles, no matter how few or how small, at least some of the liquid in the pot has begun to boil. And the liquid can reach 211 degrees — way too hot — without a bubble in sight. You should be able to lay your hand on the pot cover for a couple of seconds without discomfort (do this carefully, of course, especially if your pot has a thin cover). Another good sign is absolute quiet in the pot — no sizzling, hissing, or rocking noises. Steam is yet another useful indicator.

When you remove the lid, the steam should curl around the meat in lazy wisps. If there is a great deal of steam, and if the steam bursts out of the uncovered pot, the liquid is probably well above 190 degrees, much too high.

Broad, flat roasts should be turned every 20 minutes to prevent the side that is flush against the pan from overheating. Loaf-shaped roasts can be turned every half hour. Flat chuck roasts will, on average, take two hours, plus or minus a half hour. Loaf-shaped chuck roasts and rump roasts usually take two and one-half to three hours, though they should be checked a bit sooner. To test for doneness, pierce the roast in several places with an ordinary table fork. The roast is done when it yields to moderate pressure (don't expect the fork to glide right in or to slide right out) and the juices bubbling up through the holes are clear, or just tinged with pink. To be sure, cut two very thin slices from the end and taste the inner one. It will have a little chew but should not seem tough. The flesh should be faintly rosy, compact, and nicely juicy — not dry, stringy, or falling apart. Remember to carve pot roast in the thinnest possible slices, against the grain if possible.

BEEF 101: BUYING A POT ROAST

It's easy enough to say that chuck cuts are best for pot roasting, but once you're in the supermarket you will likely find a dozen differently named, different-looking pieces of chuck and round. Here's a guide to help you find the best chuck cuts; with one exception (*see* illustration, below), forget the cuts from the round.

Beef Chuck Top Blade Roast Boneless (which, confusingly, is sometimes given the vague label of Top Chuck Roast) is broad and flat, and weighs a little over three pounds in its entirety. It is the most tender, juicy, and flavorful of all pot-roasting cuts, and, just as important, the most forgiving of overcooking.

Beef Chuck Mock Tender Roast is a solid, conical piece of meat that suggests a section of tenderloin. This cut is somewhat dry and fine-grained, and is less flavorful than either shoulder or top blade; it is also less tolerant of overcooking. However, as long as it is not overdone, the mock tender is tender indeed, and, because it is compact and without seams, it does make beautiful slices.

The only round cut worth considering for pot roast is Beef Bottom Round Rump Roast. Weighing five to six pounds altogether, rump roast is thick and squared at the end where it was separated from the rest of the bottom round, but pointed at the sirloin end. The tapering end, which contains some of the sirloin muscles, is markedly more tender, so you should always choose a pointy-looking piece if you need only a portion of the whole roast.

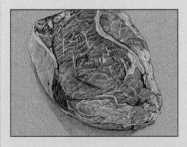  

One common pot-roasting cut, which you may find in any of the three forms pictured above, is Beef Chuck Shoulder Pot Roast Boneless (also called Chuck Roast Boneless or Chuck Shoulder Roast). This cut is taken from the muscle that covers the back of the cow's foreleg (or arm) and extends over the ribs. Depending on how it has been cut, it may resemble a steak (above, left), a conventional roast (middle), or a split roast (right). All make tender, juicy, and flavorful pot roast.

ILLUSTRATIONS BY TONY DELUZ

When you must cut with the grain, do so on the bias.

Allowing a cooked pot roast to sit in the pot indefinitely is not a good idea — the meat will dry out. Twenty or thirty minutes will cause only minimal damage; if the delay is longer, take the roast out of the pot, wrap it tightly in foil, and put it in a warm spot in the kitchen. Thick roasts will retain a temperature above 110 degrees, which is warm enough for serving, for better than two hours and even thinner, steak-shaped roasts will stay warm for at least an hour, and probably longer. (Remember, too, that a slightly cool roast will be fine if the slices are arranged on a warmed platter and masked with piping-hot gravy.) If the wait is longer still, wrap the meat in foil, let it cool, then re-heat it in barely warm gravy. A slight warmed-over flavor is not a problem where pot roast is concerned; in fact, I rather like it.

MASTER RECIPE FOR POT ROAST
Serves at least 6
If you do not have a spice grinder, substitute three-quarters teaspoon ground black pepper and one-sixteenth teaspoon ground cloves for the peppercorns and whole cloves, and simply put the bay leaves in the pot.

- 1 medium or 2 small bay leaves
- ½ teaspoon dried leaf thyme
- 2 whole cloves
- ¾ teaspoon black peppercorns
- ¾ teaspoon salt
- 1–2 large cloves garlic, peeled and sliced very thin (about 16 slices)
- 1 boneless beef pot roast (about 3 pounds; *see* "Beef 101: Buying a Pot Roast," page 8, for preferred cuts), patted dry with paper towels and tied with twine (*see* "Tying the Roast," page 7)
- 2½ tablespoons lard or oil
- 1 medium onion, chopped fine (1 cup)
- ½ small carrot, diced fine (¼ cup)
- ½ small celery stalk, diced fine (¼ cup)
- ½ medium turnip, diced fine (¼ cup), optional
- 2–5 tablespoons water, black coffee, or dry red or white wine
- 1 cup homemade stock or low-salt canned beef broth
- 2 tablespoons all-purpose flour
- 2–3 tablespoons chopped fresh parsley for garnish

1. Grind herbs and spices to a fine powder in a spice grinder or small food processor. Add salt; pulse to mix. Transfer to a small bowl, add garlic slivers, and toss to coat with spice mixture. Using a paring knife, poke 16, ½-inch deep slits in meat; stuff each with a garlic sliver. Rub remaining spice mixture over meat.

2. Heat oil in a heavy pot (about 4 to 6 quarts, preferably enameled cast iron) over medium-high heat. Put roast in pot; brown thoroughly on all sides, maintaining heat so fat sizzles briskly but does not smoke, 15 to 20 minutes. Make sure to brown meat well, then remove to a plate. Sauté vegetables until brown and crispy around edges but not blackened, 10 to 15 minutes.

3. Pour in enough liquid of choice just to film bottom of pot; scrape with a wooden spoon to loosen browned bits. Reduce heat to lowest point; cover burner with a flame-taming device. Cover pot and wait 5 minutes. If liquid steams rather than simmers, return roast to pot. The temperature should be maintained at this point throughout cooking. Using spoons rather than forks to minimize juice loss, turn steak-shaped roasts every 20 minutes, loaf-shaped roasts every 30 minutes. The meat is done when it can be pierced with a table fork and juices run clear or only faintly tinged with pink, about 1½ to 2½ hours for flat roasts, and be-tween 2 and 3 hours, or as long as 4 hours, for thick roasts. To test for doneness, cut 2 very thin slices off end and taste inner one. The meat should taste juicy and firm-tender, and appear faintly rosy. If meat is still tough, cook a bit longer. (On the other hand, if flesh tastes dry and has a stringy, shredded look, you have overcooked it — just make gravy, slice meat, and return it to pot, set over the lowest possible flame. Let it sit in gravy 10 minutes before serving.)

4. Remove meat; wrap in aluminum foil. Tilt pot and skim fat from surface; set aside. Pour juices and vegetables into a blender jar or workbowl of a food processor fitted with steel blade; process to a coarse puree. Pour into a 2-cup measure; add enough stock or broth to make 2 cups. Return juices to pot; bring to a simmer. Mix 1½ tablespoons reserved cooking fat with flour. Whisk flour mixture into sim-mering juices, 1 teaspoon at a time, adding only as much as is necessary for the gravy to coat a spoon. Simmer to fully cook flour, about 2 minutes; adjust seasonings.

5. Unwrap meat, pouring accumulated juices into gravy. Cut meat into very thin slices — ⅛-inch, if possible — and arrange on a platter. Pour some of gravy over meat; sprinkle with parsley. Serve immediately with gravy passed separately.

SAUERBRATEN
Be careful when browning meat — the sugar in the marinade makes the meat especially prone to blackening. Serve the sauerbraten with noodles or potato pancakes.

Follow Master Recipe for Pot Roast, adding 1 teaspoon ground ginger and ¾ teaspoon each of ground caraway seed and ground coriander seed to spice rub. Mix ¾ cup each red wine and red wine vinegar and 2 tablespoons sugar in a bowl until sugar dissolves. Put the meat in a zipper-lock plastic bag; add wine mixture and all vegetables except turnips. Press air out of bag and seal; refrigerate 2 to 4 days, turning bag occasionally. Drain and reserve meat and vegetables and marinade separately. Dry meat and cook it and turnip and vegetables, follow-ing Master Recipe. Use reserved marinade as liquid of choice in Master Recipe, reducing it to a few syrupy tablespoons before returning roast to pot. Whisk ½ to ¾ cup sour cream into the finished gravy; avoid simmering after adding sour cream.

POT ROAST IN RED WINE
Follow Master Recipe for Pot Roast, putting garlic-studded meat in a zipper-lock plastic bag. Add all vegetables except turnips, 2½ cups of fruity red wine, 6 peeled garlic cloves and/or a 3-inch strip of orange zest. Press air out of bag and seal; refrigerate 2 to 4 days, turn-ing bag occasionally. Drain and reserve meat and vegetables and marinade separately. (Garlic cloves and orange zest can be added to braising liquid or discarded; remove zest be-fore pureeing vegetables for gravy.) Dry meat and cook it and turnip and vegetables, follow-ing Master Recipe. Use reserved marinade as liquid of choice, reducing it to a few syrupy tablespoons before returning roast to pot.

SOUTHWESTERN POT ROAST
Feel free to stud the meat in this recipe with ex-tra slices of garlic. Try Red Pack brand whole tomatoes — they are packed in a thick puree and require virtually no reducing.

Follow Master Recipe for Pot Roast, adding 1½ tablespoons chili powder, 2 teaspoons ground cumin, 1½ teaspoons ground cinna-mon, and ½ teaspoon cayenne pepper to the spice rub. Use 1 pound of canned whole toma-toes, crushed with your hands, for liquid of choice, boiling them over high heat until thick. Cook meat according to Master Recipe, but in-stead of making a gravy with beef broth and flour, simply degrease the juices and reduce them somewhat, if watery. Sauté 1 cup chopped seeded green peppers (sweet, hot, or a mixture) in 2 tablespoons of the skimmed fat until softened and browned around the edges. Add peppers to the sauce; simmer to blend fla-vors, about 5 minutes. Substitute minced cilantro for the parsley garnish.

POT ROAST WITH PORCINI MUSHROOMS
Follow Master Recipe for Pot Roast, soaking 1 ounce (or more, if desired) dried porcini mush-rooms in 2 cups fruity white wine (such as Chardonnay) until softened, about 1 hour. Strain mushrooms, pressing to extrude most of the liquid, and chop fine; cover mushrooms and set aside. Strain wine through cheesecloth or coffee filter and use as liquid of choice in Master Recipe, reducing it to a few syrupy tablespoons before returning roast to pot. After making gravy, stir in reserved chopped porcinis and, if desired, ½ cup heavy cream; simmer to blend flavors, about 5 minutes. ∎

Stephen Schmidt is the author of *Master Recipes* (Ballantine, 1987).

How to Roast Root Vegetables

Roasting concentrates the flavor and caramelizes the exterior of root vegetables such as parsnips, carrots, potatoes, onions, and turnips.

∽ BY STEPHANIE LYNESS ∽

Roasting vegetables evaporates much of their water, concentrating their natural sugars and yielding a rich, sweet taste and meaty texture. Roasting also gives root vegetables a crisp, golden skin that makes a wonderful contrast to their soft, moist interior.

I wanted to find an easy way to roast a lot of root vegetables at one time — cut them to size, throw them into the oven, and, aside from an occasional stir, forget about them until they're cooked. I experimented with a variety of cut-up root vegetables: potatoes, sweet potatoes, white turnips, rutabagas, carrots, and parsnips. I added onion, shallot, and garlic for flavor. (I also experimented with beets, but found that they roast best when left whole.)

Different vegetables have different ideal cooking temperatures, so I devised a master recipe,

Most of us are used to eating roasted root vegetables exclusively as an accompaniment to roasted meat or poultry. But with this recipe, you can enjoy their sweet, concentrated flavor and meaty texture any time you want.

roasting at 400 degrees, that represents a compromise. Potatoes and sweet potatoes cooked beautifully at 400 degrees, browning well on the outside and staying soft and luscious on the inside. Turnips, rutabagas, carrots, and parsnips, however, shriveled a little at that temperature; they do better at 375 degrees for 30 minutes to cook them through, with a final roasting at 425 degrees for 15 to 20 minutes to brown them (*see* below for recipes for individual vegetables). I also tried roasting at 450 degrees for 15 minutes, then reducing the temperature to 350 degrees for the remainder of the cooking time, but none of the vegetables browned well.

The rules that apply to roasting meats also apply to roasting vegetables: You need high, dry heat and a low-sided roasting pan that is large enough to accommodate the vegetables without crowding. In addition, the vegetables, with some exceptions, must be cut to roughly the same size for even cooking. What the pan is made of is much less critical than its size; vegetables brown well in aluminum, Pyrex, enameled steel,

and even porcelain, but a too-small pan will enormously inhibit browning. This browning, or caramelization, is important for reasons of both sight and taste: not only is the golden brown color attractive, it is evidence that the natural sugars in the vegetables have caramelized, adding a rich, deep, concentrated sweetness.

You also need some fat to roast vegetables well. For about a pound of vegetables, I use at least one tablespoon of butter, vegetable oil, or olive oil; chicken or duck fat is especially wonderful. You can, of course, combine more than one fat. I found that vegetable oil (I used canola) gave the lightest, crispest crust; olive oil browns a little less well but adds a nicer flavor. Butter keeps the vegetables moistened and makes a softer crust; it also lends a superior flavor. A combination of butter and oil browns better than butter alone but not as well as oil alone; the butter flavor is not particularly noticeable. My recommendation: for visual appeal, choose vegetable oil; for flavor, olive oil or butter. You can hardly go wrong, regardless of your choice.

This recipe is devised for roasting any combination of the following root vegetables: carrots, parsnips, all-purpose or boiling potatoes, sweet potatoes, rutabagas, and turnips, along with yellow or red onions, shallots, and garlic. Do not go overboard, however; too many vegetables muddy the flavor. I usually limit the mix to two or three root vegetables. Cut all vegetables, as necessary, so that they are about one and one-quarter inches thick.

If you wish to parboil the vegetables before roasting, follow the procedure described in "Parboiling: Is it Worth It?," on page 11 before beginning the Master Recipe. Season the vegetables with pepper only after roasting — pepper becomes strong and bitter with prolonged cooking.

When roasted individually, carrots, parsnips, rutabagas, and turnips should cook at a lower temperature to start; at higher temperatures, they dehydrate and shrivel. (The roasted turnip and carrot recipes that follow give specific cooking times and temperatures.)

MASTER RECIPE FOR ROASTED ROOT VEGETABLES
Serves 4

1　head garlic
1½–2　pounds root vegetables, peeled and cut into 1¼-inch pieces
1　medium onion or 4 to 6 shallots, peeled
2　tablespoons melted butter, vegetable, or olive oil, or a combination
　　Salt and ground black pepper

1. Heat oven to 400 degrees. If roasting garlic cloves in skins, simply break head into individual cloves. If you wish to roast cloves out of skins, put whole, unpeeled head in a small saucepan with water to cover. Bring water to

boil, then simmer to soften cloves and loosen skins, about 10 minutes. Drain and refresh garlic head under cold water. Separate cloves and peel.

2. Put vegetables (excluding garlic) into a roasting pan large enough to hold them without crowding. Toss vegetables with butter and/or oil and sprinkle with salt. Roast, stirring or shaking vegetables every 15 minutes, until tender and evenly browned, 45 to 50 minutes. Add unpeeled garlic cloves during final 20 minutes; add peeled garlic during final 15 minutes. Sprinkle with pepper; taste and adjust seasonings. Serve hot or at room temperature.

ROASTED TURNIPS, SHALLOTS, AND GARLIC WITH ROSEMARY
Serves 4

Follow Master Recipe, using turnips or rutabagas, shallots, and garlic for vegetables. Add 1 teaspoon crumbled dried rosemary or thyme leaves (or 2 teaspoons fresh) when tossing vegetables with salt and fat. Decrease roasting temperature to 375 degrees for first 30 minutes, then raise heat to 425 degrees and continue with Master Recipe, adding garlic at appropriate time.

ROASTED CARROTS AND RED ONION WITH BALSAMIC VINEGAR
Serves 4

Follow Master Recipe, using carrots and a medium red onion for vegetables. (Omit garlic, if you like.) Add 3 tablespoons balsamic vinegar when tossing vegetables with salt and olive oil. Decrease roasting temperature to 375 degrees for first 30 minutes. Increase temperature to 425 degrees and continue with Master Recipe.

ROASTED SWEET POTATOES WITH CHIVES
Serves 4

Follow Master Recipe, using sweet potatoes and shallots for vegetables; omit garlic. Toss roasted potatoes with 1 tablespoon snipped fresh chives.

ROASTED POTATOES WITH ONION, BACON, AND THYME
Serves 4

This preparation is superb with potatoes, but it works nicely with other root vegetables as well. Remember to follow the oven temperatures in the roasted carrot and turnip recipes if you choose those vegetables.

Cook 5 slices of bacon (¼ pound) in a roasting pan over medium-high heat or in a 400-degree oven until crisp. Remove bacon, crumble, and set aside. Leave about 2 tablespoons of bacon fat in roasting pan. Follow the Master Recipe, using potatoes and onions for vegetables: toss vegetables with 1 teaspoon crumbled dried thyme leaves in the bacon fat (rather than fats listed in Master Recipe). Garnish roasted potatoes with crumbled bacon and serve. ∎

Stephanie Lyness is a freelance food writer and cooking teacher living in New York City.

CUTTING ROOT VEGETABLES FOR ROASTING

When roasting several types of root vegetables together, it is important that all the vegetable pieces be about the same size, so that they cook evenly. Note that the accompanying recipe is timed for vegetables cut about one and one-quarter inches thick.

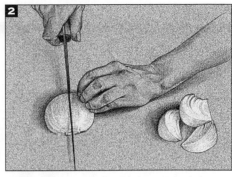

1. Cut oblong vegetables such as carrots and parsnips into two-inch lengths, then cut the fatter tops in half lengthwise. (Carrots take longer to cook than the other vegetables, so cut them slightly smaller.)

2. Peel onions and cut into one-inch to one and one-quarter-inch wedges through the root end.

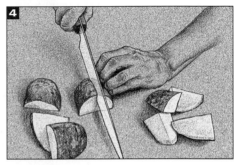

3. With round vegetables such as turnips, cut in half, then in quarters, then in eighths.

4. Cut white or sweet potatoes in half or thirds crosswise to make two and one-half to three-inch chunks. Cut each chunk in half lengthwise, then cut in half again.

PARBOILING: IS IT WORTH IT?

Some cooks parboil root vegetables before roasting them. Since one of my goals in these experiments was to devise a simple method, I wasn't especially keen to add more pots and more technique to the process. At first I tried a compromise, covering the vegetables in the roasting pan with aluminum foil for half of the roasting time to allow them to steam partway before they began to brown. This was a failure: the vegetables took much longer to cook than they did when simply roasted, they didn't brown as well, and the flavor wasn't as good.

So, in my second experiment, I parboiled carrots, potatoes, and turnips, simmering them until they were about halfway cooked; then I roasted them at 425 degrees. The result was interesting; because the vegetables absorb water during parboiling, they don't dry out as much as they do when simply roasted, and they end up plumper and juicier — especially turnips and carrots. On the other hand, the parboiled vegetables did not have the ultra-concentrated flavor and chewy texture of those vegetables that were simply roasted. In their favor, parboiled vegetables had a thinner, more delicate crust. The preliminary parboiling gives a slightly more refined result than roasting alone, but it requires an extra step that I am unwilling to perform when ease of execution is chief among my goals.

If you do choose to parboil, start the vegetables in cold, salted water and simmer them until they are about halfway cooked, about ten minutes. Drain the vegetables well, toss them in the fat as in the Master Recipe, and then roast them at 425 degrees until cooked through, 40 to 50 minutes. Sweet potatoes, onions, and shallots needn't be parboiled because they roast absolutely exquisitely with no added fuss; garlic, on the other hand, can be parboiled (see *Cook's Illustrated*, September/October, 1993, for details).

Making Crisp, Long-lasting Biscotti

The good news: The most flavorful biscotti are made with a small amount of fat.

~ BY STEVE JOHNSON ~

Despite their elegant appearance, the twice-baked Italian cookies known as biscotti are easy to make. A longer-than-average baking time yields a uniquely crunchy texture and also gives them an unusually long shelf life. Together, these factors make biscotti an excellent choice for home bakers. To find out how to make the very best biscotti, I decided to test and compare the dozens of traditional recipes that I have encountered during my cooking career. The results were surprising.

Varying the "Fat Factor"

The many biscotti recipes with which I experimented had a fairly constant ratio of sugar to flour to flavorings. The major difference among these recipes was the type and quantity of fat used, which varied dramatically. It was this "fat factor," I discovered, which most dramatically affected the taste, texture, and shelf life of the resulting biscotti.

Most traditional biscotti recipes include egg yolks as the only source of fat, but some include butter as well, while others contain virtually no fat at all, and use only the white of the egg. In the matter of texture, I found that recipes containing butter produced a satisfyingly crunchy biscuit, but were somewhat softer and richer, more cookielike, compared to those not containing butter. I also discovered that recipes using whole eggs only, without additional yolks, turned out to be noticeably less cakelike, with a more straightforward crunch. On the other end of the scale, the biscotti made with egg whites only — no butter or yolks — produced the driest and crispiest cookies, reminiscent of hard candy. In fact, these cookies were so hard that they might present the risk of cracking a tooth if eaten *sans* dunking.

In the matter of taste, the fresh-baked biscotti containing sweet cream butter provided a superior and irresistible rich flavor. My favorite combination of ingredients, however, included whole eggs, with no additional yolks or butter, because it resulted in the truest delivery — lean and direct — of the flavors in these cookies.

I found that storage and shelf life were also directly affected by fat content. As I experimented with different doughs, I noticed that recipes using butter initially had the best taste and texture, but lost their full flavor and satis-

SHAPING BISCOTTI

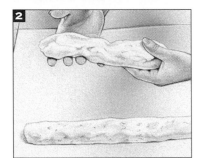

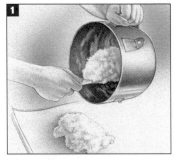

2. Using floured hands, shape the dough masses into two rough logs, each about 13 inches long and roughly 2 inches in diameter.

1. Biscotti dough is rather sticky; use a rubber spatula to divide the dough into two portions for shaping.

3. Reflour hands, then pat the logs into smoother shapes. Because the dough is rather heavy, the logs will be oval, rather than perfectly round.

4. When the logs have been cooked once and have cooled slightly, use a serrated knife to cut into ⅜-inch slices, then replace on cookie sheet for second baking.

fying crunch after only one day, as the butter baked into the cookies began to go stale. Recipes including no butter, but with whole eggs plus yolks, came in second in the taste and texture evaluation when eaten fresh, but held up better in both categories as the days went by. The biscotti recipes using whole eggs, however, seemed to get even better with time; they tasted great and remained very crisp after a week and, if stored properly, would keep for several weeks.

Baking Them Twice

Whatever the amount and type of fat they contain, all biscotti recipes share the common characteristics of quick preparation time and a relatively long baking time. For most recipes, preparation involves simply mixing the wet ingredients with a whisk in one bowl, sifting the dry ingredients together in another bowl, then folding the dry into the wet, while adding flavorings. Because they are baked twice, however, the total baking time for biscotti is a bit

longer than for regular cookies; first they are baked in flat loaves for 30 to 40 minutes, then sliced and baked again for an additional 10 to 15 minutes. This double-baking technique ensures a very low moisture content, contributing enormously to biscotti's great potential for storage — the primary reason for bakers to have gone to all this trouble in the first place.

As for flavorings, there are literally dozens of different combinations used in biscotti, since the plain dough adapts beautifully to various pairings. Some of the best flavor combinations date from the late Middle Ages, when sea trade became very active and many new and varied ingredients became available to cooks and bakers. Medieval sailors and explorers such as Columbus and Marco Polo relied upon these biscuits for energy and nourishment. Zests of citrus fruits, native to southern Italy and other parts of the northern Mediterranean, were combined with exotic dry spices such as cinnamon, clove, and ginger. Dried and candied fruits were used, along with local and foreign vari-

ILLUSTRATIONS BY MICHELE AMATRULA

eties of nuts such as walnuts, hazelnuts, almonds, pistachios, and sesame seeds. I offer variations on these flavor combinations in my recipes.

When organizing your first batch of biscotti, make sure that you allow enough time for both of the baking steps. Use their long shelf life to your advantage: make large batches and save them, or, if you're incorporating them into a complete menu, go ahead and prepare them early on in the process. The batter may at first appear rather sticky, but resist the urge to dust with flour: too much and they will become heavy and dense. It is preferable to use a rubber spatula, waxed paper, or plastic wrap if you have trouble handling the dough. One final note: biscotti must be completely cooled before storage, to ensure that all the moisture has escaped.

LEMON-ANISE BISCOTTI
Makes 3–4 dozen

A Sicilian specialty, this recipe produces a relatively hard biscuit — perfect with an afternoon cup of coffee.

```
2    cups unbleached all-purpose flour
1    teaspoon baking powder
¼    teaspoon salt
1    cup sugar
2    large eggs
¼    teaspoon vanilla extract
1    tablespoon minced zest from 1 lemon
1    tablespoon anise seed
```

1. Sift first 3 ingredients together in a small bowl.

2. Whisk sugar and eggs in a large bowl to a light lemon color; stir in next 3 ingredients. Sift

dry ingredients over egg mixture, then fold in until dough is just combined.

3. Adjust oven rack to middle position and heat oven to 350 degrees. Halve dough and turn each portion onto an oiled cookie sheet covered with parchment. Using floured hands, quickly stretch each portion of dough into a rough 13-by-2-inch log, placing them about 3 inches apart on the cookie sheet. Pat each dough shape to smooth it. Bake, turning pan once, until loaves are golden and just beginning to crack on top, about 35 minutes.

4. Cool the loaves for 10 minutes; lower oven temperature to 325 degrees. Cut each loaf diagonally into ⅜-inch slices with a serrated knife. Lay the slices about ½-inch apart on the cookie sheet, cut side up, and return them to the oven. Bake, turning over each cookie halfway through baking, until crisp and golden brown on both sides, about 15 minutes. Transfer biscotti to wire rack and cool completely. (Biscotti can be stored in an airtight container for at least 1 month.)

Variation: Follow the mixing, baking, and slicing instructions for Lemon-Anise Biscotti, substituting ½ cup of unhulled sesame seeds for the anise seeds in the recipe. Brush the top of each loaf of dough with an egg wash and sprinkle with additional sesame seeds.

HONEY-LAVENDER BISCOTTI
Makes 4–5 dozen

Based on the flavors of a popular Provençal ice cream, these honey-lavender biscotti are best made with an assertive honey, such as a spicy clover. Dried lavender blossoms, also an ingredient in *herbes de Provence,* can be found in spice or herbal stores, or *see* Sources and Resources, page 32.

```
2¼   cups unbleached all-purpose flour
1    teaspoon baking powder
½    teaspoon baking soda
¼    teaspoon salt
⅔    cup sugar
3    large eggs
3    tablespoons honey
½    teaspoon vanilla extract
2    tablespoons minced zest from
       1 orange
1    tablespoon dried lavender blossoms
       (optional)
```

1. Sift first 4 ingredients together in a small bowl.

2. Whisk sugar and eggs in a large bowl to a light lemon color; stir in next 3 (or 4) ingredients. Sift dry ingredients over egg mixture, then fold in until dough is just combined.

3. Follow steps 3 and 4 in Lemon-Anise Biscotti.

SPICED BISCOTTI
Makes 4–5 dozen

If desired, substitute three whole eggs for the two eggs and two egg yolks in this recipe.

```
2¼   cups unbleached all-purpose flour
1    teaspoon baking powder
½    teaspoon baking soda
¼    teaspoon salt
¼    teaspoon ground white pepper
½    teaspoon ground cloves
½    teaspoon ground cinnamon
¼    teaspoon ground ginger
1    cup sugar
2    large eggs plus 2 yolks
½    teaspoon vanilla extract
```

1. Sift first 8 ingredients together in a small bowl.

2. Whisk sugar and eggs to a light lemon color; stir in vanilla extract. Sift dry ingredients over egg mixture, then fold in until dough is just combined.

3. Follow steps 3 and 4 in Lemon-Anise Biscotti.

Variations: Macerate ¾ cup currants, chopped raisins, or dates in ¼ cup brandy or marsala for at least 1 hour. Drain and fold into the dough in step 2, adding a teaspoon or so of the macerating liquid to the dough.

ORANGE-ALMOND BISCOTTI
Makes 3–4 dozen

The addition of a small amount of butter produces a richer, more cookielike texture. Although they will keep at least two weeks in an airtight container, these biscotti are especially good when eaten the same day they are baked.

```
2    cups unbleached all-purpose flour
1    teaspoon baking powder
¼    teaspoon salt
4    tablespoons unsalted butter
1    cup sugar
2    large eggs
½    teaspoon vanilla extract
¼    teaspoon almond extract
¾    cup whole almonds with skins;
       toasted, cooled, and chopped coarse
2    tablespoons minced zest from 1
       orange
```

1. Sift first 3 ingredients together in a small bowl.

2. Beat butter and sugar together in bowl of electric mixer until light and smooth; add eggs one at a time, then extracts. Stir in almonds and zest. Sift dry ingredients over egg mixture, then fold in until dough is just mixed.

3. Follow steps 3 and 4 in Lemon-Anise Biscotti.

Variations: You may substitute toasted hazelnuts for the almonds in this recipe. A combination of hazelnuts and almonds also works very well. ∎

Steve Johnson is the *chef de cuisine* at Hamersley's Bistro in Boston.

Raspberry Charlotte Royale

The secret of this dessert — a sliced jelly roll filled with mousse — is a flexible cake that's a cross between a genoise and a classic sponge.

~

While standard charlottes depend on bread, ladyfingers, or plain cake, the impressive Charlotte Royale uses spirals of jam-filled jelly roll to encase a mousse filling. Despite its impressive appearance, though, this dessert is not particularly difficult to make. To simplify it even further, Susan Purdy, author of *A Piece of Cake* (Macmillan, 1989) and *Have Your Cake and Eat It, Too* (Morrow, 1993), created a cake specifically designed to hold its shape while being rolled up.

Like the classic French genoise, Purdy's cake relies on beaten egg foam for its light, airy texture. Nevertheless, there are differences between the two cakes. To begin with, a genoise is made by warming whole eggs with sugar and beating air into the whole mass. In Purdy's cake, the egg yolks and whites are beaten separately with sugar; this process builds elasticity and flexibility in the batter, resulting in a cake less likely to crack during rolling.

This cake also differs from conventional American sponge cakes, which use baking powder to achieve a high rise and a rather coarse crumb. To give her cake a denser, stronger texture more suitable for rolling, Purdy relies solely on the egg foam for rise, omitting chemical leaveners. In addition, Purdy adds cornstarch to the cake flour in the recipe, creating a very low-protein mixture that yields an extremely tender crumb. The resulting delicacy of the batter makes it important to fold in the dry ingredients gently, by hand, to avoid breaking the air bubbles in the egg foam. By adding the dry ingredients in small amounts, the cook can incorporate each portion with minimal mixing.

To promote tight rolling, trim the crisp edges and roll the cake in a sugared tea towel as soon as it comes out of the oven (*see* illustrations 1 and 2, page 15). Once the cake has been unrolled, coated with preserves, and rerolled (illustration 3), slices are used to enclose a gelatin-based mousse enriched with whipped cream (illustrations 4 through 6). The mousse can be made with one cup of any fruit puree, including mangoes, passion fruit, cherries, or berries of any type. If you choose to make your mousse with a fruit other than raspberries, be sure to use a complementary jam in the cake (apricot is fairly neutral and can be used with tropical fruits), and serve the dessert with a sauce made from the same fruit that is used in the mousse.

For additional variations, instead of vanilla, the cake can be scented with an equal amount of lemon or orange extract or one tablespoon citrus juice plus the grated zest of one fruit.

If you wish, you can use this versatile cake as a simple jelly roll, rather than as the base for a Charlotte Royale. To do so, simply follow the recipe instructions through step 5, then dust the top with sifted confectioner's sugar and garnish with whipped cream.

RASPBERRY CHARLOTTE ROYALE
Serves 8–10

The entire charlotte can be prepared and refrigerated a day in advance of serving. Or, freeze the unsliced jelly roll until you are ready to assemble the charlotte. You can speed up the process of setting the gelatin for the mousse by chilling it in an ice-water bath, which takes about 15 minutes, as opposed to one hour in the refrigerator. If the mixture becomes too stiff, place the bowl in a hot-water bath and whisk briefly until the consistency of soft pudding is achieved.

Raspberry Jelly Roll Cake
- ½ cup sifted cake flour
- ¼ cup sifted cornstarch
- 4 large eggs at room temperature, separated
  Pinch of salt
- 10 tablespoons sugar
- ¾ teaspoon vanilla extract
- ¼ cup confectioners' sugar
- ⅔ cup raspberry preserves

Raspberry Mousse Filling
- 1 tablespoon unflavored gelatin
- 1½ tablespoons juice from ½ lemon
- ¼ cup sugar
  Pinch of salt
- 1 pint fresh raspberries or 12 ounces frozen, unsweetened raspberries, thawed, pureed, and strained (1 cup)
- 3 tablespoons fruit liqueur, such as Framboise (optional)
- ¾ cup chilled heavy cream

Raspberry Sauce
- 1 pint fresh raspberries or 12 ounces frozen unsweetened raspberries, thawed, pureed, and strained (1 cup)
- 3 tablespoons sugar
- 1 tablespoon juice from ½ lemon
- 2 tablespoons fruit liqueur to match filling (optional)

  Fresh raspberries for garnish

1. *For the jelly roll,* adjust oven rack to low position and heat oven to 350 degrees. Sift flour and cornstarch together; set aside. Beat egg whites and salt in bowl of electric mixer on medium speed until frothy. Gradually add 6 tablespoons sugar, beating constantly, until mixture is stiff and glossy but not dry; set aside.

2. Without washing beaters, beat yolks and remaining 4 tablespoons sugar until thick and light in color, stopping machine and scraping down bowl and beaters twice. Add vanilla; beat on medium-high speed until yolks form a flat ribbon that falls back on itself when beaters are lifted, 3 to 5 minutes.

3. Fold ⅓ of whites into yolk mixture. Sprinkle about 3 tablespoons of dry ingredients over batter; fold in gently. Repeat with small additions of dry ingredients. Near end of folding in dry ingredients, alternate with some of whites. Finally, fold in remaining whites to form a light, smooth batter.

The cake recipe that Susan Purdy developed for this showy Charlotte Royale can also be used for a simpler jelly roll. Simply dust the finished roll with confectioners' sugar and top with whipped cream.

PHOTOGRAPH BY ERIC ROTH

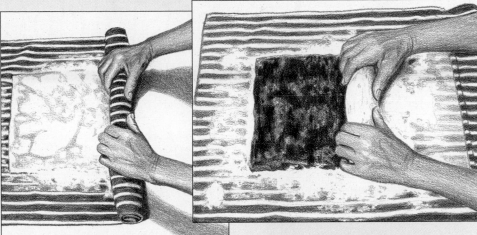

1. Crisp edges can prevent smooth rolling and should be removed. With a serrated knife, trim a scant one-eighth-inch strip of crust from all four sides of the cake.

2. Fold one end of the sugared tea towel over a short end of the cake and roll them together. Set the cake on a rack to cool, seam side down.

3. Unroll cooled cake and evenly spread a thin layer of preserves over the entire top so that the jelly roll will stick together. Reroll cake.

ASSEMBLING THE CHARLOTTE

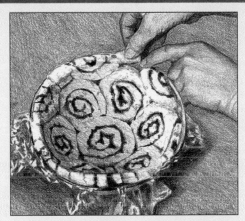

4. With plastic wrap, line a one-and-one-half-quart bowl that measures about seven and one-half inches across at the rim. Press the plastic against the inside of the bowl and let several inches drape over the outer edge. Place one slice of cake in the bottom of the bowl.

5. Surround the first piece of cake with a circle of six more slices. Then place six cake wedges between the curves of this circle to form the top ring. Place the cleanest side of each slice facing down. Fill the holes along the top of the bowl and between the slices with small pieces of cake. (This prevents any mousse from seeping through.)

6. Spoon the mousse into the bowl lined with the jelly roll slices. Cover the mousse with the remaining slices and scraps of cake.

4. Turn batter into a greased 15-by-10-inch jelly-roll pan lined with greased and floured parchment; smooth batter with a rubber spatula. Bake until top is golden and feels springy to the touch and edges begin to pull away from pan, 12 to 15 minutes. (Do not overbake or cake will be dry.)

5. Meanwhile, sift confectioners' sugar over a tea towel measuring at least 15-by-10-inches. Immediately invert baked cake onto sugar-covered towel and peel away paper. Follow illustrations 1 through 3 to make jelly roll.

6. Set finished jelly roll seam side down. With a serrated knife, cut cake into ⅓-inch thick slices, and cut 3 slices into half-circle wedges, cleaning knife after each cut to keep preserves from smearing cake. Line a 1½-quart bowl with plastic wrap (*see* illustration 4). Line bowl with cake slices (illustration 5); use another slice to fill holes.

7. *For the mousse,* combine gelatin and ¼ cup cold water in a small saucepan; let stand to soften gelatin, about 2 minutes. Stir in ½ cup hot water, lemon juice, sugar, and salt; cook over low heat, stirring constantly, until sugar and gelatin dissolve. Stir in berry puree and liqueur; refrigerate or set in ice-water bath, whisking occasionally, until mixture thickens to consistency of raw egg whites.

8. Whip chilled cream to soft peaks; fold into mousse. Spoon filling into cake-lined bowl; cover top with remaining cake slices and scraps (illustration 6). Bring draped plastic wrap (illustration 4) over cake pieces, then cover with another piece of plastic. Refrigerate at least 3 hours or overnight.

9. *For the sauce,* mix all sauce ingredients together in a small bowl; refrigerate until ready to serve.

10. To unmold charlotte, remove plastic wrap and fold back flaps of inner wrapping. Cover charlotte with a cake plate and flip charlotte onto plate. Peel off plastic and garnish with berries. Cut charlotte into wedges and serve on individual plates with sauce. ∎

Preparing Tropical Fruit

Although many tropical fruits are available year-round in U.S. supermarkets, the widest selection is available during midwinter. By following the steps below, you can easily prepare these exotic fruits for eating or cooking.

PAPAYA

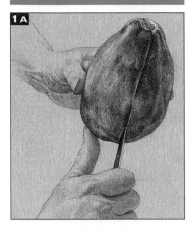

1A. Using a paring knife, score the fruit lengthwise in quarters, cutting just through to the flesh.

Elizabeth Schneider, author of *Uncommon Fruits and Vegetables* (Harper & Row, 1986), suggests this method of removing bitterness from slightly green papayas.

1B. Place the papaya, stem end down, in a glass and allow to stand for 24 hours so that the bitter papain enzyme drips out.

1C. Peel the papaya, halve it, and scoop out the core of black seeds and gelatin.

CARAMBOLA (STARFRUIT)

3A. Using a paring knife or vegetable peeler, peel off the hard ridges on top of the five ribs. The remaining portion of the peel is edible.

3B. Slice the fruit crosswise into star shapes.

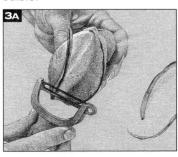

PASSION FRUIT

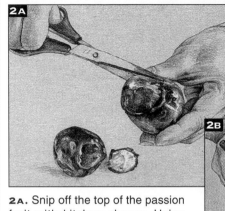

Passion fruit has a thick, stiff rind encasing very liquidy pulp the color of mustard.

2A. Snip off the top of the passion fruit with kitchen shears. Using shears instead of a knife allows you to hold the fruit upright as you remove the top, thus avoiding spilling any of the pulp inside.

2B. Holding the fruit over a bowl, scoop out the pulp, then strain it to remove seeds.

KIWI

Jill Nelson of Chicago, Illinois, and L. Scott Fitzpatrick of Medford, Massachusetts, both suggested this method of peeling kiwis.

4B. Push the spoon down and carefully move it around the fruit, separating flesh from skin.

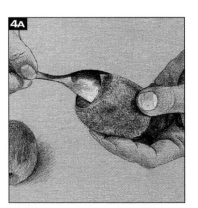

4A. Trim off the ends of the fruit, then insert a spoon between the skin and the flesh, with the bowl of the spoon facing the flesh.

4C. Pull skin away from flesh.

ILLUSTRATIONS BY ALAN WITSCHONKE

R̲ipe (black) fruit can be peeled like a banana. For green fruit, follow these directions:

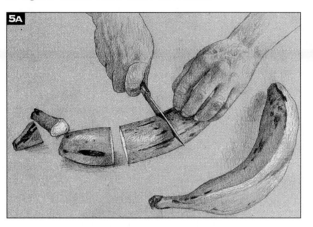

5A. Trim off ends and cut plantain into sections about two to three inches long.

5B. Slide a thin-bladed knife under each side of the skin (there are four sides), peel the skin away from the flesh, and remove.

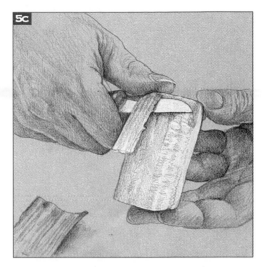

5C. Slice off any woody fibers that remain on the fruit.

CHERIMOYA

6A. Cut the fruit into quarters. Flick out the large seeds with the tip of a paring knife and cut out the fruit's central fiber, which resembles that of a pineapple.

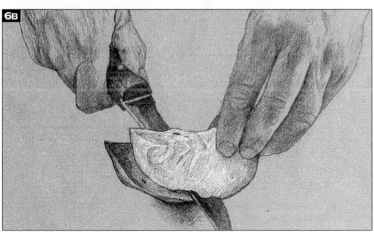

6B. Slide the knife under the flesh to free it from the skin.

PRICKLY OR CACTUS PEAR

A̲lthough spines have usually been removed from these fruits, it is best to avoid handling the exterior in case any spines remain.

7A. Jab the fruit with a fork to use as a handle, then trim a quarter-inch slice from each end.

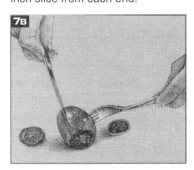

7B. Still holding with the fork, make a slit one-quarter inch deep the length of the fruit. Use the knife to pry up one edge of the skin along the cut.

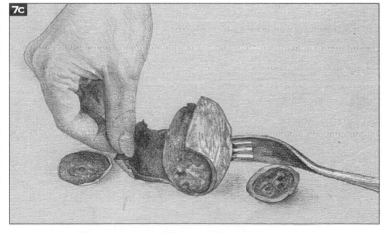

7C. Use your fingers to pull back and remove the remaining peel.

How to Make Mustard at Home

Homemade mustard is infinitely variable; here's how to make special mustards in minutes.

∾ BY LYNN ALLEY ∾

When making mustard at home, remember to allow your concoctions to rest for at least an hour or two before judging them.

Not only is making mustard simple, it allows you to create exactly the condiment that you like best. There are three main variables in the process: the type of mustard seeds you use; the texture to which you grind these seeds; and the liquid or other flavorings with which you combine them.

Mustard, a brassica related to cabbage and broccoli, produces three main kinds of seeds. Of these, black are the most pungent; these were commonly used for commercially prepared mustards in the first half of the century. Brown mustard seeds, which are slightly less spicy, are used for most modern commercial mustards, because they are larger and therefore more easily harvested by mechanical means. Mildest of the three varieties are the white or yellow seeds — these are the main ingredient in bright yellow hot-dog mustard.

Mustard can be prepared in a variety of textures. Preground or dry mustard powder, a common ingredient in oil and vinegar salad dressings, is used not only for its flavor contribution, but because it acts as an emulsifying agent. Mustard powder mixed with a liquid will produce a very smooth, but also a very hot, mustard (the "heat" of the mustard seed is contained in the endosperm, not in the hull). A mixture of mustard powder — which is simply finely ground seeds — and coarsely ground mustard seed will produce a coarse-grained, country-style mustard. Finally, a very coarse mustard can be made by using only coarsely ground mustard seeds.

You can grind mustard seeds in a mortar and pestle, or you can process them in an electric coffee mill. (I use one electric coffee grinder exclusively for grinding spices, since the oily residues give an off flavor to coffee.) There is no correct texture or degree to which you should grind your seeds — experiment until you find the texture that suits you best.

You can add almost any flavoring you like to mustard, but the most common variables are liquids. Try vinegars of all types, Champagne, wine, sherry, stout, beer, liqueurs, and plain grape juice for openers.

Keep in mind that any mustard you make at home is likely to be a bit more runny and considerably more pungent than any commercially prepared version. You should also allow your mustard to rest for a couple of hours before passing judgment on it, and at least 24 hours before serving, to allow the flavors to meld; when first mixed, many mustards taste unbalanced. And remember that brown and black powders and seeds yield more pungent mustards than yellow powder and seed.

COUNTRY-STYLE MUSTARD
Makes about ⅔ cup
If this grainy mustard seems dry, you can add another tablespoon or so of vinegar. Some spice stores may confuse brown mustard seeds with black. Either one can be used in the recipe.

- 2   tablespoons brown or black mustard seeds, coarsely ground
- 2   tablespoons yellow mustard seeds, coarsely ground
- ¼   cup brown or yellow mustard powder
- ¼   cup cold water
- 3   tablespoons white-wine or cider vinegar
- 1   teaspoon salt

1. Mix mustard seeds, powder, and water together in small bowl. Let stand for 10 minutes.

2. Stir in vinegar and salt; cover and refrigerate overnight. (Can be refrigerated at least 3 months in a sealed container.)

HOT-AND-SWEET CREAMY MUSTARD
Makes about ¾ cup
This mustard needs 24 hours for the flavor to develop properly.

- ½   cup yellow or brown mustard powder
- 3   tablespoons orange-flavored liqueur
- 3   tablespoons white-wine or cider vinegar
- ¼   cup dark brown sugar
- 1   teaspoon salt

Mix all ingredients in small bowl; cover and refrigerate to allow flavors to blend, about 24 hours. (Can be refrigerated at least 3 months in a sealed container.)

HOT-AND-SWEET MUSTARD VINAIGRETTE
Makes about ½ cup
This piquant vinaigrette is a good choice for hearty, flavorful greens.

- 2   tablespoons Hot-and-Sweet Creamy Mustard (*see* recipe, above)
- 1   tablespoon sherry vinegar
- ½   teaspoon grated fresh gingerroot
- ⅓   cup vegetable oil
     Salt and ground black pepper to taste

Whisk first 3 ingredients in small bowl. Whisk in oil until emulsified. Season with salt and pepper. Refrigerate in covered container overnight. (Can be refrigerated 1 week.) ∎

Lynn Alley, a San Diego–based food writer, is the author of *Herban Kitchen.*

HEAT MAKES MUSTARD COOL

The element that makes brown mustard flavorful and hot is its essential oil content, while the predominant flavoring agent in yellow mustard is a sulfur compound. Using cold water or liquids to mix with mustard "develops" these flavor compounds, thus intensifying their flavor and pungency. Using hot water or applying heat to the mustard will somewhat dissipate its intensity, making a milder mustard, but also tending to dissipate the more delicate nuances of flavor. Although there are many recipes that call for cooking or heating mustard while making it, cooking is not for the mustard purist. If you intend to use your prepared mustard as an ingredient in a recipe, you may want to keep this in mind and add it during the last few minutes of cooking.

Three Hand-Formed Pastas

Make this simple, egg-free dough in a food processor, roll it into a rope, and you can quickly cut and shape fusilli, cavatelli, and orecchiette.

~ BY MICHELE SCICOLONE ~

To most of us, homemade pasta means long sheets of sheer, eggy dough either rolled out with a rolling pin or cranked out of a pasta machine. But in Apulia, the region located in the heel of the Italian boot, the typical homestyle pasta is made only with flour and water, then hand-molded into shell shapes called *cavatelli;* ear shapes known as *orecchiette;* or spirals called *frusuiddati,* a local dialect term for fusilli.

These three pastas can be made with either semolina or whole wheat flour, depending on the flavor or texture you want to achieve. Semolina flour produces a creamy white, smooth pasta, while dough made with whole wheat flour is medium brown and has a rough texture. Both pastas are chewy and substantial, a good match for hearty vegetable, meat, and seafood sauces based on Apulia's delicious golden green extra virgin olive oil.

Since these doughs are rather stiff, a food processor or heavy-duty mixer is a better choice than mixing by hand. You will also find that shaping the pasta on a wooden cutting board or a plastic board with a slightly rough surface gives the pasta a rougher surface texture, an advantage in that sauce will adhere to the noodles more easily.

The pasta can be used immediately, allowed to dry slightly, or frozen for up to one month. Unless you plan to use the pasta at once, have ready two sheet pans, jelly-roll pans, or trays with a shallow border — the borders will allow you to stack the pans crosswise so that air can circulate around the pasta without taking up too much counter space. Line the pans with clean, dry dish cloths or napkins, and dust the cloths lightly with all-purpose flour. Do not let the pieces of pasta touch each other on the pans, or they may stick together.

Complete drying of these pasta shapes may take several days, depending on the weather, and results in very hard pasta that takes a long time to cook. Therefore I have found that it's best either to use the pasta within a day or so or to freeze it for later use. To freeze, simply place the pasta on the pans directly in the freezer, freeze until solid (about an hour or

Save delicate cream and butter sauces for egg pastas; these substantial pasta shapes from southern Italy match best with hearty, chunk-style sauces.

two), then transfer the individual pasta shapes to plastic freezer bags, seal, and freeze.

On a recent trip to Apulia, I stayed at Il Melograno (The Pomegranate), a sprawling resort and health spa in Monopoli where the chef demonstrated how to make orecchiette and cavatelli. Throughout my stay, the chef created many dishes based on the unusual pastas of the region. The recipes given here are my interpretations of these wonderful dishes.

SEMOLINA DOUGH
Makes 1 pound fresh pasta (4 servings)

1¾ cups unbleached all-purpose flour
¾ cup semolina flour

Place flours in workbowl of a food processor fitted with a steel blade; pulse to mix. With machine running, add just enough hot water

(about ¾ cup) to form a stiff dough that forms a ball. Remove from processor and knead on a lightly floured surface until dough is smooth and elastic, about 1 minute. Wrap in plastic until ready to use.

WHOLE WHEAT DOUGH
Makes 1 pound fresh pasta (4 servings)

1½ cups whole wheat flour
1 cup unbleached all-purpose flour

Follow instructions for Semolina Dough.

CAVATELLI WITH WHITE BEANS AND CLAMS
Serves 4–6

In Apulia, the mussels used in this recipe are no bigger than the cavatelli and beans, about one-half inch to three-quarters of an inch long.

Shaping Three Pastas

FOR ALL THREE PASTA SHAPES

1A. Cut the dough into eight pieces. Roll one piece into a half-inch thick rope, keeping remaining dough pieces covered with a bowl so they do not dry out.

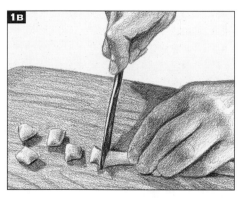

1B. Cut the dough rope into half-inch lengths.

FOR THE ORECCHIETTE

3A. Holding a dull-bladed knife with a rounded tip in one hand, press the index finger of the other hand against the blade of the knife to flatten each piece of dough; drag the dough across the work surface just enough to form a shallow concave disk.

3C. Push the disk down over the tip of your thumb, turning it inside out.

FOR THE FRUSUIDDATI (FUSILLI)

2A. Press a thin chopstick or wooden skewer of equivalent thickness against a dough piece. Rock back and forth until the dough almost wraps itself around the chopstick.

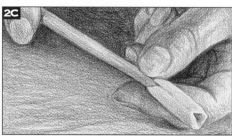

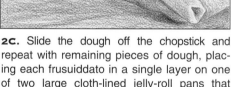

2C. Slide the dough off the chopstick and repeat with remaining pieces of dough, placing each frusuiddato in a single layer on one of two large cloth-lined jelly-roll pans that have been dusted with flour.

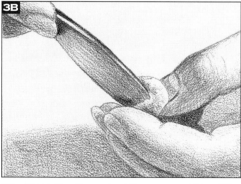

3B. Place thumb against the convex side of the disk.

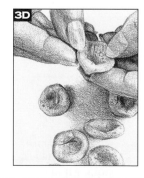

3D. The finished orecchiette should be deeply concave in shape; place them in a single layer on one of two large cloth-lined jelly-roll pans that have been dusted with flour.

2B. While continuing to rock chopstick back and forth, use your fingertips to help dough ends meet and form a tube shape.

FOR THE CAVATELLI

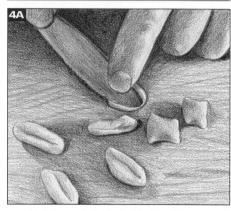

4A. Holding a dull-bladed knife with a rounded tip in one hand, press the index finger of the other hand against the blade of the knife to flatten each piece of dough.

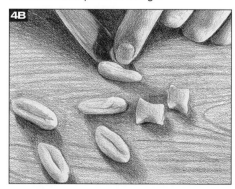

4B. Pull the knife toward you, keeping it pressed against the dough so the dough drags across the work surface and curls itself around the tip of the knife to form a shell shape. Place in a single layer on one of two large cloth-lined jelly-roll pans that have been dusted with flour.

ILLUSTRATIONS BY ANGELO

Larger mussels, the only kind available in my area, just won't do, so I have substituted small clams with great success. If you can find small mussels, however, by all means use them.

½ cup dry cannellini or great northern beans, soaked overnight in cool water to cover by 3 inches and then drained
1 medium carrot
1 rib celery
1 small onion
1 bay leaf
   Salt
2 pounds small clams, such as Manila, littlenecks, or cockles, scrubbed and soaked in water for 30 minutes
⅓ cup olive oil plus more for seasoning
2 large cloves garlic, minced
4 medium tomatoes, peeled, seeded, and chopped (or 2 cups canned Italian peeled tomatoes, chopped)
¼ cup minced Italian parsley
   Ground black pepper
1 recipe Semolina Dough, formed into cavatelli (*see* illustrations 4A and 4B, page 20)

1. Place first 5 ingredients in a medium saucepan; add cold water to cover by 1 inch. Bring to a simmer and cook over low heat until just tender, 45 to 60 minutes, adding ½ teaspoon salt after first 30 minutes. Drain, reserving liquid for another use.

2. Bring clams and ½ cup water to simmer in a medium saucepan. Cover and steam over medium heat until shells open, about 5 minutes. Remove clams from shells; strain liquid through a paper coffee filter or cheesecloth to eliminate sand; set both aside.

3. Heat ⅓ cup olive oil over medium heat in a large saucepan; add garlic and cook until fragrant, about 30 seconds. Stir in drained bean mixture; cover and cook to blend flavors, about 5 minutes. Stir in tomatoes and parsley. Add clams and about ½ cup of their liquid. Season to taste with salt and pepper; cover and set aside.

4. Meanwhile, bring 5 quarts water to boil in a large pot. Add cavatelli and salt to taste. Boil, stirring occasionally, until almost tender, 6 to 8 minutes.

5. Drain cavatelli and return to pot; stir in clam sauce; cook over medium heat, stirring constantly, until cavatelli are tender, about 1 to 2 minutes. If mixture seems dry, add more clam liquor. Transfer to a warm serving bowl, drizzle with olive oil if you like, and serve immediately.

FUSILLI WITH ARUGULA AND TOMATO SAUCE
Serves 4

3 tablespoons olive oil
2 cloves garlic, peeled and crushed
1½ pounds ripe plum tomatoes, peeled, seeded, and chopped, or 1 can (28 ounces) Italian peeled tomatoes with their juice
   Salt and ground black pepper
1 recipe Semolina Dough, formed into fusilli (*see* illustrations 2A through 2C, page 20)
2 ounces ricotta salata, shredded (about ½ cup) or ¼ cup grated Pecorino Romano and ¼ cup grated Parmigiano Reggiano
1 bunch arugula, stemmed and washed, and cut crosswise into thin strips (about 2 cups packed leaves)

1. Heat oil with garlic over medium heat in a large saucepan until garlic is golden and fragrant. Add tomatoes (crushing with back of a spoon if canned) and salt and pepper to taste. Bring sauce to a simmer and cook until tomatoes thicken to a sauce consistency, about 20 minutes; remove and discard garlic.

2. Meanwhile, bring 5 quarts of water to boil in a large pot. Add salt and fusilli. Cook until pasta is tender yet still firm to the bite, 6 to 8 minutes.

3. Drain pasta and return to pot. Stir in tomato sauce and half of cheese. Transfer to a large serving bowl; top with arugula and remaining cheese and serve immediately.

ORECCHIETTE WITH CAULIFLOWER AND BACON
Serves 6

   Salt
1 medium head cauliflower (about 2¼ pounds), trimmed and cut into 1-inch florets
2 tablespoons olive oil
1 medium onion, minced
8 ounces thick-sliced lean bacon or smoked pancetta, cut into ¼-inch strips
   Ground black pepper
1 recipe Whole Wheat Dough, formed into orecchiette (*see* illustrations 3A through 3D, page 20)
½ cup freshly grated Pecorino Romano cheese

1. Bring 5 quarts of water to boil in a large pot. Add salt to taste and cauliflower florets. Return to boil and cook florets until tender, 3 to 4 minutes; remove with a slotted spoon. (Reserve water for cooking pasta.)

2. Heat oil over medium heat in a large skillet. Add onions; sauté until soft and golden, about 5 minutes. Add bacon; cook, stirring frequently, until crisp around edges, about 7 minutes. Push onions and bacon to one side and carefully tip pan. Spoon off all but ⅓ cup of fat and discard or reserve for another use; stir in cauliflower and season with salt and pepper to taste.

3. Meanwhile, return water to boil; add orecchiette and boil until just tender, 6 to 8 minutes. Drain well, reserving 1 cup cooking liquid.

4. Return pasta to the pot; add cauliflower mixture. Cook over medium heat, stirring in some of the pasta water if dish seems dry, until ingredients are well combined. Stir in cheese and serve immediately.

Alternate Breadcrumb Topping: Heat 2 tablespoons olive oil in a small skillet. Add 4 anchovies (or more to taste). Sauté, stirring constantly, until the anchovies dissolve, less than a minute. Add ½ cup fine dry bread-crumbs (preferably homemade from non-sweet Italian or French bread). Cook, stirring, until the crumbs are lightly toasted, about 1 to 2 minutes. Sprinkle over the pasta instead of stirring in the cheese.

ORECCHIETTE WITH BROCCOLI RABE
Serves 4

You may substitute broccoli florets or any winter green, such as kale or collards, for the broccoli rabe in this recipe.

   Salt
1 pound broccoli rabe, washed, trimmed, and cut into 1-inch pieces
1 recipe Semolina dough, formed into orecchiette (*see* illustrations 3A through 3D, page 20)
⅓ cup olive oil
4 cloves garlic, minced
½ teaspoon hot red pepper flakes
½ cup grated Parmigiano Reggiano

1. Bring 1 quart of water to boil in a large pot. Add salt to taste and broccoli rabe. Return to boil and cook until broccoli rabe is bright green and almost tender, 2 to 3 minutes. Drain broccoli rabe and plunge into cold water to stop the cooking process; drain broccoli rabe again and set aside.

2. Bring 5 quarts water to boil in a large pot. Add salt to taste and orecchiette; boil until just tender, 6 to 8 minutes. Drain well, reserving 1 cup cooking liquid. Return pasta to pot.

3 Meanwhile, heat oil with garlic in a large skillet until garlic is golden and fragrant; add hot red pepper flakes, then broccoli rabe; sauté over medium-high heat until heated through, 3 to 4 minutes.

4. Pour broccoli rabe mixture over pasta and toss, stirring in some of pasta liquid if dish seems dry. Stir in cheese and serve immediately. ∎

Michele Scicolone is the author of *La Dolce Vita* (Morrow, 1993) and *The Antipasto Table* (Morrow, 1992).

Foolproof Brown Rice

It takes a rice steamer, or a combination of boiling and steaming, to make brown rice with the best flavor and texture.

∼ BY JACK BISHOP ∼

Brown rice is valued for its nutrients as well as for its satisfying texture and nutty flavor. But the traditional cooking method — in a covered pot on the stove — is unreliable and frequently results in gummy rice and burned pots. In the course of my experiments, however, I discovered two techniques that yield consistently excellent results.

Many cooks avoid brown rice because it takes so long to prepare — 45 minutes versus about 20 for white rice — so I first decided to see if I could reduce the cooking time. I tried using "quick cooking" or "precooked" brown rice. This is rice which has had the bran roughed up so that water can penetrate more quickly, and which has also been partially cooked and then dried. The results were unsatisfactory — mushy, starchy, and unappealing.

Next I tried presoaking rice for eight hours before cooking. This process cuts 15 minutes off the total cooking time, but doesn't solve the get-dinner-on-the-table-quickly dilemma.

I then moved on to various cooking methods. Looking to cut cooking time and still end up with superior rice, I tried boiling, steaming, microwaving, pressure cooking, baking, the traditional stove-top method, and a rice cooker. The cooking times varied considerably, ranging from 25 to 60 minutes. The differences in time, however, paled in comparison to the differences in taste and convenience.

The Cooking Methods

Treating rice like pasta — boiling and draining it in a colander — is relatively quick (35 minutes), but the rice is mushy and tastes waterlogged. Steaming it (about 45 minutes) is gentler and yields separate grains that are nicely *al dente*. The problem is that most steamer set-ups run dry before the rice is cooked — adding boiling water is a nuisance, and the probability of ruining a good pot is quite high (I did it).

Microwaving saves little time (it takes about 40 minutes) and involves changing the power from high to medium after 5 minutes. More importantly, microwaved brown rice tends to be sticky. Pressure cooking, while fast (just 25 minutes), results in starchy rice better suited to a stir-fry with plenty of sauce than to a salad or pilaf, where you want separate grains. Baking rice in a covered casserole was quite good, and easy enough, but it takes about an hour. I recommend it only if you are using the oven for something else anyway.

This left the conventional method and the rice cooker. Traditional recipes say to bring rice and water to a boil, reduce heat to low, cover, and simmer until water is absorbed, about 45 minutes. Simmering at a higher temperature can cut cooking time by 5 minutes but increases the risk of sticky rice. Very low heat generally works better, but I still had less than perfect results. Try as I might, I could not develop a foolproof variation on the traditional technique. I threw out sticky, soggy, starchy, or burned rice on several occasions.

Without a doubt, the easiest, most reliable method for preparing brown rice is the rice cooker; besides turning out the best brown rice (it's fluffy, separate, and still has a nice bite), rice cookers are easy to clean, especially models with a nonstick surface on the cooking pot. If you are serious about cooking rice, whether white or brown, then spending $60 on a rice cooker is a wise investment (*see* Sources and

A staple in Japanese home kitchens, rice cookers are the best way to cook brown rice.

Resources, page 32).

Most rice cookers consist of a large chamber with an electric heating element on the bottom. A cooking pot slips into the holding chamber and is covered with a lid. The heating element brings the rice and water to a boil and maintains a constant temperature. When the temperature inside the cooking chamber rises above 212 degrees — a sign that there is no more steam and all the water has been absorbed — the rice cooker automatically shuts off. Many models actually switch to a "keep warm" mode, which holds rice for several hours without damage.

At this point, the results of my extensive testing left me a bit disappointed. Although the rice cooker is a great invention, not everyone wants another appliance — no matter how useful — in the kitchen. Was I missing something in my original tests?

After rereading my notes, I realized that steaming yielded good results and was problematic only because of the long cooking time and the danger of the pot running dry. I decided to do most of the cooking in boiling water, but to finish rice in the steamer. Boiling the rice until it is almost tender (about 30 minutes), draining it, then steaming it until done (another 5 or 10 minutes) is by far the best stove-top method for brown rice. Steaming dries out boiled rice and gets rid of the watery taste. The slight loss of nutrients in the boiling water makes this method a second choice behind the rice cooker. However, the superior results place boiling/steaming far ahead of traditional covered cooking.

BASIC BROWN RICE
Makes 3 cups

Use long, medium, or short grain rice in this recipe. If you own a rice cooker, follow the variation below, using less fat and salt due to the reduced quantity of water.

> 6 cups water
> 1 cup brown rice
> 2 teaspoons olive oil or butter
> 1 teaspoon salt

1. Bring water to boil in a large pot. Stir in rice, oil or butter, and salt. Simmer briskly, uncovered, until rice is almost tender, about 30 minutes.

2. Drain rice into a steamer basket that fits inside the pot. Fill pot with about 1 inch water and return to heat. Place basket of rice in pot; cover and steam until tender, 5 to 10 minutes. Scoop rice into a bowl and fluff gently with a fork.

Rice Cooker Variation: Stir 2¼ cups water, 1 cup brown rice, 1 teaspoon oil or butter, and ½ teaspoon salt together in the cooking chamber of a rice cooker. Cover, and cook according to manufacturer's directions. If rice remains too crunchy for your taste, add several tablespoons water and restart cooking. Machine will automatically shut off when additional water has been absorbed.

BROWN RICE PILAF WITH BROCCOLI
Serves 6 as a side dish

Use this recipe as a guide for making brown rice pilafs with any ingredients on hand. Combine 3 cups cooked rice with roughly an equal amount of "sauce," using vegetables, nuts, legumes, and seasonings. Use enough juice, wine, vinegar, or oil to make sautéed ingredients moist without being watery.

> 2 teaspoons salt, plus more to taste
> 2 cups small broccoli florets
> ¼ cup pine nuts
> ¼ cup olive oil
> 1 small onion, minced

> 2 cloves garlic, minced
> ¼ pound mushrooms, sliced thin
> ¼ cup white wine
> 1 tablespoon lemon juice
> Ground black pepper to taste
> 2 tablespoons minced fresh parsley leaves
> 3 cups Basic Brown Rice (*see* above), preferably long grain or basmati, cooled to room temperature

1. Bring 2 quarts water to boil. Add 2 teaspoons salt and broccoli; boil, uncovered, until just tender, about 1 minute. Drain under cold running water, cool, and set aside.

2. Heat a large skillet over medium heat. Add pine nuts, shaking pan to prevent burning, until toasted, about 30 seconds. Remove from heat and set aside.

3. Return skillet to burner and heat oil. Add onions; sauté until almost softened, about 3 minutes. Add garlic and sauté until softened, about 1 minute longer. Stir in mushrooms and sauté until just wilted, about 2 minutes.

4. Stir in wine, lemon juice, and salt and pepper. Simmer for 3 minutes to cook off some of the alcohol. Stir in parsley, brown rice, and broccoli; cook until heated through, about 2 minutes. Stir in nuts and serve immediately.

BROWN RICE AND CHICKPEA SALAD
Serves 4 as a light main course

Use this recipe as a guide for making brown rice salads with any ingredients on hand. Combine 3 cups cooked brown rice with a mixture of 3 cups other main ingredients that have been chopped and cooked if necessary, such as vegetables, legumes, seafood, or chicken. Add ¼ to ½ cup toasted nuts if desired. About ⅓ to ½ cup dressing is enough to coat 6 cups of rice salad.

Cooked Chickpeas
> ⅔ cup dried chickpeas, soaked at least 8 hours and drained
> 2 cloves garlic, peeled
> 1 bay leaf
> 1 teaspoon salt

Basil-Curry Dressing
> 4 tablespoons olive oil
> 1½ tablespoons lemon juice
> 1½ tablespoons white vinegar
> ½ teaspoon curry powder
> 1½ teaspoons honey
> 3 tablespoons minced fresh basil leaves
> Salt to taste

> 3 cups Basic Brown Rice (*see* above), preferably medium grain or basmati, cooled to room temperature
> 1 large red bell pepper, cored, seeded, and diced small
> ¼ cup sliced almonds, lightly toasted

1. *For the chickpeas,* bring 1 quart water, chickpeas, garlic, and bay leaf to boil in a large saucepan; simmer until chickpeas are tender, about 45 minutes, adding the salt after 30 minutes of cooking. Drain, discarding garlic and bay leaf, and cool to room temperature.

2. *For the dressing,* whisk all dressing ingredients together.

3. Mix chickpeas with rice, bell pepper, and almonds in a medium bowl. Pour dressing over salad ingredients and toss to combine. (Can refrigerate for up to 4 hours.) ∎

Taking Stock of Chicken Broth

Campbell's soups take the four top places, while high-priced "natural" broths come in dead last. The most expensive "tastes worse than the Hudson River."

~ BY JONI MILLER ~

Other ingredients may be the building blocks, but the foundation of the classic European kitchen has always been a flavorful broth or stock. Indeed, the French master chef Escoffier proclaimed, "Stock is everything . . . without it, nothing can be done."

Although Escoffier was talking about stock as distinct from broth, the distinction has largely disappeared from popular usage these days. In fact, it is not uncommon to see recipes calling for "homemade chicken stock or canned chicken broth." The two preparations do share common ingredients — chicken, onions, carrots, celery, a bouquet garni — but, strictly speaking, there is also a difference: a stock is made with poultry bones, while a broth is made using a whole chicken or chicken parts.

Commercial product labeling, however, overlooks this distinction, and for most everyday cooking purposes the two can be used interchangeably. Therefore all versions in our tasting are referred to as broths.

American cooks' fondness for prepared chicken broth is readily demonstrated by its steady popularity at supermarkets. According to industry sources, 35 percent of all households purchase ready-to-serve canned broths and use at least five cans per year, mostly as a cooking ingredient. These figures have recently taken an upswing, in part because fewer home cooks take time to make broth from scratch, and because health-conscious consumers are finding new uses for broth. Canned broth is sipped on its own, used as a base for homemade soups, as a cooking liquid for grain and rice dishes (risotto, for example) and, increasingly, as a way to cut fat when poaching, braising, stir-frying, and sautéing.

The benchmarks of a good chicken broth are a clear golden yellow color and authentic, full-bodied chicken flavor and aroma. We looked for these qualities in eleven broths — nine canned versions, plus one made from bouillon cubes and another made with a paste base.

The hands-down winner of our tasting was Campbell's Healthy Request Ready-to-Serve Chicken Broth. This product was introduced one year ago as part of a rollout of the "Healthy Request" line of soups: fat-free, MSG-free products with lower salt and fewer calories than many others. Patented processes are guarded with fervor by the major soup manufacturers, but whatever the corporate culinary secret of this one, they've hit the nail on the head. Unlike some broths that were weakly or even mysteriously fla-

vored, this full-bodied, appealing-looking broth did what it was supposed to — it actually tasted like chicken. So much so, in fact, that tasters pointed out, "It tastes like something you would eat on its own."

In an unusual sweep, all four of the top-ranked broths are products from the Campbell Soup Company "family" of brands. This tasting also shows that healthfulness can taste good; both of the top two broths, Healthy Request and Swanson Natural Goodness Clear Chicken Broth, are reduced-sodium products without MSG. Each delivered "good" or "decent" chicken flavor without excessive saltiness. Third-ranked Swanson Ready-To-Serve Clear Chicken Broth, identified by tasters as a good, all-purpose choice, had a "buttery" chicken flavor, though it was "a tad salty."

As in previous Cook's Illustrated tastings, there was a dramatic line of demarcation between acceptable products and those that clearly and precipitously fell into the realm of the unacceptable. Six broths scored three or fewer points.

In home cooking a good broth is only as good as its ingredients, but this truism does not necessarily extend into commercial broths. For example, despite their organic pedigrees and the absence of artificial ingredients and preservatives, Health Valley 100% Natural Chicken Broth and Shelton's All-Natural Chicken Broth, both widely available in health food stores, placed poorly in the tasting, scoring only two points each. Neither had the requisite chicken flavor.

Finally — and most surprising to many tasters — Walnut Acres' version, the Birkenstock of broths from an organic farm in Pennsylvania that has run a thriving mail-order business for more than 40 years, fared even worse. Made with "minimally processed chickens raised on herbicide- and pesticide-free grains," organically grown vegetables, and "deep-well country water," it scored zero points. Not one taster discerned

the flavor of chicken; most were misled by its taste and color and guessed it was mushroom or lentil soup. (Wondering if we might have received mislabeled cans, I subsequently double-checked the production numbers with the manufacturer to confirm that we had, indeed, tasted chicken broth.) It is also worth noting that most of the low-ranked broths cost two to three times more than the top four.

Chicken Broth Blind Tasting

The tasting was held at Lola Bowla in New York City, a restaurant where everything on the menu is served in bowls. The panel for our tasting included Cook's Illustrated senior writer Jack Bishop; sous chef Toni D'Onofrio of the restaurants Lola and Lola Bowla; Jim Fobel, author of The Whole Chicken Cookbook (Ballantine, 1992); Abe Lebewohl, owner of The Second Avenue Deli, a New York City culinary landmark famous for its chicken soup; cooking teacher Stephen Schmidt, author of Master Recipes (Ballantine, 1987); chef/cooking teacher Maryann Terillo of the New York Restaurant School; Nahum Waxman, owner of Kitchen Arts & Letters; author Joni Miller; and a home cook.

Eleven chicken broths were evaluated on the basis of color, clarity, taste, and aroma. Nine of the broths were canned products, one was from bouillon cubes, and one was made from a paste-style base that requires refrigeration. This was a blind tasting in which the heated broths were sipped warm from small bowls; tasters cleansed their palates with bottled water and unsalted soda crackers.

Prices listed are per can, container, or box, the sizes of which varied. The majority of the broths were purchased in the New York metropolitan area. Two versions, not sold in stores, were purchased mail order. Prices vary nationally for the products purchased at super-

To "freshen up" canned chicken broth, Jim Fobel, author of **The Whole Chicken Cookbook** *(Ballantine, 1992), recommends adding a sliced carrot, celery rib, and onion and simmering for 10 minutes. To remove excess fat, refrigerate can, then skim hardened fat from the surface.*

markets and health food stores.

Because so many broths were deemed unacceptable, the panel members ranked only four favorites instead of seven, as is the custom in *Cook's Illustrated* tastings. Four points were awarded for each first-place vote; three for second; two for third; one for fourth. Broths given fewer than three points are listed in alphabetical order and marked with an asterisk. ■

Joni Miller, a New York–based writer, is the author of *True Grits* (Workman, 1990).

1 **Campbell's Healthy Request Ready-to-Serve Chicken Broth** (Campbell Soup Co., NJ), 16 ounces, $.83; no MSG; 118 mg sodium per ounce; use full strength; 29 points. The hands-down winner was a full-bodied broth with a "pure," pleasantly pronounced, well-rounded chicken flavor and appetizing aroma. Some panelists noted it would be equally tasty consumed alone or used in cooking. Introduced only a year ago, it had a richness and depth of flavor lacking in other versions. "It tastes like chicken!" said one taster. The golden yellow broth, somewhat thicker than others sampled, lacked clarity; it was cloudy and "murky" with a slightly tan tint. Nevertheless, "excellent," summed up one panelist. Widely available.

2 **Swanson Natural Goodness Clear Chicken Broth** (Campbell Soup Co., NJ), 14.5 ounces, $.85; no MSG; 80 mg sodium per ounce; use full strength; 19 points. With a "comfy" aroma akin to roasted chicken and a "pleasant enough," rather mild chicken flavor, this broth struck tasters as "pretty good," although a bit weak on flavor. Several guessed it to be an unsalted or low-salt version; another correctly pinpointed the brand as Swanson. As with the top-ranked broth, appearance was problematic. The "cloudy" pale yellow color suggested weak flavor. Visible "swirls of fat" puzzled some but were viewed as harbingers of good chicken flavor by others. A "decent," mildly flavorful broth. Widely available.

3 **Swanson Ready-To-Serve Clear Chicken Broth** (Campbell Soup Co., NJ), 14.5 ounces, $.89; contains MSG; 124 mg sodium per ounce; use full strength; 14 points. A sibling of the second-ranked broth, this one contains MSG and 50 percent more sodium; it struck tasters as a good, all-purpose choice distinguished by an appealing "buttery" chicken flavor and aroma, despite being "a tad salty." A particularly canny taster observed it was a saltier, stronger version of what was later revealed to be Swanson's Natural Goodness. Another broth whose appearance — "no real color," closer to tan than a golden hue — belied its acceptable flavor. As with the other Swanson broth, there was visible "fat," reinforcing to some that it "came from a live chicken." "Worthy of an unsalted matzoh ball — not great, but serviceable," summarized a panelist.

4 **Campbell's Condensed Chicken Broth** (Campbell Soup Co., NJ), 10.5 ounces, $.85; contains MSG; 89 mg sodium per prepared ounce; dilute with water; 11 points. A pale tannish-yellow broth dotted with tiny specks of "fat." The rather bland, weak-tasting chicken flavor was also slightly fatty and "greasy" tasting. Generally lacking in rich, fulsome chicken taste; nonchicken flavors predominated. "A significant vegetable component" was noted and identified as caramelized vegetable flavors of carrot and onion. A subsidiary beef taste was also noted. Singling out "a bouillon quality," unenthralled panelists likened it to reconstituted powder. The consensus: "Tastes like a bouillon cube." Widely available.

5 **College Inn Lower Salt Chicken Broth** (Nabisco Brands, Inc., NJ), 13.75 ounces, $.89; contains MSG; 79 mg sodium per ounce; use full strength; 5 points. A reduced-salt broth that tasted salty and not much like chicken. Unappealing pale brownish yellow. Medicinal, strawlike "Chinese takeout" aroma. Weak, salty chicken flavor with metallic undertones and a "chemical" aftertaste. Widely available.

6 **College Inn Chicken Broth** (Nabisco Brands, Inc., NJ), 13.75 ounces, $.89; contains MSG; 141 mg sodium per ounce; use full strength; 3 points. Clear, light sunny yellow color with a vaguely plastic or synthetic aroma suggesting vending-machine soup. Tasted of chemicals. Weak, very salty chicken flavor overwhelmed by chemical taste; hints of dried vegetables. "Not chickeny enough." Several tasters noted that the broth coated their tongues or that fat clung to their lips. The final analysis: "Barely okay in an emergency." Widely available.

7 * **Health Valley 100% Natural Chicken Broth** (Health Valley Foods, Inc., CA), 13.75 ounces, $1.99; no MSG; 59 mg sodium per ounce; use full strength; 2 points. Clear darkish caramel color that resembled beef broth. Vegetable-concentrate aroma ("chicken chow mein in a can") reminiscent of dehydrated onions. Weak yet fresh tasting; consensus that the broth needed salt. Vaguely chemical, slightly bitter aftertaste. "Not terrible tasting but nothing to do with chicken," the group agreed. Widely available at health and natural foods stores.

8 * **Knorr Chicken Flavor Bouillon** (CPC Specialty Products Inc., NJ), 2.5-ounce box of 6 cubes, $1.69; contains MSG; 150 mg sodium per prepared ounce; dissolve in boiling water; 2 points. Panelists immediately identified this as made from a bouillon cube due to the vivid yellow color with bits of dried herbs floating on the surface (as well as speckles of "phosphorescent" fat), and a "Knorr-like" aroma suggestive of dried onion dip or bouillon cubes. "Monumentally salty," with minor chicken flavor, it tasted and smelled "just plain awful," like "hot, salty water." Widely available.

9 * **Minor's No-Added MSG Chicken Base** (L. J. Minor Corp., OH), 8 ounces, $3.50; no MSG; 89 mg sodium per prepared ounce; dilute with water; 2 points. One of two broths available only by mail order, this is a granular mix with water paste used primarily in professional kitchens. The murky buttercup yellow color and highly emulsified, "slightly greasy-looking" appearance were unappetizing; several tasters commented that it coated their tongues. A distinct but mild chicken aroma was overwhelmed by a smell suggestive of artificial flavoring. Though mellow, the chicken flavor was very salty with a chemical aftertaste. Some who rather liked the flavor felt it had been "killed by the salt." "Smells like chicken, but doesn't taste like it," most agreed. Mail order only.

10 * **Shelton's All-Natural Chicken Broth with Salt & Spices** (Shelton's, CA), 14 ounces, $1.59; no MSG, 78 mg per ounce; use full strength; 2 points. A minimally processed broth made without preservatives or artificial ingredients. A watery, pale, cloudy white ("like tofu") liquid that was anonymous looking and tasting, with a peculiar sweet aroma suggestive of coconut. Rancid, unpleasant, and strange dishwater flavor. "Horrid. Worse than bad," agreed panelists. Widely available at health and natural foods stores.

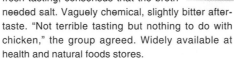

11 * **Walnut Acres Chicken Broth** (Walnut Acres, PA), 15.5 ounces, $2.59; no MSG; nutritional information unavailable; use full strength; no points. Available only by mail order, this broth comes from a highly regarded organic foods producer and is made using "minimally processed" chickens, organically grown vegetables, and "deep-well country water." Watery, unappetizing, and "strange" looking, this cloudy, dark gray-green ("like mud") liquid was a broth with nearly unidentifiable attributes. With little or no aroma, it was a "dishwaterlike" brew with the flavor of clove predominating. Very salty, sweet, and "herby"; no discernible chicken taste whatsoever. "Terrible," concurred tasters at first sip. "The Hudson River tastes better." Mail order only.

Making Bakery-Style Sticky Buns

Quick kneading and a short rise keep these "thunder buns" light.

At Cézanne Desserts in Cambridge, Massachusetts, Judy Kravitz turns out sticky buns so monumental she calls them "thunder buns." The secret of success with these extra-high, super-sticky buns is creating dough with just the right texture.

"Sticky buns should be soft and fluffy, almost cottony," Kravitz says. Overkneading the dough causes excess gluten development. To avoid this, Kravitz recommends kneading by hand; a mixer increases the likelihood of overkneading. But the hand-kneading isn't difficult, because as soon as the dough becomes smooth — just about five minutes after the flour is incorporated — it's time to stop. "It's better to underknead than overknead this dough," warns Kravitz. She offers a visual clue: the dough should be only slightly springy, not elastic and bouncy like a stiff bread dough.

"The dough should sort of flow out onto the counter when you roll it out," says baker Judy Kravitz.

It is also important not to let the dough overrise; watch it carefully after the first hour, and punch it down and roll it out as soon as it has doubled in bulk. If you allow it to rise longer, it may fail to relax properly when rolled out.

The final step in making these buns requires some extra care. When you finish, the buns will be sitting on a rich caramelized sugar syrup. Flip the pans onto a rimmed baking sheet that is deep enough to catch the hot syrup and allow to cool for at least 10 minutes before serving.

THE BEST STICKY BUNS
Makes 12

Dough
- 1 tablespoon dry active yeast
- ¼ cup sugar
- 1⅓ cups lukewarm milk
- 4 whole eggs, plus 2 egg yolks
- 1 teaspoon vanilla extract
- 2 teaspoons salt
- 6½ cups all-purpose flour
- 1 teaspoon ground cardamom
- ½ pound unsalted butter, softened

Cinnamon-Walnut Filling
- ⅔ cup packed dark brown sugar
- 1½ teaspoons ground cinnamon
- ¼ teaspoon ground nutmeg
- ¼ teaspoon ground cloves
- ½ cup currants
- ½ cup finely ground walnuts (use a food processor)
- 2 tablespoons unsalted butter, melted

Brown Sugar Glaze
- 12 tablespoons unsalted butter, melted
- 1½ cups packed light brown sugar

Honey Syrup
- 1 cup honey
- ¼ pound unsalted butter

1. *For the dough,* sprinkle yeast and sugar over milk in a large mixing bowl; let stand until yeast bubbles, about 5 minutes.

2. Whisk eggs and yolks together in a small bowl. Whisk in vanilla and salt.

3. Sift flour and cardamom together and set aside.

4. Stir egg mixture into yeast. Add butter and mix by hand until butter looks like small curdles. Mix in enough flour mixture to form a loose dough. Turn dough onto work surface sprinkled with remaining flour mixture. Knead, incorporating remaining flour, until dough is smooth and springs back slightly when touched, about 5 minutes. Place dough in a greased bowl, cover with a damp cloth, and let rise in a warm place until doubled in size, 1 to 2 hours.

5. *For the filling,* mix filling ingredients except butter; set aside.

6. *For the glaze,* grease sides of 2, 10-inch round cake pans (not springform). Pour half melted butter into each pan; sprinkle each evenly with half brown sugar; set aside.

7. Punch down dough and turn it onto a lightly floured work surface. Roll it out into an even 18-by-12-inch rectangle, about ¼-inch thick. Brush dough with melted butter (*see* filling ingredients) and sprinkle with filling, leaving a ½-inch border on long sides. Use a rolling pin to embed filling into dough (*see* illustration 1). Fold long edge of dough over twice (illustration 2) and then proceed to roll dough into a tight log. Use dental floss to slice log into 12, 1½-inch pieces (illustration 3). Place buns, cut side down, into prepared pans. Cover with a damp cloth and let rise by 50 percent, 45 minutes to 1 hour.

8. Adjust oven rack to middle position and heat oven to 375 degrees. Bake until bun tops are golden brown, 25 to 30 minutes.

9. *For the syrup,* bring honey and butter to simmer over low heat in 2-quart saucepan. Simmer until thickened slightly, 2 to 3 minutes.

10. Bring 2 burners to low heat. As buns come out of oven, pour hot syrup over them and place each pan over a warm burner. Using oven mitts to hold each pan, shake to distribute syrup and caramelize glaze, 2 to 3 minutes. Use a thin spatula to separate buns from edge of pans and each other. Immediately invert buns in each pan onto a rimmed baking sheet. Cool for 10 minutes and serve. ∎

ROLLING AND CUTTING STICKY BUNS

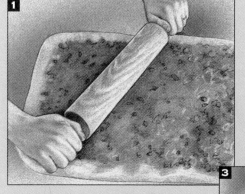

1. Use a rolling pin to embed filling into the dough. As you roll, the filling will evenly spread over the dough, as opposed to bunching at one end.

2. Fold first inch of the long side of dough over and pinch to seal. Repeat once more before gently rolling dough into a log. This keeps the log tightly coiled and prevents the buns from losing their shape in the oven.

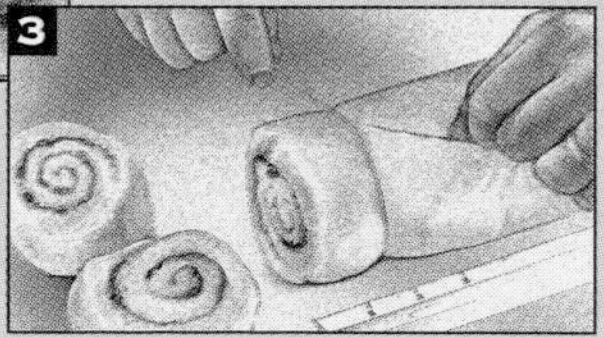

3. Use dental floss to easily and smoothly cut the rolled-up dough into individual buns.

PHOTOGRAPH BY MARK SHAW, ILLUSTRATIONS BY MICHELE AMATRULA

Culinary Uses for Homemade Juices

Juices can boost soup or form the base for intensely flavored sauces.

∾ BY JACK BISHOP ∾

Despite the associated nutrition hype, homemade juices are not just for dieters or antioxidant fiends; they also have a wide range of uses in cooking. Their pure flavors can intensify soups and act as the basis for a new kind of sauce, one that neither relies on gobs of fat nor smothers the flavor of the food it is intended to complement. Fortunately, a new generation of chefs has paved the way for us, creating a host of uses for the extracts of beets, carrots, bell peppers, cucumbers, zucchini, and more.

One way to employ vegetable juices, almost startling in its simplicity, is to add them to vegetables. Alan Harding, chef at NosmoKing in New York City, adjusts the consistency of pureed soups with vegetable juices. "If I want to thin out a cucumber soup, I'd much rather add cucumber juice than chicken stock or cream," says Harding. This clever strategy, which he also uses for potato and asparagus, boosts soup flavor instead of diluting it.

Further uptown, at the Union Square Cafe, chef Michael Romano eschews relatively bland chicken or vegetable stock and uses a mixture of carrot and celery juices to make his vegetable risotto. "I started out with just carrot juice, but it was too rich and viscous," he recalls. "Cutting it with celery juice makes risotto that's brimming with flavor." On other occasions, he makes asparagus risotto with asparagus juice, and uses cucumber juice to flavor shrimp risotto.

Charlie Trotter, chef/owner of the Chicago restaurant that bears his name, uses his Champion juicer for four or five hours each day to make flavored broths of aromatic vegetables such as fennel, celery, and bell peppers, which he uses in a variety of ways. But before proceeding, he puts the juice through a brief clarifying process: "The solids don't really have any flavor," says Trotter, "so it's important to briefly boil juices and skim off the foam with a ladle, as if you were making stock." After the surface solids have been skimmed, a quick strain removes any solids that have fallen out of the solution as it is heated.

Sometimes, Trotter reduces these strained

Some chefs cook with juices straight from the machine; others prefer to clarify them.

juices, especially those from root vegetables, to concentrate their flavor and color and to thicken their texture. He also blends the thickened juices with oil to create an emulsified sauce for drizzling directly onto plates or food, occasionally using flavored oils, such as those of ginger or basil.

Not all vegetable juices can be used in cooking. As NosmoKing's Harding says, "Leafy greens and herbs yield very strong or bitter juices that don't work well." There are, however, few other limitations; using fresh fruit and vegetable juices in cooking is a work in progress, one that will increase in importance in the coming years, as juicers become more common and cooks gain experience.

VEGETABLE RISOTTO IN CARROT AND CELERY BROTH
Serves 4–6 (about 8 cups)

Michael Romano of Union Square Cafe in New York City makes this risotto with an array of fresh vegetables. If some are unavailable, simply compensate by increasing the others; the total should be about three cups of vegetables.

2½   pounds celery, trimmed, juiced, and skimmed (3 cups)
3   pounds carrots, peeled, trimmed, juiced, and skimmed (3 cups)
¼   cup olive oil
1¾   cups arborio rice
½   teaspoon minced garlic
½   cup white wine
1   small carrot, halved and sliced thin (½ cup)
3   ounces green beans, cut into 1-inch pieces (½ cup)
½   small zucchini, halved lengthwise and sliced thin (½ cup)
4   medium asparagus, trimmed and cut into ½-inch pieces (½ cup)
½   small red bell pepper, sliced thin (½ cup)
½   cup fresh green peas or frozen, thawed
3   medium scallions, sliced thin (⅓ cup)

2   tablespoons butter
¾   cup grated Parmesan cheese
Salt and ground black pepper
1   tablespoon minced fresh parsley

1. Bring vegetable juices to a simmer in a medium saucepan; keep warm over low heat.

2. Heat oil in a large saucepan over medium heat. Add rice and garlic; stir to coat rice with oil. Add wine; stir constantly until absorbed.

3. Add carrots and green beans along with ½ cup vegetable juice; stir constantly until liquid is absorbed. Continue adding ½ cup juice at a time, stirring constantly, until each addition is absorbed. When ¾ of the juice has been used, about 20 minutes, stir in remaining vegetables and scallions. Continue adding juice in ½ cup increments, stirring constantly until rice is creamy and al dente, about 10 minutes longer.

4. Swirl in butter, ½ cup cheese, and salt and pepper to taste. Serve immediately, garnishing with minced parsley and remaining cheese.

SAUTÉED CHICKEN CUTLETS WITH BROCCOLI-BASIL SAUCE
Serves 4

¾   pound broccoli
4   chicken breast cutlets (1½ pounds), trimmed
Salt and ground black pepper
¼   cup flour
1½   tablespoons oil
2   tablespoons butter
2   tablespoons minced fresh basil leaves

1. Juice broccoli; skim foam and set aside ⅔ cup juice.

2. Sprinkle both sides of chicken generously with salt and pepper, then dredge in flour.

3. Heat oil and 1 tablespoon butter in a large, heavy skillet over medium-high heat. When butter begins to color, add chicken and cook for 4 minutes. Turn chicken and cook until cooked through, 3 or 4 minutes. Transfer chicken to a warm plate and cover with foil.

4. Deglaze hot pan with broccoli juice. Simmer briskly until juice thickens slightly, about 2 minutes. Add salt and pepper to taste along with basil and any chicken juices that have accumulated. Whisk in remaining tablespoon butter and serve immediately with chicken. ∎

Which Juice Extractor Should You Buy?

We put 17 models through their paces. Two died, and the rest varied widely in performance and percentage of juice extracted.

∼ BY JACK BISHOP ∼

Juice extractors, which have become increasingly popular in this health-conscious age, are countertop devices that separate the juice of fresh fruits and vegetables from the solid pulp. Juice extractors are actually quite simple. Most extractors house a cutting blade that rotates thousands of times every minute. As the blade spins, centrifugal force separates solids from liquids. The pulp collects inside the machine or is ejected into a separate container, while the liquid pours through a fine strainer, out of a spout in the juicer, and into a waiting glass or container.

Although the basic mechanism remains pretty much the same from machine to machine, performance varies greatly. Top-of-the-line units cost $200 or more and vie with commercial juicers for design and durability. Smaller, quite decent machines sell for as little as $40. But while the pricier models all perform admirably, many of the midpriced and bargain juicers squeeze out only a fraction of the total juice available in a carrot or peach. Given the high cost of juicing at home (it takes about one pound of produce to yield one cup of juice), low yields mean higher costs, which can really add up over time. Cheaper juicers also have smaller motors: two poorly made machines died before the testing on them could be completed. It may make sense, therefore, to consider a more expensive machine if you really intend to use the juicer; in the long run, it will pay for itself.

In my research I uncovered 17 different manufacturers of juicers, with some companies offering two or three models. For the purposes of this article, I evaluated the best juicer from each company on a number of points.

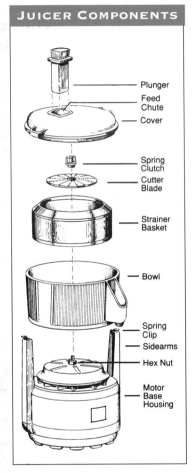

JUICER COMPONENTS

- Plunger
- Feed Chute
- Cover
- Spring Clutch
- Cutter Blade
- Strainer Basket
- Bowl
- Spring Clip
- Sidearms
- Hex Nut
- Motor Base Housing

Design and performance. I weighed all the machines and found that heavier machines tend to be more stable and work better. I also noted the size and shape of the feed tube. Machines with large rectangular or half-circle feed tubes require less chopping of produce than machines with small or odd-shaped feed tubes. I also paid attention to the noise level during operation, and measured how much produce each machine could handle before it became necessary to stop juicing and empty the pulp collector. (The average machine handles about three pounds; exceptions are noted in the accompanying chart.)

Extraction capabilities. I took six measurements for each machine. First I measured total extraction from one pound each of tomatoes, celery, apples, and carrots. Although juicers with a higher total extraction rate generally received high marks, I also wanted to see how much of the extraction was liquid as opposed to pulp, sediment, or foam. To do this, I poured apple and carrot juices into clear graduated cylinders and allowed the solids to settle out. The "liquid extraction" figure is given as a percentage of the total extraction. This measurement is an important indication of quality,

since sediment and foam should be discarded whether juice is consumed fresh or used in sauces.

Special features. Several machines come with attachments for juicing citrus. (Citrus fruits generally don't work well in regular extractors). I also have noted other unusual features where applicable.

Choose a Price, then Buy the Best

The machines divided easily into three categories based on price. The four machines with price tags between $199 and $299 all performed relatively well, although the quite similar Acme and Omega are my favorites due to their high total extraction and liquid extraction rates. The Champion, a favorite in restaurant kitchens because of its sturdy, 21-pound base and buzz-sawlike processing of produce, works well but is a bit difficult to use and clean.

The second group, with prices between $75 and $105, offers some incredible values. The Kenwood and Sanyo machines are extremely reliable and powerful juicers and both can be considered "best buys." In the inexpensive group, my top choice is the $45 Moulinex, the second cheapest juicer tested. This reliable unit outperformed several moderately priced models.

When choosing among the juicers described in the chart, decide how much money you are willing to spend and buy the best machine in that category. There is no point in buying one of the lower-rated machines in any given category, since the best model from the next-lower-priced category is a superior (and cheaper) product. If you plan on juicing 25 pounds of carrots a week, opt for a sturdy machine like the Acme, with a 10-year warranty. If you plan to juice only on occasion, then a less expensive model will meet your needs. ∎

THE ARNOLD SCHWARZENEGGER OF JUICERS

I also worked with the Vita-Mix Total Nutrition Center, an expensive and powerful blender that pulverizes produce. Unlike extractors that separate juice from pulp and therefore are unable to match whole produce in terms of nutrition, the thick "juice" from this machine squeezes out all the fiber and nutrients. However, this machine is very different from an extractor: it requires the addition of water or other liquids during blending, and the resulting beverage is not usable for cooking because it contains far too high a proportion of solids. For these reasons — and because it costs almost $400 — I decided not to include it in the ratings.

ILLUSTRATION COURTESY OF ACME WARING

RATING JUICE EXTRACTORS

Juicers are listed in order of preference within each price range. "Total extraction" measures yield from 1 pound each of tomatoes, celery, apples, and carrots. "Liquid extraction" measures juice content for apple and carrot extractions. Prices are suggested retail and will vary from store to store. *See* Sources and Resources on page 32 for information about purchasing specific units.

EXPENSIVE
Acme Supreme
Juicerator 6001

MODERATELY PRICED
Kenwood JE-600

MODERATELY PRICED
Sanyo Juicer/Blender
3020MB

INEXPENSIVE
Moulinex Juice
Extractor 753

EXPENSIVE JUICERS ($199 and higher)

Acme Supreme Juicerator 6001
Price: $299
Weight: 11 pounds
Design and Performance: Stainless-steel juicer with large rectangular feed tube. Extremely quiet and very efficient. Pulp is extremely dry. Can handle 5 pounds of produce before it's necessary to empty pulp.
Total Extraction: 6¼ cups
Liquid Extraction: 91%
Cleaning: Six parts. Optional filter paper can line machine and make clean-up very easy. Stainless bowl and cover are superior to plastic models.
Special Features: Easy-to-use citrus attachment makes great-tasting orange juice. Acme also makes a cheaper juicer (model 7001) that has the same blade, motor, and stainless-steel bowl, but with a white plastic cover. It performs just as well and retails for $199, making it a superb value.

Omega Juicer 1000
Price: $234
Weight: 10½ pounds
Design and Performance: Very similar design to less expensive top-rated Acme 7001 with stainless-steel bowl, plastic cover, and heavy base. Large feed tube and capacity; quiet operation.
Total Extraction: 6 cups
Liquid Extraction: 85%
Cleaning: Six parts. As with Acme, optional filter paper makes cleaning easier, as does stainless-steel bowl.
Special Features: Citrus attachment yields good but not great orange juice, with a bit too much pulp for my taste.

Champion Juicer
Price: $229
Weight: 21 pounds
Design and Performance: A masticating juicer that chews produce into tiny bits and yields very thick juice. Comes with fine-mesh strainer to separate out solids. A bit awkward to use but quite massive and strong. Machine extrudes pulp, but the feed and exit tubes can clog after several pounds of produce have been processed.
Total Extraction: 5¾ cups
Liquid Extraction: 86%
Cleaning: Four parts. L-shaped design makes filter screen difficult to clean.
Special Features: Machine grates as well as homogenizes to make nut butters, ice creams, and grated vegetables. Optional attachment for milling grain.

Trillium Juiceman II
Price: $225
Weight: 8½ pounds
Design and Performance: Good-size feed tube and powerful motor make for quick juicing. Ejects pulp into a separate container, although passageway can become blocked. Very quiet. Easy to use, but note lower yields.
Total Extraction: 4½ cups
Liquid Extraction: 64%
Cleaning: Five parts. Easy to clean.
Special Features: Free book offers plenty of recipes and nutrition hype.

MODERATELY PRICED JUICERS ($75–$105)*

Kenwood JE-600
Price: $90
Weight: 6 pounds
Design and Performance: Two speeds for soft and hard items. Very large feed tube. Pulp stays in machine, which is a bit loud during operation. Solid and dependable.
Total Extraction: 5 cups
Liquid Extraction: 78%
Cleaning: Four parts. Quite easy to clean.
Special Features: Excellent manual offers useful chart with tips on how to prepare various fruits and vegetables for juicing.

Sanyo Juicer/Blender 3020MB
Price: $105
Weight: 5½ pounds
Design and Performance: This versatile appliance uses the same base and motor for a juicer, blender, and wet/dry mill. Juicer has large oval feed tube and removable pulp container.
Total Extraction: 4⅞ cups
Liquid Extraction: 83%
Cleaning: Six parts. Pulp collector pops out and is easy to clean.

Panasonic Juice Extractor MJ-65PR
Price: $75
Weight: 6½ pounds
Design and Performance: Compact machine with solid performance. Large feed tube and easy cleaning.
Total Extraction: 5¼ cups
Liquid Extraction: 69%
Cleaning: Six parts. A brush with water bottle attachment can be inserted during operation to loosen debris from cutting blade.

Oster Designer Juice Extractor 323-20
Price: $94
Weight: 7½ pounds
Design and Performance: Two-speed motor with removable pulp collector. Kidney-shaped feed tube is on the small side. Smart design and good extraction make this machine a worthy option.
Total Extraction: 5 cups
Liquid Extraction: 75%
Cleaning: Six parts. Average clean-up time.

Braun Deluxe Juice Extractor MP81
Price: $90
Weight: 6 pounds
Design and Performance: Average-size, kidney-shaped feed tube; swing-out pulp receptacle. Some pulp does collect around filter and can cause juice to become excessively pulpy.
Total Extraction: 5 cups
Liquid Extraction: 68%
Cleaning: Seven parts. Too many hard-to-reach nooks and crannies.
Special Features: Comes with plastic strainer cup for separating juice from foam. Also has tray attachment for feed tube that allows prepared produce to slide into tube for juicing.

Cuisinart Juice Extractor JE-4
Price: $100
Weight: 5 pounds
Design and Performance: Small, odd-shaped feed tube necessitates extra cutting of produce. Roars like an airplane during take-off; juice spurts out of spout, causing a mess unless wide-mouthed glass is used to catch liquid.
Total Extraction: 4½ cups
Liquid Extraction: 74%
Cleaning: Four parts. Easy to disassemble and wash.
Special Features: When turned on, citrus attachment operates continually (as opposed to when pressure is applied), raising safety questions. Orange juice is very pulpy.

INEXPENSIVE JUICERS (under $65)*

Moulinex Juice Extractor 753
Price: $45
Weight: 6 pounds
Design and Performance: Solid construction with removable pulp collector. Average feed tube and noise level. Nothing out of the ordinary here, but reliable and very cheap.
Total Extraction: 5¼ cups
Liquid Extraction: 77%
Cleaning: Five parts. Has a few grooves but is not too difficult to wash.

Tefal Juicemaster 8310
Price: $40
Weight: 5 pounds

Design and Performance: Two-speed operation with one mode for extracting and one for citrus juicing. Pulp collector is quite small and must be emptied after just 2 pounds of produce are juiced. Large feed tube.
Total Extraction: 5 cups
Liquid Extraction: 70%
Cleaning: Four parts. Some narrow and hard-to-reach areas.
Special Features: Machine turns on by rotating housing, which is cumbersome and seems less safe than an on/off switch. Citrus attachment works well.

Hamilton Beach 2-Speed Juice Extractor 3920
Price: $63
Weight: 4 pounds
Design and Performance: Small 150-watt motor (with two speeds) does not have power to extract all the juice from hard items like carrots. High liquid extraction does not compensate for extremely low yields.
Total Extraction: 3¼ cups
Liquid Extraction: 82%
Cleaning: Five parts. White plastic was easily stained by carrot juice.
Special Features: Juice collection container has strainer that works well to remove foam.

Salton Vitamin Bar JC-3
Price: $55
Weight: 5 pounds
Design and Performance: Small, poorly designed feed tube and very loud operation. Just 1 pound of carrots will clog passageway to built-in pulp receptacle. Machine must be taken apart to dump pulp. Note very low liquid extraction rate.
Total Extraction: 4 cups
Liquid Extraction: 48%
Cleaning: Four parts. Average clean-up time.
Special Features: Like Cuisinart juicer, the citrus attachment runs continually when machine is on and seems a bit dangerous. Orange juice is very thick.

*One moderately priced and one inexpensive unit — the Krups VitaMight 294 ($100) and Singer Juice Giant 774 ($60) — conked out while juicing carrots, one of the toughest items on motors because of their low moisture content. I was unable to restart these juicers, even after they had cooled down. Since testing was incomplete, results are not included in chart.

Inexpensive Ports Fail Test

Professionals and amateurs agree on the best and worst Ports, but the complicated nature of this fortified wine causes disagreement in the midrange.

~ BY MARK BITTMAN ~

There was near-consensus among the *Cook's Illustrated* tasting panel of professional and amateur tasters about which Ports were best and worst: the top two wines were pretty much enjoyed by everyone, while inexpensive tawny and ruby Ports from Portugal, along with Ports made in California and Australia, finished at the bottom of the list. In the middle, however, the consensus broke down. Experienced tasters preferred vintage Ports with potential — wines that would taste better in 5 or even 10 years — while novices voted primarily for the "wood-aged" Ports designed for short-term drinking.

More than any other wine, the best Port displays little of its future charm when it is young. Vintage Port — the most cherished and most expensive — is an awkward, gangly youth when it is first bottled. By the time it reaches maturity after 20 years or more, it has become a smooth, glamorous, velvety drink that has no peer. By then it has also risen in price by a factor of at least three or four. So, to buy the best Port, you must either have patience and buy it when it is young (and tastes like alcohol mixed with grape juice), or have deep pockets. (Perhaps the most encouraging aspect of our tasting is that the top-rated Port is relatively affordable.) This limits the potential market, of course, and ties up the capital of cash-starved producers.

For these reasons, Port producers developed a number of nonvintage Ports, relatively inexpensive wines that mature quickly.

What is Port?

Port begins life as a strong red wine, usually made in Portugal's Douro region, whose fermentation is stopped by the addition of brandy before all the grapes' sugar has been turned to alcohol. The result, then and there, is a horrible drink of alcoholic grape juice. But, with time, the flavors marry and, in the best instances, the resulting drink is incomparably delicious.

From start to finish, different grapes are handled differently. The lightest wines will become the least expensive ruby and tawny Ports, which spend no more than a couple of years in wood, after which they are bottled and sold, cheap. Most are barely worth the price. Slightly more assertive wines may become aged tawny Ports, which spend much more time in wood — up to 40 years in some cases — and can be quite delicious.

Vintage Port is entirely different. For one thing, it is only made in auspicious years. For another, it only spends about 2 years in the barrel; and must mature without the help of the wood that softens the "wood-aged" Ports; aging in the bottle takes a decade or longer. In off-years, some Port producers use their best wines to make single-*quinta* (one vineyard) vintage Port, which is less expensive and matures more quickly than true vintage Port.

Late-bottled vintage Port (LBV) is usually made from wine that is not quite good enough to be true Vintage Port. It's held in wood for up to 6 years before bottling, long enough to mellow, so it is ready for drinking when bottled. Like older tawny Port, the best LBVs have some of the character of vintage Port at a lesser price. So-called "vintage-character" Port is higher quality ruby port that spends more time in wood; it, too, can offer decent value. ∎

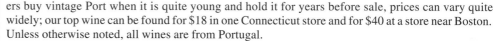

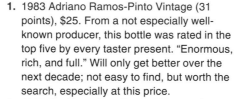

BEST WINE

PORTO
VINTAGE 1983
PRODUCE OF PORTUGAL
Shipped by
ADRIANO RAMOS-PINTO
PORTO   PORTUGAL

BEST BUY

BLIND TASTING RESULTS

As in all *Cook's Illustrated* wine tastings, the wines were tasted blind; their identities were revealed only after the poll of preferences was made. In this instance, it is safe to say that those wines finishing in ninth place or lower garnered far more negative than positive comments.

Wines are listed in order of preference. In the judging, seven points were awarded for each first-place vote; six for second; five for third; four for fourth; three for fifth; two for sixth; one for seventh. Because some retailers buy vintage Port when it is quite young and hold it for years before sale, prices can vary quite widely; our top wine can be found for $18 in one Connecticut store and for $40 at a store near Boston. Unless otherwise noted, all wines are from Portugal.

1. **1983 Adriano Ramos-Pinto Vintage** (31 points), $25. From a not especially well-known producer, this bottle was rated in the top five by every taster present. "Enormous, rich, and full." Will only get better over the next decade; not easy to find, but worth the search, especially at this price.

2. **1987 Cockburn Late Bottled Vintage** (26 points), $23. A great showing for this LBV from a top British house. "Nice, rich flavor and balance, with good depth and subtle wood tone." Roundly enjoyed, widely available, favorably priced.

3. **Da Silva Presidential Twenty-Year Tawny** (20 points), $33. Despite its light color, several tasters — including the most- and least-experienced panel members — found good character. "Sweet and delightfully creamy."

4. **1981 Smith Woodhouse Late Bottled Vintage** (19 points), $22.50. An unfiltered, quite traditional LBV with fairly broad appeal. "Big devil," remarked one admirer, who ranked it second.

5. **1980 Dow Vintage** (18 points), $30. From a light vintage, this wine is at its peak right now. Not everyone liked it, but two fairly experienced tasters put it at the top of their lists: "Big, bold, fruity, and smooth."

6. **1977 Taylor Fladgate Vintage** (16 points), $65. This was the most powerful (older tasters would say "masculine") Port, with 5 to 10 more years of aging needed. Most experienced tasters liked it; those unfamiliar with Port found it "hot, raw, and alcoholic," an accurate description for good young vintage Port.

7. **1977 Presidential Da Silva Vintage** (15 points), $40. An interesting contrast to the wine just above, this is a lighter wine from the same vintage; veterans found it "very light," novices enjoyed its "smooth, fruity" character.

8. **1990 Graham's Malvedos Centenary** (13 points), $25. Made in the style of a vintage Port, this wine may have some potential, but most tasters felt that it was in an "awkward" stage now.

9. **Fonseca Bin 27 Premium Ruby** (12 points), $16. "Nice, round fruit and not overly alcoholic," was the sole compliment this wine received. The majority of tasters found it "cloying," with a "suspicious" nose.

10. **Seppelt Mt. Rufus Barrossa Valley** (Australia; 11 points), $10. Do Australians make good Port? One experienced taster thinks so — he placed this wine second; no one else placed it higher than fifth.

11. **Sandeman Tawny** (10 points), $10. One surprising third-place vote.

12. **Ficklin Vineyards** (California; 2 points), $13. "Okay," was the nicest comment made about this wine.

13. **Sandeman Ruby** (1 point), $10. Its sole point came from a taster who called this wine "bland." Enough said.

BOOK
REVIEWS

~ BY MARK BITTMAN ~

Cooking with Daniel Boulud
Random House, $40.00

This is not the Le Cirque cookbook, and that's something for which we can be happy. Boulud, who ran what was arguably New York City's top kitchen from 1986 to 1992, is among that city's most popular and talented chefs. The food at Le Cirque, however, was never meant to be tackled at home, and the recipes would be difficult if not absurd. Now, Boulud owns his own place, Restaurant Daniel, and, there and at home, he is cooking in a more leisurely, accessible fashion. This is our gain, for his recipes here are personal, approachable, and, for the most part, quite wonderful.

They're not all French, either, nor all subtle. Crispy Chicken Cooked under a Brick is a jazzed-up version of *pollo al mattone,* a Tuscan specialty. Although you might take exception to Boulud's fussiness with this normally simple dish — he somewhat laboriously studs each chicken part with garlic and rosemary, where mixing these in with the olive oil marinade might suffice — you can't argue with the flavorings or the cooking technique, which produce stunning results.

Boulud's talent shines in dishes such as Cabbage and Lobster Soup with Chives, in which the whole is far greater than the sum of its parts. Two small lobsters are used, not only for their meat but for their flavor — the stock is made from their inedible parts — to make a dish that is intensely flavored and elegant in appearance, despite the fact that we are talking about little more than a basic cabbage soup.

Other successes include a thin Basil and Anchovy dip that could double nicely as a dressing for greens; Zucchini with Orange Zest and Rosemary, a simple side dish that's big on flavor; and Fondant au Chocolat, a gooey dessert that was easy to put together and might have been even better cold than it was warm.

There are problems here, but they are far from damning: For one thing, the back of the book, which features a nearly useless glossary ("Oregon, Texas, and Washington are the main producers of blackberries. . . ."), also contains some miscellaneous but wonderful recipes, in paragraph form; it would take luck to find these when you wanted them. For another, there are a few recipes one might consider excessive — Potato Galette with Chicken Livers, Onion Rings, and a Ricotta-Herb Mix, for example, or

Maine Sea Scallops in Black Tie, which turns out to mean fresh truffles. But the appealing recipes far outnumber the laughable ones, the organization of the book is sound, and you could happily cook from it and little else for weeks on end. A winner.

Miami Spice: The New Florida Cuisine
Steven Raichlen
Workman, $22.95 cloth; $12.95 paper

That Miami is the capital of the Caribbean; that to many Cubans, Puerto Ricans, Colombians, Dominicans, Nicaraguans, Venezuelans, Haitians, and others, Miami *is* the United States; that the food there is as interesting as any other city in the country save perhaps New York and Los Angeles — these we can take as more or less understood. That Steven Raichlen, a veteran teacher and author, was among the first food professionals to recognize this is also true.

What is not true is that there is a "New Florida Cuisine" that is somehow an amalgam of all the cultures that have come together in Miami. "If ever there was an area ripe for a culinary revolution, it is Florida," writes Raichlen, and, although I would argue that he's talking solely about south Florida, this statement is basically true. But has this given "rise to a new regional cuisine"? There's no evidence of this, nor does Raichlen really make a case for it.

Yet the fact that there is no Florida cuisine, or even a Miami cuisine, detracts not one whit from the content of *Miami Spice.* The whimsical cover, the Sunshine State hype, the cutesy design, the witty title, have little to do with what Raichlen offers here, which is nothing short of the best collection of Caribbean recipes I have seen to date. It's personalized — Raichlen feels free to add spice-scented whipped cream to calabaza soup, to invent dishes using ingredients common to Miami's ethnic communities, and even to include Mediterranean-style food, such as Pan Roasted Snapper with Raisins, Capers, and Pine Nuts — but most of the recipes have an authentic feel to them, and the ones I tried worked well in the home kitchen and were delicious.

There are two dishes I think of as essentially Miami: the watery, garlicky black beans of the omnipresent Cuban restaurants, and the crispy pork tidbits of Haitian holes-in-the-wall.

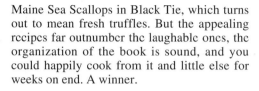

Raichlen duplicates both almost perfectly. Equally satisfying was a roast pork shoulder whose marinade, which contains an entire cup of sour orange or lime juice, I have used for things as diverse as soaking chicken and adding fat-free spark to refried beans.

Miami Spice has lots of detail, superb cooking instructions, and good sidebars. Were it entitled *Ethnic Cooking Of Miami,* or something equally drab, it might be a bit easier to take. But I recommend you ignore the glitzy packaging and enjoy the substance.

Treasures of the Italian Table
Burton Anderson
William Morrow, $18.00

Burton Anderson's latest offering is a collection of essays about the sometimes exhilarating but usually depressing state of several of the well-known artisanal products of Italy. Here we have another misnamed book, for although olive oil, truffles, espresso, pasta, pizza, parmesan, and prosciutto are indeed treasures, Anderson's brilliantly made point is that they are almost all in danger of losing their uniqueness.

"Alimentary standards have been falling throughout Europe," he writes, and "degeneracy has been hastened by the European Economic Community," which acts as a homogenizing and sanitizing agent, robbing the best of Italian (and French, and other) food of its true nature. Almost all of the foods about which Anderson writes here might be considered endangered culinary species. Today's milk is incapable of producing brilliant Parmigiano, today's techniques cannot result in perfect prosciutto, and today's *aceto balsamico* has been "overwhelmed" by industrial versions. The news is not good, but the story is terrific.

Burton Anderson has lived in Europe, primarily in Italy (he now lives in Tuscany), since he graduated from college in the mid 1960s. He worked as a reporter when he was younger, and it shows: His prose is graceful and tight, his eye is sure, his interviews succinct and personal. He tells his stories with love, care, and understanding. With *Treasures of the Italian Table,* Anderson is breaking new ground in food journalism; this is easily the most interesting book on the subject of food to be published in the last year. ∎

JUICE EXTRACTORS

The Acme Juicerator 7001, the inexpensive version of the top-rated extractor in our testing (see page 28) is available at a discounted price of $199 at Williams-Sonoma stores nationwide. To order by mail, call 800-541-2233. For information about other Acme models (including the all-stainless-steel 6001 that costs $299), contact the company directly at 203-379-0731. The second-rated Omega juicer is sold at health food stores across the country. To find an outlet near you, contact the company at 800-633-3401. As for the best buys in the moderately priced and inexpensive categories, the Kenwood ($90) is sold at J.C. Penney, Macy's, and Wal-Mart stores across the country. It also can be ordered directly from the U.S. distributor by calling 201-515-3468. The Sanyo juicer/blender combination ($105) is available at True Value Hardware. For other locations, call the company's customer service hotline at 818-998-7322. To locate a Moulinex dealer in your area, call 201-784-5137.

For information about other juicers mentioned in the testing article, contact the manufacturers at the following numbers: Champion (209-369-2154), Trillium (800-800-2641), Vita-Mix (800-848-2649), Panasonic (201-392-6875), Oster (800-528-7713), Braun (617-596-7300), Cuisinart (800-726-0190), Tefal (201-575-1060), Hamilton Beach (800-851-8900), Salton (800-233-9054), Krups (800-526-5377), and Singer (800-877-7391).

AROMATIC BROWN RICES

Most health food and gourmet stores stock a variety of aromatic brown rices, including brown basmati. Some of the best rices to pass through our kitchens have come from Lundberg Family Farms (P.O. Box 369, Richvale, CA 95974; 916-882-4551), located north of Sacramento in California's rich rice country. The company's brown basmati is distributed nationwide, as is the mahogany-colored wehani and a number of other unhulled rices in hues ranging from red to black. If you cannot locate a retail outlet in your area that carries these premium rices, contact Lundberg's customer service department.

They will ship products directly to consumers with no minimum on orders.

FLAME-TAMER

Perfect pot roast depends on gentle simmering over very low heat (see "Pot Roast Perfected," page 6). However, many stove burners are too hot, even at their lowest setting, to maintain a subsimmer. A Heat Master mutes the lowest flame on either a gas or electric range. This chrome-plated flame-tamer is about eight inches in diameter and rests just above the burner. For more information, contact Bridge Kitchenware (214 E. 52nd Street, New York, NY 10022; 800-274-3435). The Heat Master costs $5.95 plus shipping.

MESH SKIMMER

When heating vegetable juices to make oils, sauces, or broths (see "Culinary Uses for Homemade Juices," page 27), it is necessary to skim solids and foam that rise to the surface of the pot, much as if you were making chicken stock. The best tool for either task is a mesh skimmer with a long metal handle. We use a stainless-steel skimmer made in Italy. Very fine mesh that resembles a window screen covers the five-inch round skimmer, and a long, thin handle allows easy access, even into deep pots. Look for this item in local restaurant or kitchen supply shops or order it from Bridge Kitchenware (see above) for $17.95 plus shipping.

RICE COOKER

Whether preparing brown or white rice, a rice cooker with automatic shut-off ensures perfect results every time (see "Foolproof Brown Rice," page 22). The National Rice Cooker/Steamer comes in two convenient sizes and has a handy keep-warm feature that will hold cooked rice for up to five hours. A clear panel on the lid allows the cook to check on the progress of the rice without letting steam escape. The nonstick surface of the cooking chamber makes for remarkably easy clean-up. Both the large and the small rice cookers are available at Williams-Sonoma stores nationwide. To order from the company's catalog, call 800-541-2233.

The price for the smaller model, which holds about 5 cups of cooked rice, is $59. The 10-cup model costs $69. Unless you have a large family or plan on cooking rice in quantity, the 5-cup model will be adequate.

MUSTARD SUPPLIES

When it comes to paraphernalia for making your own mustard (see "How to Make Mustard at Home," page 18), the best source we know of is the Mount Horeb Mustard Museum (109 East Main Street, Mount Horeb, WI 53572; 800-438-6878). Whole and cracked brown and yellow mustard seeds are sold at the rock-bottom price of $3.00 per quart. The museum publishes a newsletter twice a year called The Proper Mustard, with mustard trivia, recipes, and folklore. The cost is $5.00 for a one-year subscription. Finally, if you want more information or ideas for making mustard at home, the museum catalog carries mustard cookbooks ranging in price from $2.95 for a simple handbook to $21.50 for an imported English title not available in American bookstores.

SEMOLINA FLOUR

Semolina flour, which is milled from hard durum wheat, is used to make sturdy pastas such as the fusilli and cavatelli on page 19. This cream-colored flour is ground quite fine for pasta — it should be about as sandy as very fine cornmeal. Look for semolina flour in Italian gourmet shops or health food stores. It also can be ordered by mail from Nancy's Specialty Market, an excellent catalog filled with ethnic ingredients — everything from chiles and morels to fish sauce and chutney. Nancy's one-and-one-half-pound box of semolina flour costs $4.50 plus shipping. For more information, call 800-462-6291.

DRIED LAVENDER

The bluish-purple buds of the lavender plant are dried and used in herbal cures and teas as well as in recipes such as Honey Lavender Biscotti on page 13. Much of the lavender sold in this country is imported from France, where it is graded according to color intensity. The highest quality buds

are the bluest and are known as "ultra." Although some health food or gourmet stores may carry lavender, it may be easier to order this special herb by mail. Top-quality dried lavender buds are available from Mountain Rose Herbs (P.O. Box 2000, Redway, CA 95560; 800-879-3337). A four-ounce container of regular lavender costs $4.00 plus shipping. Organic lavender is slightly more expensive, at $5.50 for four ounces. Larger quantities can be purchased (in either eight-ounce or one-pound bags), but four ounces is enough for numerous batches of biscotti.

MAIL-ORDER NEWSLETTER

If shopping by mail for specialty food items has become a passion, then you need to know about Mail Order Gourmet, a newsletter devoted to finding suppliers of unusual, high-quality products. The newsletter features stories about obscure regional items such as mayhaw jelly — made from a berry indigenous to southeastern Georgia — as well as more mainstream foodstuffs such as organic heirloom beans grown in New Mexico or barbecue sauce from Texas. Recipes as well as information on ordering are included. An annual subscription (six issues) costs $15 and includes a free guide to almost one hundred mail-order businesses, as well as $20 worth of discount coupons to vendors listed in the directory. For more information, contact Mail Order Gourmet, P.O. Box 1085, New York, NY 10011; 800-989-5996. Ask about obtaining a sample issue for $3.

SEEDS FOR ROLLS AND BREADS

To make your own rolls, bagels, or breadsticks with "everything" on top, try the Four Seed Baking Blend available at Williams-Sonoma stores across the country. This mixture of poppy, sesame, caraway, and fennel seeds can be used to adorn any dough that has been lightly brushed with beaten egg. The aromatic blend comes in 2.4-ounce jars and is available through the catalog (800-541-2233) in sets of two for $6 plus shipping. ∎

ASSORTED BISCOTTI
page 13

**ROASTED CARROTS AND RED ONION
WITH BALSAMIC VINEGAR**
page 11

**CAVATELLI WITH WHITE BEANS
AND CLAMS**
page 19

**VEGETABLE RISOTTO
IN CARROT AND CELERY BROTH**
page 27

RASPBERRY CHARLOTTE ROYALE
page 14

THE BEST STICKY BUNS
page 26

Poached Pears on Salad Greens with Walnuts and Stilton

Bring 6 cups water, 1 cup sugar, 12 peppercorns, and 3 strips lemon zest to simmer. Add 6 peeled pears; return to simmer. Remove from heat and cool pears in poaching liquid to room temperature; refrigerate until ready to serve. Whisk 3 tablespoons each of walnut and vegetable oil into 2 tablespoons lemon juice; season with salt and pepper and 2 tablespoons snipped chives. Pour dressing over 6 cups cleaned and torn salad greens and 2 stalks celery, sliced; toss to coat. Arrange a portion of dressed greens on each of 6 salad plates. Place a pear on each bed of greens. Sprinkle each salad with 1½ tablespoons crumbled Stilton cheese and 1½ tablespoons toasted walnuts. *Serves 6.*

NUMBER SEVEN ◆ MARCH/APRIL 1994

$4.00 U.S./$4.95 CANADA

COOK'S
ILLUSTRATED

Perfect
Leg of Lamb
How to Cook
the Entire Leg Evenly

15-Minute
Puff Pastry
Food Processor
Technique Makes Fast
Puff Pastry

Germans Win
Knife Testing
Restaurant Chefs Test
6 Different Brands

Risotto Rules
No Need for Constant
Stirring

THE BEST BROWNIES
•
HOW TO COOK WITH
FRESH COCONUT
•
INEXPENSIVE CANNED
TOMATOES WIN TESTING
•
RED RIOJA TASTING

TABLE

OF CONTENTS

"Beets"
Young beets are one of spring's pleasures. See page 11 for "How to Cook Beets."

ILLUSTRATION BY
BRENT WATKINSON

Skewered Grilled Shrimp and Artichoke Hearts, adapted from *Antipasti* (Chronicle, 1993) by Julia della Croce.

ILLUSTRATION BY
DAN BROWN

COOK'S ILLUSTRATED

Publisher and Editor
CHRISTOPHER KIMBALL

Executive Editor
MARK BITTMAN

Senior Editor
JOHN WILLOUGHBY

Food Editor
PAM ANDERSON

Senior Writer
JACK BISHOP

Managing Editor
MAURA LYONS

Copy Editor
DAVID TRAVERS

Test Kitchen Assistant
VICTORIA ROLAND

Art Director
MEG BIRNBAUM

Food Stylist
MARIE PIRAINO

Circulation Director
ADRIENNE KIMBALL

Circulation Manager
MARY TAINTOR

Marketing Manager
NANCY HALTER-GILLIS

Circulation Assistant
JENNIFER L. KEENE

Production Director
JAMES MCCORMACK

Treasurer
JANET CARLSON

Office Manager
JENNY THORNBURY

EDITORIAL

UPSTAIRS, DOWNSTAIRS

CHRISTOPHER KIMBALL

The history of food is a tale of two cities — the urban cuisine of European aristocrats married to the lesser known fare of the common laborer. Until recently, the former has dominated the culinary landscape in America. Our imagination is captured more by the haute cuisine of France and Italy than by tales of unleavened bread. As the rich indulged in luxurious ingredients they could afford — beef, butter, and cream — the poor were making do with broth, black bread, and the occasional piece of fish or pork.

For example, the history-book description of nineteenth-century England is really the story of a mere ten thousand aristocrats at the height of the Victorian period. One London dinner party described in *What Jane Austen Ate and Charles Dickens Knew* (Simon & Schuster, 1993), not atypical for the times, included turtle soup, turbot with lobster, red mullet with Cardinal sauce, oysters, chicken, sweetbreads, lamb cutlets, asparagus, peas, roast saddle of mutton, salad, beetroot — and this is merely the first course. For seconds, one tucked into goose, plover's eggs in aspic jelly, and a mayonnaise of fowl. For sweets, one confronted a macédoine of fruit, meringues a la crème, a marasquino jelly, and chocolate cream. Dessert was a separate course including two ices, cherry-water and pineapple cream, and then fruit. During the height of the social season, the diners would then adjourn to a ball which, of course, included a sit-down supper (dances with but a simple buffet were considered déclassé).

While these gentlemen and ladies were, as an English friend of mine puts it, "shoving it down the old cake-hole," the rest of England was making do with somewhat simpler fare. The poor lived on gruel made from oats or barley, bread, and onions, potatoes, or bacon. Lower-class Englishmen ate cheese rather than butter and fish rather than meat, because they were cheaper. The average farm laborer had but one hot meal per week — fuel was prohibitively expensive. On Sunday and Christmas, the poor took their geese or other meals to the local baker to get them cooked, as did the Cratchits in *A Christmas Carol*.

Although America's true culinary legacy is one of immigrant cooking, more peasant than noble (in *Joy of Cooking* one finds both Bouchées à la Reine and poached muskrat — a mind-boggling range of culinary pursuits), a majority of cookbook authors and cooking schools have, up until the 1980s, preferred the cuisine of courts and kings. Even today, many culinary academies are more likely to include Charlotte Russe in their curriculum than how to cook pot roast (*see* January/February 1994 issue, page 6) or how to roast beets (page 11). But times are changing.

Due perhaps to an interest in healthy eating, the trend in America and in Europe is finally headed downstairs. The three-star restaurants of Paris are in trouble — bistro food is gaining the upper hand. Cookbooks that offer recipes for vacherins, terrines, meat pies en croûte, galantines, or ballotines seem dated, like cigarette ads from the 1950s. Julia Child's definitive *The Way To Cook* (Knopf, 1989) devotes 112 pages to vegetables and salads. Good old-fashioned peasant cooking — more root and green vegetables, more grains, less meat, less butter — meets the needs of home cooks in the 1990s: it's easy to prepare, healthy, and satisfying.

As we simplify our approach to the culinary arts, we are coming closer to the notion of good cooking expressed in this publication — fresh, wholesome ingredients honestly prepared with attention to technique and detail. A perfectly prepared tomato sauce (*see* page 26) with fresh garlic, aromatic olive oil, good canned tomatoes (page 24), and shreds of basil is more inspiring and more of a tribute to the culinary arts than a sideboard groaning with cutlets, meringues, and ices. It isn't just that the haute cuisine of Europe is not practical for home cooks (it isn't, unless drastically modified, as with our puff pastry recipe, page 15), it's that simpler fare is often better, bringing out the true nature of foods, their natural flavors, textures, and aromas.

On the first anniversary of *Cook's Illustrated*, I can say that we have rediscovered complexity in simplicity and have been inspired by revelations found in the loving pursuit of good home cooking. I'm reminded of a well-known Italian cook's response to my question about fancy plate presentation. He said, with more than a hint of irritation, "Properly cooked food always looks good on the plate." That's exactly right. *Cook's Illustrated* is firmly ensconced, downstairs in the kitchen — and we hear footsteps on the stairs. We think it's about time. ∎

NOTES

FROM READERS

MEASURING HONEY

To get honey out of a glass measuring cup I follow this simple trick. Coat the measuring cup with vegetable oil. (Just pour some oil into the cup and then back into the bottle.) Then measure out the honey into the empty cup. The thin film of oil will make the honey slide out when poured, guaranteeing that all the honey makes it into the recipe.

T. C. AINSWORTH
Harahan, LA

WHAT IS IT?

I found this pan tucked away in the back of my grandmother's pantry. Can you tell me how this cast-iron skillet is used?

WARREN SACK
Boston, MA

This heavy cast-iron pan is called a plättar and is used to make a Swedish dish of the same name that resembles a crepe or pancake. The batter is made with flour, milk, eggs, and a bit of sugar; in the winter, a spoonful or two of fluffy snow may be added to lighten the mixture. The skillet is heated on top of the stove and a pat of butter is placed into each of the indentations. As soon as the butter foams, batter is poured into each hollow. The cook uses the handle to swirl the batter into very thin pancakes that line the entire surface of each indentation. The pancakes are served with berries or jam. Fruit-filled plättar are quite popular in Sweden as well as in Midwestern communities settled by Scandinavian immigrants.

This skillet can be used to make other thin pancakes, especially blini, and can also fry four eggs at a time. Because of the curved indentations, eggs fried in a plättar are rounder and thicker than eggs cooked in a regular frying pan. *See* Sources and Resources on page 32 for information about purchasing a plättar.

PANCETTA SUBSTITUTES

A number of recipes in my Italian cookbooks call for pancetta. How does this differ from American bacon? Also, what's the best substitute? Some recipes call for ham and others suggest bacon. Which is really better?

ELISABETH FERGUSSON
Doylestown, PA

Like American bacon, pancetta comes from the belly of a pig. While the cut may be the same, the processing is very different. Pancetta is cured with salt and spices, usually cloves and peppercorns, and then rolled into a log shape. Unlike American bacon, pancetta is not smoked, except in some northern regions of Italy near the Austrian border. In any case, the flavor of pancetta is subtle and not overly salty.

We purchased some pancetta as well as a number of possible substitutes to see which would perform best in a simple pasta sauce along with mushrooms and onions.

Salt pork proved too strong (the salt was overpowering) and fatty. We also tried boiled ham. While the mild pork flavor was closer to that of pancetta, this cut is actually too lean for most uses. The same is true of prosciutto. In many recipes, including the pasta dish we were making, pancetta serves as the base for sauces. As such, it should contribute some fat. Lean ham dried out in the pasta sauce and is therefore not the best choice in recipes where the pancetta must cook for some time. If boiled ham is the only substitute available, try to minimize the cooking time.

Next, we tried a mixture of ham and salt pork — we simply chopped the two together and then added them to the hot oil. This combination proved a close approximation of the flavor and texture of pancetta. The only drawback is convenience. In recipes that call for small quantities of pancetta, as most do, buying one-half ounce each of boiled ham and salt pork may prove impractical.

This left us with American-style bacon. Since pancetta and bacon come from the same part of the pig, the texture and fat content are right. However, you should expect a smokier flavor from the bacon than from pancetta — an advantage for those who like smokiness, a disadvantage for those who don't.

If you cannot find pancetta locally (try gourmet stores, premium butcher shops, or Italian delicatessens), the best solution may be to mail-order pancetta in bulk (*see* Sources and Resources, page 32) and then freeze it in small quantities to defrost as needed.

ALCOHOL IN COOKING

I need a definitive answer regarding cooking with wine. I frequently cook for friends who are recovering alcoholics. Is it true that alcohol burns off during the cooking process? Are there some methods of cooking that eliminate more alcohol than others? Should wine be reduced before using to ensure that no alcohol remains, and, if so, by how much? What about cooking with other alcoholic beverages?

UNSIGNED
Duluth, MN

Studies conducted at Washington State University indicate that alcohol does not completely burn off during cooking, as many cooks once supposed. In general, dishes that cook briefly will retain more alcohol than long-simmering stews. For instance, researchers found that pot roast cooked in red wine for two and one-half hours retained about 5 percent of its original alcohol content. In contrast, a chicken breast and white wine sauté still had 40 percent of its alcohol after ten minutes of simmering, and cherries jubilee kept 75 percent of its alcohol after being flambéed in brandy for one minute.

We checked with Alcoholics Anonymous and they urge recovering alcoholics to avoid all foods cooked with wine, spirits, or beer. They even suggest avoiding small sources of alcohol, such as vanilla extract, which in fact has an alcohol content equal to most spirits.

JUICING LEMONS

What's the best way to juice a lemon? Should lemons be stored at room temperature or in the refrigerator?

NANCY ROWELL
Tallahassee, FL

Several factors may influence the amount of juice that can be extracted from a lemon, including the size, temperature, and softness of the fruit. Large lemons with very thick skins may actually contain less juice than medium, thin-skinned lemons. Also, very soft, ripe lemons will give up their juice more easily than unripe lemons that are as hard as rocks.

ILLUSTRATION BY ALAN WITSCHONKE

We devised a number of tests to see how temperature and softness of the fruit affect juice extraction. For each test, we juiced three medium lemons that weighed exactly 10 ounces in total. We first squeezed lemons straight out of the refrigerator and obtained 110 ml of juice, about 3.7 ounces. Many cookbook authors suggest softening the lemons to release more juice. The best way to do this is by rolling the lemon on the counter as you exert a fair amount of pressure on the fruit. The pressure breaks some of the internal membranes in the fruit that hold in the juice. However, when tested on cold lemons, this trick did not work well. We squeezed out just 109 ml, essentially the same amount as without rolling.

To investigate the effects of temperature on juice extraction, we squeezed three room-temperature lemons. They gave up 119 ml of juice, a significant increase over cold fruit. When we rolled room-temperature lemons we were able to extract 129 ml of juice, an increase of more than ½ ounce over cold lemons.

With such good results at room temperature, one might expect an even better yield from placing lemons in the microwave for thirty seconds (Sunkist recommends this) or in a two-hundred-degree oven for five minutes. The results were mixed. Lemons that were warm but not hot to the touch gave up the same amount of juice as room-temperature lemons that had been rolled before juicing. Rolling heated lemons did not help, either. It seems that either rolling or heating will maximize juice extraction, but combining the two processes yields no further improvement.

Since lemons stored in the refrigerator will stay fresh for weeks longer than those stored at room temperature, there are two options to optimize juice extraction. Remove lemons from the refrigerator several hours before juicing them and let them come to room temperature, then roll them briefly before juicing. The other option is to use the microwave. If you forget to warm lemons naturally, pop cold fruit into the microwave on high for thirty seconds, or until they are warm to the touch, and juice.

GREASING COOKIE SHEETS

H ere is an easy tip for greasing cookie sheets and baking pans without greasing yourself. Put your hand inside of a small plastic bag. With your hand still inside the bag, break off a piece of butter. Grease the pan, holding the butter through the plastic.
SONYA SONES
Santa Monica, CA

DRIED FRUIT

I really enjoy eating dried fruit, especially raisins and apricots, and was wondering how they compare nutritionally to fresh fruit. Also, how much is one serving of raisins?
JAKA OKORN
Alexandria, VA

Because dried fruit has very little moisture, it contains more nutrients than an equal amount of fresh fruit. In addition to higher amounts of minerals such as iron and potassium, dried fruit has more fiber. For example, one-half cup of grapes has about one-half gram of fiber; the same amount of raisins contains four grams of fiber. On the downside, raisins and other dried fruits are higher in calories because the fruit sugars become concentrated as moisture is removed. Also, most of the water-soluble vitamin C is lost when fruit is dried.

The U.S. Department of Agriculture considers one-quarter cup dried fruit as one serving in the new food pyramid, in contrast to one-half cup diced fresh fruit.

AVOIDING A FLOURY MESS

M y favorite kitchen trick is to use a large piece of freezer paper, plastic-coated side up, on which to knead bread, shape rolls, and roll out dough. When I am done, I roll up the scraps and flour in the paper and discard it, with no floury mess to clean up.
FLORENCE MCCANN
Middletown, RI

CHALLAH

L ast week I ate dinner at a friend's house, and he served a delicious and beautifully braided challah. It was very high in the middle and slightly tapered at the ends. Could you please provide me with a recipe and braiding instructions?
NANCY BROOKS
Tucson, AZ

We did a little research and found this recipe from Phyllis Kirigin of Croton-on-Hudson, New York, who also provided the braiding instructions pictured on page 4.

BRAIDED CHALLAH
Makes 1 large loaf
This dough can also be mixed and kneaded in a large heavy-duty food processor. Using the steel blade, process until the dough is smooth and satiny, about thirty seconds. Also, you may use regular rather than rapid-rise yeast, but increase the rising time.

2   packages rapid-rise yeast (about 5 teaspoons)
1   tablespoon sugar
5   cups bread flour
2   teaspoons salt
3   eggs, lightly beaten
8   tablespoons butter, softened

1   egg yolk
2   tablespoons milk
1   tablespoon poppy seeds

1. Mix yeast, ½ teaspoon sugar, and 1 cup warm water in a 2-cup glass measuring cup; set

aside until foamy, about 5 minutes.

2. Mix remaining sugar, flour, and salt in large bowl of electric mixer; add eggs, butter, and yeast mixture. Using dough hook attachment, knead at low speed until smooth and satiny, 6 to 8 minutes.

3. Form dough into a ball and let rise in large, lightly buttered bowl covered with damp towel until approximately doubled in size, about 1 hour. Deflate to original size; re-form into a ball, cover, and let rise again until doubled in size.

4. Deflate dough again and turn onto lightly floured work surface. Press dough into a rough square; cut into 4 equal pieces, preferably with a blunt object to seal in gases (a wooden spatula works well). Let rest for 10 minutes.

5. Roll each portion of dough into an 18-inch rope that is thicker in the middle than at the ends, stretching dough as you roll. Place ropes on a large work surface to form an X and pinch in the center to seal. To finish the braid, follow the illustrated steps on page 4 in Quick Tips.

6. Adjust oven rack to middle position and heat oven to 375 degrees. Place braided dough on a lightly greased cookie sheet; cover with damp cloth and let rise until almost doubled, 30 to 45 minutes. Beat yolk with milk; brush entire loaf with this glaze. Sprinkle with poppy seeds and bake until bread is golden brown and an instant-read thermometer registers between 190 and 200 degrees, 30 to 40 minutes. Transfer bread to wire rack to cool. Slice and serve.

GARLIC SHOOTS

O ften when I peel garlic I find small green shoots sprouting from the cloves. What are these green shoots and can I still use garlic that has them?
DAPHNE KLEIN
West Springfield, NH

Like a tulip or daffodil, garlic is a bulb that usually sprouts in the spring. The tiny green shoots that sometimes emerge from the ends of the cloves are often quite bitter and may adversely affect the flavor of the garlic. We recommend trimming and discarding the shoots. Of course, if the cloves themselves are bruised, soft, or dull, they should also be discarded.

There is a second type of garlic shoot that is somewhat rare here, although it is commonly used in Asia. During the late spring and summer, long thin shoots rise from buried garlic bulbs. These green shoots look like scallions or thin leeks, but have a distinctive garlic flavor. If you grow your own garlic, clip the shoots when quite young and then wait until the remaining piece of the stalk turns brown and shrivels before harvesting the bulbs. Garlic shoots are also sometimes available at farmers' markets. The shoots are excellent in stir fries, soups, and stocks. They also can be briefly blanched, lightly grilled, and then served as a vegetable side dish or garnish. ∎

Quick Tips

BRAIDING BREAD

This braiding method results in a very puffy braided loaf and can be used with challah or any other type of bread dough that you wish to braid.

1. Make four ropes of equal length and lay them out in the shape of a four-pointed star; pinch them together in the center to seal. Think of the points as numbered one to four. Starting with point one, fold it directly over the center, so that it lies beside point three. Then fold point three directly over the center, again creating a four-pointed star.

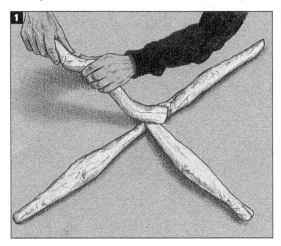

2. Now fold point four directly across the center so that it lies parallel to point two, then fold point two over the center, again creating a four-pointed star.

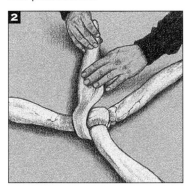

3. Continue this one-side-to-the-other braiding, making sure to keep the bread upright, until all the lengths have been folded.

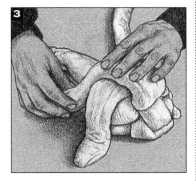

4. Pinch the end pieces firmly together at the top.

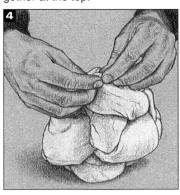

5. Lay the finished bread down on its side, glaze if desired, and bake.

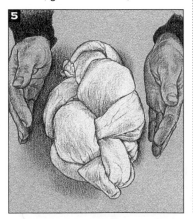

SEEDING FRESH CHILE PEPPERS

Most of the heat of chile peppers is contained in the seeds and in the membranes that connect the seeds to the pepper walls. For those who prefer peppers with only a bit of heat, follow this tip from John Dolginko of Bloomingdale, New York.

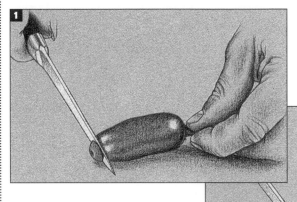

1. Holding the pepper by its stem, slice off about one-eighth inch from the tip.

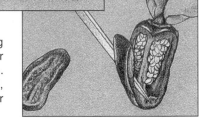

2. Place the tip end flat on a cutting board and, still holding the pepper by the stem, slice off the sides. When you have sliced all around, discard the stem, seeds, and inner membranes.

CHOPPING A BLOCK OF CHOCOLATE

To avoid ending up with nothing but chocolate shavings when chopping a large block of chocolate, follow this tip from Jim Stringer, pastry cook at The Blue Room in Cambridge, Massachusetts.

1. Hold a large knife at a forty-five-degree angle to one of the corners of the block of chocolate and bear down evenly. Repeat at each of the corners.

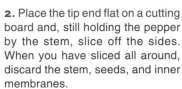

2. After you have cut about one inch from each of the four corners, you will have a block with eight distinct corners. Treat each of them as you did the original four corners in step 1. Soon you will have sixteen corners. Continue until the entire block of chocolate has been chopped.

ILLUSTRATIONS BY ALAN WITSCHONKE

MAKING A QUICK DECORATING TUBE

1. Put chocolate in a heat-safe zipper-lock plastic bag and immerse in simmering water until the chocolate melts. Snip off just the very tip of one corner of the bag.

2. Holding the bag in one hand, gently squeeze the chocolate out of the bag. Discard the bag when finished.

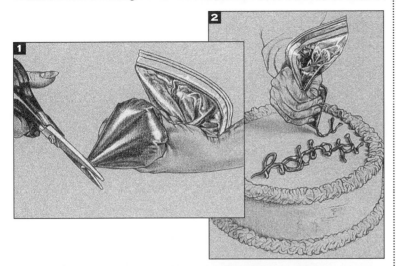

GETTING LOBSTER STRAIGHT

When lobsters are boiled, their tails tend to curl up tightly. This can spoil the appearance of the lobster in some presentations, and also makes the meat more difficult to slice or chop. To keep lobster tails straight during cooking, follow these steps.

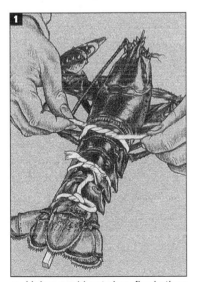

1. Using cooking twine, firmly tie a long-handled wooden spoon or chopstick along the underside of the lobster prior to cooking.

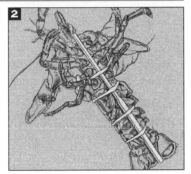

2. Be sure that the spoon or chopstick runs all the way from one end of the lobster to the other.

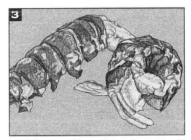

3. After cooking, the tail meat will be straight and easy to cut (left), rather than tightly curled and somewhat difficult to handle (right), as it is when a lobster is cooked in the normal way.

REMOVING THE PEELS FROM COOKED BEETS

To avoid staining towels or getting your hands messy, cradle cooked beets in a paper towel, pinch the skin between thumb and forefinger, and peel it off.

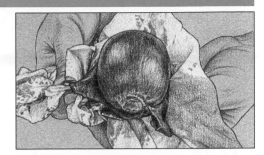

MAKING HERBED POTATO CHIPS

Herbed potato chips make attractive hors d'oeuvres. You can serve them unadorned, or add a dollop of sour cream sprinkled with minced herbs and a touch of caviar.

1. Peel potatoes and slice them into very thin rounds. Lay them out in a single layer on a well-oiled cookie sheet. Brush potato tops with oil and sprinkle with salt. In the center of each, place an herb leaf such as rosemary, thyme, flat parsley, or small sage.

2. Place another cookie sheet, the bottom of which has been very well oiled, on top of the sheet containing the potato rounds.

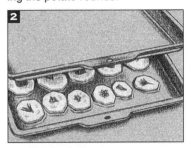

3. Bake at 375 degrees for twenty minutes. Transfer chips to a wire rack as they turn golden brown and crispy.

PREPARING PEARL ONIONS

This simple preparation prevents pearl onions from falling apart during cooking.

1. Cut off the tops and bottoms and peel off the skins.

2. Using the tip of a small paring knife, cut an X in the root end of each onion.

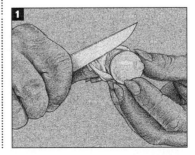

ATTENTION READERS: FREE SUBSCRIPTION FOR PUBLISHED TIPS. Do you have a unique tip you would like to share with other readers? We will provide a one-year complimentary subscription for each quick tip that we print. Send a description of your special technique to *Cook's Illustrated*, P.O. Box 569, Brookline Village, MA 02147. Please write "Attention: Quick Tips" on the envelope and include your name, address, and daytime phone number. Unfortunately, we can only acknowledge receipt of tips that will be printed in the magazine.

Scones in 20 Minutes

Traditional scones are fluffy — not hard and dense — and are worked quickly and lightly to achieve a delicate texture.

~ BY DEBORAH KRASNER ~

Scones, the quintessential tea cake of the British Isles, are delicate, fluffy biscuits, which may come as a surprise to Americans — the clunky mounds of oven-baked sweetened dough called "rock cakes" by the English are often called scones in our restaurants and coffee shops. Unlike rock cakes, in which dough is dropped from a spoon onto a baking sheet, traditional scones are quickly rolled or patted out and cut into rounds or wedges.

Ingredients and Proportions

Almost all scone recipes call for the same proportion of dry to liquid ingredients — two cups of dry to three-quarters cup of wet. I started testing scone recipes using organic unbleached white flour with the bran still in it, which I had been using for all of my baking with good results. I thought the scones tasted fine until I tried the same recipe with Gold Medal all-purpose flour. The difference was astonishing: these scones were lighter and much more flavorful. I tried the recipe again, substituting cake flour, and was disappointed — although the scones were golden, they were doughy in the center, with a raw taste and poor texture.

Why did the choice of flour make such a difference? Most all-purpose flours have a greater proportion of soft wheat flour than the unbleached white flour I'd been using. Soft wheat makes baked goods tender, whereas hard wheat gives them body and texture. Obviously, a blend that contains more hard wheat is excellent for breads, and a soft wheat flour is just right for cakes. A scone is closer to a cake on the scale of baked goods, so flour that has a greater proportion of soft wheat to hard increases its lightness and tenderness. Too much soft wheat, however, as in the cake flour, fails to provide enough body. For scones, all-purpose flour is ideal.

After trying scones made with butter and with lard, I prefer the rich flavor of butter. (If I made scones commercially I might reconsider that; day-old scones made with lard hold up better. The preservative effects of different fats, along with lower cost, may be why store-bought scones are often made with margarine or other hydrogenated fats.) Although the amount of solid fat can be varied, most recipes use one-quarter cup of fat to two cups of flour, and I found that proportion to be just right.

The choice of liquid can also profoundly affect the flavor of a scone. It is possible to use skim milk, but if you're cooking with butter, why bother? Whole milk is a traditional and delicious component of scones. Equally traditional and much richer scones are made with heavy cream and eggs; increasing the fat in a recipe makes for a moister, more tender crumb, because the fat coats the starch granules. But although fattier scones are more tender, they are also heavier; milk-and-butter scones are light and refreshing, perfect for a snack.

Other possible liquids include orange juice and buttermilk, as well as small amounts of fortified wines such as sherry or marsala. All make for leaner but unusually flavored scones; I quite like many of these variations.

Basic scones can be further enlivened and varied with the addition of nuts, dried and fresh fruits, sweets, and a range of savories. In Britain, common additions include dried fruits, such as raisins or currants; small, soft, fresh fruits, such as raspberries; or chopped nuts. Typical American additions may include blueberries, chopped crystallized ginger, or chocolate chips.

As for leavener, I have found that commercial double-acting baking powder can have a harsh flavor, and can often be tasted as a separate note in some baked goods. It also tends to be used in too much quantity. Therefore I use homemade, single-acting baking powder, made with two parts (one teaspoon) cream of tartar to one part (one-half teaspoon) baking soda; it produces a scone that is sweeter and less soapy-flavored than those made with commercial double-acting baking powder.

Finally, all scones can be glazed before baking with a brush dipped in a little beaten egg or milk. Glazes don't contribute to flavor, but they do deepen the color and make the scones

At their peak of flavor when fresh from the oven, scones are often served with clotted cream in England. American substitutions for this type of cream include crème fraîche, mascarpone, and whipped cream. Jam is also an excellent accompaniment.

look most appetizing. Glazing also makes it easier for sugar to stick, if sprinkling the surface appeals to you. In addition to milk or beaten egg, scones may also be glazed with heavy cream.

Technique

The line from "Patty-cake, Patty-cake" that goes "make me a cake as fast as you can" *must* refer to scones. The secret to making a good scone is to work the dough quickly and lightly, and to immediately bake it in a preheated oven. Speed is of the essence to prevent toughening of the dough; it is also important when using a homemade single-acting baking powder for a leavener, since you want the powder to do its work in the oven, not before baking. The whole process shouldn't take more than twenty minutes, from mixing the ingredients together to pulling the finished scones out of the oven.

Scones can be mixed by hand or with a food processor. I've given both mixing methods in the Master Recipe, for those who prefer to do most (but not all) of the mixing by machine. The processor is used to cut fat into flour; with minimal hand-mixing afterwards, machine-made dough is identical to that made entirely by hand.

Do remember to thoroughly preheat the oven, as it is the intense heat that makes the leavening pop. Other guidelines are to have the dough as wet as you can handle and, when using a scone or biscuit cutter, *don't wiggle it* — just place it on the dough and push straight down.

MASTER RECIPE FOR SWEET-MILK SCONES
Makes 8 or 9 scones

Work the dough quickly, don't overmix, and put the dough rounds into the heated oven as soon as possible. The process — from mixing to pulling the finished scones out of the oven — shouldn't take more than twenty minutes. Scones are best served warm and fresh, split open, and topped with thick homemade strawberry or raspberry jam and clotted cream (or crème fraîche, mascarpone, or whipped cream). This recipe can be doubled.

2	cups all-purpose flour
1	teaspoon cream of tartar
½	teaspoon baking soda
½	teaspoon salt
1–2	tablespoons sugar (optional)
4	tablespoons unsalted butter, chilled and cut into ½-inch pieces
¾	cup whole milk

1. Adjust oven rack to middle position and heat oven to 450 degrees.

2. Sift first 4 (or 5) ingredients into large bowl, or measure into workbowl of a food processor fitted with steel blade; pulse until blended. With a pastry blender, 2 knives, or steel blade of a food processor, cut or process butter into flour mixture until mixture resembles coarse meal with a few slightly larger butter lumps.

3. If making by hand, make a well in the center and pour in milk. Working quickly, blend ingredients together with a rubber spatula into a soft, slightly wet dough. If using a food processor, pour milk though feed tube; pulse until dough just starts to gather into a rough ball (do not overprocess or scones will be tough). Turn dough onto a well-floured work surface.

4. Quickly roll dough to ½ inch thick, or follow illustrations 1 through 3 for alternate shaping method. Use a lightly greased and floured 3-inch biscuit cutter to stamp dough with one decisive punch, cutting close together to generate as few scraps as possible. Dip cutter into flour as often as necessary to keep dough from sticking. Push scraps of dough together so that edges join; firmly pinch edges with fingertips to make a partial seal. Pat this

 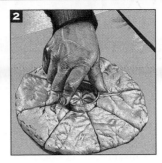 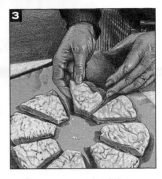

1. Form the dough into a disk and cut the disk into eight pieces.

2. Use a one and one-half-inch diameter cookie cutter to cut out the center of the circle.

3. Separate each of the sections and bake according to the directions in the recipe.

remaining dough to ½ inch thick; continue to cut 3-inch rounds. Place dough rounds 1½ inches apart on a greased baking sheet. Bake until scones are lightly brown, 10 to 12 minutes. Serve immediately.

Traditional British Additions: Add ⅓ to ½ cup dried fruits, such as raisins or currants, or small, soft, fresh fruits, such as raspberries.

New World Additions: Add ⅓ to ½ cup chocolate chips, chopped crystallized ginger, or blueberries.

Savory Additions: These make an excellent accompaniment to salads or soups. Omit the sugar and stir or pulse in ½ cup grated aged cheddar or Cheshire cheese just before adding wet ingredients; *or* add 1 tablespoon dry or 2 tablespoons minced, fresh herbs with wet ingredients; *or* sauté one small onion, minced, in 1 tablespoon bacon fat or oil until transparent, about 5 minutes. Cool slightly and add with the wet ingredients.

CITRUS HONEY-NUT SCONES
Makes 9 or 10 scones

Follow Master Recipe for Sweet-Milk Scones, adding ¼ cup finely chopped walnuts and 2 tablespoons minced lemon zest to the dry in-gredients. If using a food processor, pulse walnuts with dry ingredients, then pulse in the minced lemon zest just before adding the butter. Substitute 2 tablespoons honey for the optional sugar; substitute ¼ cup orange juice for ¼ cup of the milk. Mix honey, orange juice, and milk together and proceed with recipe.

CREAM AND CURRANT SCONES
Makes 9 or 10 scones

If currants are old and dry, plump them in one-quarter cup heated sweet sherry or sweet marsala for ten minutes. Drain, reserving liquid (which can be substituted for some of the heavy cream, if desired). If the currants are wet, add them just after wet ingredients have been added. If currants have not been macerated, toss them in with the dry ingredients.

Follow Master Recipe for Sweet-Milk Scones, making sure to add the optional sugar, adding ⅓ cup currants at the appropriate time (*see* note, above), and substituting 2 eggs and ¾ cup heavy cream for the milk. The dough tops may be brushed with beaten egg and sprinkled with a bit of sugar. ■

Deborah Krasner is the author/illustrator of the forthcoming *Kitchens for Cooks* (Viking Studio Books, 1994).

Scones are still scones whether sweetened with molasses, honey, or brown or white sugar. In Britain, a sweetener called golden syrup is also used, as is black treacle, which is similar to molasses (*see* Sources and Resources, page 32). Each sweetener adds a different flavor — molasses is the strongest, white sugar the most neutral. Different sweeteners can also alter the keeping properties of baked goods — honey and molasses, for example, act as preservatives because they are hydroscopic, or water-attracting, and thus help to keep baked goods moist over time.

For traditional scones, one to two tablespoons of any sweetener are added to the Master Recipe, depending on taste preferences. But you can also add more, up to one-quarter cup, if you wish. American scones tend to be far sweeter than the British versions, which are usually sweetened with toppings such as jam. Americans seem to eat their scones like muffins, without anything more than a smear of butter, so they like their sweetness baked in.

Roast Leg of Lamb Perfected

Here's how to roast a leg of lamb evenly, without having either raw or overcooked portions.

~ BY STEPHEN SCHMIDT ~

The main problem I have had with roast leg of lamb is that it cooks unevenly. In the past, no matter what I have tried, the outer part became dry and gray, while the meat around the bone remained almost raw. Since the leg is reasonably priced and feeds a lot of people, I have continued to serve it on casual occasions, but for fancy dinners, or when I am catering a party, I have long chosen the rack or the loin, which are easy to cook to perfection.

It turns out, however, that the leg can indeed be made nicely medium-rare and juicy throughout. A little extra work and attention are required, but the results are well worth it.

The uneven thickness of the leg is the most formidable obstacle to even cooking. At the thicker sirloin end, the meat surrounding the flat, twisting hipbone is very thin. The center of the leg, which comprises the top half of the thigh, is fleshy, but the thigh then tapers dramatically toward the knee joint, and the shank itself is a mere nub of meat.

The only way to deal with this problem is to remove the hipbone entirely and then tie the leg into as compact a shape as possible (*see* illustrated steps on this page and page 9). Once you have done this, by the way, you will understand why it is not smart to buy the sirloin end of the leg as a separate small roast, no matter how attractive the price. After the hipbone has been removed, there is barely enough meat at the sirloin end to serve two people.

Boning and tying, however, do not by themselves guarantee even cooking, as I discovered. Special procedures must be followed in roasting the leg to ensure that all parts are exposed to the same amount of heat and will thus reach similar internal temperatures at the same time.

Why Rack Roasting Works

I started out by roasting a seven-and-one-half-pound leg at 400 degrees, with the meat resting directly on the roasting pan. This is my usual method, and I got my usual and not-quite-satisfactory results. After approximately one hour, the top of the leg, which had been facing up, registered 120 degrees on a meat thermometer, which to my taste is underdone for leg of lamb (*see* "When is Lamb Done?" page 10). The meat around the thigh bone, meanwhile, was practically raw, while the bottom of the leg, which had been resting on the hot pan, had reached a temperature of around 135 degrees, which is a little overcooked for my taste.

I have always resisted roasting on a rack be-

TYING THE ROAST

After you have seasoned the exposed inner portions of the meat, tie the roast as follows.

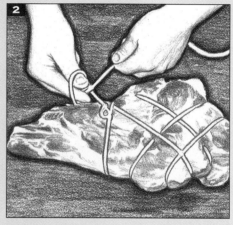

1. Set the leg top side up and smooth the flap of meat at the sirloin end so that it folds over and neatly covers the tip of the thigh bone. Using a sixteen-inch length of twine, tie a loop diagonally around the top of the leg. Bring the ends of the twine around and tie a second diagonal loop perpendicular to the first. Repeat the process, producing a "double-x" effect.

2. Beginning at the narrow top end of the leg, tie loops of twine across the leg at one-inch intervals.

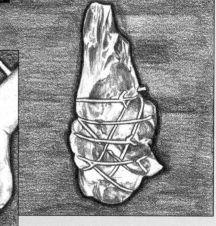

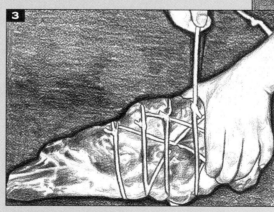

3. Continue tying loops all the way down the leg.

4 When you are finished tying the leg, it should resemble a giant turkey drumstick.

cause, when cooked only to rare or medium-rare, meat produces virtually no brown bits for gravy unless it rests directly on the pan. With leg of lamb, however, I surmised that a rack might be useful, for it would protect the downward-facing side of the leg from becoming overcooked by the heat of the pan.

To test this theory, I rack-roasted two legs simultaneously, one USDA Prime and one

Choice. After cooking at 500 degrees for thirty minutes (high initial heat promotes browning) and then at 300 degrees for about forty-five minutes longer, the legs were done on the top side; the thermometer registered a consistent 130 degrees whether inserted sideways, into the exterior portion of the top side, or poked deep into the middle. Alas, the bottom sides of the roasts proved undercooked. Evidently the

ILLUSTRATIONS BY ANGELO

REMOVING THE SILVERSKIN

Lamb fat is strong-flavored and hard to digest, and the membranous silverskin covering the leg (often called fell) is unattractive and unpleasant to chew. Remove as much of the fat and membrane as possible.

1A. Poke a sharp knife under the fat at the sirloin end of the leg. Pulling up on the flap of fat with one hand, slash at the membrane that connects it to the meat, always taking care to hold the blade against the membrane and not against the meat.

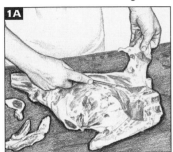

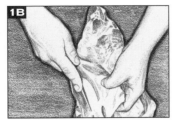

1B. Turn the leg over and continue to slash the membrane and pull off the fat with the other hand. Continue to the end of the leg.

1C. As you proceed toward the knee, you will find that some of the fat and membrane will not come away in neat chunks. This must be cut away in slabs, holding the knife parallel to the surface of the meat.

REMOVING THE HIP (AITCH) BONE

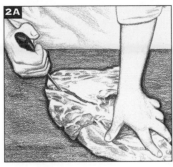

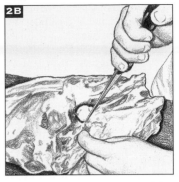

2A. Cut down along the bone of the leg, then pull apart the incision to expose the tip of the hipbone.

2B. Scrape around the tip of the hipbone proper, always holding the blade of the knife against the bone.

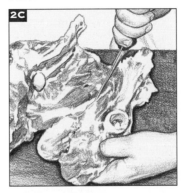

2C. When you have exposed the hipbone nearly to the thigh joint, hoist the leg onto its shank end and bend the hipbone down while at the same time cutting through the tendons around the joint. Lay the leg flat on the work surface and cut around the part of the hipbone that extends beyond the joint until the bone is completely free.

REMOVING THE LYMPH NODE

The fat and other material surrounding the strong-tasting popliteal lymph node should be removed.

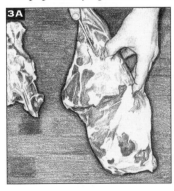

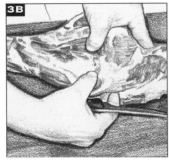

3B. Use both hands to widen the incision, exposing the popliteal lymph node and surrounding fat.

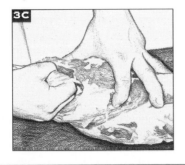

3A. Set the leg top side up, and cut down into the area that separates the broad, thin flap of meat on one side of the leg and the thick, meaty lobe on the other.

3C. Reach in and grasp the nugget of fat. Pull while cutting the connective tissue, being very careful not to cut into the gland itself. Pull the fat and other matter free.

CARVING THE LEG

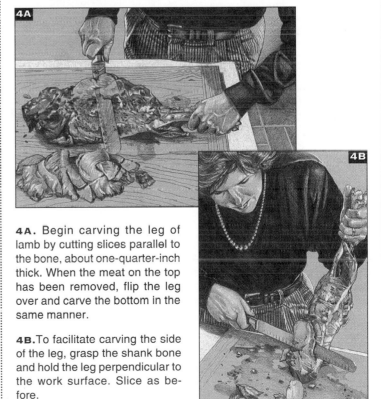

4A. Begin carving the leg of lamb by cutting slices parallel to the bone, about one-quarter-inch thick. When the meat on the top has been removed, flip the leg over and carve the bottom in the same manner.

4B. To facilitate carving the side of the leg, grasp the shank bone and hold the leg perpendicular to the work surface. Slice as before.

rack had been *too* effective in keeping the bottoms of the legs cool.

But this experiment, while only partially successful, pointed toward a solution. Perhaps turning the leg during cooking would promote more even cooking by allowing the top and the bottom sides equal exposure to both the cool rack and the hot oven roof. I further reasoned that setting the pan on the bottom shelf of the oven would slightly heat up the rack side, which was too cool, while mitigating the glare from the oven roof.

This is how I roasted my next lamb leg, and the results were near perfect. The outermost slices were a little closer to medium than to medium-rare and the bone meat was still a bit underdone, but most of the roast was the way I wanted it, deep pink and juicy. While I would never suggest that you abandon the luxury of lamb rack or loin, I think you will find that the leg, when carefully boned and trimmed and cooked according to the method outlined below, makes wonderful eating.

ROAST LEG OF LAMB WITH PIQUANT CAPER SAUCE
Serves 8–10

Whole legs of lamb generally weigh seven to seven and one-half pounds, untrimmed, but they may weigh as little as five and one-half pounds or as much as ten pounds. If you are roasting a leg weighing between five and one-half and six and one-half-pounds, decrease the twenty-minute cooking intervals at 325 degrees to fifteen minutes each and check the temperature after forty-five minutes. If you have a leg weighing eight and one-half pounds or over, increase the cooking intervals at 325 degrees to twenty-five minutes each and check the temperature after one hour and fifteen minutes. Also adjust the seasoning slightly if you're cooking smaller or larger legs. If the butcher prepares your lamb, bring seasoning so that he or she may sprinkle some over the exposed inner portions of the meat, before tying the roast securely. Roast the leg on a large cake rack or a mesh roasting rack (*see* Sources and Resources, page 32) rather than the perforated "broiler tray" that comes with some pans. Broiler trays become too hot, causing the lamb to cook unevenly.

The Roast Lamb
Salt and ground black pepper
1 teaspoon finely minced fresh rosemary leaves, or ½ teaspoon dried rosemary, finely crushed
1 whole leg of lamb (7 to 7½ pounds), cleaned, boned, and tied (*see* illustrations), hip or aitchbone cut into 1-inch pieces and meat scraps reserved
2 medium cloves garlic, each peeled and cut lengthwise into 8 slivers
2 tablespoons olive oil

The Caper Sauce
1 tablespoon olive oil
1 medium onion, coarsely chopped
2 cups canned beef broth, preferably low-salt
⅓ cup dry white wine or dry Vermouth
2 tablespoons unsalted butter, softened
2 tablespoons all-purpose flour
⅓ cup (3 ounces) small capers, drained, bottling liquid reserved
1 teaspoon balsamic vinegar

1. *For the lamb,* mix 2 teaspoons salt, 2 teaspoons pepper, and rosemary in small bowl.

2. Follow steps on page 9 to clean and bone lamb, sprinkling portion of seasoning over inner surface. Follow steps on page 8 to tie lamb.

3. Cut slits into roast with point of paring knife; poke garlic slivers inside. Rub remaining seasoning onto all surfaces of meat, then coat with olive oil. Place leg top side up on roasting pan fitted with wire or mesh roasting rack; let stand for 30 minutes.

4. *For the sauce,* in large, heavy-bottomed saucepan, heat olive oil over medium heat until it is hot but not smoking. Add reserved bones

and meat scraps, and onion; sauté, turning bones several times, until well browned, about 10 minutes. Add broth, scraping pan bottom to loosen browned bits; bring to boil. Reduce heat to low; simmer, partially covered, until bones and meat have given up their flavor to broth, about 1 hour, adding a little water if bones are more than half-exposed during cooking.

5. Meanwhile, adjust oven rack to lowest position and heat oven to 450 degrees. Roast lamb for 10 minutes. Grasp shank bone with paper towels; flip leg over, and roast 10 minutes longer. Lower oven temperature to 325 degrees. Again, turn leg top side up and continue roasting, turning leg every 20 minutes, until instant-read thermometer, when inserted in several locations, registers 130 to 135 degrees, 60 to 80 minutes longer. Transfer roast to another pan; cover with foil and set aside in a warm spot to complete cooking and to allow juices to reabsorb into the tissues, about 15 to 20 minutes.

6. Set roasting pan over medium heat; add wine and scrape with a wooden spoon until brown bits dissolve. Pour mixture into lamb stock, then strain everything into a 2-cup glass measure. Let sit until fat rises, then skim. Add water, if necessary, to make 1½ cups of liquid. Return to saucepan; bring to boil. Mix butter and flour to a smooth paste; gradually whisk into stock. Stir in capers, vinegar, and accumulated juices; simmer to blend flavors, about 3 minutes. Add more vinegar or caper bottling liquid to achieve a piquant, subtly sharp-sweet sauce.

7. Remove string from roast and carve following illustrations 4A and 4B. Transfer sliced lamb to a warm serving platter with caper sauce passed separately. ∎

Stephen Schmidt, is the author of *Master Recipes* (Ballantine, 1987).

WHEN IS LAMB DONE?

At the risk of splitting hairs, I would describe my preference for roast lamb as "dead-center medium-rare." I define this as the point where the grain of the meat has become distinctly visible, the juices flow copiously, and the color is bright pink but no longer quite red. By contrast, well-medium-rare meat has become just a tad dry and fibrous; it has lost all reddishness and faded to pale rose. Rare-medium-rare meat shows only a trace of grain and is soft nearly to the point of being squashy; it is deep-red and seems silky-moist rather than truly juicy when cut.

If you prefer your lamb the way I do, the right remove-from-oven temperature is around 130 degrees; after resting for fifteen to twenty minutes, the temperature will rise to a little over 135 degrees. For well-medium-rare lamb, take the roast out of the oven when the thermometer registers around 135 degrees; post-rest, the temperature will near 145 degrees. Rare-medium-rare meat needs to be removed from the oven at 120 degrees; the temperature will rise to about 125 degrees during resting. If you happen to prefer rather rare lamb, be sure to choose a USDA Prime leg, or splurge and buy a rack or a loin roast. Choice leg of lamb, you will find, is unpleasantly chewy and pulpy when very lightly cooked.

How to Cook Beets

Instead of boiling them, steam, roast, or grate beets for less mess and more flavor.

~ BY ERIC WOLFF ~

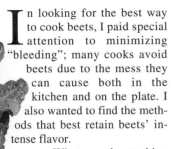

In looking for the best way to cook beets, I paid special attention to minimizing "bleeding"; many cooks avoid beets due to the mess they can cause both in the kitchen and on the plate. I also wanted to find the methods that best retain beets' intense flavor.

Whatever the cooking method, you can minimize bleeding by not peeling the skin and by not slicing off the tops of the beets. Peeling after cooking is simple; the skin slips right off with a paper towel (*see* Quick Tips, page 5).

Boiling Gets the Boot

Although most people boil beets, I no longer do; it causes too much bleeding, creating a mess and leeching out flavor. Instead, I opt for either steaming or roasting.

Steaming produces beets that are moist enough to use in any recipe. It also minimizes bleeding and concentrates flavor in much the same way that roasting does (although to a somewhat lesser degree). Beets steam in thirty to forty-five minutes, depending on size; it's best to quarter very large beets in order to cook them within this time period.

Beets are rarely roasted in batches with other root vegetables (*see* "Roasting Root Vegetables," *Cook's Illustrated,* January/February 1994), because bleeding results in a pan of pink vegetables. But beets make an excellent side dish when roasted on their own. To find the best roasting method, I tried roasting beets both wrapped in foil and unwrapped with oiled skins. I found that foil-wrapped beets were moister, but naked beets had more roasted flavor. Whichever way you choose to roast them, it is important to use absolutely fresh beets to ensure tenderness — even slightly aged beets did not become fully tender with this method.

Grating beets is simple and not terribly messy, so don't be intimidated by the thought of beet stains. Grated raw beets are a wonderful addition to salads; you can also toss grated beets with your favorite vinaigrette and serve them as a small side dish; or you can form grated beets into the fla-cakes known as roesti, as in the recipe below.

MASTER RECIPE FOR STEAMED BEETS
Be careful not to let the pan run out of water during this long steaming process. To make sure you don't forget, place marbles below the steamer basket before steaming — they will stop jiggling when the pan is dry.

> 1 bunch of beets (about 2 pounds), greens removed and reserved for another use, leaving a 1-inch beet top; beets washed thoroughly

Place beets in steamer basket set in large saucepan with 1 inch of water. Bring to boil; steam over high heat until beets can easily be pierced with thin knife, 30 to 45 minutes, depending on beet size. Drain, cool slightly, and remove skins. Serve or continue with recipes that follow.

MASTER RECIPE FOR ROASTED BEETS
Roasted beets bleed very little when cut, so they can also be used in recipes. Just remember that the dish will take on a sweet and very distinct roasted flavor.

> 1 bunch of beets (about 2 pounds), greens removed and reserved for another use, leaving a 1-inch beet top; beets washed thoroughly
> 1 tablespoon olive oil (if roasting without foil)

Heat oven to 350 degrees. Wrap beets in foil or brush with olive oil and place in small roasting pan. Roast until beets can easily be pierced with thin knife or trussing needle, about 1 hour for small to medium beets. Cool slightly and remove skins; serve.

PICKLED BEETS WITH ORANGE AND ROSEMARY
Makes about 2 quarts
Use small beets, about the size of a golf ball, if available. Bigger beets should be quartered or sliced after steaming.

> 2 Master Recipes for Steamed Beets
> ½ cup sweet vermouth
> ⅔ cup red wine
> ¼ cup cider vinegar
> ¼ cup honey or brown sugar
> 1 teaspoon whole cloves
> 1 3-inch cinnamon stick
> 1 medium sprig fresh rosemary
> 2 ¼-inch-thick slices from 1 orange, seeds removed
> Salt and ground black pepper

Place beets in medium bowl. Bring next 8 ingredients to boil; simmer to blend flavors, about 3 minutes; add salt and pepper to taste, then pour mixture over beets. Cool to room temperature, cover, then refrigerate until ready to serve. (Can be refrigerated up to 1 month.)

BEETS ROESTI
Serves 4
One teaspoon minced fresh rosemary can be added to the beet/flour mixture.

> 4 medium beets, peeled and coarsely grated (about 4 cups)
> ½ cup flour
> 4 tablespoons butter
> ¼ cup oil
> Salt and ground black pepper

1. Heat oven to 200 degrees. Toss beets with flour in medium bowl.

2. Heat 1 tablespoon each butter and oil in an 8-inch sauté pan or omelet pan. When butter stops foaming and oil is very hot, measure 1 cup of beet mixture into pan and quickly spread and press it flat with back of fork.

3. Cook over medium high heat until bottom is well browned, about 2 minutes. Loosen carefully with spatula, put plate over pan, and invert. Slide cake back into pan; cook until remaining side is well browned, 1½ to 2 minutes longer. Carefully loosen and slide onto an oven-proof platter; add salt and pepper to taste. Reserve in a warm oven; repeat 3 more times to make 4 cakes. Serve immediately. ■

Eric Wolff has been cooking since he was seven and now cooks and writes in Manhattan.

BEET BASICS

Always buy beets with the tops on if you can; fresh tops mean fresh beets. Loose beets may simply be recent "break-offs" or they may be old and therefore quite tough and lacking in flavor. With the exception of certain varieties of baby beets, I did not find a great difference in flavor and texture between small and medium-sized beets. Very large beets, on the other hand, are sometimes tough.

PHOTOGRAPH BY ERIC ROTH

Gubana: Italian Easter Bread Filled with Nuts and Fruit

Italian-baking expert Carol Field demonstrates how to make this unusual dessert bread from Friuli.

Carol Field, author of *The Italian Baker* (Harper & Row, 1985) and *Italy in Small Bites* (HarperCollins, 1993), tells an anecdote that illustrates the intensely regional nature of Italian breads. Some years ago, it seems, a member of the Bulgari family was kidnapped and ransomed. "After he was released, he led police to the region, eventually to the exact town, where he had been held," recounts Field. "He knew exactly where he had been imprisoned because of the bread his captors gave him."

Although the Tuscan panforte and the Milanese Christmas panettone are familiar sights in this country, few Americans have ever tasted *gubana,* the traditional Easter bread of Friuli, a region northeast of Venice near the Austrian and Croatian borders. Gubana is a buttery brioche dough filled with a mixture of several nuts, raisins, apricot jam, candied orange peel, cocoa, marsala, grappa, and rum. The result is a dense, sweet bread with a swirl of rich filling, usually served as dessert.

The technique for making a gubana is actually quite simple, but has a slight twist that may be unfamiliar to many American bakers. After the dough has been formed and is put in a bowl to rise, softened butter is placed on top of it. This is common practice with Italian sweet breads, says Field, adding that it causes the dough to rise more quickly than if the butter were worked into the dough before the rise. In addition, it gives the butter time to soften even further, which makes it easier to incorporate

"To me, bread is a measure of the quality of life," says cookbook author Carol Field.

into the dough just prior to the second rise.

As with other breads, the dough for gubana rises best when it is at seventy-five degrees. When making the bread on a cold morning, Field recommends placing the bowl containing the dough in a warm water bath of about eighty-five degrees. This technique is also useful on warm mornings, when it shaves about thirty minutes off each rise.

Field also recommends that you rise the dough in a straight-sided plastic container and mark the sides with tape or a pen to show where it starts. This technique makes it easy to measure when the dough has doubled, which helps prevent either under- or over-rising.

Once the dough has risen and is ready for shaping, a metal dough scraper (*see* Sources and Resources, page 32) becomes a particularly useful tool. Field recommends that you use this simple tool as an aid if the dough sticks when rolled out; to do so, simply fold back part of the dough, scrape the surface clean, flour the clean surface, unfold the dough, and continue working the dough. Field also uses the scraper to square the edges of the dough; a knife can pull and stretch the dough, while a scraper slices (*see* illustration 2, page 13).

Just before baking, the dough is brushed with an egg wash and sprinkled with sugar. Field recommends turbinado, also called raw sugar (*see* Sources and Resources, page 32), because its coarse texture does not melt in the heat of the oven.

Field also employs one final prebaking technique to prevent sogginess in this very sweet bread. Using a cake tester, she makes about ten one-inch-deep holes in the gubana. This process releases trapped air pockets, in which steam could otherwise condense.

The name gubana is thought to refer to this bread's snail-like shape (from guba, *the Slavic word for snail) or to the wealth of flavors and textures in the filling (*bubane *means abundance in Friulian dialect).*

GUBANA: ITALIAN EASTER BREAD WITH NUTS AND FRUIT
Makes 2 loaves

Because of the grappa in the filling, gubana is best served at dessert. A refreshing sorbet — lemon or other citrus flavors are good choices — makes a nice accompaniment to this not-too-sweet bread. Coffee, grappa, or dessert wine may also be served with the bread. Field uses Pepperidge Farm hazelnut cookies in the filling, but crumbs from any quality vanilla or nut cookie may be used.

Sponge

¾	cup milk, warmed to 75 or 80 degrees
2	tablespoons plus 2 teaspoons active dry yeast
1	cup plus 1 tablespoon unbleached all-purpose flour

Dough
- 2 large eggs plus 2 yolks
- ½ cup plus 2 tablespoons sugar
- 3–4 tablespoons milk
- 3¾ cups unbleached all-purpose flour
- 1¼ teaspoons salt
- Grated zest of 2 lemons (about ¼ cup)
- 2½ teaspoons vanilla extract
- ¼ pound unsalted butter, at room temperature, cut into 8 pieces

Filling
- 2¾ cups hazelnuts, toasted, skinned, and chopped
- ¾ cup walnuts, toasted and chopped
- ⅓ cup pine nuts, lightly toasted
- 2 tablespoons blanched almonds, chopped
- 1½ cups crumbs from vanilla or nut cookies
- 1 cup raisins
- ½ cup plus 1 tablespoon apricot jam
- ½ cup candied orange peel, chopped, or grated zest of 4 oranges, or 1 teaspoon pure orange oil (*see* Sources and Resources, page 32)
- Grated zest of 1 lemon (about 2 tablespoons)
- 1½ tablespoons unsweetened cocoa powder
- 1 teaspoon ground cinnamon
- 3 tablespoons marsala
- 3 tablespoons grappa
- 3 tablespoons plus 1 teaspoon rum

- 1 egg white, beaten
- 2 tablespoons turbinado sugar

1. *For the sponge,* pour milk into large bowl of electric mixer; stir in yeast. Let stand until creamy, about 10 minutes. Stir in flour with wooden spoon until smooth. Cover with plastic wrap; let rise 30 minutes to 1 hour.

2. *For the dough,* using paddle attachment, mix eggs, yolks, sugar, and 3 tablespoons milk into sponge until smooth. Mix in flour and salt until smooth. Mix in lemon zest, vanilla, and 1 tablespoon milk if needed to form a rough dough. Change to dough hook; knead until dough is velvety, supple, and blistered, 3 to 4 minutes.

3. Place dough in lightly buttered bowl. Place butter pieces on top of dough. Cover bowl with plastic wrap and let dough rise until doubled in size, 2 to 3 hours.

4. *For the filling,* meanwhile, mix together all filling ingredients; set aside.

5. Work butter into dough; turn dough onto well-floured surface and cut in half; set aside one half. Roll other half into an 18-by-12-inch rectangle, long side facing you. Spread half of filling evenly over dough rectangle, leaving a 2-inch border on all sides. Use a dough scraper to square dough edges. Brush border with beaten egg white, reserve remaining egg white. Starting from long side, use dough scraper to lift and roll dough. Finish rolling dough by hand into a log. Fold ends under and pinch to enclose filling. Twist log into a spiral. Repeat process with remaining dough and filling. Use dough scraper to lift each dough spiral into a buttered 2-quart soufflé dish or 8-inch round cake pan, 3 inches deep. Cover with plastic wrap or towel and let rise until well puffed and very tender but not yet doubled in size, 2 to 2½ hours.

6. Heat oven to 375 degrees. Brush dough tops with remaining egg white; sprinkle with turbinado sugar. Poke 8 to 10 1-inch-deep holes in dough tops with a thin skewer or cake tester to release trapped air. Bake 25 minutes; reduce heat to 325 degrees. Bake until breads are golden brown and an instant-read thermometer inserted into center of bread registers 190 to 200 degrees, about 20 minutes longer. Unmold and cool breads completely on wire rack. Cut into slices and serve. (Can be wrapped in towel or brown bag and stored at room temperature for 2 days, or wrapped in foil, placed in a zipper-lock plastic bag, and frozen for several weeks. Heat frozen foil-wrapped bread in a 200-degree oven until defrosted, 30 to 35 minutes.) ∎

FILLING AND SHAPING A GUBANA

1. Roll out half of the dough into a rectangle measuring eighteen by twelve inches. Spread the filling evenly over the dough, leaving a two-inch border uncovered on all sides.

2. Use a dough scraper to square the edges of the dough and to form the corners into right angles.

3. Brush the uncovered border with the beaten egg white.

4. Starting at the long side facing you, use the dough scraper to lift and roll the dough into a log.

5. Use your hands to finish rolling the dough into a log. Fold the dough under and pinch the ends to enclose the filling.

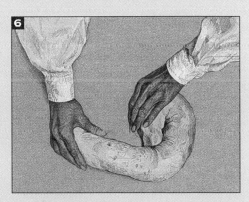

6. Twist each log into a spiral that resembles a big snail.

Quickest Puff Pastry

Using a food processor and a new "jelly-roll" folding method, home cooks can now make puff pastry easily and quickly.

∼ BY NICK MALGIERI ∼

Pastry made with Quickest Puff Pastry can be either sweet or savory, depending on the filling or topping you choose to use. Classic twisted pastry straws, for example, can contain either Parmesan-Paprika Seasoning or Cinnamon-Nut Seasoning, page 15.

Making classic puff pastry requires planning, time, and lots of work. You must first make a dough, then soften butter, combine it with flour, and form the butter into a square. Next you wrap the dough around the butter and roll and fold (or "turn") the dough four to six times, depending on whose method you are using and just how many layers you want your pastry to have.

Traditional "quick" puff pastry combines the dough and the butter and reduces the number of times the dough must be "turned." The butter is mixed with the flour to make a very rich dough containing many irregular layers of butter — a somewhat less arduous process. Nevertheless, it takes a great deal of will and

effort. Still, many good cooks gather their strength to make a batch every now and then in order to enjoy treats such as homemade Napoleons, palmiers, cheese straws, and tarts with the ultimate in flaky crusts.

I have been working on making *really* quick puff pastry for years, and recently wondered if I could eliminate the repeated rolling and folding by handling the dough only once. I eventually came up with an idea that I thought might accomplish this goal while at the same time making the dough into many layers: folding the dough and rolling it up, jelly-roll style. I also decided to try speeding up the process further by using a food processor to mix the dough.

I was delighted to find that both of these

time-saving adaptations worked well. The dough puffed as well as any quick puff pastry I've ever made. Not only that, it definitely lived up to my hopes for saving time; the whole process — from measuring the flour to wrapping the dough and refrigerating — it took only fifteen minutes.

My Quickest Puff Pastry works in the same way that all puff pastries do: the relatively large amount of butter falls into many strata when the dough is rolled and folded (or rolled and rolled up, as here). The dough is then chilled so that the butter remains separate, rather than being incorporated into the dough. As the dough heats in the oven, the butter melts and steam forms, filling and inflating the spaces previously occupied by the layers of butter. This causes the pastry to puff dramatically as it bakes.

To make sure that your dough comes out correctly, there are certain rules that you should follow. These rules apply not only to Quickest Puff Pastry, but to puff pastry made by the traditional and "quick" methods, as well.

Before using the dough, always make sure that you chill it until it is firm. This will usually take about one hour in the refrigerator. Also, if the dough softens and becomes sticky while you are working with it, slide it onto a cookie sheet, cover it with plastic wrap, and refrigerate it until it firms up. Again, this will take about an hour. Whatever you do, do not try to work with soft puff pastry; the butter will melt, and your pastry will not puff when baked.

While working with the dough, flour the work surfaces and the dough often to prevent sticking, but be sure to use only a light dusting of flour each time. Adding large amounts of flour will make the dough too tough.

If possible, chill the dough for an hour or two after forming it into pastry shapes, but before baking. This final chilling relaxes the strands of gluten in the dough, which prevents excessive shrinkage during baking and makes for more tender pastry.

Make sure that puff pastry is baked all the way through before you remove it from the oven. It should be a deep golden brown on the outside, and the inside of the dough should be white, rather

Smoked Salmon and Chive Mille Feuille

than grey. To check the interior, simply use the tip of a paring knife to poke a small hole to peek inside when you think the pastry is done.

In traditional puff pastry the layers are many and even, so properly made dough puffs tall and straight. In Quickest (and traditional "quick") Puff Pastry, the layers of butter are thin, but there are fewer of them and they are not as even — the dough puffs well, but it does not rise as high or quite as straight. As with quick puff pastry, my version may be used for 90 percent of the creations usually made from puff pastry, but for five-inch tall (or taller) vol-au-vents, gâteau Pithiviers (a round almond-filled cake, usually about three to four inches tall), and similar grand structures, you must use traditional puff pastry.

This still leaves a large range of impressive pastries, both sweet and savory, that can be easily and quickly made using Quickest Puff Pastry. By following the step-by-step illustrations on pages 16 and 17, you can make five such pastries.

Several of the recipes on pages 16 and 17 use a partial recipe of Quickest Puff Pastry. This way, you can either create a variety of shapes and tastes, or freeze a portion of the dough for later use. To do so, wrap the dough tightly in plastic wrap and then seal in a zipper-lock bag. The dough will keep in the freezer for at least three months. To thaw, simply place in the refrigerator overnight.

QUICKEST PUFF PASTRY
Makes about
1½ pounds of dough

2 cups unbleached, all-purpose flour (about 9 ounces)

20 tablespoons cold unsalted butter, cut into ½-inch dice (4 tablespoons kept separate)

1 teaspoon salt

6 tablespoons cold tap water, plus a tablespoon more, if necessary

1. Place flour in workbowl of food processor fitted with steel blade; add the 4 tablespoons butter; pulse until butter is absorbed, about 10 to 12 pulses of 1 second each.

2. Add remaining butter; pulse once or twice to distribute. Dissolve salt in water and add to flour mixture; pulse 3 or 4 times, until dough just starts to form a rough ball (*see* illustration 1, below) — do not overprocess. If mixture remains very dry, add a teaspoon of water at a time and pulse again.

3. Turn dough onto floured work surface and shape into rough rectangle, then place on top of sheet of well-floured plastic wrap measuring at

The multiple layers of Quickest Puff Pastry are created by folding dough once and then rolling it up like a jelly roll. When baked, the dough puffs dramatically.

least 12-by-18 inches. Lightly flour top of dough and cover with another sheet of wrap. Press dough with rolling pin to flatten, then roll back and forth several times with rolling pin to make 12-by-18-inch rectangle of dough.

4. Peel away plastic wrap and invert dough onto floured work surface, long side facing you. Peel away second piece of wrap. Fold top third of dough down and bottom third up (illustration 2), to make 4-by-18-inch rectangle, then roll up dough from one end (illustration 3). Press dough into square, wrap in plastic, and refrigerate 1 hour, or until firm. Proceed with any of the recipes on pages 16 and 17. Use the following seasonings to create the puff pastry straws and palmiers on page 16.

Parmesan-Paprika Seasoning: Mix together 1 cup grated Parmesan cheese, 1 teaspoon kosher salt, and 2 teaspoons paprika (Hungarian, if possible).

Cinnamon-Nut Seasoning: Mix together 1 cup sugar, ½ cup ground almonds (or other nut), and 1 teaspoon cinnamon. ∎

Nick Malgieri directs the baking program at Peter Kump's New York Cooking School and is the author of *Perfect Pastry* (Macmillan, 1989).

MAKING QUICKEST PUFF PASTRY

1. Use a food processor to mix the dough. After several pulses, the dough will start to gather into a rough ball, ready to be worked.

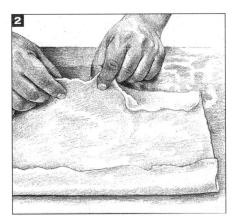

2. After forming the dough into a rough rectangle measuring about 12-by-18 inches, fold the top third of the dough down and bottom third up to form a rectangle approximately 4-by-18 inches.

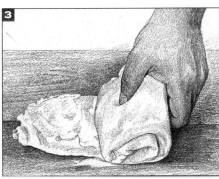

3. Starting at one end, roll the dough up like a jelly roll.

Palmiers

Making Puff Pastries

STRAWS

Makes 5–6 dozen

On a floured surface, roll 1 completed recipe of Quickest Puff Pastry into a 12-by-18-inch rectangle. Slide onto a pan and refrigerate until firm, about 1 hour. Brush dough with egg beaten with a pinch of salt. Sprinkle 1 teaspoon kosher salt and 2 tablespoons caraway seeds *or* Parmesan-Paprika *or* Cinnamon-Nut Seasoning over half the dough's surface, then fold dough over topping to form a 12-by-9-inch rectangle (illustration 1). Lightly flour surface and dough; roll dough back into a 12-by-18-inch rectangle. Refrigerate dough, if necessary. Cut the dough into about 36, 12-by-H-inch strips (illustration 2). Twist each strip into a corkscrew shape (illustration 3). Transfer twisted dough strips to parchment-lined jelly-roll pans. Press the edges of the twisted strips of dough to the edges of the pans. Chill until firm and cold, about 1 hour. Bake in a 375-degree oven until golden, about 20 minutes. Remove pan from oven and trim ends. Halve straws to make 5-inch lengths.

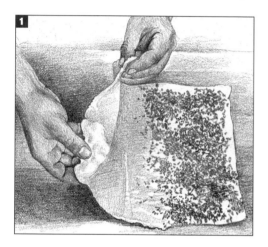
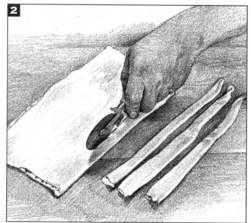
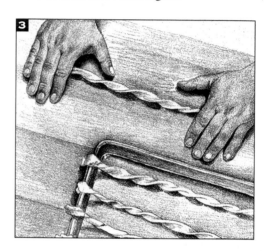

PALMIERS

Makes about 2 dozen

For Parmesan-Paprika Palmiers, on a floured surface, roll H recipe Quickest Puff Pastry into a 12-by-9-inch rectangle. Brush dough with egg beaten with a pinch of salt. Sprinkle Parmesan-Paprika Seasoning over dough surface. *For Sweet Palmiers,* sprinkle H cup sugar on work surface; on sugared surface, roll H recipe Quickest Puff Pastry into a 12-by-9-inch rectangle. Scatter another H cup sugar over dough and press with rolling pin to embed sugar. *For both types,* fold each long side about 1H inches in toward the center (illustration 1). Repeat folds so that folded edges meet in center (illustration 2), then fold in half at center. Wrap in plastic and chill until firm, about 1 hour. Using a sharp, thin knife, cut dough into H-inch slices (illustration 3); arrange cut side down on 2 parchment-lined cookie sheets, about 2 inches apart on all sides. Bake at 350 degrees about 20 minutes, until golden and crisp. Cool on pans and serve at room temperature or reheated.

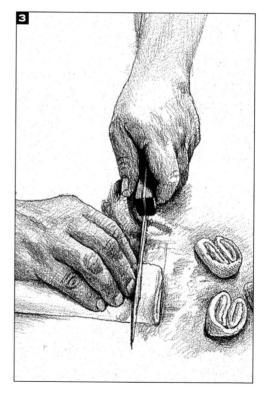

ILLUSTRATIONS BY ANATOLY

PUFF PASTRY TARTLETS

Makes 12–15, 3-inch tartlets

On a floured surface, roll ½ recipe Quickest Puff Pastry into a 15-by-10-inch rectangle. Cut into 3- to 3½-inch disks, squares, or diamonds (illustration 1). Arrange on a parchment-lined cookie sheet, about 2 inches apart on all sides, and prick with a fork (illustration 2). *For Tomato-Basil Tartlets,* top each dough shape with a thin slice of tomato (illustration 3), season with salt and pepper, and drizzle with olive oil. Sprinkle each with minced basil, then with grated Parmesan cheese. *For Apple Tartlets,* top each dough shape with paper-thin apple slices and a sprinkling of cinnamon sugar. Bake either variety at 350 degrees until golden and crisp, 25 to 30 minutes. Cool slightly; serve warm.

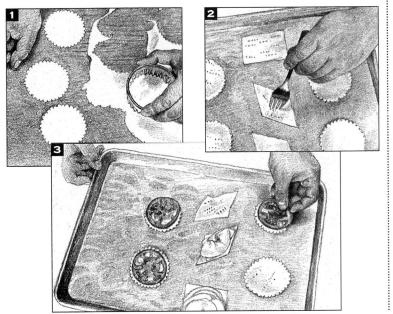

BISTRO APPLE TART

Serves 2–4

Shape ⅓ recipe of Quickest Puff Pastry into a somewhat even disk (illustration 1). Place on a lightly floured surface, flour the dough, and roll into a 10-inch disk. Slide onto a cookie sheet, cover with plastic wrap, and refrigerate until firm, at least 1 hour. Using a 10-inch plate, cut dough into an even disk (illustration 2). Prick dough with a fork at ½-inch intervals to prevent puffing during baking. Arrange thin apple slices from 2 tart apples in concentric rows, overlapping the slices slightly and leaving a ½-inch border around the edge (illustration 3), and sprinkle with 1 teaspoon sugar. Bake on the middle rack in a 450-degree oven until dough is baked through and apple slices have colored at the edges, 15 to 20 minutes. Heat 2 tablespoons apple jelly in a small pan; brush over slightly cooled tart. Serve immediately.

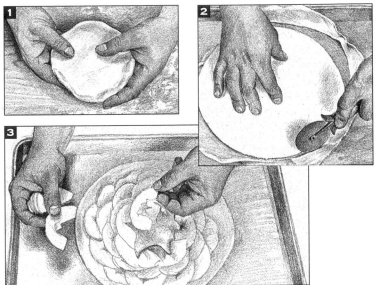

SMOKED SALMON AND CHIVE MILLE FEUILLE

Makes about 2 dozen

On a floured surface, roll ½ recipe Quickest Puff Pastry into a 16-by-11-inch rectangle. Slide onto a pan and refrigerate until firm and rested, about 1 hour. Prick dough with a fork (illustration 1) and place on a parchment-lined pan. Cover dough with another piece of parchment and another pan (illustration 2) and bake at 350 degrees, turning pans occasionally to ensure even browning, about 30 minutes. Remove dough from oven and cool between pans to prevent warping. Meanwhile, beat 8 ounces cream cheese together with 8 tablespoons softened butter until smooth and light. Beat in 1 tablespoon minced lemon zest and salt and pepper to taste. Stir in 2 to 3 tablespoons snipped chives. Cut baked pastry lengthwise to make 2, 8-by-11-inch pieces. Spread each piece with half the filling. Arrange 6 ounces thin-sliced smoked salmon over one piece, then invert the other piece on it to cover the salmon (illustration 3). Slide onto a pan; press to adhere. Refrigerate until firm, about 1 hour. Cut into strips 1 to 1½ inches wide, then cut diagonally to make diamond shapes (illustration 4) and serve.

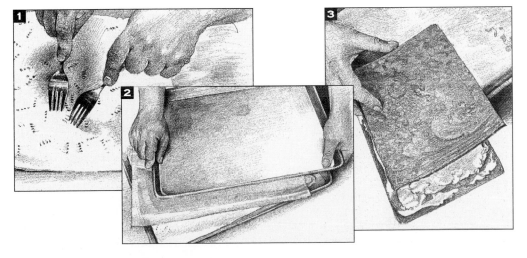

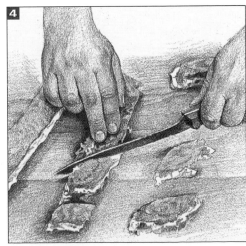

Risotto Rules

Surprise! You can forget about constant stirring the next time you make risotto.

~ BY SARAH FRITSCHNER ~

Perfect risotto is like great art — difficult to define, but you know it when you see it. Depending on the cook, this classic Italian rice dish may be thick enough to scoop or thin enough to pour; redolent of smoked meat and vegetables or gently seasoned with saffron and a little onion; chock full of chunky vegetables and meat or a simple dish of cooked, seasoned rice.

About the only thing that everyone agrees on is that risotto is an Italian short-grain rice dish. I would add two other qualities that make a rice dish undeniably risotto: First, the cooked rice grains must be discreet, but loosely bound by a sauce that appears spontaneously when you cook the rice, due to the type of starch molecules (amylopectin) abundant in the rice. Second, risotto must be served *al dente*, with a substantial firmness.

When it comes to cooking risotto, though, disagreement reigns. Some cookbook authors of stellar reputation insist upon a whole set of immutable rules, but others repudiate these guidelines. So what's the truth?

After systematically producing dozens of risottos over the last three months, I have learned that traditional methods of making the dish are not sacred, and can be varied to accommodate a busy schedule and a concern for health. But I also found that the best risotto still requires time, at least *some* stirring, and top-quality ingredients.

Let's consider each step in making this dish, looking at the traditional rules and considering their validity.

The Rice

The first rule of risotto says that the cook must begin with a certain type of rice (arborio) that grows only in northern Italy. Nothing else will do.

It is true that, in Italy, most cooks use *superfino* (top-quality) arborio rice to make their risotto dishes. However, this is not essential.

Arborio designates a short-grain japonica (Japanese) rice. It is not surprising that Italians insist on using Italian rice in an Italian dish, but there are other japonica-type rices that may be substituted in a risotto recipe. Japanese short-grain rice and California-grown medium-grain rice (both widely available in U.S. supermarkets) substitute adequately, if not perfectly, for the more expensive Italian varieties. The taste is a little different, to be sure; these medium- and short-grain rices lack the subtle "grainy" flavor you get from arborio. Also, because the grains are not the same size as arborio, they

Traditional risotto uses **arborio**, *a short-grain Italian japonica rice. We found that Japanese short-grain rices, or even California-grown medium-grain rices (shown here), are acceptable substitutes.*

don't turn over in your mouth exactly the same way, so it's a somewhat different aesthetic experience. Finally, these substitute rices can overcook more easily, passing through the *al dente* stage with much less of a grace period than arborio has.

Despite all this, my conclusion is that, while arborio is the preferred rice, other japonica varieties will do. I would not hesitate to use the medium-grain rice from my supermarket, or the short-grain rice from my Asian grocery.

The Seasoning

The second rule of proper risotto technique requires that you start with seasoning — traditionally onion cooked in butter — then stir in rice until it is translucent and covered with fat.

This rule is both true and not true. The fat is there to season the onion, so it is the first thing to go into the pot. You must add rice before you add broth, but you do not have to stir the rice in the fat and you certainly don't need to cook it for five minutes, as some recipes call for.

This type of sautéing is called for in many pilafs because it keeps the kernels separate and because the heat gelatinizes the starchy coating of the rice. Keeping kernels separate is not a problem with risotto, and gelatinizing the starch before the water hits it is certainly not in the spirit of risotto making. Cooking briefly on top of the stove is fine.

As for the type of fat, I use olive oil instead of the traditional butter because my risotto usually contains strong-flavored ingredients that overwhelm the flavor of butter and because

olive oil cuts down on the amount of saturated fat.

The Liquid

After the rice and seasonings are in the pot, tradition calls for a hot liquid to be added intermittently, about one-half cup at a time. The liquid is always flavorful: broth or wine or a combination of both.

Most cooks do bring the liquid to a simmer and add it in small amounts. This process keeps the risotto under your constant scrutiny, which is crucial because the water shouldn't boil vigorously and the rice needs to be *al dente* and no softer. The slow-adding technique definitely works — but others do too.

In fact, the best risotto I ever ate was prepared by an Italian chef who started with arborio and proceeded to break every other rule of risotto making. He combined one kilo of rice with one liter of cold tap water and brought them to a boil as he walked around the kitchen gathering other ingredients. Only after the rice had boiled nearly dry did he begin to add broth. But the risotto was better than any of the laboriously stirred versions I ever tasted.

As for the type of liquid, I always use homemade chicken broth. I prefer it to canned broth because its subtlety allows for mistakes — if you reduce homemade broth too fast, it doesn't go tinny or salty on you and ruin the dish.

But I am not a stickler for chicken broth; I use it because inexpensive chicken pieces are readily available. If I could find inexpensive beef bones I might use those. I've also used fresh tomatoes, wine, and water for a vegetarian stock. When I run out of chicken broth, I add tap water. Generally all these liquids are added at room temperature.

The Stirring

The most immutable rule of risotto making is that it must be stirred constantly for the twenty to thirty minutes it cooks (the length of time determines the firmness of the rice).

I have found that, while constant stirring does make an excellent risotto, it isn't required. Some stirring is essential both to prevent burning and to liberate the amylopectin molecules that float into the liquid and swell to make the sauce. But you don't have to stir constantly.

Let's rejoin our Italian chef who combines the tap water and the arborio. He doesn't stir at

RISOTTO ADDITIONS

Risotto is distinguished from other rice dishes by type of rice and cooking technique, not by any hard-and-fast rule about what goes into it. Even in Italy, the dish changes from place to place, as regional products dictate its personality. In the truest spirit of good home cooking, I recommend that you use what's freshest, what's grown locally, and what you have in the refrigerator.

You can add vegetables and meat to risotto after cooking your onion or at the end of cooking the rice. The first way will give you tender, limp vegetables and fully cooked meat. Cured meats and sausage should be added at the beginning, while seafood should be added with only enough time to cook through.

As for toppings, I love strong, hard, aged cheeses, particularly Parmesan, Asiago, or hard goat or sheep cheeses such as pecorino. These cheeses can be grated and added at the end of cooking (remove the pan from the heat, then stir) or sprinkled on top before serving. You can also stir in mascarpone, soft rind cheeses such as Camembert, or blue cheese such as Gorgonzola, which will add creaminess and flavor to the rice.

all until the initial liter of water has evaporated quite a bit and he can see the bottom of the pan when he drags a spoon through the rice. At this point he adds saffron, starts to add broth intermittently, and stirs vigorously.

This deluge-and-stir method works great at home, and it is one variation on tradition that I found completely acceptable. If you decide to use this method, be sure to use a heavy nonstick skillet or saucepan. Otherwise, you will have to stir constantly just to avoid sticking.

Serving the Dish

The final rule of risotto tradition is that the dish must be served immediately upon completion. Under no circumstances can it be reheated.

With a final peek into the kitchen of our Italian chef, we see him spreading fourteen-minute crunchy risotto on a wide baking sheet so that it cools quickly. Then he refrigerates it. When a patron orders risotto, the chef scoops the rice off the baking sheet and into a skillet with olive oil (the first fat he's added to the dish), a little more broth, and huge chunks of shrimp or wild mushrooms or whatever the risotto *du jour* might be.

This is not risotto the way Grandmama Rosa would fix it, but even Marcella Hazan begrudgingly admits that the partial-cooking method works for cooks who cannot make the entire risotto at the last minute.

Beware, however, that reheating partly cooked rice works best in the small portions typical of single servings in restaurants. When you reheat a large amount of risotto, you may end up overcooking the rice before the sauce is heated through sufficiently.

MASTER RECIPE FOR BASIC RISOTTO
*Serves 4 as a main course or
6 as a first course*

When the rice is done, stir in a little extra liquid, as the sauce will set up a bit when served.

    3   tablespoons olive oil
    1   medium onion, peeled and diced
  2–4   ounces country ham, pancetta,
        prosciutto, or other flavorful cured
        meat, minced
    2   cups arborio or medium-grain rice
        Salt
    5   cups homemade chicken broth (or
        1 can broth mixed with 3 cups water),
        at room temperature
   ½   cup dry white wine
   ½   cup grated Parmesan or Asiago
        cheese, plus extra for passing

Heat oil in a heavy pot, 10 to 12 inches in diameter. Add onions and ham; sauté, stirring occasionally, until onions soften, 3 to 5 minutes. Stir in rice and 1 teaspoon salt or to taste. Add 3 cups broth and bring to boil, stirring occasionally. Reduce heat to simmer and cook, stirring occasionally, until pan bottom is dry when rice is pulled back with spoon, 8 to 10 minutes. Add wine, stirring frequently until absorbed. Then add ½ cup broth at a time, stirring constantly, until each addition is absorbed; cook until rice is creamy but still somewhat firm in center (add water in ½ cup increments if broth runs out), 10 to 12 minutes longer. Stir in cheese. Serve on a wide platter or individual plates with additional cheese passed separately.

RISOTTO WITH CABBAGE AND COUNTRY HAM
*Serves 4 as a main course or
6 as a first course*

Follow Master Recipe for Basic Risotto, adding ½ small cabbage, shredded, to the pan after the onions have softened. Cover pan and cook over medium heat, stirring occasionally, until cabbage is very soft, limp, and beginning to brown, about 15 minutes. Continue with Master Recipe.

RISOTTO WITH ASPARAGUS AND WILD MUSHROOMS
*Serves 4 as a main course or
6 as a first course*

Heat 2 tablespoons butter in a large skillet. Add 4 ounces fresh wild mushrooms, trimmed and sliced thin, and ½ pound thin asparagus, trimmed and cut into 2-inch pieces; sauté until asparagus pieces are almost tender, about 7 minutes; set aside. Follow Master Recipe for Basic Risotto, omitting ham from the recipe. When risotto is done, stir in asparagus-mushroom mixture and serve.

RISOTTO WITH TOMATOES AND BASIL
*Serves 4 as a main course or
6 as a first course*

Follow Master Recipe for Basic Risotto, adding 1½ pounds peeled, seeded, and chopped plum tomatoes to the pan after the onions have softened. Cover and cook over medium heat until tomatoes start to look like a thin sauce, about 10 minutes. Continue with Master Recipe, sprinkling each serving of risotto with 1 tablespoon of shredded basil leaves. ∎

Sarah Fritschner is the food editor of the *Louisville Courier-Journal*.

TRYING THE ALTERNATIVES

In addition to testing the assumptions about cooking risotto on top of the stove, I also investigated the unconventional cooking methods that various cooks had suggested. After my testing, I recommend that you stick to your stovetop.

Microwave: Enthusiasts insist that microwaving risotto is a miracle just shy of virgin birth. It's not. The amylopectin molecules in arborio are inclined to get sticky when they cook, so even microwave risotto will have a little sauce. But microwaves do not, repeat, do not, make great risotto. The grains need friction to produce a really good sauce, and the broth needs longer cooking so it can evaporate, developing and concentrating the flavors that make it interesting.

Baking: Some cooks bake risotto in the oven, stirring only occasionally. The oven method requires longer than the stovetop method, dirties more dishes, and you don't get a maximum creaminess from the rice. But it does have advantages: you can walk away from it and, if you're heating the oven anyway, it's an efficient use of energy and the risotto tastes decent.

Pressure cooking: Pressure cookers are definitely quick. They will, however, turn your two-dollar rice, your homemade chicken broth, and your high hopes for dinner into a nearly inedible mush. If you like pressure cookers more than you like risotto, you can use them to cook your arborio. The rice doesn't turn to poison, it just turns into the most insipid substance I've eaten in a long time, and I'm a fan of soupy starch. As far as I'm concerned, there's very little you can do to a grain cooked in water to make it inedible, but pressure cooking comes close.

When Only Fresh Coconut Will Do

Here's how to open, clean, and shred fresh coconut for cooking.

~ BY NANCIE MCDERMOTT ~

Although coconuts are readily available in American supermarkets, the challenge of cracking one open and preparing it for use remains an intimidating prospect to many cooks. The process is definitely worth the effort, though; while packaged coconut is widely available, the freshly grated version adds an incomparable, moist richness to many dishes, from relishes to desserts. I've narrowed down a variety of recommended methods for handling fresh coconuts into a simple, straightforward procedure.

Opening the Coconut

Many experts recommend baking a drained coconut in a hot oven for fifteen to thirty minutes prior to opening it. I avoid this technique for several reasons. The heated meat does indeed shrink and pull away nicely from the shell on its own, and a large crack generally appears in the shell. Unfortunately, the oven cooks the sweet white coconut meat in the process, turning it gray and drying it out — a detriment to any intended culinary use. The initial heat-induced crack still requires follow-up blows from a hammer, so that step isn't really eliminated. Then there's the extra inconvenience of working with a very hot coconut.

I find the method developed ages ago by folks with tons of coconuts to crack and few ovens to rely on to be superior in every way. You must whack the coconut with, or on, something hard; I use a hammer. (If you wish to save the juice — *see* Granny's Speckled Coconut Cake, page 21 — cracking a coconut involves a little more care. Work over a bowl, and be sure to strain the juice before you use it, passing it through a fine mesh strainer, clean cloth, or coffee filter to remove fibers and bits of shell.)

Examine the outer shell before you begin. You will see that one end has a slightly pointed tip and the other sports three eyes, and that three faint but distinct ridges run lengthwise from the pointed tip to between the eyes on the base. When hitting the coconut along its equator (*see* illustration 1, page 21), pay particular attention to where these ridges intersect the equator, as that is where the shell is weakest and most easily cracked.

Don't be discouraged if nothing seems to happen when you begin to hit the coconut. Note the sounds — when you make that first pure, cracking contact, the sound will deepen to a thud, and cracks will appear.

After breaking the coconut in half with your hands, hammer it into a number of smaller, more manageable pieces (illustration 2). Next, separate the hairy, dark brown outer shell from the meat using a dull table knife (illustration 3). Avoid the temptation to use a paring knife; if does make for slightly faster work, but the potential for accidental injury is high.

For pure white coconut, the final step is to pare off the thin brown skin on the outer side of the chunks of shelled meat (illustration 4). This step is no fun, whatever tool you use, and you might consider whether to do it at all. My grandmother, who lived where coconuts are plentiful, considered the brown peel an acceptable, edible substance which was often more trouble to remove than it was worth, the end result being merely whiter rather than better.

Grating or Shredding the Meat

Once you have removed the coconut meat from its shell, you very often need to grate or shred it for use in recipes. I had always rejected a food processor as a coconut grater because the resulting meat was too coarse. California cooking teacher Phillis Carey, however, taught me to rinse the meat, cut it into half-inch dice, and drop the chunks through the processor's feed tube onto the steel blade, with the machine running. With one or two interruptions to scrape the interior, the result was a mound of beautiful, soft, fine moist coconut in a minute or two.

My second choice is to work by hand on a box grater, using the large, rounded holes for shreds or the sharp, tiny holes for thin fluff. The result is longer and more delicate shreds than a machine can produce, but the cost is high both in time and in painful scraped knuckles. If you plan to use a box grater, keep the meat in large chunks, putting more distance between your knuckles and the blades of the grater.

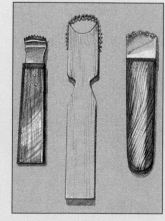
SOUTHEAST ASIAN-STYLE COCONUT CHUTNEY

Makes about 1½ cups (6–8 servings)
This chutney, adapted from *Thrill of the Grill* (Morrow, 1990), is a particularly good accompaniment to meaty fish, such as mackerel or tuna.

- 1 cup grated meat from 1 coconut
- ¼ cup roasted, unsalted peanuts, coarsely chopped
- ¼ cup minced lemongrass from 2 stalks (optional)
- 2 tablespoons minced fresh ginger
- ½ cup juice from about 4 limes
- 2 tablespoons honey
- 2 tablespoons minced fresh mint leaves
- 2 tablespoons minced fresh cilantro leaves
- 1 jalapeño pepper, seeded and minced

Mix all ingredients in medium bowl. Serve. (Can be refrigerated in an airtight container up to 4 days.)

ILLUSTRATIONS BY TONY DELUZ

GRANNY'S SPECKLED COCONUT CAKE
Serves 14–16

The recipe in Prudence Hillburn's *A Treasury of Southern Baking* (HarperPerennial, 1993), is a dead ringer for the coconut cake my grandmother used to make. The cake improves with age and is best eaten a day or two after baking. Reserve the liquid that comes from the fresh coconut, it also will be used in the frosting. If you do not want to use the self-rising flour called for in the recipe, you may use three cups all-purpose flour, one and one-half tablespoons baking powder, and one teaspoon salt.

Simple Vanilla Cake
    1   cup shortening
    1¾ cups sugar
    1   teaspoon vanilla extract
    3   large eggs
    3   cups self-rising flour
    1   cup milk

Speckled Coconut Frosting
    1   cup sugar
    3   tablespoons all-purpose flour
        Juice from 2 coconuts, plus enough
        milk to equal 1½ cups
    4   tablespoons butter
    4–5 cups grated but not peeled meat from
        2 coconuts

1. *For the cake,* adjust oven rack to center position and heat oven to 350 degrees. Cream shortening and sugar in large bowl of electric mixer until light and fluffy. Beat in vanilla, then eggs, one at a time. Beat in ⅓ of flour at a time, alternating with milk.

2. Divide batter evenly among 3 greased and floured 9-inch cake pans. Bake until a toothpick comes out clean when inserted into center of layers, 20 to 25 minutes. Cool cakes in pans for 10 minutes, then turn onto wire rack and cool completely.

3. *For the frosting,* bring all frosting ingredients to boil in a large heavy saucepan. Cook over medium-high heat, stirring constantly, until thickened to consistency of a thick sauce, 5 to 7 minutes. Cool to room temperature, then spread between each layer and on top and sides of cake.

AMBROSIA
Serves 12–15

Bananas are a delicious addition, but they're best included only if this dessert is assembled shortly before serving.

    8   large oranges, skinned and sectioned
        Confectioner's sugar (up to ¾ cup)
    1   pineapple, peeled, cored, and cut into
        medium dice, juice reserved
    2   cups grated meat from 1 coconut

Arrange about ¼ of orange sections like spokes of a wheel in a 3-quart serving bowl. Then dust with about 3 tablespoons confectioner's sugar (amount of sugar depends on sweetness of fruit). Top with ¼ of pineapple and its juice. Sprinkle about ½ cup grated coconut over pineapple. Continue layering process, ending with coconut. Cover and chill until serving time. (Can be made 1 day in advance.) ∎

Nancie McDermott is the author of *Real Thai: The Best of Thailand's Regional Cooking* (Chronicle Books, 1992).

OPENING AND CLEANING A COCONUT

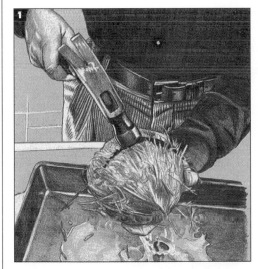

1. *If you wish to save the juice,* hold the coconut in the palm of your hand with the pointed tip facing away from you over a rimmed pan or bowl. Strike the coconut firmly on its equator with a hammer. Rotate slightly and strike it again. Continue until the coconut cracks open completely.

2. Pull the two halves apart with your hands, then crack each half into two or three smaller pieces with firm hammer blows.

4. If desired, remove the thin brown skin from the meat with a paring knife or a Chinese cleaver.

3. Insert the blade of a dull table knife between the hard, hairy shell and the meat, and work it in horizontally, wiggling both the knife handle and the coconut. Once the knife is in about an inch, twist the handle vertically to separate the meat from the shell. Repeat at several points around the piece until the meat separates.

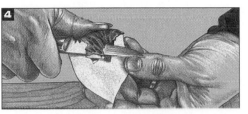

5. *If you don't care about the juice,* put the coconut in a plastic garbage bag and hit it forcefully and repeatedly with a hammer until you can feel that it has broken into several pieces. This will also separate the meat from the hard, hairy shell. *See* illustration 4 to remove the thin brown skin, if desired.

Basic Brownies Are Best

The best brownies use cake flour and baking powder for a moist, light texture.

~ BY JACK BISHOP ~

After baking almost three dozen varieties of brownies, I can report with confidence that the simplest brownie is the best. I tried every trick in the book — and there are numerous cookbooks devoted exclusively or mostly to brownies — and most were a waste of time (*see* "Tricks Without Treats," below). The ingredients for perfect brownies are easy to find and the technique is uncomplicated.

Even novice bakers know how to make brownies — just combine chocolate, butter, sugar, eggs, and flour. However, few cooks know which type of flour to use, or whether they should melt or cream the butter. In the course of perfecting my recipe I addressed some of these fundamental issues.

The Wet Ingredients

Brownies begin with melted chocolate that has been cooled slightly so as not to "cook" the eggs. However, some recipes call for the butter to be melted along with the chocolate, while others instruct you to cream softened butter and sugar and then add eggs and melted chocolate.

In recipes without leavening, creaming the butter does create a slightly fluffier brownie; the sharp sugar crystals separate fat molecules in the butter, adding more air to the batter.

At an informal sampling of brownies made with melted and creamed butter, a majority of tasters (myself included) preferred the latter. The improvement was so slight, however, it hardly seemed worth the loss of spontaneity. Brownies are spur-of-the-moment baking at its best. By the time butter softens, the craving may pass. I decided to throw my lot with the impulse crowd and melt the butter, then see if there were other techniques I could use to compensate for the slightly heavier texture.

After the melted butter and chocolate have cooled a bit — they don't need to be at room temperature, but should not be hot either — sugar is added. At this point the mixture will appear grainy. Next, eggs and vanilla are beaten in. The batter thickens and becomes smoother with the addition of the eggs, and the teaspoon of vanilla highlights the chocolate.

Brownies may have originated as a fallen cake or as a way to "stretch" fudge by adding flour; the truth remains a mystery. Either way, these half-cake, half-fudge squares date back to about the turn of the century.

The final step is to combine and add the dry ingredients.

The Dry Ingredients

The most unusual ingredient in my recipe is baking powder. Many classic recipes omit chemical leavening, and I was initially adverse to adding any. My brownies, however, were a bit leaden, especially when I decided to melt the butter and not cream it, and the addition of one-half teaspoon baking powder provided the contrasting textures I associate with the perfect brownie — a crackly top that lifts gently from the fudgy center.

I also compared brownies made with all-purpose and plain (not self-rising) cake flour. All-purpose flour yields taller brownies that are more cakey and tough. In contrast, brownies made with cake flour have a tender, melt-in-your-mouth quality, which I prefer.

I found recipes that call for as little as one-fourth cup of flour and as much as one and one-third cups for an eight-inch pan. Brownies made with less than two-thirds cup cake flour were too greasy for my taste, while those made with more were too dry.

In tests with and without salt, I found the presence of one-quarter teaspoon helps balance the sweetness. A brief whisk of the dry ingredients — sifting is unnecessary — distributes them evenly and provides a bit of aeration.

A final word about tampering with greatness. If you feel the need to jazz up brownies, fold a half cup or so of chopped pecans or walnuts into the batter along with the dry ingredients, but avoid bizarre embellishments such as Marzipan Raspberry Brownies.

Final Refinements

With my recipe in hand, I had only a few remaining questions. As I expected, brownies baked in a glass pan burned around the edges. I tried lowering the oven heat, but without success — the edges still dried out. Changing pans worked better: a greased metal pan conducts heat evenly and is the best option.

A greater challenge is determining when brownies are properly cooked. Even a few extra minutes in the oven can turn the best batter into dry and listless brownies. The problem is

---

complicated by the imprecise results of the "toothpick test." Batter around the outer edge of the pan cooks much faster and can appear dry after only fifteen minutes. The center of the pan can remain moist even after thiry minutes, when the brownies are way overdone.

I recommend using two visual clues to determine when brownies should be removed from the oven. First, check to see if the center is set. After fifteen minutes, the center should still wobble or jiggle when the pan is moved. After twenty minutes, however, the center should be gently set. At this point, stick a toothpick or cake tester into the batter halfway between the center and edge of the pan — the middle of the pan should always remain fairly moist. If the toothpick comes out clean (a few fudge crumbs are okay, but the batter should not be liquidy), the brownies are done.

In many cases, the brownies will not be completely cooked after twenty minutes. This early-bird test is really designed for ovens that run a bit hot. If the toothpick comes out covered with batter, bake the brownies another two to four minutes. However, if a toothpick comes out moist after twenty-four minutes, resist the temptation to keep baking. The ideal brownie is moist — even slightly underdone — and never overdone or dry.

THE BEST BROWNIES
Makes 12 bars
Make sure to cool the melted chocolate and butter for about ten minutes — it can be warm to the touch but not hot. Batter can be doubled and divided evenly between two eight-inch pans or poured into one thirteen-by-nine-inch pan. If using one large pan, bake for about twenty-six minutes.

```
8   tablespoons (1 stick) unsalted butter
2   ounces unsweetened baking
    chocolate
⅔   cup plain cake flour
½   teaspoon baking powder
¼   teaspoon salt
1   cup sugar
2   large eggs
1   teaspoon vanilla extract
½   cup chopped nuts (optional)
```

1. Adjust oven rack to center position and heat oven to 350 degrees. Melt butter and chocolate together in a medium saucepan set over simmering water or in a bowl in a microwave on medium power, set aside to cool.

2. Measure flour, baking powder, and salt into a small bowl and whisk briefly to combine; set aside.

3. Whisk sugar into cooled chocolate mixture. Whisk in eggs and vanilla, then fold in flour mixture (and nuts) until just combined.

4. Pour batter into greased 8-inch square metal pan, 2 inches deep; bake until toothpick inserted halfway between center and edge of pan comes out with a few fudgy crumbs, about 20 minutes. If batter coats toothpick, return pan

to oven and bake 2 to 4 minutes more. Cool brownies completely in pan set on a wire rack. Cut into squares and serve. (Pan can be wrapped in plastic, then foil, for up to 2 days — to preserve moistness, cut and remove brownies only as needed.)

LOWER-FAT COCOA BROWNIES
Makes 12 bars
This recipe can also be doubled and divided evenly between two eight-inch pans or poured into one thirteen-by-nine-inch pan. If using one large pan, bake for about twenty-five minutes.

```
½   cup plain cake flour
½   cup unsweetened cocoa powder
½   teaspoon baking powder
¼   teaspoon salt
¼   cup sour cream
2   teaspoons vanilla extract
4   tablespoons unsalted butter, melted
    and cooled slightly
1   cup sugar
1   large egg plus whites from 2 large
    eggs
```

1. Adjust oven rack to center position and heat oven to 350 degrees.

2. Whisk flour, cocoa, baking powder, and salt together in medium bowl and set aside.

3. Whisk sour cream and vanilla into cooled butter. Beat in sugar, then eggs. Fold in cocoa mixture until well combined.

4. Pour batter into greased 8-inch square metal pan, 2 inches deep; bake until toothpick inserted halfway between center and edge of pan comes out with a few fudgy crumbs, about 22 minutes. Cool brownies completely in pan set on a wire rack. Cut into squares and serve. (Pan can be wrapped in plastic, then foil, and stored overnight at room temperature — to preserve moistness, cut and remove brownies only as needed.) ■

CHOOSING THE RIGHT CHOCOLATE

After preparing dozens of brownies with Baker's unsweetened baking chocolate, I wanted to see if I could improve on my recipe by changing chocolates. I prepared two trays of Best Brownies — one with Baker's and the other with unsweetened Callebaut, an expensive Belgian chocolate favored by many professional bakers.

Brownies made with Callebaut had a deeper, richer chocolate flavor. The change was akin to drinking wine after a mild head cold has cleared; while everything

before had tasted fine, flavors now seemed truer and more intense. In defense of brownies made with Baker's, they are quite good — nine and one-half on a scale of one to ten. Nevertheless, if you want to substitute more expensive European or American chocolate, you won't be wasting money.

After this test, I wondered whether expensive semisweet or bittersweet chocolates would make even better brownies. Fancy semisweet chocolates certainly are easier to locate than unsweetened premium brands. For

this test, I prepared three batches of Best Brownies — one with Baker's unsweetened, one with Baker's semisweet, and one with Ghiradelli semisweet, a topnotch gourmet chocolate from California and normally one of my favorites.

To my surprise, brownies made with Baker's unsweetened were the clear winner. Both batches made with semisweet chocolate had a jarring candylike flavor. Although not sweeter than brownies made with baking chocolate, they lacked a true chocolate punch.

Which Canned Tomatoes Should You Buy?

When it comes to making sauces, our tasting panel finds inexpensive California tomatoes have better flavor than pricey Italian imports.

~ BY MARK BITTMAN ~

When vine-ripened tomatoes are unavailable, the canned variety often make a better substitute in sauces than the rock-hard orbs found in many supermarkets.

Does it matter where tomatoes hail from? Do we care that once-common San Marzano tomatoes from Italy are now difficult to find, and even more difficult to afford? How good are canned organic tomatoes? These are the questions that we wanted to answer when we compared eleven brands of canned tomatoes at a taste test held at Angelo's restaurant in New York's Little Italy. We found out that neither organic nor Italian tomatoes could compare to California tomatoes that have been properly grown and packed.

The long-standing assumption of many cooks and chefs is that Italian tomatoes are better than domestic ones — sweeter, plumper, and redder, with fewer seeds and liquid and more pulp. The difference has been attributed to the varieties used, the growing climate, the ideal length of time on the vine, and better methods of picking, skinning, and packing. But in January 1989, in response to the refusal of the European Community (EC) to import hormone-treated American beef, the United States imposed tariffs on various EC imports, including canned tomatoes. The cost of the tariff went from a virtually negligible 13.6 percent to 100 percent of value. Thus, Italian tomatoes that had been priced competitively with those from California — about one dollar for a twenty-eight-ounce can — suddenly doubled in price, and sometimes went even higher.

The effect has been dramatic. Five years ago genuine Italian plum tomatoes, often from the prime San Marzano area, were sold side-by-side with domestic brands such as Hunt's and Redpack; home cooks could choose a brand and stick with it. Now it is difficult to find real Italian tomatoes outside of specialty stores, and the cost often approaches three dollars per can; consequently, sales of Italian tomatoes have dropped by 90 percent. An importer we spoke with said, "Canned tomatoes just aren't worth it anymore for the Italian companies; peeling whole tomatoes isn't all that profitable to begin with." For this reason, importers of Italian foods are focusing their efforts on products such as olive oil and balsamic vinegar, which are not successfully mass-produced in the United States.

National and Regional Variations

Americans eat a lot of tomatoes — eighty pounds per person per year. Among vegetables (as the ripened ovary of a seed plant, the tomato is technically a fruit, but the Supreme Court in 1893 legally declared it a vegetable), only potatoes are consumed at a greater rate. Ninety percent of the domestic crop comes from California; Ohio is a very distant second. Canned tomatoes also come from Israel and Turkey, and from Chile, Argentina, and other South American countries.

We don't all see the same tomatoes when we go shopping. Hunt's, Del Monte, and Contadina are the only national products with significant market share, and even they are not sold everywhere. "Specialty" brands such as Progresso and the relatively new Muir Glen are also sold nationally, but, depending on where you live, you may find the former only in Italian markets and the latter, which are organic, only in health food stores. Regional brands can also be important: Redpack, our top finisher, is strong in the Northeast but not elsewhere. That doesn't mean, however, that you cannot find tomatoes just like Redpack in your store, because Tri-Valley, a company which packs for Redpack, Libby's, and S & W, also sells to supermarkets for private label products.

Since canned tomatoes are a seasonal and relatively unprocessed product, what's in the can is likely to vary from one year to the next, according to variables such as temperature and rainfall. Still, our tasting demonstrates certain constants: there is little reason to go out of your way to buy expensive Italian tomatoes; if you are buying organic tomatoes because you think they taste better (rather than because they are grown without chemicals), you may be making a mistake; supermarket brands are certainly worth trying; and Redpack tomatoes (which have been a standard in certain New York food circles for years) really are quite good.

There were also differences among the tomatoes that were not evident at the tasting, ones you might want to observe the next time you make a sauce. Some had far more seeds than others (you can easily see this if you use Julia della Croce's technique for removing most of the seeds from canned tomatoes before cooking; *see* "Tomato Sauces for Pasta," page 26). Some had more tomato and less water than others; a twenty-eight-ounce can of one variety, for example, yielded just over a cup of tomato pulp, while others measured nearly two cups (generally, the more watery varieties did poorly in the tasting). Finally, some tomatoes were mushy when coming out of the can, others quite hard. This is likely to be inconsistent even within brands, and is difficult to interpret: "mushiness" might result from extremely ripe tomatoes, not necessarily a flaw, or from overcooking during processing. Some mushy tomatoes (most notably Redpack) did well in the tasting; others fared poorly.

We sampled eleven brands of canned tomatoes, including the nationally available brands (Hunt's, Del Monte, Contadina), the dominant regional brands (Redpack, S & W, Libby's), one of the largest supermarket brands (Townhouse, by Safeway), and some specialty brands (Progresso Italian-Style, Muir Glen). We went out of our way to include two types of imported

PHOTOGRAPH ABOVE LEFT COURTESY OF TRI-VALLEY GROWERS, ABOVE BY ERIC ROTH

Italian tomatoes (Pastene, Progresso Genuine Italian), although they are no longer widely available, in the event that they might be worth the extra expense and hassle of finding them if they ranked very high in the tasting; this was not the case.

Canned Tomatoes Blind Tasting
The tasting was held at Angelo's, a 103-year-old restaurant on Mulberry Street in New York's Little Italy. Tasters included the author; Anna Teresa Callen, cooking teacher; Arthur Schwartz, food writer and radio host; Anna Amendolara Nurse, widely respected teacher of homestyle Italian cooking; Iris Carulli, home cook who once lived in Sicily; Julia della Croce, cookbook author; Tina della Croce, Julia's mother; Tina Aprea, member of the family that owns Angelo's; and Jack Bishop, *Cook's Illustrated* senior writer.

Tomatoes were tasted blind in two ways. Each was displayed in a glass bowl exactly as it came from the can; tasters cut off pieces of the tomatoes in the bowls. Each was also made into a light, quick sauce, based on Julia della Croce's Quick-Cooked Tomatoes with Olive Oil (*see* recipe, page 26). We seeded the tomatoes, measured two cups, crushed them with a potato masher, and cooked them with one-half teaspoon of salt in two tablespoons of pure (relatively tasteless) olive oil for exactly twenty minutes. We did not adjust cooking times for tomatoes that produced thin sauce.

Unless noted, all tomatoes were grown in California and came in twenty-eight-ounce cans; prices may vary. They are listed in order of preference (an asterisk indicates that the tomato tied with the one immediately below). In the judging, seven points were awarded for each first-place vote; six for second; five for third; four for fourth; three for fifth; two for sixth; one for seventh. ∎

CANNED TOMATOES LISTED IN ORDER OF PREFERENCE

 1 Redpack Italian-Style Tomatoes with Tomato Puree

 2 Progresso Italian-Style Peeled Tomatoes

 3 Townhouse Whole Peeled Tomatoes

 **4** Libby's California Whole Peeled Tomatoes

 5 S & W Premium Sun-Ripened Peeled Tomatoes

1 **Redpack Italian-Style Tomatoes with Tomato Puree**, $1.09; 38 points. When the results were revealed, one Italian-American scoffed, "No Italian would ever use these," until she realized she had put them in fourth place — after three American brands. The comments: "Deep red color, both raw and in the sauce," "sweet," and "good-tasting." Some people objected to the puree pack: "Too thick," said one, and "Must be cooked very briefly," said another (not necessarily a disadvantage). One panelist found the taste "bitter." Three first-place votes out of nine.

2 **Progresso Italian-Style Peeled Tomatoes**, $1.29; 27 points. The tomatoes in this can were from an undisclosed location. "Somewhat salty," wrote one taster, although he ranked them second for their "very tomato-y, rich flavor." The saltiness was noted by others, but most tasters found them "rich," "sweet," and/or "fruity." Six tasters placed these among the top three; one found them "unpleasant."

3 **Townhouse Whole Peeled Tomatoes** (Safeway supermarket private label) $.99; 23 points. Here there was much dissension: One taster found these "thin and watery," another "salty, thin, flat, and without much flavor." But their admirers said the sauce was "dense and dark, with excellent flavor," "vivid," and "delicate and good-tasting." Ranked in the top four places by five tasters.

4 **Libby's California Whole Peeled Tomatoes**, $1.09; 22 points. The majority of our tasters found these at least "acceptable" — seven of nine tasters ranked them in the top five. Most found them salty, but also said that the flavor was "good." "I would definitely use these," said one.

5 * **S & W Premium Sun-Ripened Peeled Tomatoes**, 14.5 ounces; $.89; 18 points. Two first-place votes and one second for this popular West Coast brand. The admirers: "Good, sweet flavor"; "excellent flavor and texture." The detractors: "Thin and bland"; "acidic and strong."

6 **Hunt's Whole Peeled Tomatoes**, $1.09; 18 points. The best-selling canned tomato in the United States had one strong admirer, a veteran sauce-maker who ranked it second (after Redpack), saying that it made "very good, intense sauce." But most tasters had problems with the flavor, finding it "overly salty," "raw and tough," even "tinny."

7 **Muir Glen Organic Whole Peeled Tomatoes**, $1.79; 16 points. A casual survey before the tasting found many people who had switched to this organic entry in recent months; the results, then, were somewhat disillusioning. Three admirers (one ranked it first, one second, one third) raved about the tomatoes: "Beautiful intensity," said one, "full of flavor," another, "very meaty," the third. But they were also called "mushy," "bitter," and "full of salt."

8 **Contadina Whole Peeled Tomatoes**, $1.19; 12 points. Comments ranged from "good, rich flavor" (from a taster who ranked these second) to "raw and stringy, with no flavor." Assessments were generally positive, but not strong enough to translate into good rankings; only three tasters rated it among their top five.

9 **Pastene Italian Peeled Tomatoes**, $2.79, 11 points. One taster put these San Marzano tomatoes first ("great — excellent and fresh tasting") but the next highest votes were for fifth place. Other comments ranged from "lack flavor" and "watery" to "thin," and even "stale-tasting."

10 **Del Monte California Premium Whole Peeled Tomatoes**, 14.5 ounces; $.79; 3 points. The second biggest-selling national brand did not elicit even marginal excitement, with comments such as "blah," "bland," "tasteless," and "do not like."

11 **Progresso Genuine Italian Peeled Tomatoes**, 35 ounces; $2.49; no points. An Italian import that was "too soft," "awful," "bitter," "watery," and "sour."

 6 Hunt's Whole Peeled Tomatoes

 7 Muir Glen Organic Whole Peeled Tomatoes

 8 Contadina Whole Peeled Tomatoes

 9 Pastene Italian Peeled Tomatoes

 10 Del Monte Premium Whole Peeled Tomatoes

 11 Progresso Genuine Italian Peeled Tomatoes

Tomato Sauces for Pasta

These four sauces made from canned tomatoes are easy, cook quickly, and showcase the flavors of the basic ingredients.

~ BY JULIA DELLA CROCE ~

Making sauce with canned tomatoes is a straightforward process, but there are a few techniques to keep in mind. First, remove the excess seeds, which are bitter and have an unappealing texture, by pushing the core of seeds out with your fingers. Next, crush the tomatoes evenly, using a potato masher, your hands, or a fork.

With those preliminaries done, there are two basic approaches to cooking sauces. In the first, crushed tomatoes are quickly cooked in oil, with or without a combination of vegetables and aromatics — any combination of garlic, onion, carrot, celery, parsley, basil, and so on, depending on the season, the dish, and regional and personal preferences. In the second method, the ingredients are combined "*a crudo,*" that is, raw, in a cold pot with no oil or butter. The sauce is simmered until the proper consistency is achieved. After cooking, extra virgin olive oil or butter is added for flavor.

A good tomato sauce can consist of just three ingredients — tomatoes, olive oil or butter, and salt — or it can include aromatics, as well. More elaborate sauces may contain wine, cream, or a variety of meats; essentially, complex sauces are built on the foundations of the simple ones given here. Each ingredient contributes something different: Vegetables add body and flavor; tomato paste concentrates the flavor (but too much imparts a sharp, even bitter taste; a good rule of thumb is to use no more than three tablespoons of paste to two and one-half cups of tomatoes). Butter or cream gives sweetness and smoothness; wine deepens the flavor.

How long to cook a sauce is another important consideration. Only tomato sauce that includes meat should undergo long, gentle simmering, which is necessary to tenderize the meat and to blend flavors. But nonmeat tomato sauces, such as the ones I offer here, are best when cooked relatively quickly, to retain the fresh, fruity flavor of the tomatoes. In general, cooking times should be no longer than are necessary to evaporate excess liquid; quick sauces can be made in about twenty to forty-five minutes.

Finally, there is the question of texture: some Italians strain their sauces, using a food mill to create a smooth, uniform consistency; others do not. Whether you strain is usually a matter of personal preference.

QUICK-COOKED TOMATOES WITH OLIVE OIL
Makes 3 cups
You can substitute one small minced onion for the garlic, if you like. This is a chunky sauce.

- 4 large cloves garlic, bruised
- 6 tablespoons olive oil, plus extra for drizzling
- 2 cans (28 ounces each) tomatoes, juice reserved for another use, tomatoes seeded then crushed
  Salt

In a large saucepan, warm garlic in oil over low heat until golden. Add tomatoes and salt to taste; simmer to blend flavors, about 15 minutes. Remove garlic, if you like; toss sauce with pasta and drizzle with additional olive oil.

ALL-PURPOSE TOMATO SAUCE
Makes about 2 cups
This chunky, rustic, and pungent sauce goes well with dried pasta as well as with fresh gnocchi and ravioli.

- 1 large clove garlic, minced
- 3 tablespoons olive oil
- 2 tablespoons tomato paste
- 1 can (28 ounces) tomatoes, juice reserved, tomatoes seeded then crushed
  Salt and ground black pepper
- 2–3 fresh basil leaves, shredded (or ½ teaspoon dried)

In a large saucepan, warm garlic in 2 tablespoons oil over low heat until soft but not colored. Stir in tomato paste, then the tomatoes and their liquid. Simmer, uncovered, until sauce coats the back of a spoon, about 25 minutes. Season to taste with salt and pepper; before serving, stir in basil and remaining 1 tablespoon oil.

AROMATIC TOMATO SAUCE
Makes 2½ cups
This elegant, fragrant sauce is suitable for fresh, dried, or stuffed pasta. If you do not have a food mill, the sauce can be pureed in a food processor, although the result will be less refined.

- 4 tablespoons butter
- 1 small white or red onion, minced
- 1 medium carrot, peeled and minced
- 1 medium celery stalk, minced
- 3 tablespoons tomato paste
- 1 can (28 ounces) tomatoes, juice reserved, tomatoes seeded then crushed
- ¼ cup dry red wine
  Salt and ground black pepper

Heat 3 tablespoons butter in a large saucepan. Add onion, carrot, and celery; sauté gently until softened, but not browned, about 10 minutes. Stir in tomato paste, then tomatoes and juice and wine. Simmer, partially covered, and stir frequently, until thickened to sauce consistency, about 45 minutes. Puree by passing through a food mill. Return to simmer; season to taste with salt and pepper; before serving, stir in remaining butter.

STEWED TOMATO SAUCE WITH BASIL AND OLIVE OIL
Makes about 3 cups
In this recipe, tomatoes are simmered slowly without garlic, onion, or oil to keep intact their sweet, clear flavor. If tomatoes in puree are unavailable, strain tomatoes and add back only one cup of liquid. The full strength of the olive oil comes through in this sauce, since it's added just before serving. If you do not have a food mill, you can puree this sauce in a food processor, as long as you carefully seed the tomatoes before cooking them.

- 2 cans (28 ounces each) tomatoes in puree, puree reserved, tomatoes seeded then crushed
- 1 medium carrot, peeled and minced
  Salt and ground black pepper
- 3 tablespoons olive oil
- 2 tablespoons minced fresh basil or mint leaves

Put tomatoes, puree, and carrot in a large saucepan; bring to simmer; continue to simmer, partially covered, and stir occasionally, until thickened slightly, about 45 minutes. Puree tomato sauce by passing through a food mill. Return to simmer; season with salt and pepper to taste. Before serving, stir in olive oil and basil. ■

Julia della Croce is the author of *Pasta Classica* (Chronicle, 1987) and *Antipasti* (Chronicle, 1993).

PHOTOGRAPH BY ERIC ROTH

Slicing through Knife Myths

Two expensive German knives take top honors, but an inexpensive Swiss blade outdices the other pricey entries.

∼ BY JACK BISHOP ∼

Ask a group of professional chefs to name the most essential piece of kitchen equipment and most will reply "a good knife." For home cooks, quality knives are just as important.

So what exactly separates a good knife from an inferior one? Is an expensive, hand-crafted knife always better than one made by a machine? And why on earth does a single knife sometimes cost close to one hundred dollars?

To answer these questions we enlisted the services of seven restaurant chefs whose livelihood depends on good knives (*see* "The Testers," page 28). We asked them each to evaluate six popular brands of eight-inch chef's knives (the standard size of the most versatile piece of cutlery). Each chef spent more than a month working with the knives, conducting specific tests we had designed as well as routine kitchen chores. A five-page evaluation form was completed for each knife, detailing its strengths and weaknesses. By the end of the test, we had accumulated 150 pages of raw data, judging knives on everything from comfort to their ability to peel a rutabaga. (For specific results, *see* "Rating Chef's Knives," page 29.)

The conclusions were quite clear. The German standard-bearers, Henckels and Wüsthof, outperformed the other knives on everything from design to sharpness. Surprisingly, however, two expensive forged knives (one French, the other American) did not fare so well. All four knives have suggested retail prices between eighty and eighty-five dollars. The conclusion: High cost does not guarantee premium performance.

Just as intriguing were the rankings of the two inexpensive machine-made knives in the group. The entry from Chicago Cutlery, a leading American company, was ranked last by the panel of chefs. However, the Forschner by Victorinox, the makers of Swiss Army knives, came in third. With a suggested retail price of twenty-four dollars (we found it discounted for even less; *see* Sources and Resources, page 32), this knife represents a tremendous value and is the best choice for cooks on a budget.

Knife Construction

To understand these surprising results — who would have thought that an inexpensive machine-made knife would outscore an expensive handmade blade — it helps to know something about how knives are constructed.

The first pieces of cutlery were made about four thousand years ago with the discovery that iron ore could be melted and shaped into tools. The creation of steel, a combination of 80 percent iron with 20 percent other elements, led to the development of carbon steel knives — the standard for three thousand years. Although this kind of steel takes and holds an edge easily, it also stains and rusts. Something as simple as cutting an acidic tomato or living along the salt-air coast can corrode carbon steel, making it a high-maintenance material.

In this century, new alloys have given cooks better options. Stainless steel, made with at least 4 percent chromium and/or nickel, will never rust. Used for many cheap knives, stainless steel is also very difficult to sharpen. The compromise between durable but dull stainless steel and sharp but corrosive carbon steel is something called high carbon stainless steel. Used by most premium knife manufacturers, including all six brands we tested, this blend (the exact formula varies from company to company) combines sharpness with durability.

Until recently, all knives were hot drop forged — that is, the steel was heated to two thousand degrees, dropped into a mold, given four or five shots with a hammer, and then tempered (cooled and heated several times to build strength). At some factories this process re-

DULL vs. SHARP

With use, a knife blade flattens out and develops nicks and burrs.

Steeling (see page 28) removes burrs and nicks and restores the knife's true edge.

GETTING A GOOD GRIP

Richard Czack, author of *The Professional Chef's Knife* (Van Nostrand-Reinhold, 1978) states, "There is no such thing as the best way to hold a knife." There are, however, two standard knife grips used by most pro fessionals. The handle grip (far right) is often favored by cooks with smaller hands. Czack notes that cooks using this grip are less likely to build up calluses on their hands. A blade grip (below) is often used by cooks with larger hands who find it difficult to fit four fingers under the handle. This grip requires a bit more strength in the wrists and fingers and, because the hand is moved slightly forward, can give the suggestion of more control over the blade.

In the handle grip, all four fingers are wrapped around the handle and the thumb is placed on the bolster.

 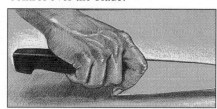

For the blade grip, hold the heel of the blade between the thumb and index finger, and wrap the remaining three fingers around the handle.

quires as many as one hundred separate steps, many of them done by hand, accounting for the high cost of forged knives. Among those tested, the Wüsthof, Chef's Choice, and Sabatier are fully forged.

A second manufacturing process feeds long sheets of steel through a press that punches out knife after knife, much like a cookie cutter cutting dough. Called stamped blades, these knives require some hand finishing but are much cheaper to produce, as a machine does most of the work. Both the Forschner and Chicago Cutlery knives have stamped blades.

Henckels uses a new patented process that is neither forging nor stamping. It takes three pieces of steel — one each for the blade, bolster (between blade and handle), and tang (the portion of the knife that extends into the handle) — especially designed for each part of the knife. The pieces are then fused together. Henckels says this process allows them to use the perfect steel for each section of the knife as opposed to using a compromise material that will work for all three parts.

While competitors have argued that this process (which relies on a stamped blade) is inferior to traditional hot drop forging, our testers certainly did not detect a difference. Taken with the strong performance of the stamped Forschner blade, we conclude that forged knives are not necessarily better than well-made stamped knives — virtual heresy in the parochial knife world.

A New Design for Handles

Once the knife has been either forged or stamped, the handle must be attached and the blade must be sharpened. Until 1976, two handles — either wood or a plastic and wood blend — were attached to the back of the knife with rivets. In that year, Henckels introduced a line of knives with a single piece of molded plastic as the handle. Because these new knives don't have any grooves or rivets that can trap bacteria, they are generally preferred in professional kitchens and are enjoying increased sales to consumers because the handles provide a better grip. In fact, they now account for more than half of all knife sales. For this reason, we chose to test only knives with molded handles.

The weight of the handle is influenced by the tang. Knives with a full tang — the Henckels, Wüsthof, Chef's Choice, and Sabatier models we tested — are generally considered the best, and are usually heavier than knives with a half or partial tang. However, the Forschner does not have a full tang and we could not detect any diminishment in quality, other than to point out that the knife is about two ounces lighter than most of the knives with a full tang.

Again, our tests shattered a knife myth. While a full tang may be preferable (many cheap knives are made with partial tangs that just barely secure the blade to the handle), it is not essential so long as the knife is as well constructed as the Forschner. ■

STEELING MADE SIMPLE

Unpack a knife from the factory and the edge should be razor sharp. However, as soon as you begin to cut, dice, or chop, the edge begins to dull. The force of repeated cutting bends microscopic pieces of the blade to either side. Instead of a thin, sharp edge, the knife edge has thickened and cuts more slowly and with more effort.

A sharpening steel — a bit of a misnomer since the steel "corrects" or "trues" the edge but does not really sharpen it — can return the blade to its original condition by pulling off burrs and smoothing the edge. In addition, metallic sharpening steels are magnetized so as to realign the molecules of the blade as you work. During normal use, the structure of steel can deteriorate. A few strokes at the correct angle on a magnetized steel will remedy this.

Despite what many cooks believe, proper steeling requires very little pressure. Listen to the steel as you work. A harsh rasping noise indicates that too much pressure is being applied. A quiet ring is a sign that a proper featherlike stroke is being used. Also, do not bang the knife against the finger guard since this can damage the edge. Perhaps most important is the angle between the blade and steel — twenty degrees is perfect.

Although steeling can be accomplished in any number of positions, the method described below makes it particularly easy to maintain the proper angle and is also quite safe since the blade is not moving toward either your hands or body.

1. Hold the steel perpendicular to a cutting board with the metal end resting on the board. Place the heel of the blade against the top of the steel and point the tip slightly upward. Hold the blade at a twenty-degree angle away from the steel.

2. Begin sliding the blade toward the counter. Maintain a light pressure and a twenty-degree angle. As the knife glides down the steel, gradually pull the back of knife toward your body so that the middle of the blade is in contact with the middle of the steel.

3. Finish the motion by passing the tip of the blade over the bottom of the steel. Repeat the motion on the other side of the steel with the other side of the blade at a twenty-degree angle. Four or five strokes on each side of the blade (a total of eight or ten alternating passes) should true the edge. When finished, wipe the steel with a cloth dipped in vinegar to remove any invisible metal shavings that may have accumulated.

THE TESTERS

We asked five restaurants to help us with this article. In some kitchens, evaluating the knives became a collaborative effort and in others it was a solo operation. Each restaurant returned one set of scored evaluations. Thanks to the following chefs who devoted much time and effort.

Brian Holleman and Jose Martinez, night and day chefs at Morrison-Clark in Washington, D.C., collaborated on the knife tests and gave Henckels their top rating. Although Jose has shied away from pricey knives in the past, he says "I'll be buying better knives now that I've seen how they make my work easier."

Andy Husbands, chef at East Coast Grill in Cambridge, Massachusetts, preferred the Henckels knife — "it performs with the greatest of ease" — but thought the Wüsthof was "a close second."

Keith Mahoney and Marlene Minor, sous chef and kitchen manager at Criolla's in Grayton Beach, Florida, gave Henckels the nod in their testing. Despite the long hours of work, they kept their sense of humor. Writing about the oh-so-dull Biocurve, they said, "Steeling is a waste of time. It's like waxing a Ford Pinto."

Thierry Raymond, executive chef at Restaurant Jean-Louis in Greenwich, Connecticut, gave Wüsthof his top ranking, followed by Sabatier. A native of France, he was the only chef to show much allegiance to the Gallic knife.

Susan Wu, executive chef at Chinois East/West in Sacramento, California, was wowed by the Wüsthof knife. "It feels as natural as holding a pen in my hand."

ILLUSTRATIONS BY ALAN WITSCHONKE

GERMAN KNIVES STEAL FIRST PLACE, WHILE AN INEXPENSIVE BLADE SLICES ITS WAY TO THIRD.

In order to evaluate chef's knives, we asked chefs at five top restaurants to use six brands for over a month during their prep work. We chose knives with eight-inch blades and molded handles. Note that the scores for Henckels and Wüsthof are almost identical and both can be considered the winners of this test. As for a best buy, the Forschner is the hands-down favorite for cooks on a tight budget. Prices are suggested retail and will vary greatly. (*See* Sources and Resources, page 32, for specific discount outlets.) The total score is the sum of the testers' rankings, each of whom graded the knives on a scale from one to ten.

CHEF'S KNIVES IN ORDER OF PREFERENCE

J. A. Henckels Four Star 31071-200

Slices through tough stuff "like butter."

Score: 44.5 points
Price: $85
Weight: 7.75 ounces
Handle: Small, light handle gets high marks. Most chefs liked smooth surface material — "feels terrific," "secure," and "not slippery when wet." All testers praised both comfort and fit.
Blade: Slightly curved blade was sharp out of the box but "lost edge quickly." Two chefs complained about need for "frequent light steeling." Fairly straight shape is good for rocking and deemed "very practical."
Peeling a rutabaga: Light pressure cuts through rind and fibrous center.
Mincing an onion: "Glides through onion with ease." "Great for chopping because blade is so thin."
Slicing a tomato: Sharp tip is good for piercing skin on ripe fruit. "Does good work with a tomato."
Mincing parsley: Raves for chopping such as "knife performs this task with the greatest of ease." High contact with board due to relatively straight blade.
Comments: Design, construction, and the comfortable handle earned accolades. Two chefs complained that blade dulls rather easily and requires frequent steeling.

Wüsthof-Trident Grand Prix 4587

"Blazes through onions so fast I hardly had time to cry."

Score: 44 points
Price: $80
Weight: 9.75 ounces
Handle: "Sturdy, thick handle" drew mostly positive comments, "exceptionally balanced" and "extremely comfortably," although testers were divided about the rough, pebbled surface. Comments ranged from "too slick" to "a definite plus when wet or greasy."
Blade: Moderately curved blade was "sharp enough to split hairs" when unpacked. Kept edge during tests and was easy to realign on steel. "Blade is perfect for all tasks."

Peeling a rutabaga: Heavy weight of knife "moves it pretty easily through hard vegetables," requiring "less force than other knives."
Mincing an onion: One chef sings this knife's praises: "Blazes through onion so fast I hardly had time to cry."
Slicing a tomato: One chef rated Wüsthof the top knife for this job. Thin tip is best part of blade for piercing skin.
Mincing parsley: Rocks well for mincing herbs with "good contact" on cutting surface.
Comments: "Thin, razor-sharp blade" earned highest praise, with comments like "perfect for all tasks." Chefs liked "great weight," although a few felt the textured grip came in second to the smooth Henckels handle.

Forschner (Victorinox) Fibrox 830-8

Some design flaws, but it makes the cut at a fraction of the price.

Score: 37.5 points
Price: $24
Weight: 7.25 ounces
Handle: Light, textured handle deemed generally comfortable, although a few chefs complained about its thinness. Near universal concern expressed about small gaps between handle and blade where bacteria could accumulate.
Blade: Sharp when unpacked and kept its edge with minimal steeling. No bolster or finger guard and "it needs one" to prevent knuckle cuts.
Peeling a rutabaga: Thin blade does job with "average force."
Mincing an onion: Thin blade minces without mashing.
Slicing a tomato: High praise, although chefs say that ripe tomatoes may require a gentle stroking motion.
Mincing parsley: High marks, with comments such as "excellent for chopping" and "does not mash leaves."
Comments: Light, dependable knife gets kudos for low cost and high performance. Remarking on its flimsy appearance, one chef wrote, "I learned you cannot judge a knife strictly by looks." Another noted, "I had so much faith in this knife I even filleted a whole fifteen-pound salmon with it." Gaps between handle and blade are a potential problem — as is the lack of a blade guard — so wash thoroughly and work with care.

Chef's Choice Trizor Professional 10X

A matter of taste: some loved it, others hated it.

Score: 36.5 points
Price: $85
Weight: 10.25 ounces
Handle: Two chefs felt knife was "handle heavy," while three others called it "solid" and "secure." Slightly raised texture called "a plus" when wet or greasy, but several testers felt handle was too thin to achieve a proper grip. One even suggested wrapping tape around handle to increase its width.
Blade: "Razor sharp when unpacked" and edge held up "as well or better than most knives." "Highly curved" edge deemed good for rocking motion by most but not all testers.
Peeling a rutabaga: Handle weight and sharp cutting edge are advantages for strenuous tasks, although curved blade drew some criticism.
Mincing an onion: Some chefs felt curvature of blade made this task more difficult, while others focused on the ability of the very sharp blade to mince without bruising.
Slicing a tomato: Sharpness of blade won raves for piercing and slicing.
Mincing parsley: Three chefs were able to achieve a good rocking motion, while two felt "too little of the blade was on the board at one time."
Comments: Everyone agreed this knife is sharp. Testers either loved or hated the curved blade and heavy handle, which was downgraded by two chefs with small hands.

Cuisine de France Commercial Sabatier 80312

Well made, but poorly designed.

Score: 26.5 points
Price: $84
Weight: 9 ounces
Handle: Heavy handle that "seems out of balance with blade" and causes "cramping" during long work periods. Some liked the smooth material, others felt it became slippery.
Blade: Relatively straight, narrow blade was the cause for much criticism. "Too little room" between bottom edge of blade and handle. "My knuckles touch

the board before the blade does." Also reports of a dull factory edge.
Peeling a rutabaga: Narrow, dull blade posed challengess. Two chefs appreciated the heavy handle.
Mincing an onion: Some bruising and mashing reported, although two chefs reported excellent results.
Slicing a tomato: Again, some positive remarks, but several complaints about a dull edge that was difficult to sharpen.
Mincing parsley: Straight blade doesn't rock, making this task "a pain." More "mashing of herbs" than with other knives.
Comments: Blade shape drew generally negative reviews. "Because of the fairly straight shape I feel like I'm doing more work during certain tasks." Some chefs were more positive: "One of my favorites." Most, however, were disappointed. "High-quality construction," but "needs a redesign."

Chicago Cutlery Commercial Quality Biocurve BR42L

It slices, it dices — not!

Score: 14 points
Price: $20
Weight: 8 ounces
Handle: Ergonomically designed curved handle with textured finish is uncomfortable. "I would have to build up small calluses on my thumb and forefinger if I wanted to use this knife all the time." More succinctly, "This biocurve thing is bogus."
Blade: Dull blade does not take or hold an edge well. "Good for grunt chopping" but little else. Unlike other blades, tip is quite thick and hard to sharpen. "Steeling is a waste of time. It's like waxing a Ford Pinto."
Peeling a rutabaga: Light knife is trouble on tough jobs.
Mincing an onion: Some chefs reported that thick blade bruises onions.
Slicing a tomato: Again, dull blade caused setbacks. "An effort just to pierce the skin."
Mincing parsley: Three chefs were unable to achieve a good rocking motion.
Comments: "Poor design," "cheap construction," and "mediocre performance" were all criticisms. "One of my worst knife experiences during fifteen years of restaurant work." "No self-respecting cook would like this knife."

BEST WINE

Rating the Bargains of Spain

Red Riojas are often pleasant but undistinguished; we found one that drew almost unanimous raves.

∽ BY MARK BITTMAN ∽

Winemaking is as old a craft in the Rioja region of Spain as it is in France. But Rioja's style changed dramatically about one hundred years ago, when the vines in Bordeaux were struck by the destructive phylloxera virus, inspiring French producers to head to Rioja, a couple hundred miles south.

As a result, extremely long wood-aging — several years or more — became standard in Rioja. When used for tempranillo, the dominant grape featured in all Rioja reds, this treatment can produce big, soft wines that complement the same kinds of foods as well-aged wine from Bordeaux, which typically spends less time in wood and more in the bottle. This makes many Riojas quite friendly: you walk into a wine store, pick a bottle of five- or six-year old Rioja off the shelf, take it home, and often encounter a soft, pleasant wine. Moreover, even very good Rioja rarely costs more than fifteen dollars a bottle, and it doesn't take much luck to find a quite decent one for seven or eight dollars, no mean feat with French wine. Thus, Rioja wines are seen as a less expensive but equally full-bodied alternative to Bordeaux.

But, as shown in our tasting of a variety of favorably priced, widely available Rioja wines, there is more than one style of wine called Rioja. One school accentuates the region's "traditional values" of using extended aging in oak barrels to produce approachable, relatively inexpensive wines. It should be emphasized, however, that this strategy works only when the wine is both fruity and well-made — inferior wines display a vegetal oaken quality that few people really like.

A second school is producing a lighter, almost Beaujolais-like product, by minimizing the time spent in wood. We only encountered a couple examples of this type of Rioja in our tasting, and neither of them did very well.

The third and final group of Rioja producers are decreasing wood-aging times and increasing time spent in the bottle. The best of these, including our winner, are using expensive single-vineyard grapes and French oak, generally considered superior to less expensive barrels from the United States. Although production details were not available, it's likely that our top five wines were made this way; all were described as

fruity *and* oaken, a pleasant combination for red wines that will be served with food.

Wines were tasted blind by a panel composed of both wine professionals and amateur wine-lovers. Although we usually designate a best buy, it seemed superfluous in this instance: most of the wines were quite reasonably priced (some of the best cost ten dollars and under), and the best — the Contino Reserva — sells for just fifteen dollars a bottle. At this tasting, which was conducted at Meson Galicia, a Spanish restaurant in Norwalk, Connecticut, those wines finishing in ninth through fourteenth places garnered more negative than positive comments. ∎

BLIND TASTING RESULTS

Wines are listed in order of preference (an asterisk next to a wine indicates that it tied with that immediately below it). In the judging, seven points were awarded for each first-place vote; six for second; five for third; four for fourth; and so on. The wines were purchased in the Northeast; prices will vary somewhat.

1. **1986 Contino Reserva (38 points), $15.** The comments you'd expect about a crowd-pleasing Rioja: "Soft and full-bodied," "pleasant," "excellent texture," "wonderful fruit complemented by oak." Three first-place votes; rated in the top five by seven out of ten tasters.

2. **1982 Campo Viejo Marquis de Villamagna (27 points), $20.** Although this wine garnered no first-place votes, six tasters ranked it among their top five. Comments: "Weak nose but smooth, full flavor"; "fruity with real presence."Campo Viejo is the largest producer of Rioja, and this is one of their best wines, from a very good vintage.

3. **1990 Marquis de Murietta Ygay (25 points), $13.** From a well-known, century-old producer once regarded as Rioja's best, this wine was declared "rich and concentrated" and "high-quality stuff."

4. ***1988 Marquis de Riscal Reserva (24 points), $10.** Though young-tasting, this wine garnered two first-place votes ("rich, full, and lovely — easily the best"), but only a smattering of others. Some found it "a bit tannic" or "slightly stinky."

5. **1988 Marquis de Murietta Ygay Reserva (24 points), $16.** "Nice fruity wine," said one taster; another called it "lively." Again, found "too tannic" by some.

6. **1988 Montecillo Vina Cumbrero (21 points), $7.** Montecillo consistently prices its wines lower than the competition. (Although we did not choose a best buy from this tasting, at $7 this wine must be considered a bargain.) Its admirers found it "Burgundian," its detractors, "muddy."

7. **1987 Viña Mayor Peñascal Tudela de Duero (20 points), $6.** This wine, along with the Mauro (*see* below), is from a region just west of Rioja that

also vinifies the tempranillo grape. Three third-place votes: "Soft, with good mouth-feel but not enough fruit" is the comment that sums it up. Note price.

8. ***1989 Viñas de Gain (19 points), $11.** This wine had "too much tannin" for most of the tasters. Two of the professionals liked it a great deal, however: "Complex, not over-oaked, tannic but young — good," wrote one. A well-made Rioja that should do better with age.

9. **1981 Sierra Cantabria Reserva (19 points), $13.** This heavily oaked wine, from what may have been the best vintage of the decade, received two first-place votes ("fresh, well-made, lively") and little else. Most tasters found it "too light." "Where's the fruit?" asked one.

10. **1989 Mauro Tudelo de Duero Vallodolid (15 points), $15.** A wine of great reputation that received one first-place vote ("rich, wonderful, and berry-like"). But many tasters felt that it "lacked complexity" or was "thin."

11. **1989 Muga Reserva (13 points), $13.** Another surprisingly poor showing from a good estate. Typical comments: "Mushroomy," "lightweight," and "good, but not impressive."

12. **1987 Conde de Valdemar Reserva (11 points), $12.** Some tasters found this light wine "soft" or "pleasant." Others called it "garbage-y."

13. ***1989 Marquis de Caceres (8 points), $8.** From a producer that is currently better known for its white wines. "Undistinguished," wrote one taster; "no interest," another.

14. **1986 Viña Tondonia (8 points), $12.** Occasionally, Tondonia is a stunning wine; this was not one of those occasions.

BOOK
REVIEWS

The Heart of Sicily
Anna Tasca Lanza
Potter, $40

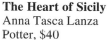hat do you call a cookbook with warm, evocative prose, breathtaking photography, and unusual, authentic recipes? A winner — and that's the term for Anna Tasca Lanza's story of Regaleali, her family's Sicilian estate. Through food, *The Heart of Sicily* chronicles the kind of life most of us can only dream of — one in which sustenance is based on beautiful land, but one without most of the hardships inevitably borne by true farmers.

In working my way through *The Heart of Sicily,* I felt a smidgen of envy along with a fair amount of gratitude — this book made me smile, and I am generally happy that Lanza decided to share her life with us. Without her, I would have to look far and wide to find Potatoes, Pizza Style (in which mashed potatoes serve as the crust), Risotto with Citrus Fruit, and the incomparably delicious Chickpea Chips, which I had tasted but never made. There are simpler, more common recipes here, too, such as Chicken with Tomatoes, Eggplant Caponata, and Blancmange (or *biancomangiare*).

But the overall effect is of a very exotic, foreign cuisine and an exotic, beautiful life, one led in a style that is for all intents and purposes disappearing — even the very rich cannot or will not live this way in the twenty-first century. Making sun-dried tomatoes by actually drying tomatoes in the sun may seem strange enough, but this is nothing compared to Lanza's description of making *estratto di pomodoro,* translated here as sun-dried tomato extract — in which two tons of fresh sauce are dried in the sun to form two hundred pounds of intense paste.

Tomato essence; it would sell for the price of truffles, I'd guess. Will you ever make it? Unlikely. On the other hand, you may make Seasoned Black Olives, Grapefruit Marmalade, or Pasta with Tuna; each of these recipes worked well, and each was delicious.

Judged strictly as a cookbook, *The Heart of Sicily* is a qualified success (and probably not as useful as a couple of the less magnificent Sicilian cookbooks that have appeared recently). It was never intended as a daily kitchen companion, and many recipes are tossed off loosely, as in, "For Roast Chicken with Orange, we put the chicken into the pan with one thickly sliced onion, the juice of two or three oranges, half a cup of wine, and rosemary, salt, and pepper to taste and roast it in a hot oven, basting often." But its invaluable glimpse into Sicilian life and cuisine more than compensates for the occasionally obscure references.

—*Mark Bittman*

Red Hot Peppers
Jean Andrews
Macmillan, $25

This book, from the author of the pioneering *Peppers, the Domesticated Capsicum* (University of Texas Press, 1984) is divided into two major parts: information about chile peppers and recipes that use the peppers. Many of the recipes are from some of America's best-known hot-cooking chefs, but a significant portion are the author's own creations. I found the latter relatively mild and somewhat old-fashioned; nevertheless, they were so satisfying that I made three of them again.

New World Pie, for example, is a rich chocolate-coffee confection with just enough ancho chile to add a beguiling trace of heat, yet subtle enough that a guest couldn't quite put a finger on the unusual taste. Andrews's version of Khatta Aloo, on the other hand, is an Indian-inspired potato dish with enough heat to send you to the antidote cupboard, and Frijol Soup is a tasty if rather basic bean soup pleasantly spiced with chiles de arbol.

But the appealing and concise collection of recipes is not the most compelling reason to buy this book. That honor goes to the wealth of facts and lore about chile peppers that Andrews has marshaled, including botanical information; advice on choosing, storing, and peeling; illustrated descriptions of seventeen individual peppers; theories about why people like them; the history of their spread from the Americas through the rest of the world; and — perhaps most fascinating — assessments of their influence not only on food, but on cuisine as part of culture.

In this department Andrews shines, as she deftly assesses, within the context of European imperialism, class stratification, religion, and gender roles, such questions as "Why did chiles become more popular in some countries than others?" I can't think of a better example of a book that, without being boringly pedantic, demonstrates how food provides not only pleasing sensory experiences, but also a revealing window on social history and behavior. Who would have thought a little chile pepper could tell so much?

—*John Willoughby*

Soup Suppers
Arthur Schwartz
HarperPerennial, $15

There should be more cookbook authors like Arthur Schwartz. He reviews restaurants in New York City, so he sees the development of nearly every cooking trend; he hosts a daily radio talk show completely devoted to food, which reinforces his current knowledge; and he loves to cook.

Soup Suppers offers us a premium collection of simple, fairly low-fat, delicious soups. Some are vegetarian, some are not; few contain cream. Most are high-flavor without being either complicated (few begin with stock) or overwhelmingly spicy. I made Russian Sweet and Sour Cabbage Soup with beef, tomatoes, and onion that would have made my grandmother cry with joy; Potato, Onion, and Tomato Soup that was far greater than the sum of its parts; Moroccan Harira with Chickpeas, Beans, and Lentils, thickened with rice and spiced — quite subtly — with saffron; and Iota, a soup of sauerkraut, beans, bacon, barley, and potato, which was a tremendous hit with my family, kids included.

The timing here, especially in those soups that contain beans, is necessarily imprecise, but all of Schwartz's recipes work well, and his sense of seasoning is on the money: I made three soups in one day without using a clove of garlic, and thought something must be wrong. But the flavor of each was full and complex.

In short, this is a fine collection of soup recipes, few of which I have seen elsewhere. I could complain about the dearth of Asian soups but, again, *Soup Suppers* is a bowlful of the soup world, not the entire pot. It contains about one hundred recipes for soup, along with a smattering of the author's favorite dishes to complete soup-based meals — salads, breads, and desserts. This is a worthwhile addition to your cookbook shelf, one that will stay current for some time. ∎

—*Mark Bittman*

SOURCES
AND RESOURCES

CHEF'S KNIVES AT A DISCOUNT
We found two excellent discount sources for knives while researching the testing article (*see* page 27). Sur La Table (84 Pine Street, Pike Place Farmers' Market, Seattle, WA 98101; 800-243-0852) sells the top-rated Henckels Four Star 31071-200 for $65.60, a substantial savings over the suggested retail price of $85.00. Sur La Table also carries the Chef's Choice Trizor Professional 10X for $85.00. One of the most complete selections of cutlery comes from Professional Cutlery Direct (170 Boston Post Road, Suite 135, Madison, CT 06443; 800-859-6994), a company that sells to consumers at professional prices. The Wüsthof-Trident Grand Prix 4587, which ordinarily retails for about $80.00, is available for just $64.00 through PCD. Their catalog, which also contains an informative newsletter, carries the Cuisine de France Commercial Sabatier 80312 for $67.00 as compared to the suggested retail price of $84.00. At press time the company was running a special on this knife for just $49.00. PCD also carries the best buy in our testing, the Forschner (Victorinox) Fibrox 830-8 for $20.88, reduced from the suggested retail price of $24.00. The catalog also features steels, sharpening stones, knife blocks, and the best book we've seen on cutlery use, *The Professional Chef's Knife* by Richard Czack. This book costs $22.95 and is worth every penny.

SWEDISH PANCAKE PAN
In Sweden, pancakes are made in a heavy cast-iron pan called a plättar. A plättar can be used to make other thin pancakes, such as blini, and cooks may find it handy for frying four eggs at a time. A sturdy plättar is available from A Cook's Wares (211 37th Street, Beaver Falls, PA 15010; 412-846-9490) for $45.

EASTER BREAD INGREDIENTS
The Italian gubana (*see* page 12) requires a couple of ingredients that can be easily ordered by mail if you cannot find a local source. King Arthur Flour Baker's Catalogue (P.O. Box 876, Norwich, VT 05055; 800-827-6836) carries a variety of candied fruits imported from Australia, including candied orange peel. A 3.5-ounce bag costs $1.95. Another good option for intense orange flavor is Boyajian orange oil, available at Williams-Sonoma stores nationwide or from the catalog by calling 800-541-2233. The gubana recipe also calls for coarse turbinado sugar. Often sold in supermarkets as "raw sugar," these tan crystals don't melt as quickly as regular granulated sugar. A Cook's Wares (*see* above) sells a one-pound bag of turbinado sugar for $2.70.

EXOTIC TEAS BY MAIL
The Republic of Tea (2165 East Francisco Boulevard, Suite E, San Rafael, CA 94901; 800-354-5530) offers a large selection of full leaf loose teas and herbs. The attractive color catalog features dozens of mainstream and exotic items, from Earl Greyer (black tea leaves with natural oil of bergamot) to Cinnamon Plum (a blend of black tea leaves, spices, fruit, and blossoms) and Sky Between the Branches (a rare green tea from China known for its delicate chestnut flavor). Teas are sold in colorful 3.5-ounce canisters (enough to brew 60 cups) that cost between $8 and $20, depending on the variety. The catalog also offers a number of gift packs and samplers as well as a good selection of pots and brewing equipment.

METAL DOUGH SCRAPERS
A metal dough scraper (also called a bench knife) is the best tool for handling sticky dough. Bridge Kitchenware (214 E. 52nd Street, New York, NY 10022; 800-274-3435) sells two bench knives. The model with a wooden handle and stainless-steel blade costs $8.95; a dough scraper with a white plastic handle that is dishwasher safe also costs $8.95.

ITALIAN PANCETTA
Pancetta, unsmoked Italian bacon, is available at most Italian delicatessens or specialty stores. Many butchers and supermarkets, especially in areas with large Italian-American populations, also carry this item. If you have trouble locating this ham product, you can order pancetta from Balducci's, the leading New York gourmet store. The cost is $7.99 per pound. There is no minimum on orders, but it's a good idea to order several pounds to compensate for the cost of overnight shipping. For more information, contact the store's mail-order division at 800-225-3822.

BUTCHER TWINE
When tying a leg of lamb (*see* page 8) or any roast, butcher twine made from white linen is the best choice because it won't brown or burn in the oven. Williams-Sonoma sells a ninety-two-yard spool that comes in a handy clear plastic dispenser with a built-in cutter for $6. Visit their store or call their catalog (800-541-2233) to order this item.

MESH ROASTING RACK
We found that roasting a leg of lamb on a flat rack prevents the underside from overcooking on the hot pan surface (*see* page 8). A mesh rack is the best candidate to support a heavy roast. The one we like is actually designed for icing cakes and candies. This icing grate has a tightly set, cross-woven mesh as well as three sturdy metal supports with six half-inch-high legs. We also use this rack to cool baked goods. Unlike flimsy cooling racks, the mesh supports heavy pans and is tight enough to prevent small candies from slipping through. Bridge Kitchenware (*see* above) carries an excellent icing grate in three sizes. For roasting lamb, we recommend the medium-sized rack that measures ten and one-quarter by eighteen inches and costs $14.95.

PREMIUM POTATOES
New Penny Farm (P.O. Box 448, Presque Isle, ME 04769; 800-827-7551) in northern Maine grows seventeen varieties of potatoes that can be shipped in five-, ten-, or twenty-pound bags. The farm plants a number of yellow potatoes (including popular Yukon Gold and tiny Bintjes which are native to Holland) as well as a variety of low-, medium-, and high-starch tubers for specific culinary uses. High-starch potatoes, like Green Mountain and Carola, are best for mashing: low-starch varieties such as Katahdin and Red Cloud (with a red skin), are best for soups and salads. A five-pound bag of any variety costs $19.50 plus $2.00 for shipping west of the Mississippi. Ten-pound bags cost $24.50 plus $3.00 for shipping out West; twenty-pound bags are priced at $34.50 plus $5.00 for shipping to Western addresses. New Penny Farm also packages samplers such as all-Maine potatoes, four yellow varieties, and a high-starch assortment.

BRITISH SWEETENERS
When the British make scones they often use one of two English sweeteners instead of sugar or honey. Golden syrup is a thick, pure cane syrup that looks like honey (it's amber in color) but has a much stronger flavor, reminiscent of caramelized sugar. Black treacle is comparable to the darkest American molasses and is still called for by name in many British cookbooks. Both products have been made for more than a century by a company called Lyle's. The King Arthur Flour Baker's Catalogue (*see* above) carries these liquid sweeteners that come packed in handsome sixteen-ounce tins. Lyle's Golden Syrup costs $4.95; Lyle's Black Treacle is $5.95.

DIGITAL THERMOMETER
If you find reading tiny lines on a dial a chore, you might be interested in a new digital pocket thermometer from Taylor, the leading manufacturer of culinary thermometers. The dial is about one and one-quarter inches across and has a large readout that displays any temperature between 14 degrees and 230 degrees to the nearest tenth. The four-inch stainless-steel stem slides easily into meat or poultry. It also can take the temperature of warm water used for a yeast sponge or of baking bread to see if the inside is cooked. A Taylor digital thermometer costs $25 and comes with a watch battery. Look for it at Williams-Sonoma stores nationwide or order from the catalog by calling 800-541-2233. ■

**PICKLED BEETS WITH
ORANGE AND ROSEMARY**
page 11

**GUBANA: ITALIAN EASTER BREAD
WITH NUTS AND FRUIT**
page 12

RECIPE INDEX

ASSORTED SAVORY PUFF PASTRIES
pages 15 to 17

**RISOTTO WITH ASPARAGUS
AND WILD MUSHROOMS**
page 19

ROAST LEG OF LAMB WITH PIQUANT CAPER SAUCE
page 10

GRANNY'S SPECKLED COCONUT CAKE
page 21

Skewered Grilled Shrimp and Artichoke Hearts

Soak 16 large shrimp, peeled and deveined, in 1 quart ice water mixed with 2 teaspoons salt for ½ hour. Drain, dry, then marinate in 3 tablespoons olive oil, 1 minced garlic clove, and pepper to taste for at least ½ hour. Using a paring knife, trim the tough stem skin from 2, 8-ounce artichokes, then pull off tough outer leaves until you reach leaves with yellowish-white bases; cut off tough upper dark green section of remaining leaves. Drop prepared artichokes into boiling water seasoned with 2 sliced garlic cloves, 1 bay leaf, and 1 small quartered onion. Simmer until tender, about 20 minutes. Drain, then halve each artichoke lengthwise, removing hairy choke and tough inner purple leaves. Cut each half lengthwise into 4 wedges. Thread 2 shrimp and 2 artichoke pieces on each of 8 skewers, brushing artichokes with marinade. Grill over a medium-hot fire or broil, turning once, until lightly charred but still moist, about 4 minutes. *Serves 4 as an appetizer.*

NUMBER EIGHT ◆ MAY/JUNE 1994

$4.00 U.S./$4.95 CANADA

COOK'S
ILLUSTRATED

Perfect Pound Cake
New Mixing Method
Yields Ideal Texture

Rediscovering Fried Chicken
Crisp, Tender, Juicy...
but *Not* Greasy

How to Cook Artichokes
Steam, Don't Boil

Rating Bread Machines
10 Models Tested
Plus Foolproof Bread
Machine Recipes

AMERICAN PASTAS
WIN TASTING
•
QUICK GRANITAS
•
EASY SAUCES FOR SEAFOOD
•
FREE-FORM FRUIT TARTS
•
TASTING SAUVIGNON
BLANCS

TABLE
OF CONTENTS

"Artichokes"
For best results, steam, don't boil. See page 10.

ILLUSTRATION BY
BRENT WATKINSON

Yogurt-Creamed Oats with Berries and Apples, adapted from *The Art of Anton Mosimann* (Waymark Publications) by Anton Mosimann

ILLUSTRATION BY
CAROL FORTUNATO

COOK'S
ILLUSTRATED

Publisher and Editor
CHRISTOPHER KIMBALL

Executive Editor
MARK BITTMAN

Senior Editor
JOHN WILLOUGHBY

Food Editor
PAM ANDERSON

Senior Writer
JACK BISHOP

Managing Editor
MAURA LYONS

Copy Editor
DAVID TRAVERS

Test Kitchen Assistant
VICTORIA ROLAND

Editorial Intern
SHARON K. BARRETT

Art Director
MEG BIRNBAUM

Food Stylist
MARIE PIRAINO

Circulation Director
ADRIENNE KIMBALL

Circulation Assistant
JENNIFER L. KEENE

Production Director
JAMES MCCORMACK

Publicity Director
CAROL ROSEN

Treasurer
JANET CARLSON

Office Manager
JENNY THORNBURY

Customer Service
CONNIE FORBES

Cook's Illustrated (ISSN 1068-2821) is published bimonthly
by Natural Health Limited Partners, 17 Station Street, Box
569, Brookline, MA 02147. Copyright 1994 Natural Health
Limited Partners. Application to mail at second-class
postage rates is pending at Boston, MA, and additional
mailing offices. Editorial office: 17 Station Street, Box 569,
Brookline, MA 02147; (617) 232-1000, FAX (617) 232-
1572. Editorial contributions should be sent to: Editor,
Cook's Illustrated, 17 Station Street, Box 569, Brookline,
MA 02147. We cannot assume responsibility for
manuscripts submitted to us. Submissions will be returned
only if accompanied by a large self-addressed stamped
envelope. Subscription rates: $24.95 for one year; $45 for
two years; $65 for three years. (Canada: add $3 per year;
all other countries: add $12 per year.) Postmaster: Send all
new orders, subscription inquiries, and change of address
notices to *Cook's Illustrated*, P.O. Box 59046, Boulder, CO
80322-9046, or telephone (800) 477-3059. Single copies:
$4 in U.S., $4.95 in Canada and foreign. Back issues
available for $5 each. PRINTED IN THE U.S.A.

EDITORIAL

MUCH DEPENDS ON DINNER

CHRISTOPHER KIMBALL

In 1963, President Kennedy invited Harry Truman back to the White House after a long and bitter absence during the Eisenhower administration. A white-tie dinner was arranged in Truman's honor. The after-dinner entertainment ended with Truman, an amateur but enthusiastic pianist, taking a turn at the Steinway, "as pleased as a man could possibly be." For Kennedy it was a dinner party; for Harry Truman it was a homecoming.

Dinner, like furniture or clothing, says a great deal about us as a culture. At its highest stage of evolution, the dinner party is a platform for discussion — a state dinner at Camelot bustling with an exchange of ideas and personalities, an eclectic mixture of Oscar Wilde and William F. Buckley, a mixed stew of showmanship and intellect.

But in its passion for the details of human activities, dinner also exudes a reverence for life. My favorite scene in *The Godfather* shows the men preparing a pasta dinner. In the midst of a gang war, they cooked — the mincing of garlic transforming chaos into order. Dinner slows the clock, allowing us a moment to catch our breath, to savor the stillness of the moment; the first taste of a family recipe connecting us instantly to each other, to our past and future.

Maybe that is why cooking is what most cultures do during extraordinary life events. We cook for weddings and funerals. We make cakes for birthdays and anniversaries. We commemorate great events in the life of our nation with roast turkey or barbecue. On a trip to central Africa in 1969, for example, I spent the night feasting and drinking in a small village in Cameroon during a local three-day celebration of the death of an elder — a whirl of dancing, cooking, and brewing.

Around my own dinner table in Boston, my wife and I try to sow the first seeds of civilization by teaching our two young girls how to hold forks (although the area under their chairs is a wild anthropological record of our family's culinary history). That same table hosts business dinners, family reunions, neighborhood action groups, and the annual *Cook's Illustrated* Christmas party. That table has heard the kids singing "This Old Man," heated political discussion, and debates about General Lee's strategy at Gettysburg, all thrown into the mix of standard family fare, from "What did you do at school today?" to weekend plans, career anxieties, even the preferred method for dispatching kitchen mice. But it is all done over food.

In some deep, primitive manner, food and conversation are inextricably linked. In Western culture, this notion has been taken to the extreme. In most other societies, one eats and then talks or vice-versa. We, on the other hand, are taught how to dine and converse at the same time, a feat that requires elaborate social customs to avoid choking to death. In the rereleased 1961 classic, *Tiffany's Table Manners*, ninety-three pages of do's and don'ts assist teenagers to navigate the murky social waters of mixing eating with speaking. The author, Walter Hoving, offers the reader the opportunity to avoid "dinner-table insecurity later in life" by following such strictures as, "Don't smack your lips," Learn "to talk with a little in your mouth," and Don't hold your soup spoon like "a mashie niblick." Social intercourse, not consumption, is the overriding philosophy.

But dinner also serves a deeper purpose — it connects us to the continuity of life when that continuity is broken. A few summers ago, we were in the middle of a dinner party at our farmhouse during a terrible thunderstorm. The phone rang. It was bad news — a close friend of ours had died suddenly. We stayed up late that night, around the table, drinking, eating, and telling stories about personal moments, the little details of life that become so important when they have no future. We shared those stories together as we had shared dinner. It made his passing part of our lives.

A few days later, my wife and I packed up our young daughter and drove down to New Jersey for the funeral. The service was difficult — he was to be married that October. Afterwards, we all met downstairs in the basement for something to eat. It was simple food, honest and homemade. At first it was awkward, but the food was good and was eaten, strangers were introduced, and there was conversation. As I walked out into the sunlight holding a sleeping one-year-old, I could even hear a few strains of tempered laughter. It felt just like a homecoming. ■

NOTES
FROM READERS

FOAM ON BEANS AND STOCK

The other day I was preparing chicken stock, and then last night I made black beans. In both cases, I noticed the same phenomenon — foamy bubbles. What is the foam that rises to the top when cooking beans? Is it related to the scum that rises to the surface when making chicken stock?

SETH PARK
Lawrenceville, NJ

All foams, whether on the surface of simmering stock or mixed with ocean waves as they crash along the shore, are nothing more than tiny pockets of air surrounded by a thin layer of water. These bubbles are stabilized by proteins that are dissolved in the water. In the case of the ocean, the protein comes from plant and animal material.

When making beans or stock, the protein comes from the foods being cooked. As these foods are heated (beans soaking in cold water do not produce foam), they leach protein molecules into the water. The agitation of molecules caused by the application of heat causes air to become trapped in bubbles. The proteins given off by the beans or chicken unwind and embed themselves in the thin layer of water that surrounds each air bubble. This network of unfolded proteins acts to stabilize the foam.

Bean or chicken scum has little culinary value — we skim stock to make it clear. However, a related foam made from protein-rich egg whites is responsible for a number of important dishes, everything from soufflés to angel food cake. In this case, the agitation does not come from heat but from a mechanical source. A whisk or electric mixer creates the bubbles and the egg proteins stabilize the foam.

MIREPOIX

I have seen the term mirepoix *in various recipes. What is it?*

RICHARD SCHUBERT
Lexington, KY

Mirepoix, a mixture of diced carrots, onions, and celery, is the basis of many French sauces, stocks, soups, and braises. These aromatic vegetables are sometimes browned in fat (often butter) before liquid (often stock) is added to make a sauce. The vegetables may be strained out (when this is done you should press them against the sides or bottom of the strainer to release all their juices) or pureed to give a sauce some body and thickness.

A mirepoix is also used in a number of braised meat, poultry, or seafood dishes. In many cases, foods (pot roast is a good example) are braised on top of a bed of browned vegetables. As the vegetables simmer in the liquid, they become quite tender and impart their flavor to the sauce.

For preparations with a short cooking time, such as fish stock, the vegetables should be finely diced to give up their flavor quickly. For dishes that cook slowly, a larger dice is acceptable. Some recipes may call for a mirepoix with diced ham or bacon, but mirepoix is traditionally meatless. Other versions may use leeks, turnips, fennel, or even parsnips in place of, or with, the celery. But unless the recipe says otherwise, assume that mirepoix means equals amounts of diced carrots, onions, and celery.

CLAY ROASTERS

Could you please discuss the advantages and disadvantages of cooking in a clay roaster? I understand that clay pots can be hard to clean and that sudden cooling might crack them. However, I have also heard that clay pots do a superb job of roasting chicken. What's the truth and what's just hype?

MRS. EUGENE DAVIS
Raytown, MO

The low-fat craze seems to be fueling renewed interest in this ancient cooking vessel. The principle is quite enticing — foods cook in their own juices in a sealed but porous pot. Before using a clay pot, it must be submerged in cold water for fifteen minutes. The water absorbed by the pot is released into the cooking chamber as the pot warms in the oven, essentially steaming the food.

To test the effectiveness of clay roasters, we decided to prepare whole split chicken breasts — a favorite cut because they cook quickly and have plenty of lean white meat. We placed two breasts in a covered three-quart clay pot and two breasts in a metal roasting pan. The breasts were rubbed with olive oil and salt, but nothing else was added to either pan.

A clay roaster will crack if exposed to sudden changes in temperature. For this reason, the pot should be placed in a cold oven. For electric ovens, set the desired temperature and the pot will gradually warm as the oven preheats. In gas ovens, it is best to set the oven to low heat to warm the pot slowly, then raise it to the desired cooking temperature. When removing a clay pot from the oven, place it on a wooden board or on towels rather than directly on a cold counter or sink.

In our tests, we placed both the metal roasting pan and the clay pot in a cold electric oven and then set the heat to 450 degrees. We chose such a high temperature because the instruction booklet that came with our clay roaster warned that the pot insulates foods and requires higher temperatures to cook efficiently. After twenty-seven minutes, the chicken in the metal pan registered 160 degrees on a meat thermometer and was removed from the oven. The chicken in the clay pot measured only 130 degrees. Ten minutes later, the chicken in the clay pot reached 160 degrees and was removed.

The differences were immediately apparent. Chicken cooked in the clay pot did not have a chance to brown. As might be expected, the skin was pale and rubbery tasting. In contrast, the skin on the chicken cooked in the open roasting pan was golden and crisp. The meat on the breasts cooked in the metal pan was juicy and tender; the meat cooked in clay was dry and chewy. The juice — there was about one tablespoon — in the metal pan was thick, dark, and rich tasting. In contrast, the clay pot held one-third cup of a pale, flavorless liquid. While browned juices had reduced and concentrated in the open pan, juices in the closed clay pot remained watery.

Perhaps most telling were the weight measurements taken before and after each piece of chicken was cooked. As the pan juices indicated, chicken prepared in the clay pot had lost 22 percent of its original weight. Chicken roasted in the metal pan lost just 18 percent of its weight.

As for washing the clay pot, a stiff brush did the cleanup with average effort. Our conclusion is that nothing cooked in a covered clay pot will ever brown and therefore will always lack the rich, caramelized flavor that searing and browning convey. For this reason, a clay pot does not really roast foods. It's more of an oven steamer. It may have benefits, for instance, when baking fish — by keeping delicate fillets or steaks moist, it will prevent them from overcooking in the intense heat of the oven. Just don't spend fifty dollars on a clay "roaster" for chicken.

PARMESAN CHEESE DEBATE

In response to your November/December 1993 issue (see Notes from Readers, page 3), it is with good reason that most experts warn against pregrating Parmesan cheese. As a teacher of northern Italian cooking, I demonstrate frequently not only the difference in taste and texture between freshly grated Parmigiano-Reggiano and pregrated cheese, but also the differences between the various methods of grating. If Parmesan is properly grated to begin with, using either a metal grater for a fine texture or a mouli grater for shaving, the difference between fresh and pregrated cheese is usually quite apparent, even to a nonexpert.

The use of a food processor, which finely chops the cheese, destroys the character of Parmesan. It is my guess that the cheese samples you were comparing were improperly grated, or you could not possibly have come to the conclusion that it is acceptable to pregrate Parmesan cheese several weeks in advance and store it in either the refrigerator or freezer until needed. The notion of "freshly grated" is not just an affectation by food experts.

EMILY RESTIFO
New Canaan, CT

You were not the only food professional who wrote us regarding our comparison of pregrated and freshly grated Parmigiano-Reggiano. We, too, were surprised by the results of this test, so we repeated the experiment twice. As you suggest, we grated by hand, with a metal grater, both times. Our experienced tasters were able to detect a slight difference when the cheeses were tasted alone, but when tossed with hot pasta any advantage for freshly grated cheese disappeared.

As mentioned in the original report, our tests were conducted with buttered pasta. When competing with strong flavors, such as tomatoes or garlic, the difference between freshly grated and pregrated cheese would be even harder to detect.

We do recommend freshly grated Parmesan in room-temperature dishes such as a salad. But for use on pasta, feel free to keep small batches of grated Parmesan in the refrigerator or freezer for several weeks. Store cheese in an airtight container to help retain moisture.

CAPPUCCINO COMMENTS

"Secrets of Homemade Espresso" (September/October 1993) caught my attention. I would like to mention two items. I've owned the Krups Novo 964 for many years. Last year the machine died. I called the company and was told to send the body back to them. Within one week, I received a completely rebuilt machine and a bill for fifty dollars. I consider this to be money well spent.

Second, I gladly share my favorite cappuccino variation. Into a five-ounce cup, add one teaspoon sugar and a scant ounce of half and half. Insert the steam nozzle into this mixture to melt the sugar and froth the cream until its volume expands to half the cup's capacity. Add the steaming espresso, filling the cup so the froth just reaches the top. Insert the nozzle back into the cup and froth once more, essentially stirring the mixture and adding back a little more froth. I have received numerous compliments on this simple brew.

DWIGHT RUDISILL
Waleska, GA

WHAT IS IT?

I wonder if you could tell me what this device is used for. It has a sharp blade so I assume it is some kind of slicer.

ELAINE GOLD
New York, NY

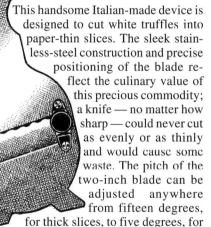

This handsome Italian-made device is designed to cut white truffles into paper-thin slices. The sleek stainless-steel construction and precise positioning of the blade reflect the culinary value of this precious commodity; a knife — no matter how sharp — could never cut as evenly or as thinly and would cause some waste. The pitch of the two-inch blade can be adjusted anywhere from fifteen degrees, for thick slices, to five degrees, for the thinnest possible slices.

If you are lucky enough to purchase fresh white truffles, slice them directly over a bowl of steaming pasta or risotto. This tool can also be used to slice chocolate into very thin shavings to garnish cakes and other desserts. *See Sources and Resources on page 32 for information about where you can purchase a truffle slicer.*

KEEPING THE RISING TEMPERATURE OF DOUGH CORRECT

To create an environment that is the perfect temperature for rising bread dough, simply place a small lightbulb in your oven and close the door. This is easily accomplished using an extension cord with a lightbulb socket on the end, available at any hardware store. To be sure you are using the right size bulb for your oven, measure the temperature in the oven with an instant-read thermometer while you try different size bulbs — about forty watts is a good place to start. The bulbs made for use in refrigerators come in small wattages and are also able to take a bit of knocking about. When you hit the size bulb that keeps the oven at a steady eighty degrees, you are all set.

JIM CHADWICK
Hercules, CA

MORE PLANTAIN TIPS

The steps on "Preparing Tropical Fruit" in your January/February 1994 issue were excellent, but here is an additional tip for peeling green plantains. Using a paring knife, make three equally-spaced lengthwise cuts just through the peel of the fruits. Then place the plantains in boiling unsalted water for one to one and one-half minutes. Remove, cool, and peel as directed. You will find that the peel will come off much more easily.

ANDY HUSBANDS
Chef, East Coast Grill
Cambridge, MA

EGG GRADES AND SIZES

Are eggs graded AA really any better or fresher those graded A? Also, is there some formula for substituting jumbo eggs for large eggs in recipes?

SANDY RAY
Darien, CT

Egg grading and sizing are two independent evaluations. Although the process is not mandatory, most supermarket eggs are graded according to shell appearance and the quality of the liquid interior. Eggs with stained or misshapen shells are marked grade B, the lowest quality.

Most eggs sold to consumers are grades AA or A, with grade B eggs being used in some commercial products. The difference between AA and A is the thickness of the white and firmness of the yolk. Most eggs are put through a candling process (they are held up to a bright light) to evaluate the quality of the yolk and white. An egg with a thick, tight white and well-defined yolk is graded AA. If the white is somewhat thinner and spreads more when cracked or if the yolk membrane is weaker, the egg is graded A.

In some instances, such as when poaching an egg, a higher grade will make a discernible difference in the finished dish. We recommend buying the highest quality eggs, those graded AA, for all purposes.

While only some eggs are graded, all eggs are sized. Depending on the breed of the hen and her size, a chicken egg can weigh as much as three ounces or as little as one ounce. Size is not necessarily a reflection of quality. The average weight of one egg for each of the most common sizes is as follows: jumbo (two and one-half ounces), extra-large (two and one-quarter ounces), large (two ounces), and medium (one and three-quarters ounces).

As you can see from these numbers, a recipe that calls for four large eggs (about eight ounces) should be made with three jumbo eggs (about seven and one-half ounces), and not four jumbo eggs (ten ounces). Likewise, a recipe that calls for three extra-large eggs (six and three-quarters ounces) should be made with four medium eggs (seven ounces).■

Quick Tips

MOVING PIE PASTRY

Follow this tip from J. Wilkes of Issaquah, Washington, to easily move a pie crust from rolling surface to pie pan.

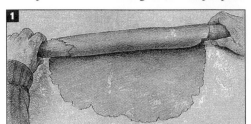

1. Being careful not to break the dough, roll it up around the rolling pin like a scroll.

2. When the dough is completely wrapped around the rolling pin, move it to the pie pan.

3. Drape the end of the dough over one side of the pie plate, then carefully unroll the dough onto the plate.

GRATING CITRUS PEEL

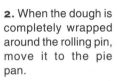

When grating citrus peel, tiny bits of peel often stick to the areas of the grater between the holes. Rather than wasting this peel, you can quickly and easily brush it off onto waxed paper, using a clean toothbrush kept especially for this purpose.

AVOIDING SPLATTERS WHEN MIXING

To avoid splatters when using an electric mixer, follow this tip from Judith Cobbs of Davie, Florida.

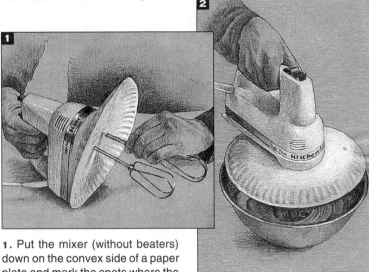

1. Put the mixer (without beaters) down on the convex side of a paper plate and mark the spots where the holes for the beaters hit the plate. Punch holes through the plate at those two spots, then insert the beaters through the holes and into the mixer.

2. Proceed to mix, keeping the surface of the plate approximately even with the top of the bowl. Any food that is kicked up by the beaters will splatter onto the paper plate.

CHOPPING GARLIC WITH HERBS

When you are making a recipe that calls for both garlic and herbs, you can combine tasks and make both of them easier.

1. When chopping garlic by itself, the garlic often sticks to the knife, riding up on the sides of the blade as shown here.

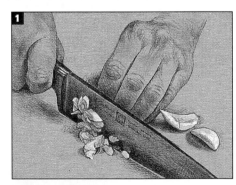

2. If you chop the garlic and herbs together, the garlic sticks to the herbs, rather than to the knife.

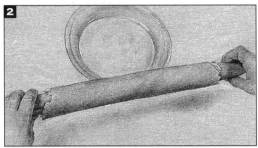

ILLUSTRATIONS BY ANATOLY

SLICING OVAL ROOT VEGETABLES

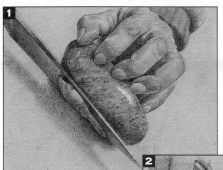

1. When slicing oval or round root vegetables such as potatoes, begin by cutting a small slice off one side to create a flat surface.

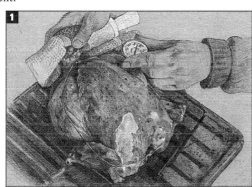

2. Then, place the vegetable on the cutting board with the cut surface down so that the vegetable will not roll. Continue slicing.

TAKING POULTRY TEMPERATURE

When using a thermometer to judge poultry doneness, it is important to insert the thermometer at the proper place on the bird. There are two options for placement:

1. The thermometer may be inserted into the leg pit, as shown here.

2. Alternatively, you may test at the neck end, inserting the thermometer into the breast as deeply as possible without touching a bone.

SCALING FISH

To scale a fish without getting scales all over your kitchen, follow the advice of Yvette M. Cortez of San Francisco, California and hold the fish under water while scaling it.

CUTTING BUTTER FOR PASTRY

When cutting butter into flour for pastry dough, the process is made much easier by cutting the butter into small pieces before adding it to the flour.

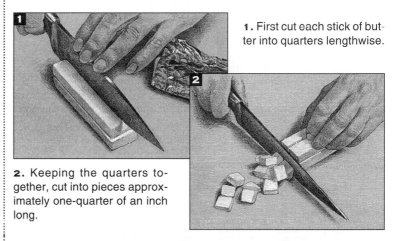

1. First cut each stick of butter into quarters lengthwise.

2. Keeping the quarters together, cut into pieces approximately one-quarter of an inch long.

BUTTERFLYING A CHICKEN BREAST

For quick, even cooking, a chicken breast may easily be butterflied so that it is half of its original thickness. This is particularly useful when grilling.

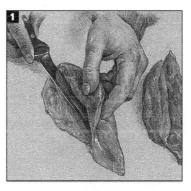

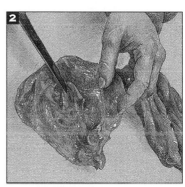

1. Starting on the thickest side of the breast, slice the breast crosswise almost in half.

2. Open the breast up, as if you were opening a book, creating a single flat piece.

ATTENTION READERS: FREE SUBSCRIPTION FOR PUBLISHED TIPS. Do you have a unique tip you would like to share with other readers? We will provide a one-year complimentary subscription for each quick tip that we print. Send a description of your special technique to *Cook's Illustrated*, P.O. Box 569, Brookline Village, MA 02147. Please write "Attention: Quick Tips" on the envelope and include your name, address, and daytime phone number. Unfortunately, we can only acknowledge receipt of tips that will be printed in the magazine.

Rediscovering Fried Chicken

For tender fried chicken with a skin that is crispy instead of greasy, use a hefty skillet, a buttermilk bath, and vegetable shortening.

~ BY PAM ANDERSON WITH KAREN TACK ~

With the help of the fast-food industry, many of us have lost our taste memory of good fried chicken — and even more of us have forgotten, or never learned, how to make it. I know, because it happened to me.

When I was about eight years old, my matriarchal aunt in Alabama announced to all her younger sisters that she had discovered how to duplicate the fried chicken of a local fast-food chain. The key was to dip chicken parts in flour, then in water, then back in flour. The flour followed by water formed a glue, which in turn caused the second round of flour to form an unusually thick coating that fried up hard, thick, and crispy. Of course, the fast-food chicken was deep-fried, so we replaced our skillets with Dutch ovens, our solid shortening with oil. And this is how my family has fried chicken ever since.

I was fairly certain that my method of double-dredging and deep frying produced a blue-ribbon bird. As I researched recipes for this story, however, the older, more authentic ones that scoffed both at deep-frying and at newfangled coatings jarred my memory and took me back to before age eight, to my grandmother's kitchen. I remembered her cast-iron skillet and the glass lid she had borrowed from another pot to cover the frying chicken. I recalled the way she cut the chicken into ten pieces — the standard eight, plus the pulley (or wish) bone piece and the meaty lower back piece. I remembered, just barely, the crispy yet somehow smothered quality of my grandmother's fried chicken.

It had been so long. I couldn't remember what pan-fried chicken tasted like. Is it better — or was I romanticizing the past?

Frying chicken involves more than just purchasing the right skillet. There are other issues to consider. What size chickens are best? Should the chicken parts be soaked before frying and, if so, in what? What kind and size of pan, and what fat or combination of fats is best for frying chicken? Is all-purpose flour the best coating, or could corn flour or even self-rising flour produce a better crust? Is it best to dredge the chicken parts in a pan of flour to coat the chicken, or is a paper bag better? Should the cook season the chicken, the flour, or both? Some recipes recommend air-drying the chicken before frying for an extra-crispy effect. Is this worth the time? During frying, should the pan be covered, partially covered, covered part of the time, or not at all? How should the fried chicken be drained — paper towels, paper bags, or is there something to learn from the fast-food restaurants after all?

By using only enough fat to come halfway up the sides of the pieces of chicken, you can achieve perfect texture — so long as the fat is hot enough so that it is not absorbed by the chicken.

Sizing It Up

I've always thought frying chicken to be a time-consuming project, mainly because it had to be cooked in two batches. I discovered, though, that if the bird is small enough and the pan big enough, you can fry a whole chicken at one time. Birds weighing 2½ to 3 pounds work best, but these smaller birds are often not easy to find. Call your butcher or grocery meat department to check on availability.

I wanted to like the 13⅜-inch cast-iron skillet I had specially purchased for this fried chicken, because it was large enough to hold all ten pieces of chicken in one frying (see "Butchering the Bird," page 7). But I soon found that its size was a handicap because the perimeter of the pan sat off the burner. Getting the fat temperature right for frying chicken around the edge of the pan meant scorching the chicken in the center, while properly cooking the chicken in the center of the pan meant blond-skinned, greasy chicken around the edges. The skillet I came to prefer was a 12-inch cast-iron skillet (a modest fifteen-dollar investment), though I'm certain that any heavy-bottomed 12-inch skillet would work. (*See* Sources and Resources, page 32 for information on where to purchase a skillet.)

Soaking: Buttermilk Is Best
Of all the stages — buying, butchering, seasoning, coating, and frying — I found the greatest recipe diversity in the soaking period. After testing thirteen different soaking methods (*see* "Finding the Best Soaking Method," page 9), I discovered that dairy-soaked chicken displayed the most beautifully textured and richly colored skin.

This is not surprising. Since milk is thicker than water, these dairy-based soaking liquids tend to cling better to the slippery, raw chicken parts, which, in turn, attract more flour during dredging. The end result is a thick, even coating. Lactose, the sugar found in milk, caused the chicken to develop a deep mahogany color during frying. Heavy cream also coated the chicken beautifully, but the resulting fried chicken was too rich. The milk and lemon juice combination gave the chicken a clean, heightened flavor, but since it was thinner it didn't adhere as well and offered a less impressive coat. The buttermilk, on the other hand, was as viscous as cream and as tangy as the milk with lemon juice, with none of the liabilities. This became my favorite soaking medium.

BUTCHERING THE BIRD

There are not too many ways to cut up a chicken. You can't play around much with the legs, thighs, and wings, but you do have options with the back and breasts. I've always disliked the chicken breasts overpowering the other parts, so I like the technique of shaving off a portion of the breast before it's split thus creating the wishbone piece. This step makes the chicken pieces more evenly sized and the breasts more manageable during cooking. I like the idea of frying up the meatier half of the back, but I found it crowded the frying pan. I ultimately sent it to the stockpot with the other back piece and giblets. If you're partial to this piece, though, fry it up.

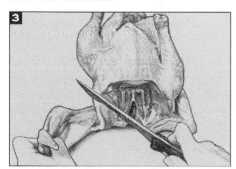

1. Remove giblets and excess fat from the cavity. Place the chicken on a cutting board and run your fingertip along the breastbone until the bone ends and you feel a sudden drop.

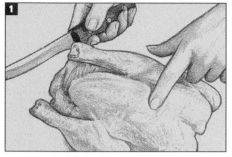

2. Cut straight down about one and one-half inches, then turn the knife toward the neck end at a slight angle and continue cutting until this wishbone piece is completely severed from the breast.

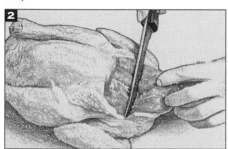

3. At this point, the wing joints are more or less exposed. With neck end toward you, cut off each wing, then sever the wing tips and reserve for stock.

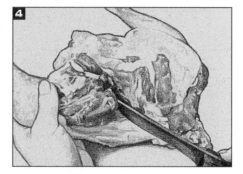

4. With the neck end toward you, cut the skin between the breast and leg, simultaneously pulling the leg away from the breast to expose the thigh joint. Bend the leg back so that the joint snaps; then cut the whole leg from the breast at this joint. Turn the chicken, with the cavity end toward you, and repeat with the other leg.

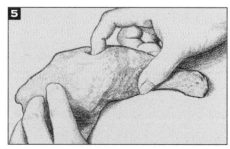

5. To locate the leg/thigh joint, position drumstick with the base toward you and place your finger at a right angle where the leg and the thigh meet. You will feel a slight indentation where the cut should be made.

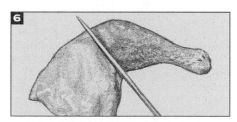

6. Using the identification mark in step 5, sever the leg and thigh at the joint. Repeat with the remaining leg.

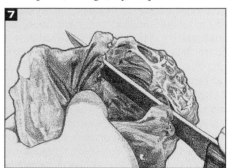

7. Turn the chicken, cavity end up, and cut through the thin flesh between the back and the breastbone.

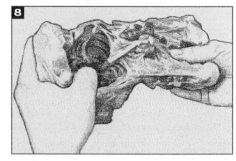

8. Bend the lower back away from the breast; it will snap at the point where it should separate. Cut the lower back portion away from the breast and the upper back. Reserve the upper back for stock.

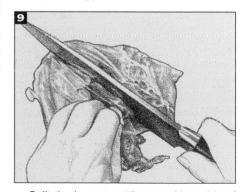

9. Split the breast, cutting on either side of the large center bone, rather than trying to halve it.

ILLUSTRATIONS BY ANGELO

You Can't Beat Flour

With the soaking issue resolved, I moved on to coatings. I was particularly intrigued by two coatings that I found in my research — self-rising flour and a combination of corn and all-purpose flour. After putting these and other coatings to the test, I found that none surpassed all-purpose flour; in fact, most alternatives were inferior.

The self-rising flour produced a coating that ballooned, then deflated during frying. Once cooked, this crumbly chicken shed its coat. A cornstarch coating produced disastrous-looking and -tasting chicken. It fried to an unpleasant white with scattered hard spots, and tasted pasty, like uncooked starch. I cut the cornstarch with flour, which proved more successful but did not surpass the plain flour. I then tried various combinations with all-purpose flour — cornmeal, whole-wheat flour, corn flour, and bread crumbs. The cornmeal coating was pleasant, but didn't bind as well as straight flour. The whole-wheat coating displayed flecks of unabsorbed grain on the skin's surface. Both the cornmeal and the whole-wheat coatings had a coarse, raw taste to them. And although the corn flour sounded like a good idea, it was barely discernible on the fried chicken. Bread crumbs mixed with flour delivered a respectable crust — nice dark brown, fairly crispy — but I wouldn't recommend it over plain flour.

Several recipes recommended drying the chicken on a rack for a couple of hours to allow the flour to adhere. I found that this extra step produced a brittle, thin, shell-like crust, not unpleasant but certainly not worth the wait. On the other hand, if you want to coat your chicken and let it sit for a couple of hours before frying, it certainly won't hurt it.

Brown Bag It

I was also intent on finding the best way to get the coating on the chicken. I compared dredging the chicken parts in a flour-filled pie tin to shaking the chicken and flour in a brown paper bag. After only one try with each, I quickly declared the bag method the winner in both consistency of coating and easy cleanup. I have to add, however, that after shaking a thin dusting of flour over the kitchen floor and watching heavy chicken parts threaten to break the bag, I quickly switched to a double brown bag.

I also wanted to determine at what point the chicken should be seasoned. After a number of experiments, I decided that seasoning only the flour or the soaking liquid wasn't enough — the sound culinary principle of seasoning all along the way produced the best fried chicken. I started off with small amounts of salt, but discovered that the soaking liquid must be generously seasoned for the chicken to absorb the salt. And, since only a portion of seasoned flour clings to the chicken parts, it's important that it is heavily seasoned as well.

Into the Frying Pan

I tested every conceivable fat and combination of fats for frying, and found less dramatic results in this area. Lard produced gorgeous, deeply tanned chicken, but I disliked the heavy, porky smell it produced during frying. Also, while this fat seemed to enforce and enhance the chicken's meatiness, it overpowered the skin and crust. I appreciated its rich, heavy taste, but tired of it after only a few bites. Even when I cut the lard with shortening, the crust was still tainted with a distinctive lard flavor.

Chicken fried in a combination of butter and vegetable oil was sweet and mild, but too rich for my taste. It was also lighter in color than any of the other chickens I fried, and the fat foamed nonstop during frying. This combination is also more perishable, making it difficult to store and use again like other fats. Plain vegetable oil worked only relatively well; the resulting chicken, although pleasant and fast-food-like, was a bit splotchy.

My overall preference turned out to be straight shortening. Chicken fried in this medium had a consistent mahogany color, and shortening also turned out to be the most odor-

free of all the fats (*see* "Shortening: The Long and Short of It," below).

A few recipes called for flavoring the shortening with bacon drippings. I tried this, but was unimpressed. Although I could distinctly smell bacon as the chicken was frying, I could barely identify it during tasting.

The Frying Game

Pan frying, in my opinion, produces superior fried chicken. Deep-fried chicken, simultaneously attacked on all sides by hot oil, quickly develops a brittle, protective shell right down to the meat. Pan-fried chicken, on the other hand, is more complex. It has the same crunchy exterior, but when the pan is covered, the half of the meat not submerged in oil is exposed to a sort of steaming process. This creates a moist sublayer that offers a nice contrast to the crisp exterior.

I then moved on to the next frying question: Should the chicken be covered during frying and, if so, when? The point of covering the pan during frying is to trap moisture; the chicken I left uncovered during the entire frying time did not develop the soft undercoating I came to like. Yet I found that covering the chicken during the entire process created too much steam, leaving the coating too soft. In some cases the oversteaming caused the skin to separate from the meat and fall into the hot oil. Covering the chicken during the first half of the cooking time allows the chicken to steam and fry; leaving it uncovered for the second half keeps the already browned side from getting soggy.

Chicken drained on paper towels gets soggy faster than chicken drained on a paper bag, but both were inferior to a wire rack set over a jelly-roll pan. The pan and wire rack mimic the draining system used by so many fast-food restaurants. In the prefrying stage, the rack offers the ideal resting place for the coated chicken. After frying, it keeps the chicken grease-free and crisp. The pan and rack sit safely on a stovetop as well as in a warm oven — not true for either paper towels or bags.

BUTTERMILK-FRIED CHICKEN
Serves 4

1   whole chicken (2½ to 3 pounds), cut into 9 or 10 pieces (*see* "Butchering the Bird," page 7), neck, giblets, wing tips, and back reserved for stock

1½ cups buttermilk
    Salt and ground black pepper

2   cups all-purpose flour

3–4 cups vegetable shortening for frying

1. Place chicken pieces in a gallon-size zipper-lock bag. Mix buttermilk with 1 teaspoon salt and ½ teaspoon pepper. Pour mixture over chicken; seal bag, then refrigerate for at least 2 hours and up to 24 hours.

2. Measure flour, 1 teaspoon salt, and ½ teaspoon pepper into a large double brown paper bag; shake to combine. Drop half of chicken pieces into flour mixture and shake thoroughly to completely coat with flour. Remove chicken from bag, shaking excess flour from each piece. Place coated chicken pieces on a large wire rack set over a jelly-roll pan until ready to fry. Repeat coating with remaining chicken pieces.

3. Meanwhile, spoon enough shortening to measure ½-inch deep into a 12-inch skillet; heat to 350 degrees. Place chicken pieces, skin side down, into hot oil; cover with lid or cookie sheet and cook for 5 minutes. Lift chicken pieces with tongs to make sure chicken is frying evenly; rearrange if some pieces are browning faster than others. Cover again and continue cooking until chicken pieces are evenly browned, about 5 minutes longer. (Be sure oil continues to bubble; oil temperature at this point should be between 250 and 300 degrees, and should be maintained at this level until chicken is done.) Turn chicken over with tongs and cook, uncovered, until chicken is browned all over, 10 to 12 minutes longer. Remove chicken from skillet with tongs and return to wire rack set over jelly-roll pan. ∎

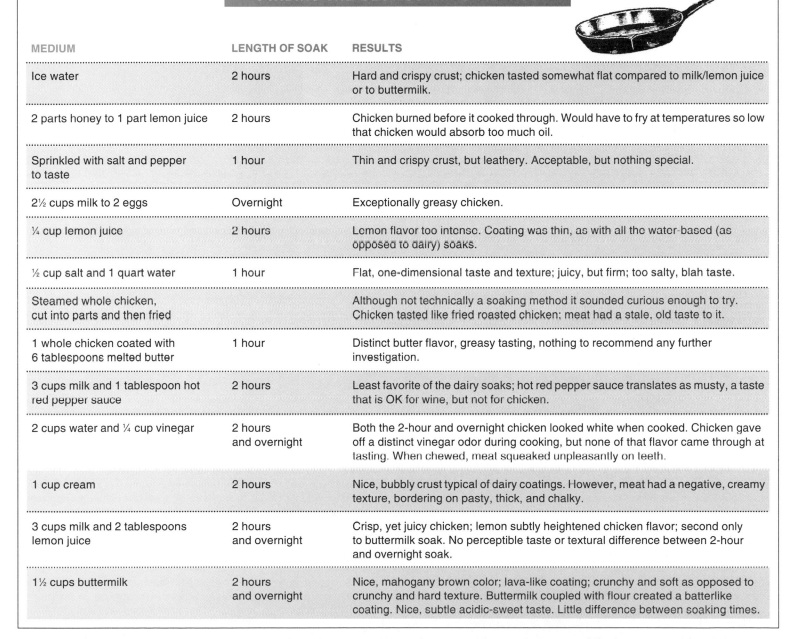

FINDING THE BEST SOAKING METHOD

MEDIUM	LENGTH OF SOAK	RESULTS
Ice water	2 hours	Hard and crispy crust; chicken tasted somewhat flat compared to milk/lemon juice or to buttermilk.
2 parts honey to 1 part lemon juice	2 hours	Chicken burned before it cooked through. Would have to fry at temperatures so low that chicken would absorb too much oil.
Sprinkled with salt and pepper to taste	1 hour	Thin and crispy crust, but leathery. Acceptable, but nothing special.
2½ cups milk to 2 eggs	Overnight	Exceptionally greasy chicken.
¼ cup lemon juice	2 hours	Lemon flavor too intense. Coating was thin, as with all the water-based (as opposed to dairy) soaks.
½ cup salt and 1 quart water	1 hour	Flat, one-dimensional taste and texture; juicy, but firm; too salty, blah taste.
Steamed whole chicken, cut into parts and then fried		Although not technically a soaking method it sounded curious enough to try. Chicken tasted like fried roasted chicken; meat had a stale, old taste to it.
1 whole chicken coated with 6 tablespoons melted butter	1 hour	Distinct butter flavor, greasy tasting, nothing to recommend any further investigation.
3 cups milk and 1 tablespoon hot red pepper sauce	2 hours	Least favorite of the dairy soaks; hot red pepper sauce translates as musty, a taste that is OK for wine, but not for chicken.
2 cups water and ¼ cup vinegar	2 hours and overnight	Both the 2-hour and overnight chicken looked white when cooked. Chicken gave off a distinct vinegar odor during cooking, but none of that flavor came through at tasting. When chewed, meat squeaked unpleasantly on teeth.
1 cup cream	2 hours	Nice, bubbly crust typical of dairy coatings. However, meat had a negative, creamy texture, bordering on pasty, thick, and chalky.
3 cups milk and 2 tablespoons lemon juice	2 hours and overnight	Crisp, yet juicy chicken; lemon subtly heightened chicken flavor; second only to buttermilk soak. No perceptible taste or textural difference between 2-hour and overnight soak.
1½ cups buttermilk	2 hours and overnight	Nice, mahogany brown color; lava-like coating; crunchy and soft as opposed to crunchy and hard texture. Buttermilk coupled with flour created a batterlike coating. Nice, subtle acidic-sweet taste. Little difference between soaking times.

Steam, Don't Boil, Artichokes

Forget the classic method of snipping each leaf, trussing, and then boiling for an hour. Just slice the stem and top, then steam.

~ BY PAMELA PARSEGHIAN ~

My first encounter with artichokes came when I was working as an apprentice at a classic French restaurant in California. On one of my first days, I was given a few sketchy instructions and handed a huge case of raw artichokes. I choked, and after a few spastic attempts asked the French chef for help.

His technique was laborious, to say the least. It entailed trimming the stem and top tips of the artichoke, snipping off the tip of each leaf, then tying a slice of lemon to the stem and trussing the artichoke as if it were a gift package. The artichokes were then boiled for more than an hour. To test for doneness, the chef pulled off leaves, a technique which caused us apprentices to burn our hands every time.

After this introduction, I shied away from cooking artichokes for years. Recently, however, I decided to find out for myself if all of those tedious steps were actually necessary. After many hours of slicing, snipping, tying, boiling, microwaving, braising, and steaming, I found that artichokes are in fact relatively simple to prepare and that they are best when cooked using the easiest method — steaming.

Preparation Shortcuts

My first simplification was to stop trussing the artichoke, a technique necessary only when ar-

tichokes are overcooked to the extent that they would otherwise fall apart. Then I wondered if I could eliminate the lemon, or if, as I had been taught, it really affected the color of the cooked artichoke.

I tested cut artichokes, rubbing them with lemon and cooking them, boiling them in water acidulated with lemon juice, and finally using no acid at all in preparation and cooking. I learned that whole artichokes turn the same drab olive green whether cooked with or without acid.

Another time-saving tip came from Mary Comfort of the California Artichoke Advisory Board, who suggested eliminating the step of cutting off each leaf's pointy tip because the tip softens when cooked and will not pierce eaters. I tested the suggestion and found she was right. When cooked properly, the tips were not sharp. I happily put away my scissors.

At the end of the tests I realized that whole artichokes need very little advance preparation. In fact, the only preparation they need consists of two slices — one to trim the stem and one to slice off the top quarter.

There are, however, some dishes that require more elaborate advance preparations. For example, when stuffing a whole artichoke without prior blanching, you need to remove the inedible choke first. Personally I did not find the resulting dish to be worth the effort, but if you decide to remove the choke prior to cooking, the easiest method I found was to split the artichoke in half from tip to stem, and then to use a sharp-edged spoon to scrape away the inedible center.

Trimming the artichoke down to the totally edible heart prior to cooking also requires more work. (For this technique, *see* "Getting to the Heart," page 11.) For this preparation, I found it helpful to use lemon juice. After trimming several artichokes down to the heart, my fingertips and nails were stained brown, and the hearts also turned brown after a few minutes of standing. The cause of the unsightly staining, according to Tina Seelig, food scientist and author of *The Epicurean Laboratory* (W. H. Freeman, 1991) is oxidation, the same process that causes apples to turn brown when cut. Artichoke cells contain enzymes that help to cause the discoloration. Acids, such as lemon

Artichokes are actually a form of thistle. The inedible choke is composed of flowerets that turn a deep blue-violet if allowed to bloom.

juice, inactivate the enzymes and slow the oxidation. Once I rubbed my hands as well as the artichoke with lemon juice, the stains didn't reoccur.

Steaming Wins for Ease

After eliminating much of the cumbersome preparatory routine, I went on to test various methods of cooking artichokes, including roasting, microwaving, boiling, steaming, and braising.

Roasting was the first method I discarded. It simply did not work for this rather long-cooking vegetable. In fact, when I added halved baby artichoke hearts and quartered large artichoke hearts to a roasting chicken, they burned and became tough before they were done, even when stock was added to the roasting pan for extra moisture.

I then moved on to microwaving, but found it to be more of a nuisance than it was worth. Checking the artichoke's state of doneness required repeated stopping and starting of the machine; the artichokes occasionally shriveled and became unsightly by the time they were done; and the cooking time was not significantly reduced from other methods.

I next compared steaming to boiling in acidulated water, the method I had most often used in the past. Both methods were superior

PHOTOGRAPH BY ERIC ROTH

and each resulted in very evenly cooked artichokes that looked almost identical. The steamed artichokes, however, had a more intense, richer flavor. In addition, heating one inch of water for steaming took less time than heating water for boiling, and steamed artichokes cooked a few minutes faster. Add to this that the nutritional value is somewhat higher for steamed than boiled vegetables, and steaming was the clear winner.

Steaming is an easy method for cooking any size artichoke, from whole, giant globes to tiny babies as well as trimmed hearts. I put whole artichokes, stem end up, in about an inch of water in a heavy-gauge, nonreactive pot with a tight-fitting lid. A steaming rack was useful but not necessary; I tried steaming both with and without the rack, and got similar results.

I should add that braising, which combines browning and simmering, also produces very flavorful artichokes. However, this method involves more work than steaming, since you first have to sauté the artichokes, then deglaze the pan, then simmer the artichokes in liquid.

Are They Done Yet?

To me, scraping uncooked artichoke leaves on my teeth is as unpleasant as hearing fingernails scratching on a blackboard. For this reason, I paid particular attention to methods of checking for doneness.

Whole artichokes are cooked when the outer leaves pull away from the base without much effort. The inner leaves, however, which are smaller and thinner, are easy to remove even before the thistle is thoroughly cooked. For added assurance, I taste-tested the leaves to be sure they were well cooked.

This testing method, although foolproof, can be difficult to execute when you are working with steaming hot artichokes. Fortunately, there is another trustworthy method, which works especially well for hearts: Insert a toothpick or skewer into the stem end. If it is easy to insert, the artichoke should be tender.

MASTER RECIPE FOR STEAMED WHOLE ARTICHOKES
Serves 4

A steaming apparatus, such as a collapsible basket or bamboo rack, is helpful but not necessary for whole artichokes. Simply make use of the artichoke's tips and trimmings as a rack. Artichokes can be served warm with melted butter or at room temperature with one of the vinaigrettes that follow.

> 4 large *or* 12 baby artichokes, rinsed
> and trimmed
> Salt

1. Place steaming apparatus (optional) in large nonreactive pot with tight-fitting lid; bring 1 inch of water to boil.

2. Place artichokes, stem end up, in steaming apparatus or in water. Sprinkle with ½ teaspoon salt; cover and steam over medium-high

1. Using a chef's knife, cut off the stem.

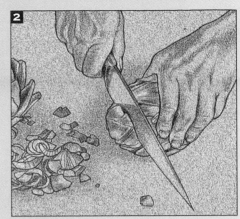

2. Next cut off the top quarter of the artichoke.

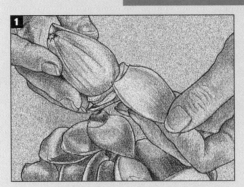

1. First, cut off the stem and top quarter as shown above. Then, to get to the heart of the artichoke, bend back and snap off the outer leaves, leaving the thick bottom portion attached to the base. Continue snapping off the leaves until you reach the light yellow cone at the center.

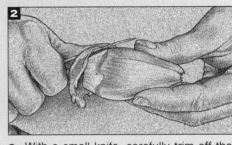

2. With a small knife, carefully trim off the dark green outer layer from the bottom of the artichoke.

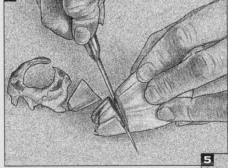

3. Cut off the dark section of the top.

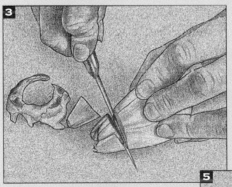

4. The raw heart can be halved to remove the inedible center or it can be cooked first, then halved and dechoked.

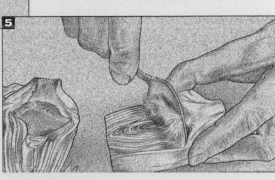

5. In either case, remove the purple leaves and the fuzzy choke with a sharp-edged spoon. This step is not necessary if using baby artichokes.

To get the best artichokes, pay attention to the following characteristics:

SIZE: The size of the thistle depends on where on the plant it grew. The artichoke growing on the center stalk is the largest. Those growing where the leaves meet the stem are widely and incorrectly referred to as babies; they are actually mature, but they grow in the shade of the leaves and are smaller. Artichokes that cook together should be as uniform in size as possible so they finish cooking at approximately the same time.

COMPACTNESS: Tightly packed artichokes are ideal. The leaves seem to have more edible flesh, they cook better, and the inedible chokes are smaller.

FRESHNESS: Leaves should look plump and not shriveled. When bent back, they should snap, not tear. A small amount of brown discoloration at the stem and tips is fine, but avoid shriveled brown stems and leaves. Choose those that feel heaviest. According to Julia Child, "Very fresh artichokes will talk to you when you squeeze the head — squeaky fresh, in other words."

SEASONALITY: Artichokes are available year-round, but they are at their peak in California in the spring, from March to May, when the price often drops.

heat until tender, about 40 minutes for large whole artichokes, about 25 minutes for babies; outer leaves should pull away easily and the stem end should be thoroughly tender.

3. Gently remove artichokes with tongs. Serve immediately or cool, stem end up, to room temperature. (Can be covered and refrigerated overnight; bring to room temperature before serving.)

MASTER RECIPE FOR STEAMED ARTICHOKE HEARTS
Serves 4
Toss warm artichoke hearts with butter and lemon juice and serve as a vegetable. Or, cool hearts to room temperature and drizzle with one of the vinaigrettes that follow; serve as an antipasto or salad.

    4   large *or* 12 baby artichokes, rinsed and trimmed to the heart (*see* "Getting to the Heart," page 11), large hearts halved, de-choked, and, if desired, quartered; baby hearts left whole or halved
          Salt

1. Place steaming apparatus in large nonreactive pot with tight-fitting lid; bring 1 inch of water to boil.
2. Place artichoke hearts in steaming apparatus. Sprinkle with ½ teaspoon salt; cover and steam over medium-high heat until tender, about 30 minutes for large hearts (20 minutes, if halved; 10 minutes, if quartered), and about 15 minutes for baby hearts (10 minutes, if halved).
3. Carefully lift steaming apparatus from pot. Use tongs to gently remove hearts. Serve hearts immediately or cool to room temperature. (Can be covered and refrigerated overnight; bring to room temperature before serving.)

LEMON-CHIVE VINAIGRETTE
Serves 4
Other fresh herbs, such as dill or parsley, can be substituted for the chives in this citrus sauce.

  4½   tablespoons lemon juice
       Salt
  ⅔   cup olive oil
   2   tablespoons snipped fresh chives

Whisk lemon juice and ½ teaspoon salt in a small nonreactive bowl. Gradually whisk in oil so that mixture emulsifies. Just before serving, stir in chives. Serve in small individual bowls to accompany steamed artichokes.

BALSAMIC VINAIGRETTE
Serves 4
This vinaigrette can be served as a dipping sauce for large whole artichokes. Artichoke hearts can be tossed in some of the vinaigrette and served on Bibb lettuce with a complementary salad of grated carrots and thin-sliced scallions; drizzle some of the vinaigrette over the carrot salad and the lettuce.

  ¼   cup balsamic vinegar
   2   tablespoons sherry or wine vinegar
      Salt and ground black pepper
  ⅔   cup olive oil

Whisk first 2 ingredients with ½ teaspoon salt and ¼ teaspoon pepper in a small bowl. Gradually whisk in oil, so that vinaigrette emulsifies. Serve.

SPAGHETTI WITH ARTICHOKE-LOBSTER SAUCE
Serves 6
This pasta dish makes an especially nice first course. If you prefer, you can substitute for the lobster one pound boneless, skinless chicken breast, cut into one-by-one-and-one-half-inch pieces, seasoned with salt and pepper and quickly sautéed.

   2   1½ pound lobsters, or 2 cups cooked crabmeat
   1   pound spaghetti
  ¼   cup olive oil
      Salt and ground black pepper
   6   tablespoons juice from 2 lemons
  16   baby artichoke hearts, halved and steamed (*see* Master Recipe for Steamed Artichoke Hearts)
   3   tablespoons minced fresh parsley

1. Bring 1 inch water to boil in large pot. Add lobsters; steam until done, 10 to 12 minutes. Cool slightly, then remove tail and claw meat. Cut lobster meat into bite-size pieces and set aside.
2. Bring 1 gallon of water to boil in a large pot. Add 1 tablespoon salt and the spaghetti; boil until al dente.
3. Meanwhile whisk olive oil, ½ teaspoon salt, ¼ teaspoon pepper, and the lemon juice in a medium bowl.
4. Drain pasta, but do not shake dry; return to pot. Add dressing; toss to coat. Add lobster, artichoke, and parsley; toss carefully. Serve immediately.

BRAISED ARTICHOKES WITH TOMATOES AND GARLIC
Serves 4 as an appetizer or side dish
I found an enamel-coated cast iron pot works best for sealing in the moisture and ensuring even heat distribution.

   2   tablespoons olive oil
  12   baby artichoke hearts, halved, or 4 large hearts, halved, dechoked, and quartered (*see* "Getting to the Heart," page 11)
   3   cloves garlic, minced
  ½   small onion, minced
  ⅓   cup dry white wine
  ¼   cup water
   1   can (16 ounces) plum tomatoes, juice drained and reserved for another use; tomatoes halved and seeded
  ¼   teaspoon dried thyme leaves
      Salt
   2   teaspoons minced fresh parsley

1. Heat oil in large, heavy-gauge nonreactive soup kettle. Add artichokes and sauté over medium heat, stirring frequently, until light brown, about 7 minutes.
2. Add garlic and onion; sauté until softened, about 4 minutes. Stir in white wine; simmer until reduced by half, 2 to 3 minutes. Add water, tomatoes, thyme, and salt to taste. Cover and cook over low heat until artichokes are tender, about 25 minutes.
3. Uncover and simmer until juices thicken, about 5 minutes. Sprinkle with parsley. Serve hot or at room temperature. ■

Pamela Parseghian is the food editor of *Nation's Restaurant News*, a trade journal based in New York City.

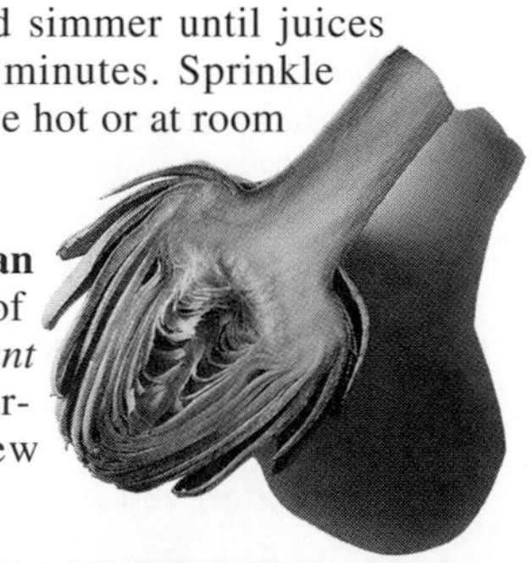

PHOTOGRAPH BY ERIC ROTH

Five Easy Sauces for Fish

Quick, flavorful accompaniments for grilled or broiled fish.

~ BY MARK BITTMAN AND STEVE JOHNSON ~

Mastering the basics of grilling fish is pretty straightforward, but there are a few simple rules worth following. First, don't build a super-hot fire; you should be able to hold your hand above the grate for two or three seconds. Preheat gas grills at the highest setting for at least ten minutes.

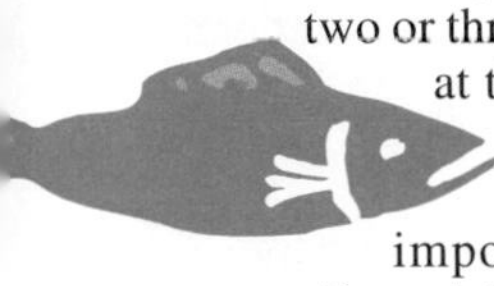

A clean grill rack is also important; use a wire brush to scrape off any debris. Before putting the fish on the rack, oil it lightly. Too much oil will cause an instant flare-up, however, so be careful.

Finally, place the fish on the grill (skin-side down, if you have the option) and let it sit for at least two minutes before turning. This allows the fish to build up a firm crust, which helps it to release from the grill rack without sticking.

Broiling fish is even easier than grilling. Because you can adjust the distance from the heat source to the food, it gives you greater control. You can broil thin fillets just two inches from the heat source, allowing them to brown before they overcook. You can also broil in a nonstick pan or on a nonstick cookie sheet, so there are fewer problems with sticking.

Whether you grill or broil your fish, though, you can be sure that when you match the proper fish with one of these accompaniments, you will have a summer meal that is quick, flavorful, and light enough for hot weather dining.

WARM CUCUMBER/RED ONION RELISH WITH MINT
Serves 6 (about 2 cups)
Salmon is the most logical choice to serve with this relish, because of its traditional and well-known affinity to mint and cucumbers. But this somewhat delicate sauce also works nicely with broiled or pan-cooked lighter fish, such as cod or flounder.

- 5 tablespoons olive oil
- 2 cucumbers, halved, seeded, and sliced thin (peeled if thick skinned)
- 1 medium red onion, halved and sliced thin
   Salt and ground black pepper
- 2 tablespoons red wine vinegar
- 2 tablespoons chopped fresh mint

Heat 2 tablespoons oil in large sauté pan. Add cucumbers; sauté until lightly colored, about 2 minutes. Add onion and salt and pepper to taste; sauté until vegetables just turn translu-cent, about 2 minutes longer. Turn cucumber mixture into medium bowl; stir in vinegar, mint, and remaining olive oil. Check season-ings and serve.

LIME-GINGER VINAIGRETTE
Serves 4 (about ½ cup)
This sauce is delicious with any firm white- or light-fleshed fish such as halibut, monkfish, shark, or swordfish, whether grilled or broiled. If you grow your own cilantro or have ac-cess to fresh green berries, substi-tute them for the coriander seeds listed below, and use parsley in place of cilantro.

- 2 tablespoons juice from 1 lime
- 1½ teaspoons minced or grated ginger
- 1 teaspoon dried coriander seeds, crushed
- ¼ teaspoon crushed red pepper flakes
- 1 tablespoon Vietnamese fish sauce (nuoc mam)
- 1 tablespoon chopped fresh basil
- 1 tablespoon chopped fresh cilantro
- ⅓ cup canola oil
   Salt and ground black pepper

Mix first 3 ingredients in small bowl; let stand for 15 minutes. Whisk in next 4 ingredients, then the oil. Season to taste with salt and pep-per. Let stand for 1 hour before serving.

ONION, BLACK OLIVE, AND CAPER COMPOTE
Serves 6 (about 2 cups)
This intensely flavored, high-acid sauce com-plements fatty fish such as bluefish, mackerel, and tuna.

- ½ cup olive oil
- 2 medium onions, halved and sliced thin
- 6 cloves garlic, sliced thin
- ½ cup black olives, such as Kalamatas, pitted and chopped coarse
- ¼ cup capers
- 2 anchovy fillets, rinsed and minced
- ¼ cup balsamic vinegar
- 1 teaspoon minced fresh marjoram, or ½ teaspoon dried
- 2 tablespoons minced fresh parsley
   Salt and ground black pepper to taste

Heat 2 tablespoons oil in large sauté pan. Add onions and sauté over medium heat until soft-ened, about 5 minutes. Add garlic; sauté until fragrant, about 1 minute longer. Turn onion mixture into medium bowl; stir in remaining ingredients. Serve compote warm or at room temperature.

PLUM TOMATO SALSA WITH SHERRY VINEGAR
Serves 6 (about 2 cups)
One of the classic accompaniments for grilled shrimp and other shellfish (including grilled or roasted clams), this salsa also cuts the richness of tuna, swordfish, and bluefish. For a milder salsa, substitute a jalapeño for the serrano chile.

- 6 plum tomatoes, peeled, seeded, and cut into ½-inch dice
- 1 medium shallot, sliced thin
- 1 serrano chile, seeded and sliced thin
- 2 tablespoons sherry vinegar
- ⅓ cup olive oil
- ½ teaspoon chopped fresh thyme, or ¼ teaspoon dried
- 1 tablespoon chopped fresh cilantro
- 1 tablespoon chopped fresh parsley
   Salt and ground black pepper to taste

Mix all ingredients together in medium bowl. Serve within 2 hours.

HOISIN-SESAME SAUCE
Serves 4 (about ½ cup)
This dense, rich sauce is best with rich-textured fish such as grilled shrimp or scallops; it's also great with salmon. Just before serving, you can sprinkle thin sliced scallions and toasted sesame seeds over the sauce.

- 2 tablespoons sesame oil
- ¼ teaspoon crushed red pepper flakes
- 1 tablespoon minced ginger
- 1 medium clove garlic, minced
- ¼ cup hoisin sauce
- 2 tablespoons balsamic vinegar
- 2 tablespoons soy sauce
- 2 tablespoons fresh orange juice
- 1 teaspoon ground coriander
- ½ teaspoon Chinese 5-spice powder

Heat oil with pepper flakes in small skillet. Add ginger and garlic; sauté until softened, 1 to 2 minutes. Pour this flavored oil into small bowl; stir in remaining ingredients. Serve warm or at room temperature. ■

Steve Johnson is the *chef de cuisine* at Hamersley's Bistro in Boston.

Free-Form Fruit Tart

Proper rolling and chilling creates a tender crust that you can form into any shape, mask with pastry cream, and then top with fresh, seasonal fruits.

~ BY NICK MALGIERI ~

The elements of a fruit tart are the same, no matter what fruit is used: A tender, fragile, and slightly sweet crust is spread with a small amount of pastry cream which is in turn covered with a selection of fresh, raw fruit. A glaze, although not essential, may be used to highlight both the flavor and appearance of the fruit.

A free-form tart, such as the one here, simplifies the process by eliminating the need for a tart pan with removable sides. Instead, you simply form the dough into the shape that you wish; edges are created with the crimping maneuver familiar to bakers of pie crusts.

Tart doughs are usually wrapped and chilled, or at least rested, at two stages (see "Chilling Out," right). In both cases, resting helps to limit gluten development in the dough and to hydrate the starch in the flour, which prevents toughness and excessive distortion in the baked dough.

Because of the high butter content of this dough, docking (piercing the dough with holes before baking) is important. During baking, water trapped in the dough begins to evaporate, causing steam to accumulate in the tiny spaces previously occupied by the butter, which has melted. These spaces inflate and distort the tart crust if the crust is not docked. This is particularly important with a free-form crust, such as the one used here, which has no pan to help maintain its shape.

If the quantity of pastry cream we specify seems small, remember that too much pastry

cream makes the tart overly rich; excess pastry cream will also ooze out between the fruit, making the tart look sloppy.

In this recipe we eliminate the painstaking process of thin-slicing fruit and arranging it in careful concentric circles. Instead, a variety of fruits are simply tossed together and then spooned on top of the pastry cream layer.

Any fruit normally served uncooked will be perfect in this type of tart, with the exception of those that discolor quickly, such as apples, pears, bananas, peaches, and apricots. Good candidates include blackberries, blueberries, raspberries, strawberries, seedless grapes, kiwis, oranges, mangoes, and papayas. The first three berries can be simply rinsed and dried prior to use; strawberries should be hulled and halved; grapes should be halved if large; kiwis peeled, halved, and sliced; oranges peeled and sectioned; and mangoes and papayas peeled, pitted, and sliced thinly.

FREE-FORM FRUIT TART
Serves 8

Although the crust can be baked and pastry cream can be made a day ahead, a fruit tart is best assembled just before serving, ensuring a crisp crust and a fruit juice-free custard.

If you prefer, you can fashion the dough into a square or rectangular base, rather than a disk.

In that case, rotate the dough ninety degrees rather than forty-five degrees when flattening and rolling it (see steps 2, 3, and 4, page 15).

Free-Form Pastry Shell
- 1¼ cups all-purpose, bleached flour, about 5½ ounces (spoon flour into measuring cup and level off with a spatula)
- 2 tablespoons sugar
- ⅛ teaspoon salt
- ⅛ teaspoon baking powder
- 7 tablespoons cold, unsalted butter, cut into ½-inch pieces
- 1 egg beaten with 1 tablespoon water

Easy Pastry Cream
- 3 tablespoons sugar
- 2 tablespoons all-purpose bleached flour
- Pinch of salt
- ¾ cup milk
- 1 egg
- 1 egg yolk
- 1 teaspoon vanilla extract
- 1 tablespoon unsalted butter, softened
- 2 teaspoons orange liqueur or Kirsch

- 6 cups mixed fruit
- ¼ cup apple jelly

CHILLING OUT

Is it really necessary, we wondered, to chill tart dough before and after rolling it out? If so, what is the perfect length of time for chilling, and can you speed up the process by using the freezer?

To answer these questions, we tried chilling the dough in the refrigerator both before and after rolling; using the freezer for both chilling periods; using the refrigerator for one chilling period and the freezer for the other; skipping both of the periods; and finally skipping first one and

then the other of the two chilling periods.

Some of the test results were as expected: Dough that hadn't been chilled at all, for example, was too sticky to roll easily and required extra flour, making it tougher. All the doughs that weren't chilled enough looked blistered after baking, because the too-soft butter bubbled out. Doughs that sat in the freezer for twenty minutes before rolling seemed to get too cold on the outside, so that the edges cracked early in the rolling — but then they

warmed up too fast and required extra flour and delicate handling by the end of the rolling.

We got the best shell by refrigerating the dough for an hour before rolling, then freezing it for twenty minutes after rolling but before baking. This shell was tender, browned evenly, and held its shape well. Although the shell that rested in the refrigerator for an hour both before and after rolling was nearly as good, why wait the extra forty minutes?

— *Sharon K. Barrett*

1. *For the shell,* mix flour, sugar, salt, and baking powder in workbowl of food processor fitted with steel blade, or in medium bowl. Scatter butter over dry ingredients. With fingertips, a pastry blender, or steel blade of food processor, mix, cut, or pulse until mixture resembles coarse cornmeal. Add egg; stir with a fork or pulse until dough starts to form a rough ball, adding additional water 1 teaspoon at a time if necessary.

2. Remove dough from bowl and place on lightly floured work surface; pat dough into 5-inch disk shape. Wrap in plastic and chill until firm, at least 1 hour. (Can be refrigerated up to 5 days or double-wrapped and frozen up to 1 month; defrost overnight in refrigerator before using.)

3. Place dough on 14-inch square sheet of lightly floured parchment. To flatten dough, use rolling pin to press dough in a series of lines parallel to paper edge nearest you. Rotate paper about 45 degrees and continue pressing dough in series of parallel lines. Continue rotating (45 degrees) and pressing dough to flatten to ⅜-inch thick.

4. Starting at edge of dough nearest you, roll to far edge, but do not roll over edge itself. Without lifting rolling pin, roll back to edge nearest you. Rotate paper 45 degrees and continue to roll back and forth as described above, lightly sprinkling flour under and over dough when necessary, until dough is a 12½-inch disk.

5. Slide parchment paper and dough onto cookie sheet. Using a plate or cardboard disk as a guide, trim dough to a 12-inch disk. Fold dough about ½ inch under perimeter of disk. Flute edge of tart dough by pressing thumb and index finger of one hand about ½ inch apart on the outside lip while using index finger (or knuckle) of other hand to lightly press an indentation into space between thumb and finger; repeat around the perimeter of the dough. Using a table fork, prick dough at ½-inch intervals. Cover with plastic wrap; place in freezer until firm, about 20 minutes. (Can be refrigerated up to 3 days or frozen up to 4 weeks.)

6. Adjust oven rack to center position and heat oven to 400 degrees. Bake shell, lowering heat immediately to 350, until golden brown, about 20 minutes. Slide tart shell on parchment to a wire rack; cool to room temperature. (Can be wrapped in plastic and refrigerated up to 3 days or frozen up to 1 month. Reheat at 350 degrees about 10 minutes, then cool before filling.)

7. *For the pastry cream,* whisk sugar, flour, and salt together in a 1- to 1½-quart nonreactive saucepan. Whisk in milk, then egg and yolk. Heat mixture over low heat, whisking constantly, until pastry cream thickens and comes to a boil. Boil, whisking constantly, for 15 seconds.

8. Remove from heat; whisk in vanilla and butter. Scrape pastry cream into a nonreactive bowl and press plastic wrap against the surface.

Refrigerate until cold, at least 1 hour. (Can be refrigerated overnight.)

9. Stir liqueur into pastry cream, then spread pastry cream evenly over tart shell. Toss fruit in a bowl, then spoon over pastry cream.

10. Heat jelly in a small saucepan. Using a funnel if necessary, pour warm jelly into a heat-safe atomizer. Mist fruit evenly with apple glaze. Serve immediately. ∎

Nick Malgieri is the author of *Great Italian Desserts* (Little, Brown, 1990). He directs the baking program at the Peter Kump Cooking School in New York City.

MAKING THE FREE-FORM PASTRY SHELL

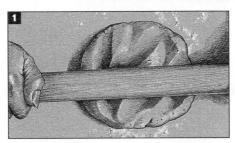

1. To flatten the dough, use a rolling pin to press the dough in a series of parallel lines. Rotate the paper forty-five degrees; continue pressing the dough in a series of parallel lines. Continue rotating (forty-five degrees) and pressing to flatten the dough to ⅜-inch thick.

2. Starting at the edge of the dough nearest you, roll toward the far end, without rolling over the edge. Roll back again from the far end to the near end. Rotate the paper forty-five degrees and continue in this manner until the dough is a 12½-inch disk.

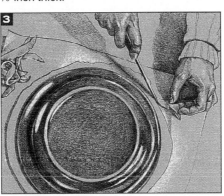

3. Using a plate as a guide, trim the dough to a 12-inch disk.

4. Fold dough about ½ inch under the perimeter of the disk.

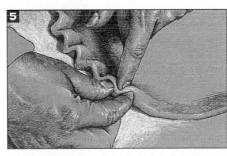

5. Flute the edge of the tart dough by pressing the thumb and index finger of one hand about ½ inch apart on the outside lip while using the index finger (or knuckle) of the other hand to lightly press an indentation into the space between the thumb and finger. Bake the shell as directed in step 6, left.

6. Spread the pastry cream evenly over the baked tart shell.

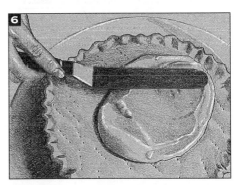

7. Spoon the fruit over the pastry cream. Using a funnel if necessary, pour the warm apple jelly into a heat-safe atomizer; mist the fruit with the apple glaze.

ILLUSTRATIONS BY TONY DELUZ

Cleaning Shrimp, Squid, and Soft-Shell Crab

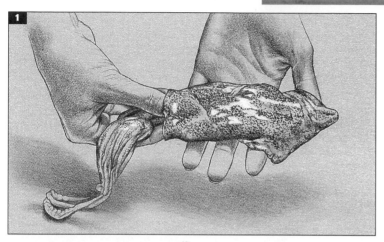

1. Reach into the squid's body with your fingers, grasping as much of the innards as you can.

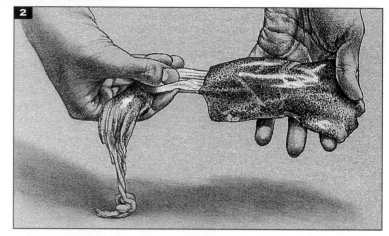

2. Gently pull out the head and innards.

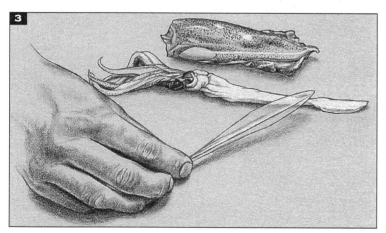

3. You may have to make a second incursion to remove the hard, plastic-like "quill"; it will come out easily once you find it.

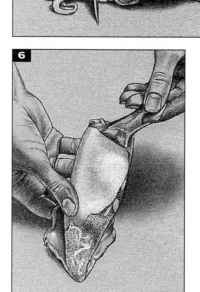

4. Cut the tentacles just above the squid's eyes. Be careful of the black ink (which can be reserved for sauce); it does stain.

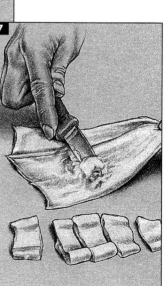

6. The thin, membranelike skin of the squid is perfectly edible; you can, if you prefer, peel it off easily.

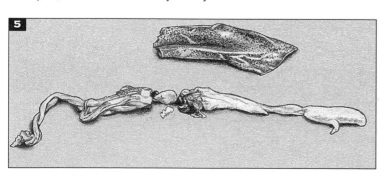

5. From the left: The edible tentacles (you may trim the two longest ones for the sake of appearance); the inedible "beak," which you should squeeze out of the tentacles if it doesn't fall out of its own accord; the inedible head and innards. In the rear: the edible body, or mantle.

7. Front: You can wash the interior of the mantle, then cut the mantle into rings. Rear: Or you can slit the mantle lengthwise, scrape off any remaining innards as shown, then rinse and cook.

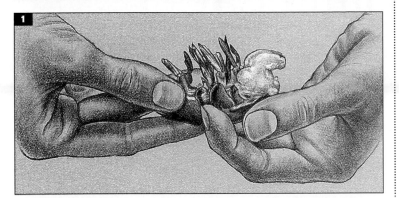

1. Hold the shrimp in one hand, with the legs facing up. Grab as many of the legs as you can with your other hand, and peel downwards.

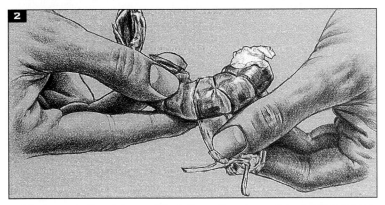

2. Moving your thumb toward the tail, continue to peel. In most instances, you will be able to remove most of the shell in one piece.

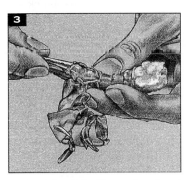

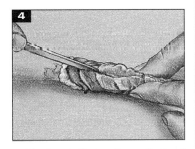

3. Pinch the tail with one hand and gently pull the body away from the tail; the tail meat will come out easily.

4. To devein first make a slit about one-eighth-inch deep along the length of the shrimp's back. Note that deveining is optional, as many shrimp have veins so pale that you can barely see them

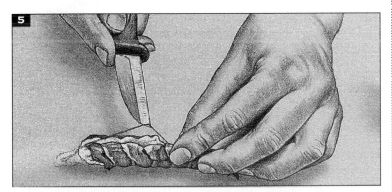

5. Lift out the vein with the point of a knife and discard.

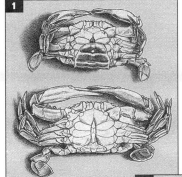

1. Female soft-shell crabs may contain roe and may be somewhat meatier and more flavorful than males. You can distinguish them in two ways: the tips of their claws are redder and their "apron" (the flap of shell on their belly) is much broader than that of the male. In this picture, the female is the top crab.

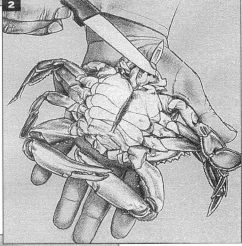

2. To clean, lift up the apron of the crab and twist or cut it off.

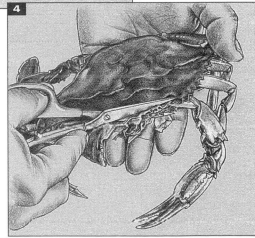

3. Lift the shell on each side of the body and, using your fingers or a small knife, remove the gray gills and discard.

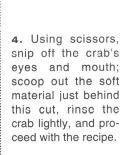

4. Using scissors, snip off the crab's eyes and mouth; scoop out the soft material just behind this cut, rinse the crab lightly, and proceed with the recipe.

The Best Pound Cake

After trying thirty-one pound cakes, we found that the perfect version varies the "pound-of-each" formula and relies on an unusual mixing method.

⁓ BY STEPHEN SCHMIDT ⁓

Pound cakes formed the bridge between the heavy fruit cakes of Medieval times and the lighter cakes of today. The right proportion of ingredients plus careful mixing can still produce a great pound cake with no chemical leavening.

Unlike their modern descendants, classic pound cakes contain no chemical leavening. Instead, they depend for lightness on the innate puffing power of eggs and on the air incorporated into the batter through beating. This gives these cakes a wonderful flavor, but can cause problems with texture. After testing thirty-one old-style pound cake recipes, however, I have found one that is perfect in every regard — and, because the cake is made without a speck of baking powder, it tastes of pure butter and eggs.

Problems with Texture

I embarked on my orgy of baking knowing that the main difficulty with pound cakes of the classic type is textural. Cakes might be said to have five "texture points": moist/dry; soft/hard; dense/porous; light/heavy; rich/plain. To the contemporary taste, cakes *must* be relatively moist and soft; the three remaining texture points are negotiable.

The problem with pound cake is that we ask it to be moist and soft, on the one hand, but also dense, light, and rich on the other. This is an extremely difficult texture to achieve — unless one resorts to baking powder, with its potent chemical magic. Air-leavened cakes that are light and soft tend also to be porous and plain, as in sponge or angel cakes; those that are moist and dense inevitably also come out heavy, as in the various syrup-soaked bundt cakes currently so popular. From pound cake we ask all things.

The Mixing Method

In my early experiments, my interest was in comparing the merits of the three major mixing methods for pound cake. Accordingly, I prepared all of the cakes with exactly one-half pound each of flour, sugar, butter, and eggs. When I got what looked to be a promising result, I also tried adding varying amounts of liquid in the hope of achieving perfection.

The first mixing method I tried is probably the most common and it produced good cakes, but not great ones. It entails creaming the butter, sugar, and egg yolks into a fluff, adding flour, and then folding in the stiffly whipped egg whites. But the cakes were a little tough, dry, and heavy, and they did not taste quite rich enough. I next tried adding some of the sugar to the egg whites during beating, in order to give the whites more strength and puffing power. This did make the cakes lighter and more tender, but I still found them dry and insufficiently rich. Adding one-quarter cup of liquid, as older cookbooks recommend, made the cakes moister but also turned them rubbery.

In French cookbooks, pound cake is generally mixed like genoise. The eggs and sugar are first whipped into a fluffy mass, and then the flour and butter (melted or softened to the consistency of mayonnaise) are folded in. Although I tried several variations on this method, adding liquid at different points in the process, beating the yolks and whites separately, I got generally similar results. All the cakes were good — moist, soft, and fairly light — but they were also crumbly and coarse-grained, a little, in fact, like genoise. In short, all of the cakes failed the density test. This may well be the French understanding of pound cake, but it is not mine.

The simplest, most straightforward method of making pound cake involves beating the butter and sugar to a fluffy cream, adding the eggs (whole) one at a time, creaming the batter some more, and then mixing in the flour. No matter how I tried this method — with and without liquid, beating the batter after putting in the flour

TEMPERATURES AND MEASURES

Emulsification of butter and eggs is crucial to producing a pound cake with proper texture. For optimal emulsification, both the butter and eggs should be at around seventy degrees. At this temperature, the butter will be just firm enough to come cleanly away from the wrapper; the beaten eggs will feel slightly cool when you dip a finger in. Butter that has become too warm should be returned briefly to the refrigerator. Since eggs separate best when cold, leave them in the refrigerator until just before you use them, then, as you beat them, immerse the bottom of the cup in tepid water. If your kitchen is very hot, use butter the consistency of firm clay (around sixty degrees) and distinctly cool eggs.

Careful flour measurement is crucial if you are to end up with seven ounces in your cake. Before your begin, your flour should be turned into a canister or other container and shaken a few times to settle it. When measuring, dip a half-cup measure into the flour, filling it completely, and sweep off the excess with the back of a knife. Do not tamp the flour down or shake the cup. And do not spoon extra flour in: if you do not fill the cup completely the first time, dump the flour back into the canister, give the canister a little shake, and try again.

(as some old cookbooks recommend) — I got simply awful results. The cakes were rubber doorstops. How could any conscientious cookbook author possibly print a recipe of this type? I wondered indignantly. I still believe that this method, if dispatched without important adjustments in both ingredients and technique, is very poor. However, once I'd learned a few more things about pound cake, I actually adopted a modified version of this method.

The Ingredients

Having thus far failed to make a perfect pound cake with any mixing method, I turned my attention to the ingredients themselves. In my readings of old cookbooks, I had long noted that pound cake, in the period of its greatest popularity, was rarely made with precisely one pound each of flour, sugar, butter, and eggs; nor were these necessarily the only ingredients used. For example, Eliza Leslie, the Julia Child of the 1830s and 40s, specifies a "small pound of flour" (around fourteen ounces, I believe), "a large pound of sugar" (perhaps eighteen ounces), and somewhat better than one-half cup of liquid (eggs plus brandy, sherry, or rose water). Leslie's fiddling with the flour and sugar are atypical, but her use of one-half cup liquid is virtually *invariable* in pound cake recipes written before 1850. Meanwhile, other authors play around with the eggs. In *The Virginia House-Wife* (1824), Mary Randolph specifies a dozen eggs; in her time, ten eggs were generally considered to weigh one pound. Susannah Carter, an English author whose cookery book was published in America in 1772, calls for six whole eggs and six yolks. Carter's idea to use extra yolks eventually proved a cornerstone in my own recipe.

Before tinkering with the sacrosanct pound formula, I decided to consult some modern cookbooks. I could hardly believe what I found in Flo Braker's *The Simple Art of Perfect Baking* (Morrow, 1985). Her classic pound cake is mixed in a way very similar to the third method I had tried, the one that I had found disastrous! Now, Flo Braker's baking is indeed perfect, and I knew that she could not be in error. So I made her pound cake exactly as directed, and it turned out, indeed, to be the very best one I had baked so far. What made the difference?

First of all, Braker has refined the mixing method. Instead of adding whole eggs one at a time to the creamed butter and sugar, she directs that the eggs first be lightly beaten in a bowl and then added by tablespoons to the butter mixture. The butter and sugar mixture is evidently incapable of absorbing whole eggs; the mixture "curdles" and all the air is let out, resulting in tough, shrunken, wet pound cakes. But dribbling in the egg a little at a time preserves the emulsion — Braker cannily compares the process to making mayonnaise — and allows all the air to be retained, making for a light, soft, tender cake. In baking, everything is in the details.

I also noted that Braker has slightly modified the one-pound-each proportions. Her recipe, a "half-pound" cake like the ones I had been working with, calls for roughly seven ounces of flour, nine ounces of sugar, and five eggs (ten ounces weighed with the shells, the usual method of computation, or eight and three-quarters ounces weighed without). She calls for eight ounces of butter, the standard amount, and no added liquid other than almond and vanilla extracts. What a brilliant formula this is. Decreasing the flour makes the cake moister; increasing the sugar makes it more tender and, of course, sweeter; and adding an extra egg adds both moistness and lightness while at the same time compensating for the loss of structure caused by removing a little of the flour.

For many people, Flo Braker's Viceroy Pound Cake will prove to be the only pound cake recipe they will ever need. It is a truly wonderful cake. I was hoping, however, to make a slightly denser cake, to suit my personal tastes. Adding liquid to Braker's pound cake turned it rubbery; increasing the butter by a mere two tablespoons made it heavy. I tried any number of other small modifications, all to no avail, until finally I remembered Susannah Carter's recipe, with those extra egg yolks. Because they contain lecithin, yolks are good emulsifiers and thus help the batter retain air, making the cake light. Their fattiness contributes richness, tenderness, and moistness, while tamping the batter down a bit and thus militating against too fluffy an effect. Finally, the deep yellow of egg yolks gives the cake a beautiful golden color. Herewith is my own version of the perfect classic pound cake, inspired by gifted bakers living two centuries apart.

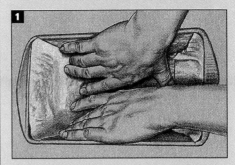

LINING THE PAN

1. To cover the ends: Cut two pieces of parchment paper large enough so that they cover the ends and overlap both the bottom and corners of the pan by about one-half to one inch. Fit securely into the ends of the pan.

2. To cover the sides and bottom: Cut one piece of parchment paper large enough to run down the side of the pan, across the bottom, and up the other side, overlapping the top edges by about one inch. Fit securely into the pan, making sure to cover the overlapping portions of the end pieces.

OLD VS. NEW POUND CAKE

Cakes made with one pound each of flour, sugar, butter, and eggs began to emerge in England in the mid- and late seventeenth century. Originally, these cakes seem to have been conceived as richer, moister, more tender alternatives to the various yeast-leavened fruit cakes, similar to today's stollen and Gugelhopf, that had been the only type of cake known since the Middle Ages. Thus the earliest pound-type cakes always contained dried or candied fruit, almonds, or seeds. Around 1720, the basic batter began to be baked without additions, and the term pound cake arose.

The heyday of the pound cake was relatively brief — in 1854, American cookery author Eliza Leslie declared that "pound cake is not so much in use as formerly, particularly for weddings and large parties" — but its influence on American baking was enormous. Today's standard American butter cake, of which yellow, white, and most chocolate cakes are offshoots, grew directly out of the pound formula. (The French also make a type of pound cake, which they probably borrowed from the English. Interestingly, though, they took *biscuit,* or sponge cake, as their basic cake

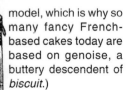

model, which is why so many fancy French-based cakes today are based on genoise, a buttery descendent of *biscuit.*)

Ironically, American bakers eventually reinvented pound cake as a chemically leavened butter cake, simply adding a little extra flour and sugar for the requisite density. The father became the son. Mrs. S. R. Dulle dubbed the new hybrid Twentieth-Century Pound Cake, and she found it lighter, moister, and more tender than the original. Ever since, a lively controversy has raged: which is better, classic pound cake or the modern kind?

THE BEST POUND CAKE
Serves 8–10

Before making this cake, read "Temperatures and Measures," page 18, to make sure butter and eggs are at the right temperature and flour is measured properly.

Be careful not to overbeat the butter-sugar mixture, especially on a hot day — you could rupture the air cells and cause the batter to be heavy. It's important to beat in the eggs very slowly. If you don't think you can pace yourself, set a timer or watch the clock. When you are folding in the flour, fold up from the very bottom of the bowl, otherwise some of the batter will have little flour in it, and this will either rise to the surface, never cooking through, or settle in hard, dense streaks near the bottom of the cake. You may double the recipe and bake the cake in a large nonstick bundt pan (fourteen cup capacity); the baking time remains the same. The recipe also makes four miniature pound cakes; use four two-cup pans and reduce baking time to forty minutes. Though best when freshly baked, the cake will keep reasonably well for four to five days.

1	cup (2 sticks) unsalted butter, softened (8 ounces)
1⅓	cups sugar (9 ounces)
3	large eggs (5.25 ounces, without the shells)
3	large egg yolks (2 ounces)
1½	teaspoons pure vanilla extract
1½	teaspoons water
½	teaspoon salt
1½	cups plain cake flour, measured by dip-and-sweep (7 ounces)

1. Adjust oven rack to center position and heat oven to 325 degrees. Grease a 9-by-5-by-3½-inch loaf pan (7½-cup capacity) with vegetable shortening or spray. Follow illustrations in "Lining the Pan," page 19, to line bottom and sides of pan with parchment.

2. Beat butter in bowl of electric mixer set at medium-high speed until smooth and shiny, about 15 seconds. With machine still on, take about 30 seconds to sprinkle in sugar. Beat mixture until light, fluffy, and almost white, 4 to 5 minutes, stopping mixer once or twice to scrape down sides of bowl.

3. Mix eggs, yolks, vanilla, and water in a 2-cup glass measure with a pour spout, set in a pan of tepid water until mixture is about 70 degrees (*see* "Temperatures and Measures," page 18). With mixer set at medium-high speed, take 3 to 5 minutes to add egg mixture to butter/sugar mixture in a very slow, thin stream. Finally, beat in salt.

4. Remove bowl from mixer stand. Turn ½ cup of flour into sieve or shaker; sprinkle it over batter. Fold gently with rubber spatula, scraping up from bottom of the bowl, until flour is incorporated. Repeat twice more, adding flour in ½-cup increments.

5. Scrape batter into prepared pan, smoothing top with a spatula or wooden spoon. Bake

until cake needle or tester inserted into crack running along top comes out clean, 70 to 80 minutes. Let cake rest in pan for 5 minutes, then invert onto wire rack. Place second wire rack on cake bottom, then turn cake top side up. Cool to room temperature, remove and discard parchment, wrap cake in plastic, then in foil. Store cake at room temperature.

Ginger Pound Cake: Add 3 tablespoons very finely minced candied ginger, 1½ teaspoons ground ginger, and ½ teaspoon mace along with the salt.

Citrus Pound Cake: Add any of the following along with the salt: the grated zests of 2 lemons, the grated zest of 1 orange, or the grated zest of 1 lemon and 1 orange. You may replace the water and vanilla extract with 1 tablespoon orange or lemon blossom water.

Rose Water Pound Cake: Replace vanilla extract and water with 1 tablespoon rose water and add ½ teaspoon ground mace along with the salt.

Seed Cake: Turn 1 teaspoon anise seed and ½ teaspoon caraway seed into a mortar and crush to a coarse powder. Add the seeds along with the salt. You may replace the vanilla extract and water with 1 tablespoon of brandy. ∎

Stephen Schmidt is the author of *Master Recipes* (Ballantine, 1987).

IN SEARCH OF LOW-FAT POUND CAKE

I spent a good deal of time trying to create a low-fat pound cake. I found, however, that significant quantities of both butter and egg yolk were required to make a cake with the qualities that I think make pound cake most attractive: lightness, moistness, and good flavor.

Pound cakes made without chemical leavener need to have a significant amount of air incorporated into them, or they will be heavy little bricks. The baker has several choices as to how to beat in the air: whip the butter and sugar, or beat the eggs to a foam, or combine both methods. In the course of my experiments, I found that I preferred the texture of pound cakes aerated through the whipping of the butter and sugar. Thus, in my recipe, fat plays an important part in leavening the cake.

I did find it possible to raise pound cake using a slightly reduced quantity of butter (in ratio to flour). Butter is heavy. Therefore, while lowering the butter content decreases the number of air cells that can be incorporated into the batter, it also decreases the need for these cells because the batter starts out lighter. Unfortunately, when I lowered the amount of butter, my cakes, though still light, came out dry. In common with other fats, butter helps to create an impression of moistness by promoting a melt-in-the-mouth sensation.

In some cakes, liquid can be added in lieu of fat to increase moistness, and I indeed attempted this strategy in a number of my pound cakes. I consistently found, however, that adding more than a tablespoon of liquid caused my cakes to become rubbery and chewy, no matter what other tricks I tried. In the worst instances, hard, dense streaks appeared in the crumb, a problem that is often warned of in old recipes, which typically call for up to one-quarter cup of liquid in the proportions I used. I did find that I could prevent the streaks by increasing the flour, but then my cakes turned hard and compact. Liquid was not the answer.

In addition to the butter, an appreciable amount of the fat in my pound cakes is derived from the six egg yolks called for. The quantity of yolks may strike some as high, but I believe the results more than justify it. In my early experiments, I stuck with the classic proportions of four eggs to roughly one-half pound each of flour, butter, and sugar. Nevertheless, no matter how I mixed my cakes, and no matter what adjustments I made in the weights of the other ingredients, my four-egg cakes consistently came out heavy and tough. When I added a fifth egg, my pound cakes became lighter — and a good deal better — but they also lost some of the requisite density and moistness. Eventually I discovered that substituting three yolks for the fourth and fifth whole eggs produced the lightness I was seeking without also bringing on the fluffiness and dryness that I did not want.

Finally, I will add that my pound cakes, fat-laden though they might seem, are not appreciably richer than many other cakes. Go through the recipes in any sophisticated baking book and add up the weights of fat (.5 ounce per tablespoon) and egg yolks (.65 ounce for each large) in relation to flour (4 to 5 ounces per cup depending on type, measured by dip-and-sweep) and egg whites (1 ounce each). In my pound cakes, the butter and yolks weigh 11.9 ounces altogether and the flour and egg whites 11 ounces, a ratio close to 1:1. You will find that the proportions called for in many recipes for other fine-quality butter cakes are much the same.

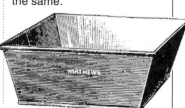

American Spaghetti Tops Tasting

American pastas take four of the top five spots in a blind tasting; the most expensive Italian import comes in dead last.

~ BY JONI MILLER ~

Get ready to change your thinking about dried pasta: Standard American brands are actually better than many pricey Italian imports. This was the surprising (and near-unanimous) conclusion of a *Cook's Illustrated* taste-test of eight leading brands of domestic and imported spaghetti.

With Ronzoni beating out every import, and ordinary American brands like Creamette and Mueller's near the top of the list, at first we thought something must be amiss with our test. After rechecking the results, it seems that our thinking — and that of most of those in the food world, since the superiority of Italian pasta is largely taken for granted — is out of step. Just as Europeans once thought the earth was flat, most Americans now believe that good pasta must come from Italy. It seems that both perceptions are false.

American Success Story

Dried pasta is nothing more than semolina flour and water. Despite this simplicity, there are large differences among commercial pastas. Until recently, American pastas were mushy and starchy. As the popularity of pasta began to explode in this country, however, the leading manufacturers and agricultural interests decided it was time to compete with the Italians.

"Fifteen years ago, Italian pasta was better than most of the small, regional brands made in this country," says C. Mickey Skinner, president of the Hershey Pasta Group, which makes Ronzoni and several other top brands. "Consolidation in the American pasta business has allowed manufacturers to spend the money needed to upgrade equipment and improve the quality of raw materials." Skinner notes that most of the domestic pasta business is now controlled by a few food giants who can afford the best high-tech European machinery.

In both Italy and the United States, dried pastas are now produced in factories using very similar manufacturing techniques. The flour and water are kneaded together to form a smooth dough, then mechanically forced through dies (usually made of brass) to form the pasta's shape. Once extruded, the pasta is placed on racks in drying ovens. The length of drying time is key to a good-quality product. If too much moisture remains in the pasta it may spoil; if too little moisture is retained the pasta becomes brittle and breaks easily.

As for the ingredients, they still come from different sources. Italians rely on European durum wheat — the hard variety that is milled to make semolina — from Italy and France. American companies use North American durum grown in North Dakota and neighboring areas of Canada. Skinner says American pasta companies now use the finest quality durum in the world. This was not always the case.

In the 1970s, largely in response to the increasing American appetite for pasta, North Dakota State University (NDSU) in Fargo launched a program to boost the quality of the local wheat. "The key to good dried pasta is flour with strong gluten characteristics," says Jim Jacobs, technical director of the Northern Crops Institute at NDSU. "When dried pasta is thrown into boiling water, the starch in the flour starts to swell. If there is not enough gluten or if the gluten is very weak, it cannot contain the swelling starch. The starch leaches into the cooking water or onto the surface of the pasta, which makes the cooked noodles taste gummy and starchy."

Jacobs explains that if pasta contains enough high-quality gluten, the gluten expands and encases the swelling starch molecules in the center of the noodle. The result is firm pasta that does not taste starchy. In addition, strong gluten increases the rigidity of the protein structure in the flour; stronger proteins mean firmer cooked noodles.

"The big push to improve quality," Jacobs recalls, occurred during the past decade. Most North Dakota farmers now plant newly developed varieties with strong gluten profiles. "Overall quality is at a very high point and we are making only minor modifications to the gene pool," he stresses. Along with new equipment from Europe (such as high-temperature dryers that remove water more rapidly than old devices), Jacobs credits better American wheat for better pasta.

Myth-Busting Tasting Results

Given the recent advances made in the American pasta business, the results of our tasting should not come as a surprise — at least that's the party line from domestic manufacturers. However, our panelists were in disbelief after their preferences had been revealed. In an informal poll conducted after the tasting, I asked panelists to name their personal favorites. With one exception, everyone mentioned Italian brands. Asked to speculate on the reasons for the strong showing of American pastas, Italian cooking authority Anna Teresa Callen commented, "The Americans have learned how to make pasta!"

AMERICA'S SPAGHETTI HISTORY

Spaghetti's long, cylindrical strands (the name translates from the Italian as "a length of cord" or "string") are entwined with Italian culinary history stretching back to twelveth-century Sicily. By the eighteenth century the port city of Naples in the south had also established itself as a center of commercial pasta manufacturing, with an emphasis on spaghetti.

In the late 1800s and early 1900s, many Neapolitans and Sicilians were among the first great wave of Italian immigrants to America. They brought with them sustaining supplies of spaghetti tucked away in their luggage. Soon they were sending home for new supplies and the first imported dry pasta, mostly spaghetti, arrived here. It was a taste of home for the immigrants, a nutritious new foodway for Americans.

The first American pasta factory was established in Brooklyn in 1848 not, as you might expect, by an Italian but by a French flour miller named Antoine Zerega who hailed from Lyon. Using a horse-powered millstone to grind flour, Zerega produced the first stateside spaghetti, spreading it out on a rooftop to dry in the bright New World sun.

Today, the American passion for pasta continues to grow. According to the National Pasta Association, in 1991 the average American ate 19 pounds of pasta, while American pasta producers annually sent 4.8 million pounds of pasta onto store shelves.

PHOTOGRAPH BY ERIC ROTH

The pastas are listed in order of preference (an asterisk indicates a pasta tied with the one immediately below it). In the judging, five points were awarded for each first-place vote; four for second; three for third; two for fourth; and one for fifth. Prices listed are for a sixteen-ounce box or package unless otherwise noted. Brands were purchased in the New York metropolitan area from supermarkets and specialty stores with high turnover. Prices will vary nationally.

1 Ronzoni Spaghetti (Hershey Foods Co., PA), 16 ounces, $1.19; 29 points. The only pasta ranked in the top five by all tasters was judged appealing on virtually every basis. A creamy golden yellow color with a smooth surface before cooking, after cooking it seemed to retain a "fuller," slightly more substantial shape than some others. The "good" texture was "very firm," "springy," and "resilient to the bite" (it "bounced back" from the teeth), with a "wonderful chewiness." The "excellent" to  "nice" flavor was "lively tasting" with a "clean, nutty flavor of wheat." However, several tasters found "minimal" flavor. The consensus: a good all-around spaghetti that would perform well with an "assertive," "hearty" sauce. *Widely available at supermarkets in the Northeast, all Rocky Mountain states, most Western states, and Florida.*

2* Mueller's Spaghetti (Best Foods, CPC International, NJ), 16 ounces, $.79; 21 points. A light golden, relatively rough-textured  pasta that some panelists felt exhibited texture problems once it had been cooked. "Rubbery and chewy at the same time," noted one taster, while another zeroed in on a "mushy" exterior yet found the strands "pleasantly resistant to the teeth" with "decent" bite. A desirable wheat flavor, "a little nutty," was clearly present. Still, some judged it lacking in flavor ("nondescript") and two panelists noticed a "slight, unidentifiable" or "off" aftertaste. An acceptable, mildly flavorful pasta. *Available in supermarkets east of the Mississippi.*

3 De Cecco Spaghetti (De Cecco, Fara San Martino, Italy), 16 ounces, $1.69; 21 points. A good, all-around pasta that was creamy beige and cooked up much lighter in color (almost "white") than others. "Clean and smooth" feeling in the mouth with a noticeably "slick" surface and good bite,  though a shade "sticky." Mixed response on the flavor front found some tasters drawn to an almost buttery "nuttiness" and a "distinctive" wheat flavor while others felt this spaghetti was "bland" and "nondescript." One panelist, detecting a "bad flavor" of cardboard, suspected it might have been an old or improperly stored box. It's interesting to note that whatever their opinion of the flavor, half of the panel identified this pasta's taste as a two-step experience (for example, an initial flavor that was bland and unflavorful followed by a "wheaty" aftertaste). "I liked the texture but I'm not sure about the flavor," summed up one taster. *Widely available nationwide at supermarkets and specialty stores.*

4 Creamette Spaghetti (Borden, Inc., MN), 16 ounces, $1.15; 20 points. Straw-colored with visible white specks when uncooked, the texture emerged as "a tad mushy" overall and not "firm" enough in the  center when cooked, though some liked its "slick, silky feel in the mouth." "A bit bland and "undistinguished," with a hint of wheat taste. One taster noted the flavor was more floury than wheaty. "OK flavor," summarized another panelist, but "the texture doesn't do much for me." *Available in supermarkets nationwide.*

5 Contadina della Casa Buitoni Spaghetti (High-Protein Pasta) (Nestle USA, Inc., CA), 8 ounces, $1.05; 17 points. An "odd" spaghetti unlike the others in appearance, with dark brown "soba-like" color before cooking; pale beige cooked. Firm and smooth with a bite that was slightly too soft. Darker color suggested  a flavor stronger than what some tasters found. Others liked the "earthy," rather "intense," wheaty taste. Aroma of "malt" and "yeast" noted by two tasters. "Has a kind of health food store flavor," concluded one taster. A puzzling pasta. *Available in supermarkets in the Northeast, Chicago, Florida, and California.*

6 Barilla Spaghetti (Barilla Alimentare S.p.A., Parma, Italy), 16 ounces, $1.50; 16 points. Italy's best-selling pasta evoked a middle-of-the-road response,  evaluated as a "pleasant"-tasting pasta with subtle wheat flavor and a firm, springy texture that two panelists found too "rubbery." An acceptable pasta. *Available at some specialty food shops and Italian specialty stores.*

7 Delverde Spaghetti all Chitarra (Fara San Martino, Italy), 16 ounces, $1.75; 7 points. Unique, slightly flat, squarish shape immediately noticed by all tasters, with one describing it as "homey" looking. Mixed reactions from tasters, with some quite  positive about the flavor despite a consensus that the pasta was "blah" and pale colored before cooking. Tasters noticed "white flecks," suggesting poor storage, old pasta, or not 100 percent semolina. Pallid and "very white" when cooked, without much bite ("too soft, too smooth"). Divided opinion on flavor: one taster detected a full sweet wheat taste, "even a little buttery," while another panelist noted a slightly "cardboardy" taste. *Available at specialty food shops and Italian specialty stores.*

8 Martelli (Martelli F. Lli Dino, Mario & C., s.n.c., Pisa, Italy), 17 ounces, $4.29; 4 points. By far the most expensive spaghetti in the tasting. Oddly "raw," pale, "anemic" appearance uncooked. "Albino  pasta," noted one taster. "Gummy," "gooey," and "slimy" in appearance after cooking with a "bland," very mild wheat flavor and a hint of "butteriness." The taste was "insipid" and "unexceptional" given the price. *Limited distribution in specialty food shops and Italian specialty stores.*

Together with cookbook author and teacher Callen, the panel for our blind tasting, held at Caffe Bondi in New York City, included chef/caterer Robert Cacciola; cooking instructor Daniel Rosati; food writer and New York *Daily News* restaurant reviewer Arthur Schwartz; Antonino Settepani, co-owner of Caffe Bondi; Kathleen Spadaro, president of a pasta company called Unlimited Pastabilities; Iris Carulli, a home cook who lived for an extended period in Italy; *Cook's Illustrated* senior writer Jack Bishop; and the author.

The eight brands of spaghetti were evaluated on the basis of color, aroma, taste, and texture. Panelists examined uncooked sheaths of each prior to the tasting and noted the color, which ranged from off-white to brown. With the exception of the brown Buitoni — the dark hue comes from wheat germ, gluten, and yeast, all of which are added to boost the protein content by 50 percent — we found no relationship between color and flavor.

After examining the raw spaghetti, each brand was tasted, one at a time. The pasta was prepared by Caffe Bondi's chef, Francesco Crescenzo-Crescenzi, who is a native of Naples. Each was cooked until al dente, drained, and then served hot without sauce. Texture criteria included a significant degree of "chewiness" or "good bite." Panelists noted if strands maintained the integrity of their shape and whether they exhibited proper elasticity. As for taste, testers were looking for a mild yet detectable wheat flavor and perhaps a slight, nutlike aroma. Tasters cleansed their palates with bottled water between samples.

Winners and Losers

The top-ranked pasta, once listed as a favorite by every tester, was Ronzoni, a midpriced ($1.19 per pound) American brand manufactured by the Hershey Foods Company. Along with Ronzoni, Hershey Pasta Group brands include American Beauty, Delmonico, Perfection, P & R, San Giorgio, and Skinner. Hershey Foods and Borden, Inc. (which manufactures Creamette, our fourth-placed spaghetti, as well as Prince, R & F, and Anthony brands), control more than three-quarters of the domestic pasta market with their various regional brands.

American-made Mueller's (the least expensive pasta sampled, at $.79), and De Cecco, the best-selling Italian import ($1.69) tied for second in the rankings, suggesting that low price does not signify poor quality. Creamette and Contadina della Casa Buitoni followed closely in fourth and fifth places, as did Barilla, the best-selling pasta in Italy. Note the precipitous drop-off after sixth place. Delverde, a highly respected import used in many restaurants, and Martelli (an artisanal pasta that costs a whopping $4.29) both showed quite poorly in the tasting. ∎

Joni Miller, a New York-based writer, is the author of *True Grits* (Workman, 1990).

HOW TO COOK DRIED PASTA

Pasta is one of those things that is simple to cook, but hard to cook exactly right. For perfect pasta, you must pay attention to everything from the water-to-pasta ratio to the time between draining and saucing.

Pasta needs to cook in a fair amount of water, although not as much as many cookbooks specify. I recommend two quarts of water for one-half pound or less of pasta, four quarts for one-half to one pound of pasta, and six quarts for one to two pounds. If you are cooking more than two pounds of pasta, use two pots.

Many cooks add oil to the cooking water, but I don't recommend it. Oil does lessen foaming and can reduce the chance of boil-overs, but it also makes pasta slick, which can prevent it from marrying properly with the sauce. If boil-overs are a concern, a better solution is to lower the heat slightly during cooking.

After the water comes to a full rolling boil, add salt (a generous 1½ teaspoons per half pound of pasta, since most of the salt goes down the drain with the cooking water) and then the pasta. Stir several times to separate the strands and, if necessary, bend long noodles to submerge them quickly. Use a spoon to push hot water over ends if needed, then cover the pot until the water just returns to a boil.

The pasta will immediately begin to rehydrate and expand. After several minutes of cooking, it will be tender on the outside but still hard in the middle. At this stage, the partially cooked strands no longer snap easily in half, but will break if firmly squeezed. The inner core is white — not pale yellow like the exterior.

The next stage, which occurs a minute or two before the pasta is fully cooked, is the "rubber band" stage. At this point (which may occur after as little as five minutes for thin pasta such as spaghettini or as long as ten minutes for a thick, curly shape such as fusilli) the center begins to soften, the white core disappears, and the strand becomes elastic enough to quiver when gently pulled.

This is the point at which personal taste comes into play. Everyone agrees that pasta should be cooked al dente, an Italian term roughly translated as "to the tooth" and generally implying pasta that is tender not mushy, firm not hard, chewy not crunchy. However, this term means different things to different people. Southern Italians often drain pasta as soon as it quivers, leaving the pieces chewy enough that they sometimes stick to back teeth when eaten. I prefer to cook pasta for another minute or two, to the stage preferred in northern Italy. If you let the pasta go three or four minutes, however, it passes that point; it still quivers, but is now mushy and no longer *al dente* by anyone's definition.

Begin tasting after four or five minutes, especially when preparing thin noodles like spaghettini. This is the first point at which the white center may disappear and the pasta may start to quiver. (Cooking times on pasta boxes are often wrong so ignore them.) Keep checking the pasta every minute or so from then on. As soon as the noodles seem almost al dente — they should still have some chewiness, but the center should no longer be hard or gummy — remove the pot from the heat and drain the pasta. The pasta continues to cook after it is drained so you need to compensate by draining when it is a little underdone.

Never shake pasta bone dry. Instead, pour it into a colander, allow the cooking water to flow out, and then shake the pasta once or twice to remove excess liquid. The small amount of cooking water that remains on the pasta helps spread the sauce and is especially useful when tossing pasta with relatively dry oil-based sauces. Also, never rinse drained pasta under running water. This only cools it down, makes it taste watery, and removes some of the starch coating.

Once the pasta is drained, you have less than a minute to sauce it; otherwise, even premium brands may stick together. If your sauce is not done (I never throw pasta in the pot until the sauce is almost cooked), toss the pasta with a tablespoon or two of oil to slow down the clumping. Consider this an emergency measure.

To keep pasta hot, sauce it in the cooking pot or in the pan used to make the sauce, rather than in a separate bowl. After mixing the sauce and pasta together, immediately transfer individual portions to warm bowls. I prefer wide soup bowls, which provide an edge against which noodles can be twirled.

The whole process of draining, saucing, and serving should be accomplished as quickly as possible — no more than two minutes. Great pasta waits for no one.
— *Jack Bishop*

Quick Granitas

A new food-processor technique replaces the tedious scraping demanded by traditional granita recipes.

～ BY JACK BISHOP ～

Granitas, the icy Italian dessert, are simple stuff: a flavorful fruit puree or liquid — juice, espresso, herb-infused tea, or wine — is combined with sugar and flavorings and then frozen. Traditionally, the liquid is frozen in a bowl and scraped every thirty minutes for several hours to produce a shimmering, granular dessert made up of individual ice crystals.

This traditional scraping technique, which has been used in Italy for centuries, poses two problems for today's cooks: it requires hours of off-and-on attention, and it cannot be prepared in advance because it must be served just as the crystals of freezing liquid harden to the proper consistency. Fortunately, an excellent version of granita can be made using that most modern of tools, the food processor.

Food-Processor Technique

To make granitas in a food processor, simply pour the flavored liquid into ice-cube trays. A few hours later, when they have hardened, you can store them in a zipper-lock bag (to prevent freezer burn) for up to a week, or transfer them immediately to the workbowl of a food processor and pulse them into tiny ice shavings. The texture, a bit creamier than that of traditional granitas, is often preferred by people accustomed to the texture of sorbets and ice creams.

The biggest challenge in making granitas with this method is obtaining the right texture. Granitas can become too slushy when pureed too long, or contain hidden mini-icebergs if the processing is too quick. The trick is to chop the ice cubes evenly and finely without making an icy shake. I have found through testing that limiting the number of cubes processed at one time is the best solution. As a rule, do not process more cubes than can fit comfortably in a single layer in the food processor. Use the pulse button, turning the machine on and off ten or twelve times to ensure even grinding. Generally, bursts of two or three seconds are most effective.

Preparation Shortcuts

Most granita recipes call for hot sugar syrup to be added to fruit juice or puree. I have found, however, that this slows the freezing process and unnecessarily complicates the recipe. In most cases, brisk stirring suffices to dissolve the sugar used in granitas. The amount of sugar and other flavorings in each recipe varies with the sugar and acid content of the puree; strawberries obviously need less sugar than lemons, for example. You can, of course, alter recipes to suit your taste and the sweetness level of the fruit you are using.

When making fruit purees for granitas, you will find that soft fruits do not have to be precooked (see Mango Granita recipe, below). Simply puree berries, mangoes, and papayas, for example, with just enough water for the food processor to do its job. Harder fruits, such as fresh pears, must first be simmered in sugar syrup and then pureed, along with the syrup, to obtain a smooth texture (see Plum Granita recipe). Thick purees should be thinned with water or juice until they can be poured easily.

MIMOSA GRANITA
Master Recipe for Liquid-based Granitas
Serves 4

This recipe is typical of granitas made from liquids rather than purees. Fresh-squeezed juice and good-quality sparkling wine will make all the difference in the final product.

- 1   cup juice from 3 medium oranges
- ½   cup sugar
- 1¼   cups sparkling wine
- 1   tablespoon lime juice

1. Whisk orange juice and sugar in large bowl until sugar dissolves.
2. Stir in wine and lime juice and pour mixture into 2 ice-cube trays.
3. Freeze mixture until firm, at least 2 hours. (Can transfer frozen cubes to zipper-lock plastic bags and freeze up to 1 week.)
4. Just before serving, place a single layer of frozen cubes in workbowl of food processor fitted with steel blade. Pulse 10 or 12 times or until no large chunks of ice remain. Scoop crystals into individual bowls. Repeat with remaining ice cubes and serve immediately.

PLUM GRANITA
Master Recipe for Poached Fruit-based Granitas
Serves 4

Follow the poaching and pureeing technique used in this recipe for harder fruits such as apples, cherries, peaches, and pears. With the exception of citrus, all fruits should be strained to remove pulp and/or seeds.

- 1   pound ripe plums, pitted and sliced thin
- 1¼   cups water
- ⅓   cup sugar
- 1   cinnamon stick
- 1   tablespoon lemon juice

1. Bring first 4 ingredients to boil in medium saucepan. Simmer until fruit is tender, about 5 minutes. Turn off heat, remove and discard cinnamon stick, and stir in lemon juice.
2. Transfer mixture to food processor fitted with steel blade; puree until smooth. Strain mixture through fine-mesh sieve; discard peel and pulp. Pour flavored liquid into 2 ice-cube trays. For freezing and grinding, follow steps 3 and 4 in Mimosa Granita.

MANGO GRANITA
Master Recipe for Raw Fruit-based Granitas
Serves 4

- 1   pound ripe mangoes, pitted, sliced thin, and peeled
- ¾   cup water
- ⅓   cups sugar
- 1   tablespoon lemon juice

1. Combine mango and water and puree in a food processor or blender until smooth. Strain through fine-mesh sieve and discard pulp.
2. Add sugar and lemon juice and stir briskly until sugar is dissolved. Pour into 2 ice-cube trays. For freezing and grinding, follow steps 3 and 4 in Mimosa Granita. ■

After mixing, liquids are frozen into cubes, then processed to make granita.

GRANITAS MADE EASY

BASIC INGREDIENT	FLAVORING LIQUID OR PUREE	SUGAR	WATER	OPTIONAL INGREDIENTS	SPECIAL TECHNIQUES
APPLE JUICE	2 cups juice	¼ cup	✳	1 tablespoon lemon juice and/or 1 tablespoon apple brandy	
BERRIES	1½ cups fresh fruit or 1 12-ounce bag, frozen	⅓-½ cup	¾ cup	1 tablespoon lemon juice	Puree berries in food processor with water. Strain seeds (or skin, as with blueberries) if necessary.
CAFFE LATTE	1 cup strong espresso	3 tablespoons	✳	1¼ cups milk	
CHERRIES	1½ cups pitted fruit	¾ cup	✳	1 tablespoon orange liquer or Kirsch	Simmer cherries in sugar syrup 5 minutes; puree with syrup; strain out skins.
ESPRESSO	2 cups strong espresso	¼ cup	✳	¼ teaspoon ground cinnamon, 2 tablespoons sweetened cocoa, or 1 tablespoon Amaretto, Frangelico, or Sambuca	Stir sugar into hot espresso, then cool to room temperature before proceeding.
GRAPEFRUIT	1½ cups juice from 2 medium pieces of fruit	⅓ cup	½ cup	If using pink grapefruit juice, add 1 tablespoon Campari to boost color and flavor.	
LEMONS OR LIMES	½ cup juice from 2 medium-large fruits	⅓ cup	1½ cups	2 teaspoons grated zest	
ORANGES	1½ cups juice from 4 medium fruits	¼ cup	½ cup	1 tablespoon Cointreau	
PAPAYAS	1 pound fruit	⅓ cup	¾ cup	1 tablespoon lemon juice	Puree peeled and pitted papaya with water until smooth; strain out pulp.
PEARS	1 pound fruit	½ cup	1¼ cups	1 tablespoon lemon juice and/or 1 tablespoon pear brandy	Simmer peeled and sliced pears in sugar syrup until soft, about 10 minutes. Puree with syrup; strain out pulp.
PINEAPPLE	1½ cups juice	¼ cup	½ cup	1 tablespoon lemon juice	
TEA	2 cups hot tea	⅓ cup	✳	2 tablespoons lemon juice	Steep 4 mint sprigs in hot tea; remove before freezing. Honey can be substituted for sugar.
WATERMELON	2 cups juice from 2½ pounds fruit	¼ cup	✳	1 tablespoon lemon juice and/or 1 tablespoon Campari to boost flavor and color	Puree peeled and seeded watermelon; strain out pulp.

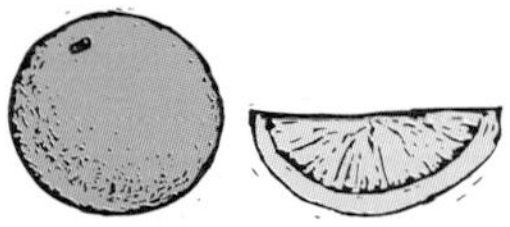

✳ If desired, water can replace some of the flavoring liquid for a mellower flavor.

Are Bread Machines Worth the Dough?

For the best results, choose a machine with a long baking cycle, a large baking pan, and multiple setting options.

~ BY JACK BISHOP ~

Five years ago when I first tested automatic bread machines, then the newest Japanese high-tech wonders, I found them so useless I threw them out. After making fifty loaves in ten of the new-generation bread machines, however, I have upped my estimation of them considerably. They are never going to replace bread made by hand, but these "smart" machines are much improved.

The automatic bread machine is slightly larger than a bread box. It contains a chamber with a baking pan; a small kneading arm inside the pan attaches to a motor in the base. Ingredients are placed in the pan, which is then snapped into place.

A computer chip runs a program that leads the machine through the various stages of mixing, kneading, rising, punching down, and rising again. When the bread is ready to be baked, a coil in the machine heats to around 275 degrees. The whole process takes anywhere from two and one-half to seven hours, depending on the machine and the specific cycle.

Bread machine loaves have a number of intrinsic disadvantages: First of all, there is the squat, unattractive shape; among the machines I tested, only the National has a "normal" loaflike shape, which helped it to gain its top ranking. Second, loaves from a machine have a hole in the bottom — sometimes small, sometimes gaping — left by the dough blade.

Most important, however, is the crust. Bread baked on a stone or a hot baking sheet comes into contact with very hot temperatures, and experienced bakers add moisture by dropping ice cubes on the floor of the oven or spritzing with water, which further improves the crust. But bread baked in a machine sits directly against the pan at a lower temperature for a longer period. The result is a thick, chewy crust; the thin, crackly crusts of good French bread are impossible to achieve.

On the positive side, of course, the bread machine is incredibly convenient and can, with the right recipes (*see* page 29), produce quite a tasty loaf. All the machines I tested are equipped with a timer that allows ingredients to be placed in the pan up to thirteen hours in advance. For instance, you can dump everything in the pan in the morning (making sure that yeast and water are separated, to prevent early fermentation) and come home to fresh-baked bread for dinner. The appeal of this convenience cannot be overrated, especially for cooks who work away from home.

Buying Recommendations

To find out which of the available machines produces the best bread, I ran ten machines through a series of tests to evaluate their relative advantages. I made the standard recipe from each manual, the white and wheat bread recipes on page 29, and a basic cinnamon-raisin bread. The white bread was made with the timer function to judge its effectiveness. Each bread was judged on the quality of its crust and crumb as well as its flavor. In the case of the raisin bread, the distribution of the fruit was an important consideration.

The most significant variable I found among machines (and one not often considered) is the size of the bread pan. The manufacturers and most cookbook authors have tried to write two standard recipes, since some machines have a capacity of one pound, others, one and one-half pounds. But I found that the maximum volume the larger machines can handle varies greatly, from eight cups to twelve cups. If you stick with the manufacturer's recipes, the small "large-capacity" machines, using smaller amounts of yeast, produce adequate if dense loaves. But if you use a "generic" recipe in those machines, the loaves may overrise, stick to the lid, then collapse during baking. For this reason, I severely downgraded the Sanyo, Regal, and Breadman.

In my testing, I also found that the tremendous differences in the length of the machine's standard cycle markedly affected the quality of the bread produced. Machines with shorter cycles did not allow enough time for the bread to rise twice before baking; those with longer cycles — such as the National and Zojirushi — made bread that tasted better. In a machine or on the counter, making bread takes time; you can only cut so much before the quality suffers.

In general, machines with more options made better bread. I did find some machines with bogus cycles — the French bread setting on the Maxim, for instance, was exactly the same as the standard setting. Of course, meaningless options don't help make better bread, but machines with longer cycles for whole-grain breads or with cycles that beep when it is time to add raisins or that automatically trim baking time to prevent overcaramelization of the crust generally produced superior loaves. Sweet breads didn't burn, raisins weren't mashed, and breads with lots of whole-wheat flour still rose well.

Machines were also distinguished by an array of special features, including a dough setting (that kneads and rises dough in a controlled atmosphere); power interrupt (machines remember where in the cycle they are for up to ten minutes without power); automatic cooling (loaves made in machines without this feature become soggy after baking unless immediately removed); and lock button (to prevent accidental resettings during operation).

One final note: Even if you buy a top-ranked machine, don't expect a perfect loaf on the first shot. Many recipes tested from manuals were unacceptable. The recipes on page 29 are far superior but you may still need to make slight changes as suggested in "Troubleshooting Guide," page 28. Each machine has its own peculiarities and kinks and you will need to compensate for them to make perfect bread.

Customer assistance is available from manufacturers during business hours. Most hotlines are staffed by baking experts who should be able to lead you through any pitfalls. ■

Dozens of improvements in design and function separate today's sleek bread machines (left) from the very first model introduced into the U.S. seven years ago by Welbilt (right).

PHOTOGRAPH BY ERIC ROTH

1 National Bread Bakery
SD-BT65N

*Best-shaped loaves
with great crust.*

2 Zojirushi Home Bakery
BBCC-S15

*Bread machine
with most powerful
computer chip.*

3 West Bend Automatic
Bread Maker 41040

*Better-than-average
performance at a
low price.*

4 Welbilt Bread Machine
ABM2200T

*Basic model with
very strong
performance.*

National Bread Bakery SD-BT65N

Price: $375
Capacity: 12 cups (1½-pound loaf)
Standard Cycle: 4 hours
Design: Five bread cycles, two crust controls, no viewing window. Separate dispenser holds yeast away from other ingredients until proper time. Biggest asset is the normal loaf shape — instead of tall and narrow, long loaves from this machine look like they were baked in a standard loaf pan.
Performance: Superb white and wheat breads with thick, chewy crusts. Tops of loaves are particularly impressive — taut, domed, and crisp. Raisins added up front became mashed and barely visible. (To remedy this, add nuts and fruits after the first knead.) Recipe from manual is only so-so.
Special Features: Dough setting, power interrupt, and automatic cooling. Exactly the same machine as Panasonic model number SD-BT65P.
Customer Assistance: National 714-373-7757/Panasonic 201-348-9090
Overall Rating: A-

Zojirushi Home Bakery BBCC-S15

Price: $339
Capacity: 11¾ cups (1½-pound loaf)
Standard Cycle: 3 hours, 25 minutes (plus cooling)
Design: Fully loaded machine with four bread cycles, three crust controls, large viewing window, and memory storage for programming custom recipes.
Performance: White and wheat breads have dark, thick, chewy crust and tender, moist crumb. Good distribution of fruit in raisin bread but top fell just a bit. Recipe tested from manual was disappointing.
Special Features: One of two machines (*see* West Bend) to preheat ingredients before kneading. Only machine with clock as well as timer that shows estimated finish time. Only machine with programming capabilities. Dough setting, power interrupt, and automatic cooling.
Customer Assistance: 800-733-6270
Overall Rating: B+

West Bend Automatic Bread Maker 41040

Price: $200
Capacity: 11 cups (1½-pound loaf)

Standard Cycle: 3 hours, 40 minutes
Design: Five bread cycles, three crust controls, and viewing window. Digital display is hard to read. Bread pan is a bit smaller than top machines so you may need to cut back yeast to two teaspoons in some recipes.
Performance: Wheat bread had pale, sunken top but decent crumb and side crust. Very good white and raisin breads with not-quite-taut tops. Excellent results with recipe from manual.
Special Features: One of two machines that preheats ingredients before kneading. Dough setting, automatic cooling, lock button, and instructional video.
Customer Assistance: 800-367-0111
Overall Rating: B

Welbilt Bread Machine ABM2200T

Price: $170
Capacity: 8 cups (1-pound loaf)
Standard Cycle: 3 hours
Design: Stripped-down model with start/stop buttons, two crust controls, but no viewing window. Pan yields loaves with five-inch-round base (not rectangular, as in other machines).
Performance: Beautiful loaves with dark brown, domed tops and thick, chewy crusts. Crumb is tender in white and wheat breads. Raisins well distributed and recipe in manual is fine. Only drawback is circular shape of slices.
Special Features: Dough setting is only extra on this no-frills machine.
Customer Assistance: 516-365-5040, ext. 344
Overall Rating: B

Hitachi Automatic Home Bakery HB-B201

Price: $360
Capacity: 12½ cups (1½-pound loaf)
Standard Cycle: 3 hours, 50 minutes (plus cooling)
Design: Three bread cycles, three crust controls, and small viewing window.
Performance: Thick, chewy crusts but frequent problems with crinkly (not taut) tops that are often pale and undercooked. However, rest of crust and crumb are quite good. Some bunching and burning of raisins on the bottom. Poor results with recipe from manual.
Special Features: Dough setting, power interrupt, automatic cooling, and lock button.
Customer Assistance: 800-241-6558, ext. 720
Overall Rating: B-

Toastmaster Bread Box 1152U

Price: $200
Capacity: 8½ cups (1¼-pound loaf)
Standard Cycle: 3 hours, 15 minutes (plus cooling)
Design: Three bread cycles, three crust controls, and small viewing window. Machine designed to produce 1¼-pound loaves. Since all recipes (other than those in manual) are written for loaves of either 1 or 1½ pounds, this model can be difficult to work with. Poor recipe in manual doesn't inspire confidence.
Performance: Crusts are thin and somewhat pale, especially on top. Crumb in white and wheat is fairly good. Decent raisin bread.
Special Features: Dough setting, power interrupt, and automatic cooling.
Customer Assistance: 800-947-3744
Overall Rating: C+

Maxim Accu-Bakery BB-1

Price: $275
Capacity: 8 cups (1-pound loaf)
Standard Cycle: 3 hours, 30 minutes
Design: Three bread cycles (French setting is a gimmick since it takes the same time as standard setting), two crust controls, but no viewing window. Flimsy plastic kneading blade is not coated with nonstick material (blades in other machines are), so bottoms of loaves stick and are marred by large holes.
Performance: Very good results with white and wheat breads. Taut, domed tops with dark brown crust and tender, moist crumb. Pulverizes raisins if added at the start as manual suggests. Along with National, only machine without special indicator that tells when to add ingredients during kneading. Poor results with recipe from manual.
Special Features: Dough setting.
Customer Assistance: 800-233-9054
Overall Rating: C+

Regal Automatic Breadmaker K6773

Price: $330
Capacity: 10 cups (1½-pound loaf)
Standard Cycle: 2 hours, 30 minutes
Design: Four bread cycles, two crust controls, but no viewing window. Along with Breadman, this is only machine that does not indicate what cycle (knead, rise, or bake) the machine is operating.
Performance: Good wheat bread with crust that is a bit thinner than top ma-

chines but still impressive. A good number of raisins burned on the bottom of the loaf. Very good recipe in manual. Problem caused by undersized pan that is really better for smaller recipes, especially when using timer or making white bread.
Special Features: Dough setting. Instructional video included.
Customer Assistance: 800-998-8809
Overall Rating: C

Breadman (Trillium Health Products) TR-500

Price: $199
Capacity: 10 cups (1½-pound loaf)
Standard Cycle: 2 hours, 30 minutes
Design: Three bread cycles, three crust controls, and tiny viewing window. The Breadman is marketed to health-conscious consumers and is designed to bake whole-grain breads.
Performance: Wheat bread rises perfectly to top of pan with thick, dark, chewy crust. White and raisin breads are disasters as is recipe tested from manual; all three breads rose up to lid and then sunk during baking. Tops were deep, pale craters that had curled around pan at edges. Especially with timer function (where breads already have a tendency to overrise), this presents a major problem and a tremendous clean-up. Very noisy rocking during operation.
Special Features: Dough setting. Instructional video included.
Customer Assistance: 800-800-9885
Overall Rating: C-

Sanyo Bread Factory Plus SBM-15

Price: $200
Capacity: 8 cups (1½-pound loaf)
Standard Cycle: 3 hours, 20 minutes
Design: Four bread cycles, three crust controls, and small viewing window that tends to fog during use.
Performance: White, wheat, and raisin breads were total disasters. This machine has a serious flaw — an undersized bread pan. As a result, regular recipes for 1½-pound loaves rise to the lid, then pour down the sides of the pan, and smoke during baking. White bread tested from manual is fine — recipe calls for very little yeast, which keeps the rise down.
Special Features: Dough setting, power interrupt, and automatic cooling.
Customer Assistance: 800-421-5013
Overall Rating: D

Foolproof Bread Machine Recipes

Extensive testing yields improved recipes for bread machines plus troubleshooting tips for problem loaves.

~ BY TOM LACALAMITA ~

Traditional bread baking is a hands-on experience — no two loaves knead, rise, or bake quite the same. The accomplished baker knows when to add a little more flour and when dough has risen enough. In a machine, such flexibility and adjustments are possible (you can open the lid and feel the dough), but that's not really the point. If you want to throw in ingredients and then walk away, the initial recipe better take potential problems into account.

The key ingredient to good bread from a machine is bread flour. Certain grains, including wheat and rye, contain a protein called gluten. When flour made from these grains is hydrated and kneaded, the gluten forms fine elastic strands that eventually give bread its height and chewy texture. Flour milled from hard wheat, called bread flour, has the highest gluten content. This is the only flour that works well in a machine.

Most bread flour contains a small amount of ascorbic acid (vitamin C) to boost the flour's effectiveness. I have found that some bread flours are still a bit weak. So, I add lemon juice to boost the flour and give the dough greater elasticity. The amount of lemon juice — just a teaspoon — does not affect flavor.

The Right Ingredients for Machines

Breads made from 100 percent whole-grain flours do not always fare well in bread machines, often yielding stubby, overly dense loaves. Although whole-wheat flour has a higher gluten content than white bread flour, the gluten cannot be as easily broken down during kneading. Therefore, whole-wheat dough is rarely as elastic and does not rise as much.

When making whole-grain breads by hand, bakers compensate with longer rises. While some bread machines offer longer cycles for whole-grain breads, many do not. My advice is to mix whole-grain flour with white bread flour to ensure proper texture and rise in your loaves. This also solves the problem of bitterness caused when supermarket whole-wheat flour (made from red wheat) is used straight. When mixed with a larger amount of white bread flour (*see* Master Recipe for Basic Wheat Bread for proportions), whole-wheat flour performs and tastes better.

Liquid ingredients are added in varying amounts according to the time of year and ambient temperature in your kitchen. During the summer, flour picks up moisture from humid air (its weight

Since the baker can't easily intervene in the process, recipes for bread machines must anticipate potential problems and contain ingredients carefully designed to counteract them.

can increase by as much as 10 percent), so you may need less liquid. On cold winter days flour will be dry, so use the full amount of water. Always use room-temperature liquids (between sixty-eight and eighty degrees). Excessive heat can kill yeast, while cold may delay its action.

Regular active dry yeast is the best choice for bread machines. I do not recommend fast-action yeast because the dough can overproof, especially during warm, humid weather. If you must use fast-action yeast, reduce the amount by one-half to one teaspoon. The one exception to this rule is recipes that contain large quantities of sugar or other ingredients (such as fresh garlic or a lot of cinnamon) that can impede gluten formation.

Besides enhancing the flavor of the bread, salt also acts as an inhibitor for the yeast. By preventing yeast from multiplying too fast and losing steam too early, salt ensures an even rise and proper dough development. To avoid inhibiting the yeast too much when using the timer function on your bread machine, impose a layer of flour between salt and yeast.

TROUBLESHOOTING GUIDE

Some of the most common problems with bread machines are listed below, along with possible causes and solutions. Of course, proper measurement of ingredients, including the use of large eggs, is essential.

Problem: *Dough appears dry and bread machine labors during kneading.*
Cause: Absorbent ingredients such as oatmeal were used with timer. Flour contains very little moisture.
Solution: Do not use timer when making breads that contain oats, cracked wheat, or other dry ingredients that will rapidly absorb moisture. Gradually add more liquid until dough comes together.

Problem: *Dough appears very sticky. Top of loaf is wrinkled and/or sunken when baked.*
Cause: High humidity or too much liquid.
Solution: Reduce liquid by one to three tablespoons.

Problem: *Dough rises too quickly and appears foamy. Dough touches lid and top of bread has collapsed.*
Cause: High ambient temperature (above 80 degrees).
Solution: Use bread machine when temperature is lower. Reduce yeast by a quarter or a third.

Problem: *Dough does not rise enough.*
Cause: Cool ambient temperature (below 68 degrees). Ingredients were cold. Yeast was not fresh.
Solution: Raise kitchen temperature. Use room-temperature ingredients. Check expiration date on yeast packet.

PHOTOGRAPH BY ERIC ROTH

In addition to flour, water, yeast, and salt (the ingredients found in most bread recipes), my recipes contain a number of ingredients designed to guarantee optimum performance in a machine.

Sugar gets the yeast started, allowing it to begin multiplying before the natural starches in the flour are converted to sugar. Since bread machines have preprogrammed cycles, this is quite important. Loaves that rise on the counter can take as long as they need to rise. In a machine, the yeast must start working immediately. Use at least one-half teaspoon of sugar per cup of flour and no more than two teaspoons per cup. Too much sugar can overfeed the yeast and burn the crust.

Bread machine recipes also often contain dairy, usually in the form of nonfat dry milk, which won't spoil when using the timer function and doesn't contain any fat that can sometimes darken the crust. Milk gives white bread an ivory crumb and promotes softness in either white or wheat breads. I usually add four teaspoons of nonfat dry milk per cup of flour.

Fat, whether solid (butter) or liquid (oil), coats flour molecules and promotes a soft crumb. Fat also helps prolong freshness. I usually add about one teaspoon per cup of flour.

The addition of sugar, milk, and fat makes American-style breads (such as those baked in loaf pans) among the best choices for bread machines. When making sourdough or European-style breads, the presence of sugar and dairy can be a bit jarring. The recipes below are especially suited to bread machines.

MASTER RECIPE FOR BASIC WHITE BREAD
Makes 1½-pound loaf

1¼	cups water
1	tablespoon butter
1	teaspoon lemon juice
¼	cup nonfat dry milk
1	tablespoon sugar
1	teaspoon salt
3	cups bread flour
2¼	teaspoons active dry yeast

Add ingredients in order suggested in owner's manual; continue process with machine on basic/standard bread setting.

Variation for One-Pound Loaf:

¾	cup water
2	teaspoons butter
1	teaspoon lemon juice
2	tablespoons plus 1 teaspoon nonfat dry milk
2	teaspoons sugar
¾	teaspoon salt
2	cups bread flour
1½	teaspoons active dry yeast

SWEET BREAD WITH ALMONDS AND DRIED CHERRIES
Makes 1½-pound loaf

Follow the Master Recipe for Basic White Bread, making the following changes: Reduce water to 1 cup; increase sugar to 2 tablespoons; add 1 large egg and 1½ teaspoons almond extract. Continue process with machine on raisin bread setting. Add ⅔ cup dried cherries and ⅔ cup toasted slivered almonds at the appropriate time, depending on bread machine.

Variation for One-Pound Loaf: Follow the Master Recipe for Basic White Bread, making the following changes: Reduce water to ½ cup; increase sugar to 4 teaspoons; add 1 large egg and 1 teaspoon almond extract. Continue process with machine on raisin bread setting. Add ½ cup dried cherries and ½ cup toasted slivered almonds at the appropriate time, depending on the machine.

MASTER RECIPE FOR BASIC WHEAT BREAD
Makes 1½-pound loaf

1	cup water
1	large egg
3	tablespoons honey
1	teaspoon lemon juice
1	tablespoon butter
¼	cup nonfat dry milk
1½	teaspoons salt
2¼	cups bread flour
¾	cup whole-wheat flour
2¼	teaspoons active dry yeast

Add ingredients in order suggested in owner's manual; continue process with machine on basic/standard or whole-wheat bread setting.

Variation for One-Pound Loaf:

½	cup plus 1 tablespoon water
1	large egg
2	tablespoons honey
1	teaspoon lemon juice
2	teaspoons butter
2	tablespoons plus 2 teaspoons nonfat dry milk
1	teaspoon salt
1½	cups bread flour
½	cup whole-wheat flour
1½	teaspoons active dry yeast

APPLE-WALNUT WHEAT BREAD
Makes 1½-pound loaf

Follow the Master Recipe for Basic Wheat Bread, adding ¾ teaspoon cinnamon. Continue process with machine on raisin bread setting. Add ½ cup chopped dried apples and ½ cup chopped toasted walnuts at the appropriate time, depending on the machine.

Variation for One-Pound Loaf: Follow the Master Recipe for Basic Wheat Bread, adding ½ teaspoon cinnamon. Continue process with machine on raisin bread setting. Add ⅓ cup chopped dried apples and ⅓ cup chopped toasted walnuts at the appropriate time, depending on machine. ∎

Tom Lacalamita is the author of *The Ultimate Bread Machine Cookbook* (Simon & Schuster, 1993).

ADAPTING YOUR FAVORITE RECIPES

You can modify most bread recipes by using the following guidelines. Although you may have to make adjustments for some machines (*see* "Troubleshooting Guide," page 28, and individual instruction manuals), the approximate ratios and rules below will get you started.

The order in which ingredients are added to the pan varies with each machine. Follow the manufacturer's recommendations, which have been developed with the operation of that model in mind.

Size of Loaf	Bread Pan Capacity	Flour	Yeast	Liquids
1 pound	8 cups	2 cups	1½ teaspoons	¾ cup plus 1 tablespoon
1½ pounds	12 cups	3 cups	2¼ teaspoons	1¼ cups

HELPFUL HINTS

1. Vegetable oils (but not butter), liquid sweeteners (honey, maple syrup), and eggs are considered liquids, so reduce the water, milk, or other liquid by the amount added. One large egg equals one-quarter cup.

2. See text for recommendations regarding sugar, nonfat dry milk, and fat. You may want to add some if recipes without any are not working well in a machine.

3. If you are unsure about the exact proportions, add a little less water than you think might be necessary. If the dough appears dry and crumbly (like pastry) during kneading, add additional liquid, one tablespoon at a time. Simply open lid and drizzle water along the sides of the pan until dough is smooth and elastic.

Lively (and Inexpensive) Sauvignon Blancs Sweep Tasting

~ BY MARK BITTMAN ~

1992 Duckhorn Vineyards

BEST WINE

BEST BUY

1992 Chateau Bonnet

Sauvignon Blanc, after Chardonnay the second-best-selling white wine in the United States, is still seeking its identity. The talk in the trade is that people buy it because it isn't Chardonnay — not a very compelling reason. This leads some California winemakers, who would prefer a pro-Sauvignon over a non-Chardonnay attitude, to vinify their wine to taste just like Chardonnay. They are counting on little more than a different name to sell their wine and, to some extent, this works. Other vintners emphasize Sauvignon Blanc's unique — and not always pleasant — characteristics, such as a "grassy" nose and a "vegetal" flavor. People who enjoy wine can rejoice that this approach is waning.

Increasingly, as with many other varietals, California Sauvignon Blanc is becoming more French in style: restrained, almost austere, with citrus overtones, lots of acid, and very little wood. At its best, sauvignon blanc grapes make a *very* dry wine — almost flinty, in the manner of Chablis — but one in which the fruit remains evident because the use of oak or other wood has been limited. And, until recently, its highest and best expression was found in Graves, a part of Bordeaux, where the grape is traditionally blended with the softer semillon, or in the northern towns of Sancerre and Pouilly-sur-Loire. Here it is unblended and sold as Sancerre and Pouilly Fumé (the grape is locally known as blanc fumé).

The one Sancerre we tasted finished a sad eleventh, and the Pouilly Fumé did not fare much better, which leads me to conclude that our tasters, as a group, did not enjoy the super-dry, ultracrisp expression of the sauvignon blanc grape found in the Loire valley. At the same time, the tasters rejected the heavily oaked Sauvignon Blancs that were so reminiscent of Chardonnay. Rather, they preferred the softer style in which sauvignon blanc is lightly tempered, either by the addition of semillon (as in the Chateau Bonnet) or by vinification that results in a gentler wine, as in those from Duckhorn and Frog's Leap.

Regardless of the style in which it is made, Sauvignon Blanc is wine to be drunk cold, accompanying summer food; this is among the best wines for picnics. It should also be consumed when it is young; note that only four of our wines were more than two years old. Even the best Sauvignon Blancs gain little from aging and in fact begin to fall off in quality within a few years of the vintage. ∎

BLIND TASTING RESULTS

As in all *Cook's Illustrated* tastings, the wines were tasted blind by a panel composed of both wine professionals and amateur wine-lovers. One unusual aspect of this tasting is that most of the tasters enjoyed most of the wines; only those finishing in the last two places garnered more negative than positive comments.

1. 1992 Duckhorn Vineyards (Napa) Sauvignon Blanc (38 points), $13.50. From a winery best known for its Merlot, this wine was placed in the top three by almost every taster. Even one detractor called it "full and pleasant." One taster who ranked it first said it was "beautiful, clean, and elegant."

2. 1992 Chateau Bonnet (28 points), $7.00. Although this is a favorite of retailers, who have long sold it as the best of the cheap whites from France, few would have predicted this strong a finish. A solid best buy: "Pleasant, floral nose; not powerful but eminently enjoyable."

3. 1992 Frog's Leap (Napa) Sauvignon Blanc (24 points), $11.00. This winery does every thing right, and this wine is no exception. "Clean, soft, and very fine."

4. 1992 Caliterra (Chile) Sauvignon Blanc (22 points), $5.50. Good seller in the past year, and the combination of price and decent showing tells why. "Good, bright fruit," wrote one admirer. Worth sampling.

5. 1991 Dry Creek (Alexander Valley) Fumé Blanc (20 points), $9.00. From a winery best known for its reds. No one found this wine exceptional, but many liked it: "Lively, acidic, and nicely integrated," wrote one taster.

6. 1991 Cloudy Bay (New Zealand) Sauvignon Blanc (19 points), $15.00. One of the favorites coming into the tasting, the current wisdom being that New Zealand is producing brilliant Sauvignon Blanc. Not this one: it got one first-place vote from a taster who found it "subtle, quiet, smooth." One other taster found it "flat," perhaps a less kind view of "quiet."

7. 1990 Ladoucette Pouilly Fumé (18 points), $22.50. Among the best-known (and most expensive) of the Loire valley wines made from sauvignon blanc, this wine did not show well except to one taster, who ranked it first and said: "Very tart and austere — the way this wine *should* taste." Few others agreed.

8. 1992 Murphy Goode (Sonoma) Fumé Blanc (17 points), $9.50. "Nonvarietal," said one taster, and most agreed; this heavily oaked wine tastes like Chardonnay. But *good* Chardonnay: "Lively and full," wrote one.

9. 1992 Matanzas Creek (Sonoma) Sauvignon Blanc (16 points), $13.50. One of three varieties on which this winery focuses. Again, many people liked it, but no one loved it: "Crisp and fresh, but fruit is restrained."

10. 1990 Chateau Carbonnieux (Graves) (14 points), $23.00. Widely considered to be among the best whites of Graves, this wine stood out in a way that some disapproved of: "Full, rich, and opulent," wrote one taster, who found those qualities inappropriate. Its admirers found it "rich and vanilla-ish."

11. 1992 Henri Bourgeois Sancerre (12 points), $13.00. A well-known and much-liked (usually) Loire valley wine. One first-place vote: "Light, zippy, and bone-dry." Others found it "too acidic" and even "harsh."

12. 1992 Caymus Napa Valley Sauvignon Blanc (11 points), $10.00. "A heavily oaked wine that lacks character," wrote one, but another, who ranked it first, said, "Toasty, ripe, and delicious."

13. 1991 Robert Mondavi Woodbridge Sauvignon Blanc (6 points), $5.25. The second label of the famous Napa winery, about a million cases are sold each year. Name recognition and price must count for a lot; two fourth-place votes was all this wine could muster.

14. 1992 Kendall-Jackson Sauvignon Blanc (4 points), $9.00. A surprisingly weak entry from a solid Lake County winery. "Lacks intensity," wrote one; "boring," another.

BOOK
REVIEWS

All Around the World Cookbook
Sheila Lukins
Workman, $27.95 cloth; $18.95 paper

When xeroxed pages from Sheila Lukins's *All Around the World Cookbook* arrived in our office, our excited staff dropped everything to check it out. We wanted to see where the other half of the Silver Palate team had gone in recent years, especially after our disappointment with Julee Rosso's *Great Good Food* (*Cook's Illustrated,* July/August 1993). Within a few days, we had tested some 30-odd recipes from the 450 included in the book, and had perused the pages with care.

Sadly, we were underwhelmed. Although the recipes in this book are collected from Lukins's recent world travels, some of them feel tired (coq au vin), many are underseasoned (one-quarter teaspoon of salt for a salad that serves ten?), and others just don't work. In general, most seem like lowest-common-denominator food, as if Lukins had gathered authentic recipes but then, rather than transferring what she'd discovered to us, tried to interpret them to make them appealing to the broadest possible audience. The result is recipe names that often sound exciting but dishes that, when they are not downright problematic, still fail to deliver on their names' promise.

Mexican Lentils with Pineapple and Bananas, for example, turn out to consist of lentils cooked with aromatics and tomatoes, then combined with canned pineapples, golden raisins, and bananas to create a sweet mush with a juxtaposition of tastes that is more jarring than pleasing; Rigani, White Bean, and Garlic Slather is a fancy name for a not-so-great hummus-like spread (rigani, by the way, is oregano); the Pao-doce — Portuguese Sweet Bread — never cooked all the way through, but even if it had worked well, this cakelike bread wouldn't join our repertoire; Caribbean Coconut Tart also has technical problems, but even allowing for those, the taste of coconut is overwhelmed by the sugar.

Some recipes are worse: Lemon Wafers not only disappoint the taste buds but are impossible to lift from the wax paper on which they are cooked; Beet Bread Pudding tastes like a sweet and rather soggy loaf of rye bread layered with beets; a Cream of Wheat-based dessert is as gloppy as it sounds; and one of our tasters announced that she was skipping the dessert sec-

tion entirely "because it's really quite weak."

There were some high points among the recipes we tested, and it seemed to us that they came when Lukins herself was excited about a recipe: a sort of Tunisian *salade nicoise* is beautiful and quite delicious, as is a Swiss chard-based salad from Andalusia. Stuffed Cabbage from Lukins's grandmother is a real winner, and we'd certainly make Indian-Style Spinach again.

But these moments were unfortunately rare. In general, the food here lacks excitement as well as the authenticity that we had anticipated and that the recipe titles promise.

— *Mark Bittman*

Food Lover's Tiptionary
Sharon Tyler Herbst
William Morrow, $15.00

Spike homemade ice cream with too much rum and it won't freeze; add lemon juice to broccoli as it cooks and the vegetable turns an unattractive grayish-green; heat hollandaise over high heat and the sauce curdles.

These are a few of the culinary problems Sharon Tyler Herbst addresses in this compendium of 4,500 culinary tips. For the most part, she offers sensible advice that can save novice cooks from many pitfalls. Occasional tips are even ingenious — she places a slice of bread in the bottom of a broiler pan to soak up grease and prevent fires, for example.

However, readers may at times be thwarted by the book's organization. For example, the tip about not adding too much rum to ice cream appears under the heading "alcohol" and not "ice cream." Likewise, the cook who wants to know how to revive a curdled hollandaise has to wade through an omnibus section on sauces before finding the answer — number fourteen in a list of twenty. Grouping tips in categories from A to Z is fine, but a good index or a better system of cross-referencing is badly needed.

In fact, my advice to seasoned cooks is to pass on this book. Much is old hat here and the intriguing nuggets are often too cryptic to believe. For instance, I would love to know why Herbst suggests transferring milk in a paper carton to a glass container to extend shelf life.

My advice to novice cooks is more positive. This book distills much essential cooking information into one compact volume. You will sometimes have to hunt around to find the right

tip, but I can't think of another source that provides rudimentary answers to so many culinary questions.

— *Jack Bishop*

A World of Curries
Dave DeWitt and Arthur J. Pais
Little, Brown, $16.95

In *A World of Curries*, Dave DeWitt, editor of *Whole Chile Pepper* magazine, teams up with Indian-born Arthur Pais to survey curries around the globe. While I have minor quibbles with the book — I disagree with the authors, for example, on their definition of the historically complex notion of a curry — in general I found it both enjoyable and rewarding. It is filled with fascinating and accessible information about curries, and the recipes, organized by geographic region of origin, are for the most part excellent.

As you might expect from a book devoted to curries, many of the dishes call for a long list of spices, or include as an ingredient a paste or spice mix for which the recipe is given elsewhere. However, the flavorful results justify this modest effort.

Spinach Curry, one of the book's many vegetarian recipes, was at once light, simple to make, and layered with many contrasting flavors. Spicy Yogurt Salad, with its strong ginger tones, was a far more complex and interesting dish than similar, raita-related recipes I have tried from other cookbooks. Swimming Chicken Curry, a Burmese wet curry, was milder than expected — next time I would ignore the advice to seed the single serrano pepper the recipe calls for — but for many readers the level of heat would probably be just right.

In short, *World of Curries* is a fine addition to the library of any cook interested in exploring the flavorful, spicy cuisines of the hot countries of the world, where curries in all their complex variety abound. ∎

— *John Willoughby*

Note: We are pleased to announce that this spring marks the publication of three cookbooks by *Cook's Illustrated* staff members: *Fish* (Macmillan, $27.50), by Mark Bittman; *Lasagna* (Contemporary, $8.95), by Jack Bishop; and *Born Under a Hot Sun* (Morrow, $24.95), by John Willoughby, with co-author Chris Schlesinger.

SOURCES
AND RESOURCES

BREAD MACHINES

The National Bread Bakery machine, which received the top rating in our testing (*see* page 26), is available at Williams-Sonoma stores nationwide. It can also be ordered from the company's catalog by calling 800-541-2233. The cost is $375. The highly rated Zojirushi machine is available from the King Arthur Flour Baker's Catalogue (P.O. Box 876, Norwich, VT 05055; 800-827-6836) for $300, a discount of about $40 from the suggested retail price. Expert bakers at King Arthur will answer questions about the Zojirushi and discuss any problems with recipes made in this machine. Technical support is available during business hours at 802-649-3717. The West Bend unit is available from the Bennett Brothers Catalog (30 East Adams Street, Chicago, IL 60603; 312-263-4800). The cost of the unit is $204. The Welbilt is sold at various department stores across the country. For an outlet in your area, contact the manufacturer at 516-365-5040, ext. 321.

BREAD BOX

Unlike commercial bread, the homemade variety contains no preservatives. Before the rise of commercial bakeries, therefore, most American kitchens were equipped with bread boxes to prevent half-eaten loaves from becoming stale. Once you start making loaves in an automatic bread machine, you, too, will need a place to keep your bread protected and fresh. Williams-Sonoma stores carry an attractive stainless-steel bread box with white enamel finish and chrome trim. Made in Belgium, this box holds two loaves and has a sliding door for easy access. To order this item, which costs $45, call 800-541-2233.

TRUFFLE SLICER

For paper-thin slices of everything from white truffles to fine chocolate, use a specially designed truffle slicer (*see* page 3) from Bridge Kitchenware (214 E. 52nd Street, New York, NY 10022; 800-274-3435). The pitch of the two-inch blade can be adjusted anywhere from fifteen degrees, for thick slices, to five degrees, for the thinnest possible slices. The cost is $22.50.

CAST-IRON SKILLET

A heavy cast-iron skillet is the best choice for pan-frying chicken (*see* page 6). We like a sturdy skillet, such as the version made by Lodge. This pan has pouring spouts on either side and can be purchased with a matching cast-iron lid with loop handle. La Cuisine Kitchenware (323 Cameron Street, Alexandria, VA 22314; 800-521-1176) sells the Lodge skillet for $22. The matching lid also costs $22.

SPRING-ACTION TONGS

When turning fried chicken in hot oil, you need a sure hand to prevent splattering. We recommend using restaurant-quality metal tongs with a strong internal spring that keeps the tool open unless you pinch the two arms closed. The stainless-steel construction and scalloped grip is great for plucking fresh corn on the cob from boiling water or for turning any meat without piercing the flesh and causing the loss of moisture. Look for this handy item at well-stocked kitchen stores. Sur La Table (84 Pine Street, Pike Place Farmers' Market, Seattle, WA 98101; 800-243-0852) carries a set of three tongs — measuring nine and one-half inches, twelve inches, and sixteen inches long — that together are good for just about any job. The set costs $16.95.

CALIFORNIA ARTICHOKES

Almost 80 percent of the artichokes grown in this country come from the California town of Castroville, about thirty miles south of Santa Cruz. While artichokes may only make occasional appearances at markets in other parts of the country, they are a year-round staple in Castroville. Giant Artichoke Company (11241 Merritt Street, Castroville, CA 95012; 408-633-2778) will ship fresh artichokes anywhere in the country. Best of all, instead of traveling by truck for days or weeks to your local market, fresh artichokes arrive at your home in just two days. Home cooks can order the small pack (about nine pounds) that features as few as ten large artichokes or as many as eighty baby artichokes, depending on the size you request. The cost, including shipping, is $30 east of the Mississippi, $28 in the West, and just $25 within California.

GRAPEFRUIT SPOON

A small spoon with serrated edges is the best tool for removing the fuzzy choke from an artichoke. We found a grapefruit spoon — although designed to perform a different purpose — the best choice for this task. The sharp cutting edge loosens the choke from the artichoke heart and the spoon scoops and lifts the fuzzy hairs for easy removal. Look for this item (and not a long, thin grapefruit knife) at kitchen-supply shops. The version made by Henckels, with its black polypropylene handle that ensures a good grip, is particularly well suited to this job. A Cook's Wares (211 37th Street, Beaver Falls, PA 15010; 412-846-9490) carries this item in its catalog for $9.60.

ASIAN INGREDIENTS

The sauce recipes for fish (*see* page 13) call for a number of ingredients that were once exotic and are now fairly easy to obtain, especially if you live near an Asian market or good gourmet shop. However, two items may require a bit more searching. Fish sauce, the basis of many Southeast Asian dishes, is used in Thai and Vietnamese cooking much as soy sauce is used in Chinese and Japanese kitchens. Nancy's Specialty Market (P.O. Box 327, Wye Mills, MD 21679; 800-462-6291) carries a twenty-four-ounce bottle of fish sauce, also called *nuoc mam,* for $3.75. The company also offers a wide array of spices, including Chinese five-spice powder, which is a mixture of ground star anise, cloves, fennel, cinnamon, and Szechwan peppercorns. A three-quarter-ounce supply costs $3.25.

FLORAL WATERS

The recipe for Rose Water Pound Cake (*see* page 20) relies on rose water, a floral liquid made from rose petals. This floral water, which is particularly popular in Indian and Middle Eastern cooking, is made by the same process employed to create orange blossom water, an optional ingredient in Citrus Pound Cake. In both cases, flowers — usually pink damask rosebuds or bergamot orange blossoms — are macerated in warm water and then distilled to make a powerful extract that lends a gentle flavor and bouquet to desserts. Nancy's Specialty Market (*see* above) carries both items in three-ounce bottles that sell for $3.25.

MINI-LOAF PANS

The batter for perfect pound cake (*see* page 20) can be baked in any number of pans. A single recipe can be scraped into a seven and one-half-cup loaf pan or a double recipe can be baked in a bundt pan. Either of these pans can be found at a kitchen supply shop. However, mini-loaf pans with a two-cup capacity can be harder to locate. We like the non-stick pans made by Chicago Metallic. Williams-Sonoma sells a set of four pans that measure five and one-half inches long by three inches wide by two inches deep for just $8. Their dark surface promotes even browning and the Silverstone coating makes for easy release. To order, call 800-541-2233.

KITCHEN SCALE

In Europe, most baking recipes list ingredients by weight rather than volume. In this country, professional bakers use the European system of weighing ingredients to ensure proper measurements. Home cooks might want to follow their example, especially when it comes to making pound cake. For instance, measuring flour on a scale is always a good idea, since one cup of flour by volume can vary from as little as three and one-half to as much as five ounces, depending on how it is packed into the measuring cup. Of course, your kitchen scale must be accurate. We like the Terraillon scale carried by Williams-Sonoma. This scale holds up to ten pounds and has an easy-to-read dial. The plastic housing and weighing tray are easy to clean. The scale costs $26. To order, call 800-541-2233. ■

THE BEST POUND CAKE
page 20

**STEAMED WHOLE ARTICHOKES WITH
LEMON-CHIVE DIPPING SAUCE**
pages 11-12

THREE SAUCES FOR FISH
page 13

**PINEAPPLE, STRAWBERRY, AND TEA
FLAVORED GRANITAS**
pages 24-25

BUTTERMILK-FRIED CHICKEN
page 9

FREE-FORM FRUIT TART
page 14

ALL PHOTOGRAPHS BY ERIC FOTH

Yogurt-Creamed Oats with Berries and Apples

Soak ¼ cup quick-cooking oats in 5 tablespoons warm skim milk until swollen, about 5 minutes. Stir in ⅔ cup plain yogurt, ¼ cup toasted, skinned, and chopped hazelnuts, 3 to 4 tablespoons honey, and 2 tablespoons lemon juice. Coarsely grate 2 crisp, peeled apples; mix into the yogurt mixture, then carefully mix in 1 pint mixed berries. (Hull and halve or quarter strawberries, depending on size.) Spoon mixture into each of 4 goblets or bowls. Garnish with thin apple slices and mint sprigs and serve. *Serves 4 for breakfast, brunch, or dessert.*

COOK'S
ILLUSTRATED

Authentic Homemade Barbecue
The Secret of Tender, Flavorful BBQ Ribs

6 Best Chocolate Cakes
Light and Airy to Dense and Fudgy

Perfect Potato Salad
Ultimate Recipes for 3 Distinct Styles

How to Cook Shrimp
New Technique Dramatically Improves Texture and Taste

~

CHOOSING A MINI FOOD PROCESSOR

•

RATING CHENIN BLANCS

BREYERS WINS ICE CREAM TASTE-OFF

$4.00 U.S./$4.95 CANADA

"Stone Fruits"
See page 20 for a variety of relishes based on stone fruits.

ILLUSTRATION BY
BRENT WATKINSON

Baked Peaches with Amaretti Cookies, adapted from *Look and Cook: Fruit Desserts* (Kindersley, 1992) by Anne Willan.

ILLUSTRATION BY
CAROL FORTUNATO

Publisher and Editor
CHRISTOPHER KIMBALL

Executive Editor
MARK BITTMAN

Senior Editor
JOHN WILLOUGHBY

Food Editor
PAM ANDERSON

Senior Writer
JACK BISHOP

Managing Editor
MAURA LYONS

Editorial Assistant
KIM RUSSELLO

Copy Editor
INGRID SCHORR

Test Kitchen Assistant
VICTORIA ROLAND

Art Director
MEG BIRNBAUM

Food Stylist
MARIE PIRAINO

Circulation Director
ADRIENNE KIMBALL

Circulation Assistant
JENNIFER L. KEENE

Production Director
JAMES MCCORMACK

Publicity Director
CAROL ROSEN KAGAN

Treasurer
JANET CARLSON

Office Manager
JENNY THORNBURY

Customer Service
CONNIE FORBES

Special Projects
FERN BERMAN

Cook's Illustrated (ISSN 1068-2821) is published bimonthly by Natural Health Limited Partners, 17 Station Street, Box 569, Brookline, MA 02147. Copyright 1994 Natural Health Limited Partners. Application to mail at second-class postage rates is pending at Boston, MA, and additional mailing offices. Editorial office: 17 Station Street, Box 569, Brookline, MA 02147; (617) 232-1000, FAX (617) 232-1572. Editorial contributions should be sent to: Editor, *Cook's Illustrated*, 17 Station Street, Box 569, Brookline, MA 02147. We cannot assume responsibility for manuscripts submitted to us. Submissions will be returned only if accompanied by a large self-addressed stamped envelope. Subscription rates: $24.95 for one year; $45 for two years; $65 for three years. (Canada: add $3 per year; all other countries: add $12 per year.) Postmaster: Send all new orders, subscription inquiries, and change of address notices to *Cook's Illustrated*, P.O. Box 59046, Boulder, CO 80322-9046, or telephone (800) 477-3059. Single copies: $4 in U.S., $4.95 in Canada and foreign. Back issues available for $5 each. PRINTED IN THE U.S.A.

EDITORIAL

MY DAUGHTER THE CRITIC

Every night I undergo a sauce-curdling assessment of my culinary prowess from our two daughters. The four-year-old, shocked at that night's menu, slips under the table and bursts into tears. The five-year-old uses a rating system based on colors: brown (the color of meat and chocolate) and white (potatoes and pasta) get thumbs up; serving anything green, however, is like sprinkling holy water on the undead.

After one particularly dreadful dinner hour, it occurred to me that it would be delightful to subject a professional chef to the savage culinary whims of our older daughter, Whitney. I chose Hamersley's Bistro in Boston, and made reservations for an early dinner.

Whitney Kimball, age five, reviewing one of Boston's finest, Hamersley's Bistro, attended by chef/owner Gordon Hamersley (center) and wait staff.

6:00. We arrive. Gordon, the chef/owner, comes over to Whitney and tries to gather some intelligence. "Do you like fish?" "No." "Vegetables?" "No." "Mushrooms?" "No." Things were going just fine.

6:05. A plate of steamed mussels arrives. Whitney yanks two of them out with her fingers and stuffs them into her mouth. I ask hesitantly, "You must have liked the mussels. You ate two." "I just ate them because I wanted to pretend that I liked them." That's my girl.

6:20. Gordon has a special appetizer sent out: Roasted Beet Terrine with Smoked Salmon and Horseradish Sauce. Whitney takes a bite and considers: "Salmon is a kind of fish. I don't like fish. I guess I don't like salmon."

6:30. Root Vegetable Ravioli with Brown Butter and Asiago and one of Gordon's signature dishes, Grilled Mushroom and Garlic Sandwich on Country Bread arrive together. Whitney ignores the mushrooms and dives into the pasta. "This is good. Real good. Mmmmm. Can I have more?" I give her another piece, this time with lots of filling. She looks like she just ate a broccoli floret. "There's stuff inside! Yuck!" A close call. She tries a taste of mushroom sandwich and manages to keep it down.

6:40. We're served Crisp Duck Confit with Peppers and an Aged Sherry Vinegar Sauce, an exquisite dish. "I like it. It tastes just like bacon." Score one for Gordon.

6:50. The table is cluttered with six markers, two half-eaten orange slices, two thin strips of duck confit, a balled-up cocktail napkin that has been dunked into a water glass, a ramekin of butter littered with shards of bread, and drawings of six tulips and a rainbow. Whitney wipes her hand on the edge of the tablecloth. "When are we going to have dessert?"

7:00. The Whole Grilled Bass with Onions and Fennel Flamed with Pernod is placed in front of Whitney. She notices the intact head. "My goodness!" She picks up the head and looks at it. "Excuse me, I don't think I'll have any fish."

7:05. The Sautéed Scallops with Orange and Beets and then the Roast Chicken with Garlic, Lemon, and Parsley arrive. Whitney tucks into the chicken and potatoes. "The potatoes taste just like french fries." She starts to make high-pitched sounds like a mauled rabbit. "I have to go to the bathroom."

7:10. She returns singing a song from the movie *Oliver & Company*. She sits sideways on the chair and rocks back and forth. She makes faces at the woman in red at the table behind us. I ask her what she is thinking about. "Nothing nice."

7:20. Desserts arrive. Layered Mexican Chocolate Terrine. Apple Bread Pudding with Crème Anglaise. Warm Pecan Pie with Vanilla Ice Cream and Southern Comfort. Warm Apple and Prune Tart with Crème Fraîche. Andrew's Favorite Cookies. She starts in on the chocolate terrine and discovers that she likes the chocolate but not the coffee buttercream layers. She strips away the buttercream with the skill of a plastic surgeon. I ask how the chocolate terrine is. "Great."

7:25. The terrine is history. She picks up every cookie and licks the confectioner's sugar off the top. She starts drawing pictures of Gordon Hamersley. "Is it midnight yet? I want coffee. What else can I eat?"

7:30. The table is cleared and the bill is paid. I ask Whitney if she likes this restaurant. "I like it but I don't like the food. The food is yucky." "Is your daddy a better cook?" "Yes." Then she adds with a sigh, "I love you daddy." That's my girl. ∎

— Christopher Kimball

NOTES FROM READERS

FREEZING AND PEELING TOMATOES

*A*t this time of year there are always more tomatoes than can be eaten right away. I like to freeze them, which is much quicker and easier than traditional preserving methods. Just wash the tomatoes, remove the stem ends and any damaged or bruised parts, place whole tomatoes in a plastic bag (a bread bag holds just the right amount), close the bag, and place it in the freezer. There's no need to peel skins, prepare jars, or boil vats of hot water.

Once frozen, tomatoes can be removed individually for use. They are easily peeled by running them under warm water for several seconds to loosen their skins.

STEVE KILKUS
Winona, MN

BETTER WAY WITH BREAD TOPPINGS

*B*read recipes that include a topping like poppy or sesame seeds usually instruct the baker to brush the dough with a mixture of egg whites beaten with water, then sprinkle with the seeds. However, we find that when we use this method the wet coating usually spills over the side of the dough and sticks to the baking sheet or pan. Also, the seeds usually do not stick all that well.

We have developed a better way to apply seeds to loaves. If you lightly beat the egg white without water and then add the seeds, you can easily spread the thick mixture with a teaspoon over the risen loaf. You will find that the topping will not drip as much and the seeds will be less likely to fall off after baking.

DOUG AND LENORE ADLER
Columbus, IN

ORDERLY BUBBLES

*I*n college I stumped my organic chemistry professor with this question, and I still have not found the answer to it after several years of casual thought.

I have noticed that the bubbles in Champagne rise to the surface, single file, in neat little rows. The bubbles in good beer and naturally fermented cider act in the same way. On the other hand, the bubbles in cheap sparkling wines and industrially produced beer form haphazardly on the surface of the glass, and rise at random. These bubbles are often different sizes too.

For some time, I assumed this phenomenon had something to do with natural versus artificial carbonation. However, just recently someone poured me a glass of flat, warm Sprite and guess what — the bubbles rose to the surface single file, just like Champagne. Can you explain my observations?

MEG TOCANTINS
Brooklyn, NY

We spoke with a number of wine experts, and the most plausible explanation comes from Robert Beelman, a food scientist at Penn State University who teaches classes in wine making. Premium sparkling wines, including Champagne, rely on yeast and sugar to produce carbon dioxide. After many months and sometimes years of aging, the yeast undergoes a process called autolysis. In effect, "the yeast spills its guts," says Beelman. The yeast dies and the cellular material, including many proteins, is released into the wine.

The remains of the yeast form a sediment that is removed from the wine by a process called disgorging. However, many of the yeast components are still dissolved in the wine. Eventually the dissolved proteins break down into peptides, molecules that increase the Champagne's ability to hold onto carbon dioxide.

This same process may occur with slow-fermented and aged beers and ciders. However, industrial beers and cheap sparkling wines are produced by a different method. The yeast is not given enough time to decompose since it is usually introduced for only a matter or hours or days, not months or years. Most of the carbonation in these beverages is mechanically injected.

When you open a bottle of industrially made beer or soda, most of the carbon dioxide is immediately released into the air. This is because there are no yeast components to grab hold of the gases. This is also why sodas have large bubbles that rush to the surface in a haphazard manner. With premium Champagne, however, the carbon dioxide is released much more slowly. Often bubbles will slowly rise in vintage Champagnes for fifteen or twenty minutes, hence the appearance of small bubbles floating to the surface in an orderly fashion.

This answer does not explain your observation with the flat, warm Sprite. Beelman's best guess is that you saw the soda after it had released most of its gas. If just a small amount of carbon dioxide was being released, the appearance might be similar to that of just-opened Champagne. However, any just-opened soda, including Sprite, should fizz quite rapidly.

COCOA POWDER

I have a recipe that calls for unsweetened alkalized cocoa powder. What is this? Are unsweetened alkalized cocoa powder and unsweetened non-alkalized cocoa powder interchangeable?

ALBERT AITKEN, JR.
San Bernardino, CA

To understand the differences between these two types of cocoa, it helps to know how cocoa is made. Beans from *Theobroma cacao*, an evergreen that grows in tropical regions, are first roasted to bring out flavors and then cracked open. The meaty kernels, or nibs, are separated from the shells, which are used as animal feed. The nibs contain about 55 percent cocoa butter, and when they are ground up and heated they form a thick liquid called chocolate liquor, the basis of most chocolate products.

To make cocoa powder, much of the cocoa butter must be removed from the chocolate liquor. This step brings the final fat content down to between 10 percent and 25 percent. With the removal of so much liquid fat, the resulting cocoa is dry and powdery. At this point, unalkalized cocoa, a style preferred by most U.S. companies, is finely ground, sifted, and packaged. (Cocoa powders used expressly for hot chocolate often have added sugar, but most baking recipes call for unsweetened cocoa.)

During the early nineteenth century, a Dutch inventor named Conrad van Houten developed a process called dutching that has been used for over a century by most European companies to make Dutch-processed or alkalized cocoa. To dutch chocolate, an alkaline solution, usually potassium carbonate, is added to the chocolate liquor as it is refined. The alkali raises the pH of cocoa, which is normally acidic, from around 5.5 to 7.5. Raising the pH has the effect of darkening the color of the cocoa, mellowing its sometimes harsh flavor, and improving its solubility in liquids.

The results in cooking, however, are more muddled. (*See* "Six Chocolate Cakes," page 22, for a comparison of cakes prepared with the two types of cocoa.) Which type of cocoa to choose depends on the specific recipe and the leavening agent used.

Regular unalkalized cocoa is acidic and therefore reacts with alkaline baking soda to form carbon dioxide. This reaction is important for the leavening of many cookies and cakes, especially traditional recipes from the United States. European-style alkalized cocoa, being less acidic, does not work as well in recipes with baking soda. Baking powder, however, is more acidic than baking soda, so in recipes in which powder is the main leavening, alkalized cocoa becomes the better choice. The general idea is to balance the pH level in the cocoa and the leavening agent.

CHERRY PITTING

While harvesting a bumper crop of cherries at my sister's home in Massachusetts, I developed a method for cherry pitting that is much faster than using a hand-held cherry pitter. The best way to get this potentially messy job done is as follows: Use your thumb to gently press down on the stem end of the cherry to dislodge the pit. Then, with the index finger and thumb on your other hand, gently squeeze the sides of the cherry slightly below the bottom of the pit. The pit comes right out of the top of the cherry with minimal loss of pulp or juice.

SUSAN BROUGHTON
Clarksburg, WV

SCALDING MILK FOR BREAD

I thought your answer to the question about why some bread recipes call for scalded milk was incomplete (see Notes from Readers, January/February 1994). The scalding of milk is necessary to alter milk serum proteins that otherwise interact with flour protein and produce a weak dough. It is an ancient practice among bread bakers and it was necessary in the past. However, since virtually all milk is now pasteurized at temperatures that are high enough to alter serum proteins, scalding milk, at least for this reason, is no longer necessary. Warming the milk is still beneficial for faster yeast action but is not essential.

GEORGE ERDOSH
Sacramento, CA

MUFFIN TOPS

A bakery near my home sells large muffin tops. My favorite part of a muffin is the crisp cap, so I love to buy these special treats. I was wondering what they do with the rest of the muffin. Do you think they throw it out, or are there special tins for making muffin tops?

SUSAN FELDMAN
Parsippany, NJ

If your bakery plans on staying in business, it probably uses tins specially designed to bake thin, domed muffin caps. Chicago-Metallic

makes a small nonstick version of this pan for home use. The pan has six cups that are four inches wide and just one-half inch deep. Fill cups to the rim and pop the pan in the oven for just a few minutes — regular muffins take much longer to bake. The result is a high-rising, extra-large muffin top with an extremely shallow base. This pan is available at Williams-Sonoma stores nationwide. It also can be ordered from the company's catalog by calling 800-541-2233. The cost is $16.

CHICKEN BROTH QUESTIONS

The article on chicken broth (January/February 1994) was interesting but with some shortcomings. When doing taste tests, if there is a standard to compare something against, it should be used. In this case, the comparison should have been with homemade stock.

When I cook, it is not only for pleasure but also for the added bonus of better health. We all know there are massive amounts of chemicals in our food supply. These chemicals are mostly used for the benefit of the producer and do not improve the nutritional value of food. In the case of the chicken broths tested, I feel that there should have been at least a small commentary on the health aspect. I know that a large amount of salt (as well as other chemicals) is used in most commercial broths. I can't help wondering if the flavor the testers found so delightful came out of a chemist's lab.

A. C. NEAL
Tampa, FL

You make several good points worth addressing. Although not explicitly stated in the article, there is no comparison between homemade chicken stock and the best canned broth. Not even an inexperienced taster could fail to detect the difference. Broth out of a can will never have the texture or rich flavor of homemade stock. The overall poor quality of canned broths was indicated in the article by the fact that testers refused to give positive comments to the vast majority of samples. Even the top brands elicited only modest praise like "pleasant enough" and "decent."

Your point about salt is also correct. Most canned brands are loaded with sodium, often as much as 1,000 mg per cup — almost half the recommended daily allotment. The saltiness of many canned broths can become a real problem during cooking, especially if the broth is reduced substantially. Lower-salt brands are better — Campbell's Healthy Request, the winner of our taste test, contains 470 mg of sodium per cup. Of course, when making broth at home, salt levels are much easier to control.

Lastly, your point about chemicals is interesting. As noted in the article, we tested several "all-natural" broths sold in health food stores. We found all three leading brands to be unacceptable. In fact, two of three ranked dead last in the tasting. It may be that canned broth needs

some added ingredients, like preservatives and flavorings, in order to survive the distribution process. And while some of the top brands do indeed have fairly long ingredients lists, Swanson Natural Goodness, the second-place broth in our tasting, contains just chicken broth, chicken fat, salt, dextrose (a type of sugar), and natural flavoring. This may not be your grandmother's recipe for chicken stock, but the label on this canned broth does not read like a chemical textbook, either.

For all of the reasons you mention, homemade stock is always preferable to canned broth. That said, there are times when canned broth is simply more convenient. Especially in recipes that call for small amounts of stock, even devoted cooks sometimes turn to canned alternatives. This is a personal choice that we realize many cooks are making due to time constraints. Our article was designed to help them make the best choices among canned broths.

REMEDY FOR GARLIC ODOR

When chopping or handling garlic, you can remove the smell from your hands instantly by rubbing a piece of stainless steel over your fingers under gently running water. Try it — it really works!

TOBY MANUEL
Larkspur, CA

We did try this suggestion, which was also sent to us by June Seelman of Nichols, New York, and it works like a charm.

WHAT IS IT?

I found this odd pumplike contraption in a secondhand store. The owner wasn't sure what its purpose was. Do you know?

KAREN SKEFFINGTON
Peoria, IL

It is the Bel Cream Maker, a unique appliance made in England since 1934. To use it, simply combine melted butter and warm milk in the chamber and work the pump vigorously, and in a few minutes the emulsification process will produce cream. It's a rich cream, too — about 40 percent butterfat, compared with 36 percent butterfat for heavy cream and 30 percent butterfat for "whipping" cream. Cream made with the Bel is not ultrapasteurized, as is most store-bought cream, so it whips very quickly and makes great crème fraîche. This little device is ideal when you need just a bit of cream, have none in the house, and don't feel like running to the store. ∎

Quick Tips

PEELING AND SEEDING MELONS

To easily peel and seed honeydew, cantaloupe, or other round melons, follow this method suggested to us by Nancy Hoffman of San Rafael, California.

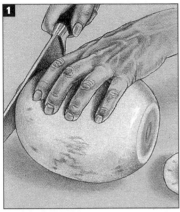

1. Cut a small slice off each end of the melon so that you can work with a flat surface.

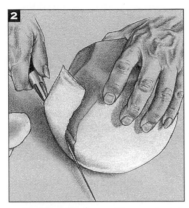

2. Holding the top with one hand, carefully slice off the peel in sections from top to bottom, rotating the melon as you go.

3. Once the melon is peeled, cut it in half and scoop out the seeds.

SOFTENING BUTTER FOR MIXING

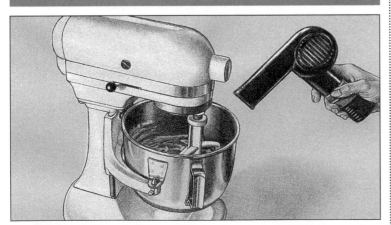

To soften butter quickly for creaming, cut the butter into large cubes, place the cubes in a mixing bowl and, with the mixer running, use a blow dryer to direct hot air into and around the mixing bowl until the butter just begins to soften.

SEEDING A WATERMELON

The great majority of seeds in a watermelon are found in a concentric ring a few inches from the center of the melon. You can take advantage of this fact to remove most of the seeds, following these steps.

 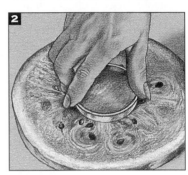

1. Cut the melon into circular slices of the desired thickness.

2. Use a biscuit cutter or a cookie cutter to remove the seedless melon center.

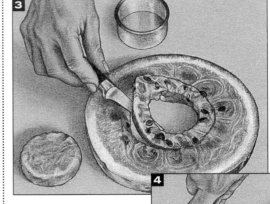

3. With a paring knife, cut out the concentric ring that contains most of the seeds.

4. Use the paring knife to cut along the inner boundary of the rind.

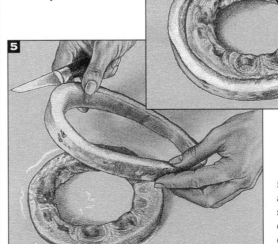

5. Lift off the rind and cut the now-seedless fruit, including the melon center, for whatever use you desire.

ILLUSTRATIONS BY ALAN WITSCHONKE

PEELING RIPE TOMATOES

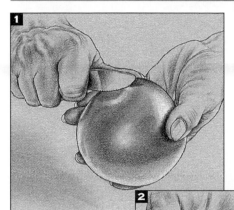

To quickly and easily peel a vine-ripened tomato without having to drop it into boiling water, follow this tip from Isabelle Wolters of Scituate, Massachusetts.

1. Run the blade of a table or butter knife over the entire surface of the tomato without cutting or piercing the skin.

2. With a paring knife, remove the core of the tomato and use the sharp end of the knife to start lifting off the skin. You can then pull it off easily with your fingers.

CUTTING BACON EASILY

When you need to cut bacon, especially just one or two pieces, kitchen scissors perform the task more easily than a knife.

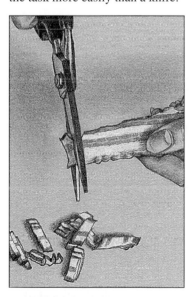

READING A MEAT THERMOMETER

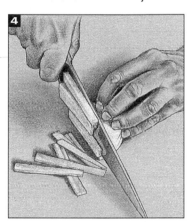

Jerry Seaward of Pasadena, California, points out that meat thermometer numbers are difficult to read when you are peering into the oven. To make this task easier, he recommends putting a paper clip on the thermometer at the desired temperature mark.

PREPARING JICAMA

Jicama is a tuberous root vegetable with a crisp, crunchy texture and a taste that lies somewhere between an apple and a potato. It is widely used in Latin and Asian cuisines and has become increasingly popular in the United States over recent years. Follow these steps to prepare jicama for dishes such as the Apricot-Jicama Salsa on page 20.

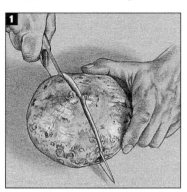

1. Slice the jicama in half.

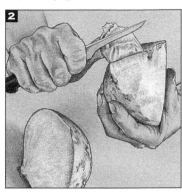

2. Use a paring knife to peel the brown outer skin from the jicama.

3. Slice the crisp flesh into half-circles.

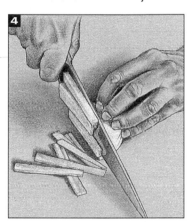

4. Stack the half-circles and slice them lengthwise into matchsticks.

MEASURING CAKE BATTER

To ensure that you end up with equal amounts of batter in each pan when making layer cakes, use a kitchen scale to measure the weight of filled pans.

ATTENTION READERS: FREE SUBSCRIPTION FOR PUBLISHED TIPS. Do you have a unique tip you would like to share with other readers? We will provide a one-year complimentary subscription for each quick tip that we print. Send a description of your special technique to *Cook's Illustrated*, P.O. Box 569, Brookline Village, MA 02147. Please write "Attention: Quick Tips" on the envelope and include your name, address, and daytime phone number. Unfortunately, we can only acknowledge receipt of tips that will be printed in the magazine. In case the same tip is received from two readers, the one postmarked first will be selected.

Perfect Potato Salad

For the best potato salad, use low-starch potatoes, boil them in their skins, and drizzle vinegar both on the potatoes and in the dressing.

~ BY PAM ANDERSON WITH KAREN TACK ~

There are certain dishes you just grow up making. You don't need measuring cups and spoons — you're comfortable just eyeballing it. Vegetable soup is one of those dishes for me; potato salad is another. In fact, I don't think I've ever followed a recipe for potato salad in my life. But I recently deviated from my usual method and learned that there are good ways and there are better ways of making even a dish as seemingly straight-forward as potato salad.

After analyzing well over a hundred recipes, I limited myself to French-, German-, and American-style potato salads. Before compiling a shopping list for what appeared to be a massive project, I wondered what I had gotten myself into. How many recipes would I have to test to determine the best way to make the dish? Was it possible to come up with a best salad in each category? It seemed pretty presumptuous, considering all the regional variations in the United States alone.

However, when I actually put together the list, it wasn't nearly as long as I thought it would be. Though all the recipes seemed dramatically different, they all had four things in common — potatoes, of course; fat (usually bacon, olive oil, or mayonnaise); an acidic ingredient to perk things up; and flavorings for distinction. Though these salads were very different in character, the issues affecting all of them, as it turns out, were much the same.

Four issues concerned the main ingredient, the potato. First, what type of potato should be used? Recipes writers seemed split down the middle between starchy and waxy potatoes, with starchy praised for being more absorbent and waxy admired for their sturdiness.

Next was the issue of how to cook the potato. I had always just boiled mine with the skin on, so I was surprised to find others steaming, microwaving, roasting, or baking all kinds of potatoes, from skin-on to peeled and cut. One recipe suggested boiling the potatoes in chicken stock; another, in milk — but would either liquid infuse and enrich the potato?

Then, when should the potato be peeled? On the assumption that hot potatoes are more absorbent, some thought it worth scorching fingertips to get the cooked potatoes peeled and cut immediately. Other recipe writers were more casual — "peel when warm enough to handle." Still others instructed to refrigerate the cooled potatoes, then peel and cut the next day. And of course you wonder whether you really need to peel them at all.

Finally, should potatoes be seasoned when still warm, assuming that they do absorb flavorings better in this state? Is it worth the two-step process of seasoning the potatoes with vinegar (or vinaigrette), salt, and pepper first? Or should you toss everything together at the same time?

High-Starch Spud: The Dud
After boiling, steaming, baking/roasting, and microwaving four different varieties of potatoes — Red Bliss, russets, all-purpose, and Yukon Golds (*see* "Finding the Best Cooking Method," page 8) — we found that boiling was the cooking method of choice. However, that was true only if using *low-starch* boiling potatoes such as Red Bliss or new potatoes. For the most part, we found high-starch potatoes — russets, all-purpose, and Yukon Golds — not sturdy enough for salad making. They fell apart when cut and looked sloppy in salad form. A few cooking methods, however, made these potatoes more suitable for salad. Although the microwave cooked up a disastrous boiling potato (gummy and sticky), it seemed to firm up the russet potato's texture. And while the Yukon Gold and all-purpose potato boiled up soft and mealy, it was amazing how ten minutes in a 275-degree oven firmed them up. Because of the varying starch quantity in each potato, it seemed the cooking method that proved successful for one kind of potato produced negative results in the others.

Before giving up on high-starch potatoes for salad making, we wanted to test their absorption power, a selling point to many cooks. A number of French, German, and American potato salad recipes suggested an initial drizzling of either vinegar or vinaigrette over warm or hot salad potatoes, so that they would taste seasoned from within as well as dressed from without. To check their ability to absorb oil as well as vinegar, we tossed each variety of potato with vinaigrette.

We found that high-starch potatoes do indeed absorb better than the lower-starch — to a fault. When tossed with the same amount of

Low-starch potatoes such as Red Bliss provide the sturdy texture needed to stand up to whatever dressing you choose.

dressing, the high-starch potato salads tasted dry, sucking up all the dressing and asking for more. These mealy high-starch potatoes, we determined, were great for mashing or baking, but not for salad. The low-starch boiling potatoes successfully absorbed the vinegar and most of the oil. We liked the firm yet creamy texture of this potato. Though some of the oil went unabsorbed, we didn't see this as a negative. If the purpose of drizzling the potatoes was to flavor them, and they were to be tossed with some form of fat at the second tossing, why make them more fatty than was necessary?

Impenetrable Skin
So far, we had settled on a potato and found that oil was not necessary at the first flavoring session. Next we wanted to see if we could boost flavor at the cooking stage by boiling the potatoes in chicken broth and in water heavily seasoned with bay leaves and garlic cloves. (We ruled out simmering them in milk, since the idea of drizzling vinegar over milk-coated potatoes just wasn't appetizing.) The chicken stock may as well have been water — there wasn't even a scent of evidence that the potatoes had been cooked in stock. The bay leaves and garlic smelled wonderful as the potatoes

cooked, but while the potato skin smelled faintly of garlic, the potato itself was still bland.

The fact that nothing seemed to penetrate the potato got us wondering: Does the potato skin act as a barrier? We performed yet another experiment by cooking two batches of unpeeled potatoes, the first in heavily salted water and the second in unsalted water. We rinsed them quickly under cold running water and tasted. Sure enough, both batches of potatoes tasted exactly the same.

We tried boiling potatoes without the skin, but none of the varieties benefited from this method. The outer flesh of both the Idaho and the all-purpose flaked off into the boiling water, and the Yukon Gold practically disintegrated. The Red Bliss held up the best, though all were waterlogged compared to their skin-on counterparts. In salad form all the potatoes had a sloppy, broken look and tasted watery. Our conclusion: Potatoes should be boiled skin-on in unsalted water.

Put a Lid on It

We observed that the potatoes that sat close to the water's surface cooked more slowly than those at the bottom of the pan. This was most noticeable when the lid was off. We found that covering the pot, as well as giving the potatoes a gentle stir once or twice during cooking, helped to cook the potatoes more evenly.

We also confirmed that when pricking the potato to check for doneness, the thinner the utensil, the better. A fork, which is frequently the quickest thing to grab, is actually the worst testing tool; it visibly damages the potato, sometimes causing it to split. A thin-bladed knife or a metal cake tester works best.

Although we might not want to eat the skin of a boiled Idaho in a salad, we found the paper-thin skin of the boiled red potato not unpleasant to taste and certainly pleasant to look at in what is often a monochromatic salad. Although this saved the peeling step, we found the skin tended to rip when cutting the potato. Since this was especially true when the potatoes were very hot, we solved the problem in two ways. First, we cut the potatoes with a serrated knife, which minimized ripping, and second, we found it wasn't necessary to cut them when they were hot, since warm ones are just as absorbent. Although the high-starch potatoes tended to fall apart most readily, even boiling potatoes had a tendency to fall apart when tampered with hot off the stove.

At this point we had learned that warm potatoes absorb vinegar, but we weren't necessarily sure where we wanted the acidity: Should it be in the potato, in the dressing, or in both? To find out, we made three mayonnaise-based salads. In the first, we drizzled all the vinegar on the potato; in the second, half the vinegar went on the potato and the other half was mixed with the mayonnaise; and in the third salad, we mixed all the vinegar with the mayonnaise. The results were clear. Too much vinegar on the

potatoes make them taste pickled. The other extreme produced a zesty salad dressing, with creamy but bland potatoes. Using vinegar in moderation both on the potatoes and in the dressing provided the right balance.

To sum up: Use low-starch potatoes; boil them in their skins; don't salt the water; don't peel them unless you really want to; and use a serrated knife to cut the potatoes after boiling, once they have cooled down slightly. Then, while the potatoes are still warm, drizzle them with a splash of vinegar. After this, proceed with one of the salad recipes we've developed. If you think we've left out the green pepper, Tabasco, or white wine, we have. That's where you take over.

MASTER RECIPE FOR BOILED POTATOES

2 pounds Red Bliss or new potatoes (about 6 medium or 18 new), rinsed; scrubbed if not peeling them

Place potatoes in a 4- to 6-quart pot; cover with water. Bring to a boil, cover, and simmer, stirring once or twice to ensure even cooking, until a thin-bladed paring knife or a metal cake tester inserted into the potato can be removed with no resistance (25 to 30 minutes for medium potatoes and 15 to 20 minutes for new potatoes). Drain; cool potatoes slightly and peel if you like. Cut potatoes (use a serrated knife if they have skins) while still warm, rinsing knife occasionally in warm water to remove gumminess. Proceed as directed in one of the following recipes.

FRENCH-STYLE POTATO SALAD WITH TARRAGON VINAIGRETTE
Serves 6

If fresh tarragon is not available, increase the parsley to three tablespoons and use tarragon vinegar for drizzling and in the vinaigrette.

2 pounds Red Bliss or new potatoes, boiled (*see* Master Recipe), peeled if

---

To find out which mayonnaise makes the best potato salad and to find out if any of the light and fat free varieties are worth consideration, we made American-Style Potato Salad with seven different national brands: Hellmann's, Hellmann's Light, Hellmann's Reduced Fat, Kraft, Kraft Light, and Kraft Free. The informal tasting was blind, and the order of preference follows:

Hellmann's Real Mayonnaise (11 fat grams per tablespoon). Unanimous number one choice. Unquestionably identified as real mayonnaise. All noted that this salad looked and tasted creamy — fat complimented the acid for a well-balanced taste. Although we did not include homemade mayonnaise in this tasting, we later compared salads made with Hellmann's Real Mayonnaise with those made using homemade. Most felt homemade and Hellmann's were of equal quality, while others actually preferred the Hellmann's to the homemade. No one preferred homemade over Hellmann's.

Hellmann's Light Reduced Calorie Mayonnaise Dressing (5 fat grams per tablespoon). Though not the number one choice, most tasters thought this salad was dressed with real mayonnaise — quite a compliment since it scored higher than Kraft Real Mayonnaise and has 6 fewer fat grams. Salad looked and tasted creamy.

Kraft Real Mayonnaise (11 fat grams per tablespoon). The biggest surprise of the tasting was that this mayonnaise trailed Hellmann's Light. No one identified this salad as one dressed with real mayonnaise.

Hellmann's Reduced Fat Cholesterol Free Mayonnaise Dressing (3 fat grams per tablespoon). Although this salad received a higher taste score than those dressed with Kraft Light and Kraft Free, tasters could tell they weren't eating salad made with the real thing.

Kraft Light Reduced Calorie Mayonnaise (5 fat grams per tablespoon). A step up from Kraft Free. You have the sense that there's some fat in the salad. One taster commented that the salad looked like it had been dressed with white sauce, without the sheen of real mayonnaise. Like the Kraft Free salad, this one was also too acidic.

Kraft Free Fat Free Cholesterol Free (0 fat grams per tablespoon). All tasters noted that this salad was sour — there was no fat to round out the acid in the salad. "It's just a facade," noted one taster. Salad was not much moister than before it was dressed.

desired, and cut into ¼-inch slices
¼ cup white wine vinegar
½ teaspoon salt
½ teaspoon ground black pepper
1 tablespoon Dijon-style mustard
1 medium shallot, minced
6 tablespoons olive oil
2 tablespoons minced fresh parsley
1 tablespoon minced fresh tarragon

1. Layer warm potato slices in medium bowl; sprinkle with 2 tablespoons vinegar and the salt and pepper as you go. Let stand at room temperature while preparing dressing.

2. Combine remaining 2 tablespoons vinegar, mustard, and shallot in small mixing bowl. Gradually whisk in olive oil so that mixture is somewhat emulsified. Pour over potatoes; toss lightly to coat. Refrigerate salad until ready to serve. Bring to room temperature; toss in parsley and tarragon and serve.

AMERICAN-STYLE POTATO SALAD WITH EGGS AND SWEET PICKLES
Serves 6–8

2 pounds Red Bliss or new potatoes, boiled (*see* Master Recipe), peeled if desired, and cut into ¾-inch cubes
2 tablespoons red wine vinegar
½ teaspoon salt
½ teaspoon ground black pepper
3 hard-boiled eggs, peeled and cut into small dice
2–3 scallions, sliced thin (about ½ cup)
1 small celery stalk, cut into small dice (about ½ cup)
¼ cup sweet pickle (not relish), cut into small dice
½ cup mayonnaise
2 tablespoons Dijon-style mustard
¼ cup minced fresh parsley

1. Layer warm potato cubes in medium bowl; sprinkle with vinegar, salt, and pepper as you go. Refrigerate while preparing remaining ingredients.

2. Mix in remaining ingredients; refrigerate until ready to serve.

GERMAN-STYLE POTATO SALAD WITH BACON AND BALSAMIC VINEGAR
Serves 6

For salads like this German-style one, the smaller new potatoes are more attractive. The slices are smaller and tend not to break up like the bigger potatoes do.

2 pounds Red Bliss or new potatoes, boiled (*see* Master Recipe), peeled if desired, and cut into ¼-inch slices
¼ cup balsamic or cider vinegar
½ teaspoon salt
½ teaspoon ground black pepper
4–5 slices bacon (about 4 ounces), cut crosswise into ¼-inch strips

1 medium onion, cut into medium dice
2 tablespoons vegetable oil
½ cup beef broth
¼ cup minced fresh parsley

1. Layer warm potato slices in a medium bowl; sprinkle with 2 tablespoons vinegar and the salt and pepper as you go. Let stand at room temperature while preparing dressing.

2. Fry bacon in a medium skillet over medium heat until bacon is brown and crisp and fat is rendered, 7 to 10 minutes. Transfer bacon with a slotted spoon to bowl of potatoes. Add onion to bacon drippings; sauté until softened, 4 to 5 minutes. If bacon is fairly lean, onions will absorb most of drippings, so you will need to add up to 2 tablespoons vegetable oil to yield 2 tablespoons unabsorbed fat. Add beef broth and bring to a boil; add remaining 2 tablespoons vinegar. Remove from heat and pour mixture over potatoes. Add parsley; toss gently to coat. Serve warm or tepid. ■

FINDING THE BEST COOKING METHOD

In the hundred or so potato salad recipes I analyzed for this story, I noticed virtually every imaginable cooking method applied to just about every kind of potato. So we put four different varieties of potatoes to the test — Red Bliss or boiling potatoes; Idaho, a type of russet; chef's or all-purpose; and Yukon Gold. We boiled, baked/roasted, steamed, and microwaved each representative. As I suspected, boiling was the cooking method of choice, and the Red Bliss, boiled skin-on, was our favorite potato. However, there were also a few surprises.

BOILING

Potatoes peeled first, then boiled: None of the potatoes benefited from this method. The outer flesh of the Idaho and all-purpose flaked off into the boiling water; the Yukon Gold practically disintegrated. The Red Bliss held up the best, though all were waterlogged compared with their skin-on counterparts. In salad form all the potatoes had a sloppy, broken up look and tasted watery.
Boiled skin-on, then peeled and cubed: All varieties peeled with equal ease, although we noted that some of the meat on the all-purpose potato peeled away with the skin. The Idaho, and to some extent the all-purpose and Yukon Gold, tasted tender and fluffy, a texture begging

for butter and sour cream — not sturdy enough for cubing or slicing. The Red Bliss stayed firm yet creamy and held its cubed shape well.
Boiled, dried in a 275-degree oven for ten minutes, then peeled and cubed: For all four types the skins were slightly more difficult to remove. This drying technique, which we thought might help all the potatoes, actually had a negative affect on the Idaho. It accentuated the potato's fluffiness, a texture ideal for mashed potatoes but not for potato salad. We could feel the Idaho literally expand in our mouth. Oddly, the oven time caused the Yukon Gold and the all-purpose to resemble the Red Bliss — the texture of both was smoother, firmer, and creamier than the fluffy, mealy Idaho. The Red Bliss was neither helped nor hindered by the drying time.

STEAMING

Steamed, peeled, then cubed: Steaming whole potatoes took forty-plus minutes, and we had to add water once during the process. If you do not watch the pot carefully, you run the risk of burning it, and the odor will permeate the potatoes. The all-purpose, Idaho, and Yukon Gold were firmer when steamed than with any of the boiling methods, while the Red Bliss was gummy.
Steamed cubed potatoes: Certainly the fastest method,

with potatoes steaming to tenderness in about twelve minutes, even faster than with the microwave. However, the potato cubes were totally waterlogged — too soft and mushy for potato salad, or for much of anything for that matter. The Red Bliss, once again, held up the best.

MICROWAVE

Microwaved one of each variety together on high power for fifteen minutes, rotating them every five minutes, then peeled and cubed: Got the most varied result of any of the cooking methods. The Idaho and Yukon Gold were both nice and firm. If I were making salad and only had Idaho or Yukons on hand, I would cook them in the microwave. The cooking method that worked for these starchier potatoes proved disastrous for the Red Bliss, producing a gummy, gluey potato that tasted as if it had been pureed in a food processor. The all-purpose potato was mushy.

ROASTING/BAKING

Baked at 400 degrees until tender, peeled, then cubed: All the potatoes smelled and tasted more potatoey, but all the potatoes were harder to peel. A fair amount of the flesh peeled away with the skin, and the exterior flesh left behind was leathery.

Real Tabbooleh

For the best version of this classic Arabic salad, use a high proportion of parsley and presoak the bulgur in lemon juice.

～ BY ANNE MARIE WEISS-ARMUSH ～

Perhaps the best-known Arab dish in the United States is tabbooleh. However, the tabbooleh typically served here is very different from the original. In its Middle Eastern home, this dish is basically a parsley salad with bulgur, rather than the bulgur salad with parsley that is frequently found here.

In addition to finely minced parsley, a perfect tabbooleh includes morsels of bulgur — crushed, parboiled wheat — tossed in a penetrating, minty lemon dressing with bits of ripe tomato. While these principal ingredients remain the same, a variety of preparation techniques exist, each Arab cook being convinced that her method produces the finest version. I decided to examine the various ingredients and preparation methods recommended by Lebanese and Syrian friends to determine which produced the best tabbooleh.

Selecting the Ingredients

The variety of parsley used in the Arab Mediterranean is the flavorful, flat-leafed plant that is usually labeled "Italian parsley" in American markets. Once rare in the United States, this variety is widely available today. The other option is curly-leafed parsley, which is more delicately flavored and less fragrant than flat-leafed. Either will make an acceptable salad. If you particularly like the parsley flavor to shine through, use flat-leafed; if you don't mind a more mellow tabbooleh in which the flavors blend together, the curly is a good choice.

One advantage of curly-leafed parsley is that its tougher leaves can be minced — with care — in the food processor. To do so, snip off the crisp stems and pinch off the branches of green leaves. Fill the bowl of your machine lightly with the leaves, and briefly pulse. Instead of packing in a large quantity of parsley, it is better to repeat this step two or three times until all the parsley is lightly minced. Unless you have removed every bit of stem before processing, some noticeable lengths will remain. These should be removed. Contrary to popular belief, the stems are not more bitter than the leaves, but they are much more fibrous and can create an unpleasant texture in the salad.

Flat-leafed parsley, more delicate than the curly variety, should be chopped by hand in the traditional manner. Simply pinch off the leaves and mince them.

The bulgur (or burghul) used in tabbooleh in the Middle East is an earthy homemade product, boiled until it is just about to crack open, then set out to dry on sheets in the hot sun. A more commercial version of bulgur can be found in ethnic groceries and natural-food stores throughout the United States, as well as in supermarkets in many parts of the country. When buying this product for use in tabbooleh, be sure to look for fine grain (often labeled #1). Medium grain (labeled #2) is an acceptable substitute. Just be sure that you do not get the coarse version, which needs to be cooked rather than just soaked. Medium bulgur is about the same size as couscous, while fine is even smaller. Never substitute cracked wheat, which is an uncooked and totally dissimilar grain. Similarly, avoid boxed tabbooleh mixes, which usually consist of irregularly sized bits of bulgur with a few flecks of dried parsley.

Processing the Bulgur

Arab cooks have developed many different methods of processing the bulgur for tabbooleh, each method sworn to by its adherents as the only acceptable one. I tried processing the bulgur in the five most commonly used ways. First I rinsed the grain, combined it with the minced tomato, and set it aside to absorb the tomato juices. With this method, the bulgur remained unacceptably crunchy.

Next I tried marinating the bulgur in lemon juice and olive oil dressing. This approach produced bulgur that was tasty but slightly heavy. The third method, soaking the grain in water until fluffy and then squeezing out the excess moisture, produced an equally acceptable — but equally heavy — nutty-flavored wheat.

Next I discovered that, if I first soaked the wheat in water for about five minutes, then drained the liquid and replaced it with the lemon–olive oil dressing, the wheat's texture was good and the flavor superior.

But the all-out winner came as a surprise. I first rinsed the bulgur, then mixed it with fresh lemon juice. I then set the mixture aside to allow the juice to be absorbed. When treated in this way, bulgur acquires a fresh and intense flavor, but without the heaviness that the added olive oil produces.

To complete the dish, combine the bulgur with the parsley, finely chopped scallions, fresh mint, and tomatoes. Toss with the remaining dressing ingredients and serve within a few hours. Letting the mixture sit for an hour or so blends the flavors nicely, but after five or six hours the onion tends to become too strong and overpower the other flavors.

I enjoy a touch of Middle Eastern red pepper in this salad but find that other spices overpower its fresh flavors. (Allspice is sometimes added in Syria, while Egyptians favor cumin.) In the Tripoli region of Lebanon, minced cucumbers are added, and I have also seen the dish prepared with a bit of chopped romaine lettuce.

The final question is the proportion of parsley to bulgur. Although some Lebanese restaurateurs present a nine to one ratio of parsley to bulgur, I find that the wholesome goodness of the wheat is lost unless it is in a more harmonious balance. While Arab cooks continue to debate the topic, it remains a matter of individual taste. For myself, I recommend that the finished dish contain five parts parsley to three or four parts wheat.

TABBOOLEH
Makes 4–6 servings (about 1 quart)

Middle Eastern cooks frequently serve this salad with crisp inner leaves of romaine lettuce, using them as spoons to scoop the salad from the serving dish.

- ½ cup fine-grain bulgur wheat, rinsed under running water and drained (you may substitute medium-grain if necessary)
- ⅓ cup juice from 2 lemons
- ⅓ cup olive oil
- Salt
- ⅛ teaspoon Middle Eastern red pepper or cayenne (optional)
- 2 cups minced fresh parsley
- 2 medium tomatoes, halved, seeded, and cut into very small dice
- 4 medium scallions, green and white parts, minced
- 2 tablespoons minced fresh mint leaves (or 1 rounded teaspoon dried mint)

1. Mix bulgur wheat with ¼ cup of the lemon juice in medium bowl; set aside until grains are tender and fluffy, 20 to 40 minutes, depending on age and type of bulgur.

2. Mix remaining lemon juice, olive oil, salt to taste, and red pepper if desired. Mix bulgur, parsley, tomatoes, scallions, and mint; add dressing and toss to combine. Cover and refrigerate to let flavors blend, 1 to 2 hours. Serve. ∎

Anne Marie Weiss-Armush is the author of *Arabian Delights* (Lowell House, 1994).

How to Make Authentic Barbecued Ribs at Home

By following these seven steps — including one that uses tinfoil and a paper bag — you can make real barbecued ribs in your own backyard.

~ BY A. CORT SINNES ~

All food is personal. Some food, however, is more personal than others. Whip up a great bowlful of mashed potatoes, and you're likely to get agreement around the table (no matter where your guests are from) that they are, indeed, mighty good mashed potatoes.

Ribs — and we're talking barbecued pork spareribs here — are another matter. A summit conference couldn't settle the fierce loyalties people feel about barbecued ribs and all their infinite variations. Luckily, however, that wasn't the question I set out to answer. Instead, I wanted to know whether it was possible to produce "authentic" ribs (as in the kind you love to eat at your favorite barbecue joint) at home.

After a lot of grill work and a trip to Kansas City, I can report that the answer is an enthusiastic yes. It is indeed possible to produce tender, full-flavored, succulent barbecued ribs without having to leave the backyard.

Early Advances

The culinary path that led to this conclusion was not, however, a direct one. As a child of the 1950s, I, like countless others of my generation, thought that ribs were those charred, dry-as-a-bone *things* liberally swabbed with a sweet, mass-market, bright red "barbecue" sauce. This conclusion was not helped by growing up in northern California, a region not known for its expertise in the barbecued rib department, nor by a father who judged whether grilled food was done by checking not the food, but the level of the libations.

Once on my own, with my own family and barbecue grill, I continued to labor under the notion that ribs could be cooked directly over a bed of hot coals, a holdover, no doubt, from the days when I would ride grillside shotgun for my father, dousing every lick of flame that arose from the coals with a shot from a large plastic squirt gun.

Somewhere along the way, however, it became more generally known, even out in the Far West, that the sugars in barbecue sauce caramelize in the presence of high heat, then quickly char. The general recommendation was to wait until the last few minutes of cooking before basting the sauce onto the ribs, and then serve additional, warmed-in-a-pot-on-the-stove sauce at the table.

Duplicating the deep, smoky flavor and tender texture of classic Southern barbecued ribs requires a good dry rub, some foil-wrapped smoking chips, and a last-minute rest in a paper bag. Sauce is optional, but in any case should be added after cooking.

Coinciding with this new technique was the immense growth in popularity of the covered kettle grill, and with it, the advent of indirect cooking. This meant piling the coals under one side of the cooking grate, putting the food on the other, and cooking with the lid in place so that heat and smoke surrounded the food. At last there was a way to charcoal-cook food without burning it — especially naturally fatty foods, such as chicken and ribs.

When I began using these advances, the ribs I pulled off the grill not only looked better, but tasted much better, too. But I still had miles to go and a lot to learn. It wasn't until I moved to

Kansas City, Missouri, that several other pieces of information fell into place.

Kansas City was, quite literally, my first experience with a slower way of life and a slower way of outdoor cooking. Back home in California, I may have been cooking the ribs using the indirect method, but I was still using a large bed of coals, essentially cooking the ribs with high heat. The first time I watched a Kansas City local cook ribs, it seemed an excruciatingly slow process. Even more amazing was that *everyone* seemed to cook ribs this way — with just a few coals and plenty of hickory smoking chips — and no one seemed to mind how long the ribs took to get done. After I tasted the results, it didn't matter to me anymore, either.

Somewhere along the way, I learned about dry rubs. The concept was completely foreign to me, but once I got with the program, it made complete sense. Quite simply, a dry rub flavors the food without burning in the process, as barbecue sauce does.

My authentic-barbecue-ribs-at-home journey culminated only recently, with one final secret — one that not even all the folks in Kansas City (and other points south) know. It was overheard at a butcher stall in, of all places, Berkeley, California, shortly after I had moved back home. And, as one of those sweet mysteries of life, it was a secret I had heard rumors of only the week before in a long-distance telephone call from Kansas City.

The Kansas City Experiment
Somehow it just didn't feel right performing a barbecue rib experiment in California. So I packed my bags and headed back to Kansas City, having lived there previously for seven years — long enough to know that no one would be pulling my leg when it came to opinions on ribs.

Ribs are, by their very nature, good-time food, designed to please a crowd. So on a very cold, snowy night, I gathered a crowd at the infamous Charlotte Street Mission for an impromptu rib tasting. The panel included assorted musicians, carpenters, artists, cooks, writers, and a deejay — in short, a group that takes its barbecue seriously. The Kansas City rib experiment included cooking ribs three different ways: over indirect heat, on a rotisserie, and (somewhat reluctantly) parboiling first, then finishing over direct heat. All three variations used covered kettle grills.

The ribs cooked over indirect heat were, hands down, the favorite — by consensus, no less (no mean feat in that group). I thought the ribs cooked on the rotisserie would have fared better, but they were not nearly as tender as the ribs cooked over indirect heat. The parboiled ribs came in last, tasting, as one observer put it, "suburban." But more on parboiling later.

First, let's get down to the winning recipe. Count on about four hours, from start to finish, for this process. Assemble the following:

AUTHENTIC BARBECUED RIBS

- *A covered kettle grill.* Although it doesn't have to be a "kettle" grill, a covered grill is a necessity for this process.
- *Charcoal briquettes.* For purposes of consistency, all cooking was done over premium-quality charcoal briquettes; if you prefer lump, natural charcoal, by all means use it, although it may affect cooking times slightly.
- *Hickory smoking chips.* Hickory is absolutely the favored type of wood — use other types at your own risk.

MAKING HOMEMADE BARBECUE RIBS

1. To provide extra smoky flavor, wrap about two cups of hickory or other hardwood smoking chips in foil.

2. Poke several holes through the top of the foil packet with a fork to allow smoke to escape.

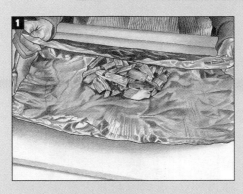

3. After lighting the briquettes, mound them on one side of the fire grate. When all the briquettes are covered with light gray ash, lay the foil-wrapped smoking chips on top.

4. When placing the ribs on the grill grate, make sure that they are on the part of the grate that is not over the fire.

5. When the ribs are done (see recipe, page 12), remove from the fire and immediately wrap in aluminum foil.

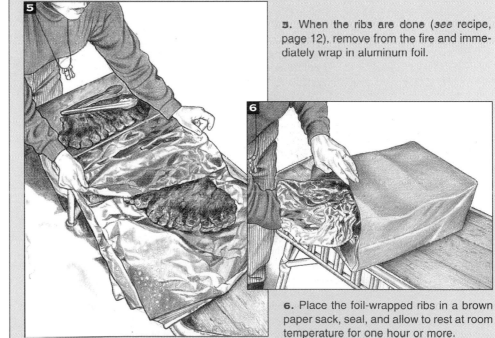

6. Place the foil-wrapped ribs in a brown paper sack, seal, and allow to rest at room temperature for one hour or more.

- **Two slabs of pork spareribs,** about 6 pounds total (serves about 4).
- **Your favorite dry rub** (*see* "Dry Rubs," page 13).
- **Your favorite barbecue sauce** (page 13).
- **Aluminum foil** (extra-wide, heavy-duty, if you have it on hand).
- **A large brown paper bag.**

1. Pick your ribs. Strangely, there's not much disagreement here: Aficionados from all quarters seem to agree it's the old-fashioned spareribs you want — not the baby back ribs, not the country-style ribs, just the plain old, under-three-pounds pork spareribs, in one big slab. (When I brought up the fact that other types of ribs were meatier, one knowledgeable friend quickly said, "But I don't want my ribs *meaty*.") If there is a large amount of extraneous fat on the ribs, trim it before cooking. The amount of fat trimmed from ribs varies, somewhat mysteriously, from one part of the country to another.

2. At least an hour before cooking the ribs, concoct the dry rub (*see* "Dry Rubs," page 13) and rub a generous amount (a scant three tablespoons) onto each side of the ribs. The ribs can sit at room temperature for up to an hour; wrap them in plastic wrap and refrigerate if you plan to hold them any longer that. An hour is plenty of time for the dry rub to flavor the ribs. If you want the meat more intensely flavored, this step can be done the night before you plan on cooking.

3. Start with a grill that's free of any leftover ashes or coals. Light forty or so charcoal briquettes (if you're using one of those metal chimney starters, fill it approximately two-thirds full). Push all the coals to one side of the fire grate, arranged in a mound two or three briquettes high. Keep the bottom vents of the grill completely open. The coals will be just right when they are covered in a light gray ash. Meanwhile, wrap two large handfuls (about two cups) of hickory smoking chips in foil (*see* illustration 1, page 11). Poke small holes in the top of the foil packet with a fork (illustration 2). Contrary to popular practice, there's no real benefit to be had by soaking the chips first. Note: Some folks swear by having a source of moisture inside the grill, most often an aluminum pan of water shoved up next to the coals. As much as this sounded like a good idea and seemed to make culinary sense, no discernible difference was noted each time it was tried. But since it doesn't hurt, feel free to employ it, if desired.

4. Once the coals are ready, lay the foil-wrapped smoking chips on top of the charcoal (illustration 3). Put the cooking grate in place. Position the ribs on the cooking grate opposite the fire; on a twenty-two-inch kettle grill, you should be able to cook two full slabs of ribs, side by side, at one time (illustration 4). Put the lid on the grill, with the top vents two-thirds of the way open, directly over the ribs. This will help draw the heat and hickory smoke past the ribs. Initially, the heat inside the grill will probably hover around 350 degrees. Over the two-hour cooking period, it will drop a hundred degrees or so — all of which falls into the acceptable slow-cooking range.

5. Turn the ribs every thirty minutes for a total cooking time of two to three hours. There is no need to baste the ribs with anything, unless basting happens to be part of the way you learned how to cook ribs. In other words, basting doesn't make much difference in the quality of the final product, but it doesn't detract from the ribs, either. In all but the most extreme of weather conditions, the ribs will be done in two hours. In normal weather conditions (say, above 60 degrees) the coals will begin to lose some of their vigor toward the end of the cooking time. Don't worry. They still produce enough heat to cook the ribs thoroughly.

In cold weather, prepare for a longer cooking time. Depending on just how cold it is, when you turn the ribs at the one and one-half hour point you'll probably need to add an additional fifteen coals to keep the cooking temperature more or less constant. As a way of gauging how outside temperatures can affect cooking times, it took me four hours to cook the ribs in 17 degree weather.

Signs of doneness include the meat starting to pull away from the ribs (if you grab one end of an individual rib bone and twist it, the bone will actually turn a bit, separate from the meat) and a distinct rosy glow on the exterior.

6. If there is a secret to producing authentic

TO PARBOIL OR NOT TO PARBOIL

Although I have a natural, unfounded bias against parboiling any food — let alone ribs — before grilling or barbecuing, as long as we were performing an experiment I figured we might as well go all the way and give parboiling its due.

First of all, why would anyone even think about parboiling ribs? There *are* a few advantages: The ribs can be parboiled and dry-rubbed the night before barbecuing them; it cuts the time on the grill down to about fifteen minutes; and there are some who would claim parboiling renders most of the fat from the ribs.

In the first go-around I parboiled the ribs in a large kettle of water for approximately twenty minutes, with the water held somewhere between a simmer and a rollicking boil for the entire time. The ribs were then cooked using the method below, to — as previously mentioned — less than enthusiastic reviews. Still good, mind you, but not great.

On my way home to California, I remembered a time some years ago when I tried to cook boiled beef (using a brisket) and had the meat "seize up" on me — that is to say, toughen. No amount of cooking would tenderize it. The texture of the parboiled ribs reminded me of that poor brisket, and then I remembered reading Stephen Schmidt's *Cook's Illustrated* article ("Pot Roast Perfected," January/February 1994). In that article, Schmidt suggested (with plenty of gastronomic science to back up the assertion) that too high a cooking temperature is the culprit for tough meat.

Armed with this knowledge, I gave parboiling another chance. This time the results were far superior, producing very succulent barbecued ribs that some folks may actually prefer to the traditional variety. Here's how to make them:

1. Place the ribs in a large kettle and completely cover with cold water. Place kettle, uncovered, over medium heat and allow to come almost to a simmer. At this point, carefully adjust the heat so that the water never really simmers, but moves just a little, under the surface (approximately 160 degrees). Cook, uncovered, for one hour, occasionally removing the scum that comes to the surface.

2. Drain the ribs. Allow to cool slightly and rub both sides (a scant three tablespoons per side) with your dry rub. Allow to sit for thirty minutes at room temperature, or wrap in plastic wrap and refrigerate overnight.

3. Light approximately fifty charcoal briquettes (enough to cover an area slightly larger than the slab of ribs, in a single layer, sides of the briquettes not quite touching). Leave the bottom vents of the grill completely open. Wrap two large handfuls of hickory smoking chips in foil. Poke holes in the top of the packet with a fork.

4. Allow the coals to burn past the hot stage to "medium." Medium is when you can put your hand directly over the coals and spell "M-I-S-S-I-S-S-I-P-P-I" without discomfort. Place the foil-wrapped hickory chips on top of the coals. Put the cooking grate in place.

5. Place the ribs on the cooking grate, directly over the coals. Put the lid on the grill, with the top vent two-thirds open, directly over the ribs. Do not leave the scene after this point!

6. Turn the ribs after five to six minutes. Cook five to six minutes on the opposite side. Turn; cook for two to three minutes. Turn the ribs again, and cook for a final two to three minutes, for a total cooking time of approximately fifteen minutes.

7. Remove the ribs from the grill and immediately wrap in foil. Place the foil-wrapped ribs in a brown paper sack, and fold the sack over the ribs. Allow to rest at room temperature for one hour or more. Serve with warm barbecue sauce.

barbecue-joint-style ribs at home, it is this step: Immediately after taking the ribs off the grill, completely wrap them in aluminum foil (illustration 5). Put the foil-wrapped ribs in a brown paper sack, and fold the sack over the ribs (illustration 6). Allow to rest at room temperature for one hour or more. Although it's difficult to say exactly what happens inside that foil-wrapped, brown-paper-sacked package, whatever it is, is good. My unscientific guess is that the moist, enclosed heat allows some of the juices to return to the meat, further flavoring and tenderizing it.

7. Finally, heat up your favorite homemade or store-bought barbecue sauce, unwrap the ribs, swab on the sauce, chop into individual ribs, and then chomp. You may find yourself agreeing with a couple of folks in Kansas City on that cold and snowy night who had the temerity to suggest, "These ribs are so good, they don't need no sauce!"

Barbecue Sauce

An entire book could be written on the countless variations of barbecue sauce, but I'm not sure what purpose it would serve, as everyone seems to already have a personalized variation. And then there's the burgeoning array of bottled sauces that seems to take up more space on the grocery store shelves each year, some of which are first-rate, as is, right out of the bottle. Should you decide to create your own customized barbecue sauce, the list of possible ingredients would contain just about everything from the herb and spice section of your local market. Three variations follow.

MASTER RECIPE FOR BARBECUE SAUCE
Makes 2–2½ cups

4   tablespoons butter
1   small onion, chopped
2   cloves garlic, minced
1   teaspoon paprika
1   tablespoon ground black pepper
2   tablespoons juice from 1 lemon
1   teaspoon dry mustard
½   teaspoon hot red pepper sauce
½   teaspoon salt
¼   cup cider vinegar
1   can (16 ounces) tomato sauce

Heat butter in a medium saucepan. Add onions and garlic; sauté until onions soften, 3 to 4 minutes. Stir in next 6 ingredients; cook over medium heat to blend flavors, about 5 minutes. Add vinegar and tomato sauce; bring to simmer. Simmer uncovered until sauce thickens slightly, about 15 minutes. Brush over ribs and serve. Serve additional sauce passed separately for those who want it.

KENTUCKY SMOKED BARBECUE SAUCE
Follow Master Recipe for Barbecue Sauce, making the following changes: Increase lemon juice to ¼ cup; increase paprika to 2 teaspoons; add ½ teaspoon liquid smoke with the lemon juice; dissolve 2 tablespoons firm-packed brown sugar in the vinegar and add with the tomato sauce.

LOUISIANA SWEET BARBECUE SAUCE
Follow Master Recipe for Barbecue Sauce, making the following changes: Increase vinegar to 6 tablespoons; dissolve 1 tablespoon firm-packed brown sugar in the vinegar. Add it along with ¼ cup molasses and 2 tablespoons sweet sherry when you add the tomato sauce.

SPICY RIO GRANDE BARBECUE SAUCE
Follow Master Recipe for Barbecue Sauce, making the following changes: Increase garlic to 4 cloves; increase lemon juice to ¼ cup; increase hot red pepper sauce to 1 teaspoon; add 1 can (7 ounces) diced mild green chiles along with the lemon juice. For an even hotter sauce, add ⅛ to ¼ teaspoon cayenne pepper. ■

A. Cort Sinnes is the author of over twenty books on outdoor living, gardening, and cooking, including *The Grilling Encyclopedia* (Grove/Atlantic 1992).

RIB CUTS

Spare ribs come from the underbelly or lower rib cage of the pig. A full slab contains thirteen ribs and weighs three pounds or less. These are the favorite of most barbecue enthusiasts.

Baby back or loin ribs do not come from a baby pig, as I thought once upon a time. Instead, they come from the upper end of the rib cage, where all the expensive cuts of pork are located. They are smaller than spare ribs and can be cooked to tenderness in a shorter period of time.

Country-style ribs are also from the upperside of the rib cage, but from the fatty end of the loin (the other end of the loin produces the lean pork tenderloin). They contain a small section (as compared with a loin chop) of loin meat.

DRY RUBS

Dry rubs are made of a variety of dry seasonings and are meant to be rubbed into the meat before grilling. Because they will not burn (as will marinades that contain sugar, fruit, or tomato), dry rubs are the favored method for flavoring any food that requires a long cooking time on the grill, such as brisket of beef or pork spareribs.

It's not unusual for years of experimentation to go into the creation of the "perfect" dry rub. Indeed, there are many annual competitions held across the country that award big prizes for the best barbecue chicken, ribs, or what-have-you, with the secret to success almost always in the rub. More often than not, dry rubs have a southwestern flair to them, with at least a hint of chili powder, cumin, or paprika.

You can create a wonderfully herby crust on grilled food by using a dry marinade or paste. This can be as simple as dusting with powdered herbs, such as ground black pepper, paprika, cayenne, or garlic powder, one layer over another, which is the method preferred by two of the winningest members of barbecue contests, the Schroeger brothers. Or it can involve a mortar and pestle, an electric spice grinder, or some other method of grinding the various dry ingredients into a uniform mixture. Some aficionados add a tablespoon of oil to a mixture of herbs and flavorings and vigorously rub the paste into the food.

There's something about creating a dry rub that brings out the alchemist in even the most levelheaded of cooks. Faced with a long list of potential ingredients and infinite variations, most adults are immediately transported back to being a kid with their first chemistry set. While there are no hard-and-fast rules regarding the makeup of a dry rub, the following recipe will at least give you an idea of the proportions. After that, you're on your own. Don't be afraid to experiment — the perfect rub may be just a teaspoon of paprika away.

BARBECUE-STYLE DRY RUB
This dry rub is a fairly traditional combination of flavors. Feel free to adjust amounts, or to add or subtract ingredients. To prepare the rub, simply mix all ingredients together. This rub yields about one and one-half cups — enough to coat about four slabs. Store leftover rub in an airtight jar or in the freezer.

1   tablespoon ground black pepper
2   teaspoons cayenne pepper (optional)
2   tablespoons mild chili powder
2   tablespoons cumin
2   tablespoons packed dark brown sugar
1   tablespoon white sugar
1   tablespoon ground oregano
4   tablespoons paprika
2   tablespoons salt
1   tablespoon ground white pepper
3   tablespoons celery salt
3   tablespoons garlic powder

Fresh Corn Tamales with Tomatillo-Chile Sauce

Chef and cookbook author Rick Bayless demonstrates how to make a classic Mexican snack that is rich with the earthy flavors of both fresh and dried corn.

~ BY JOHN WILLOUGHBY ~

Fresh corn husks are used not only to line the pan and steamer basket but also to enclose the tamales, which helps give the dough inside a unique fresh flavor.

The wrapped snacks called tamales are traditional throughout Mexico, widely popular in that country since pre-Columbian times for their rich, earthy flavors. Tamales are also a favorite of Rick Bayless, author of *Authentic Mexican* (Morrow, 1987) and chef/owner of Frontera Grill and Topolobampo in Chicago, widely regarded as the top Mexican restaurants in the United States.

A tamale may consist of almost anything that is wrapped in a leaf and steamed. However, the primary ingredient is usually *masa*, a dough made from dried field corn that has been boiled briefly with slaked lime, hulled, and then coarsely ground.

To take advantage of the fresh corn available at this time of year, Bayless makes a tamal filled with a combination of sweet corn and masa, an innovation he first discovered at a restaurant in Chiapas. "These tamales have a wonderful, moist, corny flavor, and are a little cakier than other fresh corn tamales," explains Bayless. "They are sold on the streets in Mexico, and you can easily pick them out because they have the green tint of the fresh corn husk."

Despite the rather heavy corn dough, these tamales are surprisingly light. Bayless attributes this not only to the baking powder used as leavening, but also to the way the lard is incorporated. "When you beat the lard together with the masa, it is pliable enough to trap quite a lot of air," Bayless says. "This causes the dough to expand as the tamales steam, so they become much fluffier."

Though fresh corn husks are normally used for fresh corn tamales, dried ones may also be used. Either type will impart a distinctive flavor to the tamales. Dried husks, which are more consistent in size and have a slightly sturdier texture than fresh, come in packets that often look like a single husk, but in fact produce at least five husks when rehydrated. Fresh husks, on the other hand, have the distinct advantage of coming along with the corn used in the filling. If you use fresh husks, you may need two for each tamal, overlapping them about one inch in the center.

In this recipe, the slight sweetness of the tamales is balanced by a tart tomatillo salsa. For additional flavor, the tamales can be topped with sour cream and roasted Anaheim or poblano chiles.

"Making tamales is a fair amount of work, so in Mexico people tend to make them for special occasions," says Bayless. "Fortunately, both the prepared dough and the finished tamales keep very well." In fact, fresh masa may be frozen for several months, and cooked tamales may either be wrapped tightly and refrigerated for several days or frozen, then defrosted and reheated for about fifteen minutes in the steamer before eating.

FRESH CORN TAMALES WITH TOMATILLO-CHILE SAUCE
Makes 12 tamales
(Serves 4 as a light main course or 6 as an appetizer)

The special fresh masa for tamales (more coarsley ground than the masa used for tortillas) is available at many grocery stores that carry Latino food products. If you cannot easily locate masa, you can make an acceptable substitute by combining masa harina and quick-cooking grits with water (*see* below). The result, says Bayless, will be be slightly coarser and not quite as homogenous as fresh masa, but will still make fine tamales.

If you decide to use dried corn husks, drop husk "packets" into boiling water; cover and simmer until husks soften throughout, about 10 minutes. Cool slightly, then separate husks. Choose some of the small inner husks for shredding into ties and lining steamer basket.

Fresh Corn Tamales
- 2 large ears fresh sweet corn (plus extra husks if needed)
- 2 cups (1 pound) fresh masa *or* Substitute Masa (*see* recipe that follows)
- 2 ounces unsalted butter, cut into half-inch cubes and softened slightly
- ¼ cup fresh lard, cut into half-inch cubes
- 2 tablespoons sugar
- ½ teaspoon salt
- 1½ teaspoons baking powder

Quick-Cooked Tomatillo-Chile Sauce
- ½ pound fresh tomatillos, husked and washed *or* two 13-ounce cans tomatillos, drained
- 1 jalapeño chile pepper *or* 2 serrano chile peppers, stemmed (and seeded if you prefer a milder sauce)
- Salt

PHOTOGRAPH BY ERIC ROTH

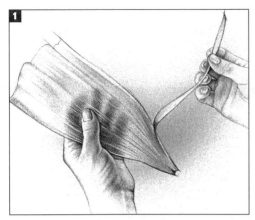

1. Tear one husk into small strips to use as ties. Set aside.

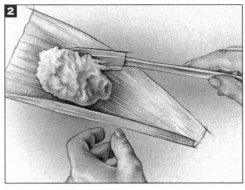

2. With the tapering end of the husk facing you, place a scant one-quarter cup of dough onto the husk, leaving at least a one and one-half-inch border of husk at the tapered end.

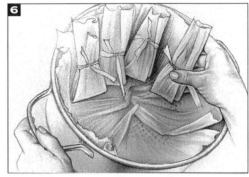

3. Fold the two long sides of the corn husk in over the corn mixture.

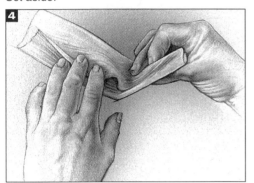

4. Fold the tapered end up, leaving the top open.

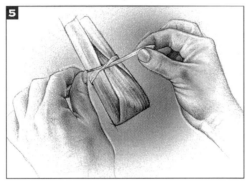

5. Secure the tamale by tying with a strip of the husk.

6. Meanwhile, line the steamer with husks. Stand the tamales up in a row around the edge of the steamer.

---

 2 tablespoons chopped fresh cilantro
 ½ small onion, chopped coarse
 1 small clove garlic, peeled and roughly chopped
 1½ teaspoons lard or vegetable oil
 ½ cup chicken or beef stock or low-sodium chicken or beef broth

1. *For the tamales,* if using dried husks, see note above. If using fresh corn husks as wrappers, cut through each ear of corn, just above the base, with a large sharp knife. Carefully remove husks without tearing. Shred two small husks to make ties; wrap husks and ties in plastic, and set aside. (If husks start to curl, blanch very briefly in boiling water to relax.) Remove and discard corn silk from corn.

2. Slice kernels off cob and scrape each cob with back of knife to remove remaining bits of corn and juice. Place corn in food processor; pulse to a medium-coarse puree. Add remaining ingredients (except husks); pulse several times to mix, then process until mixture is light and very smooth, about 1 minute.

3. Measure about 1 inch of water in a large saucepan. Set a collapsible vegetable steamer into saucepan. Line steamer and pan sides with corn husks. Follow illustrations above to fill and form tamales. As the tamales are made, stand them in prepared steamer. Cover and steam, checking water level frequently and replenishing with boiling water as needed, until

tamales easily come free from husks, about 1 hour for tamales made with fresh masa and 1¼ to 1½ hours if made with substitute masa.

4. Meanwhile, *for the sauce,* place tomatillos and chiles in a small saucepan; add water to cover. Bring to boil; simmer until barely tender, about 10 minutes.

5. Remove tomatillos and chiles with a slotted spoon; cool. Transfer to a food processor fitted with a metal blade. Add cilantro, onion, and garlic; pulse to a coarse puree.

6. Heat lard or oil in a medium skillet. When a drop of puree causes oil to sizzle, add puree all at once; cook over medium-high heat, stirring constantly until mixture darkens and thickens, about 5 minutes. Add broth; bring to boil. Simmer until mixture thickens enough to lightly coat the back of a spoon, 10 to 15 minutes. Season with salt. Serve warm on top of unwrapped tamales.

SUBSTITUTE MASA FOR TAMALES
Makes about 2 cups
While masa harina may look like fine-ground cornmeal, it is very different in taste and application, so you should not try to substitute one for the other. Masa harina can be located in many supermarkets across the country under Quaker, Maseca, or Goya brand names.

 ⅔ cup quick (not instant) grits
 ¾ cup masa harina

1. Pulverize grits in a spice grinder (in batches) or blender, then transfer them to a medium-size bowl.

2. Whisk in 1¼ cups boiling water (don't worry if grits lump a bit; mixture is eventually pureed in food processor); let stand 10 minutes. Stir in masa harina; cover and cool to room temperature. ∎

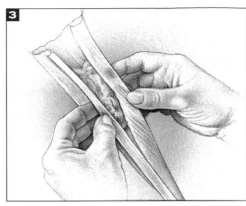

"Tamales are ideal for large, informal parties," says chef and cookbook author Rick Bayless, "because making them often becomes a sort of party-before-the-party."

How to Cut Vegetables

The techniques illustrated below can be used for cutting up a wide range of vegetables. Notice that when one hand is using the knife and the other is holding the food, the holding hand is formed into a sort of claw, with the tips of the fingers pulled back and the knuckles leaning toward the knife. This allows you to firmly hold the item being cut while keeping your fingertips away from the knife.

HOW TO MAKE A CHIFFONADE

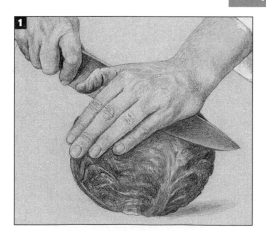

1. To make a chiffonade of basil or other leafy greens, begin by stacking the leaves with the largest at the bottom.

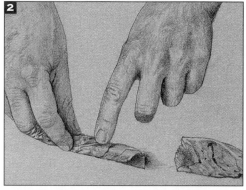

2. Roll the stack of leaves tightly.

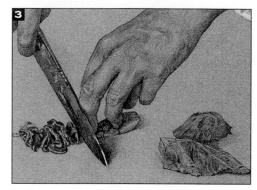

3. Cut across the rolls to produce ribbons, or chiffonade. As when slicing vegetables, keep the tip of the knife in contact with the cutting surface; cut with a rapid rocking motion.

HOW TO JULIENNE LONG VEGETABLES

1. Since cutting a whole carrot is unwieldy, cut the carrot into thirds or other manageable pieces.

2. Cut a thin slice off each carrot section so that it will lie flat.

3. Cut "panels" off each carrot section, slicing as thinly as you can. As you cut, keep the knife blade in contact with the cutting surface and cut with the full length of the blade, using a rocking motion.

4. Stack the panels and slice them thinly to make a julienne. This technique can be used to julienne any long vegetable.

HOW TO SLICE LARGE VEGETABLES

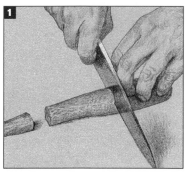
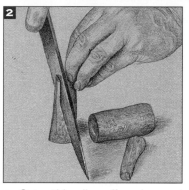
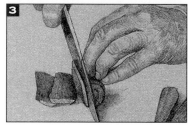
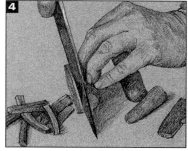
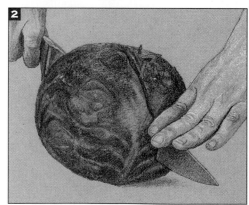
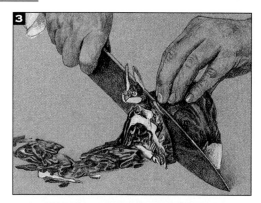

1. Place the heel of your palm on the back of the knife, a little in front of the center, and apply pressure toward the tip of the knife.

2. When the top of the knife blade is below the top of the cabbage, move your fingers to the top of the front section of the knife and apply pressure, finishing the cut.

3. As with other vegetables, press the tip of the knife against the cutting surface while you hold the cabbage with fingers bent out of the way. Rock the knife back and forth to slice through the cabbage.

ILLUSTRATIONS BY ANATOLY

SLICING ON THE BIAS

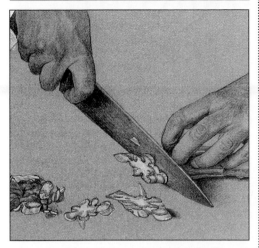

To make an atttractive shape from broccoli, celery, scallions, or other long vegetables, cut them on the bias by holding the knife at a 45-degree angle to the vegetable.

HOW TO SLICE ROUND VEGETABLES

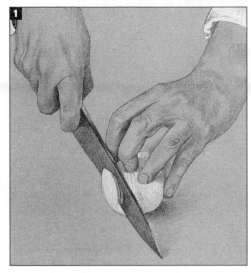

1. Cut a thin slice off the side so that the onion will lie flat.

2. Slice the onion. For maximum control, always keep the tip of the knife in contact with the cutting surface. Cut in a rocking motion, using the full length of the blade, so that the knife slides through the onion, rather than sawing it. This technique can be used to slice any round vegetable.

HOW TO JULIENNE OVAL VEGETABLES

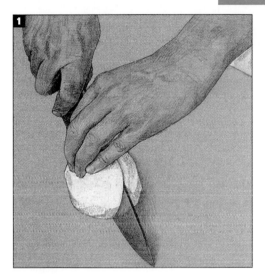

1. Cut the potato in half to so you have a flat surface.

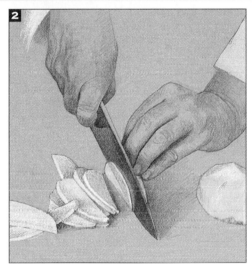

2. Cut half-moon panels from the potato halves; you can use the slices as they are at this point.

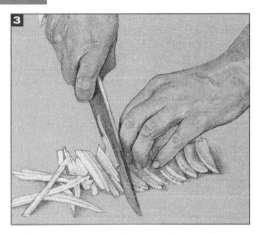

3. Stack the potatoes in accordion fashion and move the knife down the row, keeping the tip in contact with the cutting surface, to produce a julienne. This technique can be used to slice or julienne any oval vegetable.

HOW TO DICE

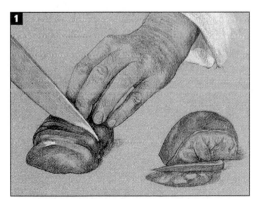

1. Halve the tomato. Draw the tip of the knife back through the tomato halves to make quarter-inch slices, leaving one end intact to hold the slices together.

2. Create a grid by cutting through the tomato halves horizontally, holding onto the top of the tomato with the fingertips of your other hand.

3. Complete the dice by cutting through the tomato crosswise. This technique can be used to dice any round vegetable.

A New Way to Prepare Shrimp

Brining before cooking dramatically improves taste and texture.

~ BY MARK BITTMAN ~

One day last summer I was in a hurry to defrost a two-kilo brick of shrimp; I was going to a party and had agreed to bring something to grill.

I knew from experience that if you defrost fish (or any other animal protein, for that matter) in a warm, dry environment, such as on the kitchen counter or in the microwave, the frost-damaged cells lose liquid and flavor. The industry calls this "drip loss," and you've seen it: that puddle of water underneath the meat you're defrosting for dinner. That's why it's best to defrost frozen food in a refrigerator: slowing the process reduces drip loss.

I had no time for this, though, so I went for the second-best and much faster method: defrosting in cold water. I decided to try brining it at the same time; I had recently found that brining foods usually changes their taste and texture, often favorably. Since my shrimp were not a prime variety, I decided to take a chance.

In a large bowl, I dissolved a few fistfuls of salt in a cup of boiling water. Then I added ice and cold water to make a gallon or so and plunged the shrimp right in. After a couple of hours I rinsed the shrimp, doused them with olive oil and garlic, and headed out to my party. Once there, I dumped them unceremoniously on the grill, cooked them for three or four minutes, and served them to the other guests. The reviews were unanimous: These were the greatest shrimp ever.

I talked about my brining technique but was discreet enough to avoid mentioning that, far from being the greatest shrimp ever, these were an inferior variety.

Over the next few months I explored different combinations of brine with just about every variety of shrimp I could find. Although the results varied in degree, they were always positive. All gained plumpness (sometimes as much as 10 percent in weight) and firmness. At its most successful, the brining changed a rather mushy shrimp into one that had the chewy texture of lobster tail. I could still tell a top-quality shrimp from a lesser variety, but the differences became quite subtle.

The reasons behind this transformation are detailed in "The Holiday Turkey Perfected" (November/December 1993). By denaturing protein strands, salt changes the structure of the flesh and allows it to trap more water. This excess water gives us the sensation of plumper, firmer, and juicier meat — or shrimp.

I now defrost and brine shrimp frequently. About 98 percent of the shrimp sold in this country is frozen to begin with. Because some drip loss is inevitable — even if you defrost in the refrigerator or under running water — I believe that, by counteracting drip loss, brining may benefit shrimp more than it does other foods.

There is one more asset to brining and defrosting simultaneously: It encourages you to buy frozen shrimp. Since the shelf life of previously frozen shrimp is not much more than a couple of days, buying thawed shrimp gives you neither the flavor of fresh nor the flexibility of frozen. Stored in the freezer, however, shrimp remain top quality for several weeks, deteriorating only gradually and remaining usable for some months.

In the past few months I have brined perhaps seventy-five batches of shrimp. Once I settled on the brining technique I liked best, I varied the procedure to answer some of the many other questions that arise in preparing shrimp. Primary among these was whether marinating shrimp was worth it and, if so, under what conditions. I theorized that it would be more effective to marinate peeled shrimp; after all, not much of the marinade could get through the shell.

But after trying a couple of basic, nonacidic marinades (a marinade with lemon juice or vinegar cooks the shrimp as surely as heat, toughening it in a rather unpleasant fashion) with brined shrimp, I changed my mind. Shrimp has a full, assertive flavor, and, even when it is peeled, a marinade doesn't affect it much. In fact, I found that basting peeled shrimp as it grilled, or sautéing it in oil or butter and aromatics such as garlic, was just as effective as marinating and far less time-consuming.

But basting, sautéing in fat, or marinating shrimp *in the shell* has more of an effect on flavor than following the same procedures for peeled shrimp. The reason is not that the marinade mysteriously penetrates the meat through the shell, but rather that much of the marinade or basting liquid remains on the shell during cooking. When you peel the shell off to get to the meat, you coat your fingers with flavorful liquid, which is in turn transferred to the meat as you eat it (and directly to your mouth as you lick your fingers clean).

What effect does peeling before cooking have on the flavor and texture of shrimp? Using the kinds of cooking methods I'm considering here — grilling and sautéing — it has only

Whether you peel shrimp before cooking depends on the cooking method to be used.

negative consequences. When the shell remains on shrimp, the meat itself is shielded from the intense heat of the grill or sauté pan and remains moist and tender inside, assuming you don't overcook it. But try as I might, I could not get peeled shrimp to cook properly on the grill; even removing it the moment it turned pink, it seemed quite dry throughout. Using lower heat only made matters worse; the meat became uniformly tough and dry. The only thing that worked was to intentionally undercook the shrimp; but that left the inside a little gooey, a texture that almost no one seems to enjoy.

Unpeeled shrimp, however, is easier to cook than sirloin steak. Whether I skewered it (which does make it easier to turn and serve), dumped it on the grill, or used one of those grilltop screens (to prevent losing shrimp through the grates), when the shrimp turned pink — after about two minutes on the first side and a minute or so on the second, for medium to large shrimp — the meat was done. Varying the heat mattered little; although a good, hot fire is surest and easiest, a medium-hot fire isn't bad. Stay away from cool fires, though; if shrimp remains above the heat for too long it will become unpleasantly tough.

(When you cook shrimp in liquid — a stock or a sauce, for example — the tables turn and it becomes worthwhile to peel before cooking, for three reasons: The shells themselves make a terrific stock; cooking shrimp in liquid does

PHOTOGRAPH BY ERIC ROTH

not dry it out as much; and finally, it's nearly impossible to peel shrimp that is sitting in a piping hot sauce without both making a mess and burning your fingers.)

No article about shrimp could be complete without a discussion of deveining. Although some people won't eat shrimp that isn't deveined, others believe that the "vein" — actually the animal's intestinal tract — contributes to flavor. In most medium to large shrimp, the vein is so tiny that you have to look for it in order to find it, and after cooking it virtually disappears. In larger shrimp, the vein stands out. But I never devein shrimp, not because I feel that the vein contributes anything, but because I can only rarely detect the presence of the vein when it is left in (unless I am looking for it) nor notice its absence when it is removed. Basically, I choose to ignore it. Anyone who cares is welcome to remove the veins at the table — along with the shells.

MASTER RECIPE FOR BRINED SHRIMP

I tried brining shrimp in literally dozens of combinations — with varying amounts of salt, added sugar, and different lengths of time. Almost regardless of the solution and technique, the shrimp were improved by the treatment. Some combinations, however, resulted in overly salty shrimp, some minimized the effect of the brining, and some took longer than they needed to. In the end, I settled on soaking the shrimp in a fairly strong salt solution for about forty-five minutes; if you're in a rush, you can soak it in a 50 percent stronger solution for twenty to twenty-five minutes; the difference in taste is almost nil.

2 cups kosher salt
2 pounds frozen shrimp

Pour 2 cups boiling water in large bowl; add salt and stir until almost dissolved. Add 3½ quarts cold water (along with some ice if ambient temperature is over 70 degrees); stir until salt completely dissolves. Add shrimp and let stand about 45 minutes. Drain and rinse thoroughly under cold running water; proceed with your recipe or one of the two that follow.

SEARED SHRIMP WITH LEMON
Serves 4–6
These shrimp are delicious as they are, but you can also serve them with a vinaigrette or sauce for dipping, such as Piquant Plum Sauce with Sesame Oil and Ginger, page 20.

2 pounds large shrimp, brined (see Master Recipe for Brined Shrimp), and deveined if desired
½ lemon

Heat a large skillet (nonstick or cast iron works well) over high heat until very hot. Place single layer of shrimp in pan. Cook until shrimp shells turn spotty brown, 1 to 2 minutes. Turn shrimp

as they brown; cook until remaining side turns spotty brown, 1 to 2 minutes longer. As shrimp are done, transfer them to medium bowl. Repeat process with remaining shrimp. Squeeze lemon juice over shrimp and serve warm or at room temperature.

GRILLED SHRIMP WITH SPICY GARLIC PASTE
Serves 4–6
To keep the shrimp from dropping through the grill rack onto the hot coals, thread them onto skewers or (see illustrations below) use a perforated grill pan (see Sources and Resources, page 32).

2 pounds large shrimp, brined (See Master Recipe for Brined Shrimp), and deveined if desired

1 large clove garlic
1 teaspoon salt
½ teaspoon cayenne pepper
1 teaspoon paprika
2 tablespoons olive oil
2 teaspoons juice from 1 lemon
Lemon wedges

1. Mince garlic with salt; mix it with cayenne and paprika in small bowl. Add olive oil and lemon juice to form thin paste. Toss shrimp with paste until evenly coated. (Can be covered and refrigerated up to 1 hour.) Thread shrimp onto skewer, if desired (see illustrations below).

2. Heat grill or broiler. Grill or broil shrimp, turning once, until shells turn bright pink, 2 to 3 minutes per side. Serve hot or at room temperature with lemon wedges. ■

PREPARING SHRIMP FOR THE GRILL

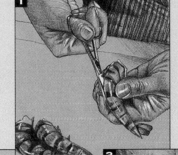

Shrimp may be deveined (if you wish) and threaded onto single skewers, or they may be butterflied and threaded onto two skewers.

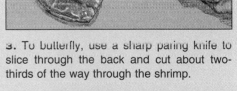

1. If you choose to devein shrimp, manicure scissors cut them open quickly and easily.

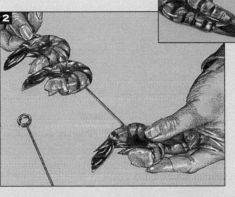

2. Shrimp may be threaded by passing the skewer through the body near the tail, folding the shrimp over, and passing the skewer through the body again near the head.

3. To butterfly, use a sharp paring knife to slice through the back and cut about two-thirds of the way through the shrimp.

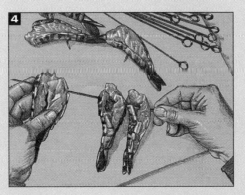

4. Push one skewer through both sides of the butterflied shrimp near the head.

5. Push a second skewer through the shrimp near the tail.

Stone Fruit Relishes

Stone fruits such as peaches, nectarines, plums, and apricots can be used to create highly flavorful relishes and savory salads.

~ BY ANDY HUSBANDS ~

Stone fruits — simply defined as fruits with a pit at the center — are familiar to most cooks as ingredients in desserts or as simple pleasures eaten out of hand. However, these fruits also combine very well with herbs, spices, and citrus to make a wide variety of savory accompaniments.

These recipes provide a range of tastes, textures, and treatments using stone fruits, the common denominator being strong flavors in combination.

When choosing fruits for these dishes, it makes the most sense to select those that are just ripe or slightly underripe, rather than fully ripe, since they tend to hold their shape better when mixed with other ingredients. If covered and refrigerated, these dishes will keep for three to four days.

CURRIED FRUIT CHUTNEY WITH LIME AND GINGER
Makes about 4 cups

Although this chutney works well with other meats, beef is a particularly fine choice. Grilled beef tenderloin offers the richness and simplicity that anchors these curried fruits.

- 1 tablespoon olive oil
- 1 small white onion, sliced very thin
- 1 tablespoon minced fresh ginger
- 1 large clove garlic, minced
- 1½ teaspoons ground coriander
- ½ teaspoon ground cinnamon
- 1 teaspoon curry powder
- ½ teaspoon hot red pepper flakes
- ½ ripe mango, peeled and cut into ¼-inch dice
- 1 peach, peeled, pitted, and quartered
- 1 plum, pitted and quartered
- 1 apricot, pitted and quartered
- 1 nectarine, pitted and quartered
- 1 tablespoon juice from ¼ orange
- 2 tablespoons juice from 1 lime
  Salt and ground black pepper

Heat oil in large saucepan over medium-high heat. Add the onion slices; sauté, stir frequently until onion browns, about 4 to 5 minutes. Add ginger and garlic; sauté until fragrant, about 1 minute longer. Lower heat to medium; add remaining ingredients; cook until fruits start to soften, but have not fallen apart, about 5 minutes longer. Adjust seasonings. (Can be set aside at room temperature for several hours; heat before serving.)

PIQUANT PLUM SAUCE WITH SESAME OIL AND GINGER
Makes about 2 cups

Serve this dipping sauce with soy sauce — marinated, grilled boneless chicken thighs. For appetizers, cut the chicken into bite-size pieces and thread them onto a skewer. If you have a low tolerance for hot dishes reduce the amount of red pepper flakes called for in the recipe.

- 2 tablespoons sesame oil
- 1½ tablespoons minced fresh ginger
- 2 medium cloves garlic, minced
- 1 pound plums, pitted and halved
- ¼ cup rice wine vinegar
- 2 tablespoons juice from 1 lime
- ¼ cup water
- 1 teaspoon hot red pepper flakes
  Salt

1. Heat oil in medium saucepan over medium-high heat; add ginger and garlic and sauté, stirring constantly, until golden, about 1 minute. Add remaining ingredients, including salt to taste; simmer, stirring frequently, until plums just begin to break down, about 10 to 12 minutes.

2. Cool for 10 minutes, then puree in food processor fitted with steel blade. Adjust seasonings. (Can be stored in an airtight container and refrigerated up to 3 days; return to room temperature before serving.)

APRICOT-JICAMA SALSA
Makes about 4 cups

Serve this clean, crunchy salsa with grilled fish such as tuna steaks. If you like, dredge the edges of each tuna steak in ground coriander seeds before cooking. *See* Quick Tips, page 5, for instructions on preparing jicama.

- ½ pound jicama, peeled, sliced thin, then cut into ¼-inch strips
- 4 apricots, pitted and cut into ½-inch slices
- 2 tablespoons minced fresh cilantro
- ½ small red onion, halved and sliced thin
- ½ small red bell pepper, cored and sliced thin
- 1 tablespoon minced chipotle peppers (*see* Sources and Resources, page 32 for description and source)
- 2 tablespoons juice from 1 lime
- 1 tablespoon olive oil
  Salt and ground black pepper

Mix all ingredients, including salt and pepper to taste, in large bowl; toss lightly. Refrigerate until ready to serve.

DRIED PEACH AND APPLE SALAD WITH ALMONDS AND CUMIN
Makes about 4 cups

Dried apricots, plums, or nectarines can be substituted for the dried peaches in this North African–style salad. Although this salad would seldom be eaten with pork in North Africa (Muslim dietary law prohibits pork consumption), its ingredients are a perfect match for this meat. Any mild-flavored tropical fish such as mahimahi can also be paired with this salad.

- 6 ounces (2 cups) dried peaches, cut into ¼-inch strips
- ¼ cup dry red wine
- ¼ cup warm water
- 1½ teaspoons minced fresh ginger
- 2 small tart apples, sliced thin
- ¼ cup blanched, slivered almonds, toasted
- 2 tablespoons brown sugar
- 1½ teaspoons coriander seeds, toasted and ground
- 1½ teaspoons cumin seeds, toasted and ground
- ¼ teaspoon cayenne pepper
- 2 tablespoons juice from 1 lime
- 2 tablespoons juice from ¼ orange
- 2 tablespoons minced fresh cilantro
  Salt and ground black pepper

In medium bowl, rehydrate peaches in wine and water for at least 15 minutes. Mix next 7 ingredients in separate medium bowl, then add peaches and their liquid, lime and orange juices, cilantro, and salt and pepper to taste. (Can be refrigerated for several hours; return to room temperature before serving.) ∎

Andy Husbands is the chef at East Coast Grill in Cambridge, Massachusetts.

The Best Granola

Here's how to make granola that is chewy, crisp, and crumbly.

⮌ BY DANA JACOBI ⮌

After testing twenty-three versions of this hearty, intense food, I have found that the keys to making great granola are choosing the right ingredients and combining them in the proper proportions.

Grain flakes are the foundation of granola. Oats, wheat, and rye are used in various recipes, but to my taste buds, wheat flakes leave a bitter aftertaste, while rye flakes lessen the nutty impact of oats without adding a positive note of their own. I find only oat flakes (also called rolled oats) to be satisfactory.

When buying oat flakes, it is crucial to get the right type — small, thickly rolled, golden-beige ovals just over a quarter-inch long. These chubby flakes are chewy and have a pleasant sweetness, unlike most commercially made oat flakes, which taste dry and are so thinly pressed that they crumble when handled. Look for these thick rolled oats at natural food stores.

The total volume of nuts, seeds, and dried fruits you choose to include should be equal to or slightly greater than the volume of grain flakes (*see* chart below). These proportions ensure that every mouthful will have the interplay of flavors and textures, the combination of crunch, chewiness, and sweet and tart tastes, that is the essence of granola.

Almonds are the best choice for nuts, especially when combined with hazelnuts, walnuts, pecans, or cashews. For the right crunch, halve almonds, skin and halve hazelnuts, and break other nuts into one-quarter to one-half-inch pieces. Leave out small particles of nuts — they cook too fast and can impart a burned taste to the mixture.

Sweeteners affect both the flavor and texture of granola. Honey is more intensely sweet than maple syrup, and also produces a more clumpy version. I recommend using equal amounts of both, for a granola that is slightly crisp, slightly clumpy, and also perfectly moist.

In recipes such as Toast and Roast Granola, below, the oil in the seeds and nuts is sufficient to crisp the granola as it roasts and to provide richness. Other recipes, however, do need added oil; canola is best because its mild taste will not mask that of other ingredients.

For a final touch, a bit of vanilla extract or grated citrus zest blended into the liquid ingredients gives a nice complexity. I find these additions particularly good in honey-sweetened granola. You might also try adding a scant half-teaspoon of ground cinnamon or cardamom to the sweeteners when warming.

CUSTOM BLEND GUIDE

Follow these proportions when making your own personal blend of Classic Granola.

Ingredient	Quantity
Rolled oats	3 cups
Walnuts, cashews, hazelnuts, pecans, blanched almonds	1½–2 cups total
Unsweetened shredded coconut	½ cup
Sesame seeds, sunflower seeds	½ cup total
Honey, maple syrup	½ cup total
Canola or safflower oil	⅓ cup
Regular or golden raisins, apricots, prunes	1 cup total
Vanilla extract or grated citrus zest	1 teaspoon
Cinnamon or cardamom	½ teaspoon
Raw wheat germ	¼ cup

CLASSIC GRANOLA
Makes 7–8 cups

- 1 cup walnuts, broken into ¼- to ½-inch pieces
- 3 cups rolled oats
- ½ cup unsweetened shredded coconut
- ½ cup blanched almonds, halved
- ¼ cup sesame seeds
- ¼ cup sunflower seeds
- ¼ cup maple syrup
- ¼ cup honey
- ⅓ cup canola oil
- 1 cup raisins

1. Adjust oven rack to center position and heat oven to 325 degrees. Mix first 6 ingredients together in large bowl.

2. Heat maple syrup and honey together with oil in small saucepan, whisking occasionally, until warm. Pour mixture over dry ingredients; stir with spatula until mixture is thoroughly coated. Turn mixture onto an 11-by-17-inch jelly-roll pan, spreading into an even layer.

3. Bake, stirring and respreading mixture into an even layer every 5 minutes, until granola is light golden brown, about 15 minutes. Immediately turn granola onto another jelly roll pan to stop cooking process. Stir in raisins, then spread granola evenly in pan; set on a wire rack and cool to room temperature. Loosen dried granola with a spatula; store in airtight container.

TOAST AND ROAST GRANOLA
Makes 5½ cups

Make sure not to toast the ingredients at too high a temperature — you run the risk of scorching them. For clumpy granola, right after you remove the mixture from the oven, press it into a three-quarter-inch layer with even edges, then press a single layer of paper towels onto the granola. When the granola is cool, remove the towels. Remove the cereal in sections and place in an airtight container. When ready to use, crumble granola to desired chunkiness.

- ½ cup blanched almonds, halved
- ½ cup cashews, broken into ½-inch pieces
- 2 cups rolled oats
- ⅔ cup unsweetened shredded coconut
- ¼ cup sunflower seeds
- 2 tablespoons sesame seeds
- ¼ cup honey
- ½ cup raisins

1. Adjust oven rack to center position and heat oven to 325 degrees. Toast nuts in large, heavy-bottomed skillet over medium heat, stirring often, until they just begin to color, about 3 minutes. Stir in oats and coconut; toast until oats color lightly, about 2 minutes. Add sunflower and sesame seeds; toast, stirring constantly, until mixture turns an even beige, about 1 minute. Remove pan from heat; stir in honey until mixture is well coated.

2. Turn mixture onto a 10-by-15-inch jelly-roll pan; spread into an even layer. Bake, stirring and respreading mixture into even layer every 5 minutes, until granola is lightly browned, about 15 minutes. Immediately turn onto another jelly-roll pan to stop cooking process. Stir in raisins, then spread granola evenly in pan. Set on wire rack and cool to room temperature. Store in airtight container. ∎

Dana Jacobi is a New York–based food writer and natural foods cook.

Six Chocolate Cakes

Starting with a Velvet Devil's Food Cake, the author tests each ingredient to produce the best six chocolate cake recipes, from a sour cream layer cake to a low-fat, low-guilt variation.

~ By Stephen Schmidt ~

Recipes for chocolate cake can be maddening. One promises an especially fudgy and rich cake, the next guarantees a light and tender one, the third pledges the best-ever devil's food cake — whatever precisely "devil's food" might be. The secret to the recipe, we are told, is Dutch-process cocoa, or dark brown sugar, or sour cream, or buttermilk, or some special mixing method — so on and so forth. If you've made as many chocolate cakes as I have over the years, you can fill in the blanks yourself.

Finally, you make the cake, and you think, well, it is a *little* fudgy, or tender, or devil's food–like, or whatever. But isn't it also very much like the chocolate cake you made just the other week, from a recipe that called for very different ingredients and promised some very other kind of result?

I set out to make sense of this muddle. After baking and comparing dozens of different chocolate cakes (I lost count somewhere in the thirties), I have devised a master recipe and five variations that produce six truly distinctive chocolate layer cakes. In the process, I discovered a couple of general principles that apply to whatever type of chocolate cake you are making. Perhaps more important, I also learned a great deal about how various ingredients function and what results they produce, so that each of these recipes delivers exactly the type of chocolate cake it promises.

The Basic Recipe

To carry out these experiments, I needed a base from which to begin. I chose as a master recipe my personal favorite among all chocolate cakes, which I call Velvet Devil's Food Layer Cake.

This cake appeals to me not only because it is extremely soft and tender, as well as pleasantly sweet (I find very bitter chocolate cakes hard to swallow — literally), but also because it delivers a potent chocolate punch. The "velvet" in the title suggests the cake's texture as well as distinguishing it from what I take to be a more classic devil's food, which is sweeter and decidedly spongy, even a tad chewy. I also chose Velvet Devil's Food Layer Cake because it is basically a standard yellow butter cake with some of the flour replaced by cocoa. Because it follows a simple, familiar pattern, the recipe is easy to change by varying ingredients and techniques.

Testing Cocoa and Chocolate

Bakers can (and do) argue endlessly over whether cocoa-based chocolate cakes are best made with standard American cocoa, such as Hershey's, or with a European-style cocoa, such as Droste, that has been alkalized, or "Dutched," to neutralize some of the natural acid (*see* Notes from Readers, page 2).

To settle this question for myself, I prepared several recipes using both types of cocoa — and found that, to my palate, there was not an enormous difference. Cakes made with Hershey's were a little blacker and had a slight bitter edge; in the Droste cakes, the chocolate flavor was perhaps a bit mellower, but also fainter. But these distinctions were minor, and the bottom line was that I liked both cocoas just fine.

A second cocoa experiment, however, proved much more conclusive. In cakes made with cocoa and water, the chocolate flavor was much stronger and the color twice as dark when the cocoa was first dissolved in boiling water rather than simply being mixed into the batter dry. I therefore recommend following this procedure in any cocoa-based chocolate cake in which water is the liquid.

Next, I sought to discover the effects of substituting unsweetened baking chocolate or semisweet chocolate for cocoa. Following standard substitution tables, I prepared the master recipe using three ounces of unsweetened chocolate in place of the cocoa, subtracting three tablespoons of butter to compensate for the fat in the chocolate. I also made the master recipe with five ounces of semisweet chocolate in lieu of cocoa, cutting the butter by two tablespoons and the sugar by six tablespoons.

In my first set of experiments, I simply melted the chocolate over boiling water. Both the unsweetened and the semisweet chocolates produced terrible cakes: pale, dry, hard, and lacking in flavor. I remembered, however, that Rose Levy Beranbaum, author of *The Cake Bible* (Morrow, 1988), counsels actually *cooking* the chocolate over boiling water for several minutes in order to rupture the cocoa particles and release the flavor. A second round of experiments substantiated the wisdom of this advice: Both unsweetened and semisweet chocolate responded dramatically, producing cakes with a much richer, darker flavor.

Even when made with cooked chocolate, however, my cakes were neither as moist nor as flavorful as when made with cocoa. I will therefore venture a rule: In butter cakes, at least (if not necessarily in chocolate cakes of other types), cocoa is always better than chocolate.

Liquid Ingredients

My second — and most extensive — set of experiments concerned the effect of dairy liquids on the cake. I checked out everything from sweet milk to buttermilk to yogurt to sour cream.

Sour cream and buttermilk have a seductively mouth-watering ring in chocolate cake recipes, but I have long had reservations about using milk products when baking with chocolate. Hot chocolate prepared with water (with a spoonful of cream added for richness, if you wish) has a far more intense flavor than hot chocolate made with milk. If milk is a flavor-blocker in hot chocolate, I reasoned, why wouldn't dairy products have a similar effect in chocolate cakes? My experiments prove that they do — but the whole business turned out to be surprisingly complicated.

When I replaced the water called for in the Master Recipe with milk, I got a cake that I liked a great deal. As I had predicted, the chocolate flavor was somewhat muted, but to some tastes (and to mine in certain moods), this would be for the better. The cake was a little less tender and more crumbly than the one made with water, but on the plus side, it also felt pleasantly substantial in the mouth. Milk produced the kind of chocolate cake that I remember from childhood, so I call my milk-based variation Old-Fashioned Chocolate Layer Cake.

Further experiments revealed that neither dissolving the cocoa in hot milk nor cooking the cocoa and milk together made for an appreciably stronger flavor than simply adding the cocoa to the batter dry. Evidently, dissolving the cocoa in boiling liquid only improves its flavor if the liquid in question is water.

Buttermilk and yogurt, which I use interchangeably in baking, proved to be far more problematic ingredients. In my myriad tests, both had a paradoxical effect on texture, on the one hand velvetizing the crumb and adding a nice moistness (this, say various authorities, is due to their lactic acid content), but on the other compacting the cakes and making them seem a little hard and chewy and also a bit pasty. Taste, though, was the real issue. While milk had a gentling effect on the flavor of chocolate, buttermilk and yogurt nearly killed it.

By testing various cookbook recipes, I eventually learned how to use buttermilk in such a way as to maximize its tenderizing qualities without obliterating all chocolate taste. One solution is to make your cake with a great deal of sugar; sugar speeds melting, and rapid melting intensifies flavor. Thus my Classic Devil's Food Layer Cake, which like other standard devil's food recipes is high in sugar, derives a lovely moist sponginess from buttermilk while retaining a good chocolate pungency. I discovered that extra fat also mitigates the chocolate-blocking effects of buttermilk, though fat seems at the same time to undercut buttermilk's tenderizing properties, resulting in a fudgy texture.

Finally, if you actually prefer a chocolate cake with a mild flavor, buttermilk can be very helpful, for the velvetiness it imparts reinforces the flavor impression you are trying to create.

The trick, I think, is to use the buttermilk in sparing quantities. My German Chocolate–Style Layer Cake is a reconfiguration of a cake popularly made with German sweet chocolate and a cup or more of buttermilk. I am not particularly fond of the cake made according to the standard recipe, but when the buttermilk is reduced, the cake turns out quite nicely.

Having tested the Master Recipe using buttermilk in place of water, I next tried replacing some of the water with sour cream, at the same time decreasing the butter to compensate for the milk fat in sour cream. Like buttermilk, sour cream made for a more velvety crumb, but there was a marked difference in degree — the sour cream cake was so feathery soft as to seem almost puddinglike.

The effects of sour cream on flavor were complicated. It did make for a less pungent chocolate taste, but at the same time it imparted a pleasing, lingering mellowness. Strangely enough, it seemed to sweeten the cake rather than making it more tart, as buttermilk had. Sour cream and buttermilk, of course, are two very different things, so perhaps I shouldn't have been so surprised by the results. In my fifth variation, Sour Cream–Fudge Layer Cake, I use the unique properties of sour cream to produce a cake with a dense yet melting texture and a rich taste.

Leavening

My final set of experiments concerned leavening, which presented me with a fascinating set of problems. In several of the earlier tests, I had noticed that the Master Recipe and the Old-Fashioned Chocolate Layer Cake developed a slight hump during baking, which subsided upon cooling. This phenomenon often results from insufficient leavening, so I tried increasing the baking soda from one-half teaspoon to three-quarters teaspoon.

Sure enough, the cakes rose higher and were more level, and they were also lighter and

QUICK AND EASY WAYS TO DECORATE A CAKE

FROSTING THE CAKE

1. Use a long metal spatula to spread a portion of the frosting on the first cake layer. Top with the second layer; frost the top of this layer, then the sides.

2. Once the sides are frosted, use the metal spatula to smooth the frosting on the cake top. Proceed to decorate as desired.

COMBING

Use a cake comb to create concentric furrows on the cake top and/or sides. This technique can be used with Whipped Cream, Coffee Buttercream, or Chocolate Cream Frosting.

SWIRLING

Use the back of a tablespoon to make decorative swirls on the cake top and sides. This technique can be used with all frostings.

USING A PASTRY BAG

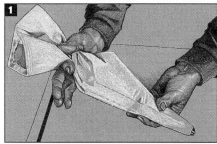

1. To decorate the cake with a pastry bag and tip, fill the bag, fitted with a star tip, with the remaining frosting. Holding the tip end of the bag with one hand, twist the open end with the other hand until the frosting just begins to come out the tip. This may be used with all frostings except meringue.

2. For a simple shell shape, pipe swirls around the base of the cake. (The bigger the tip, the simpler the piping process, and the more dramatic the presentation.)

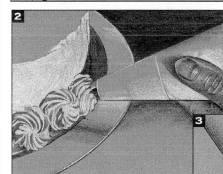

3. Repeat this piping process around the perimeter of the cake top, if you like.

STIPPLING

The tip of a metal spatula may be used to stipple the top and sides of the cake. This technique is best with Meringue Frosting.

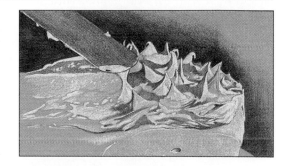

softer in texture without seeming excessively crumbly or porous. I also noted that the cakes were considerably darker. A little research revealed why: As pH increases, the pigments in cocoa turn from blondish to brownish to black; if you add enough soda, you will eventually induce a reddish cast in cocoa cakes, which is how the name devil's food arose.

Initially I was pleased by the results of adding extra soda, but then I noticed something else. Tasting one of the cakes, I detected a musty, peculiar flavor. At first I thought I had merely become oversensitized to the taste of chocolate after days of testing. But then I sampled a piece of Classic Devil's Food Layer Cake, which I had also made with three-quarters teaspoon soda, and I noted that the strange off-flavor was not present.

Eventually I discerned the answer to the baking soda mystery. The musty taste, more commonly described as soapiness, is caused by using more baking soda than can be neutralized by the available acid in a batter. In both the master recipe and the old-fashioned variation, the cocoa supplies the only acid present. But in the devil's food variation, additional acid is provided by the buttermilk, which in turn neutralizes the extra one-quarter teaspoon baking soda. It is not essential to add the extra baking soda to classic devil's food cake, but you might as well, since the soda produces greater volume and also tames the slightly distracting tang of the buttermilk.

VELVET DEVIL'S FOOD LAYER CAKE WITH COFFEE BUTTERCREAM FROSTING (MASTER RECIPE)
Serves 12

This cake's texture is both soft and dense, similar to chocolate pound cake, only softer and lighter. Its flavor is intensely chocolate, yet pleasantly sweet. The substantial coffee-flavored buttercream stands up to the cake's dense texture and balances the rich chocolate flavor.

Velvet Devil's Food Cake
- ½ cup nonalkalized cocoa, such as Hershey's, measured by spoon-and-sweep
- 2 teaspoons instant espresso or instant coffee
- 1 cup boiling water
- 2 teaspoons pure vanilla extract
- 12 tablespoons (1½ sticks) unsalted butter, softened
- 1¼ cups sugar
- 2 large eggs, at room temperature
- 1¼ cups all-purpose flour, measured by dip-and-sweep
- ½ teaspoon baking soda
- ½ teaspoon salt

Coffee Buttercream Frosting
- 1 tablespoon instant coffee (preferably espresso)
- 1 tablespoon coffee liqueur
- 1 tablespoon pure vanilla extract
- ½ pound (2 sticks) unsalted butter, softened
- 2 cups confectioners' sugar
- 2 tablespoons beaten egg or pasteurized egg, or 1 beaten egg yolk

1. *For the cake,* adjust oven rack to center position and heat oven to 350 degrees. Grease two 8-by-1½-inch round baking pans with shortening. Line pan bottoms with waxed or parchment paper; grease paper as well. Dust pan with flour; tap out excess.

2. Mix cocoa and instant coffee in small bowl; add boiling water and mix until smooth. Cool to room temperature, then stir in vanilla.

3. Beat butter in bowl of electric mixer set at medium-high speed (number 4 on a Kitchen Aid) until smooth and shiny, about 30 seconds. Gradually sprinkle in sugar; beat until mixture is fluffy and almost white, 3 to 5 minutes. Add eggs one at a time, beating 1 full minute after each addition.

4. Whisk flour, baking soda, and salt in medium bowl. With mixer on lowest speed, add about ⅓ of dry ingredients to batter, followed immediately by about ⅓ of cocoa mixture; mix until ingredients are almost incorporated into batter. Repeat process twice more. When batter appears blended, stop mixer and scrape bowl sides with rubber spatula. Return mixer to low speed; beat until batter looks satiny, about 15 seconds longer.

5. Divide batter evenly between pans. With rubber spatula, run batter to pan sides and smooth top. Bake cakes until they feel firm in center when *lightly* pressed and skewer comes out clean or with just a crumb or two adhering, 23 to 30 minutes. Transfer pans to wire racks; cool for 10 minutes. Run knife around perimeter of each pan, invert cakes onto racks, and peel off paper liners. Reinvert cakes onto additional racks; cool completely before frosting.

6. *For the buttercream frosting,* mix instant coffee, coffee liqueur, and vanilla in small cup until coffee dissolves; set aside. Beat butter in bowl of electric mixer at medium-high speed until fluffy, about 1 minute. Add sugar and beat 3 minutes longer. Add coffee mixture and egg to frosting; beat until frosting mounds around beaters in a fluffy mass, 3 to 5 minutes longer. *See* "Frosting the Cake," page 23, for frosting instructions and decorating options.

CLASSIC DEVIL'S FOOD LAYER CAKE WITH WHIPPED CREAM
Serves 12

The increased sugar quantity in this recipe results in an extremely tender cake — it almost falls apart at the touch of a fork — yet when you chew it, it turns out to be resilient and spongy. Since this batter rises higher, make sure to use 9-by-1½-inch round cake pans rather than the 8-inch ones called for in the Master Recipe. Sweeter and lighter than the Velvet Devil's Food Layer Cake, this cake is appropriately paired with lightly sweetened whipped cream.

For the cake, follow Master Recipe, making the following changes: After dissolving the cocoa and instant coffee in boiling water, stir in ¾ cup firmly packed dark brown sugar and ½ cup low-fat yogurt or buttermilk; let cool and add vanilla. Decrease butter from 12 to 8 tablespoons (1 stick) and increase the baking soda from ½ to ¾ teaspoon.

For the whipped cream, beat 2½ cups cold heavy cream at medium speed in an electric mixer until thickened. Add ¾ cup confectioners' sugar and 1 teaspoon vanilla; beat until stiff. *See* "Frosting the Cake," page 23, for frosting instructions and decorating options. Decorate with chocolate shavings, if you like.

OLD-FASHIONED CHOCOLATE LAYER CAKE WITH CHOCOLATE CREAM FROSTING
Serves 12

Unlike the previous two devil's food cakes, which are almost like chocolate in the form of cake, this one resembles a traditional yellow cake with a great deal of chocolate added. The milk slightly mutes the chocolate flavor while giving the cake a sturdy, pleasantly crumbly texture. Cream enriches the frosting, making it compatible with this less assertive chocolate cake.

For the cake, follow Master Recipe, making the following changes: Omit boiling water. Whisk cocoa and instant coffee into dry ingredients until no lumps of cocoa remain. Add vanilla and 1 cup plus 2 tablespoons room-temperature milk alternately with dry ingredients.

For the frosting, break up 12 ounces semisweet chocolate and pulverize in a food processor fitted with metal blade until it is the texture of coarse sand. Bring 1⅔ cups heavy cream to boil. With machine running, pour hot cream over the chocolate. Add ¼ cup corn syrup; process until just combined. Turn mixture into a bowl and refrigerate until spreadable, stirring with a wooden spoon every 15 minutes, about 1 hour. *See* "Frosting the Cake," page 23, for frosting instructions and decorating options.

GERMAN CHOCOLATE–STYLE LAYER CAKE WITH COCONUT-PECAN FILLING

Serves 12

Buttermilk gives this cake a pleasantly mild chocolate flavor with a very light, soft texture. The pecan and coconut filling provides textural contrast. Be sure to divide batter evenly between pans (*see* "Quick Tips," page 5), as cakes will rise high.

For the cake, follow Master Recipe, making the following changes: Decrease cocoa from ½ to ¼ cup and water from 1 cup to ⅓ cup. Stir ⅓ cup nonfat yogurt or buttermilk into cocoa mixture. Increase eggs from 2 to 3.

For the filling, mix 4 egg yolks, 1 cup sugar, and ¼ teaspoon salt in a medium bowl; beat in 8 tablespoons softened unsalted butter, then gradually beat 1 cup heavy cream and 1 teaspoon vanilla into mixture. Pour into medium, nonreactive saucepan and cook over low heat, stirring constantly until mixture is puffy and just begins to thicken, 15 to 20 minutes. Pour mixture into a medium bowl and cool to room temperature. Stir in 1½ cups toasted pecans and 7 ounces (about 2 cups lightly packed) sweetened flaked coconut. Halve each cake round, crosswise. Place one of the cake bottoms on a serving plate. Spread about 1 cup filling over cake half. Place another halved cake round over filling. Repeat this stacking and spresding process with remaining filling and cake, ending with a final layer of filling.

SOUR CREAM–FUDGE LAYER CAKE WITH CHOCOLATE BUTTER ICING

Serves 12

Sour cream gives this cake its smooth, rich chocolate taste with a dense yet melting texture, almost like fudge. An equally intense chocolate icing stands up to the rich cake. Since this batter rises higher, make sure to use 9-by-1½-inch round cake pans rather than the 8-inch ones called for in the Master Recipe. It is best not to refrigerate this cake, but if you do, cut it while cold, then let slices come to room temperature before serving.

For the cake, follow Master Recipe, making the following changes: Increase cocoa from ½ to 1 cup. Whisk ½ cup sour cream into the cocoa mixture. Increase butter from 12 tablespoons to 16 tablespoons (2 sticks) and sugar from 1¼ cups to 1¾ cups. Increase baking soda from ½ to ¾ teaspoon.

For the icing, melt 9 ounces semisweet or bittersweet chocolate and 8 tablespoons (1 stick) unsalted butter in a medium bowl set over pan of almost-simmering water. Stir in ⅓ cup light corn syrup. Set bowl of chocolate mixture over a larger bowl of ice water, stirring occasionally, until the frosting is just thick enough to spread. *See* "Frosting the Cake," page 23, for frosting instructions and decorating options. ■

Stephen Schmidt is the author of *Master Recipes* (Ballantine, 1987).

LOW-FAT CHOLESTEROL-FREE CHOCOLATE LAYER CAKE

Obviously, you cannot make a cholesterol-free chocolate butter cake, but you can, it turns out, make a cake that tastes a great deal like a chocolate butter cake but does not require butter or egg yolks. The trick is to replace the butter/sugar/whole egg mixture of the typical butter cake with a combination of whipped egg whites and vegetable oil. You end up with a cake that is a little like a chocolate chiffon cake, but without egg yolks. Because it contains less fat, this cake is springier and spongier than the others, and it is not quite as rich. The egg whites, though, make the cake soft and wonderfully moist, and the absence of butter and egg yolks, both of which contain flavor-blocking protein solids, actually results in a more intense chocolate taste and a darker color.

REDUCED-GUILT CHOCOLATE LAYER CAKE WITH MERINGUE FROSTING

Serves 12

For the cake, follow Master Recipe, making the following changes: mix ½ cup oil into cocoa mixture. Add 1 cup of sugar called for in Master Recipe to dry ingredients. Mix cooled cocoa mixture into dry ingredients. Omit butter and whole eggs. At slow speed in electric mixer, beat 4 large egg whites until foamy. Add ¼ teaspoon cream of tartar, increase mixer speed to medium, and beat to soft peaks. Increase mixer speed to high; beat whites until stiff and glossy. Slowly sprinkle in remaining ¼ cup sugar called for in Master Recipe and beat 15 seconds more. Fold egg whites gently but thoroughly into cocoa batter. Follow baking directions in Master Recipe, but bake only 20 to 25 minutes.

For the frosting, beat 3 large egg whites at slow speed in electric mixer until frothy. Add 1 teaspoon vanilla, ⅛ teaspoon cream of tartar, and pinch salt and beat at medium speed to soft peaks. Raise mixer to high speed and beat whites to stiff, glossy peaks. Turn off mixer. Combine 1¼ cups sugar and ⅓ cup water in a small saucepan and bring to boil over high heat, all the while gently swirling pan by handle. Cover and boil 2 minutes, then uncover and boil until a candy thermometer registers 200 degrees (syrup will form soft, gum-like ball when dropped in ice water). With mixer at high speed, pour syrup in thin, steady stream into egg whites. Continue to beat until frosting is cool, 7 to 10 minutes. *See* "Frosting the Cake," page 23, for frosting instructions and decorating options.

Naturally Flavored Vanilla Ice Creams Win Tasting

Kids and adults alike vote down artificially flavored brands, but they disagree on the ideal texture.

～ BY JACK BISHOP ～

When it comes to ice cream, Americans are the world's experts. Each man, woman, and child in this country consumes about twenty-four quarts a year, 30 percent more than our nearest competitors in New Zealand. And vanilla is America's overwhelming favorite — it's three times more popular than chocolate.

Given the universal appeal of ice cream, we decided to run this tasting a bit differently from our custom. Instead of enlisting the services of an expert panel, we asked five adults and five children we know to sit down and try eleven leading brands of vanilla ice cream. After all, while tasting soy sauce or vinegar may required a trained palate, everyone knows good ice cream — and bad — when they lick it.

All of our tasters, who ranged in age from nine to fifty-two, agreed on one thing — artificially flavored vanilla ice cream is not worth the calories or effort. In fact, the three brands with artificial flavors ranked ninth, tenth, and eleventh.

This is not to say, however, that all naturally flavored ice creams are wonderful. Despite the presence of numerous vanilla bean specks, some brands had a conspicuously mild vanilla flavor, and naturally flavored brands that tasted mostly of sugar and cream

Children are not fooled by substitutes for real vanilla, but they do prefer fluffy texture in their ice cream.

ranked well below those samples that delivered a strong vanilla jolt.

While there was consensus on the issue of flavor, texture separated the men from the boys, or in this case the women from the girls. All of our younger tasters preferred fluffy, lighter-textured ice creams, ranking Breyers first and Edy's Grand second. Both of these brands are made without egg yolks and have a lighter, airier consistency. In contrast, the adult tasters rewarded denser, creamier brands like Ben & Jerry's (the top choice of adults) and Häagen-Dazs (tied for second place among adults) with their highest ratings. Both of these brands are made with egg yolks, which provide richness and creaminess.

Since Breyers was the top choice among the kids and tied for second in the adult rankings, it was the overall winner. Ben & Jerry's took second place overall, followed by Häagen-Dazs and Edy's Grand. There was a sharp break between fourth and fifth place, indicating a steep decline in quality. After seventh place, there was another sharp drop in the scoring.

How Much Air Is Enough?
All ice cream contains some air. As the ingredients are churned, air is pumped into the mix to make the product edible; ice cream without air would have a texture akin to ice cubes. Super premium ice creams generally contain much less air. Overrun — the industry term for the amount of air added during processing — is kept between 20 and 50 percent in these ice creams. (This means the volume has been increased by 20 to 50 percent with the addition of air.) Most less-expensive ice creams packed in half-gallon containers contain much more air — often as much as 100 percent overrun, which is the legal limit.

How can you distinguish an airy, fluffy ice cream from a dense, rich one before you buy? The best method is to weigh the package. According to federal standards, a half-gallon of ice cream (minus the carton) must weigh at least two pounds, four ounces. When we weighed samples we found that many brands just scraped by the legal limit (*see* chart for exact figures) and one (Edy's Grand) fell shy by one ounce. While top-rated Breyers weighs in at two pounds, five ounces per half-gallon, second-rated Ben & Jerry's tips the scales at three pounds, eleven ounces, and third-ranked Häagen-Dazs is the heaviest of all those tested at three pounds, twelve ounces.

So why did our kid judges like lighter ice creams? Most said they could eat more without getting full — that's because they were eating more air. On the other hand, our adult tasters preferred the silky richness of ice cream without much air. They also found they were satisfied by a smaller serving of the richer ice creams, which may help even out the nutrition scales, given that Ben & Jerry's and Häagen-Dazs contain twice as much fat as Breyers.

Low-Fat Brand Earns Modest Respect
Of course, fat content is a big concern for ice cream lovers, especially adults. For this reason we held a pretasting of the five leading lower-fat ice creams on the market. We included the top favorites from the pretasting — Mattus and Light n' Lively — to see how they would measure up against full-fat ice creams.

With its artificial flavors and extremely airy texture, Light n' Lively drew no favorable comments. On the other hand, Mattus, an all-natural ice cream recently introduced by the family that created Häagen-Dazs, was a bit more favorably received. Although deemed overly sweet, some (but not all) tasters were impressed by its creamy, rich texture, which approximated that of the "real" premium brands.

While Mattus pales in comparison with the winners of the tasting, it did beat out two best-selling regular ice creams. Dieters with self-control might consider eating a small amount of Breyers; because it contains more air, each scoop has half the fat of superrich ice cream. If quantity is more important, than Mattus makes a decent if not remarkable alternative to regular ice cream.

Are Stabilizers Needed?
The use of natural and/or artificial vanilla flavors is noted in the chart, as is the use of plant stabilizers such as cellulose gum, carrageenan, carob bean gum, locust bean gum, and guar gum. With the exception of Breyers, Häagen-Dazs, and Mattus, all of the brands tested use one of these gums to prevent iciness and prolong freshness. Many industry experts contend that ice cream made with just milk, cream, sugar, and vanilla has a tendency to go bad quickly, especially when exposed to several temperature changes. Our tasting, held during the winter, when ice cream is subjected to fewer temperature extremes during the distribution process, did not find this to be the case. ∎

Nutrition information provided in the chart is for the standard industry serving of one-half cup, an amount most ice cream eaters will find quite small. The half-gallon weight (without the carton) is provided to compare the density and amount of air in various brands. (Figures for ice creams sold only in pint containers have been multiplied by four.)

Our panel included Mark Bittman, *Cook's Illustrated* executive editor, Karen Baar, Sally Connolly, Beth Miller, and the author, as well as five children, Kate (age 16) and Emma (age 9) Baar-Bittman, Emily Forman (age 15), Abbie Goetting (age 9), and Sarah Tsalbins (age 10). Tasters were asked to rank their six favorite ice creams after a blind sampling of eleven brands. Six points were awarded for each first-place vote; five for second; four for third; three for fourth; two for fifth; and one for sixth. An asterisk indicates that the ice cream tied with the brand listed immediately below it.

VANILLA ICE CREAMS LISTED IN ORDER OF PREFERENCE

 **1**   **2**   **3**  **4**  **5**

1 Breyers Natural Vanilla Ice Cream (Kraft General Foods, Philadelphia, PA), half-gallon, $3.99; natural flavors without plant gums; 150 calories and 8 grams of fat; 2 pounds, 5 ounces; 37 points. A real crowd-pleaser listed as a favorite by every taster. Texture described as "smooth, light, and airy" with a hint of iciness noticed by some tasters. Most panelists felt this sample was "creamy without being rich or heavy." Strong vanilla flavor rated "fresh" and "clean." While several adults thought this ice cream was a tad too fluffy, kids were drawn to the lighter texture. *Available nationwide.*

2 Ben & Jerry's Vanilla Ice Cream (Ben & Jerry's Homemade, Waterbury, VT), one pint, $2.79; natural flavors with plant gums; 215 calories and 16 grams of fat; 3 pounds, 11 ounces; 31 points. All five adults ranked this ice cream in first or second place, and it also received several votes from the under-eighteen crowd. Texture described as "creamy and dense," "smooth," and "nice and soft." Several tasters noted the presence of eggs and "fresh cream flavor" but wanted a stronger vanilla punch. Sweetness deemed average, although one panelist detected a "fairly strong caramel overtone." *Available nationwide.*

3 Häagen-Dazs Vanilla Ice Cream (Häagen-Dazs Company, Teaneck, NJ), one pint, $2.79; natural flavors without plant gums; 260 calories and 17 grams of fat; 3 pounds, 12 ounces; 24 points. Pale yellow color indicates presence of egg yolks, which were picked up by most panelists. "Smooth and heavy" texture with "strong cream flavor." Two tasters who gave this entry their top rating were drawn to its "sheer decadence" and "rich vanilla flavor." Others (including several adults and all of the children) were somewhat overwhelmed by the dense texture and/or "intense" sweetness. One noted, "This ice cream is all right but would be better eaten with cake." *Available nationwide.*

4 Edy's Grand Vanilla Ice Cream (Edy's Grand Ice Cream, Fort Wayne, IN), half-gallon, $3.99; natural flavors with plant gums; 160 calories and 10 grams of fat; 2 pounds, 3 ounces; 21 points. Texture described as "both creamy and fluffy," which may explain its broad appeal. Although not ranked in first place by any taster, this entry received votes from eight of the ten panelists. As one kid tester wrote, "this tastes real." Several judges thought flavor was "very sweet" with "just a touch of vanilla." *Available east of the Rockies. Same product sold under Dreyer's label on the West Coast.*

5 Turkey Hill Premium Vanilla Ice Cream (Turkey Hill Dairy, Conestoga, PA), half-gallon, $3.99; natural flavors with plant gums; 133 calories and 8 grams of fat; 2 pounds, 4 ounces; 13 points. "Airy" texture was thought to be "too elusive." Some objections to "icy crystals," which were described as "rough and yucky" by two kids. Several adults liked the low sweetness level, while one kid downgraded the "tart, tangy flavor." In any case, most everyone felt vanilla needed to be turned up a notch or two. "Acceptable" but not especially noteworthy. *Available in the Northeast from Hartford to Baltimore.*

6 Lady Borden Premium Vanilla Bean Ice Cream (Borden, Columbus, OH), half-gallon, $3.99; natural flavors with plant gums; 160 calories and 9 grams of fat; 2 pounds, 7 ounces; 12 points. "Gummy" texture downgraded by most tasters — "It coats my tongue" or "leaves a chalklike film in my mouth." Ice cream is so firm, "you can actually bite and chew it." Vanilla flavor is quite faint — "sort of vanilla but not quite" — with a strong, unpleasant aftertaste. *Available nationwide.*

7 Kemps Premium Natural Vanilla Ice Cream (Marigold Foods, Minneapolis, MN), half-gallon, $3.99; natural flavors with plant gums; 150 calories and 8 grams of fat; 2 pounds, 6 ounces; 11 points. "Fluffy style" ice cream is "airy" as well as "a little grainy and icy." Flavor described as "achingly sweet with no vanilla presence." Another taster thought this brand tasted like "dixie-cup ice cream." Damned by such faint praise as "really unremarkable." *Available in the upper Midwest and Mid-Atlantic regions.*

8 Mattus Low-Fat Original Vanilla Ice Cream (Mattus Group, Fairfield, NJ), one pint, $2.69; natural flavors without plant gums; 170 calories and 3 grams of fat; 3 pounds, 10 ounces; 6 points. "Creamy, dense" texture received decent marks from two panelists who thought this sample had "a nice consistency." To other tasters the "gooey and chewy" texture was the tipoff that this was not regular ice cream. While some tasters felt that Mattus approximated the texture of full-fat ice cream, everyone was disappointed by the "phony vanilla" flavor and "extreme sweetness" — "so much sugar it tastes like caramel." *In the process of establishing nationwide distribution, now available in most areas.*

9 Sealtest Vanilla Flavored Ice Cream (Kraft General Foods, Philadelphia, PA), half-gallon, $2.99; natural and artificial flavors with plant gums; 140 calories and 7 grams of fat; 2 pounds, 4 ounces; 5 points. Texture is quite "airy" and "seems as if it has been pumped up." "Extremely soft, almost like whipped cream," wrote another taster. "Weak flavor" with an "odd aftertaste" garners little praise. Several complaints about "unreal," "bland," or "weird" vanilla flavor. *Available east of the Mississippi.*

10 *Blue Bell Homemade Vanilla Flavored Ice Cream (Blue Bell Creameries, Brenham, TX), half-gallon, $3.99; natural and artificial flavors with plant gums; 180 calories and 9 grams of fat; 2 pounds, 15 ounces; 4 points. Tasters were divided about the texture. Some praised "creamy and fluffy" consistency, while others thought it "icy and grainy." Everyone was in agreement that flavor is "light and bland," with some harsher criticisms such as "fake vanilla with lots of sugar." Overall reactions ranged from "inoffensive" to "not on a bet." *Available in Texas as well as southern Plains and Gulf Coast states.*

11 Light n' Lively Premium Vanilla Flavored Ice Milk (Kraft General Foods, Philadelphia, PA), half-gallon, $3.59; natural and artificial flavors with plant gums; 110 calories and 3 grams of fat; 2 pounds, 4 ounces; 4 points. "Airy, fluffy" texture that "goes down like foam." Several tasters felt this lower-fat ice milk was "kind of sticky" with "unpleasant globules" melting on the tongue. "Artificial flavor" has "absolutely no vanilla component." Aftertaste described as "sour milk" or "chemical flavor." *Available east of the Mississippi.*

 **6**   **7**   **8**  **9**   **10**  **11**

Testing Mini Food Processors

Standard food processors have trouble mincing two cloves of garlic, a small bunch of parsley, or grating a few ounces of Parmesan. Can a mini food processor do a better job?

~ BY SHARON K. BARRETT ~

Despite its usefulness, a full-size food processor is not a perfect tool. In some cases, it's just too big. For instance, garlic cloves get lost under the large metal blade in most food processors, so they never get properly minced. Other small jobs — making one-half cup of pesto or tapenade, for example, or chopping two handfuls of parsley — are often not worth the bother, since the cleanup can take more time than simply doing the job by hand. With a bowl capacity of at least ten or twelve cups and sometimes as high as twenty cups, heavy-duty machines just are not designed for small jobs.

In the mid-1980s, manufacturers sought to fill this gap with smaller machines called minichoppers. Easy to clean and with a capacity of around one cup, they seemed like the perfect tool for all those tiny but tiresome jobs. However, they just didn't work that well. The blades in these machines were too small to be capable of chopping evenly, and their weak motors burned out when given a task like grating an ounce of Parmesan.

A more recent refinement is the mini or compact food processor. In an ideal world, this machine would have the virtues of a minichopper (small size and easy cleaning) along with the power of a real food processor. After testing seven models, I can report that some actually live up to their promise.

How Small Is Small Enough?

So exactly what qualifies as a mini food processor? Ask seven housewares companies and you'll get seven different answers, as I did. I started with a definition of a processor that had a capacity of two to seven cups. That definition kept the all but useless minichoppers out of the ratings, but what I got still varied widely. In fact, the machines were so different that I have grouped them into two categories in my ratings: small capacity (a workbowl that holds between two and three cups) and large capacity (a workbowl that holds between six and seven cups). These two types of machines seem designed for different markets — the smaller capacity ones for those who already own a regular food processor, and the larger capacity for those who don't.

Despite the differences between these two categories of machines, my criteria for judging them were the same: A mini food processor should have many of the advantages and accessories of a regular food processor, but not their size. That means, preferably, a shredding and slicing disk, a feed tube, an "on" button that doesn't have to be held down to work, and a pulse setting. A mini food processor should also be able to chop and mince small batches of food quickly, batches just larger than I would care to chop on my own.

To test these machines, I used them to do a number of tasks. The first was mincing two cloves of garlic, a chore that I might do by hand unless I had other things to chop in the processor. Nevertheless I chose this test because it provided an excellent gauge of a machine's ability to handle very small quantities. Next I minced a cup of packed parsley, which again is a job usually done by hand because large food processors cannot mince evenly. I then ground a cup of pecans and grated four ounces of Parmesan to test the power of the machines' motors. Finally I pureed two cups of soup (a handy amount when pureeing part of a bean soup, for instance) to see if the machines leaked when working with liquids.

With those requirements, the winner was pretty obvious, especially given its low price: the Black & Decker Handy Shortcut ($36). Although the second-place Cuisinart performed some of the chopping and mincing jobs as well as or even slightly better than the Black & Decker, its features paled in comparison. The Black & Decker comes with a feed tube that allows you to add oils or other liquids slowly to the workbowl as the blade turns, an "on" button that stays depressed on its own to keep both hands free, and a shred/slice disk that is perfect for small quantities of carrots, cabbage, or anything else. The Cuisinart ($42) has none of these features. It works very well but in essence is nothing more than a large minichopper. On the other hand, the Black & Decker has all the features of a regular food processor squeezed into a smaller body.

The two other small-capacity processors I tested, from Sunbeam and Krups, rate far below the top two. The Sunbeam Oskar is the better of the two, but its lack of a feed tube or "on"switch is inconvenient and the food chute attachment is too much of a bother. The Krups, with its extremely loud motor and problems handling small jobs, is annoying at best and costly at worst, as when its motor burned out on four ounces of Parmesan (hardly a huge amount). Its manual says to grate no more than one and one-half ounces at a time, but I'd much prefer to do that amount by hand and have only a grater to wash at the end.

As for the three large-capacity machines (Panasonic, Moulinex, and Regal), they seem more like watered-down regular processors. Although their makers consider them mini or compact, the machines take up almost as much counter space as full-size machines. Of the three, the Panasonic is clearly the best — as well it should be, given its price of $120. It handled more liquid than the manual said it could and performed the other chopping and mincing tasks without trouble.

The Regal's design makes sense because it's tall rather than wide, so it takes up less space on a counter. Unfortunately, its performance was below average. The Moulinex performed slightly better than the Regal, but again this machine is quite large and does not handle small jobs well.

Buying Recommendations

As someone who already owns a full-size food processor, I found the mini food processors from Panasonic, Moulinex, and Regal too big for some jobs that were easier to do by hand, and too small for other jobs that I could already do in my other machine. This is not exactly a winning combination, especially given the high price tags of these machines. Despite their marketing, these machines don't really handle small jobs that well. If you are looking to complement a full-size machine, my advice is to stick with the nicely loaded Black & Decker or the highly competent if stripped-down Cuisinart.

First-time food processor buyers not willing to commit to an expensive model, as well as apartment dwellers with tight kitchen space, might consider purchasing the large-capacity Panasonic. Note that you may find better performance among regular food processors that are on the small side, but not marketed as mini or compact models. For instance, Cuisinart makes several standard food processors, the smallest of which has a seven-cup workbowl — the same size as the Panasonic. Of course, the seven-cup Cuisinart costs almost twice as much as the seven-cup Panasonic, which in the end may be the real virtue of the latter. ∎

Sharon K. Barrett recently graduated from Peter Kump's New York Cooking School.

The seven models tested were evaluated on a number of points, including mincing, chopping, grating, and pureeing as well as overall size and special features. Specific tests involved mincing two cloves of garlic, mincing one cup packed parsley, grinding one cup pecan halves, grating four ounces Parmesan cheese cut into half-inch chunks, and pureeing a carrot soup made with cooked carrots, onions, celery, and broth. The maximum volume of the workbowl is noted under bowl capacity. The height, width, and depth of each machine are listed in that order under overall size. Special features include a feed tube, a separate shredding/slicing disk, and a pulse setting.

The machines are listed in order of preference within each category. *See* Sources and Resources on page 32 for information about discount mail-order outlets that sell the top machines.

Black & Decker Handy Shortcut
Micro-Processor HMP30

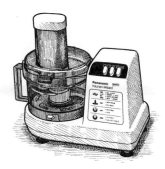

Panasonic Kitchen Wizard
MK 5070

SMALL-CAPACITY MINI FOOD PROCESSORS
(Two-to-three cup capacity)

Black & Decker Handy Shortcut Micro-Processor HMP30
Price: $36
Bowl Capacity: 3 cups
Overall Size: 9-by-4-by-6½ inches
Special Features: Feed tube, slice/shred disk, and pulse setting.
Garlic: 30 seconds; not quite as fine as Cuisinart. Sides must be scraped down once.
Parsley: 30 seconds for good mince.
Nuts: 30 seconds for a fine, mostly even grind.
Cheese: 1 minute and 40 seconds with a few small chunks still remaining.
Soup: Handles 2 cups without leaking.
General Comments: Nicely loaded machine with good but not great performance. Slice/shred disk gives even results although it does leave one big piece uncut on top of disk. Feed tube plus on/off and pulse buttons that do not have to be held down make machine easy to use. Very easy to clean.

Cuisinart Mini-Prep Food Processor DLC-1
Price: $42
Bowl Capacity: 2½ cups
Overall Size: 8-by-4-by-6½ inches
Special Features: Blade reverses for sharp/blunt edges. No pulse setting, but high/low buttons.
Garlic: Minces finely in 15 seconds.
Parsley: Evenly chopped in 10 seconds; 10 seconds more gives a fine mince.
Nuts: Blunt side of blade does job in 7 seconds.
Cheese: After 25 seconds, most of cheese was finely grated but machine began to smell like it was burning, so I turned it off. Waited several minutes and pulsed several more times to get all but seven small chunks grated.
Soup: Purees 2 cups very smoothly without leaking.
General Comments: Without a feed tube, this machine is less useful than the Black & Decker. Also, you almost need three hands for some tasks: one to hold down the on button, one to add liquid ingredients (pouring them through small holes in the lid), and one to hold the machine down, which is necessary when chopping hard items. Flipping the sharp blade can be unnerving. However, overall performance was good.

Sunbeam Oskar Food Processor 14181
Price: $49
Bowl Capacity: 3 cups
Overall Size: 10-by-4-by-6 inches
Special Features: Slicing disk and attachable food chute.
Garlic: 15 seconds for a fine chop but not very even, despite scraping down sides.
Parsley: 8 seconds for a fine, even mince.
Nuts: 10 seconds for a very even grind.
Cheese: 1 minute for a fairly fine grind.
Soup: Can handle no more than 1 cup without leaking.
General Comments: No built-in feed tube. Machine turns on by pushing lid shut — a mechanism that is difficult to use and too easy to inadvertently engage. Chute attachment is poorly designed — food flies everywhere and both hands are needed to hold chute in position and feed items into bowl. Chute is not easy to clean, either. Definitely not worth the bother.

Krups Mini Pro Food Processor 708
Price: $33
Bowl Capacity: 2½ cups
Overall Size: 8-by-4½ inches (base is round)
Special Features: None
Garlic: 10 seconds for an even chop, but despite scraping, it is impossible to get fine mince.
Parsley: 8 seconds for fine mince.
Nuts: 7 seconds of pulsing for even chop but hard to get fine grind.
Cheese: First machine burned out while grating 4 ounces of cheese; second machine grated 1½ ounces after 1 minute and 45 seconds of pure noise.
Soup: With 1½ cups I noticed a few drops; at 1¾ cup leaking began in earnest.
General Comments: I can't find much nice to say about this machine. It's loud, it leaks, and it can't handle much Parmesan. Must hold

down button to operate. Also, no feed tube, only holes in lid.

LARGE-CAPACITY MINI FOOD PROCESSORS
(Six-to-seven cup capacity)

Panasonic Kitchen Wizard MK 5070
Price: $120
Bowl Capacity: 7 cups
Overall Size: 8½-by-13-by-7 inches
Special Features: Slice/shred disk, whipping disk, pulse setting, and feed tube.
Garlic: 5 seconds to chop but no amount of scraping down could get machine to mince.
Parsley: 5 seconds for an even, fine mince.
Nuts: 15 seconds for a fine, even grind.
Cheese: 45 seconds to get an even, fine grate.
Soup: Handles as much as 5 cups without leaking.
General Comments: Although special cutting blades work, they do allow some big pieces to slip through. Whipping attachment is useless. Large size and expense of machine are drawbacks, but performance is good for all tasks except mincing garlic.

Moulinex Compact Food Processor 129
Price: $88
Bowl Capacity: 6 cups
Overall Size: 11-by-11½-by-6 inches
Special Features: Slice/grate blade, two feed tubes, whipping disk, and pulse setting.
Garlic: 20 seconds for chopping, but bowl is too big to get

a fine mince even after scraping down the sides.
Parsley: 25 seconds for an even chop — not quite a mince.
Nuts: 20 seconds of pulsing for a fairly even mince.
Cheese: 1 minute and 55 seconds for a coarse grind; machine did almost nothing for the first 30 seconds.
Soup: Handles 3 cups without leaking.
General Comments: Slicing and shredding blades work well. Small and large feed tubes are a nice touch that make small batches come out more evenly sliced. Whipping attachment is useless. Average performance at a high cost.

Regal La Machine I Food Processor K813GY
Price: $69
Bowl Capacity: 6½ cups
Overall Size: 15½-by-8½-by-6 inches
Special Features: Shred/slice disk and pulse setting.
Garlic: 20 seconds to chop; fine mince not possible even with scraping down of sides.
Parsley: 25 seconds for an even but not terribly fine mince.
Nuts: 25 seconds for an even chop; fine grind not possible.
Cheese: After 2 minutes cheese is not finely grated, small pieces remain.
Soup: Can handle at least 4 cups without leaking.
General Comments: Special cutting blades work, although a few larger pieces slip through. Below-average performance on several tests.

Tasting Finds Both Sweet and Dry Chenin Blancs Enjoyable

Our tasting of Chenin Blanc wines found two distinct styles, each of which was appreciated by at least some of the tasters

∽ BY MARK BITTMAN WITH SANDY BLOCK ∽

Chenin blanc, the white grape that produces Vouvray and other wines, has long been underrated. This is especially true in California, where chardonnay retains eminence (as it should) and sauvignon blanc is the second favorite of growers.

Yet chenin blanc is an amazing grape, one that can be made into wine that is almost dry and sweet at the same time. It can take at least three distinct forms, and does well in all of them. It can be made into quite decent sparkling wine (a category not discussed here). It can be fermented to near–bone dryness, yet remain distinctively fruity. And when it is vinified to be sweet, Chenin Blanc wine can be aged for years, even decades, becoming a luxurious dessert wine.

Medium-dry Chenin (the category into which most of our wines fell) can serve as an aperitif, or as a wine whose bold fruit-acid balance enables it to stand up to a variety of Asian foods—a quality of which few other wines can boast. And Chenin has another advantage: It is relatively inexpensive. At every level of quality, it is cheaper than comparable wines made from sauvignon blanc or chardonnay grapes.

Chenin Blanc, then, can be a bargain (one of our suppliers calls our top-ranked wine "one of the few true bargains in my store"). The trick lies in knowing your taste. For years, California winemakers made sickly sweet Chenins with low acid levels (at least one of our bottom-ranked wines meets this description). Increasingly they are producing simple but enjoyable wines that substitute nicely for pricier Chardonnays and Sauvignon Blancs, wines close in style to the drier wines of Vouvray. Unfortunately there is no way to tell the difference by reading the label (many Vouvray wines, including our winner, are labeled demi-sec when appropriate, but even this system is not completely reliable).

Hence our tasting, which covered the gamut from inexpensive, fruity, slightly fizzy West Coast Chenins to the grand demi-secs of Vouvray. Almost all the wines had their admirers; the top-ranked wine, a rich, fairly sweet Vouvray, contrasted greatly with the second-place wine, a light, silky, but much drier wine from California. Sampling each will help you determine whether you prefer one style over the other; you may well enjoy both. ∎

Our Chenin Blanc tasting was held at the Blue Room in Cambridge, Massachusetts. As usual in our tastings, the wines were tasted blind by a panel that included both wine professionals and amateur wine lovers.

In the judging, seven points were awarded for each first-place vote, six for second, five for third, and so on. Wines are listed in order of preference (an asterisk indicates that the wine tied with the one immediately below). The first six wines were enjoyed by most of the tasters. These wines were purchased in the Northeast; prices will vary somewhat.

BEST WINE

1989 Foreau Vouvray Demi-Sec

BEST BUY

1992 Pine Ridge Chenin Blanc

1. 1989 Foreau Vouvray Demi-Sec (31 points), $20. A full rich, fairly sweet wine that was the favorite of all three of our professional tasters. It was put over the top, however, by the second-place votes of the amateurs. If you like your white wines bone-dry, steer clear, but if you enjoy well-made wines with a bit of sugar, this is prime.

2. 1992 Pine Ridge Chenin Blanc, Yountville Cuvee (25 points), $8. Lighter and drier than the Foreau, this relatively acidic but still fruity wine drew raves from four amateurs and some praise from two professionals. "Nice feel — smooth but not clingy."

3. 1992 Beringer Chenin Blanc (23 points), $7. Nicely balanced wine rated first by two amateurs. "Light, smooth, clear, clean, and a little sweet," wrote one. Still a far cry from a bone-dry wine.

4. 1990 Domaine des Baumard, Savennieres (19 points), $17. "Big beautiful, world-class wine," declared one professional, who liked it almost as much as the Foreau; a couple of other tasters agreed. But several found this wine "bitter," "vegetal," and "off-putting."

5. 1991 Mondavi Napa Chenin Blanc (17 points), $7. Widely enjoyed wine that was ranked by six of eight tasters. "Good fruit, slightly sweet, nice balance of acid and fruit," wrote one. Detractors found it simple.

6. 1992 Henri Bourgeois Vouvray (14 points), $10. Another wine that was liked by the majority of tasters. Its strongest booster found it "a little one-dimensional, but good, flinty bouquet and lots of fruit."

7. 1992 Dry Creek Chenin Blanc (12 points), $8. Here the consensus begins to break down: "Smoother, fuller, and more satisfying than the others," wrote one taster, placing it first. "Dry, toasty, and fruity," wrote another, who ranked it third. But most found it "plain and common."

8. 1991 Chappellet Chenin Blanc (9 points), $9. "Complex and earthy, though bitter," wrote one taster, who ranked it fourth. But few of the others found it anything other than bitter and unpleasant. "Not something I'd seek out," wrote one.

9. *1992 Stags' Leap Chenin Blanc (6 points), $8. "Tart acidity backed by plenty of fruit," wrote one taster, who ranked this wine third. Most others agreed with the taster who said, "Thin with no finish."

10. 1989 Clos de la Coulee de Serrant, Savennieres (6 points), $50. Note price. Even the professional who admired this "older wine of high quality" could not rank it higher than fifth. Most tasters found it "flat and unpleasant." A confusing wine, as evidenced by the comment "a hint of garbage, but also a rather pleasant edge of almonds."

11. 1992 Chateau Ste. Michelle Chenin Blanc (4 points), $8. Almost everyone found this wine to be cloying and simple. "Like Asti Spumante," wrote one taster.

12. 1992 Hogue Cellars Chenin Blanc (1 point), $7. The best said about this wine was "light and mild." The consensus among all of our tasters: "Very dull."

The Cooking of the Eastern Mediterranean
Paula Wolfert
HarperCollins, $30

There are very few cookbook authors like Paula Wolfert. Take this excerpt from the introduction to her newest effort, *The Cooking of the Eastern Mediterranean*: "The recipes are merely the fruits [of my travels]; the joy is the encounters with the people, nearly always women, who prepare the dishes. The eyes of true cooks always light up when they speak about food."

Wolfert's prose lights up this book so delightfully that the recipes, while not tangential, are almost a bonus. Like her other books, this is a work that you can savor; it's a pleasure to read and to thumb through, as well as to cook from. And like her other books, this one is about a region she knows so intimately — she has been traveling and living in the Mediterranean for thirty years or more — that she writes about places other people have barely started to think about: Macedonia, for example, and Syria and Georgia.

But even if there were no prose, this would be a valuable book. Not for beginners, because Wolfert assumes a certain level of competence in her audience. There are many long, complicated dishes with relatively sketchy instructions ("stir as if making a mayonnaise . . ."). There are also many ingredients that, despite Wolfert's protestations to the contrary, are neither likely to be sitting in your pantry now nor easy to find in the neighborhood market. Pomegranate molasses certainly falls into this category, along with black lentils, Aleppo pepper, sumac, and so on. You must be dedicated to consider Wolfert, which has been true from her first book on.

The reward, however, is authentic, old-fashioned country cooking — but from a country other than ours. This is food that you can make yourself, because Wolfert's recipes always work. The dishes range from simple — Bulgur Pilaf with Toasted Noodles, a revelation — to almost ridiculously complex, such as the Baby-Size Kibbehs Stuffed with Braised Lamb Shank, Tomatoes, and Onions. (Kibbehs, if you don't know, are meat or meat-and-grain shells stuffed with more meat.)

Yet while Wolfert fans may find this hard to believe, and despite the presence of at least one recipe (Marinated Octopus) that takes one week to complete, this is a cookbook with a fair share of relatively light food fit for weeknights. Marinated pork kebabs, charred and juicy, are perfect summer grill food; creamy walnut and pomegranate sauce is an incomparable dip that will leave your guests wondering just what you did; stewed potatoes with tomato and feta is straightforward and easy; her version of hummus is superior to most; and two green bean recipes yield sweet, tender beans of unusual flavor, the more remarkable for the fact that one of the recipes requires you to cook the beans for three hours.

There are, of course, flaws and inconsistencies, bits and pieces that left us wondering. We'd be more inclined to complain about imperfections, though, if *The Cooking of the Eastern Mediterranean* weren't, well, unique. But few cookbook authors have the stamina to traipse all over southeastern Europe and western Asia for weeks at a time, collecting recipes that might otherwise go the way of the former Yugoslavia. Fewer still have Wolfert's extensive food background and discriminating palate. And even fewer still have the reputation and the clout to put these recipes in a good-looking book that will see widespread distribution. The combination deserves to be supported, and the book is wild fun.

—Mark Bittman with Sharon K. Barrett

Panini, Bruschetta, Crostini
Viana La Place
William Morrow, $20

Given America's insatiable appetite for all things Italian, it was only a matter of time before a book was written on Italian sandwiches, called *panini*. As accomplished cookbook author Viana La Place points out in her latest effort, Italians have been filling bread with chicken, olives, roasted peppers, cheese, prosciutto, tomatoes, eggs, and greens for centuries. And despite any protests from relatives of the eighteenth-century Earl of Sandwich, she convincingly claims sandwiches as Italian in origin.

Cookbook readers may already know La Place as the author of *Verdura* (Morrow, 1991) as well as the co-author of *Cucina Rustica* (Morrow, 1990), *Pasta Fresca* (Morrow, 1988), and *Cucina Fresca* (Harper & Row, 1985). With this fifth book, La Place must now be considered the preeminent proponent for California's lighter take on Italian cuisine. She approaches her subject with just the right amount of respect for tradition — there are no weird or overly Americanized combinations in this book — but does not hesitate to draw on her own background as a native of southern California.

Hence, classic Chicken and Salsa Verde Panino is just as welcome and successful as Avocado, Caper, and Arugula Tramezzini — something few Italians would recognize as their own (avocados are not widely grown in Italy) but a pleasing combination that seems Italian in spirit nonetheless. Without exception, every recipe tested from this book was excellent and extremely simple. Combinations are fresh, full-flavored, and relatively low in fat. Panino di Prosciutto e Mozzarella is so basic you may wonder why you need a recipe at all. However, Herb Frittata Panini — slices of a warm, Italian-style omelet sandwiched between slices of country bread — exemplifies the recipes that are just unusual (as well as delicious) enough to make this book worth the investment.

In addition to panini, La Place covers other Italian bread-based snacks, and the final chapter is devoted to bread with sweet fillings or toppings. Among these slightly unusual concoctions, Toasted Bittersweet Chocolate Panino (bittersweet chocolate melted between two slices of toasted bread) and Orange Marmalade Frittata Panino are both excellent.

I do have one complaint about the book. La Place gives specific bread recommendations for each sandwich — "round foccacia rolls" in one recipe, "crusty sandwich rolls with a sturdy, coarse crumb" in another — but does not provide any bread recipes. Instead, she suggests buying bread from an artisanal bakery or making your own loaves from recipes found elsewhere. For those who live far from a good bakery and must rely on their own talent, she touts Carol Field's *The Italian Baker* (Harper & Row, 1985), arguably the best book on the subject but something of a cop-out in a sandwich book.

The inclusion of a half dozen basic bread recipes would have made *Panini, Bruschetta, and Crostini* more comprehensive. But given La Place's thorough and inspired survey of Italian sandwiches, this seems like a minor quibble that is easily forgiven. ■

—Jack Bishop

SOURCES
AND RESOURCES

MINI FOOD PROCESSORS

We divided the seven mini food processors we tested (see page 28) into two groups — those with a capacity of two to three cups and those with a larger capacity, between six and seven cups. We have located discount sources for the top machines in each category. Among the smaller machines, the Black & Decker Handy Shortcut Micro-Processor HMP30 is the top choice for its good performance and array of attachments. This machine is available from Service Merchandise at a cost of $27.92, about $8 less than the suggested retail price. You can order it from the company's catalog (800-251-1212) or purchase it at any store location. It is also sold at Bradlees, K mart, and Lechmere stores across the country. The Cuisinart Mini-Food Prep DLC-1 is available at Williams-Sonoma stores nationwide. To locate a store in your area call them at 800-541-2233. The price is $32.50, a discount of almost $10 off the suggested retail price. Among the larger capacity machines, the Panasonic Kitchen Wizard MK 5070 is the clear winner. This food processor can be ordered from the Bennett Brothers Catalog (30 E. Adams Street, Chicago, IL 60603; 800-621-2626 or 312-621-1600 in Illinois). The cost is $99.95, a $20 discount off the suggested retail price.

OUT-OF-PRINT COOKBOOKS

If you are looking for an out-of-print, foreign, or otherwise hard-to-locate cookbook, try Kitchen Arts & Letters, a New York City bookstore devoted to food and wine writings. The store stocks thousands of current titles and keeps an extensive warehouse supply of out-of-print books, including *Master Recipes* by Stephen Schmidt, author of "Six Chocolate Cakes," page 22. In addition to hard-to-find American books, the store has an impressive collection of foreign cookbooks, from expected locales such as France and Italy as well as more unusual sources such as India and Australia. Unlike most other bookstores, Kitchen Arts & Letters (1435 Lexington Avenue, New York, NY 10128; 212-876-5550) conducts book searches without charge or obligation. In fact, the store will continue searching for years, if necessary, to find your book. It does not take credit card orders, but you may place an order over the phone and then send a check for the full amount.

MEXICAN INGREDIENTS

Rick Bayless's tamale recipe on page 14 requires a number of Mexican ingredients that can be found in Latino markets or ordered by mail. The Old Southwest Trading Company (P.O. Box 7545, Albuquerque, NM 87194; 505-836-0168) has a complete line of Mexican and southwestern ingredients. If fresh tomatillos are available at your supermarket, use them in the Tomatillo Sauce. However, canned tomatillos may be used with excellent results. Old Southwest Trading Company sells an eleven-ounce can of whole tomatillos for $2.50. The store also carries masa harina, which they call Corn Masa Mix. A 4.4-pound bag costs $5. The relish recipes on page 20 also use a number of Mexican ingredients. Most can be found in supermarkets, but you may have trouble tracking down canned chipotle chiles. Old Southwest Trading Company has a seven-ounce can for $2.25. Another excellent source for Mexican ingredients is the Santa Fe School of Cooking & Market (116 W. San Francisco Street, Santa Fe, NM 87501; 505-983-4511). This gourmet store/cooking school sells two kinds of masa harina — tamale grind (which is finer) and stone-ground (for tortillas) — in two-pound bags that cost $3.49 each. They also have an extensive selection of chiles. Call for a free catalog.

BULGUR FOR TABBOOLEH

Tabbooleh is a Middle Eastern parsley and bulgur salad (see story on page 9). Look for bulgur in better supermarkets as well as in many health food stores and Middle Eastern groceries. It also can be ordered by mail from Walnut Acres Farms (Walnut Acres Road, Penns Creek, PA 17862; 800-433-3998). Bulgur ground for tabbooleh is sold in one-, three-, and five-pound bags. The cost is $2.39, $6.39, and $10.29, respec-tively, with an additional $4.90 shipping charge on all orders.

CAKE-FROSTING TOOLS

If baking is your passion, then you should know about Maid of Scandinavia (3244 Raleigh Avenue, Minneapolis, MN 55416; 800-328-6722), a mail-order company that sells literally thousands of cake-decorating and cake-making tools. For instance, if you want to purchase a cake comb to create simple frosting designs (see page 23), Maid of Scandinavia has two excellent options: a plastic comb with scalloped edges for a wavy design, or a stainless steel comb with sawtooth edges for straight lines. The plastic comb costs $1.35; the metal comb is $1.45. The catalog also carries several rotating cake stands that make frosting easier. A twelve-inch cast-aluminum stand costs $43.50; a twelve-inch white plastic stand is just $9.75. Maid of Scandinavia also sells a number of offset spatulas designed for spreading frosting. One particularly useful model has a rosewood handle and a twelve-inch flexible blade that is about one and one-quarter inches wide. Finally, the catalog offers a basic decorating set called the Get Started Kit ($11.75). It comes with a pastry bag, coupler, nine tubes, a decorating nail for making flowers, a decorating book, and four paste food colors.

BARBECUE SAUCES

Commercial products rarely taste as good as homemade, but jams, sauces, dried fruits, and syrups from American Spoon Foods (1668 Clarion Avenue, Petoskey, MI 49770; 800-222-5886) are an exception. This small mail-order business is run by Justin Rashid and chef Larry Forgione. The emphasis is on high-quality regional products from Michigan's Upper Peninsula, such as dried cherries, wild rice, and rhubarb marmalade. The company also carries a number of top-notch marinades and sauces. Larry Forgione's Barbecue Sauce is made without sugar (unlike most commercial sauces) or oil — just red bell pepper, jalapeño chiles, garlic, chili powder, and oregano. A seven and one-half-ounce jar costs $4.95. In addition to the standard barbecue sauce, variations like barbecue mustard, smoky tomato catsup, pineapple-chili barbecue sauce, and tangy ginger marinade are available. Call for more information or to receive a free copy of the company's colorful catalog.

GRILL PRODUCTS

Homemade barbecue (see story on page 10) requires the use of smoking chips. Williams-Sonoma offers an assortment of wood chips made from hickory, apple, mesquite, and alder woods. Each kind comes in a separate three-pound box, and the set retails for $30. Williams-Sonoma also carries a set of rosewood barbecue tools designed for basting, lifting, and turning ribs or anything else cooked on the grill. The set includes a pair of heavy-duty tongs, a spatula with beveled edges and holes to allow grease to drip through, an angled boar-bristle basting brush, a sharp knife, and a sturdy two-pronged fork. The five-piece set costs $48.50. For more information about either product or any of the grilling equipment sold by Williams-Sonoma, call 800-541-2233. A rack with small holes prevents shrimp (see page 18), vegetables, or other small items from falling through the grill grate. Chef's Catalog (800-338-3232) carries a large (sixteen-inch by twelve-inch) steel grid that is coated with porcelain for easy release and clean-up. Small round holes let heat through but keep foods from dropping onto the hot coals. This large grill topper costs $14.99.

GRILL HOTLINE

The people at Weber, manufacturers of the kind of kettle-style grill we recommend for making barbecue at home, are operating a toll-free consumer hotline this summer. The hotline is staffed by home economists, who will answer grilling questions on weekdays from 11:00 A.M. to 9:00 P.M. CST and on Saturdays from 9:00 A.M. to 6:00 P.M. CST. Callers may request their booklet of backyard barbecue tips. For more information, call 800-GRILL-OUT (474-5568). ■

AMERICAN- AND GERMAN-STYLE POTATO SALADS AND TABBOOLEH
pages 8 and 9

OLD-FASHIONED CHOCOLATE LAYER CAKE WITH CHOCOLATE CREAM
page 24

PHOTOGRAPHS BY ERIC ROTH

GRILLED SHRIMP WITH SPICY GARLIC PASTE
page 19

FOUR STONE FRUIT RELISHES
page 20

AUTHENTIC BARBECUED RIBS
page 11

FRESH CORN TAMALES WITH TOMATILLO-CHILE SAUCE
page 14

Baked Peaches with Amaretti Cookies

Halve and pit 6 peaches; place peach halves, cut side up, in a buttered baking dish just large enough to hold them comfortably; set aside. Grind 10 whole amaretti cookies in a food processor; transfer crumbs to a small bowl. Peel and pit another peach; process to a smooth puree. Transfer puree to a medium bowl; mix in ⅓ cup sugar, 1 egg yolk, and the cookie crumbs. Spoon a portion of the filling into each peach half. Bake in a 350 degree oven until peaches are tender, about 1 hour. Serve warm with sweetened whipped cream, flavored with a bit of Amaretto liqueur if you like. *Serves 6.*

COOK'S
ILLUSTRATED

Perfect Pie Crust
We Test 35 Variations to
Find a No-Fail Master
Recipe

Secrets of
Butterflied Chicken
Refined Technique
Provides Faster, More
Even Cooking

Rating Toasters
Most Expensive Model
Bombs

How to Cook
Pork Chops
Covered Sautéing
Creates a Juicy,
Tender Chop

SPECIALTY CHICKENS
WIN TASTING
•
QUICK HOMEMADE PICKLES
•
THE WAY TO COOK
TENDER GREENS
•
VEGETABLE PASTA SAUCES

$4.00 U.S./$4.95 CANADA

TABLE
OF CONTENTS

"Assorted Apples"
See page 8 for The Best
Apple Pie recipe.

ILLUSTRATION BY
BRENT WATKINSON

Baked Apples with
Cranberries, adapted
from *Cooking with Daniel
Boulud* (Random House,
1993) by Daniel Boulud

ILLUSTRATION BY
CAROL FORTUNATO

COOK'S
ILLUSTRATED

Publisher and Editor
CHRISTOPHER KIMBALL

Executive Editor
MARK BITTMAN

Senior Editor
JOHN WILLOUGHBY

Articles Editor
ANNE L. TUOMEY

Food Editor
PAM ANDERSON

Senior Writer
JACK BISHOP

Managing Editor
MAURA LYONS

Editorial Assistant
KIM RUSSELLO

Copy Editor
KURT TIDMORE

Test Kitchen Assistant
VICTORIA ROLAND

Art Director
MEG BIRNBAUM

Food Stylist
MARIE PIRAINO

Marketing Director
ADRIENNE KIMBALL

Circulation Director
ELAINE VALENTINO

Circulation Assistant
JENNIFER L. KEENE

Production Director
JAMES MCCORMACK

Publicity Director
CAROL ROSEN KAGAN

Treasurer
JANET CARLSON

Office Manager
JENNY THORNBURY

Customer Service
CONNIE FORBES

Special Projects
FERN BERMAN

Cook's Illustrated (ISSN 1068-2821) is published bimonthly by Natural Health Limited Partners, 17 Station Street, Box 569, Brookline, MA 02147-0569. Copyright 1994 Natural Health Limited Partners. Application to mail at second-class postage rates is pending at Boston, MA, and additional mailing offices. Editorial office: 17 Station Street, Box 569, Brookline, MA 02147-0569; (617) 232-1000, FAX (617) 232-1572. Editorial contributions should be sent to: Editor, *Cook's Illustrated*, 17 Station Street, Box 569, Brookline, MA 02147-0569. We cannot assume responsibility for manuscripts submitted to us. Submissions will be returned only if accompanied by a large self-addressed stamped envelope. Subscription rates: $24.95 for one year; $45 for two years; $65 for three years. (Canada: add $3 per year; all other countries: add $12 per year.) Postmaster: Send all new orders, subscription inquiries, and change of address notices to *Cook's Illustrated*, P.O. Box 59046, Boulder, CO 80322-9046. Single copies: $4 in U.S., $4.95 in Canada and foreign. Back issues available for $5 each. PRINTED IN THE U.S.A.

EDITORIAL

OLD RECIPES, OLD FRIENDS

I first met Dorothy, the impish, fiercely independent mother of our Vermont neighbor, when she came up to me after church and declared, "Your stairs are two steps too long." It is the custom in Vermont to inspect a new house under construction when the owners are away — the neighbors drop by for a clandestine tour. It appeared that Dorothy had taken the measure of our new farmhouse and couldn't wait to speak her piece. Two years after her passing, I still remember her words every time I run upstairs. She was right. The stairs *are* too long — by exactly two steps.

CHRISTOPHER KIMBALL

Dorothy was best known in our household for her cream pie. Every Thanksgiving, she would sneak into her daughter's kitchen and whip up her secret recipe — just cream and sugar and pie crust. She cooked it for several hours at a very low temperature until the cream set; and of course, Dorothy's pie always set perfectly. When I asked for the recipe, she lit up like a schoolgirl and made me guess at the oven temperature, the ratio of ingredients, the possibility of an egg, the baking time. With each formula I ventured, she laughed so hard that her slight frame shook and tears ran down her cheeks. When she died, her secret died with her. Her daughter, Jean, claims that she has Dorothy's recipe, but I wonder. Some years her pie sets and some years it doesn't. I'd bet the last two steps of my staircase that the recipe isn't complete — like a true Vermonter, Dorothy knew how to keep a secret.

A lot of us in the food world, myself included, praise the virtues of cooking without recipes. Cooking according to what someone else has written feels like an admission of apprenticeship. But lately I've begun to re-think my feelings about this. Marion Cunningham, a well-known cookbook author, recently said to me, "You know, cooking shared recipes is like visiting old friends." In many Muslim countries, it is thought that the taking of a person's photograph is akin to stealing their soul. Like a tourist's snapshot, a shared recipe may be a kind of loss, but it's also a special gift.

Another Vermonter, Marie Briggs, was the town baker when I was a kid. In the back room of a house that had no running water (just a hand pump in the sink) and no indoor facilities (plumbing arrived in 1970), on a soot-blackened wood cookstove, she baked country breads, apple pies, and molasses cookies for the local store. After she passed away four years ago, a neighbor, Junior Bentley, gave me some of her recipes. Reading the recipes, I can remember the yeasty kitchen aroma, the taste of molasses and cornmeal in the big slabs of anadama bread, the first bite of warm spice doughnuts. I recall her bright squinty face, and the day she took me aside after I had moved back to town after a twenty-five-year absence and said in her plain-spoken manner, "It's nice to have you back again." I find myself using her recipes more and more as I get older. It isn't just the food I'm making, it's like cooking up a small batch of Marie in the rich dark doughs. The small measures of memory — her sensible square-heel shoes, oversize black-frame glasses, and the spare, measured pace of both her cooking and conversation — all come back to me.

Other recipes hold more exotic memories. On vacation in Tobago, my wife and I discovered a one-room shack in a tucked away cove. A foam-green, hand-drawn sign hung above it saying, "Jemma's Seaview Kitchen." Jemma was an enormous swirl of a cook barely contained by her galley-size kitchen. Yet out of that thumbnail of a kitchen came the best red snapper I've ever eaten (served in a ginger sauce) and a two-tiered dessert made from coconut and burnt-sugar gelatins. Jemma freely told me the secrets of her dessert. I've never made it — there was too much of her in that cooking — but I think about that recipe a lot, and I count Jemma as a friend for giving it to me.

Malvina Kinard, my first kitchen mentor, a native of Birmingham, Alabama, once told me that sharing recipes is like "sharing flowers from your garden." Many years ago she gave me her recipe for Double Chocolate Cookies, and their fudgy, chewy filling and thin flaky crust are so good that, in her words, eating one is like "dying and going to heaven." She lives far away now, and when we call she says in her luxurious Alabama drawl, "Bless my soul! You just live too far away for an old lady like me. Now what are we going to do about this?" We promised to come and visit, but that was two years ago, and it's a long drive with the kids.

We miss them all. Dorothy. Marie. Jemma. Malvina. But we make their recipes on crisp Saturday afternoons, with the oven warm and the kids helping. It's nice to have old friends stop by for a visit. ◆

NOTES

FROM READERS

UNSALTED VS. SALTED BUTTER

Why do so many recipes, including most of yours, call for unsalted butter and then tell you to add salt a few lines later? Can't I just use salted butter?

ALTA MORTON
Glen Ellyn, IL

There are a couple of reasons why most cookbooks and magazines, including *Cook's Illustrated,* call for sweet butter and salt instead of salted butter in recipes. First, some salted butters are saltier than others. This poses a problem for recipe writers and can lead to dishes with too much or too little salt. Adding salt separately makes it easier to duplicate the total amount of salt in the original recipe.

Secondly, salted butter has a different flavor than sweet butter combined with salt. Traditionally, salt was added to butter to extend shelf life. Refrigeration has made this unnecessary, but many dairies still add salt for flavor. However, we find that salt often masks the sweet creaminess associated with the finest farm-fresh butter. Especially when baking, we miss this flavor. In a blind test of sugar cookies made with salted and sweet butter, the results were quite clearly in favor of cookies made with unsalted butter.

Lastly, salted butter almost always contains more water. Water content in butter can range from 10 to 18 percent. (By law, fat content in butter must exceed 80 percent.) In baking, the butter with the lowest water content (i.e., sweet butter) is preferred, since excess water from butter can interfere with the development of gluten in the flour.

ROASTING COFFEE BEANS AT HOME

I've heard that it is possible to roast your own coffee beans at home. I thought this might be handy at my country home, which is pretty far from the nearest coffee store. What's the best way to do this?

KEN MILLER
New York, NY

The flavor of coffee beans will begin to deteriorate within days of roasting. Within weeks the change is quite noticeable. Because green coffee beans have an indefinite shelf life (some varieties even improve with age), it can be worthwhile to roast your own.

Most stores that roast coffee will sell you the green beans at a discount. To roast at home, you need good ventilation or a willingness to temporarily disconnect your smoke alarm, since the natural oil in the beans will smoke quite a bit.

We tried roasting beans in the oven, in a skillet on top of the stove, and in a stove-top popcorn popper. We found that the oven is the best and most convenient place to roast coffee, since it is less messy and doesn't call for constant stirring.

To roast beans, put four ounces of green coffee beans into a collapsible vegetable steamer, pushing them up the sides a bit, and place the basket in a preheated 425-degree oven. For the first ten minutes, there is no need to stir them. At ten minutes, the beans should begin to smell yeasty. Stir and continue roasting for another two minutes, during which time they should start to crackle. Keep checking them and stirring at two-minute intervals. After eight more minutes (a total of about twenty minutes), the beans should be dark and shiny and just starting to smell pleasantly roasted.

When the beans are just a shade lighter than you want (keep some properly roasted beans on the counter for comparison), take them out of the oven. Dump them into a colander in the sink (be careful, the beans are quite hot), and shake them under a small fan aimed at the colander. The fan is necessary because beans continue roasting, and you want to cool them down quickly to prevent scorching. Point the fan down at the beans so that the small bits of papery skin from the beans will fly into the sink and not up in the air. Store cooled beans in an airtight container on the counter or for longer periods in the refrigerator.

If your home-roasted coffee tastes raw, try roasting the beans a bit longer. In some cases, beans may look done on the outside but still need more time to cook through. If home-roasted coffee tastes burned and thin, try roasting at a lower temperature or for less time.

MEASURING SHORTENING

Years ago, when I was a mere slip of a girl, the mother of my best friend gave me a few cooking lessons. She taught me a number of very helpful tricks, including this easy method for measuring shortening using Archimedes's principle of water displacement.

To accurately measure a half cup of shortening, for example, fill a large measuring cup with one cup of water and gradually add shortening until the water level reaches one and a half cups. Presto, you have an accurate (and unstuck) half cup of solid fat. Just pour off the water, blot shortening dry, and add to other ingredients.

NANCY BALDRIDGE
Lawrence, NY

ALCOHOL-FREE WINE FOR COOKING

I read the letter about cooking with alcohol (Notes from Readers, March/April 1994) and thought you might be interested to learn about the products from Vie-Del (P.O. Box 2896, Fresno, CA 93745; 209-834-2525). This company makes a line of alcohol-free wine concentrates that are sold by mail. They take regular wine and cook off all of the alcohol and most of the water. The result is a pure wine flavor that is eight times more concentrated than the original wine. Concentrates of sherry, burgundy, and sauternes are available. A recipe booklet is included with the product.

JUDITH MILLER
Walnut, CA

SCALDING MILK

Every time I scald milk, some of it scorches and sticks to the pan. Is there any way to prevent such a mess?

ROBERTA MICK
Chapel Hill, NC

When milk is scalded — that is, heated to just below the boiling point — the whey proteins fall to the bottom of the pan, stick, and burn because of their close proximity to the heat source. Some cookbooks suggest rinsing the pan first with cold water and not wiping it dry before adding the milk.

In our tests, this trick did not help when the milk was heated very slowly over low heat. True, neither the rinsed nor the dry pan scorched, although there was a thin film (easily wiped out) in the bottom of both pans. The problem was that such low heat took almost twenty minutes to scald a half cup of milk. When we heated two more batches of milk over medium-high, rinsing the pan first did prevent scorching, but still left a heavy layer of skin that required some scrubbing to remove. It seems that high heat is the real culprit and that the presence of a thin film of water on the bottom of the pan can help disperse some of the whey that might otherwise burn.

We also tried scalding milk in a double boiler and found that this gave the best and fastest results. Simply put milk into the rinsed but not dried (this step makes clean-up a bit easier, especially if water is boiling furiously) top of a double boiler and set it over simmering water. The milk will scald in a few minutes and leave almost nothing stuck to the pan.

CORNSTARCH PROBLEMS

*R*ecently I have been having problems using cornstarch as a thickener. The mixture simply does not thicken properly even though I have used the recipe many times in the past without trouble. Is it possible that cornstarch has a limited shelf life?

ELIZABETH LELAND
Los Alamos, NM

We spoke with a home economist at CPC Foods, which manufactures Argo brand cornstarch. She assured us that cornstarch has an almost indefinite shelf life. In rare cases, high humidity can cause clumping in cornstarch, which may reduce its thickening powers, but the damage is usually visible.

Note that cornstarch's thickening powers can also be inhibited by high proportions of fat, sugar, and especially acid in a recipe. For this reason, when making lemon meringue pie, for example, the custard is usually thickened before the lemon juice is added. You may want to adopt a similar strategy and thicken sauces or other liquids before adding any highly acidic ingredients.

WET AND DRY MEASURES

*M*y husband argues that he can use any measuring cup to measure anything, regardless of whether it is a wet or dry ingredient. I think you have to use measures designed specifically for wet and dry ingredients. Who's right?

BETH BLOOMBERG
Arlington, VA

In the interests of marital harmony, we are happy to say that you are both right. Let's explain. We first tested sugar and flour, measuring them into dry cups (made from metal and plastic and capable of being leveled off) and then dumping them into wet measures — glass and clear plastic containers marked with ounces and cups. The dry ingredients came up short in the wet measures, and it was impossible to level off and accurately gauge how much sugar or flour was in a wet measure. So in terms of dry ingredients, you are right — they must be measured in cups specifically designed for dry measures.

But we also measured varying amounts of water in wet measures and then transferred the water to the appropriate dry measures. The amounts were the same, so your husband is also correct, in that liquid ingredients can be measured in cups designed for either wet or dry measures. However, we generally find wet measures easier to work with since they need not be filled to the rim.

Finally, we are often asked what is the best way to measure yogurt and sour cream. We weighed out eight ounces of yogurt and found that it fit perfectly into a one cup dry measure. However, in a wet measure it fell below the one cup line. It also was harder to gauge how much yogurt was actually in the glass measuring cup, so we recommend measuring yogurt, sour cream, and other semi-solid ingredients in dry measures.

ACHIOTE PASTE

I have seen many Mexican recipes that call for annatto seed. What is this? Is it the same as achiote paste?

SABINA CROSBY BARRETT
New York, NY

Annatto seeds come from a small tropical tree that grows in parts of Mexico, Central America, and the Caribbean. The tree bears large brown prickly pods that contain as many as fifty small, dark red seeds. The seeds can be ground to produce a brilliant yellow-orange dye. In fact, annatto is used as a natural food coloring in everything from Cheddar cheese to vanilla ice cream.

In Mexico and other parts of Latin America, the seeds are ground — usually along with a number of other ingredients — to make achiote paste. The other ingredients in achiote paste vary from region to region, but may include garlic, black peppercorns, cumin, oregano, and citrus juice. The paste can be used as a marinade for meats, poultry, or seafood. It also serves as the basis of a large variety of Mexican sauces. (*See* Sources and Resources, page 32, for a mail-order source for this and many other spices.)

SOFTENING BROWN SUGAR

*W*hat's the best way to keep brown sugar soft, or to soften it once it has clumped together?

MARK SMITH
Charlottesville, VA

When brown sugar comes into contact with air, the moisture in the sugar evaporates. This eventually causes the sugar to lump together. You can prevent this by storing brown sugar in a zipper-lock plastic bag or in a tightly covered plastic container — the latter makes scooping and measuring easier. Storing brown sugar in the refrigerator will also help keep it fresh and soft.

If your brown sugar does harden, heat or moisture can be applied to soften it. For sugar not needed right away, place a slice of bread in a container with a tight lid, add the sugar, and close. By the next day, the sugar will have absorbed the moisture in the bread and softened. Some cookbooks recommend using an apple slice in the same fashion, but we found that the apple was so moisture-laden that some of the sugar began to melt, and the apple imparted an unwelcome flavor.

If you realize at the last minute that your brown sugar has hardened, heat must be applied to soften it. The microwave on low power does the job in a minute or two, but can be difficult to control. The sugar can melt in some spots and remain lumpy in others. We found a 250-degree oven to be more reliable. Placing a measuring cup full of water in the oven to add moisture, a step recommended on some brown sugar packages, was found to be unnecessary in our tests.

Spread the sugar in a pie plate or on a square of aluminum foil. After about three minutes in a preheated oven, poke the sugar with a fork to see if it crumbles; if not, leave it in the oven for a few more minutes. In our tests, brown sugar softened in three to seven minutes, depending on how hard it had become. Cool the softened sugar, and store in an airtight container any not being used immediately.

WHAT IS IT?

*E*nclosed you will find a picture of a tool I discovered in our home. I would appreciate any information you can give me on this unusual culinary item.

JACK COOMBES
Menomonee Falls, WI

This handy item comes from France and is used by professional fishmongers and amateur sportspeople to gut and scale small and medium-sized fish like trout or bass. The sharp stainless steel tine is used to puncture the belly and begin the evisceration. The serrated edge finishes the job and also removes scales from the skin. A wood handle ensures a firm grip.

We did some checking to see if this item is still available in this country. It seems that the importer has recently dropped this particular scaler from its list. La Cuisine Kitchenware (323 Cameron Street, Alexandria, VA 22314; 703-836-4435) sells a similar fish scaler that is also from France. The design is based on the same principal, but the execution is quite different. In this version, a sharp point for piercing the skin, a beveled edge for eviscerating, and a serrated edge for scaling are all on one four and a half-inch-long blade. The cost is $12 plus shipping. ∎

Quick Tips

MAKING YOGURT CHEESE

Labne, or yogurt cheese, a soft cheese made from thick yogurt, is popular in the Middle East, particularly Lebanon. Susan Asanovic of Wilton, Connecticut, came up with this way to make yogurt cheese without special equipment.

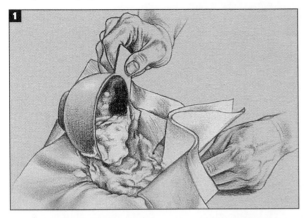

1. Pour the yogurt onto a double layer of paper toweling.

2. Gather the paper towels together at the corners, secure them with a rubber band, and place a chopstick through the rubber band.

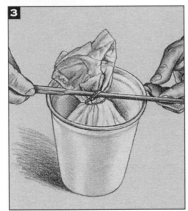

3. Suspend the yogurt from the rim of a yogurt carton until it is well drained (about four to eight hours).

REMOVING FAT FROM STOCK

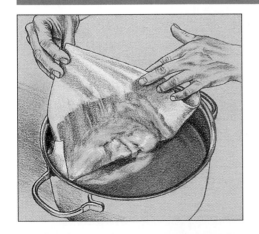

To remove the fat from stock, gently lay a paper towel on the surface of the stock for a few minutes. When you pick up the paper towel, it will have soaked up a large proportion of the fat. This is a modification of a tip from Nancy Hoffman of San Rafael, California.

SQUEEZING MOISTURE FROM EGGPLANT

To make eggplant less bitter and give it a denser texture for cooking, it should be salted, drained for an hour, and then pressed to squeeze out the moisture. William van Druten of Duluth, Minnesota, suggests an unusual but highly effective way of doing so.

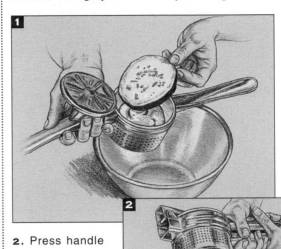

1. Place salted and drained eggplant pieces in a ricer.

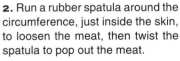

2. Press handle to squeeze out excess water.

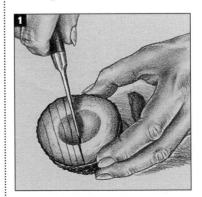

EXTRACTING THE MEAT FROM AVOCADOS

Andrea J. Morgan of Austin, Texas, provides this quick and easy way to get the meat out of an avocado.

2. Run a rubber spatula around the circumference, just inside the skin, to loosen the meat, then twist the spatula to pop out the meat.

1. After cutting the avocado in half and removing the pit, slice through the meat, but not the skin, with a paring knife.

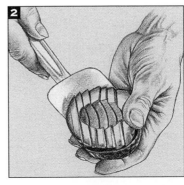

ILLUSTRATIONS BY ALAN WITSCHONKE

MOVING CAKE LAYERS

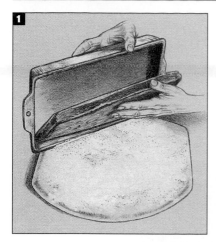

When making large or delicate layer cakes, it is sometimes hard to keep the top layer in one piece while transferring it into position on top of the bottom layer. To solve this problem, follow this tip from Pamela Czerwin of Oceanside, New York.

1. Carefully place the second layer of the cake onto a pizza paddle that has been coated with confectioners' sugar.

2. Gently slide the second layer onto the first layer as you would slide bread or pizza dough onto oven tiles.

CRUSHING GARLIC AND SPICES

The best kitchen utensils are not always the most modern. Judith Mack of Anchorage, Alaska, learned from Hawaiian cooks to use a large smooth stone rather than a chef's knife blade to smash garlic or crush spices. It works so well that our test kitchen director now keeps a "garlic rock" on her kitchen counter.

MEASURING DOUGH HEIGHT

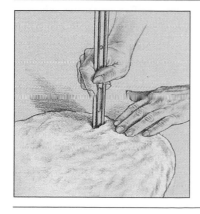

Recipes often instruct you to roll dough out to a particular height. Many cooks estimate the height of the dough "by eye," which can lead to problems later on in the recipe. It is very easy to measure the height of dough by simply rolling out the dough and sticking a ruler directly into it.

DRYING HERBS

To provide your kitchen year-round with quality dried herbs from your own garden, harvest herbs in season, then follow these steps from Kelly Fleming of Elgin, Arizona.

1. Tie the herbs together at the stem end.

2. Place the herbs upside down in a paper bag and tie the paper bag shut around the bunched stems.

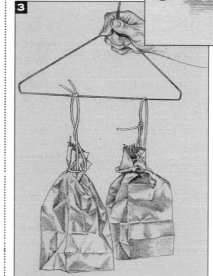

3. Hang the paper bag in a well-ventilated area. (Clothes hangers make a convenient rack.) Using this method, herbs will stay dust-free, and any leaves that fall from their stems will be caught in the bag.

MAKING COOKIE CRUMBS

To crush cookies for cookie crumbs, put the cookies in a plastic bag and run back and forth over them with a rolling pin until they are the size called for in your recipe.

ATTENTION READERS: FREE SUBSCRIPTION FOR PUBLISHED TIPS. Do you have a unique tip you would like to share with other readers? We will provide a one-year complimentary subscription for each quick tip that we print. Send a description of your special technique to *Cook's Illustrated,* P.O. Box 569, Brookline Village, MA 02147-0569. Please write "Attention: Quick Tips" on the envelope and include your name, address, and daytime phone number. Unfortunately, we can only acknowledge receipt of tips that will be printed in the magazine. In case the same tip is received from two readers, the one postmarked first will be selected.

Perfect Pie Crust

To meet the home cook's most difficult challenge, we tested thirty-five variations of all-purpose pie pastry and came up with a no-fail Master Recipe.

≈ BY CHRISTOPHER KIMBALL ≈

Making good pie crust can be a home cook's worst nightmare. Despite your best efforts, the crust can turn out hard, soggy, flavorless, over-salted, under-baked, too short, or totally unworkable. One expert tells you butter is the secret to perfect crust, another swears by vegetable shortening, still others, for health reasons, use only canola oil. Some cooks work the dough by hand, others do everything in a food processor.

After hundreds of pie crusts and twenty years of mixed results, I felt like an addicted gambler at the racetrack, seeking out that magical piece of information that would make me a winner. If only I could discover the right system, I thought. I even accosted celebrity bakers at social events, cajoling them for scraps of advice that might finally reveal some underlying theory of American pie crusts. I was desperate for the simple truth. To get at that, I consulted Stephen Schmidt, our resident expert on pie crusts, and researched a score or more cookbooks, seeking every possible theory and technique. Then I devised a list of thirty-five different pie crusts to test.

Pie Crust History

According to Schmidt, traditional English crust was "raised pastry," made by combining flour with a boiling mixture of water and butter, plus lard or shortening. This creates a soft, workable dough that can be shaped by hand into a free-form shell. When cooled, it becomes hard and holds its upright shape, hence the term "raised". In centuries past, raised pastry was not usually eaten, but used as a baking container for elk, deer, or even porpoise.

The Italians invented puff pastry, which probably came to France and England in the sixteenth century. It is made with a very high proportion of butter to flour and is referred to as a "short" crust because the amount of shortening created a pastry that could not be "raised up" like the English pies. The butter melts during baking and is replaced by steam, which slightly separates the layers, giving the pastry its puffy texture. In England, puff pastry was originally used for small, rich pastries, which were baked in pans rather than free-form.

Ordinary flaky pastry, the focus of this article, had already taken hold in England by 1600 and is descended from both the English and Italian version. The Pilgrims baked pastries surprisingly similar to today's pies — a combination of the English and Italian traditions — though they often called them by other names.

Choosing Fat, Flour, and Liquid

Armed with this historical knowledge and my thirty-five recipes, I began my tests. As my standard, I used Stephen Schmidt's recipe for pie pastry printed in the November/December 1993 *Cook's Illustrated*. This recipe calls for one and one-quarter cups of all-purpose flour, ten tablespoons of cold butter, a half-teaspoon each of salt and sugar, and three to three and a half tablespoons of water. All pastry doughs were rolled out, placed into nine-inch pie pans,

The perfect pie crust must combine flaky texture and great flavor.

and baked. The baked crusts were then compared in batches, always using the November/December recipe as a standard.

The most controversial ingredient in pastry is fat. In my tests, I found that while an all-butter crust has the best taste, it isn't as flaky as one made with shortening. On the other hand, an all-Crisco crust has a wonderful texture, but is lacking in flavor. The crust made with lard was a little heavy and too strongly flavored.

After testing a variety of combinations, I found that six tablespoons of butter to four tablespoons of Crisco was the optimum mixture for both flavor and texture.

With the fat question settled, I tested salt and sugar. A full teaspoon of salt was clearly too much for pie pastry, yet one-quarter teaspoon was too little; the one-half teaspoon called for in the original Master Recipe was just right.

However, the half teaspoon of sugar in that recipe was not enough; boosting it to a full tablespoon greatly improved the pastry.

I then moved on to consider the type of flour used. The protein content of flour is important in any sort of baking. Bread flours are very high in protein, since bread needs a strong, elastic dough. Pastry flour is low in protein, to produce a soft, tender product. To find the best flour for pie crust, I tried substituting cornstarch for part of the all-purpose flour (a cookie-baking trick that increases tenderness), adding a quarter teaspoon of baking powder to increase rise, and mixing cake flour with the all-purpose flour (again to increase tenderness). But none of these variations was an improvement on all-purpose flour (*see* "Searching for a Better Crust").

I was also intrigued with the notion of adding liquid ingredients that contain lactic acid, such as buttermilk or sour cream, because of the dramatic effects these ingredients have on batter for waffles, pancakes, and biscuits. However, I was disappointed to find that pie crust made with buttermilk was not as good as the Master Recipe, since the flavor was the same and the texture was actually slightly inferior. I then added a quarter-teaspoon of baking soda to the buttermilk version to see if it would cause the crust to rise and become lighter and flakier, but the result was terrible. It tasted like a biscuit to which too much baking powder had been added.

To test sour cream, I used one tablespoon sour cream diluted in two tablespoons water. Both the taste and texture were excellent, but still no better than the Master Recipe. I tried substituting one tablespoon of apple cider vinegar for one tablespoon of the water since acids often produce more tender baked products, but this gave a strong unpleasant aroma and flavor. The original version, using only water as the liquid, is best.

Preparation Techniques
For years, I had clung to the old methods of making pastry dough. I either cut in the shortening with a hand-held pastry blender (a D-shaped device consisting of a straight handle with a set of stiff wires or thin blades bowed from one end to the other) or I did it by hand, rubbing in the shortening with my fingers. But the results were inconsistent. I was finally converted to the food processor method when my wife, with lit-

tle experience, picked up a processor recipe and proceeded to crank out terrific pie crust. However, the food processor can easily overblend ingredients, so a precise set of instructions is still important.

After much testing, I settled on processing the butter and flour for five one-second pulses, then adding Crisco and pulsing an additional four times. To see how much difference the proper mixing makes, I also made one crust using only three and then two pulses, and one using five and then four pulses followed by twenty seconds of continued processing. The under-mixed crust shrank when baked and was hard and crackly and not consistent in texture, remarkably similar to the first pie crusts I made twenty years ago. The over-processed crust was very short and cookielike.

I also tested the effect of using different tools to mix the water into the flour and fat. I tried a food processor, a fork, a whisk, and a rubber spatula. The food processor produced good results, but was a bit hard to control.

While I was in the processing mode, I also tried adding hot water to the mixture and processing it until a ball formed (which happened almost instantly). The resulting crust was too dense. As a final test, I purposely added too much water, five tablespoons. Although the crust rolled out nicely, when baked it was heavy, gluey, tough, and damp.

Using a fork to mix in the water required an additional tablespoon of water (for a total of four tablespoons), and the result was too soft and not as flaky as the Master Recipe. The whisk proved to be entirely the wrong tool for the job — the dough clumped together and became overworked. A spatula turned out to be the ideal tool. The water is mixed into the dough with a "folding" motion, and then the mixture is pressed together with the broad side of the spatula. The folding action exposes all of the dough to moisture without overworking it, thus minimizing the water used (the less water used, the tenderer the dough) and reducing the likelihood that the dough will be overworked.

Also, since a spatula is larger, it is easier on the dough than a fork. This technique is by far the best, especially for a novice baker.

Letting The Dough Rest
Many bakers argue that allowing the dough to rest permits the gluten to relax. This is not true. A good pie pastry has very little gluten, because the ingredients are handled so gingerly. Resting, however, does provide time for complete hydration. If dough is rolled out immediately after mixing, some parts of it will be wetter than others. Proper resting lets the moisture distribute evenly throughout the dough.

Some recipes claim that pie dough must rest overnight in the refrigerator. Other cooks go ahead and roll out the dough after just a few minutes. I tested resting times of 15, 30, 45, 60, and 120 minutes in the refrigerator, as well 15 minutes in the freezer. A rest time of 30 minutes worked best. In fact, a long stay in the refrigerator can be a problem. The dough gets so cold that it must warm up before rolling. I tested this by refrigerating a batch of dough overnight. The next morning the center of the dough registered fifty degrees. After 45 minutes at room temperature, the internal temperature had risen to only fifty-eight degrees. This compares to an internal temperature of sixty-eight degrees for dough made in a seventy-five-degree kitchen and allowed to rest in the refrigerator for only 30

SEARCHING FOR A BETTER CRUST	
THE TEST	**THE RESULT**
All butter	Great flavor, good texture
All Crisco	Great texture, bland flavor
6 tablespoons butter, 4 tablespoons Crisco	Great flavor *and* great texture
Buttermilk instead of water	No change in flavor, texture suffers
1 tablespoon sour cream, 2 tablespoons water	Great taste and texture but not better than Master Recipe
Substitute cornstarch for 1/3 cup flour	Crust too short and cookielike
Use pastry flour	Less flaky, heavier crust
Under-mix shortening	Crust hard and crackly
Over-mix shortening	Crust too short and cookielike
Too much water	Crust heavy, gluey, and tough
Let dough rest overnight in refrigerator	Must warm up 1 hour before rolling
Let dough rest 30 minutes	Perfect, can roll immediately
Use hot instead of cold water	Soft, crackly, cookielike crust
4 tablespoons canola oil instead of shortening	Tough crust, off-flavor
Vegetable oil and milk instead of shortening and water	Oily, sticky, could not roll out; mealy, crumbly texture
Pillsbury All-Ready Pie Crust	Inedible; rancid, industrial taste

minutes. If you do allow the dough to rest in a refrigerator overnight, be sure to let it warm up before rolling. I suggest one hour.

The Winning Recipe

After testing thirty-five different recipes, I understand the very specific culinary niche that pie pastry fills. First and foremost, pie pastry is a container for a filling: usually a custard or fruit. It must therefore be strong enough to hold together, unlike a cookie or a biscuit. So avoid recipes that use oil instead of shortening and soft flours instead of all-purpose flours. Next, a good pie pastry needs flavor. To get this, it needs a good proportion of butter and/or lard and an adequate amount of salt and (for a dessert pie) sugar. Using the minimum amount of water is also crucial, because too much water makes for tough dough. The shortening needs to be cut in, but over-processing produces a short, cookielike result. Flakiness results from small bits of shortening remaining intact so that steam can form during baking. Under-processing, however, will create a tough dough, because the flour is not properly coated with fat. Also note that this recipe uses a high proportion of fat to flour (about 1:2, whereas some recipes use as little as 1:5), which is crucial to a tender dough. Here, then, is a precise Master Recipe for pie pastry.

As a final note, I pass along the major surprise from our days of kitchen tests. In one of our tastings, one crust came out a bit overbaked (it was a very dark brown) but with a wonderful flavor — buttery, rich, complex, and mature. By comparison, the others tasted young and undeveloped. This is due to the Maillard reaction commonly known as brown-

---

HEALTHY INEDIBLE CRUST

I eat my share of basmati rice and green vegetables, but I am quick to anger when the health police get their oven mitts on a classic recipe and try to make it healthy. It rarely works. As Oscar Wilde quipped about fox hunting (and I think this applies nicely to the current pack of culinary revisionists), it's the "unspeakable in pursuit of the inedible."

I now see "healthy" recipes for pie pastry that use canola oil in place of butter or vegetable shortening. I copied one such recipe out of a recently published cookbook and gave it a try. Although edible, the taste was off and the crust was tough and cookielike. You need butter or lard for flavor and texture. Another interesting variation that cropped up in more than one cookbook is a "pat-in-the-pan" pie crust recipe that uses vegetable oil (some also add milk) in place of butter and water. This recipe is very oily and therefore you cannot roll it out. It must be pressed into the pie tin. The result was mealy and crumbly.

THE BEST APPLE PIE

Serves 8

For this pie, baker Stephen Schmidt chooses slightly tart Granny Smith apples and macerates them in sugar so they shrink slightly before rather than during baking. This step keeps a gap from forming between the top crust and the apples. To keep the bottom crust crisp, he recommends using a glass pan and baking the pie near the bottom of the oven at a relatively hot temperature; this heats the bottom of the pie at a slightly faster rate than the rest, so it cooks through before the top burns.

2½ pounds (5 to 6) Granny Smith apples, peeled, quartered, cored, and cut into ⅜-inch slices (5 to 6 cups)
¾ cup sugar, plus 2 teaspoons for sprinkling on dough top
2 tablespoons all-purpose flour
½ teaspoon ground cinnamon
Pinch of salt
The Best Pie Dough, for a double-crust 8-inch or 9-inch pie (below)
2 tablespoons unsalted butter, cut into small pieces

1. Toss apples and next 4 ingredients in large bowl; let stand until apples soften and shrink a bit, no longer than 10 to 15 minutes.

2. Adjust oven rack to low position and heat oven to 400 degrees. Roll larger dough disk on a lightly floured surface into a 12-inch circle, about ⅛-inch thick. Transfer dough to 9-inch Pyrex pie pan, leaving dough that overhangs lip of pan in place. Turn apple mixture, including juices, into shell; scatter butter pieces over apples.

3. Roll smaller dough disk on a lightly floured surface into a a 10-inch circle. Lay it over top of pie. Trim top and bottom dough edges to ¼ inch beyond pan lip. Tuck this rim of dough underneath itself so that folded edge is flush with pan lip. Flute dough in your own fashion, or press with fork tines to seal. Cut 4 slits at right angles on dough top to allow steam to escape; sprinkle with remaining sugar.

4. Set pie on a rimmed baking sheet; bake until light brown, about 30 minutes. Reduce oven temperature to 350 degrees and continue baking until crust is a rich golden brown and apples can be easily pierced with a knife, about 30 minutes longer. If pie browns before it bakes through, cover top with foil and continue baking. Transfer pie to a wire rack; cool for at least 1 hour before serving. Serve warm with vanilla ice cream. (The pie is best when consumed within a few hours of baking, but can be stored at room temperature, covered by an inverted bowl, for a day or two.)

---

ing. Browning promotes flavor in everything from meats to cookies to waffles. The single most important factor in flavor, therefore, is how much you cook the pie crust. A good pie crust is solid nut brown, not light brown.

THE BEST PIE DOUGH
For an 8- or 9-inch single pie shell

To cut the butter into small bits, halve the stick of butter lengthwise with a large knife, rotate the stick ninety degrees, and cut again. Then cut the stick, crosswise into one-quarter-inch-pieces. Dough should be rolled about one-eighth-inch thick (about the thickness of two quarters).

1¼ cups all-purpose flour
½ teaspoon salt
1 tablespoon sugar
6 tablespoons chilled unsalted butter, cut into ¼-inch pieces
4 tablespoons chilled all-vegetable shortening
3–4 tablespoons ice water

1. Mix flour, salt, and sugar in food processor fitted with steel blade. Scatter butter pieces over flour mixture, tossing to coat butter with a little of flour. Cut butter into flour with five 1-second pulses. Add shortening and continue cutting in until flour is pale yellow and resem-

bles coarse cornmeal with butter bits no larger than small peas, about four more 1-second pulses. Turn mixture into medium bowl.

2. Sprinkle 3 tablespoons of ice water over mixture. With blade of rubber spatula, use folding motion to mix. Press down on dough with broad side of spatula until dough sticks together, adding up to 1 tablespoon more ice water if dough will not come together. Shape dough into ball with your hands, then flatten into 4-inch-wide disc. Dust lightly with flour, wrap in plastic, and refrigerate for 30 minutes before rolling.

For a 10-inch regular or a 9-inch deep-dish single pie shell, follow recipe for The Best Pie Dough, increasing flour by ¼ cup and butter by 2 tablespoons.

For a double-crust 8- or 9-inch pie, follow recipe for The Best Pie Dough, increasing flour to 2¼ cups, salt to 1 teaspoon, sugar to 2 tablespoons, butter to 11 tablespoons, shortening to 7 tablespoons, and ice water to 4 to 5 tablespoons. Divide dough into 2 balls, one slightly larger than the other, before shaping into discs.

For a double-crust 10-inch regular or double-crust 9-inch deep-dish pie, follow above variation, increasing flour by ¼ cup and butter by 2 tablespoons. ■

Pureed is Best for Parsnips

Extensive kitchen testing finds that pureeing is the best use for this often unappreciated root vegetable.

∽ BY SHARON KEBSCHULL BARRETT ∽

Many people ignore parsnips, probably because they look like dirty, anemic carrots. When I started buying parsnips for this article, people stopped me in the supermarket checkout line to ask what they were and how I cooked them. Pounds of parsnips later, I had the answer for those people. Parsnips shouldn't be thought of as a pale version of a carrot. They're sweeter, richer, and more assertive, and should be used in recipes where they can shine. For the most part, this means pureeing them.

To arrive at this culinary understanding, I tried substituting parsnips for mashed or grated potatoes and carrots in cakes, puddings, and breads. The results were disappointing (and expensive). I also tried eating parsnips raw, in salads, and blanched, with a dip. The flavor was bland and texture was unpleasantly chewy. I sautéed them and wished I had used potatoes.

I did find that parsnips responded well to roasting, becoming soft and sweet on the inside and crisp and caramelized on the outside. But in the end, my taste buds led me to understand why most good cooks puree parsnips: They taste best that way.

How to Puree Parsnips

Although many recipes call for boiling parsnips until tender before pureeing them, I found that the best flavor resulted from steaming them whole for about ten minutes and then pureeing. Use small, firm parsnips without dark spots, and with a base of no more than one to one and a quarter inches in diameter. Larger ones have a woody core that takes as long as twenty minutes to cook and offers little flavor. If you get stuck with large ones, cut out this woody core before cooking (*see* illustration).

Unless you truly despise peeling, I recommend you peel parsnips before steaming or boiling. After cooking, the skin will rub off, but a fair amount of flesh comes off with it.

Parsnips were once widely used, but are rarer — and more expensive — today.

Before cooking, quarter large parsnips and cut out the woody cores.

You can puree parsnips with any of the tools you use to mash potatoes. However, since they are not as high in starch as potatoes, they can also be pureed in a food processor without turning into a gummy mess. This is definitely the easiest and quickest method.

Parsnip purees can form the base of both savory and sweet dishes. I've developed two basic recipes. The first is rather neutral. You can use it as is for a side dish, add ginger or garlic and sauté it as pancakes, or substitute it for pumpkin in pie. The second puree, with shallots and stock, has more flavor. It makes a tasty vegetable dish, and can be thinned for a creamy, low fat pasta sauce, or turned into a rich soup.

SIMPLE PUREED PARSNIPS
Serves 4

Since the vegetables are steamed, the flavor of this puree is sweet and intense. The puree can be refrigerated for up to three days. It can also be frozen.

1½ pounds parsnips, peeled, cut into 2½-inch lengths, and halved (or quartered and cored, if necessary)
1½ tablespoons unsalted butter, softened
Salt and ground white pepper

1. Place parsnips in steamer basket in large saucepan with 1 inch of water. Bring water to boil; cover and steam over high heat until parsnips can be easily pierced with thin-bladed knife, about 10 minutes. Reserve cooking liquid.

2. Transfer mixture to food processor fitted with steel blade or to a food mill. Puree, adding reserved cooking liquid (about ¼ cup) to achieve desired consistency. Return puree to skillet and reheat, stirring in butter. Season to taste with salt and pepper.

CREAMY PARSNIP PUREE WITH SHALLOTS
Serves 4

This puree can be served as a side dish with roast pork or roast chicken. It can also be used as a pasta sauce by thinning it with one to one and a quarter cups milk. Toss the sauce with corkscrew pasta and steamed or lightly sautéed vegetables, such as carrots, yellow or red peppers, beets, broccoli, peas, or pearl onions.

1 tablespoon butter
3 shallots, chopped
1 pound parsnips, peeled, cut into 2½-inch lengths, and halved (or quartered and cored, if necessary)
¾ cup vegetable or chicken stock
¼ cup milk, or more to taste
Salt and ground white pepper

1. Heat butter in medium skillet. Add shallots; sauté until softened, about 2 minutes. Add parsnips, toss to coat with butter. Add stock; bring to boil. Simmer, partially covered, until parsnips are tender, 10 to 15 minutes.

2. Transfer mixture to food processor fitted with steel blade or to a food mill, then puree. Return puree to skillet to reheat; stir in milk and season to taste with salt and pepper.

ROASTED PARSNIPS

To roast parsnips, follow the method in "How to Roast Root Vegetables" (*Cook's Illustrated*, January/February 1994, page 10): Toss 1 pound of peeled parsnips cut into 2½-inch lengths and halved (or quartered and cored, if necessary) with 1 tablespoon melted butter or oil. Place in a roasting pan large enough to hold them without crowding. Roast at 375 degrees for 30 minutes. Increase temperature to 425 degrees and continue to roast until nicely browned, 15 to 20 minutes longer. ∎

Sharon Kebschull Barrett recently graduated from Peter Kump's New York Cooking School.

Sour Cream Pastry Strudel

In Richard Sax's updated recipe, flaky sour cream pastry evokes old-fashioned strudel dough better than the packaged phyllo favored by modern cooks.

~ BY JACK BISHOP ~

"**M**y grandmother used to roll out strudel dough over a six-foot table," says cookbook author and baking expert Richard Sax. "To work right, it has be stretched thin enough to read newsprint through, but without any tears." Not surprisingly, the dough is notoriously fickle, and working with it makes hand-rolling pasta seem easy by comparison.

Once prepared, the paper-thin dough is brushed with plenty of melted butter, then filled and rolled into a tight log to create the layering effect in baked strudel. The whole process takes several hours and is fraught with potential pitfalls.

Given the dexterity and patience required to make homemade strudel dough, modern cooks (both amateurs and professionals) have turned to commercially produced phyllo as an alternative. While these thin sheets have the flakiness of real strudel dough, they lack the tenderness and flavor. "Phyllo is little more than a crisp wrapper," notes Sax. The best praise he can muster for it is "acceptable."

What may seem like a hopeless task — approximating the rich, buttery, homemade flavor and flaky texture of traditional strudel without the back-breaking work — is just the sort of baking project that appeals to Sax, who has made a career out of breathing new life into old-fashioned desserts. His latest book, *Classic Home Desserts* (Chapters, 1994), is a collection of 350 recipes, some with roots dating back to Medieval times. Many are presented with only minor modifications for modern tastes. Others, like this strudel recipe, have been retooled in his New York kitchen.

Sour Cream as Star

"I wanted a dough with some of the flakiness of real strudel, but one that would be more tender and easier to work with," says Sax. Part of the answer, he discovered, was sour cream. The acid in sour cream takes the place of the lemon juice in traditional strudel and promotes tenderness by slowing gluten formation in the flour. It also adds a wonderful flavor.

With flavor and texture assured, Sax turned to the issue of flakiness. First, he supplemented chilled butter with shortening. The principle here is the same as with any pastry: a small amount of shortening, which is 100-percent fat, boosts flakiness, while butter is used for flavor.

After the dough has been formed, two quick turns increase flakiness. "Unlike puff pastry, these turns are done without chilling the dough first," explains Sax. "Folding and turning is very easy and really makes a difference. It can be done on any pastry or pie crust to give it a better flake." In this recipe, the turns create more layers, much like rolling a long sheet of traditional strudel dough does.

While Sax's sour cream pastry may not be quite as flaky as strudel dough or phyllo, it is much more durable. Traditional strudel dough often tears during the long stretching process. In addition, once it is baked, it can never be rewarmed. Sax's sour cream pastry, on the other hand, is quite forgiving and even stands reheating and serving several hours after baking. "Because of all the fat and sour cream, the dough is pretty sturdy. But you still should not work it more than necessary," he cautions.

Updated Mincemeat Filling

The filling is a takeoff on the classic poor folks' mincemeat. "In many old cookbooks, all-fruit mincemeat was given as a less expensive alternative to the traditional meat-based filling," says Sax, who combs libraries for rare cookbook manuscripts. "Here, I have combined several dried fruits with fresh pears to give the filling a lighter texture." Crumbled gingersnaps bind the filling and reinforce the Old World character of this strudel.

Sax's final touch is crème anglaise. In this case, the vanilla custard sauce is flavored with pear brandy and provides a rich, cool contrast to the warm strudel.

PEAR AND DRIED FRUIT STRUDEL
Serves 12

Sax chooses to moisten the dried fruit in the filling with clear pear brandy (*see* Sources and Resources, page 32), but regular brandy or dark rum can be substituted. Serve the strudel warm. (It can be baked several hours in advance and reheated in the oven for a few minutes, if desired.) Lay slices in a small pool of chilled pear brandy custard sauce.

Richard Sax has drawn on a number of old-fashioned recipes to create a thoroughly modern, no-fuss strudel with a decidedly Old World flavor.

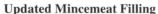

Sour Cream Flaky Pastry Dough
- 3 cups all-purpose flour
- 3 tablespoons sugar
- ½ teaspoon salt
- ½ pound (2 sticks) chilled unsalted butter, cut into ¼-inch pieces
- ¼ cup chilled solid vegetable shortening, cut in pieces
- ¼ cup sour cream

Pear and Dried Fruit Filling
- ¾ cup golden raisins
- ⅔ cup chopped pitted prunes
- ⅔ cup chopped pitted dates
- ½ cup dried currants
- 2 tablespoons grated zest from 1 orange
- 1 tablespoon grated zest and 1 tablespoon juice from 1 lemon
- ⅓ cup *poire eau-de-vie* (pear brandy), other brandy, or dark rum
- 2 large firm, ripe pears (about 1¼ pounds), peeled and cut into ½-inch dice
- 2 tablespoons honey
- 3 gingersnaps, coarsely crumbled (use 4 if pears are very juicy)

PHOTOGRAPH BY ERIC ROTH

1 teaspoon ground cinnamon
½ teaspoon ground allspice
¼ teaspoon ground cardamom
¼ teaspoon grated nutmeg
  Pinch freshly ground black pepper
1 tablespoon cream or milk
1 tablespoon granulated sugar
  Confectioners' sugar for dusting

1. *For the dough,* mix flour, sugar, and salt in food processor fitted with steel blade. Add butter; pulse 5 times. Add shortening; pulse until butter bits are no larger than small peas and flour resembles cornmeal, about 4 more pulses. Mix sour cream with ⅓ cup cold water; add to flour mixture. Pulse until dough begins to clump, adding more water, 1 teaspoonful at a time, if dough does not start to come together.

2. Gather dough together and transfer to lightly floured surface; turn pastry (*see* illustrations 1 and 2). Wrap folded dough in plastic and chill at least 1 hour. (Can be refrigerated for up to 3 days or frozen for up to 6 weeks.)

3. *For the filling,* combine dried fruits and citrus zests in large bowl. Pour brandy over fruit and stir to combine. Set aside to soak for at least 30 minutes or overnight.

4. Toss lemon juice with pears to prevent browning. Add pears to dried fruit mixture along with honey, gingersnaps, and spices. Stir gently to combine.

5. *To assemble the strudel,* roll out pastry on a lightly floured surface to form a 14-by-16-inch rectangle about ⅛-inch thick. Trim off rough edges. Divide rectangle in half, forming two 14-by-8-inch rectangles. Working with one rectangle at a time, brush short edges lightly with cold water. Spoon half of filling in a narrow strip down center of rectangle, leaving about 2 inches uncovered at short ends (illustration 3).

6. Fold one long side of pastry up and over filling. Brush upper edge lightly with cold water, then bring other side up, overlapping slightly; press gently to seal (illustration 4). With sides of your palms, press filling toward center to keep it compact. Trim off ends of pastry if necessary, leaving about 1½ inches at each end. Bring ends of pastry up and press gently onto top surface.

7. Adjust oven rack to center position and heat oven to 375 degrees. Place a baking sheet covered with parchment next to pastry. Gently ease strudel, seam side down, onto sheet (illustration 6). Repeat process with other strudel, spacing them at least 3 inches apart. Chill briefly while oven preheats.

8. Brush strudels with cream, then sprinkle with granulated sugar. Bake until pastry is golden brown, about 45 minutes. Cool strudels on baking sheet set on a wire rack until no longer hot. (Strudel can be baked up to 3 hours before needed and warmed at serving time.)

9. To serve, dust with confectioners' sugar and cut into 2-inch slices. Place slices on plates and surround with 2 to 3 tablespoons of Pear Brandy Custard Sauce.

PEAR BRANDY CUSTARD SAUCE
Makes 2½ cups

If you have time, steep vanilla beans in hot milk for one hour. Return milk to a simmer when ready to proceed with step 2.

2 cups whole milk
1 vanilla bean, split lengthwise but attached at one end, or 1½ teaspoons vanilla extract
⅓ cup sugar
5 large egg yolks
2 tablespoons *poire eau-de-vie* (pear brandy), other brandy, or dark rum

1. Bring milk, vanilla bean (if using), and a tablespoon or so of the sugar to simmer in heavy saucepan.

2. Whisk egg yolks with remaining sugar to blend. Gradually whisk half of the hot milk into egg mixture. Return mixture to saucepan; reduce heat to low. Cook, stirring constantly with wooden spoon, until custard thickens enough to coat back of spoon, about 7 minutes. Do not boil.

3. Immediately pour custard through a fine sieve into clean mixing bowl. Scrape seeds of vanilla bean into sauce or add vanilla extract; stir in brandy. Put plastic wrap directly onto custard surface to prevent a skin from forming. Cool custard, then refrigerate until well chilled. (Can be refrigerated overnight.) ■

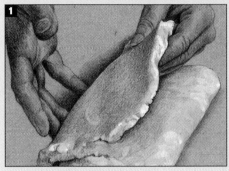

1. Roll rough dough into a twelve-by-eight-inch rectangle. Fold dough in thirds, as if folding a business letter.

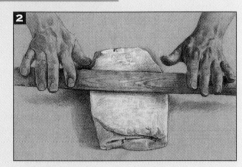

2. Rotate the dough ninety degrees so that an open side is at your right. Roll the dough again into a twelve-by-eight-inch rectangle and fold in thirds.

3. After chilling and rolling out the dough, spoon half of the filling in a narrow strip down the center of each rectangle, leaving about two inches uncovered at the short ends. Bring one long side of pastry up and over filling and brush that side lightly with cold water.

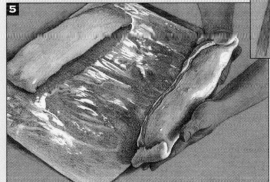

4. Bring the other side up, overlapping the first side slightly, and press it gently to seal.

5. Bring the trimmed ends of the pastry up and press them gently onto the top surface. Gently ease the strudel onto a parchment lined baking sheet, inverting it so that the seam is down.

The Way to Cook Pork Chops

For juicy, tender pork chops, sauté in a covered skillet, listen carefully to the sounds of cooking, and be careful not to overcook.

~ BY STEPHEN SCHMIDT ~

All too often, cooked pork chops turn out tough and dry. You can avoid this by selecting the right type of chop (*see* "Choosing the Best Chop," below), and by choosing the right cooking method. In my view, the best way, hands-down, is to sauté them. However, in the course of preparing this article, I also re-evaluated other cooking methods to be sure I was correct.

First, I once again attempted to broil pork chops. But regardless of how close or far from the heating element they were placed, the chops came out hard and dry. This has always been my experience with broiling pork chops, and I'm now thoroughly convinced that it is simply a bad idea.

Baking the chops uncovered on a flat tray proved little better. The chops did not brown at either low or high oven temperatures, and at the higher temperature they turned leathery.

Then there is braising. Formerly, when pork was more fatty, braising was the cooking method of choice. The long, slow cooking in liquid served to melt out some of the fat, and the fat that remained prevented the pork from being dry, especially when served with a flavorful gravy made from the pan juices. But today's leaner pork does not take well to braising: it simply becomes fibrous and dry. Actually, even old-fashioned fatty pork had a tendency to become fibrous rather than truly tender, though its fat helped to camouflage that.

In truth, pork — or at least pork loin — is inherently unsuited to braising. The purpose of braising is to break down connective tissue. In beef and lamb a good deal of the connective tissue is collagen, which turns to tender gelatin when the meat is cooked in a moist environment. Thus beef and lamb make marvelous pot roasts and stews. But most of the connective tissue in pork loin is elastin, which does not soften when heated. Instead, the meat merely shrinks and stiffens as it cooks, becoming ever more stringy the hotter it gets. To make matters worse, the shrinking and stiffening drive out the juices, and this is especially damaging to pork. Beef and lamb have fat to fall back on, but the juiciness of pork is largely a function of the water it contains. If the water is forced out, there is little pleasure left in eating the meat.

Testing Pre-Cooking Strategies

To test various preparation and sautéing techniques, I bought an entire pork loin and had it cut into twenty inch-thick chops. This way I could be sure that differences in results were caused by the way I handled the chops rather than by the meat itself.

I began by investigating the tenderizing effects of various marinades. In Volume I of *Mastering the Art of French Cooking* (Knopf, 1961), Julia Child recommends a salt-based dry marinade for pork roasts. Since I have long enjoyed great success marinating my pork roasts in this manner, I wondered if the same procedure might also prove beneficial to chops. My tests showed that it does, but there is one hitch. Even though they are much smaller, pork chops, like roasts, must be allowed to marinate for at least two days if the salt is to work its magic. In fact, three to four days proved optimal. A brief marination of an hour or two gave a lovely flavor, but I found it did nothing to improve the tenderness of the meat.

Except in the case of strongly flavored meats such as beef or lamb, I find the taste of acid-based marinades distracting, but I gave them a try. I prepared one marinade with white wine, aromatic vegetables, and herbs; and another with lemon juice and garlic. I poured the marinades into self-sealing plastic bags and added three chops to each. After twelve hours, I cooked one chop from each bag; a day later I

CHOOSING THE BEST CHOP

When buying pork chops, always look for chops that are solidly pink rather than streaked with white — the white is not fat but connective tissue, mostly elastin, which does not break down in cooking. Also be sure to buy chops that are around an inch thick. Years of experience have taught me that thinner chops always become overcooked, and thus hard and dry, no matter how careful you are.

When choosing a particular type of chop, there are five choices, illustrated at right. The two "center-cut" chops, so named because they are taken from the center of the loin, are usually considered the top choices. These two are the center rib chop, which looks like a miniature beef rib, and the center loin chop, which looks like a miniature T-bone or Porterhouse steak.

The cuts you do *not* want are generally from the ends of the loin. The first of these is called the sirloin end chop. Cut from the sirloin, or hip, area, this chop contains a slice of hip bone, and the meat appears broken into bundles.

The second undesirable end cut is the rib end blade chop, which comes from the shoulder. It is easily identified because it contains a section of the long, thin blade bone and also shows many muscle separations.

There is, however, one end cut that you might want to consider, the so-called "rib-end" pork chop. Taken from the part of the rib loin that lies closest to the shoulder, the rib-end chop looks much like a center rib chop, but the rib-eye meat is smaller, as well as coarser, fattier, and darker. Rib-end chops are also less compact and uniform in shape than center-cut rib chops. While rib ends are a little chewy, they also tend to be juicier than center-cut rib chops.

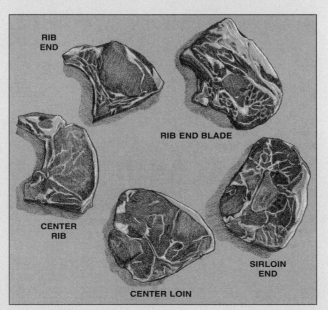

RIB END

RIB END BLADE

CENTER RIB

SIRLOIN END

CENTER LOIN

ILLUSTRATIONS BY TONY DELUZ

cooked one more of each, and three days after putting them in the marinade, I prepared the remaining ones. Predictably, I found that the longer the chops marinated, the more strongly flavored they became, and the less I liked them. The marinades' effect on texture was more complicated. The chops that were marinated for a day or less did not seem appreciably more tender. Those marinated for a full three days struck me as a being a little softer, but they also had a mushy, mealy quality. So I still don't recommend marinating pork.

Someone once told me that freezing pork before cooking yields a more tender final result. I tried this technique twice. My first test followed standard practice: the chops were allowed to thaw slowly before cooking, so as to minimize juice loss. Defrosted in this manner, the chops seemed no more tender than others that I had not frozen. So I ran the test again, this time defrosting the chops in sealed plastic bags immersed in hot water. There was no difference. Freezing is not the answer for pork.

Sautéing Techniques
Having found limited value in all these precooking strategies, I turned to sautéing techniques for my remaining experiments. To say that pork chops belong in a skillet is to tell only part of the story, for they require skillet cooking of a specific kind. First brown the chops over high heat for one minute on each side. When browning is done, cover the chops and cook relatively slowly for about ten minutes more, turning only once.

I also tried cooking chops following this general method but leaving the skillet uncovered, and was surprised by the difference it made. The chops cooked through before the meat around the bones was completely done. Worse still, the chops were tough.

Pork chops will toughen if the cooking temperature is too high or too low, so listen carefully as they sauté. Loud sputtering and hissing indicate that the heat is too high; remove the skillet from the burner for a minute, counting this as part of the cooking time. If cooking noises subside to a bare murmur, turn up the heat a bit, or the chops will poach in their own juices. Fear of illness should not prompt anyone to overcook pork chops: the trichinae parasite is killed at 137 degrees, when the pork is still medium rare. An internal temperature of around 150 degrees is my personal preference. At this temperature the meat, when cut, is ivory in color and reveals a distinct grain, but the juices still run pale pink. If you are unalterably opposed to pinkish pork juices, you can cook the chops a minute or two longer, bringing the internal temperature to around 160 degrees, but you will find that the meat is markedly drier and harder when cooked to this point.

It is impractical to use a meat thermometer with chops and other thin cuts, so you need to gauge the approximate internal temperature by other means. I press on the chops. When they feel firm but not hard, they are done to my taste. If the chops still feel a little squishy, particularly near the bone, at the end of the cooking time, or if you prefer them done to the point where the juices run clear, cook them another minute or two until the juices begin to collect on top of the chops and spill into the pan. At this point, the temperature is nearing the 160-degree mark. Don't cook beyond this point, or the meat will surely be tough.

MASTER RECIPE FOR SAUTÉED PORK CHOPS WITH WHITE WINE PAN SAUCE
Serves 4

- 4   1-inch-thick center loin or center rib pork chops (about 2 pounds), patted dry with paper towels
- ½   teaspoon salt
- ½   teaspoon ground black pepper
- 1   tablespoon unsalted butter
- 1   tablespoon vegetable oil
- 2   large shallots, minced (¼ cup)
- 1   medium clove garlic, minced
- ⅓   cup dry white wine or ¼ cup dry vermouth
- ½   cup chicken stock or low-salt canned broth
- 2–3   tablespoons unsalted butter, cut into pieces and softened
- 1   small wedge lemon

1. Season pork chops with salt and pepper. Melt 1 tablespoon butter in a 10- to 12-inch skillet over a strong medium-high heat. Add oil; swirl skillet occasionally until fat turns nut brown and just begins to smoke.

2. Lay pork chops in skillet, bony side facing toward center of skillet; sauté until browned on one side, about 1 minute. Turn chops with tongs and sauté until browned on other side, about 1 minute. Reduce heat to medium; cover and cook chops 4 minutes. Turn chops; cover and cook until firm but not hard when pressed with a finger, about 5 minutes longer. Transfer chops to a plate; set aside in a warm spot while preparing sauce.

3. Spoon all but 1 tablespoon of fat from skillet. Add shallots; sauté until softened, about 1 minute. Add garlic; sauté until fragrant, about 30 seconds. Add wine; boil until reduced by half, about 1 minute, scraping skillet with wooden spoon to dislodge browned bits. Pour in stock and accumulated juices from around chops; boil to a thin syrupy texture (about ⅓ cup), 2 to 3 minutes. Off heat, scatter butter pieces over sauce; swirl skillet until butter melts and sauce thickens slightly. Squeeze a few drops of lemon juice over sauce and swirl in. Adjust seasonings. Spoon over chops and serve.

SAUTÉED PORK CHOPS WITH MUSTARD AND CAPERS
Serves 4
Follow Master Recipe, making the following change: In step 3, reduce stock and accumulated juices to about ¼ cup and whisk in 2 tablespoons Dijon mustard and 2 tablespoons drained *small* capers. Continue with Master Recipe from that point.

MIXED HERB AND SPICE RUB FOR SAUTÉED PORK CHOPS
Enough for 4 pork chops
This mixture can be used with the Master Recipe or with the Sautéed Pork Chops with Mustard and Capers above. Let rubbed chops stand, loosely covered, at room temperature 2 to 3 hours for a pleasant herb flavor. If sealed in a plastic bag and refrigerated for 2 to 4 days, the chops will become tender as well.

Grind to a fine powder in a coffee or spice grinder ¾ teaspoon *each* dried leaf thyme, dried rosemary, and black or white peppercorns, one 2-inch bay leaf, broken up, 1 whole clove or allspice berry, and, if you wish, 2 juniper berries. Mix in ¾ teaspoon salt. Thoroughly dry chops, then rub spice mixture onto both sides. Before cooking, scrape off marinade and dry chops again. Do not add salt or pepper.

SAUTÉED PORK CHOPS WITH PINEAPPLE SALSA
Serves 4
Follow Master Recipe, making the following changes: In step 1, mix salt and pepper with 1 teaspoon ground cinnamon and ½ teaspoon ground cumin. Rub mixture over chops. Cover loosely, let stand up to 2 hours at room temperature, then proceed with Master Recipe.

Instead of making the sauce outlined in the Master Recipe, pour all fat from skillet. Add ⅓ cup dark rum; boil until reduced by half. Add ⅓ cup chicken broth and accumulated juices; boil to a thin, syrupy texture. Add 1 teaspoon sugar, and cook until dissolved. Spoon the sauce over chops; serve with Pineapple Salsa.

PINEAPPLE SALSA

- ¼   small pineapple, peeled, cored, and cut in ⅜–inch dice (about 1¼ cups)
- 1   medium-size barely ripe banana, peeled and cut in ⅜–inch dice (about ½ cup)
- 4   teaspoons juice from 1 lime
- 1   jalapeño, seeded and minced
- 1   teaspoon minced fresh oregano leaves
- ½   cup seedless green grapes, halved or quartered
- ½   firm avocado, peeled and cut in ⅜-inch dice (about ½ cup)
      Salt

Mix all ingredients including salt to taste; let stand 30 minutes to 1 hour at room temperature. (Bananas and avocados will darken if salsa is prepared much further ahead.) ■

Stephen Schmidt is the author of *Master Recipes* (Ballantine, 1987).

How to Make Asian Dumplings

Match two wrappers with three fillings, eight shapes, and four cooking methods for dozens of flavorful Asian-style dumplings.

~ BY NICOLE ROUTHIER ~

For best texture, add boiling broth to dumplings that have been sautéed until just browned.

Dumpling wrappers can be used to wrap any number of fillings for quick Asian dumplings. Usually, the first question is: Commercial or homemade? Fresh homemade wrappers and dried commercial versions are analogous to fresh and dried Italian pastas: There is no reason to think of commercial dumpling wrappers as second-rate. They let you spend your time preparing special fillings and sauces — where the extra effort really pays off.

The main advantage of commercial wrappers is that they are moisture-free and can be combined with almost any cooking method. In addition, these dried sheets are infinitely easier to work with than homemade wrappers which, because they are moist, often are sticky during rolling and can cook up gummy or mushy.

Two types of wrappers are readily available in supermarkets and Asian food stores. Wonton wrappers (also called skins) are delicate and paper-thin, usually about a thirty-second of an inch thick. They typically come in three-inch squares and are made from flour, eggs, and salt. These wrappers, which are Chinese in origin, are suitable for boiling, steaming, deep-frying, and pan-frying. They are sold fresh and can be

frozen for up to two months if not used within a week. (If you decide to freeze them, do so in small batches since they cannot be separated from each other until completely thawed, and once thawed, do not take well to refreezing.)

Round gyoza wrappers, also called potsticker skins, are usually about three and a half inches in diameter, and are made from flour, salt, and water, without the eggs used in wonton skins. These Japanese dumpling wrappers are slightly thicker and more resilient than wonton skins. Gyoza wrappers tend to dry out and harden when steamed, but can be used in recipes where dumplings will be boiled, deep-fried, or pan-fried. As with wonton skins, fresh gyoza skins can be refrigerated for a week or so. Once frozen they can be stored for about two months.

Both wonton and gyoza wrappers vary in quality from brand to brand, with thickness being the most important variable. Look for at least fifty wrappers per pound. Brands with fewer wrappers per pound should be avoided since they will be too thick and may taste doughy.

Basic Cooking Methods
Since these wrappers contain little or no fat, dumplings made with them should be cooked using moist heat methods such as steaming, boiling, or frying. (If baked, grilled, or stir-fried, they become extremely dry and unpalatable.) Each of the recommended cooking methods will yield a different result, especially in terms of the final texture of the wrappers.

Boiling in a large quantity of water allows the wrappers to absorb plenty of moisture and expand as they cook. It also keeps the exterior especially moist and tender and is the best choice if dumplings will eventually be floated in a bowl of soup. When boiling, make sure to seal the dumplings securely. Since boiled dumplings will invariably become a bit watery

no matter how tightly sealed, season the filling especially well.

Steaming yields moist but resilient dumplings with chewy skins. Unlike boiling, it does not dilute the flavors in the filling and is a good choice for protecting delicate ingredients. As an added bonus, the nutritional value is retained, since vitamins and minerals are not dissolved away.

As a third alternative, dumplings can be completely submerged in hot oil. A temperature of 350 degrees is best. Deep-frying yields crisp, tasty dumplings with an appealing golden color. And because fried dumplings brown, they develop a natural sweetness from the caramelization of sugars — a phenomenon that does not, of course, occur in steamed or boiled versions.

Somewhere between frying and steaming is pan-frying, a popular means of cooking potstickers because it combines two methods and retains the advantages of both. The dumplings are first browned in hot oil in a skillet and then steamed to tenderness. Pan-fried dumplings, which must have at least one flat side for browning, combine crispy and chewy textures, plus the rich flavor associated with browning.

Dumplings, with their rather bland dough wrappers, benefit from tangy and savory dipping sauces. Two examples of all-purpose sauces are found below. Either can be paired with any of the fillings or dumpling shapes.

Use the following fillings in one or more of the dumpling shapes outlined on pages 16 and 17. Refer to "Four Cooking Methods" on page 15. Serve with dipping sauce. All fillings may be made one day in advance.

SHRIMP FILLING WITH GINGER AND SESAME
Makes about 1½ cups, enough for 32 dumplings or 16 shao mai

- 6 ounces shelled raw shrimp, coarsely chopped
- 2 ounces ground pork
- 6 peeled water chestnuts (fresh or canned), minced
- 1½ teaspoons finely grated fresh ginger
- 1½ teaspoons dry sherry or vermouth
- 1½ teaspoons cornstarch
- 2 teaspoons oyster sauce
- 1 teaspoon sesame oil
- ½ large egg white, lightly beaten
- ½ teaspoon sugar

Any filling can be used in these dumplings, but the best cooking method to use depends on the type of wrapper.

¼ teaspoon salt
   Ground black pepper to taste
2 tablespoons minced greens
   from 2 medium scallions

Mix all ingredients in medium bowl; let stand about 30 minutes. Refrigerate until ready to make dumplings.

CURRIED CHICKEN FILLING WITH CARROTS AND BASIL
Makes about 1½ cups, enough for 32 dumplings or 16 shao mai

If red curry paste is unavailable, increase curry powder to one and a half teaspoons and add a pinch of cayenne pepper. *See* Sources and Resources, page 32, for mail-order sources for Asian ingredients.

1 tablespoon vegetable oil
1 small onion, minced (½ cup)
1 small celery stalk, minced (¼ cup)
1 small clove garlic, minced (at least ½ teaspoon)
2 medium carrots, shredded (about 1 cup)
½ teaspoon Thai red curry paste
3 tablespoons unsweetened coconut milk
6 ounces ground chicken
2 teaspoons fish sauce
½ teaspoon curry powder
2 tablespoons shredded fresh basil leaves

1. Heat oil in large skillet. Add onions, celery, and garlic; sauté until almost softened, about 3 minutes. Add carrots; sauté until vegetables soften, about 2 minutes longer. Add curry paste and coconut milk; cook over medium-high heat, stirring to incorporate curry paste, until most of coconut milk has been ab-

sorbed. Transfer vegetable mixture to a bowl; cool to room temperature.

2. Mix in remaining ingredients. Let stand about 30 minutes. Refrigerate until ready to make dumplings.

SESAME BEEF AND CABBAGE FILLING
Makes about 1½ cups, enough for 32 dumplings or 16 shao mai

¼ small Napa cabbage, finely shredded (about 2 cups)
1 teaspoon salt
4 ounces ground beef
1 medium scallion or shallot, minced (about 2 tablespoons)
1 medium clove garlic, minced (1 teaspoon)
1 tablespoon soy sauce
2 teaspoons sesame seeds, toasted
2 teaspoons sesame oil
   Pinch cayenne pepper (optional)

Toss cabbage and salt together in colander; let stand until cabbage wilts, 15 to 20 minutes. Rinse cabbage; squeeze dry. Mix cabbage with remaining ingredients. Refrigerate until ready to make dumplings.

CHILE DIPPING SAUCE
Makes 1 cup

½ cup unseasoned rice vinegar or distilled white vinegar
¼ cup plus 2 teaspoons light brown sugar
2 medium cloves garlic, minced (at least 1 teaspoon)
¼ cup fish sauce

2 teaspoons Thai hot sauce (sriracha sauce), or 1 teaspoon crushed dried red chile pepper

Bring vinegar and sugar to boil in small saucepan, stirring briefly, until sugar dissolves. Pour into bowl; stir in garlic, fish sauce, and hot sauce. Can be covered and refrigerated overnight.

SOY-GINGER DIPPING SAUCE
Makes 1 cup

¼ cup soy sauce
¼ cup unseasoned rice vinegar
2½ teaspoons sugar
½ medium scallion, minced
2 teaspoons finely shredded fresh ginger
½ teaspoon sesame oil
½ teaspoon chile oil

Bring soy sauce, vinegar, sugar, and ¼ cup water to boil over medium heat, stirring briefly, until sugar dissolves. Pour into bowl; stir in scallion, ginger, and sesame and chile oils. Can be covered and refrigerated overnight. ∎

Nicole Routhier is the author of *Cooking Under Wraps* (William Morrow, 1993).

FOUR COOKING METHODS

With all of the methods that follow, cook the dumplings in small batches to avoid overcrowding the pan and to ensure proper cooking. Serve dumplings as soon after cooking as possible, with dipping sauces passed separately.

To pan-fry dumplings: Bring ½ cup water or chicken broth to simmer in small saucepan. Meanwhile, heat 2 tablespoons vegetable oil in large skillet over medium-high heat. When oil is hot and hazy, add dumplings, flat sides down. Fry until bottoms are brown, about 2 minutes. Add simmering broth to skillet, pouring around dump-

lings. Cover and cook until liquid is absorbed, about 3 minutes longer. Uncover and let dumplings fry until bottoms are crisp again, about 1 minute.

To deep-fry dumplings: Heat 2 to 3 inches vegetable oil to 350 degrees in wok or heavy skillet. Add dumplings, a few at a time, and fry until golden, about 2 minutes. Remove with slotted spoon and drain on wire rack set over jelly-roll pan. Keep warm in 200-degree oven while frying remaining dumplings.

To boil dumplings: Bring 4 quarts water to boil; add 1

tablespoon salt and dumplings. Reduce heat to medium; simmer, uncovered, until filling is cooked through, 2 to 3 minutes. Remove dumplings with slotted spoon. Serve with dipping sauces or drop into hot broth.

To steam dumplings: Grease a collapsible steamer basket (cooking spray works best). Fill large soup kettle with enough water to come to bottom of basket. Bring to simmer over medium-low heat; lower basket into kettle. Arrange dumplings ½-inch apart in basket. Increase heat to high; cover and steam until dumplings are cooked through, about 5 minutes.

Shaping and Filling Asian Dumplings

Shao mai, wonton shapes, and pyramids should be made with square wonton wrappers. Potstickers, mandus, and pel'menis can be made with round gyoza or with square wonton wrappers that have been cut into rounds (*see* Shao Mai, illustration 1). Choose any of the fillings on pages 14 and 15 and serve with either of the dipping sauces. *See* "Four Cooking Methods," page 15, for detailed cooking instructions.

SHAO MAI

1. Use a cookie cutter to make square wonton skins round.

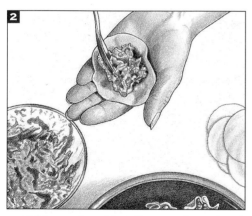

2. Hold a wonton skin in the cup of your hand; place two rounded teaspoons of filling in the center.

3. Cup your hand around the wonton skin, gathering folds up around the filling. Press the gathered folds lightly around the filling to adhere, forming a cup-shaped dumpling. Top with a fresh pea, if desired. Proceed with steaming.

TORTELLINI-SHAPED WONTONS

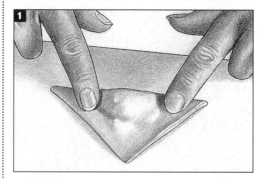

1. Position a square wonton wrapper with one point facing you. Place one rounded teaspoon of filling in the center. Fold the wrapper in half to form a triangle.

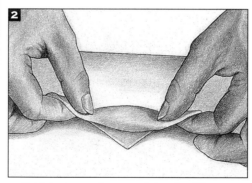

2. Fold the long edge containing the filling over, leaving the top of the triangle exposed about a half inch.

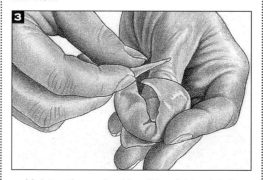

3. Moisten the underside of the right point, then bring the two points together, right over left, to overlap away from the tip of the triangle. Pinch the points together to seal the dumpling. Proceed with boiling, steaming, or deep-frying.

PURSE-SHAPED WONTONS

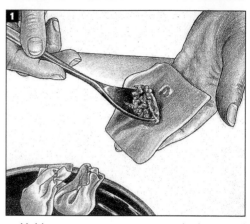

1. Hold a square wonton wrapper in the cup of your hand. Take one rounded teaspoon of filling, and place the spoon slightly off-center on the wrapper.

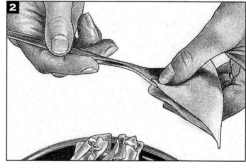

2. With your thumb, fold one side of the wonton wrapper over the filled spoon.

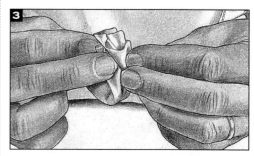

3. Trap the filling inside the wrapper between your thumb and index finger, gently remove the spoon, and seal the wonton by pinching the wrapper together. Proceed with boiling, steaming, or deep-frying.

ILLUSTRATIONS BY WENDY WRAY

PYRAMIDS

1. Place two level teaspoons of filling in the center of a square wonton wrapper.

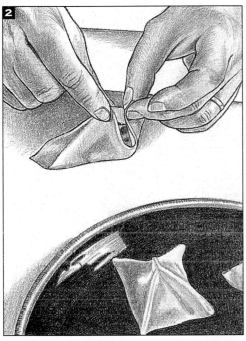

2. Moisten the edges lightly with water. Bring up two opposite corners of the wrapper and join over the filling.

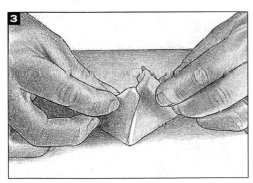

3. Bring up the two other corners and pinch all four together in a point to make a pyramid-shaped parcel. Pinch the seams firmly together to seal. Proceed with pan-frying or steaming.

PLEATED POTSTICKERS

1. Place one teaspoon of filling in the center of a round wrapper. Moisten the edge with water. Holding the filled circle in one hand, pinch the dough shut at one point on one side with the thumb and index finger of your other hand.

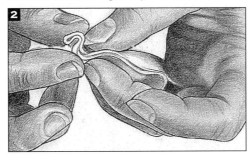

2. Still using that thumb and index finger, continue to pinch the dough to form pleats along the back edge, pressing the pleats against the front edge to seal the dumpling.

3. Pinch the dumpling shut to completely enclose the filling. Proceed with pan-frying or steaming. (Do not steam if made with gyoza wrappers.)

RUFFLED POTSTICKERS

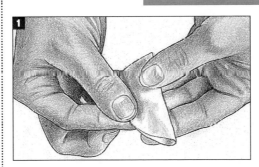

1. Place one rounded teaspoon of filling in the center of a round wrapper. Moisten the edge with water. Fold the wrapper in half, then use your index finger and thumb to pinch the edges together and seal.

MANDU OR PEL'MENI

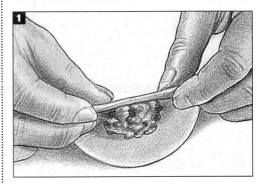

1. *For the mandu*, place one heaping teaspoon of filling in the center of a round wrapper. Fold the wrapper over the filling to form a half-moon shape. Seal edge. Proceed with boiling.

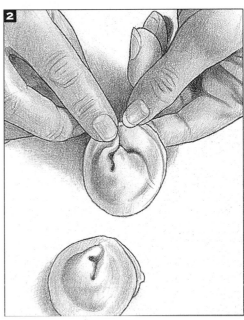

2. *For the pel'meni,* follow step 1, moistening the two corners of the half-moon shaped dough. Bring the corners together, overlapping them a bit. Pinch to seal. Proceed with boiling, deep-frying, or steaming. (Do not steam if made with gyoza wrappers.)

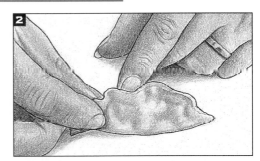

2. Lightly press the filling on the counter to form a flat base. Gather the pinched edges together to form ruffles on the top. Proceed with pan-frying or steaming. (Do not steam if made with gyoza wrappers.)

Quick Homemade Pickles

A master pickling liquid makes dozens of quick pickles without canning.

～ BY KATHERINE ALFORD ～

When making quick pickles, the texture of the vegetable determines the precise process.

Unfortunately, most commercial pickles are either too bland, too sweet, or just plain boring. So I decided to develop a quick method for making pickles that can be stored in the refrigerator and eaten within a day or two, eliminating the rigmarole of canning while keeping the wonderful pickle flavor.

Pickling basically consists of combining vegetables (in this case) with a vinegar-based solution that also contains other liquid, salt, and usually additional flavorings. Sometimes the vegetables are cooked before the pickling liquid is added, sometimes they are cooked in the liquid itself, and sometimes the liquid is simply heated and poured over the uncooked vegetables. In addition, vegetables may be salted before or after they are cooked. I decided to investigate each step systematically.

The Proper Pickling Medium
In traditional pickles, the brine must have at least a 5 percent acidity level to preserve the vegetable. If you eat these pickles right away, they taste excessively sharp and vinegary, so most pickle recipes end with the instructions "store for four to five weeks before eating." This allows the flavors to develop and the acidity to mellow. Since I wasn't trying to preserve vegetables, I didn't need high acidity. My goal was to find a liquid that would duplicate the mellow taste in a short period of time.

I first set out to find the proper vinegar. Vinegars range in acidity from 4 to 7.9 percent, with rice at the low end (4 percent), cider and plain white in the middle (5 percent), and wine vinegars near the upper end (5 to 7 percent for

white wine, 5 to 7.5 percent for red wine). Although this sounds like a small range, the tastes are dramatically different.

In my first round of pickling I tried a wide variety of vinegars on ten different vegetables. Some of the vegetables were soaked in straight vinegars: white, cider, white wine, red wine, or rice vinegar. Other vegetables were pickled in blends of vinegars with water, wine, sugar, and salt.

The results varied dramatically from pleasantly tangy to unpalatably sharp. Rice vinegar contributed a bright acidic taste without an overwhelming pucker, but it was too bland and lacked the complex taste of wine vinegars and fruit vinegars. Pickles made with straight distilled white vinegar, cider vinegar, or wine vinegar, on the other hand, were too acidic and obscured the flavor of the vegetables.

The optimum solution, I decided, would be a blend of mild and sharp vinegars diluted with water. After several more experiments, I came up with the right combination of liquids: three parts rice vinegar to three parts water to one part white wine vinegar. This had just the right mellow pickle taste, and was versatile enough for a wide variety of vegetables.

Salting vs. Cooking
While testing various recipes for the pickling liquid, I also experimented with several ways of preparing the vegetables prior to pickling. Part of the experiment was to examine the role of salt. In traditional pickles, salt has several purposes: it enhances flavor, prevents bacterial growth, and draws moisture from the vegetables to keep them firm and crisp. Because my pickles were destined for quick consumption, I was able to cut back on the amount of salt used in traditional pickling.

I tried all the vegetables both salted and unsalted. I noticed little difference in texture; for example, the cucumbers and fennel stayed crisp whether salted or not. But there was a dramatic difference in taste. In most cases, salting the vegetables made them much tastier, eliminating their raw flavor. But salting is not the answer for all vegetables. Salt did nothing, for example, for cauliflower, green beans, or okra.

I divided the vegetables into two general categories — those whose flavor and/or texture are improved by the addition of salt at the beginning of the process, and those that should be cooked without being salted. Cauliflower, for example, is best when cooked directly in the pickling solution; okra and green beans should be steamed briefly before being covered with

the hot brine; peppers are best when salted and then cooked before pickling.

Seasoning
In seasoning these pickles, the cook has a wide variety of flavorings to choose from. Mustard seeds are used in many pickles, both as a complementary flavor and as a natural preservative. Dill is great with cucumbers and adds a brightness that also complements other vegetables, from green beans to carrots. Coriander and allspice add a rounded sweetness.

Commercial blends of pickling spice vary, but generally are composed of mustard seeds, dill seeds, allspice, cloves, cinnamon, coriander seeds, ginger, black peppercorns, chiles, bay leaves, and cardamom. But in quick pickles, these blends can overwhelm the vegetables. If you use them, be careful when measuring from the jar, since the spices tend to settle apart, with the allspice rising to the top and the mustard and dill falling to the bottom. I prefer to use whole spices because they give a fuller flavor and lack the dusty look of ground spices.

Making your own pickles allows lots of room for improvisation. Add more sugar for sweeter pickles, as in the recipe for bread and butter cucumbers, or add chiles to make them spicy, as in the jicama recipe. The spices I like best are fresh thyme, coriander seeds, celery seeds, ginger, allspice, and cloves. Many different cuisines include pickles — Greek, Indian, Japanese, Chinese, Mexican, Eastern European — and seasoning reflects their traditional flavor combinations. You can change the character of any of these pickles by the flavorings you choose.

All these pickles may be stored in the refrigerator for up to two weeks.

BASIC PICKLING LIQUID
Makes about 2½ cups
To get the right sweet-tart balance, check the label on the white wine vinegar to be sure it has 6 percent acidity.

- 1 cup rice vinegar
- 1 cup water
- ⅓ cup white wine vinegar
- 3 tablespoons sugar
- 2 teaspoons kosher salt

Mix ingredients together. *See* "Quick Pickle Recipes," page 19 for further instructions. ∎

Katherine Alford is an instructor at Peter Kump's New York Cooking School.

PHOTOGRAPH BY ERIC ROTH

To prevent a reaction with the pickling liquid, use nonreactive bowls and pans. Each recipe yields about 1 quart, and all salt used is kosher. All pickles should be cooled to room temperature and refrigerated overnight before eating. They will keep in the refrigerator for up to two weeks.

Type of Pickle	Vegetable Quantity	Vegetable Preparation	Amount Basic Pickling Liquid	Additional Flavorings	Instructions
Pickled Cucumber Spears	4 kirby cucumbers, about 1 pound	Quarter lengthwise, sprinkle with 1 teaspoon salt, let stand in bowl 1 hour. Drain. Transfer to bowl.	1 recipe	2 cloves garlic, peeled and halved; ¼ teaspoon dill seed; 1 small dried or fresh red chile; ¼ teaspoon mustard seed; 1 bay leaf	Bring pickling liquid and flavorings to simmer. Pour over cucumbers.
Bread and Butter Pickles	4 kirby cucumbers, about 1 pound	Slice very thin, sprinkle with 1½ teaspoons salt, let stand in colander 1 hour. Drain. Transfer to bowl.	½ recipe	3 tablespoons sugar; ½ teaspoon mustard seed; ¼ teaspoon celery seed; ¼ teaspoon ground turmeric	Bring pickling liquid and flavorings to simmer. Pour over cucumbers.
Pickled Bell Peppers	1 each red, yellow, and green bell peppers	Cut into ½-inch wide strips, sprinkle with 1½ teaspoons salt, let stand in bowl 1 hour. Drain.	1 recipe	1 tablespoon olive oil; 1 teaspoon cracked coriander seed; 2 chopped cloves garlic; 5 allspice berries; 1 crumbled bay leaf	Heat oil in large sauté pan; add peppers, then flavorings. Sauté to soften slightly, about 1 minute. Add pickling liquid; bring to simmer. Simmer 2 minutes. Transfer to bowl.
Pickled Turnips	1¼ pounds turnips	Peel and julienne, sprinkle with 1½ teaspoons salt, let stand in colander 1 hour. Drain. Transfer to bowl.	1 recipe	6 thin slices ginger; ½ teaspoon Chinese five spice powder; pinch hot red pepper flakes (optional)	Bring pickling liquid and flavorings to simmer. Pour over turnips.
Pickled Purple Onions	3 small purple onions	Peel and cut into 8 wedges, sprinkle with 1 teaspoon salt, let stand in bowl 1 hour. Drain.	1 recipe	¼ teaspoon mustard seed; ¼ teaspoon celery seed; ¼ teaspoon coriander seed; ½ small dried or fresh red chile	Bring pickling liquid, flavorings, and onions to simmer. Simmer onions 5 minutes. Transfer to bowl.
Pickled Fennel	2 small fennel bulbs	Remove stalks and fronds, halve bulbs, slice ¼-inch thick, sprinkle with 1 teaspoon salt. Let stand in bowl 1 hour. Drain. Transfer to bowl.	1 recipe	½ teaspoon fennel seed; 4 black peppercorns; 1-inch strip orange zest	Bring pickling liquid and flavorings to simmer. Pour over fennel.
Pickled Jicama	1 medium jicama (about 1 pound)	Peel and cut into thin wedges, sprinkle with 1½ teaspoons salt, let stand in a bowl 1 hour. Drain. Transfer to bowl.	1 recipe	1 teaspoon cracked coriander seed; 1 jalapeño, seeded and julienned; 4 thin slices ginger	Bring pickling liquid and flavorings to simmer. Pour over jicama.
Pickled Green Beans With Dill	1 pound green beans	Trim. Steam to soften slightly, 2 to 3 minutes. Transfer to bowl.	1 recipe	8 sprigs fresh dill; 1 teaspoon mustard seed; 2 peeled cloves garlic; 1 small dried or fresh red chile (optional)	Bring pickling liquid to simmer. Pour over beans and flavorings.
Pickled Pearl Onions	1 pound pearl onions	Cut X into root end. Bring 2 quarts water to boil. Add onions; boil to soften slightly, about 3 minutes. Refresh under cold water. Peel.	1 recipe	⅓ cup sugar; 1 small dried or fresh red chile; 2 sprigs fresh thyme; ½ teaspoon coriander seed; 2 cloves; 1 bay leaf	Bring pickling liquid, flavorings, and onions to simmer. Simmer until tender, about 3 minutes. Transfer to bowl.
Pickled Curried Cauliflower	1 small head cauliflower	Cut into florets.	1 recipe	2 teaspoons canola oil; 2 teaspoons curry powder; ½ teaspoon cumin seed; 1 teaspoon coriander seed; 1 teaspoon minced ginger; 1 peeled clove garlic; 1 small dried or fresh red chile (optional)	Heat oil in medium skillet; add flavorings. Cook over medium heat 1 minute. Add cauliflower; coat with spices. Add pickling liquid; bring to simmer. Simmer until cauliflower is almost tender, about 5 minutes. Transfer to bowl.
Pickled Okra	¾ pound okra	Steam until almost tender, about 3 minutes. Transfer to bowl.	1 recipe	1 teaspoon packaged pickling spice; 2 peeled cloves garlic	Bring pickling liquid and flavorings to simmer. Pour over okra.

Cooking Tender Greens

For tender greens such as spinach, Swiss chard, and beet greens, a combination of wilting and sautéing yields perfect results.

∽ BY PAM ANDERSON WITH KAREN TACK ∽

Too often, greens are lumped together into one big leaf pile. Cooks use the same set of instructions for stemming, cutting, and cooking this odd mix, even though some of them are delicate enough for salads, while others seem tough as shoe leather.

After cleaning, stemming, and cooking over 100 pounds of greens, we realized that about all they had in common was their color. They couldn't be cooked, or even stemmed, the same way. However, they did split quite naturally into two categories.

Kale and broccoli rabe, as well as mustard, turnip, and collard greens, comprise the tough, strong-flavored greens. Spinach, beet greens, and Swiss chard, on the other hand, belong to the tender greens category. Because the tender greens are moisture-holding succulents, they need no additional liquid during cooking; because their leaves are delicate, they cook quickly; and because they are so mild, tender greens meld easily with other flavors.

Though many greens are available year-round, the tender versus tough categories divide them seasonally too — tough greens are more readily available from late fall to spring, while tender greens are available spring through fall. For this reason, we will focus on tender greens in this issue, and consider the more assertive winter greens in a future issue.

Cleaning Greens

The first step in cooking greens of any sort is cleaning them. The process is tedious, but as anyone who has suffered through a dinner of gritty greens knows, it is essential.

At first we threw gritty greens into a sink of clean water before stemming them, thinking that we should remove as much dirt as soon as possible. We abandoned this method, however, when we realized that working with wet, dirty greens was a cold, messy business.

It was simpler to stem dry greens, then drop them into a sink filled with clean water. Much of the dirt collects along the intersection of leaf and stem, so stem removal is actually another form of cleaning. Usually one or two more rinses — removing the leaves, emptying and refilling the sink, then swishing the leaves around again — makes them skillet-ready.

Not All Greens Stem Alike

After learning this, we investigated the best ways to stem greens. Here we found that mature spinach and beet greens — greens with tougher stems — were best stemmed by holding each leaf between the thumb and index finger of one hand while pulling back the stem with the other hand (*see* illustration 1). Much like an asparagus stalk, tough stems seem to break off naturally just at the point where they are tender enough to eat.

Younger spinach and beet greens, with stems almost as tender as the leaves, need simply to be pinched or snipped where the stem meets the leaf. For ease of stemming, we preferred bunch to loose spinach. We were able to stem a cluster at a time by holding the bunch by the root, leaf-ends down, over a sink filled with clean water. It was then a simple matter to pinch each leaf from its stem (illustration 2), dropping the leaves into the water each time we accumulated a handful.

For Swiss chard we held each leaf at the stem base and used a butcher or boning knife to slash the leaf from either side of the stem (illustration 3).

Wilting Wins

With the greens ready for the pot, we tried four different cooking methods: blanching, steaming, microwaving, and wilting. Although blanching produced the most brilliantly colored greens, it compromised the greens' taste and texture, leaving them mushy and less flavorful than greens cooked by the other methods.

Steaming produced acceptable greens, but required the cook to set up a steamer basket and boil water, unnecessary steps since these greens did not need the added moisture.

Unlike their drier leafy cousins, tender greens can be microwaved successfully, but we found no time savings with this method. One pound of tender greens could be microwaved in five minutes, the same amount of time required for wilting or steaming. If you are microwave-oriented and don't plan to sauté the greens (which would require using a skillet anyway) the microwave is an option, because it is capable of wilting tender greens.

Wilting on the stovetop, however, was the simplest, most straightforward method. We simply tossed the leaves, wet from washing, into a heated sauté pan, covered it, and cooked, stirring occasionally, until the greens were

---

STEMMING TENDER GREENS

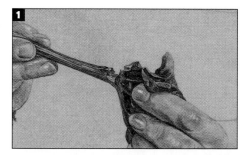

1. Mature spinach and beet greens should be stemmed by holding each leaf pointing down between the thumb and index finger of one hand, while pulling down the stem with the other hand.

2. For bunch spinach, hold a bunch by the root, leaf-ends down, over a sink filled with clean water, then pinch each leaf from its stem.

3. For Swiss chard, hold each leaf at the base of the stem over a sink filled with water, then use a butcher or boning knife to slash the leaves from each side of each stem.

ILLUSTRATIONS BY ANATOLY

wilted by the steam from their own liquid. This was accomplished in only a few minutes. Wilted greens can be used in recipes calling for blanched greens by shocking them in cold water and squeezing out the excess liquid.

When combined with sautéing, wilting becomes even more appealing, because the cook can use both cooking methods almost simultaneously. To do this, heat the oil in the sauté pan, along with spices and aromatics if you like, add the wet greens, cover, and steam until wilted. Once the greens wilt, remove the lid and sauté the greens over high heat until all the liquid evaporates. You may add other flavorings at this point.

MASTER RECIPE FOR WILTED AND SAUTÉED TENDER GREENS
Serves 4

- 3 tablespoons olive oil
- 2 medium cloves garlic, minced
- 2 pounds tender greens such as spinach, beet greens, or Swiss chard, cleaned and prepared following illustrations on page 20
  Salt and ground black pepper
  Lemon wedges (optional)

Heat oil with garlic in large, nonreactive sauté pan or Dutch oven. When garlic sizzles and starts to turn golden, add wet greens. Cover and cook over medium-high heat, stirring occasionally, until greens completely wilt, but are still bright green, about 5 minutes. Uncover, season to taste with salt and pepper. Cook over high heat until liquid evaporates, 2 to 3 minutes longer. Serve immediately, with lemon wedges if desired.

TENDER GREENS WITH INDIAN SPICES
Serves 4

- 2 tablespoons vegetable oil
- 1 small onion, minced
- 2 medium cloves garlic, minced
- 1 teaspoon minced ginger
- ½ medium jalapeño, seeded and minced
- 2 teaspoons curry powder
- ½ teaspoon cumin
- 2 pounds tender greens such as spinach, beet greens, or Swiss chard, cleaned and prepared following illustrations on page 20
  Salt and ground black pepper
- ¼ cup heavy cream
- 2 teaspoons brown sugar

Heat oil in large sauté pan or Dutch oven. Add onion, cook until partially softened, about 1 minute. Add next 5 ingredients; cook until onion softens and spices are fragrant, about 2 minutes longer. Add wet greens and follow wilt/sauté method in Master Recipe. When greens have wilted, season with salt and pepper to taste. When liquid evaporates, add cream

and brown sugar; cook, uncovered, until cream thickens, about 2 minutes longer.

TENDER GREENS WITH CUMIN, TOMATOES, AND CILANTRO
Serves 4

- 3 tablespoons vegetable oil
- 1 small onion, minced
- 2 medium cloves garlic, minced
- ½ medium jalapeño, seeded and minced
- 1½ teaspoons cumin
- 2 large plum tomatoes, seeded and chopped
- 2 pounds tender greens such as spinach, beet greens, or Swiss chard, cleaned and prepared following illustrations on page 20
- 2 tablespoons minced fresh cilantro
  Salt and ground black pepper
  Lime wedges (optional)

Heat oil in large sauté pan or Dutch oven. Add onion; sauté until partially softened, about 1 minute. Add garlic, jalapeño, and cumin; sauté until onion softens, about 2 minutes longer. Add tomatoes; cook until their juices release, about 1 minute. Add wet greens and follow wilt/sauté method in Master Recipe. When greens have wilted, add cilantro plus salt and pepper to taste. Serve immediately, with lime wedges if desired.

TENDER GREENS WITH ASIAN FLAVORINGS
Serves 4

- 2 teaspoons rice wine vinegar
- 2 teaspoons sugar
- 1½ tablespoons soy sauce
- 1 tablespoon sesame oil
- 2 tablespoons vegetable oil
- 2 medium cloves garlic, minced
- ½ teaspoon hot red pepper flakes
- 2 pounds tender greens such as spinach, beet greens, or Swiss chard, cleaned and prepared following illustrations on page 20
- 2 teaspoons toasted sesame seeds

Mix first 4 ingredients together in small bowl; set aside. Heat vegetable oil with garlic and red pepper flakes in large sauté pan or Dutch oven. When garlic sizzles and starts to turn golden, add wet greens and follow wilt/sauté method in Master Recipe. When greens' liquid has almost evaporated, add vinegar mixture. Sauté until vinegar mixture almost evaporates, about 1 minute longer. Serve immediately with toasted sesame seeds.

TENDER GREENS WITH RAISINS AND ALMONDS
Serves 4

- 3 tablespoons olive oil
- 3 medium cloves garlic, minced
- ¼ teaspoon hot red pepper flakes
- ⅓ cup golden raisins
- 2 pounds tender greens such as spinach, beet greens, or Swiss chard, cleaned and prepared following illustrations on page 20
- ½ teaspoon minced lemon zest
  Salt
- 3 tablespoons slivered almonds, toasted

Heat oil with garlic and red pepper flakes in large sauté pan or Dutch oven. When garlic sizzles and starts to turn golden, add raisins and wet greens and follow wilt/sauté method in Master Recipe. When greens have wilted, add zest plus salt to taste. When liquid evaporates, stir in almonds and serve immediately. ∎

INCREDIBLE SHRINKING GREENS

Since greens shrink so dramatically when prepared and cooked, it's hard to know how much to buy when a recipe gives ingredient amounts, such as "2 cups blanched and squeezed spinach." It's equally difficult to calculate how to substitute frozen spinach for fresh. Though based on averages, the following should help you make more accurate guesses.

Yield from 10-ounce package fresh (curly leaf) spinach, pre-rinsed and more or less stemmed:
1½ ounces stems

8½ ounces leaves
8 cups lightly packed leaves
Scant ⅚ cup wilted and lightly squeezed leaves

Yield from 1-pound bundle of flat-leaf spinach:
6 to 7 ounces stems
9 to 10 ounces leaves
8 to 9 cups lightly packed leaves
About 1 cup wilted and lightly squeezed leaves

Yield from 1-pound bundle of Swiss chard:
9 ounces stems (cut into 1-inch pieces equals 4 cups)

7 ounces leaves
6¾ cups lightly packed leaves
1 cup wilted and lightly squeezed greens

Yield from 1-pound bundle of beet greens:
8 ounces stems
8 ounces leaves
7 to 8 cups lightly packed leaves
1 cup wilted and lightly squeezed leaves

Yield from 10-ounce package of frozen spinach:
6¾ ounces or scant 1 cup thawed and lightly squeezed leaves

Vegetable Pasta Sauces

Late-harvest vegetables such as broccoli, zucchini, and bell peppers are transformed into homey pasta sauces using traditional Italian flavors.

~ BY JULIA DELLA CROCE ~

Italians have a long tradition of creating robust pasta sauces out of everyday vegetables. The strength and range of this culinary tradition is reflected in the recipes below, which use a number of techniques to bolster flavor.

In a twist on the common Italian practice of combining beans and greens, escarole and white beans are paired in a simple garlic-laced sauce. Anchovies join broccoli in another of these quick sauces, but rather than simply being added as is, the anchovies are dissolved in hot oil to become an integral part of the sauce. For a simple sauce based on red and yellow bell peppers, the peppers are chopped rather than pureed, so that they retain their distinct colors. Thyme and mint flavor a ratatouille-like sauce.

Whatever the individual ingredients, these vegetable-based sauces make it clear that meat is not necessary for rich, deep flavor.

ZUCCHINI, RED PEPPER, AND TOMATO SAUCE WITH THYME AND MINT
Sauce for 1 pound dried pasta
Serve this ratatouille-like sauce with buckwheat or corn pasta, or with egg noodles. The grainy, nutty flavor of these pastas contrasts beautifully with the soft, sweet vegetables.

- 4 small zucchini (about 1 pound), cut into 1-inch-thick rounds, then sliced thin, lengthwise
- 5 tablespoons olive oil
- 2 large shallots, minced
- 2 large cloves garlic, minced
- 1 medium red bell pepper, stemmed, seeded, and cut into medium dice
- 2 tablespoons minced fresh mint leaves
- 2 teaspoons minced fresh thyme leaves or 1 teaspoon dried thyme
- 2 teaspoon dried green peppercorns, crushed
  Salt
- 2 medium tomatoes (about 12 ounces), peeled, seeded, and sliced thin

1. Bring 2 quarts water to boil in a large saucepan. Add zucchini; blanch for 1 minute, drain, then plunge into cold water to stop the cooking.
2. Heat 3 tablespoons of the oil over low heat. Add shallots and garlic, cook until soft. Increase heat to medium, add peppers, and sauté to soften slightly, 2 to 3 minutes. Stir in the mint, thyme, peppercorns, and salt to taste. Add tomatoes and zucchini; cook until tomatoes release their juices and thicken slightly, 2 to 3 minutes. Remove from heat and stir in remaining 2 tablespoons olive oil. Adjust seasoning. Toss immediately with cooked pasta and serve.

ROASTED RED AND YELLOW PEPPER SAUCE WITH GARLIC
Sauce for 1 pound dried pasta
This sauce is compatible with almost any string or ribbon-type pasta except angel hair, and is particularly nice with *farfalle* ("bowties"). Most macaroni-type pastas are also suitable, except for small *pastine* or the large tubular varieties. Chop the peppers with a knife or *mezzaluna* ("half moon") chopper. Do not use a food processor, because it will puree the peppers, causing them to blend rather than to retain their brilliant red and yellow colors. Toss this at room temperature with hot pasta, using some of the pasta water to thin the sauce.

- 2 medium yellow bell peppers, roasted, peeled, cored, seeded, and chopped fine
- 2 medium red bell peppers, roasted, peeled, cored, seeded, and chopped fine
- 6 tablespoons olive oil
- 1 large clove garlic, minced
  Salt and ground black pepper

Mix peppers with oil and garlic in a bowl. Season with salt and pepper to taste. Cover and set aside to let flavors meld, at least 30 minutes. Toss with cooked pasta and serve or refrigerate sauce for up to 5 days.

ESCAROLE AND WHITE BEAN SAUCE WITH GARLIC AND OREGANO
Sauce for ½ pound dried pasta
Use large *ditali* ("thimbles"), not the small soup-size version of this pasta. Substitute *orecchiette* if ditali is unavailable. Either green from the chicory family can be used in this recipe; escarole is sweeter, curly endive more bitter. Because of the cannellini beans, you only toss this sauce with a half pound of pasta.

- 6 tablespoons olive oil
- 6 medium cloves garlic, minced
- 1 large head escarole or curly endive (about 1 pound), wilted outer leaves removed; remaining leaves cut crosswise into ½-inch strips and rinsed thoroughly; core discarded
- 2 teaspoons minced fresh oregano leaves or 1 teaspoon dried oregano
  Salt and ground black pepper
- 1 can (16 ounces) white cannellini beans, drained and rinsed

Heat oil with garlic over low heat in a large sauté pan. Add greens, increase heat to medium-high, and sauté until completely wilted, 4 to 5 minutes. Add ¾ cup water, oregano, and salt and pepper to taste; cover and simmer to completely cook, about 5 minutes. Add beans; cover and simmer to blend flavors, 3 to 4 minutes longer. Toss immediately with cooked pasta and serve.

BROCCOLI-ANCHOVY SAUCE WITH ZITI
Sauce for 1 pound dried pasta
This dish is a specialty of Apulia, an area in southern Italy. Don't be put off by the anchovies in the sauce. They dissolve completely in the hot olive oil.

- 1 tablespoon salt
- 1 large bunch broccoli (about 1½ pounds), head cut into florets, stems peeled, quartered, and cut into 2-inch lengths
- 1 pound tube pasta, such as ziti, penne, or rigatoni
- 1 can (2 ounces) anchovy fillets, oil reserved
- 6 tablespoons olive oil

1. Bring 4 quarts water to boil in a large soup kettle; add salt, broccoli stems, and pasta, stirring several times to prevent pasta from sticking together. After 5 minutes, add broccoli florets; cook until pasta is al dente, 4 to 5 minutes longer. Drain, leaving some of the cooking water clinging to pasta; transfer to a warm bowl.
2. Meanwhile, heat anchovies, including their oil, and olive oil together until anchovies dissolve, 1 to 2 minutes.
3. Toss the pasta and broccoli with the anchovy sauce. Serve immediately. ∎

Julia della Croce is a writer, cooking teacher, and the author of four cookbooks, including *Pasta Classica, The Pasta Book,* and *Antipasti: The Little Dishes of Italy* (Chronicle, 1993).

Secrets of Butterflied Chicken

Whether grilled, roasted, broiled, or sautéed, a butterflied chicken cooks faster and more evenly than a traditional whole bird.

~ BY PAM ANDERSON WITH KAREN TACK ~

Removing the backbone from a whole chicken — a process known as butterflying — may seem like an unnecessary and time-consuming process. But we have found that this relatively quick and simple procedure, because it leaves the bird a more even thickness, provides many benefits.

A flattened three-pound chicken cooks in half an hour or less, versus forty-five minutes for a traditionally roasted bird. In addition, since the breast isn't sticking out exposed to the heat while the legs are tucked under away from it, all the parts of a flattened bird get done at the same time. Finally, unlike a whole roasted chicken, the butterfly cut is a breeze to separate into sections. One cut down the breast with the kitchen shears, a quick snip of the skin holding the legs, and the job is done (*see* illustrations 8 and 9, page 24).

Won over by the virtues of this technique, we set out to test various methods by which butterflied chicken can be cooked. Our purpose was to work out the kinks in each method and determine if there were some general rules that applied to all of them.

The first question to ask is, where should the chicken be split? Most recipes called for the bird to be split down the back, but a few said to split the breast. Was it necessary to cut slits on either side of the breast for each leg? And did we really need to pound the chicken after we butterflied it, or was it enough to just flatten it with our hands? Was it possible to season the chicken with herbs and garlic without these burning when cooked at high heat?

Did pressing the bird down with a weight provide benefits when sautéing or grilling butterflied chicken? And if weighting was better, what was the simplest way to do it? Most recipes recommended bricks or a large can. But there had to be a better solution than scrounging the basement for dirty bricks or searching the cabinets for ten pounds of cans.

Split Backs, Tuck Legs, Then Pound

We began our research with the butterflying

Butterflying a chicken allows you to use cooking methods, such as grilling, sautéing, and broiling, that are otherwise virtually impossible with a whole bird.

technique itself. To find out if the chicken should be split at the breast or the back, we prepared one each way for roasting. From the start, the breast-split chicken looked unnatural. The back, now the center of the bird, was flanked by two towering chicken breasts. During cooking, the bird bowed and the breasts overshadowed the back which caused the juices to puddle in the middle and prevented the chicken from browning evenly. The bird split down the back was much more attractive; it stayed flat during cooking and browned evenly.

We also discovered that tucking the chicken legs under was worth the effort, if only for visual appeal. This was particularly true for the roasted and broiled chicken, where holding the legs in place with weights was not possible. Chickens cooked with untucked legs tended to bow and warp. In any case, tucking the chicken legs makes the presentation nicer. Even the weighted birds looked more attractive with tucked legs.

We thought pounding the chicken might decrease cooking time, but it made no noticeable

difference. However, it was easier to weight a chicken that had been pounded to a uniform thickness. We also liked the look of the really flattened chicken. We recommend buying a mallet with a flat side for this purpose, but whatever tool you use, make sure it is has a smooth face. A rough-textured mallet will make a mess of things.

Seasoning the outside of the chicken with herbs or garlic, regardless of the cooking method, proved to be pointless. Because each technique required high heat, the herbs charred and the garlic burned. But butterflied chickens are especially easy to season under the skin. Since the backs had been removed, access to the legs and thighs was easy. In fact, stuffing the seasoning under the skin worked beautifully for all the cooking techniques. We included salt and pepper in the seasoning mixture, and also started by adding a bit of oil or butter, but soon realized that this wasn't necessary. The garlic gave the seasoning mixture the pasty quality necessary for easy spreading. And once the cooking process began, there was enough fat from the skin and juice from the meat to moisten and transport the flavorings.

Exploring The Cooking Methods

Roasting is the simplest of the cooking methods for butterflied chicken. Once the chicken is butchered (and rubbed with seasonings, if you like), it goes in the oven, and you can forget about it until it's done.

Many of the recipes for grilling, broiling, and sautéing butterflied chicken were a bit more complicated, calling for turning the chicken several times. If possible, we wanted to turn the bird just once (especially the weighted birds).

Cooking chicken with only one turn in a skillet was a bit tricky. Our first attempts produced skin that was too dark and meat that was too pink near the bone. Two things overcame these problems: First, not heating the skillet too high before putting in the chicken (it has, after all, thirty minutes to brown); and second, reducing the heat from medium-high to a strong

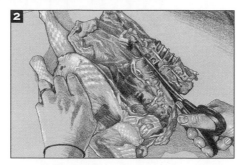

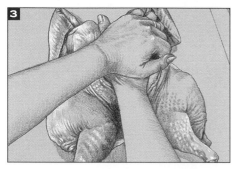

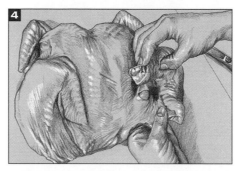

1. With the breast side down and the tail of the chicken facing you, use kitchen shears to cut along one side of the back bone down its entire length.

2. With the breast side still down, turn the neck end to face you and cut along the other side of the backbone and remove it.

3. Turn the chicken breast side up; open the chicken out on the work surface. Use the palm of your hand to flatten it.

4. Make half-inch slits on either side of each breast about one inch from the tip; stick the legs into these openings.

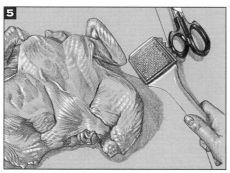

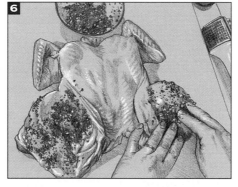

5. Use the smooth face of a mallet to pound the chicken to approximately even thickness.

6. Loosen the skin on each leg and thigh; rub the herb mixture under the skin.

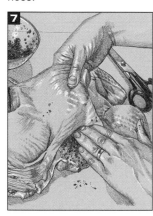

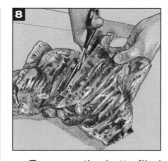

7. Loosen the breast skin; rub the remaining herb mixture under the skin.

8. To carve the butterflied chicken, use kitchen shears to cut along the breastbone. (Since the breastbone is broken and the meat is flattened during pounding, this should be easy.)

9. Once the breast has been split, only the skin holds the portions together. Separate each leg and thigh from each breast and wing.

medium, which allowed the chicken to cook through before it became too brown.

We also decided to explore the effect of weighting the birds during cooking, so we cooked two chickens — one weighted, the other simply covered. The weighted chicken browned more evenly and got done a few minutes faster than the unweighted bird.

But we hated using cans and bricks as weights. Luckily, we ran across a tip in Ed Giobbi's book *Pleasures of the Good Earth* (Knopf, 1991). He recommends using a pot of water to weight the cooking chickens. We found a soup kettle with a diameter slightly smaller than the skillet, covered its bottom with foil to protect it from spattering fat, and filled it with five quarts of water (about ten pounds). Not only was the soup kettle easier to find than bricks or cans, but it was simple to use. When it came time to turn the chicken, we just lifted the pot by its handles, flipped the bird, and returned the pot to its spot.

Unless you have an old pot that you don't mind getting smoke-damaged, you'll have to resort to bricks or stones for grilling. We used a beat-up jelly roll pan and two bricks. Since the chicken was to cook over direct heat, we thought grease fires might be a problem, but we cooked a half dozen chickens this way without a single flare-up. We suspect the combination of the grill lid and the jelly roll pan prevented oxygen from feeding the fire. As with the sautéing, we found that one turn was enough — twelve minutes breast side up, and about fifteen minutes breast side down produced a stunning-looking chicken.

Broiling is another method that took some fine tuning. Our first attempts set off smoke alarms all over the house. After experimenting, we found that the key to good chicken broiling is oven rack position. The chicken must be far enough from the heating element to cook through without burning, which means the top of the chicken must be about eight inches from the heat source (so the oven rack should be about twelve inches away to take into account broiler pan height). As with grilling and sautéing, only one turn is necessary. If you want a bread-crumb or Parmesan cheese coating, though, you do have to give it one more flip to sprinkle them on and brown them.

The following recipes provide an example of each cooking technique, but they're just to get you started. Virtually any grilled, broiled, roasted, or sautéed chicken recipe (excluding boneless, skinless chicken breast) can be tailored to one of these cooking methods. And if you adjust the cooking times, you can even substitute Cornish hens or larger chickens.

GRILLED BUTTERFLIED CHICKEN WITH ROSEMARY, LEMON, AND GARLIC
Serves 4

We tested this recipe several times with a three-pound (gross weight) chicken. Although grilling conditions vary, each time we cooked the chicken, it was done in less than a half hour — twelve minutes on the skin side and twelve to fifteen minutes on the other side. Avoid checking the chicken except when turning, or the coals will cool, increasing the grilling time. Besides, cooking a chicken this way is like grilling a steak — one turn should do it.

    1 teaspoon minced zest from ½ lemon
    1 teaspoon minced fresh rosemary
    1 large clove garlic, minced
    ½ teaspoon salt
    ¼ teaspoon ground black pepper
    1 3-pound chicken, butterflied (see illustrations 1 to 5, page 24)
    3 tablespoons juice from 1 lemon
    3 tablespoons olive oil

    1. Mix lemon zest, rosemary, garlic, salt, and pepper in small bowl. Following illustrations 6 and 7, page 24, rub garlic paste under skin. Place chicken in gallon-size zipper-lock bag with lemon juice and olive oil. Seal and refrigerate from 2 to 24 hours; return to room temperature before cooking.

    2. Light coals for grilling, spread hot coals evenly, and set grill rack in place. Cover and let grill rack heat about 5 minutes. Place chicken, skin side down, on grill rack. Set a jelly roll or other flat pan on top of chicken; put 2 bricks in jelly roll pan (see illustration at far right). Cover and grill until chicken skin is deep browned and shows grill marks, about 12 minutes. Turn chicken with tongs. Replace jelly roll pan, bricks, and grill lid, and continue cooking until chicken juices run clear, about 15 more minutes.

    3. Remove chicken from grill; cover with foil and let rest 10 to 15 minutes. Carve following illustrations 8 and 9, page 24.

BROILED BUTTERFLIED CHICKEN WITH PARMESAN, LEMON, AND RED PEPPER FLAKES
Serves 4

    1 teaspoon minced zest from ½ lemon
    1 large clove garlic, minced
      Salt and ground black pepper
    ¼ teaspoon hot red pepper flakes
    1 3-pound chicken, butterflied (see illustrations 1 to 5, page 24)
    1 teaspoon vegetable oil
    2 tablespoons grated Parmesan cheese
    1 tablespoon dried bread crumbs

    1. Mix lemon zest, garlic, ½ teaspoon salt, and red pepper flakes in small bowl. Following illustrations 6 and 7, page 24, rub this paste under skin. Transfer chicken to broiler pan, skin side up; brush with oil and lightly season with salt and pepper; let stand while broiler heats. Mix cheese and bread crumbs; set aside.

    2. Adjust oven rack so that chicken is no closer than 8 inches from heating element. Broil chicken until skin is rich brown, about 12 minutes. Turn chicken over; continue to broil

To weight grilled butterflied chicken, find an old jelly roll pan or cookie sheet and set it on top of the chicken. Put two bricks on the pan.

To weight sautéed butterflied chicken, cover the bottom of a soup kettle with foil and fill with five quarts of water; set on top of sautéing chicken.

until juices run clear, about 15 minutes longer. Remove from oven, turn skin side up, brush with pan drippings, then sprinkle with cheese mixture. Return to oven; broil until topping turns golden brown, about 3 minutes longer.

    3. Remove chicken from oven, cover with foil, and let rest 10 to 15 minutes. Carve following illustrations 8 and 9, page 24.

SAUTÉED BUTTERFLIED CHICKEN WITH MUSHROOM-SAGE PAN SAUCE
Serves 4

    4 teaspoons minced fresh sage
    1 medium clove garlic, minced
      Salt and ground black pepper
    1 3-pound chicken, butterflied (see illustrations 1 to 5, page 24)
    1 tablespoon vegetable oil
    2 medium shallots, minced
    5 ounces assorted wild mushrooms, sliced (about 2 cups)
    2 tablespoons dry vermouth
    ½ cup chicken stock
    1 tablespoon butter

    1. Mix 2 teaspoons of the sage, the minced garlic, ½ teaspoon salt, and ¼ teaspoon pepper in small bowl. Following illustrations 6 and 7, page 24, rub this paste under skin. Lightly season chicken with salt and pepper. Let stand at room temperature about 15 minutes to allow

flavors to meld.

    2. Heat oil in an 11- or 12-inch sauté pan. Cover bottom of soup kettle that has a diameter slightly smaller than sauté pan with foil and fill with 5 quarts water. Lay chicken, skin side down, in sauté pan. Set kettle on top to hold flat; cook over a strong medium heat until skin is nicely browned, about 12 minutes. Remove soup kettle; turn chicken skin side up. Replace kettle and continue cooking until juices run clear, about 18 minutes. Transfer chicken to plate; cover with foil while making sauce.

    3. Remove all but 1 tablespoon fat from pan; return pan to burner and increase heat to medium-high. Add shallots; sauté until softened, about 2 minutes. Add mushrooms; sauté until juices release and mushrooms soften, about 2 minutes. Add vermouth; cook until liquid has almost evaporated, about 1 minute. Add chicken stock; simmer until thickened, about 2 minutes. Stir in remaining sage. Remove from heat and swirl in butter. Carve chicken following illustrations 8 and 9, page 24. Serve with pan sauce.

ROASTED BUTTERFLIED CHICKEN WITH TARRAGON-MUSTARD PAN SAUCE
Serves 4

Roasting the chicken in an oven-proof sauté pan makes it easier to make a stove-top sauce right in the cooking pan. If you don't have an oven-proof sauté pan, you can substitute a roasting pan, using two burners to make the sauce.

    2 teaspoons minced fresh tarragon leaves
    1 medium clove garlic, minced
      Salt and ground black pepper
    1 3-pound chicken, butterflied (see illustrations 1 to 5, page 24)
    1 teaspoon vegetable oil
    1 cup chicken stock or low-sodium canned broth
    1 tablespoon Dijon mustard
    1 tablespoon softened butter

    1. Mix tarragon, garlic, ½ teaspoon salt, and ¼ teaspoon pepper in small bowl. Following illustrations 6 and 7, page 24, rub this paste under skin. Heat oven to 500 degrees. Transfer chicken to a large oven-proof sauté pan, skin side up; rub with oil and lightly season with salt and pepper. Let stand at room temperature while oven heats.

    2. Roast chicken until skin is nicely browned and juices run clear, about 30 minutes. Transfer to plate, cover with foil, and let rest while making sauce.

    3. Spoon off all fat from sauté pan. Place pan on burner set at medium-high; add stock and simmer until reduced by half, scraping up drippings that have stuck to bottom, 3 to 4 minutes. Whisk in mustard, then swirl in butter. Carve chicken following illustrations 8 and 9, page 24. Serve with pan sauce. ∎

Specialty Chickens Win Tasting

Premium, kosher, organic, and free-range chickens all outperform standard supermarket brands.

∽ BY JACK BISHOP ∽

Let's face it. Chicken has gotten a bad rap lately. While much of the negative press is surely deserved, we wondered if there was some good news about chicken. After all, chicken is now America's number one meat. Per capita annual consumption has doubled in the past twenty years to more than seventy pounds. We would like to think that at least some of this chicken is worth eating.

We were interested, in particular, in birds from smaller operations, many of which employ the animal-raising practices of past generations. While we applaud the principles of the back-to-basics movement, we wondered if you could taste the difference. In other words, is it worth spending the time and money to purchase a specialty chicken? The answer is a thunderous yes.

For this article, we pitted four of the leading supermarket chickens against some of the most widely available premium chickens. The results were extremely consistent. Out of a field of nine, the supermarket chickens took fifth, sixth, eighth, and ninth places. The top four birds were all specialty brands.

Best Sellers, Worst Flavor

Because chicken is so perishable, until fairly recently it was a local product. But during the 1980s, corporate mergers led to consolidation in the business and to the creation of two national brands. Tyson, which recently folded Holly Farms into its operations, and Country Pride, owned by food giant ConAgra, are the nation's largest poultry companies (in the order mentioned). Their chickens are available in almost every state. In our tasting, these birds were joined by Perdue, the largest brand in the East, and Foster Farms, the most popular chicken in California. (Perdue is the fourth largest poultry company in the country; Foster Farms is eighth.)

With the exception of the Foster Farms chicken, the supermarket entries received uniformly negative reviews. Most were so bad, panelists said they would rather swear off chicken than eat these tasteless, rubbery birds.

We don't put much stock in the notion that bigger is better, at least in the poultry business.

So why did specialty chickens dominate our tasting? There are a number of possible answers. Most small companies have invested heavily in livestock gene pool develop-

While many companies freeze and shrink-wrap chickens for shipping, the birds that won our tasting are shipped loose on ice.

ment. Some companies (D'Artagnan and La Belle Rouge) make sure that their birds have access to the outdoors, with freedom to wander a fenced-in area or stay inside as they wish. Most boutique chicken companies rely on better feeds (D'Artagnan uses a certified organic feed) and shy away from antibiotics and growth stimulants (D'Artagnan and La Belle Rouge chickens are raised without them). Other companies point to better processing (La Belle Rouge uses a European air-chilling system that it says reduces bacterial contamination caused by traditional warm-water processing baths; Empire uses cold-water processing and soaks chickens in a salt solution for about one hour to remove much of the blood). And all of these smaller companies "grow out" their birds for eight or nine weeks, instead of slaughtering at six or seven weeks like the industry giants.

The Bell & Evans Story

According to Scott Sechler, president of Bell & Evans, the oldest chicken company in America, many other poultry companies look for the "least-cost formulated diets," which change as market prices for various ingredients fluctuate. By constantly tinkering with the feed to take advantage of changing commodity prices, large poultry companies can keep costs down. However, Sechler is interested in the feed that will produce the best-tasting chickens, not the cheapest. "We have found what we think is the

best feed, and we don't change the formula every week."

Just as important, says Sechler, is the handling after processing. Most large poultry companies pre-package birds before shipping, which supermarkets like because it cuts down on their labor costs. The problem is that shrink-wrapped birds cannot "weep" — a natural process whereby blood and fluids slowly drain from the bird. Therefore, many supermarket chickens are shipped frozen at twenty-eight degrees to prevent moisture from accumulating in the packages. While shopping for this article, we ran across several "fresh" birds that were frozen in spots and still defrosting in the butcher case.

In contrast, Bell & Evans ships chickens loose on ice in forty-pound boxes at a temperature that never dips below thirty-four degrees. As Bell & Evans chickens make their way from the processing plant to the supermarket, blood and fluids are lost, reducing the net weight and hence the price per bird that Bell & Evans receives from retailers. But weeping, or the lack thereof, has a major effect on flavor. "Weeping improves the flavor," says Sechler. "If the blood and fluids coagulate and freeze in the chicken you can taste it."

In addition to this more expensive shipping method, Bell & Evans insists on making three to six deliveries per week to every store it supplies. "We don't want our chickens to spend days on end in the case," says Sechler. Some companies claim that their birds have a shelf-life of twelve or fourteen days after processing. For example, we recently saw chickens that had traveled from Arkansas to Connecticut and had "sell by" dates that were still eight days away. Sechler says common sense dictates that a ten-day-old chicken won't taste as good as one that is sold no more than a couple of days after processing, like Bell & Evans's.

While Bell & Evans was the clear winner of the tasting, the next three brands (Empire Kosher, D'Artagnan, and La Belle Rouge) were separated by a total of only one point in the scoring, and all are worth seeking out. If you cannot find one of the top-rated chickens in your area (see chart page 27 for specifics), you should still make an effort to purchase a local or regional premium brand. Small poultry farms, where attention to quality, not quantity, comes first, are in operation from coast to coast. Check out butcher shops, specialty markets, and health-food stores if your supermarket offerings are meager. ∎

Except for the Rocky (which averages five and a half to six pounds), all chickens weighed between three and a half and four pounds before cooking. Each bird was roasted plain, without fat or seasonings, to an internal temperature of 160 degrees. Half of each bird was carved, and the rest of the meat was left on the carcass so panelists could judge the bird's overall appearance. Tasters were served bread and water to clean their palates and were given access to salt.

The blind tasting was held at Restaurant Jean-Louis in Greenwich, Connecticut. In addition to the restaurant's chef/owner Jean-Louis Gerin, the panel included the author; René Chardain, a retired French chef who ran a number of restaurants in New York; cookbook author and food writer Brooke Dojny; Bob Zemmel, chef/owner of Alforno in Old Saybrook, Connecticut; Linda Giuca, food editor of the *Hartford Courant*; Dawn McLoughlin, butcher shop manager at Hay Day Country Market in Westport, Connecticut; Karen Tack, former test kitchen director at *Cook's* and a food stylist; Chris Tack, a chef for the Seagram Corporation; Mark Bittman, Executive Editor of *Cook's Illustrated*; and sixteen-year-old Kate Bittman, Mark's daughter, who demonstrated an uncanny ability to identify kosher chicken.

Judges were asked to rank their top five choices. Five points were awarded for each first-place vote, four for second, three for third, two for fourth, and one for fifth. An asterisk indicates that a chicken tied with the one listed immediately below it. The first five chickens garnered mostly positive comments from tasters; the last four chickens received mostly negative comments.

The origin of each chicken, in most cases the location of the farm, is indicated in the listings; leading poultry processors have facilities in several states to service different parts of the country, so the headquarters location is given. Per pound prices are for birds purchased in supermarkets in Connecticut, New York, and California, as well as mail-order prices, where applicable. Prices will vary, and most brands have a limited distribution area.

1 **Bell & Evans, The Excellent Chicken** (Pennsylvania), $1.59/lb; 32 points. Pale white skin described as "rough" and "a bit chewy, but not unpleasant." Many tasters noted "real chicken" flavor in both dark and light meat. "More like an old-fashioned chicken," wrote one panelist. Another thought the flavor brought this bird "fairly close to wild game." Somewhat tough texture deemed an asset by most panelists with comments like "chewy in a pleasant, meaty way" and "wonderfully firm." Available in better supermarkets and butcher shops from Boston to Atlanta and as far west as Chicago. Call 717-865-6626 for information on retail outlets in your area.

2 ***Empire Kosher, Fresh Young Broiler Chicken** (Pennsylvania), $1.99/lb; 26 points. Yellowish tinge to skin. Breast and leg meat are "very moist" and "juicy without being too fatty." Some tasters felt that the strong salt taste (which was noticed by all eleven tasters) overpowered the natural chicken flavor. "A tad too salty" or "maybe no chicken flavor to begin with," they said. Others reacted more positively to salting — "excellent bird," wrote one admirer. Available in selected supermarkets and butcher shops nationwide. Call 800-367-4734 for information on retail sources in your area. Empire birds are shipped frozen to many markets, so look in the freezer case if none are available fresh.

3 **D'Artagnan, Fresh Free Range Young Natural Chicken** (Pennsylvania), $2.95/lb; 26 points. Very pale color elicited diverse comments, from "very pretty" and "looks real" to "pinkish" and "unattractive." Texture gets raves — "breast is extremely moist," "leg meat is buttery." Mild chicken flavor too faint for some, while others detected "a hint of sweetness." Many tasters felt this chicken was a "toned-down" version of the gamier Bell & Evans. D'Artagnan chickens are raised without antibiotics or growth stimulants and are fed only organically raised grains. Available in selected retail outlets mainly in the Northeast, but with limited distribution in California and the South. Also available by mail for price listed above plus shipping. Call 800-327-8246 for information on retail sources in your area or to place an order.

4 **La Belle Rouge, Free Range Chicken** (Kentucky), $2.50/lb; 25 points. White skin is "rather pale" but flesh is "moist and buttery." Dark meat is "unctuous but not fatty" with "unusually good" texture. Most tasters felt flavor was "stronger than most." Although this chicken received only one first-place vote, eight panelists placed it among their favorites. La Belle Rouge chickens are raised without antibiotics or growth stimulants. Available in specialty stores and butcher shops east of the Mississippi, with limited distribution to the West Coast and Colorado. Call 800-242-2982 for information on retail sources in your area.

5 **Foster Farms, Fresh Young Chicken** (California), $1.08/lb; 23 points. Highest-rated supermarket chicken proves that not all "big birds" are losers. Skin has yellowish but not unnatural tinge. White meat called "tough" by some tasters, but consistency of dark meat gets better marks. "Decent chicken flavor" that is "mild but sweet." This bird was judged to be "a typical, good chicken." Widely available in supermarkets in California, Arizona, Nevada, Utah, and Hawaii.

6 **Tyson, Fresh Young Chicken** (Arkansas headquarters), $.79/lb; 14 points. America's number one chicken drew only faint praise. Skin is "gray" and "anemic-looking," although two panelists appreciated its "irregularities." White meat is "squeaky" and "rubbery." Several complained about "sour," "funny," or "musky" flavor, while others simply found the bird to be "bland" and "boring." Most favorable comment — "OK, but I wouldn't go out of my way to buy it." Widely available in supermarkets nationwide.

7 ***Rocky, The Range Chicken** (California), $1.99/lb; 7 points. "Golden, buttery-looking skin." Both white and dark meats are "too dry" and "mealy." One tester wrote that "the meat is so lean it's stringy." Flavor gets higher marks than texture, especially the dark meat, which is described as "lively," but many panelists were underwhelmed by this "bland" and "tasteless" entry. The Rocky chicken is raised without antibiotics, animal products, or growth enhancers. Available in specialty stores and butcher shops in the West, with limited distribution to major cities in the East. Call 707-763-1904 for information on retail sources in your area.

8 **Country Pride, Fresh Frying Chicken** (Arkansas headquarters), $1.19/lb; 7 points. Light golden skin covers "coarse," "grainy," and "dry" white meat. Leg meat is described as "tough" and "rubbery." Flavor is "almost nonexistent" in the breast and only "slightly better" in the leg. This "plain" bird, the second best-selling chicken in the country, was snubbed by all but a few panelists who placed it at the bottom of their list of favorites. Widely available in supermarkets nationwide.

9 **Perdue, Fresh Young Chicken** (Maryland headquarters), $1.49/lb; 2 points. "Even the flesh is yellow" on this golden-skinned bird. Texture is worst of the lot — "gag, really dry," "chalky," and "way too dry." Tasters had a number of unsavory adjectives for the flavor — "metallic," "commercial," "fake butter," and "missing in action." This popular bird makes us wonder why people eat chicken at all. As one taster wrote, "I'd rather give up chicken than have this for dinner." Widely available in supermarkets east of the Mississippi.

Building a Better Toaster

Krups and Farberware combine consistency and convenience to come out on top, while the most expensive model bombs.

⁓ BY SHARON KEBSCHULL BARRETT ⁓

In 1994 it's hard to see how making a decent toaster can be all that difficult — manufacturers have had almost a century to perfect a machine that does nothing more than darken bread. But after setting off my smoke alarm four times, tossing out dozens of pieces of charred toast, and watching other pieces go flying across my table, I realize that many manufacturers still have not figured it out.

Fortunately, however, some companies, most notably Krups and Farberware, make toasters that do just what they should — toast bread evenly from top to bottom, front to back, and do it time and again without much of a pause between batches.

I reached this conclusion after testing ten of the newest wide-slot, cool-touch toasters to evaluate their consistency and ease of use. With each machine, I first toasted two bagel halves to check whether the slots could accommodate the three-quarter inch thickness. While the halves would fit into every model, in some cases the fit was uncomfortably tight.

After the bagels popped out, I tested the doneness settings of the machines by putting in two slices of toast at a time, three times in a row, at a medium setting, followed by two slices on a light setting and two slices on dark. In evaluating the results, I relied not on specific color definitions (light, medium, and dark), but on how consistent the results were. All toasters take some getting used to, but once you've found the color you like, the settings shouldn't have to be adjusted every morning. Unfortunately, some of the toasters couldn't produce six consistent medium slices; others couldn't produce light toast once they were warmed up; and others couldn't make dark slices without burning them.

I also noted how fast the toasters worked, but that didn't turn out to be much of a distinguishing factor. Generally speaking, two (or four, depending on the model) pieces of toast took about one and one-half to two minutes to prepare on a medium setting.

Don't Use Top Settings

In the course of the tests, I noticed that — with the exception of one model that could not produce a dark slice of toast at any setting — all the toasters burned bread when set at their highest setting. To get dark toast, it was best to set the dial between four and five if the top setting was six. I also tried toasting frozen pastries; I theorized that the darkest settings, which always seemed to set off smoke alarms, must be for frozen foods. But even frozen items came out charred at these settings. The Krups, the Farberware, and the Maxim did the best job of thawing and toasting pastries.

I discovered that many of the toasters that boast of being cool-touch barely qualify as

---

WHAT MAKES A TOASTER WORK?

After days of toasting all kinds of bread, I was curious about why some machines, especially the Krups and Farberware, performed so consistently and other models were such duds. According to industry experts, the temperature sensor technology developed in the past decade makes the difference. Given this simple answer, I confess I'm still puzzled why some companies seem wedded to outdated designs.

"The world of toasters is not necessarily rocket science," says Jonathan Steinberg, group manager for market development at Farberware. He says old toasters simply measured temperature and could not differentiate between types of bread and pastries. Quartz heating elements in the Farberware and Krups machines measure the moisture level in the bread and adjust the length of the toasting cycle to ensure consistent results. For instance, dry bread needs less time than a moister slice. By measuring both temperature and moisture, the toaster automatically adjusts the length of the cycle.

The type of heating coil also seems to make a difference. Old-style toasters use coils that inevitably have hot and cold spots. But Krups now uses a straight heating bar which, combined with a curved interior top, reflects heat evenly over the bread. Farberware uses thin wires that run throughout the inner walls to distribute heat evenly.

The effectiveness of the cool-touch feature is a function of the plastic used — thick materials perform better — and the distance between the metal innards and the plastic outer wall. While the perfect toaster doesn't sound all that complicated to manufacture, my tests indicate that many companies are still playing catch-up.

such. For example, the Toastmaster is hot enough to burn skin if touched for more than a few seconds. But the Krups and Farberware excel here, with outer shells that are never more than warm to the touch.

The Krups and Farberware models also stood out for another design feature, one that all toasters should have — long cords (forty-four and forty inches, respectively) that coil up underneath the toasters for storage or to make the cord shorter, which is especially important when children are around. Contrast this with the Toastmaster's cord, at a paltry twenty-two inches.

The length of the toast slot or slots also sets a few toasters apart; once again, the Krups and Farberware came out on top with eleven-inch slots that can hold three bagel halves or two slices cut from the center of a round sourdough loaf. The width of the slots also became an issue for toasters that lacked an automatic centering device to hold slices upright in the center of the slot. Without this feature, bread falls to one side of the slot in the Black & Decker and Toastmaster, and gets considerably darker on that side. ∎

Sharon Kebschull Barrett recently graduated from Peter Kump's New York Cooking School.

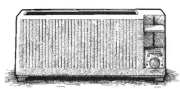

Krups Toastronic Deluxe 118

Farberware Electronic T2020

Maxim Widemouth ET-6

All ten toasters claim to have wide slots and a cool-touch housing. But as this chart indicates, not all of them lived up to their advance billing. The Krups and Farberware were the clear winners; the Maxim is the best buy for shoppers on a budget. In general, the first five toasters were deemed excellent or good. Results with the last five toasters were fair or poor, and these models are not recommended. *See* Sources and Resources on page 32 for information on buying the top-rated toasters.

TOASTERS IN ORDER OF PREFERENCE

Krups Toastronic Deluxe 118

Price: $60
Design: One extra-long slot holds up to three bagel halves. The 44-inch cord clips underneath to shorten it to about 19 inches.
Performance: Settings from one to six, with switches for rewarming toast and defrosting, both of which work well. Especially easy to clean. Consistent, even toasting with no wait between batches. Darker settings give genuinely dark, not burned, toast. Exterior gets warm but not hot.

Farberware Electronic T2020

Price: $50
Design: One extra-long slot holds up to three bagel halves. Has storage underneath for its 40-inch cord.
Performance: Light to dark settings, with cancel button to interrupt toasting, frozen button to defrost and toast, and high-rise feature to lift bread up for easier retrieval. Side crumb tray for very easy cleaning. Consistent, even toasting. Outside stays very cool.

Maxim Widemouth ET-6

Price: $40
Design: Two wide slots hold one bagel half each.
Performance: Settings from one to six. Consistent toasting, uniform on both sides and from top to bottom, except for dark setting (five), which tends to burn one edge. Light setting is especially good and fast. Easy to clean. Outside gets warm, not hot.

Rowenta Sensor Electronic TP-200

Price: $40
Design: One long slot holds two bagel halves.
Performance: Settings one to six, plus a keep-warm setting. Consistent toasting from batch to batch, although slightly darker at the top. Light setting produces barely crisp toast with no color. Outside gets warm on the bottom, hot near the top.

Salton Sonata TO-6

Price: $40
Design: One long slot holds two bagel halves.
Performance: This toaster's box yells, "It's cool! It's touchable!" Cool it's not, but it does stay touchable. Settings one to six. No crumb tray; turn it upside down over a sink to clean. Toaster clicks once, sounding like it's done — 30 seconds later, it is done (toaster comes with a warning about this). Fairly even, consistent toasting, although between settings four and five the toast still gets burned a bit.

Waring Microchip Toaster MCT-1

Price: $48
Design: One long slot holds two bagel halves.
Performance: Settings one to six, plus defrost and keep-warm functions. Edges never got toasted until I tried to make dark toast at setting six, which burned; the next batch, at setting five, came out even more charred. At lower settings, toast comes out fairly even and consistent, except for pale edges. Outside of toaster gets warm but not hot.

Proctor-Silex Coolwall T4300

Price: $40
Design: Two wide slots hold one bagel half each. Cord is only 23 inches long.
Performance: Settings one to six, plus pastry and defrost modes. It notes which slot to use if only toasting one piece of bread. Slices toasted at setting three repeatedly came out quite light on one side, barely done on the other. Between settings five and six the slices came out as medium toast. Two pieces done on the darkest setting came out barely dark enough, and on only one side. Stays cool.

Black & Decker Metropolitan Toaster T245

Price: $30
Design: Two slots barely able to hold thick bagel halves.
Performance: This toaster — which is rounded instead of sleek like the rest — looks attractive, but there's nothing attractive about the way it works. Settings from one to five, with a note on top about which slot to use if toasting only one slice. One slot adjusts to hold bread upright; the other doesn't — an odd feature that makes one slot narrower than the other. The first batch of medium toast came out OK, although darker on one side than the other. But the next two batches at the same setting popped up quickly and were very light. Toaster must cool between batches. Light toast came out barely toasted. Dark toast came out unevenly dark/burned. Housing gets barely warm.

Sunbeam Cool-Touch 4-Slice Toaster 3825

Price: $60
Design: Two long slots can hold a total of four bagel halves at once.
Performance: Settings one to six. Toaster gave uneven results with some burning even at setting three. Toast flies up out of toaster when it's done. By the third batch of "medium" toast, at setting three, the toast popped out very quickly. However, it was burnt on one side and set off the smoke alarm. It seems to work best with four pieces of toast at once, with more even toasting and no charring. Outside is warm, hot near the top.

Toastmaster Cool Steel Wide Slot B722

Price: $37
Design: Two slots barely hold bagel halves, which had to be nudged in and didn't pop up when done. The shortest cord in the test, 22 inches.
Performance: Uneven toasting that got lighter as it went along, with long pauses for the machine to cool down. Toast done on the light setting came out virtually uncooked, while the dark setting triggered the smoke alarm. Setting four produced a somewhat even, dark toast. Housing would burn skin if touched for more than a few seconds.

ILLUSTRATIONS BY DAN KROVATIN

Inexpensive Pinot Noirs Disappoint

There were some winners among the fourteen under-$15 Pinot Noirs we tasted, but we concluded that this grape does not make great inexpensive wine.

∽ BY MARK BITTMAN ∽

Our Pinot Noir tasting of a year ago (*Cook's Illustrated*, September/October 1993) yielded surprising results, with American wines, one of which sold for $6, taking the top three places. So this year we decided to refine the selection, focusing on Pinot Noirs that cost $15 or less. Once again, we drew on wines from around the world, but because there are so many inexpensive Pinot Noirs, and because the grape is so difficult to work with and the wines so unpredictable, a small pre-tasting panel chose from a group of more than thirty wines to determine which ultimately would be tasted by our larger group. Theoretically at least, our final tasting included only the cream of the inexpensive Pinot Noirs.

Which didn't stop our panel from agreeing almost unanimously that four of the wines were virtually undrinkable. After that, there was little consensus. Nine of the wines finished within just five points of each other and we had a three-way tie for first (an Oregonian and two Californians).

Yet none of this reflected especially well on the wines. Our tasters made disparaging comments about all of them — including the top finishers. Even when it came to each taster's favorite, the only striking aspect of the wines was the tasters' marked lack of enthusiasm. All of this confirmed the observation that this prized red grape of Burgundy does not readily present its charms.

It is generally agreed that the best pinot noir grapes draw much of their flavor from the soil; the lower the per-acre yield, the more intensity in the grape and in the resulting wine. But low-yield winemaking operations are obviously more expensive than those that maximize tonnage. It's fairly safe to assume, therefore, that our wines were all made from grapes grown in fairly high-yield operations. And the results showed it, with even the top-ranked wines drawing comments such as "a real lightweight" and "lacks intensity."

Still, it can be said that our tasting revealed several Pinot Noirs that, although far from earth-shattering, provide good value and an opportunity to get a sense of the charming aromas and flavors that this marvelous grape is capable of producing. One of our top-ranked wines, Saintsbury Garnet — an old reliable in the new world of American Pinot Noir — costs just $11; and although the $7 Napa Ridge, which finished second in last year's tasting, did not do as well this year, it finished well up in the pack. ∎

As usual, wines were tasted blind by a panel comprising both wine professionals and amateur wine-lovers. In the judging, seven points were awarded for each first-place vote, six for second, five for third, and so on. An asterisk next to a wine indicates that its score was identical to that of the next wine below (note the three-way tie for first place). These wines were purchased in the Northeast; prices will vary somewhat, and may be slightly higher elsewhere.

1991 Chalone Gavilan

1989 Knudsen Erath

1992 Saintsbury Garnet

1. *1991 Chalone Gavilan (24 points), $14. Most tasters agreed that this wine was fruity and enjoyable. The three who ranked it first, all of whom are wine professionals, believed it to be the closest wine to "real, mature Pinot Noir." Others found it "nice" or "pleasant," but said it was "thin" or had "no backbone."

2. *1989 Knudsen Erath (24 points), $12. "Explosive," wrote one taster, who gave this wine one of its two first-place votes. Others found it "soft," "light," and "subtle." Another called it "drinkable, but nothing more."

3. 1992 Saintsbury Garnet (24 points), $11. One who ranked this wine in first place said, "This has good fruit and nice balance; a wine with a future." But — and this is an indication of the overall lukewarm feelings our tasters had about these wines — one who ranked it second called it "pleasant enough to drink."

4. 1990 Vaiveley Cuvee Jacquelet Mercurey (23 points), $13.50. The top-ranked of the French wines tested. One who placed it second wrote, "This shows a touch of its breed." Another found it "earthy and spicy," just what you'd expect to hear in a Pinot Noir tasting.

5. *1990 Pinnacles (22 points), $15. Garnered a first-place vote from a veteran taster who wrote, "A good bit of fruit with a touch of chocolate; classy wine." But another found it "thin, tart, and lean — unacceptable."

6. 1990 Volpato Costaille Bourgogne Passetout-grain (22 points), $11. Unlike most of the wines here, this one provoked some real disagreement. It was ranked first by one taster, who said it was "rich and earthy," with "lovely fruit." Others found it "just awful."

7. *1992 Napa Ridge (20 points), $7. A new, weaker vintage from last year's second-place finisher. Still, it had its admirers: "Good quality with sweet flavors," wrote one professional, who mistook it for a French wine. Detractors found it "odd," with "little fruit."

8. 1990 Roche (20 points), $14. "Good intensity, spicy, and soft, with a good finish," wrote one of our tasters, a winemaker himself, in ranking this first. Others, unfortunately, found it "dry," with "no charm."

9. 1991 Meridian (19 points), $15. "Fruity," "with good intensity," wrote two tasters who liked this wine enough to rank it second. But others detected an "odd, metallic nose."

10. 1990 Bourgogne Clos de Chenoves (13 points), $10. Here the consensus against the weaker wines begins to build. Even the one veteran taster who called this "mature and sweet" then commented, "Too bad it stinks." Others were less kind.

11. 1990 Antonin Rodet (6 points), $9. There was general agreement that this wine was "tannic," "acidic," and "without much fruit."

12. 1990 Latour Cotes de Beaune Villages (5 points), $10.50. "Light but acceptable" was the best thing said here.

13. 1991 Menetou-Salon Morogues (2 points), $8.50. "Some body" was the best thing any of our tasters had to say about this wine. "Dreadful" was a more common sentiment.

14. 1992 Mountain View (0 points), $6. Some people found this wine "cheesy," others found it unimpressive. None found it worth ranking.

Classic Home Desserts
Richard Sax
Chapters, $29.95

At a time when half the cookbooks published have the words "low" and "fat" in their titles, Richard Sax's *Classic Home Desserts*, a book of 350 recipes in twenty-two chapters, not only has classic appeal but novelty value. It is also a gem.

Sax is an unusual character. Trained as a chef, he can also write, and well; furthermore, he appreciates the differences between home and restaurant cooking, and values them equally. None of his books has become a standard, yet many of them deserved wider attention. *From the Farmers' Market* compares favorably, in a strictly American vein, to Elizabeth David's classic *Summer Cooking*. His *The Cookie Lover's Cookie Book* is a solid work on a small subject, and *Cooking Great Meals Every Day* is a strong attempt to teach people how to do just that.

Classic Home Desserts would appear to be Sax's *chef d'oeuvre*. For ten years he has worked on it, testing and re-testing, rejecting some recipes as too "professional" and reworking others to jibe with his overall approach, which he describes quite nicely as "unadorned frankness."

Many of the recipes are perfect for people who like desserts but don't like to spend much time putting them together. We tested about a dozen — betties and buckles, puddings and simple pies and cakes — and loved them all. The food is homey rather than elegant, delicious but never pretentious.

Indiana Sugar Cream Pie, for example, is essentially a vanilla pudding made with butter, sugar, milk, cream, cornstarch, and vanilla, piled into a pie crust to create a rich, old-fashioned pie that rivals a great crème brûlée in its delicious simplicity.

A bread pudding connoisseur called Sax's Omaha Caramel Bread Pudding, dense with cream and cinnamon and topped with melted caramel, "one of the best I've ever eaten." When Sax says, in introducing the apple cake section, "Stick a bookmark right here, and leave it in," he's telling the truth; Ligita's Quick Apple Cake takes only a few minutes to put together, but produces a moist, dense, slightly gooey dessert that is bound to become a fall standard.

Equally successful are the Quintessential Coffee Cake, an unorthodox one-bowl affair in which you make the topping, scoop out a cup, then mix the batter in with the remaining butter crumbs; the Quick Chocolate Candy Cake, which takes a bit more than the six minutes Sax claims, but not much; and the tart-sweet Cranberry Crisp.

Not everything is as middle-America as we're making it sound, but make no mistake: This is an old-fashioned American cookbook. As one of our reviewers said, "It's as if you updated the recipe section from *Joy of Cooking*." Like *Joy*, it draws inspiration from all over the world. But, also like *Joy*, it has its roots in nineteenth century America.

One reason *Classic Home Desserts* is so successful is that Sax has borrowed from nearly everyone he knows. He appears to have extracted the soul of American home desserts, with the willing, eager participation of hundreds of cooks.

—*Pam Anderson and Mark Bittman*

The Mediterranean Diet Cookbook
Nancy Harmon Jenkins
Bantam, $27.95

Do not be misled by the title — this is not another book promising slimmer thighs in ninety days. Rather, it is an excellent cookbook that gracefully combines the seemingly disparate poles of epidemiology and earthy, tasty, down-home food.

The "Mediterranean diet" of the title refers not to a calorie-counting method, but to a particularly healthful regional way of cooking and eating. The term originated in the late 1950s, when researchers exploring the links between diet and health found a correlation between the foods that Mediterranean peasants ate and their relatively good health.

Simply put, the Mediterranean diet is largely plant- and grain-based, using red meat mostly as a flavoring. Other animal products are eaten sparingly, fat comes primarily from olive oil, and wine is drunk in moderation. In other words, it is a Mediterranean version of what most of us would consider healthy, sensible eating.

Through her writing and her work with the Massachusetts-based Oldways Foundation, Jenkins has been in the forefront of the movement to popularize this way of eating. But more

important for readers of her book, she has also spent twenty years traveling, eating, and cooking in the Mediterranean, and consequently has a firm grasp of the region's flavor combinations and cooking traditions.

In addition, Jenkins is an excellent writer. *The Mediterranean Diet* is full of anecdotes about her experiences, and just when you think things might be getting a bit too thick with epidemiological studies and public health statistics, you run across some reassuringly level-headed cooking advice such as: "If you can't quite master a new technique, don't tell anyone. I can almost guarantee you they won't know the difference. Flavor counts for far more than elaborate techniques and presentations."

As with almost any cookbook, the heart of this book is the recipes. Most are not meant to startle with novelty or dazzle with inventiveness. Instead, they are straightforward versions of Mediterranean cooking. When I started leafing through the book, I wanted to make just about every recipe, and every one that I did make was a hit.

Oven-Braised Leeks were a breeze to prepare, and the simple olive oil-based pan sauce was so delicious that a friend borrowed the recipe and served it over pasta. Warm Grape Leaves Stuffed with Meat and Rice was simple but flavorful, a tangy garlic-yogurt sauce perfectly balancing the richness of the lamb filling. Egyptian Lentil Soup had just the right blend of spices, heat, and earthy lentils. Tunisian Chick-Peas with Spicy Vegetables was beautiful in appearance, had a nice, mild heat, and was filling enough to satisfy even devoted carnivores. Venetian Cornmeal Cookies, a perfect dessert, were barely sweet, with a beguiling underlying flavor provided by a healthy dose of grappa.

There are also some more unusual dishes, such as Sgheena, which Jenkins defines as "a one-pot meal for the Sabbath." This hearty dish consists of wheat berries, beef, rice, white and sweet potatoes, chickpeas, and eggs in the shell, all cooked together in a huge pot and flavored with harissa, garlic, allspice, cumin, and a good dose of saffron. At first bite I thought the combination odd, but I ended up going back for seconds and thirds.

Through her recipes, Jenkins deftly makes her point: When food tastes this good, you don't have to force yourself to eat healthily. ∎

—*John Willoughby*

SOURCES
AND RESOURCES

PICKLE JARS

The Williams-Sonoma catalog features an array of wide-mouthed jars perfect for holding pickled vegetables (*see* page 18). These Triumph clamp jars from France come in three sizes — half liter, three-quarter liter, and one liter — all with wide mouths for easy pickle removal, tinned-steel clamps, and rubber gaskets to insure a tight seal. The jars come in sets of six, and cost $18 for small jars, $21 for medium, and $22.50 for large. For a more old-fashioned look, the catalog sells one-quart Wecks canning jars from Germany. These bowed glass jars come with rubber gaskets and snap-on metal clasps that attach to either side of the detachable glass lids. A set of four jars costs $16. Williams-Sonoma also sells adhesive labels with botanical prints, the centers left empty to allow for labeling of the contents. A set of forty-five stickers (in three different sizes) costs $6. For a copy of the Williams-Sonoma catalog, call 800-541-2233.

AMERICAN PEAR BRANDY

Pear brandy adds a wonderful flavor to the Pear and Dried Fruit Strudel and to the Pear Brandy Custard Sauce on pages 10 and 11. While the French are known for their clear brandies (in this case called *poire eau-de-vie*), an Oregon company has earned a reputation for fine pear brandy made from fruit grown in the Pacific Northwest. In France, the Williams pear is used to make top-quality brandy. Clear Creek Distillery (1430 Northwest 23rd Avenue, Portland, OR 97210; 503-248-9470) uses Bartlett pears, which are the same variety except carrying the name given them decades ago by an American grower. The brandy is available in 375 ml and 750 ml bottles that retail for approximately $15 and $30. Contact the distillery to find a local source or a retailer that will ship to your home.

GLASS PIE PLATE

A nine-inch glass pie plate is best for baking the pie pastry on page 8. Most cookware stores should stock a Pyrex pie plate with gently sloping sides. Corning, the company that manufactures Pyrex products, also sells directly to consumers. Its open-stock catalog carries a nine-inch glass pie plate that is one and a quarter inches deep. It comes in three colors (clear, amber, and cranberry) and costs $4.25. Corning's customer order line is 800-999-3436.

DISCOUNT SPICES

Penzeys Spice House (P.O. Box 1448, Waukesha, WI 53187; 414-574-0277) sells hundreds of whole and ground spices, including tiny red annatto seeds (*see* Notes from Readers, page 3). The cost for annatto seeds from Peru is 49¢ for a one-ounce package or $4.80 for a one-pound container. Ask for a copy of the company's free catalog, an exhaustive thirty-six-page listing of almost every known spice and herb from adobo to vanilla. Best of all, most items are sold well below supermarket prices.

TOP TOASTERS

Of the ten toasters tested for the story on page 28, we highly recommend three models. The Krups Toastronic Deluxe 118 was a top choice because its extra-long slot holds up to three bagels at once. This cool-touch toaster is available at Williams-Sonoma stores nationwide or from the catalog (800-541-2233) for $60. Krups also operates a consumer hot line (800-526-5377) that can lead you to the nearest retail source. Our other top choice is the Farberware Electronic T2020, which also holds three bagels in one long slot, operates consistently, and stays cool during use. This toaster costs about $50 and is sold at Macy's, Stern's, and Strawbridge & Clothier (or you can locate another source by calling Farberware at 718-863-8000 and asking for sales). Priced at just $40, the Maxim Widemouth ET-6 is our best buy. This toaster has two wide slots and works dependably. It is sold at Bloomingdale's, Marshall Field's, Macy's, Jordan Marsh, A & S, and other large department stores and housewares shops. Maxim operates a consumer hot line (800-233-9054) that can direct you to a retail source in your area.

ASIAN INGREDIENTS

Most of the ingredients for the dumpling recipes on pages 14 and 15 are available at Asian markets or well-stocked gourmet stores. But two items may be a bit more difficult to find, so here's a good mail-order source: Nancy's Specialty Market (P.O. Box 327, Wye Mills, MD 21679; 800-462-6291) sells both Thai red curry paste and unsweetened coconut milk, ingredients used in the Curried Chicken Filling with Carrots and Basil on page 15. The red curry paste is a blend of chiles, herbs, and spices and comes in a four-ounce jar. An even hotter green curry paste is also available; both cost $1.95. Nancy's also carries fourteen-ounce cans of unsweetened coconut milk at $3.25. The extensive catalog features thousands of food products from around the world, from fish sauce and cactus salsa to miso paste and bonito flakes. Call for a free copy.

TOOLS FOR BUTTERFLYING CHICKEN

A sturdy pair of poultry shears is essential for butterflying chicken (*see* story on page 23). Henckels makes two shears; one is all nickel, the other has plastic handles. A Cook's Wares (211 37th Street, Beaver Falls, PA 15010; 412-846-9490) carries both shears at a discount. The all-nickel shears cost $33.90 (on sale from $52) and the plastic-handled shears cost $24.90. Once the shears have been used to cut out the backbone, a heavy metal mallet is needed to pound the butterflied chicken. La Cuisine Kitchenware (323 Cameron Street, Alexandria, VA 22314; 800-521-1176) stocks a heavy meat hammer with flat sides for pounding chicken and corrugated sides for tenderizing meat. The mallet is all metal, the preferred material when working with raw chicken, since it is easy to clean and sanitize. The meat hammer costs $11.50.

MULTI-PURPOSE RICER

Few cooks would think of using a potato ricer for removing the excess moisture from raw eggplant. As reader William van Druten suggested to us (*see* Quick Tips, page 4), most kitchen shops carry a type of metal ricer with a small, round bowl that holds the food and a handle that forces the food through holes in the bowl's bottom. La Cuisine Kitchenware (*see* above) carries a sturdy Italian potato ricer that is perfectly designed for squeezing moisture from eggplant. It is made of cast aluminum and comes with two grids, one with larger and one with smaller holes. It costs $20.

SPECIALTY DRIED PASTAS

Although the pasta sauces on page 22 can be paired with standard supermarket pasta, occasionally it is worth looking for a more exotic noodle. For instance, the Zucchini, Red Pepper, and Tomato Sauce with Thyme and Mint is especially well-suited to buckwheat noodles. These can be found in most Japanese groceries or health food stores. The mail-order division at Balducci's (424 Avenue of the Americas, New York, NY 10011; 800-225-3822), a gourmet store in Greenwich Village, also sells a number of specialty dried pastas, including buckwheat pizzoccheri. This regional pasta comes from Lombardy in the north of Italy and resembles fettuccine. A one-pound box costs $4.50. Balducci's also sells its own homemade dried pastas made with Jerusalem artichoke flour or squid ink, as well as commercial spaghetti made with red bell peppers; lemon and mint; beets and onions; ginger and carrots; artichoke hearts; or tomatoes, basil, and garlic.

CHEESE GRATER

Many pasta sauces require a light dusting of grated Parmesan cheese. A Swiss-made plastic grater with a removable stainless steel drum does this pesky job with minimal effort and no scraped knuckles. Simply place a small piece of cheese in the drum, press down on the plastic clamp, and turn the handle to rotate the drum and grate the cheese directly over a bowl of hot pasta. This gadget can also be used to grate chocolate and is dishwasher-safe. The Zyliss grater is available at Williams-Sonoma stores nationwide and from their catalog (800-541-2233) for a cost of $17. ■

**TENDER GREENS WITH
RAISINS AND ALMONDS**
page 21

ASSORTED PICKLED VEGETABLES
page 19

**GRILLED BUTTERFLIED CHICKEN
WITH ROSEMARY, LEMON, AND GARLIC**
page 24

**SAUTÉED PORK CHOPS WITH
PINEAPPLE SALSA**
page 13

**PASTA WITH ZUCCHINI, RED PEPPER, AND TOMATO
SAUCE WITH THYME AND MINT** page 22

THE BEST APPLE PIE
page 8

PHOTOGRAPHS BY ERIC ROTH

Baked Apples With Cranberries

Remove zest from 1 orange. Mince half the zest, leave the other half in strips; set aside. Mix 2 cups cranberries, ¾ cup fresh-squeezed orange juice, ¼ cup firmly packed brown sugar, and 2 tablespoons melted butter. Divide this mixture in half. Stir minced zest into one half; set other half aside. From the stem end of each of 4 large Rome or Golden Delicious apples, slice off ½-inch to form a cap. Remove stem from each cap, and cut an opening large enough for a cinnamon stick. Core each apple with a melon baller. Place apples in a small baking pan and stuff each with a portion of the cranberry mixture containing the zest. Replace cap on each apple, with a cinnamon stick through the old stem opening. Pour remaining cranberry mixture around apples, stirring in remaining zest strips. Bake in a 350-degree oven until apples are tender, about 45 minutes. Transfer apples to serving plates; pour cranberry mixture from baking pan into a medium saucepan and simmer over medium heat until reduced to a thin syrup, 7 to 10 minutes. Spoon some of the thickened cranberry mixture around each apple. Serve warm with ice cream or whipped cream. *Serves 4.*

COOK'S
ILLUSTRATED

Ultimate Lemon Meringue Pie
Crisp Crust, Lush Filling, and No-Weep Meringue

The Best Way to Cook a Goose
A New Technique for Crispy Skin

Classic Lasagne Simplified
More Pasta, Less Sauce

Rating Nonstick Skillets
Chefs Test 6 Models for 3 Months

FISH STEWS MADE EASY

MODERATELY PRICED CHOCOLATES WIN TASTING

BEST CALIFORNIA SPARKLING WINES

MUFFIN TIN POPOVERS

$4.00 U.S./$4.95 CANADA

"Late Fall"
See page 14 for cranberry relishes, and page 15 for the best way to cook butternut squash.

ILLUSTRATION BY
BRENT WATKINSON

Broiled Oysters Topped with Roasted Chile-Cilantro Sauce

ILLUSTRATION BY
CAROL FORTUNATO

COOK'S
ILLUSTRATED

Publisher and Editor
CHRISTOPHER KIMBALL

Executive Editor
MARK BITTMAN

Senior Editor
JOHN WILLOUGHBY

Food Editor
PAM ANDERSON

Senior Writer
JACK BISHOP

Articles Editor
ANNE TUOMEY

Managing Editor
MAURA LYONS

Copy Editor
KURT TIDMORE

Editorial Assistant
KIM N. RUSSELLO

Test Kitchen Assistant
VICTORIA ROLAND

Art Director
MEG BIRNBAUM

Food Stylist
MARIE PIRAINO

Marketing Director
ADRIENNE KIMBALL

Circulation Director
ELAINE REPUCCI

Circulation Assistant
JENNIFER L. KEENE

Production Director
JAMES MCCORMACK

Publicity Director
CAROL ROSEN KAGAN

Treasurer
JANET CARLSON

Office Manager
JENNY THORNBURY

Customer Service
CONNIE FORBES

Special Projects
FERN BERMAN

Cook's Illustrated (ISSN 1068-2821) is published bimonthly by Natural Health Limited Partners, 17 Station Street, Box 569, Brookline, MA 02147-0569. Copyright 1994 Natural Health Limited Partners. Application to mail at second-class postage rates is pending at Boston, MA, and additional mailing offices. Editorial office: 17 Station Street, Box 569, Brookline, MA 02147-0569; (617) 232-1000, FAX (617) 232-1572. Editorial contributions should be sent to: Editor, *Cook's Illustrated*, 17 Station Street, Box 569, Brookline, MA 02147-0569. We cannot assume responsibility for manuscripts submitted to us. Submissions will be returned only if accompanied by a large self-addressed stamped envelope. Subscription rates: $24.95 for one year; $45 for two years; $65 for three years. (Canada: add $3 per year; all other countries: add $12 per year.) Postmaster: Send all new orders, subscription inquiries, and change of address notices to *Cook's Illustrated*, P.O. Box 59046, Boulder, CO 80322-9046. Single copies: $4 in U.S., $4.95 in Canada and foreign. Back issues available for $5 each. PRINTED IN THE U.S.A.

EDITORIAL

ALL HAIL RONZONI?

In our May/June issue, we did a dried pasta taste test at Cafe Bondi in New York. Among the experts were Anna Teresa Callen, Italian cookbook author and teacher; Arthur Schwartz, restaurant critic for the *New York Daily News*; Antonino Settepani, co-owner of Cafe Bondi; and Kathleen Spadaro, president of a local pasta company. The pasta was prepared by Cafe Bondi's chef, Francesco Crescenzo-Crescenzi, a native of Naples.

When I first heard the amazing result—Ronzoni was rated the number one pasta—I felt like Forrest Gump had just won a seat in the Senate. The Ronzoni I remember from childhood was limp, starchy, and without tooth. There had to be something amiss with our tastings.

CHRISTOPHER KIMBALL

I asked that the tasting be repeated with the same cook but with the entire staff of *Cook's Illustrated* as the tasting panel. We sampled the same eight pastas in a blind tasting. We agreed on the characteristics of the ideal pasta: a clean, nutty, wheat flavor; good bite; no starchiness; springiness; slight chewiness; and a pleasant, fresh aftertaste. The cooked pastas were served on individual plates, and an extra plate of each sample was left on the table for reference. We dug in and spent two hours rating pastas.

It quickly became apparent that pastas are difficult to rate. Unlike soy sauce, the variations are, for the most part, quite subtle. A pasta tasting consists of slight differences in bite, shades of wheat flavor, and degrees of color varying from manila to buff. Halfway through the tasting, I was beginning to lose my confidence. Could I really compare the bite of a pasta sampled an hour ago to the spaghetti on the plate in front of me?

Near the end of the tasting, we sampled a pasta that I thought was quite different. The color was darker than the rest—a rich hazelnut—and the first taste was lively and wheaty with an assertive, nutty aftertaste. This was a pasta that could stand up to any combination of anchovies, garlic, capers, and tomatoes; not a pasta to quietly sit in the back seat and enjoy the scenery, but a pasta with a driver's license.

After we finished up our tally sheets, the brands were identified. As the names were read aloud, I was pleased that I counted DeCecco, the number one Italian import, and Barilla, the best-selling pasta in Italy, in my top four. But when my favorite pasta was identified, I felt the hot rush of embarrassment. Ronzoni! I had picked a mass-market brand, a brand name that lived in the suburbs next to Heinz and Kraft, not in the bustling ethnic neighborhood of DeCecco and Delverde.

But after an espresso and some reflection, I realized the results were both consistent and liberating. In the second tasting, four pastas received much higher ratings than the others. Three of these (Ronzoni, DeCecco, and Creamette) were also rated in the top four in the original tasting. Also, the expensive pasta with the lowest rating in our first tasting (Martelli at a whopping $4.29 per pound, versus $1.19 for Ronzoni) came in next to last in the second round. The results were generally consistent.

Most of all, these tastings go a long way to making the basic point of this publication, which is that first-hand experience counts for a lot. I may think that Ronzoni, at just over a dollar a pound, is a pale imitation of the pricey Italian imports, but it just ain't so. There is something very American about this "show me" attitude, something that leads us away from the prevailing fascism of the gourmet police (do we really need to buy imported extra-virgin olive oil at $20 a bottle?) and moves us closer to a sane, democratic notion of good food. Why not Ronzoni?

For that matter, why not Heinz vinegar or Redpack canned tomatoes, other winners of *Cook's Illustrated* tastings? Maybe "Made in America" really counts for something in the 1990s. It seems to me that American wines, cheeses, breads, produce, and specialty foods have skyrocketed in quality since the 1970s, while Europe seems headed toward a love affair with convenience. The flaunting of the gastronomic superiority of the French peasant becomes untenable in an age when most of them quit the farm, move to Paris, get a job in the federal bureaucracy, and grab some take-out in time to catch *Larry King Live*. We import Dijon mustard and export Burger King. In my book, it's the French who are running the trade deficit.

As for Ronzoni, I will swallow my professional pride, trust in first-hand experience, and do the right thing at $1.19 a pound. I'm proud to be an American. ∎

NOTES
FROM READERS

PRESERVATIVES IN DRIED FRUITS

Is there a way to eliminate or diminish the smell of sulfur dioxide in dried fruit? This chemical is added as a preservative, and is especially noticeable in dried apricots.

SUSAN WAHL
Bozeman, MT

Sulfur compounds are added to dried fruits to prevent the natural browning caused by oxidation. (Think of a cut apple turning brown when exposed to air.) In general, the sulfur levels should be quite low and often are not detectable. However, if you find the aroma or flavor of sulfur to be unpleasant, or if you are allergic to sulfides, you have several options.

Look for sulfur-free, organically grown, dried fruits in a natural foods store. You can also order sulfur-free, organically grown, dried fruit directly from Timber Crest Farms (4791 Dry Creek Road, Healdsburg, CA 95448; 707-433-8251). In addition to dried apricots, they also carry dried peaches, pears, prunes, and apples. Instead of using chemical preservatives, Timber Crest keeps its dried fruit in cold storage and they recommend that you store their sulfur-free dried fruits in the refrigerator.

If you are using sulfur-treated dried fruit, you can soak the fruit in boiling water for a minute or two to lessen any chemical odor. Soaking in hot liquid—you can add brandy or another liqueur to the water to boost flavor—also helps rehydrate the fruit and is often recommended in bread, cake, and cookie recipes. Soaked fruits should be drained and dried on paper towels before use.

HOMEMADE CONDENSED MILK

I have a number of recipes that call for a can of sweetened condensed milk. When I bake, I like to use as many fresh products as possible. Is there a way to make sweetened condensed milk at home, or can you suggest a substitute?

ELENA LEVY-NAVARRO
Iowa City, IA

Sweetened condensed milk was one of the first canned products made in the United States. In fact, it was a staple for many Civil War soldiers, since it was a concentrated source of calories and nutrients that combined long shelf life with portability. Today, commercial condensed milk is still made by evaporating away much of the liquid in whole milk. Instead of reducing the liquid content

with heat (as you might do with a sauce), dairies use a vacuum to draw off more than half of the liquid. The addition of sugar not only makes the milk sweet, but also helps protect it against spoiling. This is why unopened cans of sweetened condensed milk last for months, and why sweetened condensed milk is used in many traditional recipes from the tropics, where refrigeration used to be unavailable.

Here at *Cook's Illustrated*, we have often avoided recipes that called for canned sweetened condensed milk, since we did not want the extra fat. However, your letter prompted us to search for a substitute. After some tinkering, we found that adding nonfat dry milk powder to regular milk increases the solid content without adding any liquid, thus mimicking commercial condensed milk. As an added benefit, depending on the type of milk used, the homemade version can contain as little as one-tenth the fat found in an equal amount of the commercial product.

To make fourteen ounces of sweetened condensed milk substitute, whisk one and one half cups of milk powder into a half cup of whole or 2 percent milk in a saucepan until it is very smooth, about one minute. Then whisk in two-thirds cup of sugar and one teaspoon of vanilla extract, and cook over low heat, continuing to whisk constantly until the sugar and milk powder dissolve, about five minutes. Cool before using, then whisk again to be sure that no graininess remains. (This can be covered and refrigerated for up to one week.)

BAGUETTE BAKING PANS

In several local kitchen shops, I have noticed curved, perforated pans for baking French baguettes. Most of these pans are built to bake three loaves at a time. Do these pans make good baguettes, and if so, why?

ERIC MANNES
New York, NY

According to the information that came with the aluminum pan we purchased, the perforations in the curved holders promote a crisp crust and even browning by allowing the oven's heat to reach the bread directly. We decided to put this claim to the test by preparing a favorite baguette recipe on a regular aluminum baking sheet, on a baking stone (which we use for pizza), and in this curved, perforated pan. The latter was lightly greased and sprinkled with cornmeal (as directed by the instruction booklet), while the stone and the regu-

lar baking sheet were simply sprinkled with cornmeal. All loaves were brushed with an egg glaze before baking to promote a rich, glossy color.

The loaves baked on the regular baking sheet clearly lost the competition. They browned unevenly and were not especially crisp. The loaves baked in the perforated pan were golden brown and pleasantly crisp. The bread baked on the stone was just as crisp and evenly browned but had one drawback—since most stones, including ours, are no more than fifteen inches across, the baguettes were a bit shorter than we would have liked. In contrast, the loaves baked in the perforated pan were seventeen inches long. While the quality of the baguettes baked in the perforated pan and on the stone were similar, the appearance of the former convinced us that buying one of these pans or a series of larger baking tiles is certainly justified. As an added benefit, the pans also make for an easier second rising.

KEEPING FOOD WARM

When entertaining or cooking a meal with several elements, I seem to have a great deal of difficulty getting everything to the table hot at the same time. Any suggestions?

JEANNENE LA BAR
Toronto, Canada

Most cooks have this problem, for which we can offer several ideas. You may want to cook the main course first and then concentrate on side dishes. For instance, roasts and many cuts of meat should rest after they are removed from the oven and before they are carved. If you cover a roast with a piece of aluminum foil, this resting period can be as long as thirty minutes, which is more than enough time to finish preparing many side dishes. Because it lacks this waiting period, a sautéed main course is much harder to incorporate into an elaborate meal.

Another good idea is to serve food on warm plates or in warm bowls. We often place heat-proof serving bowls in a 200-degree oven for ten minutes. If you take hot food off the stove and transfer it directly to warm bowls, it should stay hot for several minutes while you finish cooking. Covering bowls of hot food with foil is another good idea, but only if condensation won't affect them. Finally, you may want to think about using a microwave oven to reheat side dishes just before you serve them. A quick blast of thirty seconds or so, depending on how powerful your oven is, should do the trick. A final caveat—if you use warm serving bowls, wear oven mitts, use heat-proof trivets, and alert your guests that the bowls are hot.

KUCHEN PANS

When I make a traditional German kuchen in a springform pan, the pastry tastes metallic after a day or so. My guess is that the juice from the plum topping seeps down to the pan and causes a reaction. Is there any way, short of changing the topping, to remedy this?

GEORGIA KEBSCHULL
Raleigh, NC

Acidic fruits and their juices react chemically with the aluminum used in the most commonly available springform pans, eventually causing an off-flavor in the pastry. You have two options to prevent this: Buy a nonstick springform pan (the non-stick coating won't react with acidic juices), or line the bottom of your aluminum pan with a piece of parchment paper. If you choose to buy a new pan, you can order a nine-inch nonstick springform from the Williams-Sonoma catalog (800-541-2233) for $34.

CLAY ROASTERS REVISITED

I was extremely surprised that you gave such a poor review of clay cookers in your May/June 1994 issue (see Notes from Readers in that issue). I have used a clay cooker for about fifteen years now (I'm on my second one, in fact), and I have not experienced the problems you discussed. Contrary to your findings, when I cook chicken in my clay cooker, the skin browns and the juices are very flavorful.

I have used my clay cookers almost exclusively for whole poultry—not split chickens, as you did in your tests. I generally stuff the bird with a mixture of onions, celery, and a good dose of fresh herbs. I do not use any fat or oil on the skin. The recipe that came with my cooker advises roasting the bird at a high temperature for about one-and-a-half hours, which is considerably longer that the time in your test. By that time, the skin is brown and crispy, and the juices are thickened and very flavorful.

While clay cookers are prone to cracking, they do produce a fine roasted whole chicken. You are really missing out if you eliminate the clay cooker from your selection of cooking utensils.

DEBBIE LEE
Riverside, IL

We received several letters about our original evaluation of clay cookers. Without exception, all of the letters touted roasting whole birds (not split breasts as we had tested). So we went back into the kitchen, this time roasting a three-and-one-half pound (net weight) whole chicken.

As before, we first soaked the clay roaster in cold water for fifteen minutes. As directed by a number of readers, we seasoned the bird inside and out, stuffed the bird's cavity with half an onion and a handful of fresh herbs, and surround-ed the chicken with vegetables—halved small new potatoes, peeled and halved carrots cut into two-inch lengths, and a dozen or so peeled garlic cloves. With the chicken and vegetables in place, we put the covered clay roaster in a cold oven and turned the heat to 450 degrees. After one-and-one-half hours, we opened the pot and discovered an excellent roast chicken.

Although cooking time was considerably longer than for a bird of the same size roasted in an open pan, the skin was golden brown and crisp on top, and the meat was extremely tender and moist. (Since the chicken cooks in its own juices, the skin on the bottom half of the bird was not crisp, especially if compared to a bird roasted on a rack in an open pan.) Best of all, we had a complete meal with perfectly roasted vegetables.

After more tests, we realized that clay cookers work best when filled to capacity; several letters from readers and one from a manufacturer of clay cookers had suggested this. It seems that full cookers retain heat better than half-empty ones. We also found that it was imperative not to open the cooker to check on the chicken's progress. Removing the lid (as we did several times in our original test, to see if the chicken breasts were cooked) releases the trapped steam and heat, defeating the purpose of cooking in a covered clay pot. Therefore, cook the chicken by time—twenty-five to thirty minutes per pound for a whole chicken. If after this, the chicken does not seem quite brown enough, cook for another five or ten minutes without the lid. Exposure to direct oven heat at the end of the cooking time will crisp the skin nicely.

RISING BREAD IN THE MICROWAVE

I do not own a bread machine, because I still like to make my bread "the old-fashioned way." But I have found the perfect place for rising bread dough without having to cover it with anything, and for this, I do rely on a modern convenience.

When the bread dough is ready for rising, place it in a shallow, greased bowl and set it aside uncovered. Then pour one cup of water into a two-cup Pyrex measuring cup. Microwave the water in the cup for three minutes, or however long it takes your microwave to boil the water for between thirty and sixty seconds. Remove the measuring cup from the microwave and discard the water. Place the bowl with the bread dough in the microwave and close the door. The environment is draft-free, humid, and warm. This trick works every time.

ELIZABETH NOYES
Shoreview, MN

We find this tip to be especially helpful in chilly, winter kitchens.

MORE ORDERLY BUBBLES

I read with interest the letter in the July/August 1994 issue (see Notes from Readers, page 2) about "orderly bubbles." The reader asked why fine Champagnes exhibit orderly rows of bubbles in a glass, but cheap Champagnes and sodas do not. Since I am a chemist, I feel qualified to answer this question.

Your reply was essentially correct with regard to the speed with which bubbles are released. Since cheap Champagnes and sodas are artificially carbonated, the excess carbon dioxide is released quickly when the drink is opened. With fine Champagnes, the carbon dioxide is introduced naturally in the fermentation process and released more slowly when the beverage is poured into a glass. However, a different phenomenon is responsible for the formation of orderly rows of bubbles. Each bubble is actually an aggregate of numerous individual gas molecules that come together at something called a "nucleation site." In a glass of Champagne, the nucleation sites are provided by tiny scratches in the glass surface that contain small pockets of trapped air. Bubbles in naturally carbonated beverages keep reforming at these scratches, and this is why we see orderly rows of bubbles. Theoretically, if you mark the spots on the glass where the bubbles form, wash the glass without inducing any new scratches, and then pour more Champagne into the glass, the bubbles should form in the same spots.

DR. TRACI HOPKINS
Tucson, AZ

WHAT IS IT?

This baking utensil was given to me by an elderly aunt many years ago. I have not been able to figure out what it is for or how to use it. I hope you can tell me.

CHARLOTTE MAEDER
Park City, UT

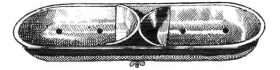

This is a German baking tool called a stollen form or stollen mold. It is used to rise and shape dough. It is especially designed for the traditional Christmas morning bread called stollen, which is made with dried and/or candied fruits, nuts, and aromatic spices. The tinned-steel mold is about fifteen inches long, five inches across, and three inches deep. After the dough has risen once, it is divided in half, and one half is placed on each side of the mold for the final rise. The metal divider, which is supposed to symbolize the baby Jesus wrapped in swaddling clothes, can also swing out away from the mold to allow for the shaping of one long loaf as opposed to two shorter loaves. The bottom of the mold is ridged to impress the stollen with markings reminiscent of a Yule log. The stollen can be baked in the form (this will make the log shape and ridged top quite pronounced) or it can be turned out onto a baking sheet. A standard stollen form will accommodate about three pounds of dough. ∎

Quick Tips

BONING A CHICKEN THIGH

In the Premier issue of *Cook's Illustrated* we showed how to bone a chicken thigh. Lee Blackwood of Olney, Maryland, suggests this alternative method, which may work better for some people.

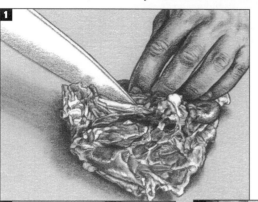

1. With the thigh skin-side down, make a lengthwise incision down to the bone. Then work the knife blade around the bone to free it from the meat.

2. Crack the thigh bone in half with the back of a large chef's knife or cleaver.

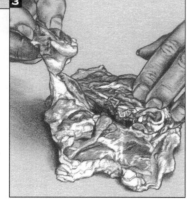

3. Pull out each half of the bone.

FREEZING FISH

Follow this quick tip from Barbara di Tulio of North Miami, Florida, to make sure that fish don't get freezer burned.

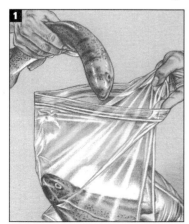

1. Partially fill a zipper-lock bag with water. Add whole fish or fillets.

2. Add more water until the fish are covered, and freeze.

BOUQUET GARNI

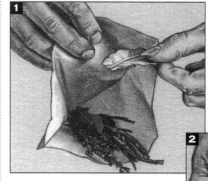

A bouquet garni is a classic French combination of herbs and spices used to flavor a wide range of dishes. Bruce Karash of Mt. Clemens, Michigan, and Cynthia A. Lay of Palm City, Florida, both suggested using a coffee filter to hold the bouquet garni.

1. Put the herbs into the coffee filter.

2. Tie the coffee filter closed, catching the stems of the thyme, etc. as you do so.

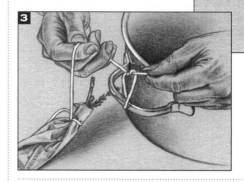

3. Tie the other end of the string to the handle of the pot or pan, so you can easily retrieve the bouquet garni.

CHOPPING A SMALL QUANTITY OF HERBS

To chop a small quantity of herbs, follow this suggestion from Barbara Nyholm of Irvine, California. Put the herbs in a small glass, and snip them with scissors until minced.

HEATING A PASTA BOWL

To easily heat a large serving bowl for your pasta, follow the advice of M. Amann of Colts Neck, New Jersey. Place a colander in the bowl, pour the pasta and water into the colander and let the hot water stand in the bowl for a few seconds to heat it. Then pour out the water, put the pasta and sauce in, toss it, and serve.

ILLUSTRATIONS BY ALAN WITSCHONKE

CREATING A VACUUM SEAL

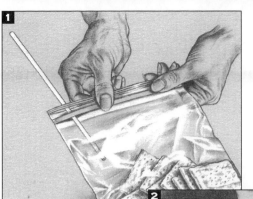

Kenneth Gray of New York, New York, suggests this method of keeping food fresh.

1. Put the food in a plastic bag and insert a straw at one side. Seal the bag around the straw.

2. Suck out as much air as possible through the straw, then remove the straw and finish sealing the bag.

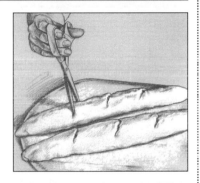

PREPARING A PERSIMMON

1. With a paring knife, cut out the large stem and surrounding leaves.

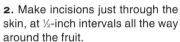

2. Make incisions just through the skin, at ½-inch intervals all the way around the fruit.

3. Peel away the thick skin, and use the fruit.

SLASHING BREAD DOUGH

Slashes in bread dough help it to expand evenly as it bakes. However, using a knife to make these slashes often pulls or tears the dough, deflating the delicate structure. Susan Asanovic of Wilton, Connecticut, has found that sharp kitchen scissors do the job quickly, cleanly, and easily.

SLICING MUSHROOMS

To slice mushrooms quickly, use an egg slicer. This tip was sent to us by Jan Mickey of Morristown, New Jersey.

CHOPPING CELERY QUICKLY

Recipes often call for a small amount of chopped celery. Rather than breaking off one or more ribs, try doing as Mary Carol Brindl of New Cumberland, Pennsylvania, suggests. Chop the entire stalk across the top. It is easier to get just the amount you need, and it makes storing the celery easier, since the whole stalk gets shorter as you use it.

DECORATING COOKIES

To make an easy garnish for cookies, place the cookies on a rack over waxed paper, dip the tines of a fork into melted chocolate, and wave the fork gently back and forth over the cookies, allowing the chocolate to drip onto them in parallel wavy lines.

ATTENTION READERS. FREE SUBSCRIPTION FOR PUBLISHED TIPS. Do you have a unique tip you would like to share with other readers? We will provide a one year complimentary subscription for each quick tip that we print. Send a description of your special technique to *Cook's Illustrated,* P.O. Box 569, Brookline Village, MA 02147-0569. Please write "Attention: Quick Tips" on the envelope and include your name, address, and daytime phone number. Unfortunately, we can only acknowledge receipt of tips that will be printed in the magazine. In case the same tip is received from two readers, the one postmarked first will be selected.

The Best Way to Cook a Goose

For a rich, flavorful roast goose with crispy browned skin, first dunk the bird in boiling water, then refrigerate for at least twenty-four hours before roasting.

~ BY STEPHEN SCHMIDT ~

Those who have never cooked a goose are in for a treat. The meat is surprisingly firm, almost chewy to the bite, yet it is also moist and not at all tough or stringy. Both the breast and legs are dark, in the manner of duck, but unlike duck, goose has no gamy or tallowy undertones. Actually, the first impression of many people is that goose tastes a lot like roast beef, and perhaps it is this rich, beefy quality that makes the bird so satisfying and festive.

Goose, however, does have a problem. Although the meat itself is not fatty, a thick layer of fat lies just below the skin. As a consequence, the skin, which looks so tempting, often turns out to be too soft and greasy to eat. I have been roasting goose for years, but I never succeeded in solving the fat problem until I began work on this article. Happily I have found a method that not only roasts but also renders.

Fat Reducing Strategies

My strategy over the years has been to periodically baste goose with chicken stock or wine as it roasts. This helps to dissolve the fat, and it also promotes a handsome brown color. In researching this article, however, I chose not to test this method, because I know from experience that the results are imperfect. A considerable amount of subcutaneous fat always remains, and worse, the basting seriously softens the skin. Last Christmas I tried a variation on this technique. During the last hour of roasting, I turned the oven heat up to 450 degrees and stopped basting. I was hoping to get crispy skin, but what I actually got was a smoky kitchen. And to no purpose—the skin was still chewy and fatty.

Among all the goose-cooking methods I had read about, I was most intrigued by the steam-roasting and closed-cover techniques recommended by various authorities. Since the best way to render fat is to simmer it in water, steaming sounded like a promising procedure.

So in my first test I set the goose on a rack over an inch of water and steamed it on top of the stove in a covered roaster for about an hour. Then I poured the water out of the pan and put the goose into a 325-degree oven, covered. After one hour I checked on the goose, and seeing that the skin was very flabby and not in the least bit brown, I removed the cover of the pan and turned the heat up to 350 degrees. Alas, an hour later the skin was still soft and only a little browner. Even though the goose tested done at this point, I let it stay in the oven for another thirty minutes, but the skin did not improve.

Despite its shortcomings, this method melted out a good deal of the subcutaneous fat, so I decided to modify it and try again. This time I poured only a few cups of water into the pan, and I put the goose directly into the oven rather than starting it on top of the stove. My plan was to roast the goose covered for about one and one half hours, and then uncover the pan, raise the oven heat, and roast for about one and one half hours longer. During the first phase, I reasoned, the goose would steam and the fat would melt; and during the second phase the dry heat of the oven would evaporate the juices in the pan and crisp the skin. Or so I hoped.

What actually happened was that I got a goose much like the first, with unsatisfactorily soft, pale skin. And tasting the goose, I realized that there was yet another problem; steaming had perhaps made the meat a tad juicier, but it had also made the texture a little rubbery and imparted a boiled, stewish flavor. The goose no longer tasted the way I thought goose should. So steaming and I parted company.

Since liquid basting and steaming had both proved unsuccessful, I thought it was time to try a simple dry roast. Some of the geese that I had bought came with instructions to roast at 500 degrees for thirty minutes and then to turn the oven down to 300 degrees and roast several hours longer. The directions said to cover the pan during the second phase of roasting, but having had poor results with covered cooking, I decided to ignore that recommendation and roast uncovered throughout. I stuffed the goose, dried and pricked the skin, and popped it into the scorching oven. As I should have guessed, within fifteen minutes the goose had begun to drip, and the kitchen had filled with smoke. I quickly turned the oven thermostat down to 325 degrees (my usual temperature for goose) and let the bird roast until it tested

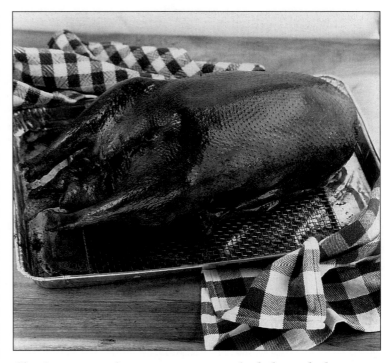

Classic accompaniments to roast goose include mashed potatoes, braised red cabbage, and Brussels sprouts. When stuffed, a ten-pound goose serves eight to ten; for more people, you will need to cook two geese.

done, about three hours. Then I increased the oven temperature to 400 degrees, transferred the goose to a large jelly-roll pan, and returned it to the oven for about fifteen minutes to brown and crisp the skin. The results surprised me. This method, the simplest of all, yielded a beautifully brown, crisp-skinned bird, with moist meat and surprisingly little unmelted fat.

Dry, open roasting looked like the way to proceed, but I wondered if the technique could be further improved. Some time ago I had read about a method for roasting duck that was adapted from the classic technique for Peking duck. The duck was immersed in boiling water for one minute and then allowed to dry, uncovered, in the refrigerator for twenty-four hours. The boiling and drying were supposed to tighten the skin, so that during roasting, the fat would be squeezed out. I tried the method with duck and found it highly effective, so I was emboldened to roast a goose using the same procedure. I loved the results. The skin was papery-crisp and defatted to the point where it could be eaten with pleasure—and without guilt.

As it happened, I wanted to do a bit more work on my stuffing, and I also needed to refine my recommendations with respect to timing and doneness. So I had to roast another goose. I boiled the bird and put it in the refrigerator, planning to roast it the next day, but something came up that prevented me from cooking it until the day after. The delay proved to be a lucky happenstance. Dried for a full two days, the goose was even crisper and less greasy than the one dried for twenty-four hours. It was perfect.

Confirming the Nature of Goose

My tests tended to confirm various observations that I have made over the years about the nature of goose meat and its reactions to cooking. As I have long noted, the breast and leg meat of a goose are not as dissimilar as the breast and leg meat of a chicken, turkey, partridge, or even a duck. Thus, while most birds require special roasting procedures—such as trussing, barding, or basting—to keep the breast at a lower temperature than the legs and prevent it from drying out, goose can simply be put in the oven and left alone except for turning it over at the halfway mark to ensure even cooking.

These tests also demonstrated to me that the doneness of goose cannot be judged solely by the internal temperature of the meat. The length of the cooking time is also an important factor. Goose generally reaches an internal temperature of 170 degrees in the thigh cavity (the usual indicator of "well done") after less than two hours of roasting. Yet the meat turns out to be tough, especially around the thighs, if the bird is removed from the oven at this point. At least forty-five minutes of additional roasting are required. The most reliable indicator of doneness, is the feel of the drumsticks. When the skin has puffed and the meat inside feels soft and almost shredded when pressed—like well-done stew meat—the rest of the bird should be just right.

Another good way to test for doneness is to make a small slit in the skin at the base of the thigh, where it joins the body. If the juices are pinkish rather than clear, the bird needs more cooking. If, on the other hand, there are no juices, the goose has been cooked enough and may even be verging on overdone. Don't panic though. One of the nicest things about goose is that it is tolerant of a little overcooking and does not readily dry out and turn stringy. This is because the particular proteins in goose tend to turn soft and gelatinous during cooking, so goose remains moist and tender even when thoroughly cooked.

ROAST GOOSE WITH PRUNE AND APPLE STUFFING AND RED WINE GIBLET GRAVY
Serves 8–10
Turning the goose in the boiling water may not be necessary if you have a stock pot large enough for the goose to be fully submerged. To make sure there is plenty of meat to go around, I make up the plates in the kitchen rather than passing platters at the table. Mound a big spoonful of stuffing on the plate and bank three to four slices of meat against it. Moisten both stuffing and meat with gravy, and lay a strip or two of skin over the top.

Roast Goose
1 roasting goose (10 to 12 pounds gross weight), neck, giblets, wing tips, and excess fat removed, rinsed, patted dry, and reserved; wishbone removed and skin pricked all over (*see* illustrations 1 through 4, page 8)
Salt and ground black pepper

Brown Goose Stock
3 tablespoons reserved goose fat, patted dry and chopped
 Reserved goose neck and wing tips, cut into 1-inch pieces; heart and gizzard left whole, all parts patted dry
1 medium onion, peeled and chopped
1 medium carrot, peeled and chopped
1 medium celery stalk, chopped
2 teaspoons sugar
2 cups full-bodied red wine
½ cup chicken stock or low-salt canned broth
6 large parsley stems
1 large bay leaf
1 teaspoon black peppercorns
½ teaspoon dried thyme

Prune and Apple Stuffing
6 ounces (about 1 cup) pitted prunes, cut into ½-inch pieces
⅓ cup sweet sherry (cream or amontillado)
8 ounces homemade-style white bread, cut into ½-inch cubes (about 4 cups lightly packed)
⅓ cup reserved goose fat, patted dry and chopped
3 medium onions, chopped fine (about 3 cups)
3 medium celery stalks, chopped fine (about 1½ cups)
3 medium-large (1½ pounds) Granny Smith apples, peeled and cut into ½-inch chunks (about 3 cups)
6 ounces Black Forest ham, minced (about 1 cup)
2 tablespoons minced fresh sage or 1½ teaspoons rubbed dried sage
 Salt and ground black pepper
¼ teaspoon ground cloves
¼ teaspoon grated nutmeg or ground mace

Red Wine Giblet Gravy
1 recipe Brown Goose Stock
½ cup sweet sherry (cream or amontillado)
½ cup chicken stock or low-salt canned broth, if needed
2½ tablespoons melted goose fat from the roasting pan
2½ tablespoons all-purpose flour
1 goose liver, cut into small dice
 Salt and ground black pepper

1. *For the goose,* fill a large stock pot two-thirds of the way with water and bring to a rolling boil. Following illustration 5 on page 8, submerge goose in boiling water. Drain goose and dry thoroughly, inside and out, with paper towels. Set goose, breast side up, on rack in roasting pan and refrigerate, uncovered, for 24 to 48 hours.

2. *For the stock,* heat fat over medium heat in a large saucepan until it melts, leaving small browned bits. Increase heat to medium-high; heat fat until it just begins to smoke. Add goose pieces and giblets to fat; sauté, stirring frequently, until meat turns deep mahogany color, about 10 minutes. Add onions, carrots, and celery; sauté, stirring frequently, until vegetables brown around edges, about 10 minutes longer. Stir in sugar; continue to cook, stirring continuously, until it caramelizes and begins to smoke. Pour in wine, scraping pan bottom with a wooden spoon to dissolve browned bits. Add chicken stock, parsley, bay leaf, peppercorns, and thyme. Bring to simmer, then adjust heat so that liquid barely bubbles; simmer, partially covered, until stock is dark and rich, about 2 hours, adding a little water if solids become exposed. (Can be cooled to room temperature and refrigerated in the saucepan up to 3 days—do not strain at this point.)

3. *For the stuffing,* soak prunes in sherry in a small bowl, at least 2 hours, preferably overnight.

4. Heat oven to 400 degrees. Spread bread cubes over large baking sheet; bake, stirring occasionally, until cubes are lightly toasted, but still soft inside, about 10 minutes.

5. Heat fat in 12-inch skillet over medium heat

HOW TO PREPARE AND STUFF A GOOSE

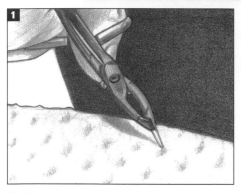

1. Use tweezers or small pliers to remove any remaining quills from the goose.

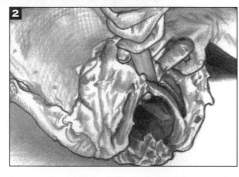

2. Pull back the skin at the neck end and locate the wishbone. Scrape along the outside of the wishbone with a paring knife until the bone is exposed; then cut the bone free of the flesh.

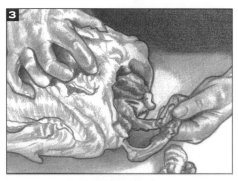

3. Pull down on the wishbone, freeing it from the carcass; add the bone to the stock pot.

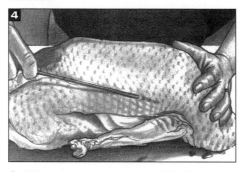

4. With a trussing needle, prick the goose skin all over, especially around the breast and thighs, holding the needle nearly parallel to the bird to avoid pricking the meat.

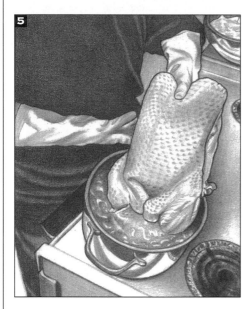

5. Using rubber gloves to protect your hands from possible splashes of boiling water, lower the goose, neck end down, into the water, submerging as much of the goose as possible until "goose bumps" appear, about 1 minute. Repeat this process, submerging the goose tail end down.

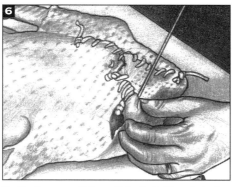

6. Pack a small handful of stuffing into the neck cavity; sew the opening shut with a trussing needle and heavy white twine.

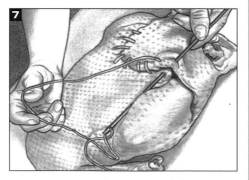

7. Pack the remaining stuffing in the body cavity, pressing it in firmly with your hands or a large spoon; sew the body vent shut.

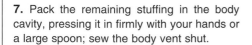

until it melts, leaving small browned bits. Leaving 2 tablespoons fat in skillet, remove and set aside remaining fat. Increase heat to medium-high. Add onions and celery; sauté until vegetables soften, 5 to 7 minutes. Scrape vegetables into a large mixing bowl. Return skillet to burner; heat 2 tablespoons reserved fat. Add apples, sauté until golden and soft but not mushy, 5 to 7 minutes. Add apples to onions and celery. Stir in ham, sage, ¾ teaspoon each salt and pepper or to taste, cloves, and nutmeg or mace, along with prunes, unabsorbed sherry, and bread cubes. (This can be covered and refrigerated a day ahead. Turn mixture into a 13-by-9-inch or comparably-sized microwave-safe pan and reheat in 325 degree oven or microwave until stuffing is warmed through before packing it into goose.)

6. Adjust oven rack to low-center position and heat to 325 degrees. Following illustrations 6 and 7, stuff and truss goose. Season goose skin liberally with salt and pepper.

7. Place goose, breast down, on heavy-duty wire rack set over a deep roasting pan; roast for 1½ hours. Remove goose from oven and bail out most of fat from roasting pan, being careful not to disturb browned bits at bottom. Turn goose breast up, and return to oven to roast until flesh of drumsticks feels soft and broken up (like well-done stew meat) and skin has puffed up around breast bone and tops of thighs, from 1¼ to 1½ hours longer. Increase oven temperature to 400 degrees; transfer goose, still on its rack, to large jelly-roll pan. Return to oven to further brown and fully crisp skin, about 15 minutes longer. Let stand, uncovered, about ½ hour before carving.

8. Meanwhile, *for the gravy,* bring reserved goose stock to simmer. Spoon most of fat out of roasting pan, leaving behind all brown roasting particles. Set pan over two burners on low heat. Add sherry; scrape with wooden spoon until all of brown glaze in pan is dissolved. Pour mixture into goose stock; simmer to blend flavors, about 5 minutes. Strain mixture into 4-cup glass measure, pressing down on solids with back of a spoon; let liquid stand until fat rises to top. Skim fat, and if necessary add enough chicken broth to make up to 2 cups. Rinse out goose stock pot and return strained stock to it. Take gizzard and heart from strainer, cut in tiny dice, and add to goose stock. Return stock to boil.

9. Heat goose fat and flour over medium-low heat in heavy-bottomed medium saucepan, stirring constantly with wooden spoon until roux just begins to color, about 5 minutes; remove from heat. Beating constantly with whisk, pour boiling stock, all at once, into brown roux. Return saucepan to low heat; simmer 3 minutes. Add liver; simmer 1 minute longer. Taste, and adjust seasoning, adding salt and lots of fresh black pepper.

10. Remove trussing, and spoon stuffing into serving bowl. Carve goose following illustrations on pages 16 and 17. Serve stuffing and carved goose immediately; pass gravy separately. ∎

Stephen Schmidt is the author of *Master Recipes* (Ballantine, 1987).

ILLUSTRATIONS BY WENDY WRAY

Popovers Perfected

To get twice as many high-popping popovers from the same amount of batter, use a preheated twelve-hole muffin tin.

～ BY DEBORAH KRASNER ～

Popovers seem like magic. Made from a simple, thin batter of eggs, flour, milk, and melted butter, they pop up in the oven to triple their original height with no help from leavening of any sort. This amazing feat is actually the result of two factors. A hot oven and a pan that is deeper than it is wide cause the steam released during baking to make a giant bubble which is contained by a structure created by the starches and proteins in the batter.

I set out to discover how to make the ideal popover: one that pops up high with a thin, crusty exterior and a relatively dry interior with threads of custardy dough. Surprisingly in a recipe so simple, this meant testing a large number of variations of both ingredients and technique.

Checking the Ingredients

First I looked for the best ratio of eggs to milk and flour. Starting with two large eggs, I worked my way up to four extra-large eggs while keeping the amount of milk and flour constant. I found that two extra-large eggs provided enough fat and protein to pop reliably and well, but without giving an overwhelming eggy flavor.

Next I tested the butter. Some recipes call for up to four tablespoons of melted butter in the pan. But after varying the quantity from less than one tablespoon up to the full four tablespoons, I concluded that only a thin film of butter was needed in the pan.

I then tried making popovers with and without melted butter in the batter. Both ways worked, and our taste panel was evenly divided on which method tasted better. Those who like a custard texture preferred the no butter version; those who prefer a crisp exterior and maximum pop liked the buttered batter. I decided that a batter with a minimal amount of melted butter (one tablespoon) gave the most consistent and best-tasting result.

With the proportions of ingredients set, I tested the recipe again to see how it would change with four different kinds of flour: bleached and bromated white flour, unbleached white flour, cake flour, and whole wheat flour. Bleached and unbleached white flour both gave good results, while whole wheat and cake flour both produced heavy muffins that never really popped.

Testing Time, Temperature, and Tins

With the ingredient list completed, I turned to other variables in the recipe—oven temperature, baking time, and baking container.

I started by sticking to one oven temperature—400 degrees. But after much experimentation I found that baking at 450 for twenty minutes created maximum height, and then lowering the temperature to 350 for another fifteen to twenty minutes ensured that the inside had the right texture.

To test the effect of the pan, I tried a six-bowl popover pan; a six-bowl crown muffin pan; deep, porcelain ramekins; and my old, tried and true, twelve-hole, blackened-by-use, aluminum muffin tin.

The surprise winner was my humble muffin tin. Deep, six-bowl popover pans (like the tinned-steel and Silverstone models) use the same amount of batter as a standard, twelve-hole muffin tin. But each "hole" in the popover pans is larger, and the batter is poured into any pan up to somewhere between the half and two-thirds mark. What I discovered was that a given amount of batter would produce the same size popovers whether it was divided between six deep bowls or twelve shallower ones! This means that the popovers cooked in the twelve-hole muffin tin popped twice as much as the other popovers. Therefore, the popovers made in the muffin tin were lighter, and when opened, their interiors were indistinguishable from the heavier popovers.

I also tried cooking popovers in both hot and cold pans, and in preheated and cold ovens. Surprisingly, all variations worked, although there is some sacrifice in pop when using cold pans in a cold oven. The best results came from room-temperature batter poured into sizzling-hot pans and cooked in a preheated oven.

THE BEST POPOVERS
Makes 1 dozen in a muffin tin
This batter can be made ahead and refrigerated for up to four days. If you're making it ahead, bring it to room temperature and stir well before pouring it into a hot pan.

- 1   cup all-purpose flour
- ¼   teaspoon salt
- 1   cup whole milk
- 2   extra-large eggs
- 1   tablespoon unsalted butter, melted, plus additional melted butter,

Many recipes recommend piercing just-baked popovers with a sharp knife and putting them back in the oven for a few minutes to dry the interior and thus prevent collapse. We found this to be unnecessary when popovers are cooked using our two-temperature method.

vegetable oil, or vegetable oil spray to grease the pan

1. Adjust oven rack to low position and heat oven to 450 degrees. Place empty muffin or popover tin in oven to heat while making batter.

2. Whisk flour and salt together in medium bowl. In a 2-cup Pyrex measuring cup, lightly whisk together milk, eggs, and butter. Pour wet ingredients into dry ingredients all at once; whisk until just blended. (Batter can be made ahead and refrigerated in sealed container for up to four days.) Pour batter into measuring cup for easy pouring.

3. Remove hot pan from oven, lightly grease interior of each cup and pan rim.

4. Fill each cup half full with batter. Bake without opening oven door for 20 minutes. Lower heat to 350 degrees and continue to bake until popovers are rich brown in color, 15 to 20 minutes longer. Serve warm. (Popovers can be frozen in airtight plastic bags, and warmed in 325-degree oven until heated through, 5 to 10 minutes.) ■

Deborah Krasner is the author of *Kitchens for Cooks* (Viking Studio Books, 1994).

Classic Lasagne Made Easy

Starting from the premise that less sauce and more pasta is better, we devise a recipe with classic tastes but without the backbreaking labor.

∼ BY JACK BISHOP ∼

I love the lasagne that my eighty-four-year-old grandmother has made every Christmas since I was kid, but I seldom make it—it contains twenty-five ingredients and takes an entire day to prepare. In fact, this dish, which is based on the cooking of southern Italy, is so time-consuming that my grandmother starts the preparation weeks before the holidays to break up the work.

I decided to explore this classic meat-and-tomato lasagne—certainly the most popular kind of lasagne in this country—in an attempt to come up with a recipe as good as my grandmother's but without the backbreaking effort. I also wanted to create a lasagne that reflected the Italian preference for restrained saucing. For inspiration, I looked to Bolognese lasagne from northern Italy. Few Americans are willing to make a ragù, a meat sauce that has to simmer for four hours, or béchamel, the classic white sauce, both of which are contained in Bolognese lasagne. However, the proportions in this dish are to my taste; it avoids the unhappy sight of mushy noodles swimming in a sea of red sauce and cheese.

Cheese, Meatballs, and Sauce

My first task was to make sense of the cheese component. Various recipes call for mozzarella, ricotta (sometimes mixed with whole eggs or egg yolks), and/or a hard grating cheese (usually Parmesan, but sometimes Pecorino). After trying the various combinations, I realized that ricotta was responsible for what I call "lasagne meltdown"—the loss of shape and distinct layering. Even with the addition of whole eggs or yolks as a thickener, I found that ricotta was too watery to use in lasagne and usually leads to a sloppy mess.

Mozzarella provides more than enough creaminess, and its stringiness binds the layers to each other and helps keep them from slipping apart when served. My grandmother uses shrink-wrapped mozzarella in her lasagne, and after a few disastrous attempts with fresh mozzarella, I now know why. Fresh mozzarella has too much moisture to be effective. When it melts, it releases so much liquid that the lasagne becomes mushy and watery. In addition, the delicate flavor of expensive fresh mozzarella is lost in the baking. I also found that a small amount of either Parmesan or Pecorino provides a pleasantly sharp contrast to the somewhat bland mozzarella.

With the cheese question resolved, I next focused on the sauce. Here again I looked to my grandmother for inspiration, then tried to simplify. Most lasagne recipes in American cookbooks call for a tomato sauce built on browned ground beef. When I tried these sauces, I thought the beef tasted bland and washed out. Before my grandmother cooks the beef, she seasons it with herbs, cheese, egg yolks, and bread crumbs—in effect making a meatball mixture. However, instead of rolling out real meatballs, which would be too large to rest snugly between the layers of pasta, she pinches off small bits of the mixture directly into hot oil. These free-form mini-meatballs don't require tedious shaping (in fact, if some fall apart that's fine) and are cooked in just a few minutes.

Since my aim was to simplify matters, I decided to add the drained meatballs to a quick-cooking tomato sauce made with crushed tomatoes. My grandmother (as well as many recipe writers) simmers whole tomatoes or tomato puree for hours to make a rich, complex sauce. However, since lasagne has so many competing elements, I found that little was gained by this lengthy process. Simmering canned, crushed tomatoes just long enough to make a sauce—about fifteen minutes—is sufficient.

Instead of large meatballs, this lasagne calls for free-form mini-meatballs, which are easy to shape, cook quickly, and fit well between pasta layers.

Putting It All Together

With my sauce and cheese combinations down, I focused on the choice of noodles and layering tricks. After much experimentation, I realized that some noodles are far superior to others (see "The Right Lasagne Noodle," page 11). Choosing either imported noodles or fresh sheets of pasta (purchased or homemade) guarantees thin, delicate layers in your lasagne.

In terms of the actual layering procedure, I find it helpful to grease the baking pan with cooking spray. (Use a thirteen-by-nine-inch metal, glass, or ceramic dish with square corners that the pasta can easily rest against.) Spread a small amount of tomato sauce without large chunks of meat over the pan to moisten the bottom layer of pasta. Then lay down the first layer of noodles (choose large, whole noodles for this layer). Spread sauce and meatballs evenly over the noodles, cover this with shredded mozzarella, then sprinkle on grated Parmesan. Build four more layers by this same process, using any broken noodles here in the middle where they won't be seen. The tomato sauce and meatballs tend to dry out when not covered by pasta so the sixth and final layer is covered only by the two cheeses, which brown during baking to give an attractive appearance.

Lasagne should be baked just until the top turns golden brown in spots and the sauce is bubbling, twenty to twenty-five minutes at 400 degrees. If you have any doubts about it being done, stick a knife into the center of the pan and hold it there

---

LASAGNE CONSTRUCTION TIPS

1. Dried Italian lasagne noodles should be layered crosswise (not lengthwise) in a 13-by-9-inch pan.
2. Lay cooked fresh noodles in the pan. Use sharp scissors to trim them to fit.

ILLUSTRATIONS BY TONY DELUZ

for two seconds. When you remove it, the tip of the blade should be quite hot.

When the lasagne is cooked, remove it from the oven and let it rest for five minutes before serving. This gives everything a chance to cool slightly and solidify a little. (Cover the pan with foil if you need to hold the baked lasagne for more than five minutes.) To serve, use a sharp knife to cut squares of no more than three inches; larger pieces are almost impossible to extract intact from the pan. A flexible plastic spatula is the best way to dig underneath the lasagne and lift the pieces out.

If you want to prepare lasagne in advance, complete the layering process and then wrap the pan tightly with plastic wrap and refrigerate it for up to one day. To cook it, take the chilled lasagne directly from the refrigerator, unwrap the pan, and place it in a preheated oven. Uncooked lasagne can also be wrapped in plastic and then covered with aluminum foil and frozen for up to a month. To cook it, at least twelve hours before baking, move the lasagne to the refrigerator. Allow it to defrost slowly, and then transfer it directly to a preheated oven.

LASAGNE WITH HERBED MEATBALLS, TOMATO SAUCE, AND MOZZARELLA
Serves 8

Herbed Meatballs
  1 pound ground beef
  2 large eggs, lightly beaten
  ⅓ cup minced fresh basil or parsley leaves
  ½ cup grated Parmesan or Pecorino Romano cheese (2 ounces)
  ½ cup plain dried bread crumbs
  1 teaspoon salt
  ½ teaspoon ground black pepper
     Olive oil for pan-frying meatballs

Simple Tomato Sauce
  3 tablespoons olive oil
  2 medium garlic cloves, minced
  1 can crushed tomatoes (28 ounces)
  2 tablespoons minced fresh basil or parsley leaves
     Salt and ground black pepper

  1 tablespoon salt
  1 pound fresh pasta sheets or 18 dried lasagne noodles
  1 pound mozzarella cheese, shredded
  1 cup grated Parmesan or Pecorino Romano cheese (4 ounces)

1. *For the meatballs,* mix beef, eggs, basil, cheese, bread crumbs, salt, and pepper in medium bowl until well blended. Heat about ¼ inch of oil in large skillet. Take a handful of meat mixture, and working directly over skillet, pinch off pieces no larger than a small grape, and flatten them slightly. Cooking in batches to avoid overcrowding, carefully drop them into hot oil (*see* illustration, page 10). Fry, turning once, until evenly browned, 3 to 4 minutes. Use a slotted spoon to transfer meatballs to a paper towel on a platter.

2. *For the sauce,* heat oil with garlic in medium saucepan over medium heat. When garlic starts to sizzle, add tomatoes, basil, and salt and pepper to taste. Simmer until sauce thickens slightly, 15 to 20 minutes.

3. Add meatballs to tomato sauce and heat through for several minutes; adjust seasonings. Keep sauce warm while preparing remaining ingredients. (Sauce can be covered and refrigerated for 2 days; reheat before assembly.)

4. Meanwhile, bring 6 quarts of water to boil in large soup kettle. Add salt and pasta. (*See* "The Right Lasagne Noodle," below, for specific cooking and draining instructions.)

5. Grease a 13-by-9-inch pan with cooking spray. Smear several tablespoons of tomato sauce (without large meatballs) across pan bottom. Line pan with a layer of pasta, making sure that noodles touch but do not overlap. Spread ¾ cup of tomato sauce evenly over pasta. Sprinkle evenly with ⅔ cup mozzarella and 2½ tablespoons Parmesan. Repeat layering of pasta, tomato sauce and meatballs, and cheeses four more times. For the sixth and final layer, cover pasta with remaining 1 cup mozzarella and sprinkle with remaining 3½ tablespoons Parmesan. (Assembled lasagne can now be wrapped with plastic and refrigerated overnight or wrapped in plastic and aluminum foil and frozen for up to 1 month.)

6. Adjust oven rack to center position and heat oven to 400 degrees. Bake until cheese on top turns golden brown in spots and sauce is bubbling, 20 to 25 minutes (25 to 35 minutes with chilled lasagne). Remove pan from oven and let lasagna rest for 5 minutes. Cut and serve. ∎

THE RIGHT LASAGNE NOODLE

There is a seemingly endless number of choices when it comes to lasagne noodles—domestic and imported dried noodles, dried no-boil noodles, fresh no-boil noodles, purchased fresh pasta sheets, and homemade pasta. After making a hundred lasagne recipes, I have come clear recommendations.

There is no doubt in my mind that fresh noodles (either homemade or store-bought) make the best lasagne. Sheets of fresh pasta are now available in many Italian delicatessens, gourmet stores, and even some of the better supermarkets. (Check with the deli manager to see if fresh noodles must be ordered in advance.) While labels on some of these refrigerated noodles claim that cooking is not necessary, I recommend that you treat them as you would homemade.

If for reasons of convenience or availability you use dried noodles, be aware that their quality varies considerably. Some are quite good, others are quite wretched. The key is thinness. Every American brand I tested was too thick. Italian noodles are generally thinner and better approximate the delicate texture of fresh pasta. The best way to judge dried noodles is by counting the number of sheets per pound. Most domestic brands have eighteen or twenty noodles in a one-pound box. In contrast, a box of my favorite Italian brand, DeCecco, has twenty-eight noodles in a pound. This brand, which is the most widely available imported Italian pasta, has shorter, wider noodles that fit just right when laid crosswise in a standard lasagne pan (*see* illustration 1). This makes for a much neater lasagne than longer noodles which never seem quite long enough to fit a thirteen-by-nine-inch pan.

Several companies have recently introduced "no-boil" dried noodles. The packages say that the noodles will "cook" in the oven and don't need to be boiled first. After trying three brands, I concluded this claim is true only if you follow the manufacturers' recipes, which call for the addition of stock or water to the pan. If you make a standard lasagne recipe, including mine, the no-boil noodles will suck all the moisture out of the sauce as they attempt to rehydrate in the oven.

As for cooking instructions, eighteen sheets of dried DeCecco noodles (enough for a six-layer lasagne) can be boiled at one time. Since it can be hard to taste whole lasagne sheets for doneness, throw in any scraps or broken pieces. You may also want to add a few extra noodles (remember, there are twenty-eight per package) in case some break as they cook. When noodles are almost *al dente*, drain them, then soak them for thirty seconds in a bowl of ice-cold water, drain them again, and lay them out on kitchen towels for up to one hour.

One pound of fresh noodles (either purchased or made with two cups of flour and three large eggs) is enough for a standard six-layer lasagne. Cook long sheets of fresh noodles in batches of three or four. When the noodles are almost al dente (after one to two minutes), gently retrieve them with a large slotted spoon and transfer them to a bowl of ice-cold water for thirty seconds. Then drain the noodles and lay them out on kitchen towels for up to one hour. Repeat the process with three or four more noodles and a fresh bowl of ice-cold water.

Authentic Panforte Di Siena

When made at home, this classic Italian holiday confection has a fresh, sweet taste and a chewy texture halfway between fruitcake and candy.

∼ BY NICK MALGIERI ∼

The Italian confection known as *panforte* is difficult to describe accurately to someone who has never tasted it. The best description may be that it is something like a cross between fruitcake, candy, and certain rather firm honey cakes from Northern Europe called *Lebkuchen* ("lasting" cakes). Like fruitcake, panforte has acquired a somewhat dubious reputation, because most people are familiar only with commercial versions. But good panforte is a wonderful holiday confection; it has a rich, complex flavor, a delicately perfumed scent, and a pleasantly moist and chewy texture.

Of course the best way to be sure that panforte has all these qualities is to make it yourself. Your homemade panforte will taste infinitely better than the imported, manufactured ones, which are very often hard and dry due to improper wrapping. Just-baked panforte has an incomparably fresh flavor and tender texture.

Panforte from your own kitchen will even taste better than the enormous panforti for sale in Siena, Italy, the home of this confection. These great wheels, usually more than a foot in diameter and about two inches thick, are sold by the piece. Though less dry than the export variety, they cannot match the freshness of homemade.

Choosing the Right Ingredients

Classic panforte is made from honey, sugar, cake flour, almonds, candied fruit, and spices, although these ingredients may be varied for different flavors. Panforte is simple to prepare, but everything that goes into it must be of the highest quality and as fresh as possible if the result is to have the right flavor.

First, since this is a confection, make sure you use the right sweeteners. For the honey, use a dark, robust variety, so that its flavor will not be obscured by the spices. A lighter-colored honey, such as orange blossom, will work well in the Blond Panforte, which has no spices. Granulated sugar is generally the sugar of choice for all types of panforti, though light or dark brown sugar will work well too, and add a different dimension of flavor to the Dried Fruit or Chocolate Panforte.

Cake flour, with its low protein content, is used to prevent the batter from becoming elastic and glutinous. As for the spices, it is best to buy them whole and grind them yourself with a spice mill, a coffee grinder, or a mortar and pestle. Fresh ground spices have a much richer and more aromatic taste than even the highest quality preground ones.

In the classic version of panforte, candied fruits of all types are used. I prefer orange peel and citron for their complementary tangy and mellow flavors. (*See* page 32 for mail-order sources for both candied orange peel and candied citron.) If you really do not like candied fruit, then light or dark figs, dried apricots, or even dark or golden raisins may be substituted for some or all of it.

As for the nuts, I like to use blanched (skinless) almonds, but leaving the skins on will not change the flavor, although the skins will muddy the color of the Blond Panforte. Hazelnuts may be substituted for part of the almonds, and walnuts are a good flavor complement in the Chocolate Panforte.

Equipment and Technique

The panforte described here is baked in an eight-inch layer cake pan either one and one-half or two inches deep. Panforte batter is very dense and extremely sticky, so the bottom of the pan must be lined with a disk of parchment paper to ensure easy removal. You may use wax paper if parchment paper is not readily available, or you may even line the entire pan with foil. But whatever you use, be sure not to pour the panforte batter into an unlined pan.

In fact, the texture of panforte requires the use of another layer of paper. If you look at the bottom of any imported panforte, you will notice that it is covered with a disk of white paper. Any attempts to peel this away will meet with failure, because the paper is baked onto the panforte. This is done to keep the slightly oozy confection from losing its shape after baking. Fortunately, this baked-on paper is edible. Called *ostia* in Italian, it is edible wheat starch paper and is also used for the outside of *torrone*, an Italian nougat candy, and to make hosts or altar breads for Mass. There are a number of substitutes for ostia (*see* "Edible Linings," page 13). Lacking any of these, you can make an acceptable substitute by scattering a mixture of one tablespoon cake flour, one tablespoon dry bread crumbs, and two tablespoons ground almonds on top of the buttered parchment paper.

A holdover from the late Middle Ages, when the use of nuts, preserved fruits, and spices signified luxury and wealth, panforte is dense, chewy, spicy, and sweet.

This mixture will provide a base that helps the baked panforte keep its shape. The top of the panforte is sifted over with cinnamon-laced flour to prevent it from becoming crusty and hard as it bakes.

A final note of caution: Be careful not to overbake the panforte; if you do, it will boil over. A little bubbling at the side of the pan is to be expected, but no more.

When the panforte has been cooled and unmolded, wrap it in several layers of plastic wrap, then cover it with foil. It can be stored for several weeks at room temperature in a tightly-sealed tin. Freeze it for longer-term storage.

PANFORTE DI SIENA
Serves 16

Butter for greasing the pan
Wheat starch paper, oblaten, Asian-
 style rice paper, *or* bread crumb
 substitution (*see* below) for lining
 the pan
½ cup plus 2 tablespoons cake flour
1½ teaspoons ground cinnamon
¼ teaspoon ground coriander
¼ teaspoon ground cloves

¼ teaspoon ground nutmeg
½ cup honey
½ cup granulated sugar
½ cup candied citron or candied melon
    (about 3 ounces), cut into small dice
½ cup candied orange peel (about
    3 ounces), cut into small dice
1 cup blanched almonds (about
    5 ounces), toasted and coarsely
    chopped
    Confectioners' sugar for dusting
    the panforte before serving

Bread Crumb Pan Lining (optional)
1 tablespoon cake flour
1 tablespoon dry bread crumbs
2 tablespoons ground almonds

1. Adjust oven rack to center position and heat oven to 300 degrees. Brush an 8-by-1½-inch round cake pan with butter. Cut a disk of parchment or wax paper to fit pan bottom. Brush paper with butter and fit into pan bottom.

2. Line pan bottom with wheat starch paper, oblaten, or rice paper, overlapping the paper by about ½ inch at seam. If substituting Bread Crumb Pan Lining mixture, mix flour, bread crumbs, and almonds; then evenly scatter it over buttered surface and pat gently into place (*see* illustration 1).

3. Mix ½ cup cake flour, 1 teaspoon cinnamon, and the coriander, cloves, and nutmeg; set this spiced flour aside. Mix remaining 2 tablespoons flour with ½ teaspoon cinnamon; set this cinnamon flour aside, as well.

4. Pour honey, then sugar into medium saucepan. Cook over low heat, stirring occasionally to prevent scorching, until mixture comes to a full boil.

5. Remove from heat; stir in candied fruit and almonds. Sift spiced flour over the mixture; stir until smooth. Scrape batter into prepared pan. Smooth top with the slightly wet palm of your hand or an oiled spoon (illustration 2). Sift cinnamon flour through strainer over the top (illustration 3).

1. If you are not using one of the edible paper linings, sprinkle the almond-flour-bread crumb mixture into the baking pan on top of the round of parchment paper.

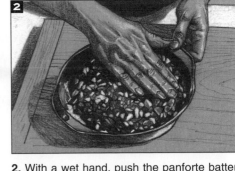

2. With a wet hand, push the panforte batter to the edges of the pan and smooth the top.

3. Sift the cinnamon flour onto the panforte batter.

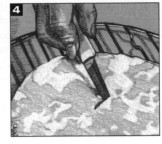

4. Use a paring knife to lift the parchment paper at the center of the panforte.

5. Peel the parchment paper off the bottom of the panforte.

6. Bake until panforte just starts to simmer around edge of pan, 20 to 25 minutes. If it begins to simmer at edge much before 20 minutes, place pan on a cookie sheet or jelly roll pan to insulate bottom, and check carefully as it bakes to be sure it does not simmer again.

7. Remove pan from oven; let cool to room temperature on wire rack. Invert pan to let cinnamon flour fall away. Loosen panforte from pan by running a small knife around perimeter. Invert onto wire rack. Use knife to peel away parchment (illustrations 4 and 5).

8. Invert panforte again and allow to cool completely. (When cool, it can be wrapped in several layers of plastic wrap and a layer of foil and stored in an airtight container for several weeks, or frozen for up to 6 months.) Before serving, dust with confectioners' sugar and cut in small wedges.

DRIED FRUIT PANFORTE
Serves 16
Follow recipe for Panforte Di Siena, making the following changes: reduce candied citron and orange peel from ½ cup to ¼ cup each. Add ¼ cup each, stemmed and finely diced dried figs and dried apricots.

CHOCOLATE PANFORTE
Serves 16
Follow recipe for Panforte Di Siena, making the following changes: Add 4 ounces chopped semisweet or bittersweet chocolate to honey and sugar mixture as it comes off the heat. Cover and let stand until chocolate melts, about 2 minutes. Add ¼ teaspoon salt to the flour and spices.

BLOND PANFORTE
Serves 16
Follow recipe for Panforte Di Siena, making the following changes: omit spices. Add ¾ cup (about 4 ounces) ground blanched almonds to the batter along with the cake flour. Omit cinnamon from the covering flour. ∎

Nick Malgieri is the director of the baking program at Peter Kump's New York Cooking School and the author of *Great Italian Desserts* (Little, Brown, 1990).

EDIBLE LININGS

If you can't locate the edible wheat starch paper known as *ostia*, try using German *oblaten* or Asian rice paper.

Oblaten, used as the base for Lebkuchen cookies, are available in several different sizes (*see* Sources and Resources, page 32). I have used all sizes with equal success—rectangular oblaten about four and one-half by eight inches are the easiest to use for lining the panforte, but the other shapes and sizes may also be used. One note of caution: The German word oblaten refers to a large variety of prepared wafers including some served on their own as cookies and others used in making cakes and cookies. Not all are made from wheat starch or appropriate to use for the panforte base.

Another substitute for ostia is Asian-style rice paper, which is available in Asian stores. Its large size makes it easy to line a baking pan without patching. Wet the paper to make it easier to cut, then trim it to the correct size with scissors. Before lining the pan, be sure the pan has first been buttered and lined with parchment paper, wax paper, or foil, so you can remove the panforte after baking.

Cut rice paper to proper shape to fit bottom of pan.

New Uses for Cranberries

Cranberries can go way beyond the standard "sauce"—try them in a flavorful confit, butter, chutney, or relish.

❧ BY KAREN TACK ❧

Along with Concord grapes and blueberries, cranberries are one of the three indigenous fruits of North America. This firm, deep red fruit is harvested in the late fall, which makes it one of America's latest-ripening fruits. Although some supermarkets have realized that cranberries can be easily frozen and sold year-round, these berries are one of the few foods that even today can be found in a fresh state for only a few months each year.

Before cooking cranberries—they are seldom eaten raw, and then only when minced and combined with other ingredients—it is important to sort through them carefully. Leave in any white berries, but discard any that are bruised, bloated, or soft.

The distinctive, tart flavor of cranberries has long made them a favorite accompaniment for game and fowl, particularly the holiday turkey or goose. However, there are many ways to use them beyond the same old sauce. Combine these seasonal berries with onions for a sweet-sour confit, or make a smooth butter of cranberries and pears. Apples, cranberries, and classic Indian spices create a spicy chutney, while bell peppers and chiles join cranberries to make a hot relish.

CRANBERRY-ONION CONFIT
Makes about 3 cups

This sweet-and-sour confit can be served with rich meats, game, pork, and even turkey. It refrigerates well but should be served at room temperature or above. Its lovely dark red color makes it an excellent gift idea.

Cranberries need not be red to be ripe—the sorting process determines their ripeness by the height they achieve when bounced.

6 tablespoons unsalted butter
4 large onions (2½ pounds), thinly sliced (about 7 cups)
½ cup sugar
2 cups whole cranberries, picked through
1 cup red wine
¼ cup red wine vinegar
3 tablespoons grenadine (optional)
1 teaspoon salt

1. Heat butter in a nonreactive soup kettle or Dutch oven. Add onions; cook over medium-low heat until onions are very soft, about 30 minutes. Increase heat to medium-high and add sugar; cook, stirring frequently, until onions are golden brown and caramelized, about 15 minutes longer.

2. Add remaining ingredients; bring to boil. Simmer, partially covered, until most of liquid is absorbed and mixture has a jam-like consistency, about 25 minutes. Serve warm or at room temperature. (Can be jarred and refrigerated for at least 2 weeks.)

CRANBERRY-RED PEPPER RELISH
Makes about 2½ cups

For a spicier dish, increase the hot red pepper flakes. In addition to the more obvious meats, this relish also complements baked ham very well.

2 red bell peppers, cored, seeded, and cut into small dice
2 cups cranberries, picked through and coarsely chopped
1 medium onion, finely chopped
½ cup apple cider vinegar
¾ cup sugar
1 jalapeño chile, minced
¼ teaspoon salt
¼ teaspoon hot red pepper flakes

Mix all ingredients in medium saucepan. Bring to boil, then simmer, stirring occasionally, until mixture thickens to a jam-like consistency, about 30 minutes. Cool to room temperature. (Can be jarred and refrigerated for at least 2 weeks.)

CURRIED APPLE-CRANBERRY CHUTNEY
Makes about 2½ cups

The curry powder in this dish is added for complexity, not heat. Serve this extremely mild chutney with roast turkey or other poultry, pork, lamb, or country pâté.

2 large Golden Delicious apples (about 1 pound), peeled, quartered, cored, and cut into medium dice (about 2½ cups)
1½ cups cranberries, picked through and coarsely chopped
¾ cup light brown sugar
4 ounces golden raisins (½ cup)
½ medium onion, minced
1 tablespoon minced crystallized ginger
1 tablespoon yellow mustard seeds
2 medium garlic cloves, minced
1 teaspoon zest from 1 small lemon
1 teaspoon curry powder
¼ teaspoon salt
⅛ teaspoon cayenne pepper

Mix all ingredients in medium saucepan. Bring to boil; cover and simmer, stirring occasionally, until apples are tender and most liquid is absorbed, about 30 minutes. Cool to room temperature. (Can be jarred and refrigerated for at least 2 weeks.)

CRANBERRY-PEAR BUTTER
Makes about 2¼ cups

Although it contains ginger, this butter is more sweet than savory, and tastes as good on your morning toast as it does on a turkey sandwich. Make sure to stir the mixture often to prevent it from sticking and scorching. Straining the mixture is not essential, but is an easy way to remove skins.

5 medium pears (about 2 pounds), peeled, quartered, cored, and thinly sliced (about 5 cups)
2 cups cranberries, picked through and coarsely chopped
1 cup apple cider
⅓ cup sugar
1 teaspoon grated gingerroot

1. Mix all ingredients in a large saucepan. Bring to boil and simmer, stirring often, until pears fall apart and mixture thickens, about 1 hour.

2. Working in batches, process mixture in a food mill or press through a fine sieve to strain out solids. (Can be jarred and refrigerated for at least 2 weeks.) ∎

Karen Tack is a food stylist and recipe developer who lives in Greenwich, Connecticut.

PHOTOGRAPH BY ERIC ROTH

How to Cook Butternut Squash

Other than conventional roasting, we discovered that the best method for cooking butternut squash is steaming.

~ BY BROOKE DOJNY AND MELANIE BARNARD ~

There are many ways to cook winter squashes, but the ideal method for one kind may not necessarily be best for another. We quickly discovered this when we set out to find the best way to cook the two most common winter squashes, acorn and butternut. After only a few tests, we found that they responded very differently. So we decided to concentrate on butternut, one of the most popular squashes for its ease of peeling and its distinctively rich, sweet flavor.

One thing that all winter squashes have in common is that, counter to the current fashion for *al dente* vegetables, they must be cooked until well-done to develop their sweetest flavor and smoothest texture. With this as the only given, we tried cooking butternut squash by microwaving, baking, roasting, steaming, and boiling to find what produced the best texture and flavor.

We began by microwaving a whole, unpeeled butternut squash, on the off chance that ease of cooking and good taste would coincide. It worked—that is, the squash did cook—but it cooked unevenly, and we also found the taste too "seedy."

Next we microwaved halved and seeded squashes, hoping this would produce a better result, but they did not fare well, either. The small end was always done before the large end, there were patches of raw squash in the center, and the flesh was watery. All in all, microwaving turned out to be a poor cooking method for squash.

So we tried a more traditional approach, baking squash halves. After some experimentation, we found that baking the unpeeled and seeded halves cut-side up gave a slightly better texture than cut-side down. However, when we began thinking about serving the squash, we realized that a baked half squash of this size—and it's hard to find butternut smaller than about two pounds—was too big for a single serving and therefore not very useful.

Roasting chunks of peeled squash proved to be much more successful. We peeled the squash and cut it into one-and-one-half-inch cubes, then roasted

it uncovered at varying oven temperatures. The ideal temperature turned out to be 425 degrees. At lower temperatures the squash was no better and took much longer to cook, and at higher temperatures it burned on the outside before it was fully cooked inside.

With the oven temperature settled, we tried parboiling the cubed squash in lightly salted water for five to six minutes until it was about half cooked, then roasting it. Squash cooked this way tasted fine, except that it was rather bland. So we tried roasting the squash chunks without parboiling them first. This took an additional twenty minutes, but the results were worth the extra time; the squash became quite caramelized, with a good chewy texture and a much sweeter and more pronounced flavor. We settled on this as one of the two best ways to cook squash.

Since sautéing also caramelizes, we decided to try sautéing diced squash in butter and oil until it became lightly caramelized and tender. This process took about twenty minutes and produced very satisfactory squash. But we found the flavor not as deep as the roasted squash, and roasting also had the advantage of requiring less attention during cooking. As a final test for sautéing, we grated the squash before cooking it. Although grated squash took about five minutes less to sauté than the squash cubes, it was less appealing in both taste and texture.

Finally, we tried pureeing squash. We prepared the squash for pureeing in two different ways: by boiling peeled cubes in lightly salted boiling water until they were tender, and by steaming cubes over simmering water. Both methods took about the same amount of time, fifteen minutes, and each method resulted in squash with good texture for pureeing, but steaming gave a somewhat stronger flavor. It seems that steaming concentrates the taste of squash, while boiling dilutes it. (We also tested putting slices of peeled fresh ginger in the water during steaming to see if it would flavor the squash, but the taste did not come through at all in the finished product.)

Once the squash was ready for pureeing, we tried mashing it with a food processor, an electric mixer, and a hand masher. To our surprise, hand mashing produced the most interesting puree—one that made an attractive presentation when

used as a vegetable, and could also be used in place of pumpkin for pies, cakes, or breads. The food processor gave the squash an ultra-smooth, silky consistency, but it was also more watery and therefore of more limited use.

For butternut squash, then, the best treatments are reflected in the recipes that follow, one for roasting and one for pureeing.

MASHED BUTTERNUT SQUASH WITH GINGER
Serves 4–6 (about 3 cups)

2 pounds butternut squash, peeled and cut into 1½-inch cubes
1½ tablespoons unsalted butter
½ teaspoon ground ginger
Salt and ground white pepper

1. Fit large soup kettle with steamer basket; fill kettle with enough water to come to bottom of basket. Bring water to boil; add squash to steamer. Cover, and cook over medium-high heat until squash is very tender when pierced with a thin-bladed knife, 14 to 16 minutes.

2. Transfer squash to shallow bowl, add butter, ginger, and salt and ground white pepper to taste; mash with fork to a coarse puree. Adjust seasoning and serve. (Squash can be covered and refrigerated overnight; reheat in microwave or double boiler.)

ROASTED BUTTERNUT SQUASH WITH SHALLOTS AND THYME
Serves 4

2 pounds butternut squash, peeled and cut into 1½-inch cubes
6 shallots, peeled
2 tablespoons vegetable or olive oil
2 teaspoons minced fresh thyme leaves
Salt and ground black pepper

Heat oven to 425 degrees. Put squash and shallots in roasting pan large enough to hold them without crowding. Toss with oil, and season with thyme and salt. Roast squash and shallots, stirring them or shaking the pan every 15 minutes, until they are tender and evenly browned, 45 to 50 minutes. Season with pepper to taste; serve warm or at room temperature. ∎

Brooke Dojny and **Melanie Barnard** are regular columnists for *Bon Appetit* and co-authors of *Parties!* (Harper Collins, 1992).

Size is not a big factor in the flavor of squash; a four-pound butternut tastes as good as a two-pounder. But choose squash with skin thick enough that it is difficult to puncture with your fingernail.

How to Carve Turkey and Goose

Carving a turkey is a simple skill, not an art. Cooking school instructor Katherine Alford offers the following instructions. If you follow them in the order given, the result will be a platter of perfectly cut meat. Although there are couple of options here—you can slice the breast while it's on the bird, or take it off first—the process is straightforward. Use a sharp, eight-inch chef's knife, a large cutting board (put a damp towel un-der it to keep it from slipping while you carve), and be careful to follow the contour of the bird. If you locate all the joints, you won't have to ex-ert much pressure at all to separate the sections.

The goose, which has a longer, trimmer shape, is carved in a slightly different manner than a turkey or chicken. *See* the special instructions in steps 14 through 18. ∎

1. Slice the skin between the meat of the breast and the leg.

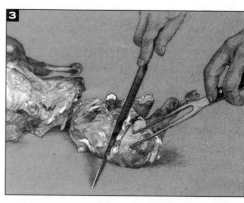

2. Continue to cut down to the joint, using the fork to pull the leg away from the bird while the tip of the knife severs the joint between the leg and breast.

3. Use the blade to locate the joint between the thigh and leg. It's right where the thigh and leg form their sharpest angle.

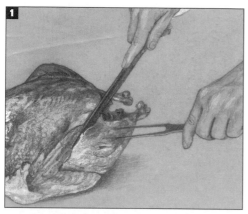

4. Cut through the joint. If you have properly located it, this should be easy, since you are not cutting through any bone.

5. Slice medallions from the leg, turning it so you can cut all the meat off.

6. Remove the large pieces of meat from the thigh bone.

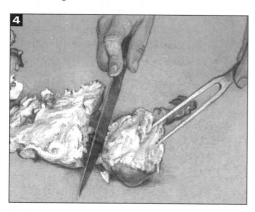

7. Slice these large thigh pieces, leaving a bit of skin attached to each slice.

8. Cut through the joint between the wing and the breast to separate the wing from the bird.

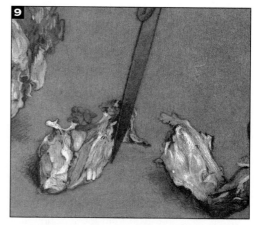

9. Cut the wing in half.

ILLUSTRATIONS BY ANATOLY

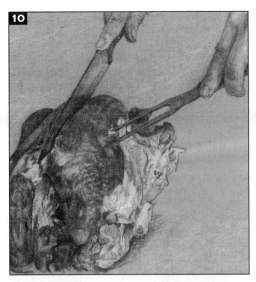

10. With the tip of your knife, cut along the entire length of the breastbone (sternum).

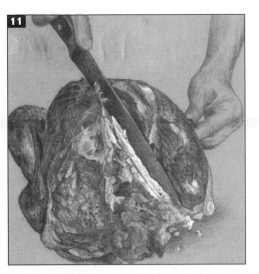

11. Angle the blade of the knife, and slice along the line of the rib cage to remove the entire breast half.

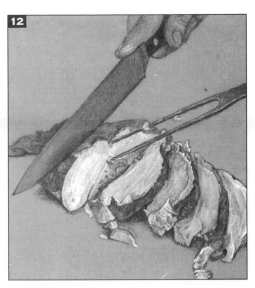

12. Cut thin slices from the breast, slicing across the grain of the meat.

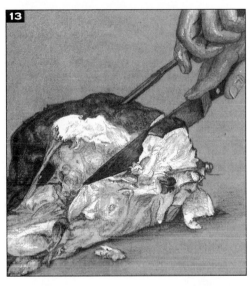

13. Alternatively, you can slice the breast without removing it from the bird.

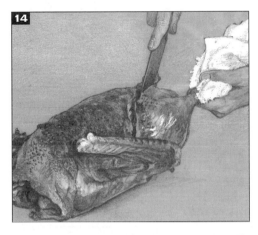

14. The goose thigh is closer to the carcass. To remove it, you must cut around the area where the breast and leg meet. Turn the goose on its side and pull slightly on the leg (hold it with a towel rather than a fork) so that you can clearly see where the muscles meet.

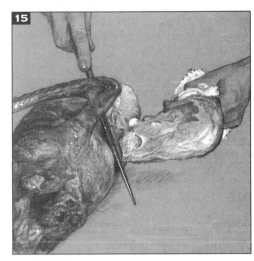

15. Remove the whole leg and thigh, making sure you get the small, delicious, boneless piece called the "oyster" on the bird's back, next to the base of the thigh.

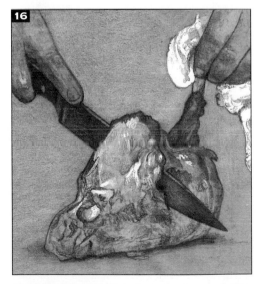

16. Separate the thigh from the leg, and slice the meat off the bone.

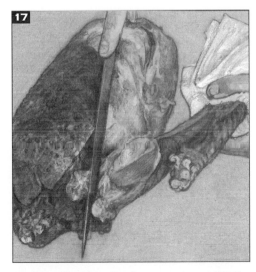

17. To remove a wing from a goose, twist the wing outwards to find the joint. It's tucked further under the breast than it would be on a turkey.

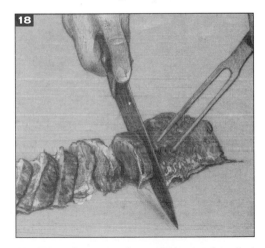

18. Although a goose breast is longer than that of a turkey, it is carved by the same method, either by cutting it away from the sternum and ribs (*see* steps 10 and 11, above) and slicing as shown, or by carving it in place (step 13, above).

Fish Stew Basics

Fish stews have just three components: the stock, the base, and the fish. Here's the best way to cook each one.

∽ BY SAM GUGINO ∽

Find a country that has a coastline, and you will find a fish stew in the culinary repertoire. *Bouillabaisse* is only the best-known of the many fish stews of France. In Italy it's *cacciucco* and *zuppa de pesce*, to name just two. Brazil boasts its Bahian *moquecas*, and the United States weighs in with cioppino and—since fish stews are often referred to as chowders—New England clam chowder.

Whatever their geographic origin, fish stews are surprisingly easy for the home cook. All you have to do is follow this simple three-step program: make the stock, make the base, and add the seafood.

Type of Stock

Some recipes for fish stew do not call for a separate stock. But since fish stew is cooked for such a short time compared to the long, slow, simmering of a beef stew, for example, it's virtually impossible to develop a full-bodied seafood flavor without starting with a good stock.

The prevailing opinion has always been that fish stocks could only be made with the bones and trimmings of firm, lean, white-fleshed fish such as cod, sea bass, sole, and the like. Oilier fish and their bones weren't to be used for stocks and stews because they were too strongly flavored. That's what I was taught in cooking school, and what I practiced as a restaurant chef.

Guess what? It ain't so.

You can make a very good, deliciously rich stock with salmon bones, heads, and trimmings. And by following the normal procedures for fish stews, you'll have a fine meal. Granted, it will be a little fishier than stock made from white-fleshed fish; not really gamy but fuller-flavored.

In addition to salmon, other unusual candidates for stock include sablefish (also known as black cod, an oily but delicious West Coast fish), and even the somewhat dark-fleshed butterfish and yellow tail. But don't carry this theory too far. Avoid very strongly flavored fish such as mackerel and bluefish (*see* "Best Fish for Stock," page 19).

The type of stock also depends on the kind of fish you're going to use in the stew. Tuna, salmon, and other strongly flavored fish can overwhelm a light broth. Conversely, mild fish such as flounder and sole would get lost in the hearty stock made with the bones of oilier fish. Always be sure to properly match the stock with the seafood to be added to it.

If you're preparing a shellfish stew such as *zarzuela*, consider a shellfish stock. This can be made using shrimp shells, the body of the lobster, and such things as crab shells and claws. When made like a standard fish stock, this produces a delicious broth that is light and sweet yet still quite flavorful. In fact, after making dozens of zarzuelas using standard fish stock, I can truthfully say that the version I made with a shellfish stock was the best ever.

Finally, if fish bones and heads are not available at your local fish outlets, you can always opt for the Cheater's Stock (*see* "In a Hurry?", page 21), which uses bottled clam juice for the seafood taste. It will have far less depth of flavor than a stock made from scratch, but it will do the job in a pinch.

Despite the fact that many fish stews originated out of the need to get rid of leftover fish or use up fish that could not be eaten whole (scraps or garbage fish, if you will), fish stews are often considered a luxury when planned in advance.

Stock Technique

A second myth about fish stocks is that fish bones and vegetables need to be sweated—cooked in a covered container over very low heat—to extract their juices before water and other liquids are added. While I've made my fish broth this way for years, I recently discovered that it isn't necessary. Indeed, it is actually an inferior method. For one thing, sweating tends to cloud the stock. In cooking fish stocks side-by-side, one made by the sweating method, one made by simply bringing the ingredients to a simmer, I found the unsweated stock to be much clearer and brighter with a more appealing yellowish cast. The sweated stock had a considerably less inviting grayish tinge. Also, the flavor of the sweated stock just wasn't as good. Though it developed more taste the longer it cooked, it never equaled the nonsweated stock.

Among cooking professionals, opinions about the length of time a fish stock should cook vary widely. I have heard respected chefs call for as little as fifteen minutes once the stock comes to a boil. Most chefs call for cooking about thirty minutes. My personal rule was forty to forty-five minutes. When stock was cooked longer than that, the prevailing belief was that it would turn bitter.

To test this, I cooked both sweated and non-sweated stocks well beyond my normal limit, checking their appearance, aroma, and flavor at five minute intervals. At fifty minutes, the flavor of the non-sweated stock deepened without loss of delicacy. It became a trifle lemony, so I threw out the lemon that was cooking in it. (I later halved the amount of lemon used.) At fifty-five minutes the flavor continued to improve. At sixty minutes it was better yet, and it finally reached its peak at sixty to sixty-five minutes. After sixty-five minutes, the flavor didn't deteriorate; it just stopped improving.

Many fish stock recipes do not call for white wine, so I made fish stocks both with and without it. The wineless stock was certainly credible, but I thought it lacked a certain spark provided by the kind of acidity that the wine added. More lemon

PHOTOGRAPHS BY ERIC ROTH

juice isn't an adequate substitute. As noted above, it just makes the stock more lemony. I would suggest always using white wine if available.

Though the fish stocks I prepared cooked longer than the conventional time, they still cooked more quickly than poultry or beef stocks. Therefore, it's important that vegetables be cut small enough to extract maximum flavor in this shorter time. Fish bones, heads, and tails should be cut into pieces no larger than three inches long and washed well under cool water. (I suspect that some bitter stocks have resulted from fish trimmings that were not well cleaned.)

There was a time when fishmongers would gladly give away bones, heads, and tails. But no longer, unless perhaps you're an especially good customer. And don't expect to automatically have bones available when you show up at the fish market, either. It's advisable to call ahead and reserve what you need. If freezer space permits, you can pack away shrimp shells, fish bones, and the like each time you buy seafood. But don't freeze them longer than three or four months; after that amount of time, it is best to go ahead and make the stock, even if you subsequently freeze it.

The Base
The prime flavoring element for most European fish stews is a seasoned tomato sauce which I call a base. The foundation of a good base is similar to that of a good stock—onions, carrots, celery, and parsley. Beyond that, the flavorings will change according to the specific kind of fish stew you want—fresh fennel (or fennel seeds) and Pernod for bouillabaisse, almonds and sweet red peppers for zarzuela, and so forth, as indicated in the recipes that follow on pages 20 and 21. But these are merely variations on a theme, easily adjusted once you have the basic concept mastered. However your base is made, it should be well seasoned, because it will be diluted with fish stock.

Must you have fresh tomatoes for a tomato base? Not necessarily, especially if you're making fish stew in November when vine-ripened tomatoes are out of the question in most parts of the country.

I tested bases made with fresh round and plum tomatoes and with canned versions of both. The fresh round tomatoes produced a base with a fresher, sweeter flavor but with no depth. A base made with fresh plum tomatoes was less sweet, but minimally more substantial. Bases made with canned round tomatoes and canned plum tomatoes had a deeper flavor, with the round tomatoes getting a slight edge. All bets are off, however, if it's late August and you're cooking with home-grown, perfectly ripe tomatoes from the backyard.

Unlike the fish stock, the base doesn't improve with longer cooking. Using canned tomatoes, I simmered the base forty-five minutes once the vegetables had been sautéed and the remaining ingredients added. I checked the progress at five-minute intervals. After twenty minutes, the base began to lose some of its freshness. Not much change occurred during the next ten minutes, but at thirty-five minutes the base started tasting old.

At forty minutes the tomatoes became noticeably more acidic, and most of their fruitiness was gone.

The Fish
As mentioned above, the stock will, to a degree, determine the types of fish used. With a strong-flavored stock, I've had good success using salmon, tuna, and butterfish. You can also consider trout, carp, and catfish.

For a stock made with lean, white fish bones or a combination of white fish and salmon bones, firm-fleshed white fish are best. Swordfish is excellent, because its firm texture holds up well. Less firm, but still firm enough, are sea bass, cod, conger eel (used frequently in bouillabaisse), halibut, monkfish, pollack, and snapper. Sturgeon is a marvelous fish for stews and has the advantage of tasting equally good in oily or lean stocks.

The biggest problem with the seafood, however, is not what kind to use, but how long it cooks. Since it's virtually impossible to undercook seafood, the problem is how to prevent it from overcooking.

Once the stock and base have been combined and brought to a boil, then reduced to a bare simmer—the liquid in which fish cooks should never boil—it is time to add the seafood, beginning with the most dense fish first, and ending with the most delicate. When shrimp and scallops are used, they should be the last ones in the pot. The temperature of the broth will plummet once you start adding the seafood, so it will be necessary to temporarily raise the heat until the broth returns to a simmer.

Fish fillets should be cut into pieces large enough to hold together during cooking, yet small enough so they do not look cumbersome when served. I've found the ideal size to be three-to-four-ounce pieces no longer than three inches. Pieces closer to four ounces will take about five minutes if they are firm-fleshed fish such as swordfish. Pieces that are three ounces or slightly less will take only about three minutes.

Clams and mussels should be put in the stew just until they open; the longer they cook after opening, the more rubbery they become. Timing for these can be tricky, especially if they aren't ready when everything else is. The solution is to put them in early and remove them as soon as they open, then keep them warm and moist in a covered serving tureen. When the rest of the seafood is cooked, add it to the tureen with the hot stock, and serve at once. This takes only minutes.

Hearty French or Italian bread is an ideal accompaniment to fish stews. Especially a country-style loaf or, in the case of cioppino,

---

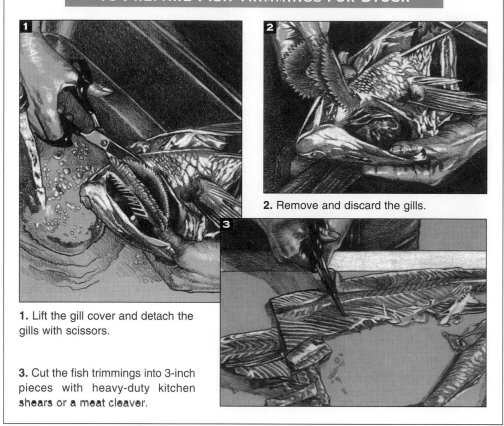

2. Remove and discard the gills.

1. Lift the gill cover and detach the gills with scissors.

3. Cut the fish trimmings into 3-inch pieces with heavy-duty kitchen shears or a meat cleaver.

MASTER RECIPE FOR FISH STEW
Serves 6

Fish is done when it feels firm and springs back to the touch. Be sure that you do not cook until the fish flakes. Serve with crusty bread or slices of toast.

- 1 Master Recipe for Fish Stew Flavoring Base
- ½ Master Recipe for Fish Stock (about 4½ cups)
  Salt and ground white pepper
  Cayenne pepper
- 3 pounds fish, preferably a mix of firm and tender white-fleshed filets (*see* "Best Fish for Stew," page 19), rinsed, patted dry, and cut into 3- to 4-ounce pieces
- 3 tablespoons chopped fresh parsley leaves for garnish

1. Mix base and fish stock; bring to boil. Reduce heat to simmer and adjust seasonings with salt, pepper, and cayenne to taste.

2. Add firmer fish pieces; simmer for 2 minutes. Add smaller, more delicate fish; simmer, stirring gently to ensure even cooking, until fish is almost cooked through, about 3 minutes longer. Remove kettle from heat; cover and let stand until fish is just cooked, about 5 minutes. Put soup in a tureen or ladle into individual soup plates. Sprinkle with parsley and serve immediately.

BOUILLABAISSE
Serves 6–8

Follow Master Recipe for Fish Stew, making the following changes in the Fish Stew Flavoring Base: increase onion from 1 to 2 medium; replace celery and carrots with 1 small fennel, bulb part only, cut into small dice; increase garlic from 3 to 6 cloves; and increase tomatoes from 2 to 3 cups. In addition to the flavorings in the Master Recipe, add ¼ teaspoon crushed saffron threads, 3 tablespoons anise-flavored liqueur such as Pernod, and 1 teaspoon grated orange zest.

Meanwhile, place 1 pound new potatoes in a medium saucepan; cover with water. Bring to boil; cover and simmer until cooked through, 15 to 20 minutes. Cut into thick slices.

To serve this stew, place a portion of the potato slices in each soup plate, top with a portion of fish, and ladle on the hot broth. Serve with slices of French bread toast and rouille (recipe follows).

ZARZUELA
Serves 6

Shellfish replaces fish in this Spanish stew. Instead of a mix of fish, use 1 lobster (1½ pounds, *see* illustrations 1 through 5, page 21, for preparation); 12 clams, scrubbed; 12 mussels, scrubbed and debearded; 12 large shrimp, shelled, tails on; and ½ pound sea scallops (halved if unusually large). Lobster bodies and shrimp shells can be substituted for part of the fish trimmings in the stock.

Follow Master Recipe for Fish Stew, making the

---

sourdough. Toasting slices with a brush of olive oil is also a fine idea. A slice of toast is often placed on the bottom of a soup plate and the broth and fish poured over it.

MASTER RECIPE FOR FISH STOCK
Makes 2–2½ quarts

Fish heads, tails, and bones are all possibilities for trimmings and can be used for the stock. An equal amount of shrimp shells and lobster or crab carcasses can be substituted for the fish bones. All are cooked according to the same procedure.

- 3 pounds fish trimmings (*see* "Best Fish for Stock," page 19), rinsed and cut into 3-inch pieces (*see* illustrations 1 through 3 for preparation)
- 1 medium onion, cut into small dice
- 2 medium carrots, cut into small dice
- 1 large celery stalk, cut into small dice
- 8 parsley stems, chopped
- 1 cup dry white wine
- ¼ lemon
- 10 whole black peppercorns
- 2 bay leaves
- 1 dried chile pepper of your choice

1. Put all ingredients in a 6- to 8-quart pot. Cover with 2¾ quarts cold water. Bring to boil over medium heat; simmer slowly for about 1 hour, periodically skimming away scum that rises to surface.

2. Strain stock through double thickness of cheesecloth, pressing out as much liquid as possible with back of a spoon. Proceed with one of fish stews that follow. (Stock can be cooled and refrigerated up to three days or frozen up to three months.)

MASTER RECIPE FOR FISH STEW FLAVORING BASE
Makes enough for 1 fish stew

- 2 tablespoons olive oil
- 1 medium onion, cut into small dice
- 1 medium celery stalk, cut into small dice
- 1 medium carrot, peeled and cut into small dice
- 3 large garlic cloves, minced
- ½ cup dry white wine
- 2 cups chopped, canned, or fresh tomatoes
- 2 large bay leaves
- ⅛ teaspoon cayenne pepper (or more to taste)
  Salt and ground black pepper
- ¼ cup flat-leaf parsley
- 1 teaspoon dried thyme or basil (optional)

Heat oil in a large soup kettle. Add onions, celery, carrot, and garlic; cook over medium heat until softened, about 10 minutes. Add wine; simmer until reduced by half, 2 to 3 minutes. Add remaining ingredients and bring to boil; simmer until thickened to a tomato sauce consistency, 15 to 20 minutes. Adjust seasonings. Proceed with one of fish stews that follow. (Base can be cooled and refrigerated up to three days or frozen up to three months.)

ILLUSTRATIONS BY TONY DELUZ

following changes in the Fish Stew Flavoring Base: increase onion from 1 to 2 medium; replace celery and carrots with 2 medium red bell peppers, cored, seeded, and cut into small dice. When vegetables are soft, add 2 ounces minced prosciutto, ½ cup coarse-ground toasted almonds, and ⅛ teaspoon crushed saffron threads; sauté to coat with oil, about 1 minute. Continue with Master Recipe for base.

Omit fish from Master Recipe for Fish Stew, and add lobster pieces and clams; simmer for 3 minutes. Add mussels; simmer for 2 minutes. Add shrimp and scallops; simmer for 3 minutes, removing clams and mussels as they open.

ROASTED RED PEPPER ROUILLE
Makes about 1 cup
Spread rouille on toast, and if you like, mix it into the stew for added flavor.

> 3 large garlic cloves, peeled
> 1 slice (about ½-inch thick) French bread
> 1 small red bell pepper, roasted, peeled, and seeded
> 1 jalapeño chile (red if possible), roasted, peeled, and seeded
> ⅛ teaspoon saffron threads, crushed
> 1 large egg yolk, at room temperature
> ½ cup olive oil
>   Salt
>   Pinch cayenne pepper

With food processor motor running, drop garlic cloves, one at a time, down feed tube. Push garlic down sides of bowl with a rubber spatula. Add bread; process to fine crumbs. Add both kinds of peppers, saffron, then egg yolk; process until pureed. With motor still running, slowly add oil until mixture thickens to mayonnaise consistency. Season to taste with salt and cayenne pepper.

SICILIAN GRILLED TUNA STEW
Serves 6
Follow Master Recipe for Fish Stew, making the following changes in the Fish Stew Flavoring Base: increase onion from 1 to 2 medium, and omit celery and carrots. When onions are soft, about 5 minutes, add remaining ingredients along with 12 pitted and halved Sicilian oil-cured olives, 2 tablespoons toasted pine nuts, and 2 tablespoons golden raisins. Substitute 2 tablespoons (or more to taste) minced fresh mint leaves for the herbs.

Substitute 6 tuna steaks (3 pounds) for the mix of fish called for in the Master Recipe for Fish Stew. Brush them with olive oil, and grill or broil until almost cooked through, about 3 minutes on each side. Add fish to simmering base and stock, remove from heat, and let stand for 5 minutes. Serve with bruschetta—slices of country-style Italian bread that have been grilled (or broiled), and then rubbed with cut garlic, and drizzled with olive oil. ∎

Sam Gugino, former food editor of the *San Jose Mercury News*, now writes about food, wine, and travel from New York, New York.

IN A HURRY?

Can clam juice substitute for a well-made fish stock? In a pinch, broth made with doctored clam juice produces stock that at least won't embarrass you. The important thing to remember with clam juice is that it is extremely salty, so don't add salt to the base until you've brought the doctored clam juice and base to a simmer.

CHEATER'S FISH STOCK
Makes 4–4½ cups

> 1 small onion, minced
> 1 medium carrot, peeled and minced
> 2 celery ribs, minced
> 8 parsley stems, chopped
> 1 cup dry white wine
> 3 8-ounce bottles clam juice
> 3 cups water
> 1 dried chile pepper

> 2 large bay leaves
> 8 whole black peppercorns
> ½ teaspoon dried thyme
> 1 tablespoon fresh lemon juice

Bring all ingredients to boil; simmer to blend flavors (no skimming necessary), about 30 minutes. Strain through cheesecloth, pressing solids with back of a spoon to extract as much liquid as possible. Use in place of regular fish stock.

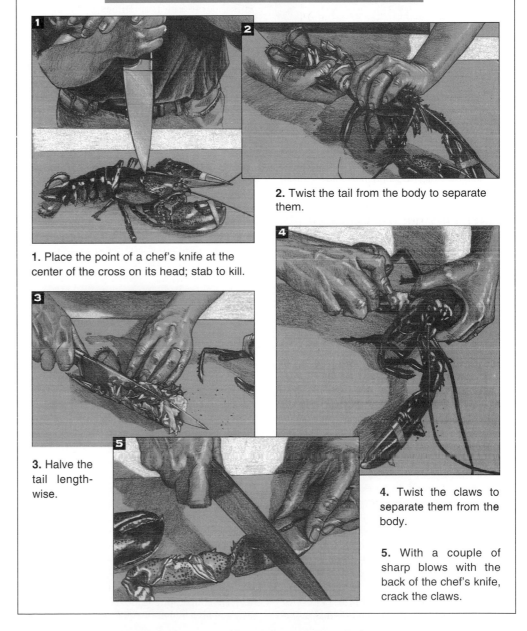

TO PREPARE LOBSTER FOR STEW

1. Place the point of a chef's knife at the center of the cross on its head; stab to kill.

2. Twist the tail from the body to separate them.

3. Halve the tail lengthwise.

4. Twist the claws to separate them from the body.

5. With a couple of sharp blows with the back of the chef's knife, crack the claws.

No-Weep Lemon Meringue Pie

This is the ultimate lemon meringue pie—a crisp crust; a firm, lush filling; and a no-weep meringue.

∽ BY PAM ANDERSON WITH KAREN TACK ∽

For perfect lemon meringue pie, use extra egg yolks in the filling, roll the crust in graham cracker crumbs, and make sure the filling is piping hot when you pour it in.

Most everybody loves lemon meringue pie—at least the bottom half of it. The controversial part, for cooks as well as consumers, is the meringue. Of all the people I've talked to about lemon meringue pie, I only know one person who adores the meringue. Most consider it penance to be endured for the pleasure of the filling and crust.

For cooks, meringue falls into the category of unsolved culinary mysteries. On any given day it can shrink, bead, puddle, deflate, burn, sweat, break down, or turn rubbery. Most cookbooks don't even attempt to deal with the problems of meringue. They follow the standard recipe—granulated sugar and cream of tartar beaten slowly into the egg whites—assuming, apparently, that there is no way around the flaws. After making thirty-something lemon meringue pies, I'm not sure I blame anyone for skirting the issue. For as easy as it was to figure out the perfect lemon filling and pie crust, the meringue remains, finally, only a manageable mystery.

My goals were clear in developing the ultimate lemon meringue pie. For me that meant a pie with a crisp, flaky crust. Of course developing the perfect crust hinged on finding a weepless meringue. Even the crispiest crust will waterlog in a puddle of sugar water. I wanted a rich filling that would balance the airy meringue, without blocking the clear, lemon flavor. And I wanted the filling to be soft, but not runny; firm enough to cut, but not stiff and gelatinous. Most importantly, I wanted a meringue that didn't break down and puddle on the bottom or "tear" on top, not even (as cook-

books and old wives' tales declare it must) on rainy days.

Filling Up

The filling in lemon meringue pie has gradually evolved over the years from a category of seventeenth-century English desserts called cheesecakes or curd puddings, according to cookbook author and food historian Stephen Schmidt. For the last century, however, the ingredients have remained constant: sugar, water (or sometimes milk), cornstarch (sometimes part flour), egg yolks, lemon juice (and usually zest), and a little butter. Though I made one old-fashioned curd-style filling, just to confirm that it was too rich for a pie, I mainly worked toward perfecting the cornstarch-thickened lemon filling, varying the proportions to determine each ingredient's role.

To start, I analyzed fifty or so recipes for lemon filling, and developed this formula I thought was representative of current fillings:

1½	cups sugar
6	tablespoons cornstarch
¼	teaspoon salt
2	cups water
3	large egg yolks
½	cup lemon juice
2	teaspoons lemon zest
2	tablespoons unsalted butter

After I tinkered with proportions and ingredients almost endlessly, the following formula evolved:

1	cup sugar
4	tablespoons cornstarch
⅛	teaspoon salt
1½	cups water
6	large egg yolks
½	cup lemon juice
1	tablespoon lemon zest
2	tablespoons unsalted butter

There are three major differences between the original and the final formula. A hefty portion of the water has been replaced with egg yolks, and the sugar and cornstarch have been decreased.

I started with the original formula, making it once with water and once with milk. As is often the case, I liked a version that, in theory, existed somewhere between the two. I liked the straightforward lemon flavor of the water-based filling, but it was one-dimensional, lacking depth. The milk-based filling was rich, mellow, and delicious, but the lemon flavor was too subdued. So I

thought a water-milk combination might be the answer. But to my surprise, the fillings made with this liquid combo came out butterscotch-colored. The flavor was fine; but the color was totally unacceptable. I had two other choices for enriching the pie—eggs and butter. While trying to fix the color, I also wanted to improve the pie's texture. The original was thick and jello-like. I had little faith that butter would solve this problem, so I focused on eggs.

I would have considered egg proportions in the filling sooner, but the meringue stopped me. Knowing how most people feel about meringue, I decided not to overdo it. I settled on a conservative, but respectable three-white meringue. Since I wanted a neat, tidy formula—equal numbers of whites in the meringue and yolks in the filling—I wanted to limit the filling to three yolks. But after making pies with four, five, and six yolks, I realized that the pies tasted progressively richer with each yolk, and this was accomplished without the lemon flavor being compromised. Also, not only did the eggs enrich the pie, unlike the milk, they also reinforced its color.

I discovered that, up to a point, the quantity of sugar had more affect on the pie's texture than on its sweetness. The fillings of pies made with one and one-half cups sugar were significantly softer than the pies made with only one cup. So by decreasing the sugar and increasing the egg yolks, I was able to cut back on cornstarch and achieve the firm yet tender filling I was looking for.

Graham Cracker Crisp

I tried four different methods to keep the pie shell crisp. I baked one shell until it was almost fully cooked, then I brushed it with beaten egg white and returned it to the oven until fully cooked. I baked another shell the exact same way, except that I brushed it with beaten yolk instead of white. I brushed a third fully baked shell with seedless raspberry jam, as suggested by a few Southern-style lemon meringue pie recipes.

The jam had nothing to recommend it. Since the filling must be poured piping hot into the shell to keep the meringue from weeping (*see* below), the jam ends up melting and bleeding into the filling. The clean layer of contrasting color that I'd hoped for turned into an ugly smudge.

The crust I brushed with egg yolk was crisper and drier than the one brushed with egg white, but neither was as impressive as the one I produced with a technique presented in *Pie Marches On* by Monroe Boston Strause (Ahrens Publishing Co., 1939), a book I would never have discovered without the help of Nahum Waxman, owner of Manhattan's Kitchen Arts and Letters, a bookstore devoted to food and wine.

This book is geared primarily to the food service industry of a half century ago. In it Strause suggests rolling pie dough in graham cracker crumbs. I tried this and discovered that the technique not only promotes browning and therefore crisps the crust, it also adds a wonderful graham flavor that complements the lemon pie without masking the character of the dough itself.

Meringue It

With each filling and crust experiment came a new meringue topping (see "In Search of the Perfect Meringue," right). But long after I had settled on the perfect filling and crust, I was still baffled by meringue. I couldn't find a consistently perfect meringue—one that was soft and billowy, yet firm enough to stipple nicely. And most importantly, I couldn't find one that wouldn't puddle on the bottom or bead on the top.

Stormy weather during the first two days of testing blew me off course. I attributed all my weeps and tears to the weather. After almost settling for a less-than-perfect meringue, I called food scientist Shirley Corriher, who slowly convinced me that my problems with meringue topping were not weather-related.

According to Corriher, the puddling underneath the meringue is from under-cooking. The under-cooked whites break down and return to their liquid state. The beading on top of the pie is from over-cooking. This near-the-surface over-cooking of the meringue causes the proteins in the egg white to coagulate, squeezing out the moisture which then surfaces as tears or beads. Although this double dilemma seemed insurmountable, Corriher offered several possible solutions, two of which worked.

To deal with under cooking, Corriher said the filling must be piping hot. To ensure this, she suggested I make the meringue first, then the filling. As a back-up plan, she also suggested I top the filling with a sprinkling of cake or cookie crumbs. This extra step would, in theory, absorb any deteriorated meringue.

Through the course of all my testing, fillings had been meringued hot. Once each filling was cooked, I covered its surface with plastic wrap to insulate it while making the meringue. Sometimes our meringues puddled; sometimes they didn't. I followed Corriher's suggestion to make the meringue first, but found that this delicate mixture deteriorated by the time the filling was made. So I tried another strategy. I made the filling and covered it as usual, but during the final minute or so of beating the meringue, I returned the filling to a simmer over low heat. I then poured this super-hot filling into the shell, promptly topped and sealed it with meringue, and immediately put the pie in the oven to bake. I followed this procedure with a number of differently prepared meringues and none of them puddled or wept. So, even if meringue beading or tearing is not an issue, you can at least make a lemon meringue pie with a dry bottom just by making sure the filling is really

IN SEARCH OF THE PERFECT MERINGUE

After baking lemon meringue pies at temperatures ranging from 325 degrees to a scorching-hot broil, I decided that lower oven temperatures produced the best looking, most evenly browned meringues. Lower oven temperatures also allow meringues to cook through before they get too brown, which reduces the chances for both puddling and beading. Here are some of the methods that I checked in my search for the perfect meringue.

INGREDIENTS	METHOD	RESULT
Granulated sugar, cream of tartar, and egg whites	Mixed sugar with cream of tartar and gradually beat into frothy whites. Beat to stiff peaks.	Lots of beading on top, nice glossy sheen; sometimes seemed deflated compared to original size.
Confectioners' sugar, cream of tartar, and egg whites	Mixed sugar with cream of tartar and gradually beat into frothy whites. Beat to stiff peaks.	Powdery, flat sweet taste instead of rich sweet taste; flat, matted look instead of glossy sheen; very tender texture; beaded less than granulated sugar meringues.
Superfine sugar, cream of tartar, and egg whites	Mixed sugar with cream of tartar and gradually beat into frothy whites. Beat to stiff peaks.	Very little difference from one made with granulated sugar; seemed to bead less, but this could have been result of oven variables.
Granulated sugar, salt, and egg whites	(Swiss meringue) Mixed sugar, salt, and egg whites in medium bowl; placed bowl over pan of simmering water. Stirred until whites warmed and sugar dissolved. Removed from heat and beat to stiff peaks.	Far less volume than conventional methods; dense and hard to spread; filling threatens to overflow when sealing meringue to crust; firm to bite.
Granulated sugar, water, and egg whites	(Italian meringue) part of sugar is heated with water to make syrup; remaining sugar beaten with egg whites; then syrup beaten into whipped whites. Beat until cool.	Very dense and stiff; inappropriate for pie meringue.
Granulated sugar, cream of tartar, calcium phosphate, and egg whites	Mixed sugar, cream of tartar, calcium phosphate and gradually beat into frothy whites. Beat to stiff peaks.	Less consistent than cooked cornstarch method; calcium phosphate not easy to locate.
Granulated sugar, tapioca flour, and egg whites	Mixed sugar and tapioca flour and gradually beat into frothy whites. Beat to stiff peaks.	Stiff and erect, not soft and billowy; very starchy and dry; tasted like powder on the outside of a marshmallow.
Ice water, egg whites, sugar, and baking powder	Ice water, egg whites, sugar, baking powder	Great volume; only meringue that browned evenly; heavy beading.
Wilton Meringue Powder, water, and sugar	Beat meringue powder, water, and part of sugar for 5 minutes. Gradually added remaining sugar, and beat until stiff.	Very dense, heavy, sweet; more like frosting than meringue; almost impossible to spread over hot filling; dries out but doesn't brown.
Cornstarch, water, granulated sugar, cream of tartar, egg whites, and vanilla	Heated cornstarch and water to a thick paste. Mixed sugar with cream of tartar and gradually beat into frothy whites. Beat to soft peaks; beat in cornstarch mixture, 1 tablespoon at a time. Beat to stiff peaks.	Cooked cornstarch didn't affect texture; only meringue that didn't bead on top; perfect.

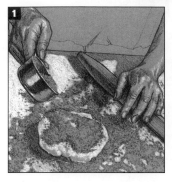

1. Sprinkle an 18-inch work area with 2 tablespoons graham cracker crumbs; place the dough disk in the center. Scatter a few more crumbs over the disk top.

2. Roll the dough from the center to the edges to form a 9-inch disk, rotating it a quarter turn after each stroke and sprinkling additional crumbs underneath and on top to heavily coat the dough.

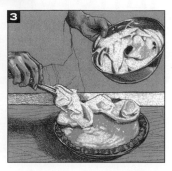

3. Distribute the meringue evenly around the edge then the center of the pie. Use a rubber spatula to spread the meringue, making sure the meringue attaches to the pie crust to prevent shrinking.

hot. I tried sprinkling the filling with cake crumbs, but the hot-filling method was so successful, the cake-crumb step was unnecessary.

To solve the problem of over-cooking, Corriher suggested that, just like the yolks in the filling, the whites in the meringue needed to be stabilized to make them more heat tolerant. Corriher said that cornstarch, the yolk stabilizer in the filling, could also be used to strengthen the whites in the meringue. Apparently a food stylists' trick, this is done by mixing cornstarch and water and cooking it until thick. Then this paste is gradually beaten into soft-peak meringue until firm peaks form.

I found that the cornstarch mixture did not affect the flavor or texture of the meringue. After a bit more tinkering—mostly with oven time and temperature—I finally got the cornstarch-stabilized meringue to produce a virtually tearless pie, even on a hot, humid day.

One really rainy day, I baked a lemon meringue pie with a cornstarch-fortified meringue, and it did tear a bit. But the same pie baked with five minutes less oven time during similar weather conditions was completely dry. So I think I finally got it right. But with meringue, even when it turns out right, you're never exactly sure why. Everything you learn about meringues doesn't guarantee anything. It just helps you manage the mystery.

I also decided two things about flavoring meringue: I didn't like the taste of even the smallest quantity of salt in it, but I found that vanilla enhanced the meringue's rather one-dimensional sweet flavor.

THE ULTIMATE LEMON MERINGUE PIE
Makes one 9-inch pie

Graham Cracker-Coated Pie Shell
1¼ cups all-purpose flour
½ teaspoon salt
1 tablespoon sugar
6 tablespoons unsalted chilled butter, cut into ¼-inch pieces
4 tablespoons chilled all-vegetable shortening
3–4 tablespoons cold water
½ cup graham cracker crumbs

Lemon Filling
1 cup sugar
¼ cup cornstarch
⅛ teaspoon salt
1½ cups cold water
6 large egg yolks
1 tablespoon zest from 1 lemon
½ cup juice from 2 or 3 lemons
2 tablespoons unsalted butter

Meringue Topping
1 tablespoon cornstarch
¼ teaspoon cream of tartar
½ cup sugar
4 large egg whites
½ teaspoon vanilla extract

1. *For the pie shell,* mix flour, salt, and sugar in food processor fitted with steel blade. Scatter butter pieces over flour mixture, tossing to coat butter with a little of the flour. Cut butter into flour with five 1-second pulses. Add shortening; continue cutting in until flour is pale yellow and resembles coarse cornmeal with butter bits no larger than a small pea, about four more 1-second pulses. Turn mixture into medium bowl.

2. Sprinkle 3 tablespoons cold water over mixture. Using rubber spatula, fold water into mixture; press down on dough mixture with broad side of spatula until dough sticks together. If dough will not come together, add up to 1 tablespoon more cold water. Shape dough into ball, then flatten into 4-inch-wide disk. Dust lightly with flour, wrap in plastic, and refrigerate for 30 minutes before rolling.

3. Generously sprinkle work area with 2 tablespoons graham cracker crumbs. Place dough on work area. Scatter a few more crumbs over dough (*see* illustration 1, above). Roll dough from center to edges, turning it into a 9-inch disk, rotating

a quarter turn after each stroke and sprinkling additional crumbs underneath and on top as necessary to coat heavily (illustration 2). Flip dough over, and continue to roll, but not rotate, to form a 13-inch disk slightly less than ⅛-inch thick.

4. Fold dough in quarters; place dough point in center of 9-inch Pyrex pie pan. Unfold to cover pan completely, letting excess dough drape over pan lip. To fit dough to pan, lift edge of dough with one hand and press dough in pan bottom with other hand; repeat process around circumference of pan to ensure dough fits properly and is not stretched. Trim all around, ½-inch past lip of pan. Tuck ½ inch of overhanging dough under so folded edge is flush with lip pan; press to seal. Press thumb and index finger about ½-inch apart against outside edge of dough, then use index finger or knuckle of other hand to poke a dent on inside edge of dough through opening created by the other fingers. Repeat to flute around perimeter of pie shell.

5. Refrigerate until firm, about 30 minutes. Prick shell at ½-inch intervals; press a doubled 12-inch square of aluminum foil into pie shell; prick again and refrigerate at least 30 minutes .

6. Adjust oven rack to lowest position, heat oven to 400 degrees. Bake, checking occasionally for ballooning, until crust is firmly set, about 15 minutes. Reduce oven temperature to 350 degrees, remove foil, and continue to bake until crust is crisp and rich brown in color, about 10 minutes longer.

7. *For the filling,* mix first four ingredients in a large, nonreactive saucepan. Bring mixture to simmer over medium heat, whisking occasionally at beginning of the process and more frequently as mixture begins to thicken. When mixture starts to simmer and turn translucent, whisk in egg yolks, two at a time. Whisk in zest, then lemon juice, and finally butter. Bring mixture to a good simmer, whisking constantly. Remove from heat, place plastic wrap directly on surface of filling to keep hot and prevent skin from forming.

8. *For the meringue,* mix cornstarch with ⅓ cup water in small saucepan; bring to simmer, whisking occasionally at beginning and more frequently as mixture thickens. When mixture starts to simmer and turn translucent, remove from heat. Let cool while beating egg whites.

9. Heat oven to 325 degrees. Mix cream of tartar and sugar together. Beat egg whites and vanilla until frothy. Beat in sugar mixture, 1 tablespoon at a time; until sugar is incorporated and mixture forms soft peaks. Add cornstarch mixture, 1 tablespoon at a time; continue to beat meringue to stiff peaks. Remove plastic from filling and return to very low heat during last minute or so of beating meringue (to ensure filling is hot).

10. Pour filling into pie shell. Using a rubber spatula, immediately distribute meringue evenly around edge then center of pie to keep it from sinking into filling. Make sure meringue attaches to pie crust to prevent shrinking (illustration 3). Use spoon to create peaks all over meringue. Bake pie until meringue is golden brown, about 20 minutes. Transfer to wire rack and cool to room temperature. Serve. ∎

ILLUSTRATIONS BY TONY DELUZ

Are Expensive Chocolates Worth the Money?

Eaten plain or in a torte, moderately priced chocolates—most of them made in America—dominated our tasting.

~ BY JACK BISHOP AND ALICE MEDRICH ~

We began research for this article with one simple question: Does the best nibbling chocolate also make the best-tasting desserts? To find out we decided to first taste the chocolates plain, then sample them again in a chocolate-almond torte with a chocolate glaze.

Before we could begin testing, however, we had to narrow the field of contestants. There's plenty of confusion when it comes to choosing a chocolate. Supermarket shoppers have a relatively limited choice: Baker's, Hershey's, and Nestle's can almost always be found, and sometimes one or two of the better-known premium brands like Ghirardelli, but that's about it. On the other hand, many pastry chefs select from pricey European imports like Valrhona, Callebaut, and Lindt. And there are also dozens of specialty brands used by professionals which have little name recognition among consumers—including Guittard, Merckens, Van Leer, and Hawaiian Vintage, the first chocolate made from beans grown in the United States.

We decided to include all of the supermarket brands in this testing, as well as specialty brands available by mail in relatively small quantities. While a professional may not mind purchasing a ten-pound block (this is how many premium brands are sold), most consumers will only buy chocolates that come in smaller bars or that can be purchased in chunks cut from the large blocks.

Besides the many choices, there is substantial confusion caused by the terms "bittersweet" and "semisweet." Although no industry or federal definitions exist for these terms (both fall under the broad category of dark chocolate), some manufacturers use them on their labels, and one company's bittersweet may in fact have more sugar in it than another company's semisweet. Therefore, when organizing this test we decided to lump together chocolates called "bittersweet" and "semisweet." In cases where a company makes more than one bittersweet or semisweet chocolate, we held an informal pre tasting to decide which chocolate would be included in the test. In general, we tried to avoid "extreme" products which might not represent a product line very well.

Consistent Chocolate Preferences

With our contestants selected, we ran the dual tasting and anxiously tabulated the results. Somewhat to our surprise, the results of these two independent tastings were extremely consistent. The chocolates that won in the initial blind tasting also came out on top in the blind tasting of chocolate tortes. Likewise, brands that fell to the bottom of the plain tasting fared poorly in the cake ratings. We had the answer to our question: The chocolate that is best for eating will also make the best baked goods.

But which chocolate was that? When the results were tabulated, four chocolates (three of them made in this country) emerged as highly recommended options. The panel's favorite was Van Leer Bittersweet, a trade brand from New Jersey sold by mail for only $4 per pound, which, if you exclude shipping costs, makes it less expensive than the last-placed supermarket chocolate.

Close behind and tied for second place were Ghirardelli Semi-Sweet, a premium brand made in California, and Callebaut Bittersweet, a top import from Belgium long preferred by pastry chefs. These two chocolates are more expensive; Ghirardelli because it is sold in small quantities, and Callebaut because of its fancy European pedigree. Rounding out this top group was Merckens Yucatan Dark, another American brand that caters to the trade. Like Van Leer, it costs about as much as the last-ranked supermarket brand.

The second group of recommended chocolates includes two more specialty American brands (Guittard and Hawaiian Vintage), and Nestle's, one of the three mass-produced chocolates generally available in supermarkets. Nestle's decent finish (seventh out of eleven) should be heartening to supermarket shoppers. If you don't have the time or inclination to order your chocolate by mail or seek it out in specialty shops, we suggest you purchase Ghirardelli (definitely the better choice) or Nestle's, which is an acceptable if not spectacular option, especially in a pinch.

The group of unrecommended chocolates contains some real surprises. Valrhona's reputation among confectioners and bakers is quite high, and its poor showing was a shock to several panelists. Most tasters thought this complex and aggressive chocolate was packed with layers of flavor. But

The selection of high quality cocoa beans is one of the many factors that determine chocolate quality.

while a few tasters appreciated the "unusual" quality, most thought its complexity detracted from the chocolate flavor. It received very low marks in both the plain and torte tastings. Lindt, another European stalwart, was deemed overly sweet, and it finished just ahead of the remaining supermarket brands. Both Baker's and Hershey's were immediately recognized by the tasters as inferior; their poor texture and off-flavors were dead giveaways.

All of the chocolates in the tasting are made with basically the same ingredients using similar manufacturing techniques. Therefore, it's probably best to think about chocolates the same way we approach wines. Some brands show better in group tastings because they have characteristics that appeal to the widest audience. "Losers" may in fact be inferior—possible factors include initial bean selection, how the beans are processed, the exact ratio of ingredients, and the length of conching, a step similar to kneading that promotes smoothness and flavor but takes many hours to do properly. However, other chocolates that landed at the bottom of the rankings may be well-made but represent a style that is harder to appreciate, even for professionals.

The tasting was held at Chez Panisse in Berkeley, California. In addition to the authors, the panel included author and pastry teacher Flo Braker; cookbook author Marion Cunningham, Fran Gage from Patisserie Francaise in San Francisco; David Lebovitz, pastry chef at Chez Panisse; Janet Rikala, pastry chef at Postrio in San Francisco; Tom Roach, owner of Tom's Cookies in San Francisco; Kathleen Stewart, of the Downtown Bakery and Creamery in Healdsburg, California; Carolyn Beth Weil, owner of The Bakeshop in Berkeley; and Chuck Williams, founder of Williams-Sonoma. ∎

Alice Medrich is the author of *Cocolat: Extraordinary Chocolate Desserts* (Warner Books, 1990) and *Chocolate and the Art of Low-Fat Desserts* (Warner Books, 1994).

Eleven chocolates were tasted both plain and cooked in a chocolate-almond torte with a chocolate glaze. The two blind tastings were conducted on the same day, but were independent of each other.

Chocolates are listed in order of preference within each category, based on their combined score in the two tastings. Chocolates that received mostly positive comments are highly recommended; those garnering mixed reviews are recommended; those earning more negative than positive comments are not recommended. Place of origin refers to the location of the corporate headquarters and/or factory. Prices are based on supermarket purchases in California and Connecticut, or on mail-order sources where indicated. Note that many mail-order outlets will not ship chocolates during the summer months. ■

HIGHLY RECOMMENDED CHOCOLATES

Van Leer Bittersweet Chocolate #1121-115 (Jersey City, New Jersey), 1-pound chunk, $4. "Blackish" chocolate that is "neither too sweet nor too bitter" with "strong espresso" overtones. While most tasters felt this chocolate  was well-balanced, a few thought it "sort of dull," leading to a fourth-place finish when eaten alone. However, it still came out ahead overall because it was the overwhelming favorite among the tortes, with comments like "good chocolate flavor comes through," and "mild but clean," *Available by mail from the Chocolate Gallery (34 W. 22nd Street, New York, NY 10010; 212-675-2253).*

Ghirardelli Semi-Sweet Chocolate (San Leandro, California), 4-ounce bar, $1.59. A third-place finish when eaten alone and a second-place showing among tortes assured this brand a high overall rating. This "glossy" chocolate is "well-rounded" with "minimal sweetness." Several tasters detected "some acidity" that was also interpreted as "fruitiness" or "winey notes." *Available in gourmet stores and supermarkets nationwide. Call the company's*  *consumer hot line (800-877-9338) for information on retailers in your area.*

Callebaut Bittersweet Chocolate (Belgium), two 17.75-ounce bars, $19.50. This import won the tasting of chocolates eaten alone by a narrow margin and finished fourth among the tortes. "Smooth and satiny" texture earned universal praise. Initial flavor was deemed "sweet" with "clean" or "slightly bitter" finish, although a few thought sweetness  made it one-dimensional. In tortes, this "flat" quality was interpreted less positively with comments like "not intense enough." *Available in gourmet stores and from the Williams-Sonoma catalog (800-541-2233).*

Merckens Yucatan Classic Dark Chocolate (Mansfield, Massachusetts), 2-pound bar, $8.40. This relatively unknown chocolate placed second when eaten plain and fifth among tortes. The flavor was deemed "somewhat sweeter" than most, with a "strong jolt of java." The texture was described as "very creamy" and "silky" with "excellent mouth-feel." In tortes, flavor was "muted" and "mild" but still "pleasant" with "some fruitiness." Again, texture earned high marks, especially in glaze. Several panelists noted this would be a good choice for candies, glazes, and mousses. *Available by mail from A Cook's Wares (211 37th Street, Beaver Falls, PA 15010; 412-846-9490).*

RECOMMENDED CHOCOLATES

Guittard Gourmet Bittersweet Chocolate (Burlingame, California), 7-ounce chunk, $1.98. A seventh-place finish among chocolates eaten alone was improved by a strong third-place showing among tortes. Several tasters thought flavor of this "extremely dark" chocolate was "too strong" and "very bitter." The  "grainy, chalky" texture received poor marks. The low sugar content worked well in the torte, with comments like "clean, chocolate flavor" with "hints of coffee" and "roasted quality." *Available by mail from Paprikas Weiss (1572 Second Avenue, New York, NY 10028; 212-288-6117).*

Hawaiian Vintage Bittersweet Chocolate (Honolulu, Hawaii), 1 pound of pistoles, $32. The only chocolate made from American-grown beans was judged very consistently, with a sixth-place finish in both tastings. Comments were also extremely consistent—"constant chocolate flavor," "no real highs or lows," "pleasant but not lots of character." Most panelists thought the texture was smooth, although a few detractors described it as "greasy" or "waxy." Again, panelists were neither wowed nor overly critical of  "vague chocolate flavor" in the torte that was "bland" and "flat" but "decent." *Available by mail from American Spoon Foods (1668 Clarion Avenue, Petoskey, MI 49770; 800-222-5886).*

Nestle's Semi-Sweet Baking Chocolate (Glendale, California), four 2-ounce bars in one box, $2.29. Highest finish among the big three supermarket brands with a fifth-place ranking among chocolates eaten alone and a ninth-place finish among tortes. The "strong, espresso-like" flavor was deemed "one-dimensional" by some tasters, while others judged it "intense" and "assertive." The "slight grittiness" and "powdery texture" were downgraded by many panelists. Although several tasters praised the torte, most were unimpressed. Overall, this chocolate can compete with some premium brands and was not immediately recognized as a mass-market product. *Available in supermarkets nationwide.*

CHOCOLATES NOT RECOMMENDED

Valrhona Le Noir Gastronomie Bittersweet Chocolate 61% Cocoa (France), 8.75-ounce bar, $6.99. The "unusual," "funny" flavor provoked mostly negative responses, which landed this premium brand in ninth place when eaten alone and eighth among the tortes. Most panelists described it as either "overly strong," "astringent," "medicinal," or "strangely fruity." A few dissenters especially liked the "exotic" quality of this chocolate but recognized that this "interesting" flavor might not be very "mainstream." Most found the chocolate flavor in the torte to be "bitter" or "odd." *Available in gourmet stores and by mail from the Chocolate Gallery (see address above).*

Lindt Surfin (Switzerland), 14-ounce bar, $9.98. Deemed "overly sweet" by a majority of tasters, this brand finished eighth when eaten alone and tenth among tortes. Comments ranged from "a little too sweet but some nice flavors" to "sweetness is overwhelming." The torte was judged "brownie-like" and "flat" because of its sweetness. *Available in gourmet stores, better supermarkets, and by mail from Paprikas Weiss (see address left).*

Baker's Semi-Sweet Baking Chocolate Squares (White Plains, New York), eight 1-ounce squares in one box, $2.25. It was immediately clear to most tasters that this was a mass-produced chocolate. A "soapy," "artificial" flavor, "dull, light" color, and "gritty, horrible" texture dropped this chocolate to last place when eaten alone. It faired slightly better in the tortes, placing seventh. Comments about the cake ranged from "too sweet" to "yeccht." *Available in supermarkets nationwide.*

Hershey's Semi-Sweet Baking Chocolate (Hershey, Pennsylvania), eight 1-ounce squares in one box, $2.29. Again "commercial" flavors were easily identified in this chocolate which ranked tenth when eaten alone and last among tortes. "Achingly sweet yet harsh" flavor earns no respect—"I would never use this chocolate," wrote one panelist. "Grainy" texture "feels like sand in your teeth." *Available in supermarkets nationwide.*

Nonstick Skillets Come of Age

After three months of use in a half dozen restaurant kitchens, All-Clad and Calphalon skillets came out on top due to excellent nonstick surfaces, even heating, and proper heft.

∽ BY JACK BISHOP ∽

Nonstick pans are obviously a great idea for cooks—not only is clean-up much easier, but you can also sauté food with much less fat than when using ordinary pans.

When Teflon-coated pans first came on the market thirty years ago, however, the idea was far better than the reality. After several months in the kitchen, the coating on these early pans would invariably begin to scratch and chip. In addition, foods would start to stick as the "release ability" of the surface literally went up in smoke. As a result, many cooks avoided these first nonstick pans, while others became resigned to replacing them every six months.

Of course, over the ensuing years new technologies have changed the way we build everything from cars to cookware. Better nonstick finishes, some of which were first engineered for the aerospace industry, have been developed, and highly respected cookware companies have applied this new generation of finishes—some of which are "guaranteed to last a lifetime"—to their top-of-the-line, heavy-duty pans.

With price tags close to $100 per pan, we wanted to see if any of these high-end nonstick skillets were worth the money. We choose to test ten-inch skillets from six leading companies. To evaluate the pans under the harshest possible conditions, we sent a set of each of the six pans to a half dozen restaurant kitchens. We asked them to perform a number of specific tests with sunny-side-up eggs, omelettes, skinless chicken breasts, and fish fillets. They also made the pans part of their daily routines over a three-month period.

We should note that the pans mentioned here are designed for home, not commercial use. We chose to conduct our testing in a professional environment for several reasons. Our panel of experts has used hundreds of pans from dozens of manufacturers over the years; this gives them a wealth of experience against which to evaluate and compare cookware. In addition, we figured if a pan could withstand a three-month stint in a restaurant kitchen, it should be able to last for years at home. Durability, even under adverse conditions, is the hallmark of well-made cookware.

After the pans had endured their three months on the line, we asked our chef/testers to judge the pans according to a number of criteria, including design, construction, heat conductivity, surface release ability, and durability. Each test kitchen filled out a six-page evaluation form for each pan.

Interpreting the Results

After reading through and compiling some 180 pages of raw data from our experts, we found that the testers agree on the ideal characteristics of a nonstick frying pan. First, the pan should be sturdy but not heavy; the consensus was that about two and a half pounds is right for a ten-inch skillet. Second, the pan must conduct heat evenly with no hot spots. Third, the nonstick surface must have excellent release ability and must resist peeling and scratching. And finally, the handles must be comfortable

---

CREATING A NONSTICK SURFACE

As our panel of experts discovered, not all nonstick coatings are the same. Teflon, the first nonstick surface, dates back to the 1930s and a laboratory at Du Pont. The first applications for this plastic made from fluoropolymers (also called fluorocarbon resins) were commercial—industrial machinery and aerospace equipment. By the 1960s, however, Teflon-coated pans began showing up in stores, with the emphasis on ease of cleaning. Busy cooks were promised scour-free clean-up.

These first nonstick coatings were extremely soft and began to wear away almost immediately. Manufacturers employed a number of tricks to improve longevity, like double and triple layering of coatings. Although these refinements led to more durable surfaces (if you scratched the top layer there still was some nonstick material between the food and the pan), the technology was still fairly primitive.

So what makes some of the nonstick surfaces we tested so much better than their predecessors? It's a combination of better pans to begin with (many early coatings were used to cover cheap aluminum skillets that did not conduct heat very evenly), stronger nonstick coatings (microscopic particles have been added to toughen the soft plastic), and better methods of applying the coatings.

Jack Kenna, the president of All-Clad (manufacturer of our top-rated skillet), says that a three-step process used to apply the Excalibur coating from Whitford ensures the surface will last "almost indefinitely." The stainless steel pan is first shot-blasted to clean and roughen the interior surface. Under high pressure a specially developed stainless steel wire is then passed through an electrical current. Molten droplets of stainless steel are propelled onto the rough pan surface by a process called "arc-spraying." This porous layer of stainless steel is particularly durable and welds to the pan, forming valleys and peaks to which the nonstick coating can attach in the final step.

Other coatings have equally complicated application techniques. Scanpan heats ceramic titanium to 36,000 degrees and then fires the liquid material at twice the speed of sound onto an aluminum pan. The company says this process, which is used by NASA on the space shuttle, creates a durable surface of microscopic peaks and valleys. Circulon takes the concept of "peaks and valleys" a step further with visible concentric grooves on the cooking surface.

The idea behind slightly rough or uneven surfaces (only the Le Creuset has a perfectly smooth cooking area) is that wear occurs at the top of the rough areas (the peaks), while the valleys remain coated with the nonstick material and preserve the release ability of the pan. John Badner, marketing manager at Whitford, says that utensils, even metal ones, "bounce across the peaks in the pan but leave the nonstick coating in the valleys untouched."

Our testers found that pans with microscopic hills and valleys (the cooking surface feels a bit rough) are better than smooth pans. However, if taken too far, this advantage becomes a liability: Pans with visibly textured cooking surfaces (like Circulon) have more surface area to which the food can stick, and food tends to collect in the deep grooves and then burn onto the pan, decreasing the release ability of the surface. Thorough scouring can mitigate this potential hazard, but our testers convincingly argued that nonstick surfaces should clean up with minimal effort.

to hold and securely attached to the pan. On the issue of the materials for the handles, our chefs preferred the versatility of metal handles, which get hot on the stove but permit use in the oven, over plastic handles, which stay cool but cannot be used in a very hot oven or under the broiler.

In terms of our chefs' preferences for individual skillets, the conclusions of our testing were also quite clear: The skillets from All-Clad (which received two first-place and three second-place votes) and Calphalon (two firsts, two seconds, and one third-place vote) were the overwhelming favorites. None of the others were recommended.

Our chef/testers also responded favorably to the classic styling of the All-Clad and Calphalon pans. Both are sturdy without being too heavy, and both conduct heat well. The nonstick surfaces were deemed first-rate when new and stood up well to many hours on the line. Although neither pan is perfect—several chefs complained about the shape of the All-Clad handle, and all felt that

the Calphalon handle became hot too quickly—they do not have the serious defects that our testers found in the other pans.

The entries from Circulon and Scanpan have heat-resistant plastic handles that our chefs liked on the stovetop, but neither handle can go under the broiler. All but one tester (who ranked Circulon first) complained about the inferior nonstick surfaces on both pans. One superhero-chef liked the Le Creuset pan (it tied for second in his ratings), but all other testers complained bitterly about its overwhelming weight. In addition, the perfectly smooth cooking surface was rated below average. The Farberware pan has the same highly rated nonstick surface as the All-Clad skillet. However, inferior heat conduction and a flimsy handle landed this pan at the bottom of the rankings. Our chefs also felt that the pan's straight sides made sautéing very difficult.

A final note about the metals used to make the skillets we tested. With the exception of copper, which is very pricey, aluminum is the most evenly

conductive material commonly found in cookware. It is also lightweight and relatively cheap. However, untreated aluminum is quite soft and prone to dents and scratching. Some top companies treat the aluminum to strengthen it. This also eliminates the metal's reactive properties which can cause off flavors in acidic sauces. The most common treatment is an electrochemical process called anodizing that hardens aluminum and "seals" its surface. Pans from Calphalon and Circulon are made with hard-anodized aluminum. The Scanpan is made from heavy-duty, pressure-cast aluminum. Our testers were impressed by the even cooking of all three pans.

Cast iron lacks the high conductivity of aluminum, but it is able to retain heat well, as our testers found with the Le Creuset pan. This durable metal makes very heavy cookware (often twice as heavy as pans made from other materials) that can take a real beating. Some cast-iron pans, including the Le Creuset skillet, are coated inside and out with colorful porcelain enamel finishes,

---

RATING NONSTICK SKILLETS

We asked six restaurants to help us with this article. Each kitchen (our two Cambridge restaurants teamed up on this project) returned an evaluation for each pan. We would like to thank the following chefs and their kitchen staffs for devoting so much effort and energy to this project. Rick Bayless, chef/owner of Frontera Grill and Topolobampo in Chicago; Johnny Earles and Keith Mahoney, chef/owner and sous chef at Criolla's in Grayton Beach, Florida; Andy Husbands and Bridget Batson, chefs at the East Coast Grill and The Blue Room in Cambridge, Massachusetts; Susan McCreight Lindeborg, chef at Morrison-Clark in Washington, D.C.; and Jamie Shannon, chef de cuisine at Commander's Palace in New Orleans.

Chefs worked with the pans for three months, performing specific tests we designed as well as their regular kitchen chores. After testing was con-

cluded, the chefs evaluated the skillets using the following criteria—design, construction, even heat conductivity, and performance of the nonstick surface (including both release ability and durability). Skillets that received mostly favorable reviews are recommended; those earning mostly negative comments are not recommended. Skillets are listed in order of preference within each category. Note that the All-Clad pan finished slightly ahead of the Calphalon skillet, but that the results were close. Also note that there was little difference in the scores of the last four skillets.

Prices are suggested retail and will vary. (See page 32 for information on purchasing specific skillets.) Actual size refers to a measurement taken from one outer edge to the other outer edge at the top of the pan (referred to as "across") and from a level counter to the top of the pan (referred to as "deep").

RECOMMENDED SKILLETS

ALL-CLAD NONSTICK STAINLESS 10" FRYING PAN #5110NS

Price: $80
Warranty: Lifetime
Actual Size: 10½" across, 1⅞" deep
Weight: 2 pounds 9 ounces
Materials: Aluminum layer runs throughout pan and is surrounded by a layer of stainless steel with Excalibur nonstick cooking surface. Stainless steel handle.
Design: "Solid," "well-made" pan is "nicely balanced" with "some heft, but still easy to carry with one hand." Smooth, thin handle elicited mixed responses—"sure grip" to "a little slippery." Testers were split on how handle performed over heat, with comments ranging from "never gets hot" to "very hot." One tester commented that handle "stays cool for a remarkable period of time, but heats

up after prolonged use," perhaps explaining the difference of opinion.
Heat Conduction: This flat-bottomed pan heats up "fairly quickly" and maintains even heat from center to edges.
Nonstick Surface: Foods do not stick on this "excellent" surface that is "very easy to clean." Manufacturer recommends use of plastic, rubber, or wood utensils, although metal is given as an option.
Comments: Few complaints about this top pan, although some division of opinion regarding the handle. Shiny exterior requires "lots of scrubbing," but otherwise few serious gripes from our picky testers.

CALPHALON PROFESSIONAL NONSTICK 10" OMELETTE PAN 1390

Price: $58
Warranty: Lifetime
Actual Size: 10½" across, 2⅛" deep
Weight: 2 pounds 11 ounces
Materials: Anodized aluminum pan coated with proprietary fluoropolymer

cooking surface called Lifetime Release System. Stainless steel handle.
Design: Most testers found pan to be "well-built," and several commented on the "great shape." One tester thought the "fold" on underside of handle is "somewhat distracting," and another thought grip was "a little slippery." More worrisome, all testers agreed that the handle "becomes scorching hot very quickly."
Heat Conduction: This heavy, flat-bottomed pan conducts and holds heat "extremely well."
Nonstick Surface: Release ability of "top-notch" surface remained quite high throughout testing with only "small scratches but nothing to worry about." Manufacturer recommends use of wooden, plastic, or coated utensils.
Comments: Biggest complaints are that the area where the handle meets the pan can trap food and that the

handle itself becomes quite hot during use. "Great pan as long as you are careful around the hot handle," one tester summed up.

NOT RECOMMENDED SKILLETS

CIRCULON 10" OPEN FRENCH SKILLET 88310

Price: $57
Warranty: 10 years
Actual Size: 9¾ " across, 1⅞" deep
Weight: 1 pound 11 ounces
Materials: Anodized aluminum pan with concentric grooves (called Hi-Low System) and nonstick cooking surface. Black plastic handle.
Design: This "lightweight" pan, smaller than others in the test, has "wild" design with tiny grooves on cooking surface, although overall shape is "traditional."  Plastic handle has a textured grip that was

ILLUSTRATIONS BY DAN KROVATIN

which eliminate the need for seasoning and prevent both rusting and the beneficial reactions between cast iron and acidic ingredients.

Good looks and durability are the chief attributes of glimmering stainless steel (it won't scratch easily or react with foods like untreated aluminum). However, stainless steel does not conduct heat very evenly, so some manufacturers sandwich a layer of another metal, such as aluminum, between two layers of stainless steel. If this layer extends across the bottom and all the way up the sides, the pan is said to be "clad," hence the name for the All-Clad pan. This approach seems to work well—our testers found that a "clad" stainless steel pan heats as evenly as an all-aluminum one. Other manufacturers choose the less expensive approach of "plating" a layer of another metal onto the bottom of their stainless steel pans. As our testers discovered with the Farberware entry, a stainless steel skillet that is simply plated with an external layer of aluminum is still prone to hot spots. ∎

deemed "an asset" by all chefs. More importantly, handle stays relatively cool ("even after 45 minutes on stove, handle only became warm") but cannot withstand high oven heat. (Owner's manual recommends maximum oven temperature of 350 degrees.)

Heat Conduction: Most chefs felt that this flat-bottomed pan distributed heat well.

Nonstick Surface: Most testers were pleased with initial quality of surface, but several felt that it lost "some of its punch" as they worked. Ridged surface "requires extra work to clean," and several reported grease and food accumulating in grooves over time. However, one chef raved about no-oil cooking, saying this pan "crisps food beautifully." Manufacturer recommends the use of plastic or wooden utensils, not metal.

Comments: Surface gets good marks for release, at least at first, but several chefs voiced strong concerns about durability: "Where did the nonstick surface go? Into my food?" In the end, the grooved surface was deemed "a gimmick and not really practical" by all but two chefs. Even one chef who felt that surface held up, thought concentric circles on foods cooked in this pan were "weird" and "unappealing."

SCANPAN 2001+ 10¼" FRYING PAN/OMELETTE PAN #4501/26

Price: $50
Warranty: Lifetime
Actual Size: 10⅝" across, 1¾" deep
Weight: 2 pounds 9 ounces

Materials: Cast aluminum pan coated with proprietary ceramic-titanium cooking surface. Black plastic handle.

Design: "Very sturdy," "solid" pan "could be a little deeper." Grip "feels really good in the hand" and stays cool during prolonged use, however pan can't go under broiler. (Manufacturer says handles are safe up to 500 degrees.)

Heat Conduction: Lightly raised 7½" external aluminum disk on bottom promotes even heating.

Nonstick Surface: Surface has average release ability with complaints that pan became harder to work with as it became hotter. "Food sticks to this pan more readily than others." Even chefs who liked this surface at the start gave it low marks on durability. One called it "scam pan" after frustrating attempts to fry an egg. Manufacturer recommends use of metal utensils.

Comments: Several chefs gave pan decent if not overwhelming marks. Others felt "cheated by good looks" that "faded after the first date." One tester described "high-tech" pan as "the Terminator," because it "seems so over-produced and over-designed."

LE CREUSET 10" TRADITIONAL FRYING PAN L2014-26

Price: $90
Warranty: 101 years
Actual Size: 10½" across, 1⅝" deep

Weight: 4 pounds 6 ounces
Materials: Enameled cast-iron pan coated with proprietary Glissemail cooking surface.
Wooden handle has metal loop for hanging pan.

Design: "Way too heavy" is the general consensus on this "out of balance" pan that is nevertheless "sturdy" and "indestructible." Very gently sloped sides leave only small cooking surface. Wooden handle stays cool, but metal loop can become "deceivingly hot." Several chefs thought handle became "slippery when wet," and noted possibility of wood scorching or burning in oven.

Heat Conduction: Slightly raised 7½" inch external cast iron disk on bottom takes some time to get pan hot, but most chefs were pleased by even distribution of heat.

Nonstick Surface: Release average-at-best, although surface proved fairly durable. One tester thought eggs cooked best on this smooth surface. Most chefs felt this surface needs more oil than others to be effective.

Comments: Size of pan ("designed for a steady, serious weight lifter") was downgraded by most chefs. "If you didn't have tennis elbow before, you would get it." On the bright side, heft means "you know this pan will never warp."

FARBERWARE MILLENNIUM 10½" SAUTÉ PAN #C2210

Price: $72
Warranty: 20 years

Actual Size: 10¼" across, 2¼" deep
Weight: 2 pounds 3 ounces without cover
Materials: Stainless steel pan with aluminum-plated base and Excalibur nonstick cooking surface. Stainless steel handle and cover.

Design: "Very lightweight" was the general consensus on this "flawed" pan. Straight sides make use of a spatula "tricky if not impossible," especially for foods that cook near edges of pan, like an omelette. "Flimsy" handle is "so light it bends." Handle gets "extremely hot in no time."

Heat Conduction: Base and lower sides of pan are coated with an external layer of aluminum plating. Testers found pan heats quickly, but were divided about whether heat was evenly distributed. Two reported that the center cooks much faster, especially over low heat.

Nonstick Surface: Superior release ability remained strong after testing, although some reported that surface was beginning to show small signs of cracking and chipping. Manufacturer recommends use of metal utensils.

Comments: Nonstick surface gets high marks (it's the same surface that's on the top-rated All-Clad), but the general design of this pan and some concerns about uneven heat conduction relegate it to last place. All testers agreed that design made true sautéing "impossible." Definitely a case of a good nonstick material wasted on a poorly conceived pan.

Finding the Best California Sparklers

Most sparkling wines from California cost about the same, but the quality varies wildly. Our tasting uncovered some surprises.

~ BY MARK BITTMAN ~

California wines did well in last year's tasting of sparklers from all over the world (*Cook's Illustrated*, November/December 1993), taking two of the top five places against generally pricier French competition. Although our conclusion was "buy French if you can afford it," we noted that the producers of California sparkling wines had made great strides while managing to hold down the costs. As a result, we organized an all-California tasting for this year's holiday issue.

The results show that, indeed, there are some more-than-decent sparkling wines from California at very attractive prices. But finding those wines is a bit of a challenge, since one of our top finishers from last year—Roederer Estate Brut—finished down in the pack this time around, and one of last year's rejects, Domaine Chandon Brut, finished a strong second.

Theoretically at least, this shouldn't happen. In France, Champagne is a blend, and each house tries to maintain an identifiable style that carries over not only from year to year but from decade to decade. Devotees of a given style can, with some assurance, buy the same brand of Champagne year in, year out. Evidently, the California houses are not dealing with a consistent enough grape supply to achieve this.

Champagne is a term rightly applied only to sparkling wines from the Champagne district in France. But there are plenty of styles of sparkling wine to choose from. The wine may be full, round, rich, and fruity; dry, yeasty, and "toasty"; or some other combination of like qualities. It should not, however, smell rubbery or otherwise foul (as many of these wines did), nor should its bubbles be overwhelming; they should titillate the palate.

The four recommended wines in our tasting were generally admired by all the tasters, amateur and professional alike. They were of two distinct styles: some were toasty, yeasty, and quite dry; others were round, full, rich, and fruity. All, however, appeared to be well-made and without serious flaws.

Our middle group comprised wines that didn't make the recommended list either because they were unremarkable or because they had outstanding problems.

The bottom group had little to recommend it, and even those tasters who ranked these wines would sooner you looked elsewhere. ∎

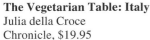

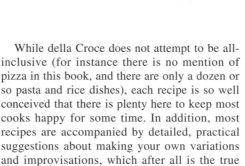

BOOK
REVIEWS

The Vegetarian Table: Italy
Julia della Croce
Chronicle, $19.95

Almost every week a Mediterranean cookbook lands at my door. Many of these new books tout the healthy aspects of the region's cooking, often relying on scientific studies and nutrition analyses to back up their claims. As I thumb through these books, I often feel that this numbers-oriented approach, which strikes me as particularly American, clashes with the recipes themselves. Information about grams of fat and HDL cholesterol does not really mesh with peasant recipes that take their cue from improvisation.

The style adopted by Julia della Croce in her new book on Italian vegetarian cooking is much subtler and, to my mind, more in tune with the region's culinary ethos. Her collection of eighty recipes—many well-known classics but some authentic Italian dishes unusual enough to be new to this reader—captures the spirit of the Italian kitchen with gutsy but simple dishes. Since all are meatless, they are generally low in fat and rich in fiber and nutrients. However, della Croce is not adverse to using eggs or roasting potatoes in plenty of olive oil.

This sensible approach translates into authentic recipes that deliver superb results. Without exception, every recipe I tested was delicious, and the directions were easy to follow and execute.

The book is divided into chapters that mirror the traditional Italian meal—*antipasti* (appetizers), first courses (soups, pastas, and rice dishes), second courses (usually meat, poultry, or fish, but here egg dishes, polenta stews, and vegetable casseroles), and *contorni* (vegetable side dishes and salads served along with the second course). Eggplant Salad, Calabria Style uses a technique common to roasting meats, but one I have never seen used with vegetables: Eggplant halves are slashed and stuffed with garlic slivers that cook along with the eggplant. When tender, the roasted eggplant (including the garlic) is cubed and tossed with mint, olive oil, red wine vinegar, and hot pepper flakes. Whole-Wheat Bread and Tomato Salad, Apulia Style is not unlike *panzanella*, the Tuscan white bread and tomato salad, but the change to whole-wheat bread adds some welcome bulk and texture. Baked Zucchini Casserole, with alternating layers of sliced zucchini, mozzarella, tomatoes, and seasoned bread crumbs, uses beaten eggs as a binding, which provides enough heft to make a hearty main course.

While della Croce does not attempt to be all-inclusive (for instance there is no mention of pizza in this book, and there are only a dozen or so pasta and rice dishes), each recipe is so well conceived that there is plenty here to keep most cooks happy for some time. In addition, most recipes are accompanied by detailed, practical suggestions about making your own variations and improvisations, which after all is the true spirit of Italian cooking.

—*Jack Bishop*

A Taste of Old Cuba
Maria Josefa Lluria de O'Higgins
HarperCollins, $25

Many "authentic" books about Caribbean cooking contain ingredients that I won't use—ketchup, margarine, evaporated milk, and canned vegetables, to name a few. I imagine that these ingredients made their way into these island cuisines for a couple of reasons. First of all, it can be difficult to get top-notch ingredients in poor, remote villages on islands visited mostly by boat. This situation was undoubtedly made worse in the postwar years, when American corporations took advantage of their marketing hegemony in the western hemisphere to push easy-to-ship, easy-to-store processed foods whenever and wherever they could.

But none of this seems to have affected the author of *A Taste of Old Cuba*, who grew up in a wealthy family (for a while, anyway) in a prosperous city during the first half of this century, long before you could find Wheat Thins on the shelves of small-town Caribbean groceries. O'Higgins (she married an Irish-American) spent her adult years traveling around the world, obviously developing a sophisticated palate and an appreciation for the cuisine of her youth. When she settled in Miami, the center of Cuban life for expatriates, she began to cook her native food rather seriously. The result is a cuisine largely based on the cooking of Spain, with lots of garlic, tomatoes, eggs, almonds, and bell peppers. This is not health food by any means, since many of the dishes are fried, and the desserts are mostly variations on custard. However, the Caribbean staples of lime juice, sour oranges, pork, black beans, and various local fish also figure prominently.

The language here is quite lovely, the information is comprehensive, and the recipes—which make up the bulk of the text—are wonderful. For the most part, this is basic, flavorful food, and although some of the recipes, such as Oven-Poached Eggs, may not add anything to either your repertoire or your reference shelf, others will do both. I tried (and loved) Eggs with Clams, an unusual dish in which clams are steamed open and poached with eggs in a broth made from the steaming liquid; Rice with Shrimp, made in a pressure cooker with shrimp-shell stock; and Cuban Creole Fried Chicken, a crispy, cumin-scented dish that made me eat more than I should have.

This is not so much a pan-Caribbean cookbook as others I've seen; it focuses almost exclusively on the Spanish-dominated cuisine of Cuba. But this focus gives it strength and clarity. *A Taste of Old Cuba* is a well-defined, well-executed work.

—*Mark Bittman*

Great Food Almanac
Irena Chalmers
Collins San Francisco, $25

Do you know the difference between almond paste and marzipan? Did you know that the tongue of a catfish has 100,000 taste buds? Would you guess that a hamburger is four times more expensive in Denmark than in Russia? If you are endlessly curious, or just want a fascinating pick-it-up-at-any-page read, then *The Food Almanac* is ideal literary snack food. Irena Chalmers has packed its 350-plus pages with great quotes ("Everyone is a pacifist between wars and a vegetarian between meals."), serendipitous factoids (sardines are named after Sardinia), good cartoons, and newsy clippings from unheard-of magazines and government publications.

Chalmers also includes recipes and sources for additional information, both of which are often superfluous—do you really want to subscribe to *The Food Insects Newsletter*? There is a low-level hiss of filler material here—a minor quibble given the abundance of cocktail party ammunition and fascinating cul-de-sacs teeming with mostly entertaining and sometimes useful stuff. It's fun, and reading it is just like having lunch with Irena. You always learn something new, she manages to combine odd facts into interesting trends (she once convinced me that the reason leather shoes are more expensive is that Americans are eating less meat), and you have a great time to boot. This is the best of Irena—and even on a bad day, she'll tell you six things you don't know. ∎

—*Chris Kimball*

SOURCES
AND RESOURCES

Most of the ingredients and materials listed here are available at your local kitchen supply or specialty food store. Following are mail-order sources for particular items. The suggested retail prices listed below are current at press time. Contact the companies directly to confirm up-to-date prices and availability.

POPOVER PAN
Popovers can be made either in a regular muffin tin or in a specially designed popover pan. The Crown Popover/Muffin Pan from Chicago Metallic is one of the best on the market. Each heavy-gauge steel pan is coated with a Silverstone nonstick coating to promote even baking and easy release. The six cups are each three and one half inches in diameter and have extra-wide collars to promote a fully puffed crown on either popovers or muffins. The Williams-Sonoma catalog (800-541-2233) sells this pan for $18.

NONSTICK SKILLETS
Our top-rated All-Clad Nonstick Stainless Ten-Inch Fry Pan is available at a discount from A Cook's Wares (211 37th Street, Beaver Falls, PA 15010; 412-846-9490). This mail-order company takes 15 percent off the list price and charges just $68. Second-rated Calphalon Professional Nonstick Ten-Inch Omelette Pan is available from the Williams-Sonoma catalog (800-541-2233) for $58. This pan was well-liked by our panel of chefs, but all of the testers found that the handle got hot very quickly. To answer this complaint, Calphalon makes stay-cool rubber grips that slip on over the metal handles of their cookware. These grips are for the stovetop only and should be removed from the pan before using it in the oven. The rubber grips come in several sizes. The six-inch grip designed to fit over the handle on the ten-inch omelet or fry pan costs $11, and is also available from Williams-Sonoma.

DRIED CRANBERRIES
Dried cranberries may not be as easy to locate as other dried fruits, but we have found an excellent mail-order source. American Spoon Foods (1668 Clarion Avenue, Petoskey, MI 49770; 800-222-5886) dries their own cranberries without sulfites, preservatives, or artificial colors. Sugar is added to make the tart fruit edible right out of the bag. Dried cranberries are available in three different package sizes—three-ounce, six-ounce, and one-pound. The smallest package is $2.50, while the two larger sizes are $4.25 and $8.50. American Spoon Foods also stocks a number of other unusual dried fruits such as blueberries, persimmons, strawberries, and cherries.

CANDIED FRUIT
The panforte recipes on pages 12 and 13 call for a number of candied fruits. While many candied fruits are overly sweet and very sticky, we found a source for tart, crisp ones. The King Arthur Flour Baker's Catalogue (P.O. Box 876, Norwich, VT 05055; 800-827-6836) sells candied orange peel and candied lemon peel imported from Australia. These thick, chewy candied fruits come in three-and-one-half-ounce packages that cost $1.95 each. King Arthur also sells a three-and-one-half-ounce bag of candied Italian citron peel for $5.50.

PANFORTE ESSENTIALS
Panforte requires an edible liner to help the confection maintain its shape. One option is a thin wheat starch wafer called oblaten. These wafers may be carried by baking supply stores with a large stock of German ingredients. Otherwise, we suggest that you mail-order round oblaten from Paprikas Weiss (1572 Second Avenue, New York, NY 10028; 212-288-6117). They sell a box of 100 oblaten for $6.99. The oblaten are ninety millimeters (about three and one half inches) in diameter, so you will need several to cover an eight-inch round cake pan. Another choice for lining the pan is Asian rice paper. Look at local Asian food stores for round wrappers that are at least eight inches in diameter. You can also mail-order rice paper wrappers from Vietnam Imports (922 West Broad Street, Falls Church, VA 22046; 703-534-9441). A package of sixty wrappers, each twenty-two centimeters (about eight and one half inches) in diameter is $1.99.

TRUSSING NEEDLES
We recommend purchasing a sturdy trussing needle and twine to sew up the cavity of a goose. Most kitchen shops should carry both items, but if you have trouble locating a good trussing needle contact La Cuisine Kitchenware (323 Cameron Street, Alexandria, VA 22314; 800-521-1176). They carry two trussing needles, both made in France from stainless steel. An eight-inch needle is fine when working with small birds like chickens. The nine-and-one-half-inch trussing needle is better for larger birds like geese and turkeys. The smaller needle costs $5.75; the larger one costs $6.50.

GENUINE SAFFRON
Known as the world's most expensive spice, saffron is a subject of confusion and mislabeling in stores. More than 70,000 hand-picked flower stamens go into every pound, which accounts for saffron's astronomical cost. Luckily, a little saffron goes a long way. While many supermarkets carry tiny vials of saffron, the origin and quality are often suspect. You should also avoid powdered saffron, which is sometimes adulterated with turmeric. We recommend that you buy real saffron from a reputable gourmet store or spice dealer. Saffron can also be ordered by mail from Penzeys Spice House (P.O. Box 1448, Waukesha, WI 53187; 414-574-0277). They sell two varieties. Kashmir Mogra Cream Indian Saffron contains 100 percent red threads and is quite rare in this country. It costs $5.95 per gram, and is best for Indian curries and rice dishes. Superior Quality Spanish Saffron is best for fish stews like bouillabaisse (see page 20). It costs $4.95 per gram.

GEESE BY MAIL
In order to avoid high shipping costs, try to order a holiday goose (see story on page 6) from a local butcher shop. Butchers that cater to a German or Eastern European clientele are probably your best bet. However, if you are unable to find a local butcher who can supply you with a bird, we recommend ordering a goose from Schaller & Weber (1654 Second Avenue, New York, NY 10028; 212-879-3047). Author Stephen Schmidt bought geese from several sources while working on his article, and found those from Schaller & Weber to be consistently excellent. Their geese range in size from ten to twelve pounds (enough to feed eight to ten people) and cost $2.98 per pound. Expect to a pay a hefty surcharge for overnight shipping.

MOLDED BAGUETTE PANS
A mini-test that we ran with a metal baking sheet, a baking stone, and a molded baguette pan (see page 2) showed that the stone and the molded pan produced the crispest, most evenly browned loaves. But unless your baking stone is quite large, the mold is a better bet, since it can produce long, slender baguettes. The King Arthur Flour Baker's Catalogue (see above) imports two baguette molds from France. They are made from black-finished metal to promote a crisp crust, and can hold loves up to seventeen inches long and just over two inches wide. The four-mold pan (capable of baking four baguettes at once) costs $28.75; the two-mold pan costs $19.25.

JAPANESE VEGETABLE SHREDDER
Several months ago we answered a reader's question regarding a Japanese mandolin (see Notes from Readers, January/February 1994), a handy device that slices and shreds carrots, potatoes, radishes, and other vegetables into numerous attractive patterns. Unfortunately, this restaurant-quality tool costs more than $300. But we recently ran across a scaled-down version called a Spiral Shredder. It also comes from Japan and is capable of creating thin, spiral-cut strands from almost any vegetable. Three interchangeable blades can also shred vegetables into straight strands that are either fine, medium, or coarse. The shredder costs $38 from the Williams-Sonoma catalog (800-541-2233). ∎

THE BEST POPOVERS
page 9

THE ULTIMATE LEMON MERINGUE PIE
page 24

RECIPE INDEX

CURRIED APPLE-CRANBERRY CHUTNEY
page 14

SICILIAN GRILLED TUNA STEW
page 21

ROAST GOOSE WITH PRUNE AND APPLE STUFFING
page 7 **WITH CRANBERRY-ONION CONFIT** page 14

CHOCOLATE AND DRIED FRUIT PANFORTE
page 13

Broiled Oysters Topped with Roasted Chile-Cilantro Sauce

Place 2 large spicy peppers (poblanos or Italian frying peppers) and 1 small hot chile pepper (jalapeño or Dutch red) that have been roasted, peeled, and seeded into a food processor fitted with a steel blade. Add 2 peeled garlic cloves and 2 tablespoons each pine nuts and fresh cilantro leaves; process until pureed. Turn mixture into a small bowl; stir in 6 tablespoons olive oil and salt and pepper to taste. Adjust oven rack to within 6 inches of heating element and heat broiler. Top each of 36 shucked oysters with about ½ teaspoon of this chile-cilantro mixture. Sprinkle about ¼ teaspoon dried bread crumbs over each oyster. Broil until bread crumbs turn golden brown and oysters are just plump, 4 to 5 minutes. Serve immediately with lemon or lime wedges. *Serves 6.*